# How
# ASIA
## CAN SHAPE THE
# WORLD

The **Institute of Southeast Asian Studies (ISEAS)** was established as an autonomous organization in 1968. It is a regional centre dedicated to the study of socio-political, security and economic trends and developments in Southeast Asia and its wider geostrategic and economic environment. The Institute's research programmes are the Regional Economic Studies (RES, including ASEAN and APEC), Regional Strategic and Political Studies (RSPS), and Regional Social and Cultural Studies (RSCS).

**ISEAS Publishing**, an established academic press, has issued more than 2,000 books and journals. It is the largest scholarly publisher of research about Southeast Asia from within the region. ISEAS Publishing works with many other academic and trade publishers and distributors to disseminate important research and analyses from and about Southeast Asia to the rest of the world.

# How
# ASIA
## CAN SHAPE THE
# WORLD

### FROM THE ERA OF PLENTY TO THE ERA OF SCARCITIES

## JØRGEN ØRSTRØM MØLLER

**LSEAS**

**INSTITUTE OF SOUTHEAST ASIAN STUDIES**
*Singapore*

First published in Singapore in 2011 by
ISEAS Publishing
Institute of Southeast Asian Studies
30 Heng Mui Keng Terrace
Pasir Panjang
Singapore 119614

*E-mail*: publish@iseas.edu.sg
*Website*: <http://bookshop.iseas.edu.sg>

*The responsibility for facts and opinions in this publication rests exclusively with the author and his interpretations do not necessarily reflect the views or the policy of the publisher or its supporters.*

ISEAS Library Cataloguing-in-Publication Data

Møller, J. Ørstrøm.
How Asia can shape the world : from the era of plenty to the era of scarcities.
1. Asia—Forecasting—21st century.
2. Asia—Economic conditions—21st century.
3. Asia—Economic policy—21st century.
4. Asia—Social conditions—21st century.
5. Asia—Social policy—21st century.
I. Title.
DS5 M72                    2011

ISBN 978-981-4311-33-5 (soft cover)
ISBN 978-981-4311-74-8 (E-Book PDF)

Typeset by Superskill Graphics Pte Ltd
Printed in Singapore by Utopia Press Pte Ltd

# CONTENTS

# FOREWORD

Professor Jørgen Møller has for years given us his trenchant thoughts on the rise of new Europe after two disastrous wars in the twentieth century. I have had the privilege of spending many hours in conversation with him, listening to his critical examination of the current travails of both Europe and the United States. He also demonstrated a keen knowledge of the troubled experiences of Asian modernization. His deep concern that there should be better understanding in the West of what is happening in Asia has often encouraged me to think afresh about what we in Asia often take for granted. At one end, those who accept the Western model of growth as inevitable, also invariably believe we must get even closer to the West and absorb all its secrets. At the other, those who are determined to go beyond that model would ask us to think, wherever possible, out of the Western box in search of some Asian way. And, in between, there are those who have begun to doubt that there is any such thing as Asian and Western today as we take in each other's washing in this small and shrinking world.

In his new book, Professor Møller depicts the nature of politics in its many dimensions, sometimes bombastic, lofty, totalistic and awesome, but, at its core, he also shows that it is all too often petty and local. He ought to know, having worked as one of his country's most senior public servants during decades of European political turmoil. He is no less objective in his assessment of his own field of expertise, that of economics. He knows that economists can often sound like housewives counting pennies and keeping good accounts, but he also demonstrates that economic ideas and policies have the capacity to make or break nations and civilizations. There is little doubt that the cumulative power of nation states and their empires and various models of rapid economic growth have, over the past 200 years, transformed every corner of the world. The rising rate of technological and material progress, and the obsession to better that rate, has dominated global discourse for so long that, now and then, this has driven poets and philosophers to wonder about the future of social cohesion and shared cultural values. I am fascinated by the way Professor Møller also wonders about that future. Indeed, many do ask if the advocates of sustainable growth and global environmental protection can really rid us of the prospect of an unending surfeit of worldly goods, cycles of economic stagnation, and relentless cultural destruction.

Professor Møller hesitates to make any forecasts, but raises similar concerns about the future world of scarce resources and suggests that group values will replace the traditions that give primacy to the individual. He has shown in his earlier writings to be a most versatile economist who can pick through the politics of high rhetoric and weave the threads of private finance into explanations of profound global change. In this book, he has drawn on his wide experience of the world of realpolitik and economic realism in European history to peer into Asia's future. By asking how Asia can shape the world, he examines the major changes of the past two decades with probing intensity. Clearly, the modern Western model has intervened at all levels of Asian political and economic development with considerable success. The most far-reaching changes in the realms of industrialization and urbanization have fundamentally changed everybody's lives, and societies and cultures that were once dominant have been systematically undermined. Now, as globalization becomes a great challenge to the whole world, what resources can Asia contribute to help the world respond?

He invites us to follow him on an exploratory and sometimes rollercoaster ride to survey Asia's uncertain but not necessarily unpredictable future. He has combed a large variety of sources to prepare a guide for the journey, warning at each step of the way that the forecasts attempted might well be sidetracked by new variables not taken into account.

This book does not allow simple answers. Professor Møller examines every effort at forecasting and each projection that has attracted attention, and subjects them to meticulous scrutiny. He persists in asking, what assets do the Asian growth centres have? What kinds of heritage have been helpful and what are likely to obstruct future development? Have they borrowed wisely from the industrialized pioneers of Europe and the United States? Are they ready to adapt, innovate, and experiment with the knowledge and skills that they have so far acquired? Have Asians educated their younger generations to build the inner strengths that will overcome current limits and reach out for zones yet to be discovered? Professor Møller has identified the achievements in various parts of Asia and does not hesitate to point to their potential as well their vulnerabilities. The overriding question is whether any Asian state that has chosen modernity can avoid taking its peoples through what the Western modern states have been through. As Europe has shown, modernity demands its pound of flesh and may be seen as a universal condition with a powerful appetite, one that all who want to have comparable standards of modernity would have to learn to satisfy.

Professor Møller surveys a variety of threats to orderly development and the best-laid plans. Some are conventional and others are new. He then suggests how Asia might deal with the evolving framework in which conflicts of an age of yet undetermined strategic changes might take place. He ends with an original final chapter on how the forces faced by the Asian states and societies could interact with each other in the years to come. On several planes, he sets out the geometry of these external pressures that call for very close reading. I am confident that, at his most persuasive, his questions will induce thinkers and planners in Asia to take careful note of what he has outlined.

*Wang Gungwu*
*Chairman, East Asian Institute*
*National University of Singapore*
*4 July 2010*

# PREFACE AND ACKNOWLEDGEMENTS

The future of Asia is like a magnet for politicians, scholars, and business people. All are fascinated by the continent obviously entering a crucial phase of its development, shaping not only its own future, but also determining the socio-economic global framework for decades even centuries to come. Around 500 years ago the pendulum started to swing from Asia to Europe and since then "the West" has dominated the world. This is coming to an end. It looks likely that a number of converging influences will gradually put Asia in the driver's seat. It remains to be seen whether Asia is ready and willing to respond and if so what kind of socio-economic model will emerge, whether it can solve Asia's many problems and at the same time constitute a framework for stable future development that may even be attractive for the rest of the world as the Western model was for centuries. There are no easy answers to these questions and when we seem to have found some, other questions arise.

As the reader will discover, my first inclination is to analyse and look at events from the perspective of an economist. There are many brands of economics; I belong to the Keynesian School. The weaknesses of economic analysis have been exposed over a number of years — not only recently and to a degree that it is questionable whether it can be classified as a science after all. This has opened the door for interdisciplinary analyses; which is what I have tried to put forward in my work, weaving many threads together. Interdisciplinary analysis is not new. In an Asian context *inter alia* the great socio-economist Gunnar Myrdal published *Asian Drama* in 1968.

My ambition is, however, to go somewhat further by including aspects beyond the social sciences, which, as I see it, makes the work fascinating, but also runs the risk of conveying the impression of superficiality. But you cannot have it both ways.

The common denominator for the book may be the emphasis of groups, working together, sharing knowledge, and grappling with the new phenomenon of burden sharing inside group frameworks. Burden sharing — either absolute or relative — becomes necessary as the world moves from two hundred years of plenty (the era of plenty) to the age of scarcities. The many new ideas of social coherence, social capital, and whatever they are called illuminate the swing in economic behaviour from focusing upon the individual to group work. To my mind this will change economic theory. Economics in the mould of Adam Smith, David Ricardo, and the other classics may no longer maintain a conceptual monopoly. They were right at their time of writing, but conditions for economic activity have changed completely and nowadays the basis for their analysis seems to me wrong. The world is going to see a new kind of economics emerge to frame future development and the message from this book is that it is likely to happen in Asia influenced by ancient Asian religions and/or philosophies. This is my starting point and I venture out from there to posit ideas about how these new conditions will look, knowing very well how dangerous such an enterprise is and how thin the ice sometimes may be.

From that basis the book goes on to discuss what future forecasting is and how it looks in an Asian perspective at the end of the first decade of the twenty-first century. Change, Asia certainly will. And changes may fall into three groups: elements that unquestionably facilitate economic growth, elements that may do so or be an obstacle depending upon how politicians tackle the issues, and elements which presumably will work against growth.

Asia needs economic growth to tackle its many challenges and problems, but the transfer of the Western style economic model based upon mass consumption will lead to a disaster that may jeopardize the future of globalization, not only in Asia but worldwide.

Writing such a book as a European is certainly a challenge, but I have enjoyed it. The main problem is that the writer to a large extent has to rely on Western sources or Asian sources translated into English or for that sake French or German. A large amount of Asian literature available only in Asian languages is out of reach. This impoverishes the book, but as I do not read Asian languages I have had to live with that constraint and so must the reader, but there is no reason to hide that the book is influenced by this limitation

— regrettably so. It strikes me, which I have often heard but never felt, how strong an influence the Anglo-Saxon world view exercises upon the rest of the world through this de facto control of much intellectual thinking. I do not criticize or voice any other kind of discontent — it is what it is — but signal this side effect. In itself it is one more reason to look upon how Asia will develop over the next twenty-five years.

My luck has been to work at the Institute of Southeast Asian Studies in Singapore (ISEAS) while at the same time teaching at Singapore Management University (SMU) and being Chairman of the advisory board to the Asia Research Center, Copenhagen Business School. This of course opens a window to the mindset of people living in Asia even if it cannot substitute for knowing Asian languages.

My first debt of gratitude goes to ISEAS and its Director, Ambassador K. Kesavapany, who from the first moment took an active interest in the project and encouraged me along the whole process. His support has been invaluable. I am also grateful for many talks with the Chairman of ISEAS, Professor Wang Gungwu that broadened my horizon and gave much inspiration. Inside the institute Arun Bala took an interest in my project and served over many meetings as a kind of sparring partner and thus helped convince me that such a book would actually be of interest. Many other colleagues offered help, assistance, and comments.

I am grateful to Professor Wang Gungwu, Chairman, East Asian Institute, National University of Singapore for having taken upon himself the task of writing the foreword pinpointing the main elements of my analysis.

A large number of friends took upon themselves the tedious task of reading all or part of the book. Louis-Francois Pau agreed to go through the text with a fine-toothed comb rescuing me from many embarrassing mistakes plus unsubstantiated statements and not the least added substance to many "loose" views. His contribution cannot be overestimated, nor can his wisdom and knowledge. Terence Chong, Aaron Maniam, Hans Peter Jensen, Pang Eng Fong, Yeo Lay Hwee, Asad-ul Iqbal Latif, and Lars Juhl Frandsen all read the text and provided feedback. S. Gopinathan and John Petersen kindly agreed to participate in a seminar organized by ISEAS to set out the main lines of the book project and S. Gopinathan helped me with the chapter on education as did Jørn Skovgaard. Daniel Saddhu gave advice about sources for outsourcing, Michael Yap helped me with the section about religions and philosophies, Jack Knetsch about some aspects concerning economic theory, Peter Newman about megacities, Ken Wye Saw about ITC, Ove Kaj Pedersen about democracy, and Zhen Yong Nian about certain aspects of social services in China. Nguyen Tho Hieu helped me to overcome IT difficulties. They all vastly improved the text and what is left of mistakes or omissions is wholly my sole responsibility.

Many other persons, knowingly or unknowingly, have helped me to form the ideas put into the book. My experience is that ideas are born as a result of interaction with other people and very rarely if at all in an isolated framework. In my own way I believe in "wisdom of the crowd". What other people say makes you respond or penetrates your brain and the words remain there for some time — a gestation period — after which they mature and emerge as a useful output. We may not always know or recognize the origins of our own thinking! In a way I feel myself as a spokesman for the many people who over the years have allocated time and effort to talk with me on subjects directly or indirectly touched upon in the book.

I do not claim "intellectual property rights" to much of the thinking, but perhaps the way I put it together may reflect some "new" thinking.

After much consideration I chose to put the conclusion as the first chapter. The reader in a hurry and only interested in the broad outline of what I term a new world view or a new model can stop there, but I hope the appetite grows sufficiently when reading to tempt the reader to find out how I came to these conclusions. The subsequent chapters present a large amount of statistical data and analyses about Asia, which many readers might find interesting and helpful. The price may be a slight degree of repetition, but I hope the reader will bear with that.

The book draws on observation over most of my life as a diplomat and academic, but the writing itself took place from late summer 2007 to autumn 2009. The manuscript was handed over to the publisher at the end of October 2009. Events or statistics after summer 2009 have accordingly not been taken into account.

My wife, Thanh Kieu Møller, has supported me with all her love. No man can ask for more.

# 1

# THE FUTURE WORLD VIEW

The dominating world view since 1750 is coming to an end. It was based upon science, industrialization, logic, rationality in philosophy, the nation state, availability of resources, and the free market model. Their interaction formed a coherent and well-functioning model. With strong growth and rising populations Asia will encounter the problems flowing from the end of the model sooner and harder than other regions. Risks or volatilities surges may happen as a result. Ancient religions and philosophies anchored in a world view of harmony between man and nature may help Asia to discover a different and new growth model reflecting scarcities of resources, mutual respect and harmony, and the need for ecological growth. The trend for objectivity as a valid, yes, undisputed, basis for arguments to give to subjectivity (rationality giving way to values) may enhance the move towards such a new world view.

Asia must transform itself from sleeping partner in economic globalization and also one of the main beneficiaries with little or no influence on decision making (and little or no wish to wield such influence), into the main beneficiary and the main playmaker of globalization. Leadership is in essence the political will to forego national or domestic benefits in order to shoulder burdens to uphold the system. To step into that role a nation or group of nations or Asia must have a clear and unequivocal concept — a grand design — of the system it wants to unfold. That will help to enrol Africa, Latin America, and the Middle East in globalization, thus keeping the fundamental skeleton of globalization intact while at the same time switching it from a Western-controlled vehicle to a genuine global one.

The encouraging and promising perspective is that it can be done. It depends fundamentally on Asia and Asians whether it will be done. To succeed

1

Asia and the Asians must "read" the Zeitgeist[1] and turn an epistemological recognition into practical and effective policies.

The scenario can be compared to what happened 250 years ago.

## THE OUTGOING WORLD VIEW

In the middle of the eighteenth century the prevailing world view started to crack. New technology using power (energy) made it cheaper and easier to extract raw materials. New agricultural methods opened the door for higher productivity. The impact of the settlements across the Atlantic had so far been of small significance for Europe, but now the number of people living in North America started to reach a critical mass where more propitious conditions delivered a rising and higher productivity from the soil.

The fruits of the Age of Enlightenment paved the way for an economic revolution in a broader sense than just the industrial revolution by highlighting objectivity — facts and logic — as the guiding principles for economic behaviour and governance. A key element was that the Enlightenment and Renaissance gave to philosophers, priests, and thinkers direct links to and influence on those in power so that there was a conceptual vision and cohesion in place. Amateurism and decisions by chance gave way to the drive for and acceptance of a philosophic and scientific foundation behind society's development.

The world moved into an era of plenty and consumerism for an unprecedented two hundred years, with easy and cheap access to raw materials, no constraints on food production, and a high economic growth interrupted from time to time by a recession, or even worse, a depression that was brushed away by an unstoppable drive for growth.

Human civilization started to change, bringing about much more civilized relations among human beings. War was still an instrument, but the underlying philosophy elucidated how human relations could be improved. The fashionable outlook was basically to improve human relations even if deviations and double standards blurred the picture somewhat.

On the other hand mankind's relations with nature worsened. Nature became an inexhaustible reservoir of raw materials. The somewhat naive and simplistic view was that there was and always would be enough, and rather primitive business people found it easy and very rewarding to prey on them. The opening up of North America unquestionably contributed to this swing in mentality. The big country with its vast resources and plentiful land promised to deliver everything without any time limit, and as there was no existing intellectual framework for this belief, a new one called capitalism was born. The European settlers kept going west to put new land under the plough and the rewards were terrific. Logistics and transport brought these to the markets in the east and in Europe.

Human beings no longer needed to compete or fight to get access to resources. There was enough, so the concept of survival changed from simple physical survival to quality of life (for most of the industrial era and for most populations, this is perceived to mean material living standard). Economics became the religion instead of the values, cultural and human relations cores of previous philosophies. Physical cruelty was not needed anymore although some (perhaps many) will take the view that psychological cruelty replaced it. Economics duly provided the tools for comparing living standards, stepping in with yardsticks, measurements, definitions, and concepts such as the consumption theory. The age of conspicuous consumption and of "keeping up with the Joneses" had arrived.

Compared with before 1750, humans started to treat one another in a more civilized manner, but broke the contract with nature for a sustainable use of nature's resources that allows them to regenerate. They also started to reproduce less, as the focus became the distribution of riches rather than making the effort to reproduce and work to keep the contract with nature.

The science of economics[2] marched on in the footsteps of industrialization to deliver an intellectual/academic base for nations and states to organize and implement industrialization, complete with the transportation and logistics involved in spreading the fruit of higher production.

Economics became a science or a tool geared to growth theories, distribution theories and availability of resources, albeit at a price, but not really subjugated to constraints. Furthermore economics never really got beyond classifying individuals as the cornerstone for theories about production and consumption, and was incapable of incorporating social relations other than as side effects. The foundation was analysis of labour productivity or capital productivity telling what one more unit of labour or one more unit of capital under the supervision of a human being could produce, how much individuals would consume more under various circumstances, and how assets were kept by individuals. Acquisition (investment theory) and the distribution of benefits and the individual formed the whole conceptual basis for the science of economics as it has developed over more than 200 years.

It is true that economics incorporated what was labelled external diseconomies and, later, elements of environmental protection, but these were always regarded as side effects that did not interfere with or crowd out growth, productivity, distribution, and consumption, which maintain their grip on the thrust of the thinking.

It fitted nicely in with Darwin's[3] theory about survival of the fittest. In the science of economics the fittest was the individual, and the survivor was the human being capable of the highest production and/or productivity.

The nation state and industrialization supported each other and were followed by globalization steered by the nation state, which transferred the nation state's political, judicial, and administrative mechanisms from the national to the international/global level.

This political infrastructure was consciously and continuously validated by the science of economics bringing out theories and proofs about growth and productivity which showed how the nation state could keep development on an upwards growth curve.

As natural resources were depleted without any consideration for their sustainability, benefits could be distributed to the expanding population, centred on consumption, which highlighted the material well-being and rising living standard for the individual and/or the family.

For people living today this model and its underlying foundation of epistemological nature seems natural. It is coherent and its various elements support and sustain each other. In a longer term perspective, however, this constitutes a new paradigm for human behaviour, people's attitude towards one another, and the human relationship with nature.

Today the question that confronts us is whether circumstances have now changed to reinstall fundamental elements of the model before 1750, or whether the materialistic economic model of the past 250 years will continue in its basic form, albeit, modified under the impact of evolution, of course.

It seems unlikely, nay, almost impossible, to see a continuation of the existing model. How can an enrolment of several hundred millions of people into a mass consumption market be sustainable with economic, ecological, and social equilibrium? What may be termed the American model could work for a limited period of time — perhaps long, but limited — and only for the United States, with its vast resources and a mindset forged by the idea that resources are unlimited. A simple calculation of increased use of resources demonstrates that something has to give, or rather, change fundamentally over the next twenty-five years to avoid an implosion. There are so many figures available showing how increased population, combined with higher income per capita, is incompatible with what nature put at our disposal. Suffice here to mention that the carbon dioxide ($CO_2$) equivalent from producing half a pound of potatoes is 0.13 pound. To produce half a pound of beef, 1.90 pounds of $CO_2$ equivalent is needed — 14.6 times as high.

The argument is often heard — and scepticism is a welcome attitude when digesting all these forecasts and calculations — that since Malthus more than 200 years ago,[4] so many theories and predictions have painted doom and gloom, so why take them seriously this time.[5]

It is often forgotten or overlooked that in the world as Malthus knew it, he was actually right and not wrong. The main reason that his thesis about shortage of food did not materialize[6] was:

- New territories were opened up in North America, Australia, New Zealand, and South Africa, as well as what is often overlooked, including Southern Russia and Ukraine, which have extremely good agricultural land, making it possible to increase agricultural production on a scale not seen before — or afterwards.
- New technologies (harvesting, self-reaping, irrigation) improved productivity phenomenally and was supplemented by breakthroughs in transport and logistics linking these new areas to the market.
- The science of economics revealing how to manage production, and the market providing tools that make it profitable for producers to produce more, consumers to buy more, and middlemen in wholesale, transport, etc. to earn their share of the emerging wealth.

The world of today is not a stagnant world, but it is difficult to see how it can deliver path-breaking changes similar to those taking place in the nineteenth century. In fact even larger scale changes are needed now, with the much higher number of people involved.

While the age of objectivity may not be entirely over, the preponderance objectivity had 200 years ago and managed to enforce on theoretical frameworks seems more contested at the beginning of the twenty-first century.[7]

Science itself, and especially philosophy, no longer holds the same illustrious place in higher education as it used to. This may yet change, but over recent decades there has been a marked decline in interest among young people in these fields. Politicians show less willingness to fund basic research in these areas, frequently questioning the use, or maybe profitability rather, of such research. Economics, with its stronger focus on short-term benefits and profitability, has worked against pure science as a guideline for budget allocations, and also seems to have served better the political ambitions or promises of decision makers. Admittedly there are many opinions about the long-term implications of these changing attitudes. But it does not seem far-fetched to fear a societal posture which turns away from a scientific and philosophical foundation for policies and attitudes, leaving objectivity defenceless against the maelstrom of emotions, feelings, and religious attitudes gaining ground all over the globe.

Science itself has since the Heisenberg uncertainty principle in quantum mechanics from 1925 moved away from pure objectivity towards as the words indicate uncertainty and more inaccuracy. In scientific terms this is obviously a watershed, but it may be even more important in implanting the fundamental philosophy that things are not so certain and accurate as science over several hundreds of years had taught. In 1958 Norwood Russell Hanson put forward his theory that what we see is not objective, but the result of observing something depends to a certain degree on the observer; what our senses receive is actually filtered sensory information.

Without an objectivity that is rooted in science, with its proofs and scientific methodology of universal validation, truth becomes a much more difficult and blurred notion which allows for the contestation of science and scientifically-supported positions without any need for evidence to explain why they are being contested.[8] The ability to think and reason in a stringent, logical, and coherent way loses ground — which is also seen in higher education under the influence of the Internet.[9]

The political steering model today suffers from this lack of stringency in the sense that the quest for facts and rational thinking behind and separated from political views, no longer seems to rule debate. Much more fluid debates are gaining ground, making it much less clear what political leaders want to do and why. Tolerance and respect for others tend to be misunderstood as being synonymous with accepting other points of views without questioning their foundation, or even shying away from contradicting others and pointing out holes in their cases for fear of offending them. Such attitudes have nothing to do with tolerance and respect, but reflect a lack of intellectual discipline.

Politics and political models have never been dominated and steered by science or sought scientific foundation, but the intellectual discipline transposed from the position of science to political thinking and behaviour in society has certainly resulted in a model repudiating solutions and decisions by chance. This does not seem to be the case anymore.

The finding that the new generation — Digital Grown Ups — is more inclined to do multitasking, scan material for what is of emotional interest and can be used here and now, and has the ability to combine inputs from various sources, means that their brains work in a different way from the way the brains of people brought up in the industrial society work. The mindset is different and if we assume that mindset steers political models, it seems unavoidable that the increasing emphasis on multitasking, emotional and role playing behaviour and other similar activities, rather than on deep, reflective skills aimed at exploring one particular subject, will lead to another model. And it seems just as unavoidable to draw the conclusion that this new political model will be less rooted in objectivity than the science-based model proved to be.

We do not know of course that politics based less on objectivity will be less successful. In fact, religions based on concepts, fiction, and some principles, are as influential as politics. We do know, however, that it would be a different model governing in a different context and anchored in a different system of selecting and electing political leaders.

But successful or not, it would be a dangerous model to say the least, for not guaranteeing fair and equal access to culture and information as emotions or policies may easily rule out such access (see the film *Fahrenheit 951* in which books are ruled out, linked by some to an idea which some believe refers to the business controls over eBook content).

What the world is seeing these past years is the end of the existing model and the attempts to forge a new model in new, unexpected, and different circumstances. This means that the rise of Asia takes place at the same time as the model underpinning industrialization, its technology, political and technical infrastructure, and international organization, breaks down.

Examining Asia's prospects in the context and light of the existing model — analysing whether the growth models, distribution models, consumption theories etc. can adjust to what is happening in Asia — is not very helpful. Such analyses can tell us where Asia is right now, but the important point here is Asia's capability not only to adjust, but to give birth to a new model that responds to the challenges of the twenty-first century.

Broadly speaking, the world, after 200 years of accumulating wealth, faces a stagnant or falling population and moves towards an economic structure respecting the United Nations' definition of sustainability,[10] basically resembling the world as it was before 1750, when living standards were a lot lower and the large majority of the world population lived at or under what is now classified as the poverty level.

The potential decline of the age of objectivity may go hand in hand with a change in economic model the same way that industrialization, with science as a driving force, and governance, calling for a mindset reflecting science and fact-based decisions, went hand in hand.

## THE CURRENT ECONOMIC MODEL

### The Starting Point

In the middle of the eighteenth century, agricultural advances saw Europe replacing old methods to maintain the fertility of land. Due to the quantity and quality of land in North America, these methods were not adopted by American farmers as there was little or no incentive for them to use them. American soil was rich and plentiful, and when yields started to fall, the American farmer simply moved further westward to put new land under the plough. To work more and spend money and time on new inventions to get more out of existing land was not profitable in a country where high quality land was plentiful. This philosophy that has probably stayed in the American mindset became known as "land butchery".[11]

When moving into the industrial age, the United States had plenty of oil (and coal) while world prices for commodities were low. Only recently has some parts of the country — and U.S. society — become aware of the need to husband resources, but fundamentally the American economy and the American way of life has not deviated from its original track. This is nowadays a completely unsuitable model as scarcities and environmental concerns force a fundamental recasting of relative prices.

China has gone through several dynasties that framed its economic development. Each dynasty brought growth and wealth, but economic progress was interrupted when the dynasty fell. The relevant economic and sociological observation here is that when this happened, wealth was destroyed and the ruling class wiped out, opening the door for a new and more competent ruling class to take over and create wealth out of the ruins. In this particular way, China swung to and fro like a pendulum instead of following a more or less unbroken path of development. Each dynasty represented an era of wealth and prosperity, but every dynasty did not build on the preceding one. Japan until the 1870s more or less also worked this way with its shogunates, and India had many fiefdoms of short and localized duration.

Walt Rostow[12] was arguably the first economist who put forward a global "growth" model — geographically and conceptually.[13] Broadly speaking he sees growth in the following stages: take-off, drive to technological maturity, and mass consumption. The beauty of his model is that it provides a tool for classifying countries to see how they are moving towards economic development. The weakness is, of course, that not all countries may follow the curve at the same speed and some countries may for non-economic reasons experience economic development without following these stages. Another weakness is that it does not address the social benefits and costs from economic development at all.

The paradigm is changing very fast. Countries cannot adopt an economic policy out of step with economic globalization. Economic growth gets more and more linked to societal foundation such as social capital and social coherence. Openness to new trends and patterns from outside move into the picture as determining factors, but fall outside most economic theoretical foundations, often disregarding foundations in philosophy, social sciences, psychology, and anthropology.

One of the great revelations of recent decades is the interdisciplinary approach as a key to understanding and explaining what drives economic growth. It is not simply a question of tax rates, depreciation allowances, etc. The effectiveness of the same economic policy instrument depends upon that country's societal structure. Many Westerners watching Asia observe that the insulation of its buildings leaves much to be desired. They argue that over a number of years savings through better insulation will actually prove profitable. This is well and good, but such advice does not take into account that many buildings in fast-growing economies in Asia will not exist for a period long enough to make the initial investment to insulate profitable. Seen from the developer's point of view, the payback period is too long and the developer cannot transfer the costs to the buyer. The advice to insulate is thus technically correct, but in many cases, useless, unless accompanied by measures that either make it profitable or obligatory in one way or another.

## Scarcities

The combination of rising populations, high growth in income for a large number of people, and the realization that resources are limited, plus the price on a clean environment, form a new quadruple of factors for economic growth that require a redrafting of most models to reflect a new price structure. Labour costs were, to a certain extent, an artificial price not reflecting the cost, but what society agreed was the relevant wage structure to ensure the politically-preferred distribution of income. The wage rate should, according to neoclassical economic theory, reflect the marginal value-added of labour, but few will maintain that this is the case. Resources were priced at costs of extraction and loan/capital financing here and now without regard to consequences for future supply. The result has been a price structure that makes labour expensive compared with resources, which raises obstacles for conserving energy and saving resources if this required the use of more manpower.

Until about the middle of the twenty-first century, a shortage of labour supply is unlikely, as populations continue to grow in South Asia and Africa. Even if labour costs in Europe and possibly also China and the United States are influenced by perhaps a reversal of past demographic trends, it is difficult to see global labour costs going up. However, there is a rising floor for wage levels unfolding globally, due to rising social, pension, housing costs, and higher taxes.

The combination of demographies and resources makes the existing economic models for growth obsolete, and calls for models using less resources and more manpower.[14] Resources should be priced in a way that takes into account their availability over a longer future time span. Even if they are cheap currently, their costs would be augmented by growing investments in new or alternative resources. Wage costs on the other hand may show exactly the opposite picture, reflecting that labour is a renewable production factor even if current manpower is not.

This calls into question the very concept of economic growth. So far conventional wisdom has classified growth as a larger quantity of goods and services because economic theory stipulates that the ultimate object of all economic activity is consumption. Investment fitted in with this picture, because, even if it does not increase consumption now, it enhances production capacity for the future thus enlarging potential future consumption.

But if demographies and resources work in tandem to show that economics no longer controls the picture and that, regardless of various theories, consumption cannot continue to rise, what then? The current model tells us not to define growth as higher production capacity at the current time, but to sketch a new model that makes it possible to deliver higher consumption over a longer time span, and maybe abandoning the current concept of consumption, and search instead for another definition that makes it more sustainable for a global economy that is reorganizing economic activity to bring it in line with limited resources. Compared with the situation pre-1750, the perception and, consequently, the relative prices of labour and resources have been reversed.

Wealth and growth may in future turn out to be measurable in terms of future production capacity, that takes into account efficiency of production, with regard to use of resources, and access to resources inside and outside the nation. A new definition may look at how efficiently a nation squeezes more production out of one unit of resource.[15] Growth can then be measured in terms of increased ability to that effect.

For some this may sound fanciful, but you need to be very optimistic to believe that China and India, with approximately a total population of 2.5 billion people by about 2050, can follow the same growth pattern as Europe did from 1800 to 1900, and the United States from 1900 to 2000.

Demographies will turn the tables even more if we dare to cast a glance on the other side of 2050. At about that time the world will enter a situation where civilization has never been before: stagnant or even falling global population.

Individual countries have tried to get out of this trap through immigration, to increase population, giving credence to the postulate that the world has never seen a growing economy with stagnant or falling population. Immigration is possible in a world with a growing global population that allows individual countries to fall back on that policy, but it cannot work with a falling global population.

The lid has been lifted from this can of worms, but this is mostly confined to the United States and seen as a generational conflict. With a smaller share of the population unable or unwilling to pay for welfare benefits to the elderly, the question arises as to how to maintain economic growth with fewer people. Should people be made to extend their working age.[16] Such analyses are useful, interesting, and to the point. They underline the fact that existing social models, in particular, schemes for welfare benefits, are unsustainable in view of the burden changing demographics brings along.[17] They forward pertinent ideas for solutions, but they all operate inside the existing model that they focus on adjustments to maintain the model. However, the fundamental issue is to shift to a new model that takes into account how falling populations and resource scarcities are now replacing the situation with rising populations and cheap resources.

## Globalization Changes the Picture

### Global Economics, but no Global Economic Policy

In the economic model dominated by the nation state, policymakers took decisions and citizens inside that particular nation state felt the pain or enjoyed the benefits. If the people thought that policymakers got it wrong, they could unseat them on the next occasion — be it an election or the appointment of a central bank governor. The system was logical and evenhanded. In the global world there is growing asymmetry between economic policymakers and those who feel the result of their decisions. No country, not even the United States, ought to map out an economic policy without regard to the effect this has abroad. But at the moment, there is no accountability for policymakers vis-à-vis the global community and/or other countries.

As the decision makers are not answerable to people outside national borders, they, of course, steer a national economic policy. This is what they are expected, asked, and paid to do. The consequence can easily be decisions good for one country, but having negative repercussions for the global economy. The global economic system is inherently unstable with policy decisions standing in the way of general equilibrium instead of moving towards it.

In a nutshell, we may have a global economy, but no mechanism for a global economic policy.

How this plays out becomes much clearer when looking at economic policy decisions and the debate in most countries. Many, maybe most, economic policy decisions are taken with a view to improve a country's position vis-à-vis other countries. So in a situation where country A and country B are in equilibrium with both doing well, everything is fine. But let us suppose that country B gets into difficulties, maybe because of labour costs that are too high. To get back to a state of equilibrium, it may depreciate its currency to improve its competitiveness, with the effect that its exports jump and production goes up. Country A's production goes down, however, because its exports cannot sell any more. Now Country A may experience inbalance and have to redress balance-of-payment disequilibrium. In this way a musical chairs game goes on. This is in fact what is happening; countries pass their burdens to other countries. The system does not work towards a state of general (global) equilibrium, but is governed by countries individually seeking equilibrium. Theoretically it should be possible to move towards general equilibrium if nation states laid down national economic policies that take into consideration their impact on other countries.[18] This is, however, not the case and the search for national equilibrium keeps the global system unbalanced.

The intellectual background for this is that fundamentally the global system is designed to further the policy objectives of the nation state and not the international/global community. If put together, the policy objectives of the majority of nation states would be irreconcilable, that is their goals for growth, employment, and balance of payments cannot possibly all be fulfilled, which precludes a balanced global economy.

Global and regional economic policy institutions such as the International Monetary Fund (IMF) and the World Bank are active in pushing and helping nation states achieve balance by stepping in with assistance. The forms of economic policy they advocate would in most cases bring about a balance for that particular country, but almost inevitably shift the burden of adjustment to other countries. These institutions shuffle production and employment around from country to country without having the competence and instruments to sketch a global economic policy.

Most observers would think that economic globalization brings about a synchronized global business cycle meaning the large majority of national economies swing in tune with one another, all going up and down at the same time. But a look at growth rates for the major economies over the last twenty years reveals that this is not, in fact, the case. There is no such thing as a global business cycle. Recently[19] there is a tendency to synchronize business cycles between groups of national economies. This may be taken as a step towards global business cycles, but it may also, and more likely, augur a splitting up of the global economy into segments, with each one living its own life. This trend seems the more likely one if recent developments of global trade is taken into account, which show more intratrade among developing countries and emerging economies, than between these groups and industrialized nations.[20]

It is exacerbated by policy stance and policy options in the wake of the global recession beginning in 2007. Between 2008–10, the budget deficit among industrialized G-20 countries is expected to grow from 4 per cent of gross domestic product (GDP) to approximately 7 per cent. For emerging G-20 countries the corresponding figures are nil for 2008, and only 2 per cent expected for 2010. Government debt among industrialized G-20 countries is expected to rise from 80 per cent to 100 per cent, but almost stable, fluctuating around 35 per cent of GDP, for emerging G-20 countries.[21] Politically the reverberating around the globe is that unsound and irresponsible policies are pursued by the industrialized world, with the United States in the forefront, while prudent policies have become the pride of emerging G-20 countries.

It is generally agreed that the wealth of nations rests upon economic globalization, but there are actually very few instruments available to economic globalization to defend itself against policies threatening to rock the boat.

### Regionalization

The triumvirate of economic globalization, the unsatisfactory performance of global governance, and the role of the nation state is likely to generate a new global steering system with less emphasis on globalization and more on regionalization. This is already seen with the European Union, ASEAN, and several other regional institutions/organizations.

Trade, services, and investment have all gone global and enjoyed the liberalization and deregulation. They are steered by the market mechanism (profits) chasing opportunities wherever they are to enhance their performance and augment their profit. Research and culture, however, have not yet taken this step, thereby holding full-scale development back.

Nation states are out of the game because — except in a few cases — they do not have the power and strength to break away from the demands of economic globalization. Even China and India are moving towards accepting a fully open and liberalized economy vis-à-vis economic globalization. There are indeed very few cases where a nation state has been able to deliberalize without paying a heavy price for doing so.[22]

The attempts to forge a "nation state" global steering system, however commendable and praiseworthy, have not succeeded. The international institutions have done their best to "govern", but events prove that it is not good enough. Nation states are unwilling to transfer sufficient decision-making powers and competences to global/international/regional institutions. Lack of confidence and trust in the abilities of international institutions to act in conformity with the exigencies of globalization holds nation states back. Many countries see these institutions not necessarily as the auxiliary arm of the United States, but of the global edition of American capitalism. Asia has seen several attempts to get out of this paradigm, i.e. the Indian model pursued under Prime Minister Nehru, but none of them has proved successful. The non-aligned movement is still alive, but has never really been able to table a viable alternative.

The likely outcome of this somewhat confused picture is a combination of continued economic globalization, regionalization instead of global governance, and further weakening of the nation state.

There are certainly chinks in the armour of economic globalization such as inequality, but at the end of the day it is the best model for economic growth, and what the world needs in the coming decades to solve its problems is quite simply growth. And that is the decisive parameter. It is unlikely that attempts to tinker with or find another model will be forthcoming, and if so, it is unlikely that they will succeed.

By choosing regionalization instead of globalization, nation states stand a much better chance of framing an international governance system that works according to the problems they face and that offers solutions which, although not approved by global economic benchmarks, take into account political, social, and cultural imperatives. The Europeans are in the forefront with the European Union, but all over the world regional organizations are popping up like mushrooms. In Asia we have ASEAN (Association of Southeast Asian Nations), the East Asian Summit, South Asian Cooperation, and APEC (Asia Pacific Economic Cooperation). In the Middle East we find the Gulf Cooperation. In Africa, there are various embryonic organizations. In Latin America, we have MERCOSUR (Southern Common Market in English) and several others. In the Western hemisphere, there is NAFTA (North American Free Trade Agreement). They are all in different stages of the life cycle of regionalization, but they have one thing in common: Nation states are gradually losing faith in the global system and falling back on regional groupings that are more malleable and more likely to be seen as "their" organization, compared with remote global institutions.

Regional bodies may produce a slightly smaller growth rate than global organizations, but may offer other advantages such as making the member states more comfortable and, above all, have a different and higher level of respect for each other. A side effect may be closer integration among adjacent nation states, which forces them into a state of higher mutual trust and confidence, thus reducing the likelihood of conflict.

It is a good question why this has not happened before. The answer is probably that until recently — apart from Europe — nation states around the world were economically too weak to break away from the politically correct line of seeking solutions inside global institutions. Now they have this strength and start to act accordingly. The impending shortages of most resources may also act as a catalyst for stronger regionalization. It may be easier to build trust among adjacent nation states than on a global level, even if conflicts normally take place among neighbours.

Nation states around the globe are at different stages of their life cycles. The European nation state is on the downward slope of the life cycle of the nation state. Most nation states in Asia are on the upward slope, having been created after decolonization mainly as a vehicle to provide infrastructure (technical and administratively) for independence first, economic development next, and to emulate what former European imperial powers had done when embarking on their development. The United States is hardly a genuine nation state in the original European mould.

In the longer run regionalization may be seen as a step towards global governance where regional organizations play the role of building blocks. When sufficient experience is gained the next step could be a link up among the regional institutions to form some kind of global governance.

## The Counter-attack of Commodity Prices, Trade Policy, Investment Policy

Relative factor prices between commodities, capital, and labour show that the highest remuneration has been allocated to labour followed by capital, with commodities at the bottom. Production processes have been designed to that effect, which means the world lives with plants that are intensive in their unconstrained use of commodities, regarded as a cheap and expendable resource, capital, less so, even if it is also classified as an expendable resource, and labour seen as a costly production factor.

Global terms of trade after having for two centuries — since industrialization — favoured industrial countries, now turn around to favour commodity exporting countries.[23] A whole range of issues, which hitherto were taken for granted, will change such as the political role of the global system, production methods, trade policies, and the supply chain.

The new paradigm turns the tables around, from distribution of benefits to burden sharing. Scarcity of commodities and the need for a clean environment mean that global growth may not continue at the same high level anymore. It will cost more to produce one unit of the end product, at least for the manufacturing sector, and probably also for other economic sectors due to sectoral interplay. At the same time allocations of resources to cope with cleaning the environment, climate change, etc. channel resources away from the individual citizen to public consumption.

Production processes that are not adjusted to this new pattern will lose competitiveness, as the higher commodity prices will price them out of the market. Countries not adjusting in one way or another will likewise lose their place in the economic ranking. Obviously this shift will benefit commodity exporting countries and put economic strains on commodity importing countries. It has been seen, however, that adjusting to such changes may open a door to growth, so it does not mean that commodity importing countries are out of the game — they are only if they do not adjust. And worst hit would be commodity importing as well as intellectual capital importing countries.

Consumer preferences may also turn in the same direction, enhancing the pressure on business and countries to adjust production processes and plants, as well as use research as a driver for intellectual property rights. The question is to what degree this will take place, not whether it does or not. When we think about the rise of the consumer mass on the scale the world has in store for us over the next twenty-five years, this question of degree may matter more than in former and existing economic models.

For more than sixty years[24] the world has laboured in the same stony vineyard of dismantling import barriers. Just when celebrations are due, a new trade policy pattern is emerging: export restrictions and export tariffs.

They are, in fact, the twins of the new age of scarcity. For more than 200 years it was a buyer's market and he could set conditions, terms and prices; the seller had little choice, but to comply. Buyers could — and did — play suppliers against one another and took advantage of the situation to exercise downward pressure on prices. Now global trade and economics are making it a seller's market, with strong repercussions on international trade policy. Asian countries are in the forefront as potential major players in this new game.

The tide is turning and those who suffered will try to get back what they lost. There is no reason to expect countries in possession of scarce goods to refrain from using their possession of scarce goods to get higher revenue through higher prices. Why should they? Trade policy will be one of several quivers in their arsenal.

Export restrictions can and will be used. Economics spell out that if supply goes down, prices go up. Raw material producers may follow in the footsteps of oil exporters to jack up the price of commodities for export, while keeping their price for domestic consumption low. Export earnings will boom and lower real wages compared with other countries will improve competitiveness.

As commodity exporters raise export prices, export earnings are given a boost. Low domestic prices on commodities financed by higher export earnings enhance competitiveness in other economic sectors.[25] Importing countries such as Europe, Japan, and the United States will see their competitiveness eroded by higher prices pushing wage levels up, and a deterioration of terms of trade eating into their national incomes. Most of Asia with China, India, and Korea in the forefront will be hit.

The world had better brace itself for a totally new paradigm for international trade and trade policy, triggered by commodity exporters starting to play the game used against them to their advantage. Winners in Asia will be most of Central Asia and, to a certain extent, some Southeast Asian nations. Paradoxically the main events may be seen outside the pure trade policy area.

*First*, fear of scarcities or rising prices may drive the main manufacturing countries such as China to seek control over supplies of commodities, buy natural resources in other countries, and interfere in takeover battles among commodity exporters. In fact it already has. It does not mean that they want to exercise price discrimination to their own advantage, but it does mean that they acquire the economic power to do so.

*Second*, according to reports, oil rich countries with no agricultural sector themselves are starting to buy farmland around the world to secure their supply of food and avoid future high food prices. This augurs a completely new pattern for international investment, with not only economic, but also political and social overtones.

It won't be long before target countries in question guess the intention of these and it is unlikely that they will accept the consequences. After all it will deprive them of what could turn out to be the family silver. But how can such investments be prevented in a world where international capital movements are free of restrictions? The answer is not far off: they may start to question the rules and opt for rolling back the global liberalization of capital movements. If, or rather when, it happens, basic elements of the existing rules for trade and international investment will be questioned.

*Third*, one of the revelations from the preceding twenty-five years has been the elimination of transport costs as a significant factor in the calculation of the price of the end product offered on the market. Of a price for a shirt selling for US$25, ocean transport costs may amount to as little as 0.85 per cent.[26] The combination of container technology and ICT (information and computer technology) as a steering system for this kind of transport has revolutionized logistics and made it possible to exploit the international division of labour fully.

What has not really been understood is that this model, like the production processes, was based on cheap commodities and, in particular, cheap oil. These two factors were the flywheel for global logistics and the global supply chain. They reduced transport costs to a negligible share of total costs.

The transport sector will unquestionably try to use new technology and modernize itself to absorb as much of the rising costs as it can, but there are limits to what can be done. Investments take time and cost a lot of money. So even if some of the costs can be absorbed, it will take time. Meanwhile manufacturing and commodity exporters will have started a reallocation of their activities to take the changed terms of trade into account, especially local or regional trade patterns. They cannot afford to wait to find out how effective the transport sector is in its endeavours to ameliorate transport productivity.

The consequence will be a shift towards production nearer to the site of commodities and/or the market to reduce transport costs, as well as a cut in the number of production sites. The threshold for determining when it is profitable to put parts of the production process in geographical places requiring transport afterwards will be higher.

Outsourcing or offshoring will not, as predicted by a number of economists,[27] start to take off in the coming years. On the contrary, the outsourcing of jobs in the manufacturing sector has probably come to a standstill. Price sensitive production has already been outsourced and what remains is manufacturing that competes on parameters other than price and these are not suited to being outsourced. It is much more likely that standard outsourcing of jobs will be shuffled around among emerging market economies and shift from countries with rising wage cost (maybe China) to countries with lower wage costs (maybe India and Vietnam, possibly Africa and parts of South America). Another story is outsourcing in the service sector, but here the picture is more blurred as most services do not compete on price to the same extent as manufactured goods. Rising commodity prices will reinforce the trend about outsourcing to be analysed in Chapter 3.

It looks like the most probable outcome will be a higher geographical concentration of manufacturing to save costs and reduce the need for transport. The supply chain will become shorter and fewer goods will be moved from place to place. Economically the benchmark for changing in competitiveness will go up, forcing countries to work harder to gain competitiveness for goods competing on costs.

## *Internationalism Exposed*

The salient lines of the old model turned around nationalism, pursuit of national interests, and defence of national sovereignty. These elements, woven together inside a philosophical and intellectual framework defined by Prussian thinker Carl von Clausewitz,[28] sketch strategies around crisis — conflict — confrontation in a nation state world that ultimately lead to war. This model hinged on the assumption, which generally speaking proved to be true over the last 200 years, that nation states strive to enrich themselves at the cost of adjacent nation states. One nation state's gain is another nation state's loss.[29]

The salient lines of a new model is guided by the emergence of transnational forces, supranational enterprises, international organizations, cross-border pressure groups, and multinational civic societies. The setting is completely new with a strategic thinking around cooperation — compromise — consensus pointing towards some kind of global governance. Such a model and way of thinking opens the door for a plus sum game in the sense that all participants stand to gain, and at the same time. Conflict in such a model will not enrich even the winner, but impoverish all; cooperation will increase wealth for all, even those appearing to be losers.

To ensure the workings of a global setting or global model, three elements need to be accepted:

*First*, interventionism or right to interfere, defined as the right of the global community to defend itself against policies by individual nation states threatening to undermine the well functioning of the global community and global economy. The tables are turned. Formerly the nation state used sovereignty to defend itself against unwarranted intervention from the outside. Now internationalism forces the door open for the global community to intervene inside a nation state to protect internationalism from unilateral national actions or policies.[30]

*Second*, institutionalization, to put in place a framework that will legitimize interventionism. Unless there are procedures for decision making, nation states cannot be expected to go along with interventionism. There must be some kind of global rule set defining what nation states are allowed and not allowed to do.

*Third*, a common set of values as the foundation for global governance and the rule of law. This is probably the most difficult item. It must not be confused with *mondoculture* (a common worldwide cultural pattern) or similar concepts. It is a common perception of how nation states and other players in the global concert see what is permissible and what is not, what acceptable behaviour is and is not.

## Main Structural Weaknesses

### Separation of Economic Powers

Montesquieu wrote his thesis about the separation of executive, legislative, and judicial powers at a time in history when power was associated with the political system. Industrialization has increased wealth thus posing the problem of power based on wealth. Borrowing from Montesquieu we can sketch a separation of economic powers by separating those who posses wealth (the owners), from those who control how the wealth is invested, and a third group — the large number of passive investors. Over the last 200 years there has been no watertight compartments between these three groups, but in reality the segregation worked. When it did not, the result was almost without exception a financial crisis leading to new control measures, which the initiators expected to be more effective and efficient.

Two major problems violate our economic equivalent of Montesquieu's theory of separation as sketched above: anonymous ownership and the blurring of the definition between services serving the public and business activities seeking to maximize profit. The fact that these have jumped from the national to the global level aggravates the threat to stable and balanced societal development. Mostly they are found in the grey area between the traditional public sector and private business, such as airports, toll roads, bridges, telecommunication services, public utilities and now gradually also in hospitals, homes for the elderly and disabled.

i) **Anonymous ownership:** Established owners transfer their ownership to investment funds, many of which are anonymous in the sense that it is difficult to find out who actually controls or owns them, except that their managers become policymakers without constituencies, and with minimal regulation, as they operate in other countries than those whose regulations they are exposed to. This manoeuvre is primarily invented to circumvent regulations aimed at controlling economic activities. It is a mystery why this traffic is allowed to take place, as it is obvious what the objective is, but the ingenuity of people to escape regulation is apparently higher and more effective than the wish of the political system to ensure that its policies are abided by. The result however is that an increasingly large number of businesses in North America, Europe, and gradually also in Asia, is owned and controlled by obscure funds outside normal rules. No economic theory has dealt with this phenomenon to clarify whether, economically, this is profitable, and even less, whether social policies are respected.

There are, however, three seminal changes to analyse.

The *first* is that the well established link between known owners and the employees of a company has broken down. Obscure owners have no particular interest in the company, and even less its employees. Very likely the company is one of many owned by the fund with the intention of selling it if or when a good opportunity arises. The employees do not feel any loyalty to a company whose owners they do not know. An unwritten social contract that has worked since industrialization — even if, admittedly, violent labour market conflicts have taken place — disappears from the scene as one of the pillars of social stability. Consequently the social contract is breaking up, with negative repercussions on nationwide social capital and coherence.

The *second* change is that the concentration of funds, combined with enhanced competition and drive for profit, leads to higher risk taking than prudent behaviour would dictate. The first fund to run a higher risk will normally get away with it because the risk is limited and it is the first to spot the opportunity without going too far in risk taking. The profit for the fund goes up; other funds see that, its stock market sees it, the stock price goes up, and its capitalization and market share go up. Competitors panic. If they do not counter-attack, the fund in question will prosper and they will not. They start to emulate the first fund, but opportunities are now more limited so to seize a profit they need to neglect the risk and sail into uncharted waters. Gradually the whole sector moves into behaviour where risks — without anybody really noticing — mount above what is sustainable. This can go on for quite a while. The fact that these funds in many cases are classified in a way that keeps them outside normal supervision means that supervisory bodies may not know what is going on. Even many of the funds engaged in the game may not themselves know this as the financial assets are sold on and on, so the original debtor has no idea whatsoever who the ultimate creditor is, and financial institutions along the line do not know how many are involved and to what extent they are part of a highly leveraged operation. The financial institutions do not care much about their risks as these are hidden and the stock market heralds the rising profit — at least on paper — and rejoice in seeing market shares *grosso modo* re-established.

Then it bursts as we have seen with the Japanese stock market in 1990, the Japanese property market in 1990, the Long-term Capital Management (LTCM) collapse in 1998,[31] the ICT bubble in 2000, and the property market around sub-prime loans in the United States, Britain, and several other countries, in 2007.

The *third* change is that conventional wisdom would say that as the risks are distributed among a large number of financial institutions, there is no reason to worry. However, it works the other way around. The involvement of many financial institutions means that as soon as signals show that something is wrong, they scramble to get out. The profit motive forces them to do this because a mere few minutes' or even few seconds' advantage in relation to competitors allows one financial institution to minimize losses by transferring them to its competitors.

Central banks step in to calm the markets by making liquidity available. This should make it possible for financial institutions to resume lending, but it does not. Financial institutions hoard the liquidity, fearing that another cycle may hit them and wishing to have enough liquidity to withstand such potential renewed onslaughts. Not only that, they cut down on normal lending and throw the economy into a credit crunch, although there is more than enough liquidity around, except that they keep their liquid assets in their vaults, instead of lending them out.

ii) **Blurring of definition of public services:** The public utility sector was for many years run on the idea that the purpose was to offer services to citizens. The notion of public utility was a part of politics and an important part. Railroads and telecommunications covered remote places; water and electricity were managed according to certain quality criteria, regardless of whether it was profitable or not. These services which have been deregulated have now fallen into the hands of private businesses that do not share these principles. You cannot blame the private businessmen. They have bought a company and they wish to make money for the company, irrespective of the repercussions on the society and community. But they end up working for the banks as many privatized utilities are deeply in debt (high leverage and at high interest rates), so our discussion about investment funds applies here also as the investors whose assets are used as security for these loans are not known.

It is clear, however, that such behaviour has at least two consequences. *First*, because it is unprofitable many sectors or groups of society or the community will not be served any longer. People living in remote places are left to see for themselves how they can maintain contact with other parts of the country. *Second*, even if it can be demonstrated that the management of a toll road or a bridge or an airport is detrimental to society or the country as a whole, there is not much citizens can do about it because ownership has been transferred out of the hands of the public.

The most crucial change may be the breakup of well-established relations between the public and the public sector. In a country such as the United States, there hardly is any public sector. Taken together these two changes will have long-run consequences for social capital and social coherence.[32]

## Shifting from Economics to a Broader Canvass

The role of economic policy was to control total demand and primarily domestic total demand. If domestic demand was too high, inflation and a deficit on balance of payments drove nation states to curb demand. If domestic demand was too low, unemployment and production below total capacity were the negative results and something had to be done to increase the nation states' production without the country falling into the trap of inflation and/or a deficit on its balance of payments.

With the 1980s came the Chinese decision to join economic globalization. That made life much easier for policymakers as Chinese production kept inflation low even if global growth soon reached a level where a comparison with the past would have indicated a risk of inflation. While in theory commodity prices should have gone up, they did not, reinforcing a golden era of high growth and low inflation.

These were fortunate circumstances that will not repeat themselves unless another miraculous age appears, and as experience shows, it is unwise to count on miracles, especially when one has already taken place.

In theory, the current economic policy seemed to work efficiently; in reality it did not. The reason the world moved on in comparative economic balance up to a few years after 2000 was that high global growth and accumulated reserves made adjustment less difficult. By reducing not the absolute figures for the various components of domestic demand, but growth rates, countries could turn this adjustment into a situation of receiving less instead of complete cutbacks. As economic policy was already tuned in with demand adjustment, most countries managed to steer a course which avoided placing heavy burdens on the population.

It became clear, however, that fiscal policy had started to lose some of its effectiveness. In a nation state economy, fiscal policy was an adequate instrument for controlling demand, but in an open economy forming part of the global economy, it was not. High import and export shares of GDP meant that a large part of the effect did not fall on the domestic economy, but on the global economy. Compared with the effect on the nation state economy, a change of one percentage point in GDP now required a much higher level of fiscal intervention to compensate for the share going into the global economy, and that raised the political and social stakes.

Monetary policy followed the same course. Tinkering with interest rates and/or money supply looked good in theory, but the spillover on free capital movement soon produced unwanted effects on the economy, particularly by complicating control over money supply, thus opening the door for credit-based asset speculation.[33]

Exchange rate adjustments did not fare much better than other instruments of economic policy. *First*, most countries preferred adhering to some kind of regional exchange rate cooperation formally or informally, thus limiting the scope for exchange rate adjustments. Experience from, among other things, the European build-up to an economic and monetary union showed how limited the effect of exchange rate adjustment was on real economic factors in the open, global economy. *Second*, most of the manufacturing that competed on price had already been hit by outsourcing. With wage levels in China only a fraction of what was the case in Europe and/or the United States, exchange rate adjustments of what was the norm, that is, 5 or 10 per cent, became rather ineffective.[34]

At the turn of the century, the three basic instruments for economic policy had demonstrated how little they were able to achieve against the backdrop of economic globalization. It might have been different if serious efforts had been put in place to set up regional or even global economic policymaking, but that was not the case.

Gradually nation states were pushed back into using microeconomic policy instruments such as productivity enhancing measures, labour market policies, education, social welfare, social coherence, and so forth. Gradually economic policymaking moved away from economics into a broader political and social context.

The challenges for economic policy and its instruments will be exacerbated in the years to come as the focus shifts from controlling demand to reducing unemployment, increasing supply, increasing productivity and helping to solve issues such as future pensions and medical care, maintaining a clean environment, and climate change. The setting will be completely different.

It is true that growth theory has always constituted a major part of economic theory, but it has been a growth theory in a world of plenty where productivity was interesting, but not decisive. Now it looks different. Growth is not the objective, growth with fewer resources is.

Distribution theory has always been one of the chapters high on the curriculum of a respectable course in economic theory. Again the focus has been on how to distribute more; actually, how to distribute what implementation of growth theories made available to society. Now it becomes a question of burden sharing, of how to allocate lesser growth, and distribute growth, not between production factors (land, labour, and capital), but between societal objectives such as health, caring for the aged, a clean environment, climate change, and a higher living standard for a majority of the population.

To a certain extent normal economic theory indirectly linked growth and distribution theories because they both revolved around production factors: growth theory is about how to use production factors; distribution theory is about how to distribute the fruit of economic activity among production factors. And both in essence were building on nineteenth century industrialization paradigms — not on what the future needed.

This is not sufficient anymore; maybe it does not make sense anymore. In the future, economic theory must offer better answers to how we distribute the fruit of economic activity, not among production factors, but among societal priorities. Fiscal policy, monetary policy, and exchange rate policy must be reoriented so that their effectiveness as instruments for achieving societal goals becomes as important, maybe even more important, than their effectiveness in influencing economic activity. It is no use anymore to say that a fiscal measure brings demand into line, if at the same time, social fabric or the state of the environment or use of resources move in the opposite direction of what is planned. And new instruments must be invented in the areas of climate (such as future Kyoto/Copenhagen agreement targets, large-scale research such as cooperative research used in the European Union for twenty years, social help as enabled by NGOs [non-profit organizations], etc.).

Recent research[35] gives an indication of how difficult it will be to maintain the "old" perspective of economic policy and its instruments with its conclusion, albeit with some reservations, that international environmental cooperation facilitates economic exchange, even if it is not an economic parameter.

This finding opens the door for a new perception of economic relations between nation states and or group of nation states. The condition sine qua non for full participation in economic globalization is not only economic activity and high competitiveness, but being in tune with the ruling perception of what is an ethically and humanely acceptable standard. It may take time for this to be acknowledged, and for some years we may hear some politicians and economists rejecting it, but the omens are clear enough. In the global world of networks and virtual relations, perceptions travel freely and, even more important, perceptions are going to shape reality more than the other way round. Be out of tune and be out of the growth circle, says the message.

## *Material Living Standard is Limited*

In 2007 a leading futurist[36] sketched seventeen great challenges for the twenty-first century. Not a single one touched on material living standard or a rise in living standard measured according to what used to be the norm in the twentieth century for traditional consumerism. Instead they focused on items such as protecting the biosphere, expanding human potential, exploring transhumanism, and bridging the skill and wisdom gap.

The current model says that an increasing number of cars is equivalent to a higher living standard. But that is because cities and geographical infrastructure in the United States and some other areas around the world are designed for the car; it is impossible to live and work without a car. If Asian cities are designed in another way so that people do not have the same need for transportation by car, the lack of ownership of a car does not mean a lower material living standard. The question then is how people perceive the car. Is it a means of transport that cuts down the time required to get to work, to leisure activities, and for holidays? If so, a different layout of the cities may reduce the need for cars. If on the other hand, the car is seen as a social status symbol that offers individual freedom to move around according to individual preferences, it will be much harder to maintain the fiction of a high living standard without the car. The escape door is that even then we may try to provide other means to meet these consumer preferences. One possibility is virtual activities conveying the same degree of freedom. There will probably be other opportunities and openings.

The key is to go behind the goods purchased by the consumer to find out what the underlying or hidden need of the consumer is. The next step is to offer consumer satisfaction in a way that does not require the same amount of resources that a high material living standard would demand.

A resource intensive activity is travelling. Why do people travel? For the most part, tourism sees people travelling to get away from their daily surroundings, to discover something new, to find out how they cope with minor challenges requiring them to take new decisions. Maybe it is a search for a combination of entertainment and excitement, and a drive for enhanced social status at home. If so, the next question is to find out whether that demand or need can be satisfied by some means other than travelling.

As consumer theory through many decades has shown, consumer preferences are not cast in stone. The consumer is susceptible to a whole range of factors, including societal norms, trends, and the behaviour of other people. A shift in consumer preferences has, for example, been noted in the Californian beer market for some years. Apparently people are willing to pay more for locally brewed beer even if it may be difficult to pin down any difference in taste. Furthermore people are willing to join hands to support local breweries for no other tangible reason than that it is locally produced.[37] The same tendency is visible in other countries. In Asia Chinese traditional medicine is gaining favour. If consumers are willing to switch to locally produced brands, they may also be willing to favour less material consumption, as obviously the preference for locally produced goods is not an economic, but a value-based phenomenon.

This line of thinking can be taken a long step further by looking at how well, or rather how badly, consumption theory incorporates non-material preferences, such as the environment and social welfare, in its charts of behaviour converted into income elasticities. The theory commonly estimates income elasticities by comparing the expenditures of people with varying incomes. In the case of environmental goods and services, as these are not usually priced in markets, those doing the study on this look at expenditures on things thought to be related to the environment — but these turn out to be things such as hiking equipment, travel to resorts, housing in nice areas, etc. Not surprisingly, these turn out to display very large income elasticities, and conventional thinking makes the strong assumption that, therefore, elasticities for environmental services (clean air, etc.) must also be large! This last assumption seems unwarranted, or, at best, not demonstrated in any convincing way.

Instead, most environmental welfare demands (and the reasons for them) involve some kind of loss, potential loss, or reductions of loss for people such as loss of clean environment from pollution, the cleaning up of pollution to prevent environmental health risks etc. And losses should rightly be assessed on the basis of what people need to be paid to accept them (willing to accept more pollution, not to have pollution reduced, etc.). On the basis of this more direct and probably more accurate measurement it is not at all clear that preferences for environmental welfare, for example, would yield high income elasticities. It might be that the rich would demand more than the poor to put up with environmental degradation, but relative to their income, it is not certain that this would lead to high income elasticities. And it is this that should be the measure for guiding policy. If this line of thinking is right the consequences for policies are significant, especially when discussing the future of Asia. It means repudiating the view that only after having got rich first are people willing to pay for the reduction of pollution. The conventional view that the world cannot expect poorer countries to do something about the environment before they have reached a certain level of GDP per capita will be wrong. Perhaps, poor Chinese peasants are after all as willing or even more willing than rich Americans or Europeans to forego income gain so as not to see his/her environment degraded.[38]

The attitude of the electorate in several countries, one of which I can mention to be my own country, Denmark, supports this view. Over the years politicians have made several attempts to offer tax reductions in their endeavour to win elections. It was in vain. The public voted constantly in favour of high taxes. There are unquestionably a number of reasons for such electoral behaviour. One of them might be that the electorate is afraid to lose the benefits flowing from a welfare system based on high taxes, with analogous consequences for income elasticities as mentioned above.[39]

The theory about growth in stages pointing towards mass consumption may no longer be valid after all.

Its replacement might be a growth theory built around a philosophy of diminishing use of resources, and consumer satisfaction without use of more resources. But diminishing use of natural resources brings down labour needed by this use, so a replacement must be found in labour terms to maintain employment. A country's way towards this state of affairs may be divided into stages, but not as defined in the existing theory. Education, health, family care, and the environment may emerge, but will Asian nation states accept growth in these sectors as drivers?

The existing economic models do not offer much help for policymakers having to tackle the problem of financing current investment, building up alternative energy sources, and removing toxic materials from agricultural and manufactured goods. As there is still some disagreement about how serious some of the environmental problems really are, it is difficult to put figures on investment, but except for a few sceptics, consensus rallies around what may, without exaggeration, be called enormous sums of money. One of the most widely quoted figure is from the Stern Report of 2006,[40] which says that one per cent of global GDP must be allocated per annum to avoid the worst effects of climate change, and if mankind does not succeed in doing so, global GDP may decrease by up to 20 per cent. The Stern Report has been criticized for being too optimistic as well as too pessimistic. In 2008 another report[41] concluded that the Stern Report was *grosso modo* (roughly) correct, but probably had slightly underestimated the problem.

The challenge for economics is to move from modelling which can be quantified and which reflect certainty, to modelling from alternatives which have a high degree of uncertainty, but which will threaten the world as we know it today should they materialize.[42]

The question is simple to ask, but difficult to answer: How will today's consumer react to reduced consumption when told that there is an X per cent risk for a major climate catastrophe ten, twenty or fifty years hence? And even more crucial, that there is a Y per cent probability that he/she will be affected? The question can also be framed another way: How will the consumer react when told there is an X per cent risk that there will be no retirement help, or a Z per cent risk that there will be no land available for building?

This new equation in economic terms can be exemplified the following way. Conventional theory says that a consumer with US$50,000 accepts postponing the buying of a new car for five years, provided that the interest rate he earns on this increases the sum to say, US$55,000. This is pure economic calculation. Consume now or later, and if later, the consumer is compensated. Behind this theory lies the assumption that the goods or services will be available five years from now without major changes in the parameters. If that is the case the consumer asks for a higher compensation — again a pure economic reasoning.

In new circumstances where resource scarcities make themselves felt as a constraint for material production, this is no longer sufficient. The equation needs to be reworked with built-in coefficients transforming uncertainty into economics.

The consumer contemplating buying a car now may have to face choices such as these:

You can buy the car now for US$50,000 or invest the money to get US$55,000 in five years' time to buy a similar car, but there is a 25 per cent probability that cars will be 50 per cent more expensive, or even worse, that cars will not be sold according to today's practice.

You can buy the car now for US$50,000 or invest the money to get US$55,000 in five years' time to buy it, but there is a 50 per cent probability that the car you look at will not be available. Maybe only cars meeting specific requirements for low consumption of petrol, or hybrid cars, or cars invested with new technologies will be on the market and they will be more expensive and perform less like a "genuine" car.

You can buy the car now for US$50,000 or invest the money to get US$55,000 in five years' time to buy a car, but in the meantime, restrictions for use of cars have been introduced, for example, one stipulating that every car must not run more than 200 kilometres per week.

In these circumstances, the consumer not only gets the choice of five years later narrowed down, but also has to forego user value in year zero until year five, which cannot be recuperated. Some kinds of user value are simply confiscated by the authorities.

Normal consumption theory would tend to look at income and price elasticities for buying (acquiring or getting something), but what may be decisive for the consumer in the future is what he/she is *not* getting, and as outlined above, the price a consumer is willing to pay for getting something is different from the price asked to give it up. Add to this the uncertainties about future consumption, and the shortcomings of the current consumption theory are obvious.

A similar line of questioning or reasoning might be applied to set out the preferences for social benefits. Where is the tilting point for an individual having to choose between paying a sum of X now in taxes for no social benefit later in life, or pay Z (a higher, maybe much higher, amount now), with the Q per cent probability of a flow of social benefits with an annual magnitude of U? For most Western countries which have had a social welfare system for many years, these equations have found solutions that are translated into politics, but that is not the case for most parts of Asia.

The necessity for adaptability becomes of critical importance in the years to come because the transition from a model based on pure economies (money, profits, etc.) to a societal model incorporating social stability, use of resources, and non-material consumption, asks for a transition not only in economic, but also in social terms. This poses problems for conventional economics in the sense that most of these investments run over a long time span and are profitable only after many years of, and often providing, benefit for society, which are not tangible.

Adaptability may compete with the other production factors as the determining factor in evaluating a society's future capability to deliver well-being for its citizens.

The virtue of a model (primarily a quantitative one) is that it constitutes a tool for feeding data into the system to get fairly accurate predictions for what is going to happen over the coming period — how long depends on the model and what we are looking for.

The crucial factor in a model are the coefficients telling us how the input of various elements transforms into output or results. The input may be, for example, a rise in oil price or a fiscal stimulus or an exchange rate adjustment, and the output (result) may be future growth rates or balance of payments.

The coefficients will in almost all cases be estimated from past behaviour even if they are used to predict future results. This is not a problem as long as the behavioural pattern among people, business, and governments is stable. If so the model works because the coefficients reflect behaviour correctly.

The problem arises when behavioural patterns change. If so, the estimated coefficients will deliver wrong results. If, for example, the savings quota among people suddenly rises, a fiscal stimulus will lead to lower consumption, higher savings, and lower growth than predicted by the model.

Another problem is the mental interaction between the model/its coefficients and policymakers. If the model has worked correctly over a number of years, policymakers start to think like the model — to take for granted that the coefficients reflect normal behaviour and that this behaviour is non-malleable, even unalterable.

The difficulty in changing the coefficients is that reference to past behaviour as the most likely future behaviour seems perfectly legitimate and sensible especially because it stands on empirically verified ground. Another obstacle is that even if powerful arguments can be advanced to substantiate a claim that the coefficients are changing, it is not easy for policymakers to adjust. Suppose that an analyst had said in 2006 that oil prices in the course of 2008 would rise to US$150 per barrel, and advocated fiscal measures to forestall the onslaught on the economy. Policymakers would respond that to implement measures to that effect, for example, higher taxes on the basis of such a prediction, would be politically tortuous. To turn expectations about change in behaviour into policies, a high degree of certainty that such changes will occur is needed and that is not always the case in future forecasting.

One more temporizing factor is the question of whether changes in the coefficients are ephemeral, temporary, or permanent. Coefficients swing over time; some of these swings are temporary, even ephemeral, and can be disregarded, while others are permanent and cannot. For policymakers faced with the decision to revise the model, it is obviously of decisive importance whether the swings observed are permanent or not. As the background for the swings is normally found outside economics, economists need to look outside their own science to find somebody giving an indication, and as seen so often, the obstacles for interdisciplinary activities are visible while the incentives to do so are small.

Given these explanations and reservations, a global model deviating from the existing one will incorporate the following points distinguishing it from the current model:

- Supply of commodities replaces global demand as the determining factor for level of economic activity.
- No modelling and goal seeking can happen without taking into account resource, social and skills constraints, with attached shadow costs.
- Growth prospects from physical goods or using only physical goods will be dominated by *produit net* defined as the capability to squeeze more manufactured goods out of a given amount of commodities.
- Growth and distribution of income among traditional production factors (land, labour, and capital) will reflect this, leading to (relatively) lower remuneration for labour and higher for commodities.
- Today's consumption will be reduced to make room for investments for reducing the negative repercussions from social and climate change. The distribution of this burden over time will be a crucial test for politics and economics.
- Profit seeking may have to be mitigated with social goals such as unemployment limits, sustainability in health, pension, and infrastructure, so in general, profit levels will fall.
- Social harmony, scientific discovery, and entrepreneurship are more than ever important engines for growth.
- New technology, in particular ICT, will emerge in economic theory as an independent production factor, with characteristics distinguishing it from established production factors: that it can be used again and again, and used by several persons at the same time (increasing returns to scale). There is a need for better modelling of ICT in the models taking these elements into account.
- Consumption patterns will shift away from material goods to having consumer and societal preferences satisfied in a less resource-intensive way.
- The global supply chain will be restructured, with fewer production places, probably nearer resources and/or markets for the end product.
- Trade policy will shift from focusing on dismantling import barriers and/or keeping markets and investment opportunities open, to restricting export barriers and/or export tariffs.

- Ownership of large companies will be increasingly concentrated, while the ownership of smaller enterprises will be more fragmented, and the link between owners and employees will be less and less visible as investment funds that often do not disclose who actually constitute the ownership will play a greater determining role.
- The social contract between owners and workers pursuing analogous objectives and knowing each other has been broken, and transformed into an opaque economic relationship thus opening the door for a different social contract or even a breakdown of the social relations keeping societies together.
- Deregulation has led to the blurring of the distinction between public services to assist the population and business transactions seeking profits.
- Regionalization with a diminished role for the nation state will emerge as the steering mechanism for economic development.

## POLITICAL SYSTEMS UNDER PRESSURE

### Main Points

In this context "political model" is perceived as comprising six elements: *first*, selection/election of political leaders; *second*, channels for communication from the people to the leaders and the way political leaders communicate directions (policies) to the people; *third*, methods to ensure uniformity among citizens with regard to behavioural patterns (attitudes, right or wrong, permissible or non-permissible); *fourth*, enforcement methods/mechanisms; *fifth*, the balance between the individual and the community; and *sixth*, right of access to knowledge and information for citizens.

Over recent years governance, governing, the political system, and democracy have been on the agenda of countries in search of an effective system that can guarantee the well-being of their citizens. Under the Bush administration the U.S. foreign and security policy was to a large degree driven by the wish to promote democracy as perceived by the United States to other countries. The underlying assumption was that the U.S. democracy model was the "best" system, and accompanying this assumption may have been the somewhat Marxian philosophy of history that says democracy is the ultimate political system which all nation states will move towards.

This book does not embark on a normative analysis of democracy, its virtues, and possible/potential drawbacks, but seeks to illustrate some of the challenges the political systems in Asia face, irrespective of whether they are labelled democracies or not.

Charles Tilly defines democracy in the following way: "a regime is democratic to the degree that political relations between the state and its citizens feature broad, equal, protected and mutually binding consultations".[43] To this can be added rules for enforcement and checks and balances.

Democracy is not, however, a uniform notion, but is like all other political systems, forged by traditions and culture. The word "consultations" sounds unambiguous, but is, in fact, perceived in different ways among nation states and societies. Various forms of political systems and various nation states have chosen their variant of democracy or used elements from democracy in setting up their own political systems.[44]

Most observers would probably agree that a starting point for defining democracy points towards the following elements:

- Guarantee against political and ethnic suppression and possible political prosecution for political reasons.
- Free elections and the existence of political choices.
- No arbitrary decisions, but a rule-based society.
- Freedom of expression as part of a number of freedoms for the individual.
- Freedom to establish political parties and/or groups.
- An independent judiciary able to stand up to, or even rule against, the political system.

All these elements seem obvious, but it is not so obvious what they really mean, particularly when some of these objectives clash with one another.[45]

How do you weigh freedom to establish political parties if these preach hatred against other groups in society? What do you do in cases where an individual acts in a way that clearly upsets a large number of other people? What do you do in cases where freedom of expression and/or the freedom to establish organizations abuse the system, and, in some cases, these organizations advocate the replacement of democracy with some kind of authoritarian rule/dictatorship?

What should the political system do in a case where a political party gets a majority of the votes with a programme saying it will dismantle democracy? At the beginning of the 1990s, an election in Algeria gave a majority to Muslim parties, and thereafter the military stepped in to prevent a government, which by all accounts, would have turned Algeria into a completely different country from what its constitution stated.[46]

In a country with a less dramatic political climate, perhaps the political system would allow a discussion of what can be done in case political parties enter a government with a programme questioning vital elements of the freedom associated with democracy.

The dilemma can also be seen when weighing political power against economic power. How democratic is a society in which money or outright violence can be used to wring decisions out of the judiciary according to the wishes of those in possession of the highest wealth?

Human security, ethnic and cultural diversity, gender equality, and protection of minorities are all key elements, but what can be done if a democratically elected government distorts these elements and does this on the basis of a mandate from the majority of the electorate?

What happens if basic rights of freedom cannot be defended by a government elected by universal vote and — as has been seen in some countries — the military steps in as the guardian of these rights? What is preferable when such dilemmas arise: To maintain and insist on a democratically elected government that cannot, and may not even wish to guarantee the functioning of society, human security, and fundamental freedoms, or accept a government not elected democratically but performing better on the scoreboard for these issues? This is not an academic question. It is actually seen around the world and is a fact of real life that policymakers have to tackle.

In the global world, another problem arises. Some organizations may be banned in their home country, but try to use other countries' constitutional rules to disseminate information to their home country. This has been seen in Europe, where the PKK (a Kurdish organization), banned in Turkey, tried to set up radio stations in European countries, pointing to the freedom of expression in these countries.

European constitutions were written many decades ago (in some cases 150 years ago) to protect the citizens in new democracies against any attempts by former rulers to quell their freedom of expression. The founding fathers of these constitutions could not have foreseen an international world where the freedom of expression granted to national citizens in a nation state world would be used by foreign citizens against the government in their home country.

So this lands an awkward problem on the political agenda of these European countries. According to their constitutions, they cannot ban the dissemination of information as long as this is done respecting the basic rules. Hence, the freedom of expression in one country can be used to undermine a legal and sometimes democratically elected government in another country.

The democratic models practised around the world are very different and each reflects the traditions, evolution, history, and challenges of that country.

This is evident when looking at the voting system. In the United States, the president is elected indirectly and there are examples where the elected president garnered fewer votes than his opponent, in an election with a participation rate of not much more than 50 per cent of the electorate, meaning that the president of the United States was actually elected by about 25 per cent of the population. In the United Kingdom, Parliament is elected by constituencies, and this produces large swings giving parties representation in Parliament that is not always consistent with their share of the votes. In some other countries, an elaborate and complicated system is applied, giving parties almost exactly the same number of seats as their share of votes. Constituencies are not always drawn by borders reflecting population size, but openly or indirectly favour selected groups of the electorate. Almost all countries apply a threshold, specifying that a minimum of say, 2 per cent or 5 per cent of the votes cast is necessary to obtain presentation in Parliament. Some countries have mandatory voting, others do not. Some countries open the door for votes cast by overseas citizens, others do not.

The interesting observation is that even in cases where the winner of the election garnered fewer votes than the opponent, few have contested its conformity with democracy. Apparently freedom of the individual and free elections seem to be of greater importance than how votes are translated into representation in Parliament.

There seems to be some kind of correlation between how well established the nation state is and how well democracy functions, even if there are exceptions to all such rules. In Europe, new nation states, such as Germany and Italy, have gone through a turbulent history towards democracy, while old nation states such as the United Kingdom, France, and the Scandinavian countries have seen few, if any, challenges to the model.

It may reflect another factor — social capital or confidence and trust among citizens and between citizens and the institutions, governmental or financial, of the nation state.

If fundamental freedoms are accepted as the foundation of democracy, the next step is to understand that rules, regulations, and laws may be less important than people's acceptance of certain unwritten norms of behaviour. If during their upbringing, people are introduced to norms, ethics, and values, they will abide by such norms without scrutinizing legislation and rules. Citizens trust the political system because it has proved itself. Financial institutions are entrusted with citizens' savings and function without being suspected of misbehaving or, worse, fraud. People find it easy to share responsibility. In societies with a high degree of social capital, various kinds of freedom can be granted because neither the institutions nor the citizens look for opportunities to deviate from the norms, but respect them by instinct.

The implication of this observation for global democracy is that unless such social capital is present or created, it will be hard, not to say impossible, to introduce or enhance democracy. It will put the state in the role of a regulatory body.

This takes us to the next observation, which is an established democracy lives in peace with its institutions, but for a newborn democracy, institutions cannot do much unless social capital is present. In other words, the introduction of democracy by institutions looks very difficult, if not impossible, if the basic behaviour of people and institutions does not reflect some, and even better, a high degree of social capital. Formalities should ideally reflect realities. Rarely, if ever, can formalities twist realities.

Following from this we see that social capital cannot be built in the short term. Experience from Europe and elsewhere points very clearly to the need for taking one step at a time and making sure that confidence and trust among citizens and institutions take root.

If this analysis is accepted, the interesting and outstanding point to note is that the election process must be weighed against social capital, mutual trust, and confidence for it to be decisive in ensuring fundamental freedoms.

## Fundamental Freedoms

### *Rights of the Individual*

The individual versus society as a whole is a well-known dilemma and different kinds of societies and/or political systems choose their own centre of gravity and way to tackle this issue.

Anecdotal evidence (conventional wisdom) suggests that the right of the individual gets a higher priority in Western political systems than is the case in many political systems in other parts of the world.

There seems to be some kind of correlation between how well structured, well established the nation state and its institutions are, and how well it has succeeded in convincing its population that the institutions are trustworthy and belong to them.

The more secure the nation is, the more confident its institutions and political leaders will be that the centre of gravity floats towards the individual.

When a nation state is young and/or heterogeneous, ethnicity and/or religion may exercise a strong pull on the individual's sense of identity. The nation state may move towards prioritizing society as a whole to make certain it functions, rather than daring to rely on a fragile national sense of identity. The identity of the individual is not sufficiently linked to society to warrant granting strong individual freedom, which may jeopardize the working of the nation state and/or society.

Another factor to take into account is how successful a large nation state has been in decentralizing political debate and decision making, hence putting the decision makers close to the people. In many Asian countries there is little public debate. The debate may take place through other channels, but not visibly, thus raising doubts as to how close politicians are to citizens. The more visible the distance between the people and decision makers is, the more likely it is that the society as a whole will get a higher priority than the individual.

When looking around the world, we will find it noteworthy that newborn nation states, often comprising several races and religious groups, try hard to protect the individual against abuses, maybe even assaults, from members of other groups inside the same nation state but adhering to another identity. This is to guarantee human security for its citizens and requires measures to prevent animosities of various kinds among groups, which lead to limitations of individual freedom.

The heart of the matter is that in well-established democracies, individual freedoms will seldom lead to abuses or assaults against citizens of the same nation state with a different identity. This risk is, however, visible in many new nation states where tribal or religious or ethnic animosities have been fermenting through centuries. In the eyes of the individuals here, human security and freedom were linked not to the nation state, which did not exist previously, but to the tribe, religious circle, or ethnic community, which has been looking after its members, and looking upon others as intruders. To transfer security and freedom (in reality a shift of identity) from one anchor to another takes time as individuals obviously do not dare to rely on the new, and for them, unknown entity, and throw away what they know as a reliable guarantor. Since individuals do not dare to transfer their identity, they stall when asked to support newborn institutions and provide them with the necessary powers to replace the old framework. It is a kind of vicious circle. The newborn institutions cannot take over because they do not have the trust and the means, and as long as that is the case, citizens withhold their support.

In many newborn nation states, human security and freedom exist inside the established framework for the members adhering to a particular tribe, religion or ethnicity. Moving outside this framework and relying on the nation state's fragile and, in some cases, embryonic instruments for human security, may prove hazardous.

The challenge is to extend the feeling of security and freedom from inside the group to all members of the nation state, regardless of which group they adhere to and whether they find themselves inside their own group or inside one of the other groups.

## Freedom of Expression

Freedom of expression is often named as one of the most important elements of democracy. But it has to be added that it is only one of several individual freedoms and has to be seen in that context. Freedom of expression is not worth much if citizens are not allowed to form political parties and create organizations, or to create and develop media channels for this purpose.

As long as we operate in a homogenous society, where the overwhelming part of the population has adopted a congruous set of values, translating freedom of expression into action may not pose insurmountable problems.

The problems arise if, or when, a nation state is composed of several cultural identities with different and, in some cases, divergent views on what is acceptable and what is not. In such societies, one cultural group may insult another cultural group by its use of freedom of expression, leading to, in the worst cases, racial or religious turmoil as the insulted party reacts, and in some cases, strongly.

Often the problems are solved by mutual recognition of values and the necessity of being understood and accepted by society as a whole. Self-discipline comes into play when something should not be said, shown, or printed, if it is known beforehand that it runs counter to values held dearly by another cultural group. This is, of course, an ideal situation, reflecting that the nation state has moved towards some kind of cultural common denominator with regard to attitudes vis-à-vis other cultural groups.

The problems arise if or when this is not the case, putting authorities in the unenviable position of having to choose between upholding freedom of expression, thus running the risk of turmoil between cultural groups, and prioritizing stability between the groups, thus making limitations for freedom of expression unavoidable.

In a global perspective, this becomes even more acute as the audio-visual world facilitates a fast transmission of reports across the world, so that what is in full conformity with norms and ethics in one country may immediately be seized upon in other countries and/or by cultural groups disagreeing with this. The ball may bounce back to the country where it started to roll, creating tensions between divergent cultural groups inside countries and between countries.

## *Freedom of Religion*

Freedom of religion is essential for a genuine democracy, and is rarely, if at all, contested either by countries moving towards democracy, or by a large number of countries with another political system.

In the prism of the globalization of democracy, at least three points meet the eye:

i) Not all religions confine themselves to religion, but some reflect a way of life with rules for believers that touch on societal norms and regulations. In such cases, either the believers of a religion may be forced to surrender not their religion, but the accompanying way of life, or the part of the population adhering to other religions may be forced into a legal system under the influence of a religion that is not theirs. A clash between the groups is regrettably also a possibility. This explains why freedom of religion is not always sufficient to produce harmony.

ii) The basic problem for some countries is to define the balance between religious freedoms and generally adopted societal norms, independent of religious adherence.

Globalization means, among other things, large immigration of people bringing their religion along and, not least, communication of minority groups adhering to a certain religion in country X, with their religious leaders in country Y where that religion constitutes a majority.

This makes it more difficult for the immigrants to adjust to rules and norms in their new home country, paving the way for parallel societies to come into existence which are based on not only another religion, but also on societal norms that the majority of the population in the new home country do not share.

The cross-border character of religion enhances these problems, opening the door for interference in a country's international set of ethical rules from outside. Individual citizens may feel a stronger loyalty towards religious leaders in their country of origin than towards the political system in their new home country, thus distancing themselves from the political process in that country.

iii) One of the most sensitive questions is the use of symbols by religious minorities to express religious attitudes, such as dress codes. The *tudung* is a case in point. It is an issue hotly disputed without anyone having any firm guidance on whether the right to express cultural and, in particular, religious attitudes forms part of the basic principles of democracy. When analysing how nation states have dealt with this problem, no uniform global pattern can be detected.

There seems, however, to be a trend. If, or when, a dress code is used by a minority group not only to express a religious attitude, but also to distance it from societal norms and what is regarded as "normal behaviour", the sentiment by the majority swings towards hostility. However, when a dress code is strictly based on religion, and is not seen or perceived as a signal of a cultural attitude beyond religion, the sentiment of the majority tends towards tolerance.

## Legal System

Legal systems must be independent. True, but the question then arises — independent of what and whom?

In some countries moving towards democracy, those in control of the legal system may not be economically independent, making them susceptible to collusion, corruption etc.

The problem may be made worse by foreign companies' possible involvement in such practices. This leads to a split between the population, including, in some cases, the political elite, and the legal system, because foreign interference thwart decisions to its advantage.

The influence on the legal system by religions and/or other sources of ethics and norms falls more or less in the same vein. As long as we operate in a homogenous society this may not be a problem, but, as experience indicates, it becomes a genuine problem in a heterogeneous country where legal rules are the same for all, but are being interpreted by members of the majority using their set of values to judge members of the minority with another set of values. In Europe, almost all countries have rules against blasphemy, etc. It is in the hands of the judiciary to interpret these rules. The judiciary, however, is formed by people from the majority, which makes it difficult for the minorities to be understood. Illustration: In a country with 3–4 per cent of Muslims, the judiciary will interpret blasphemy the same way for Muslims and Christians alike, but these two religions do not draw the same lines on blasphemy, so even if the judiciary is independent, neutral and applies the same rules, it doesn't look that way in the eyes of the minority.

In Europe, there are immigrants exercising unwritten rules towards members of their own community and indeed their own family. This is often in contradiction not only to societal norms, but also to the law. It is easy to state that every citizen must obey the law in their residing country, but the problem arises if a minority does not do so and furthermore finds that it has support for this behaviour from their own community and religious leaders there.

There are other dimensions to a well-functioning legal system: respect and enforcement of international treaties, and participation in international police collaboration. It is good to sign international treaties, but if not ratified these come to nothing. If ratified, they should be implemented and the attitude should be full cooperation with judicial systems in other countries. As the world grows global and crime in various forms proliferates among countries, the judicial system may often be kept or keep itself inside national borders. The European integration shows that out of the three core functions of a nation state — currency, army, and the judicial system — the jump to internationalization happens first for the currency, then for the army, and the most difficult one to catapult on to the international level is the judicial system.

## Minorities

Very few countries can claim they do not have one or more minority groups and consequently will face the problem, or challenge, of managing several cultural identities.

The minorities will often fear that their cultural identity cannot be maintained. The majority will sometimes feel that the minority shies away from accepting the norms and ethics of the nation state, thus jeopardizing the building of a national identity.

Europe, North America, and Australia/New Zealand find themselves faced today with the protection of the minorities and the safeguarding of their rights as an issue — and often an acute and hot one, as the examples of the Maoris in New Zealand and Aborigines in Australia show.[47] In Europe, a whole string of examples of cultural minorities can be mentioned, suffice it to point at the evolution in the United Kingdom concerning Scotland and Wales, the debate in France in the past thirty-five years over the relationship between the regions and the government in Paris. In Europe, the question of minorities has been exacerbated by the immigrants, in particular, from Muslim countries. In Asia minorities constitute a major political force and are present in almost all Asian countries in the shape of religious, ethnic, or other cultural groups.

The challenge is that in democracies with a parliament elected by free elections and a government constituted by a parliamentary majority, the government may feel it has a mandate to prioritize the cultural pattern of the majority and not incorporate the views of the minorities.

It is no foregone conclusion that the rights of minorities may be better safeguarded in a democracy, especially if it is a newborn and fragile democracy, than under a political system where the government may choose to strike a balance between different, even divergent, cultural entities more evenly.

In many multicultural, multireligious, and multiracial nation states, a strong government may emerge as the protector of the rights of the minorities, even if it is not elected in conformity with democratic principles.

A comparison of the nation states between Europe and Asia indicates that the role of the nation state may be on the decline in Europe. The strong economic integration has moved a large part of economic and industrial decision making from the national capital to the European Union, working to the advantage of the minorities and offering them the scope for loosening the grip of the central government. This has in many cases been welcomed as the central government had acted in the interest of the majority.

It is not certain that the same would be the case in Asia, where weak nation states and weak central governments may lead to less protection of the minorities and a higher degree of power exercised by the majority.

## Human Security

Human security versus human freedom is a delicate issue. While it is rarely contested that democracy opens up more freedom for the individual, interpreted in a broad sense, the unanswered question is whether human security will be at risk because of individual freedom.

In an established democracy, it is difficult to draw the line between what is permissible and what is not, which opens the door to abuses and distortions by criminals and like-minded people operating inside the formal framework, but outside the established norms.

Freedom is dependent on how those in possession of freedom use it. In a "free and democratic" society, a high degree of discipline and, in particular, self-discipline, is called for to avoid abuse and distortions.

This points back to the earlier observation highlighting common societal norms ingrained in society and accepted by the large majority of individuals.

## Knowledge and Information

The access and right to knowledge and information are essential for societal development and involvement as well as for governance.

Many nation states have been caught offguard by the strong development of knowledge flows over the Internet which ignore borders, thereby removing technical monopoly from the nation state. Both in Asia and in other parts of the world, some governments have found it difficult to accept this new state of affairs.

It is, of course, a political question whether governments will try to raise barriers for information from outside, and/or from inside, over the Internet, but several preliminary conclusions over the last decade or so seem inescapable: It is difficult to do, technology can, in most cases, be developed quite inexpensively to get the information anyway, and in the long run, the costs of imposing such barriers on society may be high as some of the advantages of ICT for economic development may be lost.

## The Electorate

### An Active Population

A genuine democracy is based on a politically active population taking part in the political debate, engaged in the policies formulated for the nation state, and able to express itself on a fair basis in the media. Such support provides at least three advantages:

- A recruiting base for future leaders is available
- The election and preceding debate focus on political issues
- Many different layers of the society take part, ensuring that the population looks on the system and the election as "theirs".

A politically engaged population is an insurance against apathy and use/abuse by peripheral forces of elections to force through a government in accordance with the votes cast, but out of tune with the population.

During the last decades, the share of votes cast in many established democracies has been falling. In the United States, participation in presidential elections comes up to about 50 per cent of the electorate. The percentage of votes cast in elections to the European Parliament hovers around the same figure, varying a little from country to country. In many nation states, participation of about 70–80 per cent of the electorate, usual a couple of decades ago, is no longer obtainable.

For countries in transition towards democracy, the percentage may be high, but the question arises as to what it actually means. With electorates that are not "educated" and who do not really understand what an election is, with political parties that are only newly established with representatives in "constituencies" who are unproven and inexperienced, votes may be subject to many other influences than political preferences.[48]

It is not uncommon to hear about vote buying, either directly by giving money to the voters, or by using the headman of a village as the channel.

The key factor in this situation is to convey the message, and instil a sense in the electorate, that the political system is "theirs". Experience indicates that a high participation rate in elections contributes to such a feeling, but is not the only one. The voters may feel that they actually influence the political process by casting their votes.

## The Young Generation

When we look at emerging values, it is interesting to incorporate recent studies from the United States.[49] Even if the United States and the American youth are not synonymous with global youth there is an indication of how young people feel and react under the influence of ICT.[50] According to these two studies, the Millennial Generation will have the following basic values governing their attitudes to politics, and accordingly, guiding their votes.

The young generation of the United States is tolerant and shows respect for other people's values without giving up their own values. It supports gay marriage, takes race and gender equality as givens, is tolerant of religious and family diversity, has an open and positive attitude towards immigration Almost two-thirds agree that religious faith should focus more on promoting tolerance, social justice, and peace in society, and less on opposing abortion or gay rights as traditional items in the American debate.

On foreign policy issues, they favour a multilateral and cooperative foreign policy more than the former generation does.

They are much more aware of the need for and accept, even expect, the government to take an active role. Ronald Reagan's famous phrase that the government is the problem is far away from the values they cherish. They want the economy to work better, help those in need, and provide more services. The ideological view that free markets always produce the best results for society does not appeal to them.

They tend to favour a more socially-balanced society, accept universal health, and support the view that workers get their fair share of economic growth. Notions such as labour unions, a minimum wage, and progressive taxation, are not anathema to them. Investment in public schools and college access are good and they believe there is a need to reduce dependence on fossil fuels and to rely more on new energy technologies instead.

Finally, millennials are neither anti-business nor anti-trade. They are, however, very clear that the government needs to regulate business in the public interest.

"Millennials are much more progressive on many issues than previous generations when they were younger. This is true not just on social issues such as gay marriage but also on issues concerning the role of government and policy goals such as achieving universal health care. In all likelihood, Millennial progressivism is here to stay" states one of the paragraphs summarizing the studies.

It may be questioned how representative the American youth is of global youth, or in our case, youth in Asia. If we accept as a working thesis that globalization promotes a drive for fundamental freedoms and knowledge, plus the fact that information flows — more or less — freely across borders, it is likely, though not certain, that Asian youth will develop analogous values.

## Multicultural Societies

The most visible risk associated with democracy and free elections arises in multicultural societies, where voters, judged on historical evolution and cultural background, can be expected to cast their votes exclusively on tribal, race, or religious relationship.

In such countries, elections may be completely free and the result may fully respect the political position of the majority of the population. If the yardstick for a democracy is free elections with no flaws, these countries may pass without a doubt.

The problem is, however, that the government constituted by parliament is composed uniquely by the majority.

Depending on the constitution, such a political system may quickly degenerate into some kind — mild or harsh — of majority rule over the minority. If the dominating political issues in society follow cultural fault lines, the majority may use the powers vested in it by the electorate to rule in accordance with its own wishes and preferences, not taking into account the preferences of the minority.

It then becomes an open question how much democracy, individual freedom, and human security a free election has delivered. It may depend on how much self-discipline the majority wishes to exercise and how much power, if any, it is prepared to award the minority.

The situation may become worse over time if the voting pattern stays frozen, preventing any attempt by the minority to ever enter into government.

Knowing that there will never be any risk of political opponents casting critical glances on its governance, the majority may assume some kind of arrogance of power and/or plunge into money corruption.

One of the virtues of democracy is the chance or possibility that another political party will come into power. What is important is not that it will necessarily happen, but that it can happen. Voting that follows cultural patterns in a multicultural society means two things:

- That a change of government is impossible
- That the party of the majority will never be faced with any change, even from its own ranks, because political issue unites the majority leaving no door open for political debate on other issues.

This can, as has been seen in several countries, easily degenerate into a divided nation where the minorities are suppressed, or emigrate having no options for changing the situation.

Many observers and politicians focus on the item of free elections as the main point of democracy, but the reality may be quite different, depending on what kind of country or society we operate in.

## Political Power, Economic Power, Media Power

Europe, North America, and Australia/New Zealand, with their strong institutionalization of society with inbuilt mechanisms for redistribution of income, and with well-developed societal norms/social capital, have seen a mingling of political, economic, and media power in democratic systems. There have certainly been flaws and some spectators of the political process will undoubtedly adopt the attitude that economic power has succeeded in dominating political power, but consensus would support the view that the three power vectors have thrived and kept one another in balance inside the system.

A stronger separation of the three power vectors can be seen in Asia, where political power is exercised by politicians, and economic power by business people, without much overlapping inside the political system.

Changes are under way in Europe, North America, and Australia/New Zealand as well as Asia, pointing to a more blurred and problematic state of affairs.

The flywheel is that the three power vectors start to make the political system less transparent and more open to influence from sources outside, which according to the textbooks, should not exercise such kind of influence.

A recent example is a headline in an Australian newspaper[51] describing how Rupert Murdoch, labelled the most powerful media mogul in America in the article, had decided to help get Hilary Clinton elected.

The media world is heavily dependent on distribution of licences, regulation, deregulation, and research and creative aids. And even if there is nothing formally wrong with media moguls taking an interest and in fact interfering in the political process, it puts into question who is actually influencing whom, and who is actually influencing the voters to obtain the preferred result of elections, and free elections at that.

With the information and entertainment business world structure growing increasingly global albeit with localized adaptations, this question is not confined to a few nation states, but arises in the form of international media moguls seeking political influence in other countries where their interests are often — but not always — exclusively of a business character.

In Asia, the former "isolation" of politics and business in their respective boxes is not so clear-cut anymore, auguring elections more prone to stronger economic influence from outside the political parties than hitherto.

These developments call for more systematic analyses of how political, economic, and media power mix, and whether a stronger separation of their power inside a democratic process should be looked at.

## Citizens and Political System: A Political and Social Contract

All political systems weigh heavily on a contract between the citizens and the political leaders. Citizens support the state (nation state or society or group) and give their loyalty (identity) in return for human security, some kind of social welfare, and economic prosperity.[52]

In the early stages of statehood, the flywheel was military service that was offered by citizens to the state, whether it was a kingdom or another form of state, in return for rudimentary human security. Those states using mercenaries were normally less successful than states relying on peasant armies because the peasants enlisted felt more loyal to the cause and had something to lose, while mercenaries could turn to another state in case of defeat. After the French Revolution the mobilization of mass armies reached a high point, with World War I illustrating this symbiosis.

In the nation state world we have lived in until recently, the equation was fairly easy to spot. Citizens spoke the same language although there were minorities and they shared the same basic culture which was synonymous with sharing the same basic values. It was possible to build on mutual trust, and trust plus social capital formed the glue of the nation state and its political system. Especially in Europe, but also in other parts of the globe, national borders followed linguistic and/or religious lines ensuring that the majority of people inside a nation state saw behavioural patterns in an analogous way.

The nation state and industrialization were born at the same time and so was democracy. In the feudal system, rulers needed the service of the people and could force the population to deliver this, irrespective of whether they were willing or not. They had nowhere else to go, literally speaking; in most parts of Europe, big masses of peasants lived under various forms of serfdom.

With industrialization political leaders needed people to be more active contributors to growth and prosperity. Social engineering to acquire a labour force presupposed or, rather, depended on mass emigration from rural districts to cities. To run reasonably smoothly a share of the growing wealth had to be diverted to workers who otherwise would have no incentive to change occupations and locality, and if forced to work, might have revolted, which in fact did happen a couple of times, interrupting the industrialization process in France (1848) and Russia (1917).

Democracy was the political instrument to make sure the population was sufficiently content with the distribution of wealth, and served as the frame for the social contract between the people and the political leaders.

The nation state ran a national economy. It was based on industrialization producing wealth distributed among social classes in conformity with voting patterns telling what was acceptable and what was not. The balance broadly speaking between farmers, the owners of the production capacity (capitalists), and workers was maintained by democracy through a voting system (consultation), conveying when adjustment of the distribution mechanism should be introduced.

The old system of loyalty to the state as a quid pro quo for services from the state to the citizens was supplemented by a political mechanism for the distribution of wealth. Military service as the major commitment was replaced by paying taxes. As more complicated services could not be delivered individually, citizens needed to pool their resources. Consultation of the people — in a democracy by voting — became indispensable for finding out what services the people asked for and what kind of burden sharing among citizens or groups of citizens was acceptable.

The nation state, industrialization, and democracy worked together inside the nation state caucus and as the development over the last two hundred years shows, it worked quite well with little disturbance from outside. Disturbance eventually entered the scene in the form of globalization.

## Global Democracy — Globalization of Democracy

Today, there is increasing equality of knowledge and information, regardless of strong inequalities in income, wealth, and opportunities, unless access to knowledge and information is deprived or restricted by policies set up to this effect. Even though around the world there is no agreement that democracy is the "ideal" or "the best possible" political model, there is today "rising expectations" among the deprived or youth, which is principally fuelled by information on fundamental freedoms. There is a growing demand for good governance, accountability, and transparency. This cuts across any "brand" of democracy.[53]

The outstanding question is whether this strong underlying trend can be reconciled with globalization as a primarily economic phenomenon. One possibility is that economic globalization would bypass democracy, which is still predominantly a national and/or domestic political system. This would bring into conflict the interests of the global economy and the interests of those seeking political control. Another possibility is a convergence of economic globalization, the above-mentioned global trends, and an emerging form of global democracy.

The dilemma is not new. It turns around the question of political control versus market forces. What is new is that market forces (economics) have gone global while control (politics) is still overwhelmingly national/ domestic, but testing the water to see whether it can and/or should take the same jump, and if it does, what are the chances that it can perform internationally.

The reading of the trend by Tapscott[54] of the Net Generation,[55] in *Grown Up Digital*, is a strong sign that indeed "rising expectations" are at hand and will prove an unstoppable push for fundamental freedoms, connected with happiness, and creativity as indispensable elements of whatever model for the selection/election of political leaders is chosen by individual countries. Any such model is labelled here as globalization of democracy even if the exact definition of democracy is left unanswered.

There are at least three hurdles ahead for global democracy and/or globalization of democracy.

The *first* is the growing threat of fundamentalism, which in some cases is harbouring terrorism. Fundamentalism runs contrary to the very principle of democracy as it is based on a self-righteous attitude that bars dialogue and, at the core of the matter, tolerance, perceived as caring about other people's destiny even if we may not agree with them. Terrorism undermines democracy by acts of violence and desperation which convey a sense of impotence of the political system to citizens, thus pushing the democracy towards implementing measures running counter to what democracy stands for. It then becomes a vicious circle. Globally this may convey an image of second best for the democratic model, especially in cases where newborn democracies that have borrowed from established democracies in other parts of the world are weighed down by the challenges.

The *second* hurdle is subtler and may in the longer run pose a higher intellectual barrier for democracy. Globalization triggers immigration, and that may cause a conflict, even a confrontation of nationally-rooted identities and cultural pluralism. Recent events in Europe undeniably support the fear that democracy and its institutions find it difficult to sketch a political solution that is adequate for the wish of a majority of the population to combine national identity with identities of the immigrants. In cases of failure, the question immediately pops up as to whether or not the way ahead is pluralism, measuring a multicultural society, and how capable democracy and/or other political systems are of facilitating this process without compromising fundamental values.

The *third* hurdle is that many of the services sought by the individual are now available outside the caucus of the nation state. Citizens can choose; there is competition. Some kind of welfare is offered by multinational companies. Working in another country — no longer a rarity — opens up the possibility of enjoying services and paying taxes there. Increasing integration (such as the European Union, but also embryonic integration such as ASEAN) creates a legal framework for citizens to move around, thus undermining the self-evident link of loyalty and identity to a particular nation state. The nation state moves into a defensive position as it strives to retain loyalty. Citizens, for their part, become increasingly baffled as to how they can influence political decision making since they are uninterested in national political processes and do not feel dependent on a particular nation state, but are at the same time cut off from international decision making due to the lack of channels for them to do so.[56]

The nation state is becoming superfluous in many respects and losing the power that made it indispensable for the individual. A more precise statement is that it has been stripped of its exclusivity and is instead forced to compete with many others to attract the attention of the individual, and deliver solutions to human security and economic welfare sought by the individual. It cannot be assumed that services offered by the nation state are cheaper or better than those offered by other suppliers, and the individual's diminished link to national identity makes it less likely that a higher price will be paid for what is offered by the nation state.

Several other trends work in the same direction. Energy supply is an example. In the traditional mould, energy supply was linked to big power stations (oil, coal, or nuclear power), making it necessary to provide large investments in installations, followed by equally large investments in a national, and later, international power grid. There was no alternative to the nation state. The trend towards renewable energy heralds a break with this concept. Many renewable energy sources are decentralized and do not require either large investments or large power grids. Houses, office buildings, and factories can be supplied with wind or solar power via links installed by citizens, not the nation state, making them less dependent on national supplies. This example can be seen in several other areas, undermining the individual's reliance on the nation state.

## Principles and Mechanisms

There are certain principles and mechanisms that are valid and applied by all political systems, be they democracies or not. That said, the next observation is that each country, or group of countries, operates models heavily influenced by their background, traditions, qualifications, the transition from another political model to democracy in some cases, and social capital.

While the systems may differ, the challenges faced by them in an Asian context are very similar. It does not mean that political systems need to or will converge, but it does mean that all Asian countries are confronted by the same basic questions. The substance or objectives of the political systems may be more important than how political leaders are selected.

At the core of selection or election processes is a mechanism ensuring rotation as the major bulwark against abuses of power — not necessarily among political parties — but this is indispensable for political leaders.

The main issues Asia's political systems are going to encounter over the next twenty-five years may be enumerated in this way:

- Freedom for the individual versus the well functioning of society as a whole. To what degree can individual freedom undermine the well functioning of society, hence eroding the capability of society to defend the individual? Individual freedom can only find its full expression inside a well-functioning society, but can individual freedom bring about a less-well-functioning society, thus undermining this essential condition for individual freedom?
- Almost all nation states have minorities and these minorities look to the state to protect them against the majority, and to secure their right to maintain their own cultural identity. In a democracy where the

government is constituted by a majority of votes, the minorities may feel less protected by the state, knowing that they have little influence — and will never have enough influence — on the composition and policy of the government.

- Free elections lead to a parliament and a government in accordance with the majority of votes, provided there is a choice, and that those offering an alternative have ways to convey their messages. In some countries with groups casting their votes based on tribal, race, ethnic, religious considerations, the cultural majority will have a monopoly of power. The minorities may be left in the political wilderness.

- A complicated constitution may be introduced, but as experience suggests, a constitution safeguarding the rights of minorities may only last as long as the majority wishes it to be so.

- One of the foundations of democracy seems to be that people are ready and prepared to move their votes according to the performance of the government and are not locked into a voting pattern determined by sacrosanct factors.

- The transition towards democracy calls for careful and meticulous preparation. Unless the foundation is established as the first step, the process may become unpredictable and uncontrollable.

- A high degree of social capital (trust among people and between people and their institutions) emerges as one of the most fundamental conditions of a democracy. It is one of the most difficult things to achieve in a multicultural society, as the gap between groups not trusting each other has to be bridged regardless of conditions. Unless social capital is present, a democracy may have to fall back on institutions and a regulatory framework, making voters less inclined to look at the political system as "theirs".

- The globalization of political, economic, and media power indicates that outside forces may interfere in domestic politics and influence elections, thus thwarting the outcome. The political picture becomes more blurred and less transparent because of such outside forces.

- Distrust directed at nation states not joining international cooperation about judicial matters.

## ASIA AS TRENDSETTER

## Principles

The triumvirate of "technology, culture, organization" sponsored the industrial revolution that took place in Europe. The drivers were steam power replacing manpower, but also philosophers driving management principles, supported by cultural creation driving innovation. Historians may discuss why it took place in Europe and not elsewhere. One explanation is the opening of North America which led to the demand for better and faster long-distance transportation. Another is that the population in Europe, in particular Britain, increased rapidly, constituting a growing market. A third is that wars favoured new technology that could also be used for other purposes (spin-off effect). This is how technology migration explains it, but it is too narrow. There is a much simpler one: the emulation in and by different countries across Europe drove technology, culture, and power structures.

Once achieved, the progress turned rapidly into a total recasting of European societies, providing a platform for their permanent and deep transition from feudal/agricultural societies to industrialized ones, with resulting synergies (there was outsourcing of work within Europe long before what we see to the emerging countries of today). These societies excelled in one activity: they were good at maintaining growth and distributing benefits, not evenly, but in a way that sponsored further growth, despite backlashes and crises from time to time. The era of industrialization over more than 200 years produced a considerable number of security, economic, and social crises, but none of them actually changed the fundamental economic system based upon accumulation of capital, distribution of labour, and consumption. Socialism did not offer an alternative model, but an alternative way of distributing benefits.

The *first* element of significance when analysing Asia in the context of the technology-culture-organization triumvirate is that societal structure in Europe, driven by philosophers as well as some religions, and later sociologically by merchants and the middle class, took a benevolent and even supportive view of higher materialistic welfare. Other societies around the globe, however, may have been less interested and more content to live in a semi-stationary society.[57]

Chinese history shows us four categories of people constituting a social hierarchy, and discloses who was ranked highly and who at the bottom. At the top we find the *shi* (gentry scholars), followed by the *nong* (peasant farmers), the *gong* (artisans and craftsmen), and at the bottom, the *shang* (merchants and traders).[58] During the Tang dynasty, examinations were introduced to form a ruling class of "civil servants". Examinations were open to all male citizens except sons of artisans and merchant classes.[59]

The social pyramid in China — and Japan — until the middle of the nineteenth century was clearly a barrier for economic growth and reflects a totally different set of values than was the case in Europe. It reveals that the basic social values and social fabric in a society may be much more important for economic growth and initiating a growth process than that set out in many purely economic works which take it for granted that people behave as *homo economicus* (economic human). They do not always do so, especially not if they have grown up and were nurtured in a social structure where earning money is not regarded as a virtue.

The *second* element in the analysis is the role of religion and its impact on how human beings look on their relations with nature.[60]

The religions in the Abrahamic tradition (Judaism, Christianity, and Islam) all focus on the morality of the human being. Nature is viewed as being of secondary importance among other things because God is regarded as above nature.[61] This attitude explains why the Europeans and, in particular, European settlers in North America and other areas around the world, did not interpret anything in their religion to stand in the way of using nature's resources.[62] Nature was there for them to use and religion or morality born out of religion did not tell them to see human beings and nature as two sides of the same coin. The initiator of this way of looking at these religions was Lynn Townsend White[63] in the middle of the 1960s, and this led to a number of counter-arguments[64] about statements in the New Testament that refer to nature. But fundamentally it is difficult to overlook the significance of the attitude to nature especially when looking at settlers who came from religious segments of society.

The great Asian religions or philosophies take a completely different approach.

Hinduism incorporates the timeless world of spirit, thus taking a certain distance from a materialistic view based on the use of resources, and Hinduism's references to sacred rivers, mountains, etc. give nature a special standing in the way of regarding it as a resource to be used/violated by human beings. The world is seen as a creative manifestation of the divine. One of the key messages in Hinduism is to see the presence of god in all and treat the creation with respect without harming and exploiting others. Such veneration of God in nature is required of Hindus to safeguard the natural harmonious relationship between human beings and nature. For the Hindus, in the ancient period God and nature were one and the same. Human beings could not assume some kind of privilege or right or authority over other creatures.[65]

Buddhism may be said to prescribe a mutual system of respect/balance for the various elements, and does not set human beings above nature. The interpretation is that these religions constitute a much stronger barrier for depreciation of nature's resources because nature is not subordinated to human beings and the disposal of resources by human beings is not facilitated by religious beliefs giving human beings the right to do so.

East Asian philosophies such as Confucianism and Taoism come closest to epitomizing the opposite of the Abrahamic view, as they view nature, human beings, and the cycles of nature as a holistic system in which human beings must not only be in harmony with other human beings, but also with nature. The interpretation is that such philosophies raise impediments to use nature's resources as if they were inexhaustible.[66]

The relevance for classical Chinese thought is analysed by J. Baird Callicott[67] who finds that the potential for the development of an explicit, indigenous Chinese environmental ethic based on classical Chinese thought is tremendous. Confucianism and Taoism point to human beings as being part of a network of ecological as well as social relationships undergoing constant change. Human beings enjoy an interdependence and mutuality with all environmental conditions. People are part of nature and do not have the right to use nature according to their own interests. This concept leads to a notion of nature based on sustainability and preservation of nature and its riches.

Daisaku Ikeda[68] defines the difference between Eastern and Western thinking by saying that Chinese thought, including that of both the Confucian and Taoist schools, adopts a peaceful approach to the struggle with nature, one that advocates harmonious relations with the natural world. This is also characteristic of Buddhism as exemplified in the concept of the "oneness of life and the environment". The Eastern view of nature is characterized by respect for the workings of nature and the maintenance of harmonious relations with its ecosystems, a view founded on the principle of harmony and non-violent coexistence. In recent centuries the West has adopted a militant approach, one in which human beings stand in opposition to nature, endeavouring to control and manipulate the ecosystems of the natural world in order to fulfil their own wants and desires.[69]

The writings of Sun Tzu on military strategy and tactics bear out this interaction between man and nature on an equal footing with an explanation of one of the principles of warfare which likens warfare to how water flows: "Now, an army may be likened to water,[70] for just as flowing water avoids the heights and hastens to the lowlands, so an army should avoid strength and strike weakness. And as water shapes its flow in accordance with the ground, so an army manages its victory in accordance with the situation of the enemy. And as water has no constant form, there are in warfare no constant conditions. Thus, one able to win the victory by modifying his tactics in accordance with the enemy situation may be said to be divine.

Of the five elements [water, fire, metal, wood, and earth], none is always predominant; of the four seasons, none lasts forever; of the days, some are long and some short, and the moon waxes and wanes. That is also the law of employing troops."[71]

In this context it is worth recalling the culture of indigenous people living in harmony with nature and its resources — normally not using more of nature's resources than sustainability warranted, and actually operating a system of recycling. Some indigenous people have, in many cases, given nature a soul thereby rejecting the Western perception of nature as an unlimited pool of resources, whereas several prehistoric populations such as those who painted the walls in the Lascaux cave in France had a different view.

Theodore Roszak in *The Making of a Counter Culture*[72] — first published in 1969, but still as readable now as it was then — recounts a Wintu (Californian) Indian describing the contrast between the relationship of her shamanistic culture and that of the modern white man with a common environment:

> The white people never cared for land or deer or bear. When we Indians kill meat, we eat it all up. When we dig roots, we make little holes … we shake down acorns and pinenuts. We don't chop down the trees. We only use dead wood. But the white people plow up the ground, pull up the trees, kill everything. The tree says: "Don't. I am *sore*. Don't hurt me." But they chop it down and cut it up. The spirit of the land hates them… The Indians never hurt anything, but the white people destroy all. They blast rocks and scatter them on the ground. The rock says "Don't! You are hurting me." But the white people pay no attention. When the Indians use rocks, they take little round ones for their cooking… How can the spirit of the earth like the white man?… Everywhere the white man has touched it, it is sore.[73]

Roszak (1969, p. 251) makes the comment that "there reside in the bowels of the earth, in concrete silos throughout our advanced societies, genocidal destructive weapons capable of annihilating our safe and secure civilization. No doubt in her (the Wintu Indian's) deeply poetic imagination the old woman would see in these dreaded instruments the vengeful furies of the earth poised to destroy the white man for his overweening pride. A purely fanciful interpretation of our situation, we might say … but maybe she realizes that the spirit of the earth moves in more mysterious ways than we dare let ourselves believe."[74]

In a fascinating book,[75] *Water Wars*, Vandana Shiva[76] reflects on water management and observes that in cases where water management has been centralized and subject to market conditions, water resources have merely been reallocated and not augmented. The result was that the poorer parts of India and the villages have faced a deterioration of water supply. She then demonstrates how decentralized water management in the villages according to traditional methods has resuscitated water supplies. She goes one step further and points out how water has a meaning, a significance, even spiritual significance, to people, and requires respect in view of the holistic relationship between man and nature, which is contrary to the industrial age outlook of seeing water as a resource, a commodity. Only if the spirit and significance of water beyond its "user value" are acknowledged, and maybe even worshipped, can man build up a solid relationship with nature that promises sustainability.

In this context, it should be recalled that Europe grew the notion of urbanized populations first, with all their bad and good. The Americas and Asia till 1900 had — with the possible exceptions of Edo, Canton, Bombay — few places that could be considered a modern city. The relation to nature of urban populations is completely different to the one of rural populations, irrespective of where in the world.

Looking at the history of at least some Asian societies and most of Asia's religions and/or philosophies, we find evidence for the view that Asians adopt a different perspective on lifestyle to that of the Westerner. It may be said with justification that developments over recent decades do not support this view as pollution, degradation of the environment, and use of resources have had little in common with the world views mentioned above. The interesting observation is, however, that basic[77] philosophies reveal other priorities than the Abrahamic ones do, and under pressure from new circumstances, Asians and Asian societies may — but not necessarily will — steer a future course more in accordance with ancient traditions, lifestyles, and philosophies.

A *third* element to add in this context to the triumvirate of technology, culture, and organization, is the question of values versus a rule-based society, or the rule of the law versus behavioural pattern making individuals act in conformity with agreed ethics, thus confining litigation and the law to the few cases where individuals and/or organizations fail to comply with common and shared values.

The Confucian Code of Rites[78] (*Liji*) controls civilized behaviour by laying down norms, ethics, and values. The law is only brought into the picture vis-à-vis those who do not respect shared values and, therefore, fall outside civilized behaviour. Relations between civilized citizens are governed by ethics and values, while the law and litigation apply to non-civilized citizens — citizens who do not know or reject common, shared values. In Japan the equivalent "glue" is the particular mix of Buddhism and Shintoism called "syncretism".[79]

The interpretation of the Confucian Code applied to today's society is that social capital is the glue holding society together. The stronger the social capital is supplemented by high mutual trust, the fewer citizens fall outside the scope of civilized behaviour.

Chinese-Confucian traditions thus have an inbuilt world view that values and ethics govern the relations among citizens in the society or community, not the law, which is relegated to an instrument only to be called into action when people do not behave in accordance with values and ethics.

The Confucian tradition prevailed in China and was instrumental under the Qing dynasty and even far into the twentieth century.[80] The Chinese ideology saying that the emperor had a mandate from heaven supported this tradition because it explained why the emperor and the people he chose knew how to define values, ethics, and morals.[81] In Japan the emperor was the living god.

A comparison of the "Rule of law" in China and India[82] in the past offers very similar pictures. Until British India emerged in the nineteenth century, the rule of men governed India. The rule of law became synonymous with British India, with its message that rules were applicable to all and were the same for all, instead of the hitherto practice based on "personal discretion" — in reality, meaning the rule of men.

For both China and India the history of the rule of law has to be seen in the context of building a state to establish and maintain sovereignty. The rule of the law served as the legitimization of the authority exercised and was closely linked to the state and sovereignty. Before the notion of state and sovereignty came to Asia — and when this happened is a good question in itself — the norm was the rule of men rooted in ethics, values, and behavioural norms. Furthermore the rule of men was seen as a moral principle to be upheld by the governing elite, based on shared, common values, while the law — its texts and the written prescriptions — was directed at the people not in possession of these values.

The world has discussed Asian values for years. Suffice it to say here that when we look at Asian traditions, three observations seem to offer themselves for a simple, almost crude, definition: a less money-oriented social behaviour defining status and social strata, a more balanced relationship between man and nature, and a different perception of whether it is values or the law that governs society. These three observations uncover fundamental differences in the cultural background of Asia and the United States, as well as to a certain extent European societies albeit the picture here is more nuanced.

Three questions to answer looking ahead at the world's future and, in particular, Asia's future are:

- Is the model — global and Asian — of 1750 to 2000 coming to an end? A large part of the preceding paragraphs in this chapter leads to an affirmative answer. Yes it is.
- What is the plinth for a new model? The conclusion of this study is that it is shortages, even scarcities, of resources, higher prices for resources, and burden sharing; societies instead of individuals, self-actualization and esteem (Maslow's hierarchy more than materialistic consumption); and values plus ethics crowding out rules as the anchor of identity for individuals.
- Where will a new model emerge, why, and how will it look?

The answer to the third question is Asia.

Original values embedded in the great Asian religions/philosophies, if rejuvenated and spread again, enunciate a holistic view of the relationship between man and nature. They cannot be separated, they support each other, and one cannot continue to live without the other. Neither has the supremacy or privileges or authority to undermine the existence of the other. It is in reality a religious and/or philosophical expression of sustainability long before that word was coined. And this is how many of the Asian societies survived until they crossed paths with Western countries and, in particular, were incorporated into the industrialization process. Looking at Asia today, we realize that the analysis should not omit the fact that most Asian societies have deviated from that world view in their drive towards industrialization. The explanation is, however, not that the foundation from ancient religions/philosophies has changed, but that Asian societies have adopted Western values instead of sticking with their own traditional Asian values.[83]

Therefore a philosophical world view pre-exists in Asia for it to swing around from exploitating nature to establishing a growth model based on harmony. It will take time and there is no certainty that it will happen, but in a philosophical context it means that Asian societies can break away from temporarily adopted Western values and go back to original Asian values.

Callicott[84] goes one step further saying that "Western philosophers initially turned to traditional Eastern wisdom for help in their search ... for an environmental ethic located in a deep ecological consciousness.... The transcendentalism of Ralph Waldo Emerson and Henry David Thoreau — who was among the first American thinkers to look on nature as something more than an obstacle to progress and a pool of natural resources — was inspired by Hindu thought. In the mid-twentieth century, the emerging contemporary environmental movement was profoundly influenced by Japanese Zen Buddhism."[85]

Analytical thinking was indispensable for the industrial age and it was based on science and technology, supported by the nation state as the political infrastructure. The Western mindset was simply suited for that way of thinking. The price paid was the neglect of segments of society other than the one industrialization addressed, and nature, which led to an unbalanced world. This opens up the opportunity for a new world view based on synthetic thinking which sees objects as part of a universal relationship, where one object cannot be addressed without consequences for other objects. This line of thinking is more in conformity with Eastern tradition than Western tradition.

The transition taking place is:

*from* a civilization based on the nation state, rising populations, economic growth, growing materialistic welfare, mass consumption, relative prices making resources cheap and labour expensive

*to* a civilization with societal networks as the political infrastructure (norms being more important than laws, rules, and regulations), stagnant or even falling populations, economic growth perceived and measured completely differently to what we have grown used to, question marks about the virtues of materialistic welfare and mass consumption, and relative prices reflecting expensive resources and cheap labour.

Just as the world saw interaction between technology, culture, and organization further the course of industrialization, the world may now see a new economic and political model(s) born in Asia framed by:

- Burden sharing instead of distribution of benefits
- Incentives for, and abilities of, individuals to share knowledge with others, thus replacing productivity of the individual with productivity of groups
- The importance of social groups, social capital, and coherence as catalysts for change
- Adaptation to economics of survival of the fittest perceived as groups and not individuals
- Ecological productivity instead of economic productivity — how much more output can be achieved without using more resources?
- A theory of consumption under scarcities, instead of plenty
- Concentration of capital in fewer hands making genuine competition and the free market a thing of the past
- A political system grappling with the difficulty of ensuring transparency,

accountability, and legitimacy with the decline of the nation state and the rise of gigantic concentration of economic wealth/powers
- Accommodation of the rising expectations about fundamental rights of freedom in the countries which harbour scepticisms about adopting the mechanism for the selection of political leaders used in Western-style democracies
- The Clautzewitzian model of crisis-conflict-confrontation replaced by a model of cooperation-compromise-consensus which reaches beyond economics to pave the way for a new interaction between politics and economics, thus pointing to better understanding of the need to share

The apparent weaknesses for which solutions remain difficult to see are essentially:

- The will to replace domination of people by people, with more institutionalized models — the political system
- Structural ability and willingness to deal with people, who for various reasons, voice discontent with existing systems
- The sense for science which runs counter to the sense for subjectivity
- Respect for innovation, creation, and diversity

## Elements Forging a Future Political System

The main pillars in a future political system/model are institutions, and the weakened nation state making room for a number of other players offering services to the citizens.

### *Institutions, Political Leadership, and Civil Servants*

Western or Western inspired political systems herald principles — which in many cases are regarded as almost sacrosanct — on the mechanism for selecting political leaders: the election engineered for a change of leadership as the rule, and not the exception. This mechanism also guarantees fundamental rights of freedom for the individual. Fortunately for Western countries and Western societies, this model, for a variety of reasons, has produced results — it has worked. For more than a century, and in some countries even longer, it has been the framework for the unprecedented creation of wealth and prosperity. It was strong enough to mobilize millions of people to go to war to defend the model, society, or nation state — regardless of which label was chosen for it, citizens found it attractive enough to die for it.[86] Sometimes it is overlooked that in the European democracies in 1870, 1914, and 1939, and in the United States, people could have ended the commitment to war via the ballot box. They did not, choosing instead to support the politicians' argument that war in the circumstances was necessary. This speaks volumes about the legitimacy enjoyed by the political system.

When discussing and analysing political systems in Asia and the Asian countries/societies, it must be borne in mind that in fact they differ widely from country to country.

Asia may be less interested in principles and more focused on how effective a political system is, how good it is in delivering solutions and improving living conditions for its citizens. In a nutshell, does it work?[87]

In that way Asia may adopt one of the virtues of the American society, albeit not the American political system: meritocracy. European countries among others were dominated by social strata inhibiting a large part of the population from assuming leadership positions which were reserved for a privileged segment of the population. A part of the success of the American model is to be found in the repudiation of these privileges and the adoption of meritocracy.[88]

There are strong barriers for meritocracy in all Asian societies as nepotism, ideology, and corruption often attest to, but the point here is that in many, perhaps most Asian nation states, the political system finds its legitimacy in its ability to deliver. Political leaders are chosen from criteria prioritizing meritocracy, competence, and ability, ahead of many of the principles governing the selection of Western political leaders.

Attention is focused on what works and what does not. Even if most Asian nation states do not refer to it, the famous phrase spoken by Deng Xiaoping — "it doesn't matter if a cat is black or white, so long as it catches mice" — has become the leitmotif in Asia.

Institutions and the civil service system constitute the backbone of any political system. Strong institutions, especially if accompanied by a robust civil service system, point towards continuity and a sense of the state functioning, irrespective of the course chosen by political leaders, but in conformity with the directions they give. Some observers would add that they serve as a barrier for changing political course. That may be true to a certain degree as is probably the case in Japan and India — you cannot have continuity and change at the same time.

In most of the European nation states, in particular those with a long history, institutions and the civil service system serve as mechanisms for selecting political leaders. The institutions work effectively and efficiently regardless of who the political leaders are, and those at the top are forged by the system, whether they like it or not, and they govern with the consent of the institutional system. When they have run out of steam, the system replaces them with new leaders chosen and forged the same way, albeit not always having analogous policies. Broadly speaking policies may change, but within a relatively narrow band of political preferences.

In the United States the institutions serve in the same way, but the civil service system does not. Institutions shape leaders whether they are then put into Congress or into the role of governors. Civil servants have, however, a much weaker role because political leaders appoint politically nominated officials to a large number of posts, thus breaking continuity, which serves as a strong point in the European model.

In Asia institutions work as catalysts for selecting political leaders in several countries among which we find China, India (less so), and Japan — all the three powerful Asian nation states. But the civil service system operates quite differently in these three nation states. In several other Asian nation states, institutions do not breed political leaders, but are used by political leaders emerging through other channels to legitimize their power and frame political decisions in particular legislation. If or when political leaders are replaced, institutions such as political parties may likewise fade and the large majority of parliamentarians may also change.

The virtue of institutions is primarily the enhanced possibilities for transparency when citizens select political leaders, and, with some of them, enhanced possibilities for some part or all of the population to have an influence on the selection process. Institutions increase the credibility of political leaders, thus enlarging the scope for trust between political leaders and the population. This is not the same as saying that it will work that way, but chances are better with, than without institutions. A civil service system working with the same ardour, irrespective of who is in charge becomes more likely to achieve this, while arbitrary or, even worse, deliberately biased decisions resulting from not having a civil service system, are in principle less likely to do so.

Institutions and a civil service system are of paramount importance in Asia's endeavours to move towards better governance in the next twenty-five years. Many Asian nation states are already there, in an embryonic or more mature state, but generally speaking, a more solid, robust, even vibrant, institutional framework is desirable for achieving their economic and societal objectives. Asia is dichotomized between a model where institutions breed political leaders (India is an example), and a model where institutions legitimize decisions taken by political leaders emerging from outside the institutions (several nation states in Southeast Asia).

Another acute, assiduous, and painstaking problem is that while Europe (with France through L'Ecole Nationale de l'Administration [ENA] as a possible exception) and the United States separate the selection process for political leaders and the civil service system, this is not the case for all Asian nation states. If political leaders and civil servants are the product of the same selection channel, for example in China, the risk for abuse of power grows, either explicitly as nepotism and corruption, or implicitly through cronyism/cliquishness and this may become an impediment to a smooth running machinery. Outsiders may also marginalized.

The other side of the coin — to the advantage to citizens this time — is the role of institutions as a feedback channel, and one for exercising control over and offering insights into the political system. Samuel Huntington[89] pointed to the role of institutions as absorber of conflicts, but this is hardly sufficient in this context. Institutions serve as a guarantee that voters and/or the people cannot be denied voicing their opinion in between elections, and/or other arrangements for tapping political leaders. Transparency again becomes key as people know how to contact politicians. The risk of the arbitrary cutting out of groups or individuals from feeding their views into the system diminishes. Even more important, proper institutions arrange it so that voters/people outside the governing party or organization for political leaders are also offered possibilities for putting their views forward. In short, institutions work both ways. They channel decisions from policymakers to the people and they organize feedback from the people to politicians.

## The Weakened Nation State

The nation state, industrialization, the current form of institutions, and the civil service system, constitute a complex of ideas forged into one single model. If one of these "pillars" starts to crack — and that is certainly the case for the nation state and industrialization — the others cannot continue to function as if nothing has happened.

The fundamental problem is that a large number of people do not really feel that the nation state is either meeting their demand for services, or providing them with a cultural identity. When that is the case, the current embryonic trend for citizens to seek their identity or take their demand for services "somewhere else" starts to gain momentum.[90]

Developments leading to this trend are: The cornerstone in the mechanics of the nation state is that all citizens rely on its services, use them, and contribute financially to the tax bill. If some groups stop identifying with the nation state, and switch loyalty, turning for services to non-state institutions, the financial base weakens with the almost inevitable consequence that the quality of services deteriorates further. A self-reinforcing economic process takes over. The lower quality of services pushes other groups to look for alternatives.

Three groups of citizens then emerge:

The *first* comprises those from the weak social strata, who do not have any alternative to using public services. However, they harbour grievances towards the nation state, which they do not think has offered them suitable opportunities. They tend to look for groups outside the nation state framework to identify with while at the same time using its public services. In the European context, a large number of the weakest immigrants are found in these social strata, making it even more complicated.

A *second* group comprises those in the strong social strata, who rely on non nation state services instead of public services, and pay for them. They do not really see themselves as economically dependent on the nation state and try to avoid the tax burden using the argument that they should not pay high taxes to finance services they do not use (they reject the concept of solidarity). They may still maintain some sense of identity with the nation state, but increasingly as a matter of convenience to be together with people speaking the same language, etc. rather than because they share a genuine common identity. They are more dependent on corporations or organizations than the nation state. Others in the same strata, even if they speak the same language, are also dependent on corporations, institutions, but not the same ones.

In between these two groups we find a *third* one comprising those neither sufficiently strong to break out of the system or weak enough to rely exclusively on the nation state. They becomes victims, so to speak, of the two other groups as they are the ones who cannot escape high taxes and do not have the financial strength to go elsewhere for education, health care, etc. This group is becoming the backbone of the European nation state, but is not able to lead or reform the system, thus keeping the European nation state on a steady course towards a growing discrepancy between objectives and the means to achieve them. They accept or are driven to accept public services run on private criteria, and may feel cheated when solidarity schemes they believed in (public services, pensions, etc.) are fiddled with by politicians in need of either cash, or because of political ambitions.

The first and second groups think — to a certain extent — beyond borders, but quite differently. The first group looks for identity in similar angry segments of society either in comparable nation states or if they are immigrants, in countries they or their parents have left. They nourish one another's grievances and build up a strong animosity towards the very nation state whose public services they use. Some of them go so far as to join extremist groups wanting to destroy the nation state in which they live.

The second group moves towards some kind of international or global identity, finding it in the company with people in the same category, irrespective of their nationalities. They do not contribute either to the functioning of the nation state or to the international community.

The third group is trapped and starts to look at international integration, economic globalization, etc. as the reason for the difficulties they meet in their daily life.

In the nation state/industrialization system/model, society was dominated by a few large groups such as workers, farmers, craftsmen, soldiers, lawyers, and academics, linked by their nationality. The individual belonged to the group reflecting his social status and nationality and radiated this belonging through a dress code, the local newspaper, etc. Gradually we have seen how this has changed fundamentally. Instead of a few large groups, societies are dominated by many small, or at least, smaller groups, putting aside the old class system. People do not show their identity through a dress code, etc. anymore, but by symbols, often small ones telling who they are and whom they want to associate with. Nationality is being replaced by ethnicity, levels of ambition or self branding, religious or regional, and/or local communities inside nation states.

If elements other than nationality, such as religion, media exposure, and ethnicity grow in importance, the way is open for groups to interact on the basis of shared values. This will be a looser, less rigid, and less rule-based interaction than between nation states and inside nation states, but that does not mean that it will be weaker. If people and organizations move together sponsored by common ethics and values, a fairly solid common behavioural pattern may emerge between the groups and inside groups. In fact some kind of social capital may be built up to govern the system by including those who act in accordance with the shared values and excluding those who do not.

The nation state model locked the individual and, to a large degree, also enterprises and organizations in their identity and loyalty. It was a big step to shift allegiance and in many cases simply not possible. This will be different in the model/system sketched above based on values and ethics. If the adherents of a group feel that the values do not attract them anymore, they can in principle shift their adherence to another group. Unlike a shift of citizenship, this does not require a physical move. How much change will take place is uncertain and will depend on several factors, among which one of the most interesting is what steers the choice of values, and also the tolerance level by others to such change. If people tend to stick with values over a lifetime, the number of changes will be limited. If, on the other hand, groups and values are susceptible to some kind of social engineering, it may be more common.

For Asia (with the possible exception of Japan and Korea), such a value-based model is more likely than in many other parts of the world where identity and loyalty are predominantly linked, and will presumably continue to be linked, to nationality, tribalism, or other elements posing high barriers to a shift of allegiance.

Asia is home to several large religions, which are neither confined to one nation state nor one ethnicity, but which cross borders and offer shared and common values to those who like to embrace them. Most of them are fairly loose in their organizational structure, making them less of a "threat" for nation states jealous or even fearful of potential political alternatives. Asia already has experience with diasporas stretching across the continent. One of them is the Chinese diaspora, estimated at 55 million; another is the Indian diaspora estimated at 20 million.[91] Asian multinational companies have not yet grown to a size and adopted attitudes that make them candidates for offering identity to their staff, but it may come as they spread their wings across the continent.

From a historical perspective, the third leg of the French revolution, "fraternité",[92] has not really been appropriated by any nation state in Asia, while it is to be found in the family and now in wider communities. Nation states in Asia do not see this as a threat/problem as long as these families and communities have no physical and financial capabilities. However, through connections and information, they are now building stronger physical and financial capabilities.

A new form of globalization that is not only for economics, logistics, and transport, but also for ideas and identities and cultural sentiments with technology opening the door for cross border communication among individuals, and the right to express values among groups sharing values, irrespective of nationality, seems to be the driver in a new political infrastructure.

Social capital becomes the crucial point because it rests on trust that will generate competences and capabilities to solve the four fundamental challenges political systems will confront in the twenty-five years ahead:

- How to reconcile fundamental freedoms to express identity with the necessary (self)discipline to make groups work together
- How to operate an economic model based on the sharing of knowledge instead of competition to acquire knowledge for exclusive use (monopolize knowledge)
- How to exercise burden sharing required of communities because of "ecological" productivity, with less materialistic consumption
- How to operate a cultural model based on the sharing of creativity and mutual tolerance

There will still be national laws, regulations, and rules and there will still be international or global rule sets governing economic life and some parts of private life, but individuals will gradually feel freer to act more in accordance within the set of values chosen by them, than a formal rule set imposed by a nation state with which they do not wish to link their identity. In practice that will mean enhanced difficulties for nation states and international bodies enforcing rules, which some of their population do not want to adhere to. They will not formally break away from the nation state, but their support and even financial contribution in form of taxes will gradually be channeled elsewhere. The key here are that values will determine the identity, and consequently, the political adherence, of the people and the citizens.

It can be done inside the nation state without pulling it apart, provided that the nation state reads the developments correctly and opens the door for its citizens to operate a kind of dual identity, splitting their identity so that it belongs partly to the nation state, and partly to some kind of community operating across borders. The nation state capable and/or willing to do this may survive relatively unscathed, while nation states trying too hard to clamp down on attempts by their citizens to split cultural allegiance between networks or organizations outside the nation state and the nation state itself will run into difficulties.[93]

The nation state is losing on three accounts. *First* citizens are shifting identity according to values and culture instead of nationality. *Second*, citizens get access to services from other sources than the nation state. *Third* — and probably the most important[94] — burden sharing means that the world is moving into an era of international, even global, regulatory framework. This is the driver for the evolution and the fundamental difference compared with the previous state of affairs. With fewer resources, what is available may not be allowed to fall under the control of market forces because policymakers do not trust that distribution vehicle. An omen of what is to come is global warming/climate change where the world, perhaps without knowing or realizing it, is fast moving towards global regulation on distributing quotas. The same may happen for fishing — it is in fact already happening for certain fish species. The nation state can no longer determine the amount of resources at its disposal; it is done in international negotiations where it might not even negotiate alone, but often as part of a regional integration or association. It is left in the role of distributing the result among its citizens. If citizens find that they may get a larger share by joining other institutional set-ups taking part in this, they lose the incentive to stay with the nation-state and start to look for other players.

## New Players

The list of new actors/players looks like this:

i) Coalitions of nation states emerging where nation states find themselves together pursuing analogous political objectives, but still wishing to preserve full freedom of sovereignty and not be bound by a rule-based organizational structure. Economic integration means that nation states have chosen to stick together. A coalition of nation states means that nation states temporarily stick together, keeping the window open for changing partners.

ii) Civic societies (communities) both inside the nation states and of an international, even global, character, offering channels for voicing opinions, and an organizational structure to give it clout. While a coalition of nation states can be expected to work in accordance with established rules, civic societies may be expected to break the rules or shape new rules, reaching out to citizens and/or organizations that do not find themselves comfortable with using existing and established channels inside the framework dominated by nation states.

iii) Cross-border regions as have already been seen in Europe, on both sides of the Rhine, the Danube, the Baltic region, and several other examples. The regions break out of the nation-state framework — not totally, but in pursuance of defined objectives — seeking partners across borders, knowing that they have more in common with regions on the other side of the border than with regions in the same nation state, but geographically far away.

iv) Megacities/Megaregions feeling that their economic weight and political significance warrant more independent behaviour than the nation state is disposed to offer them and therefore breaking out of the mould. This is seen when regions or states in federal nation states pursue their own industrial policy by attracting foreign direct investment, even in competition with other megacities/megaregions inside the same nation state.

v) Enterprises adopting the role of political enterprises, taking not only entrepreneurial decisions, but also political ones, and moving in as a potential anchor for identity, social stability, loyalty, and value-based adherence for their staff. Over the last decades the public sector has gradually withdrawn from financing many activities hitherto under its auspices, such as universities and cultural manifestations/activities.[95] Enterprises may have entered this arena to gain in reputation, but it is an illusion to postulate that in a longer-term perspective financing can and will be kept separate from decisions about the use of money — political decisions that shift politics and political decision making from the public sector to private enterprises in areas hitherto classified as under public authority.[96]

vi) Non-governmental organizations, some of which act along the same lines as civic societies, but the real discovery are the big private funds geared to operate globally and with an agenda that cannot avoid being political. Their activities mean that private funds or foundations take over activities hitherto under government control, such as development assistance, or organized by international institutions, such as sponsoring green technology. There is nothing wrong in this, but efforts, knowingly or unknowingly, to mould the international mindset, means the making of policies and laying down of political guidelines shift from being solely governmental to involving private organizations and/or persons, with obvious repercussions on accountability and transparency. Examples are Richard Branson's Virgin Green Fund,[97] The Bill and Melinda Gates Foundation,[98] and The Open Society Institute[99] under George Soros' auspices. These funds command money many times bigger than almost all governments are willing to channel into relevant activities, and consequently, assume a leading role in shaping the global mindset and provide the conditions (read money) for implementing policies.

vii) Religious groups that feel that as value-based organization they are better able to offer a "sanctuary" for people than nation states which frequently focus on materialistic living standards not realizing that values have gained in significance for individuals.

What we see emerging is a much more pluralistic political system where the hitherto "command" system based on written rules (legislation) and enforcement of rules by authorities gives way to values and enforcement through self-discipline inside groups/communities. The actors/players in this pluralistic system violate existing frames and compete for the individual's attention and identity. What is emerging may be the political counterpart to the velcro concept for business structure.[100] Citizens do not link their total identity to one player or one supplier, but split it among several players.

## Elements Forging a Future Economic System/Model

The drivers in changing the economic foundation are the consumption theory, production theory, perception of wealth, reactions to shortcomings of the market mechanism, the measurement of production and wealth, and the search for general equilibrium.

Much of the existing terminology such as free market, competition, and the price mechanism is still being used, but when analysing today's economy one should remember that it bears little resemblance to the economic condition when these terms were coined.

The free market is supposed to set prices guided by Adam Smith's invisible hand, but in today's world the free market is an illusion. A free market in economic terminology means that no supplier can influence the price and supply for the goods or services in question. The observer, however, has to search hard to find a market where that is the case. The large majority of goods and services are traded in markets with a limited number of suppliers (oligopoly), and this rules out genuine competition and instead makes the price setting opaque and elusive, which turns it into more of a negotiating process than of competition.

Competition is rarely found because a small number of suppliers control the market. Theoretically newcomers could enter the market, but this is so costly that it is fast becoming more theory than practice. If a newcomer looks like a real threat to one or several of the established companies, a bid to take it over through an acquisition is set in motion, aimed at transferring innovative skill, managerial know-how, and other non-material assets to one of the established companies. This is usually done as an explicit bid (or siphoning manoeuvre). From 1994 to 2000, the 150 biggest companies operating in free market economies increased their share of global capitalization from 25 per cent to 40 per cent.[101]

Research[102] looking at the impact of large corporations and the change in the list of large corporations supports the view that the low turnover among large corporations acts as a barrier for high growth. The analysis indicates that a big business sector with a low turnover works through institutional factors to impede the rise of new large corporation, thus inhibiting competition whic in turn means lower productivity and growth. The study adds that these findings serve to validate Joseph Schumpeter's theory that long-run growth at a high level requires new upcoming corporations to topple existing ones ("creative destruction").[103]

## The Consumption Theory

The consumption theory is the obvious starting point and will also turn out to be the litmus test of whether a value-based society and economy is actually going to materialize. If we work on the basis of Maslow's hierarchy of needs, which moves from physiological needs to self-actualization,[104] it cannot and should not be ruled out that as a large part of humanity jumps out of poverty, the incentive to express their identity through materialistic consumption is gradually replaced by non-materialistic ways (based on values and ethics).

Consumption satisfies our needs and, to a large extent, this is being done by comparing ourselves with other individuals to underline how we are different from or similar to them — there are only these two possibilities. Maslow did not speak about identity, but for individuals, this may be decisive, with values guiding them in their pursuit of identity and expressing it by consumption patterns (plural because of multiple identities).[105]

Maslow's insights have always been acknowledged, but never really taken as a warning that the consumption theory would have to change, because the large majority of consumers around the globe are still found in the lower economic bracket and are still looking to satisfy their basic physiological needs.

Much will depend on the strength of social capital and what will emerge as decisive parameters for keeping group members together, be it shared values or more materialistic consumption. If the preference for human security, expressing identity, plus economic and social welfare — not necessarily materialistic consumption — prevails, then it is likely that a value-based consumption pattern will emerge. As will be seen in later chapters (in particular Chapters 2 and 4) high social capital and trust open up for the consumer the option of deriving satisfaction from doing something for others even if it does not benefit the consumer him-/herself.

A society based on weak social capital — where individuals have to create conditions for their own human security and economic welfare — is much more likely to opt for a high materialistic consumption. Money will be an important part of identity and money, instead of group solidarity, will determine whether individuals and families are able to cope with the challenges in their daily life. Moves towards a value-based society will be blocked and consumption will be frozen by materialistic attitudes.

## Production Theory: Sharing

Production will increasingly be steered by science and knowledge as a production factor. It differs from conventional production factors (land, labour, and capital) in several decisive ways: it can be used again and again without any need for reinvestment, it delivers increasing returns to scale with the number of person using it, and most important of all, it can be used by several persons at the same time. Knowledge is the typical production factor underlining the switch from individual or small group based production to production by large groups with productivity dependent on the capability to work together.

Some writers argue that there is another difference, which is that knowledge is free. It is based on two assertions. The *first* is that you are given access to knowledge in the first place (not the case yet for billions of people in Asia) and the cost of transmitting knowledge from one user to another is extremely low. The *second* is that the user does not pay directly for accessing webpages, etc. on the Internet. The fact, however, is that the perception of freely available knowledge is wrong. The real tangible costs of creativity, innovation, content creation, and content transmission are covered in a way other than the conventional price mechanism still operating in the paradigm of the industrial age and not capable of incorporating knowledge.

The fundamental revolution comes from the third observation — that of it being used by several persons at the same time and, therefore, sometimes enhanced. This is because it puts the finger on what is determining the shift compared with the conventional production theory: sharing of the performance, skill, or output embedded in a production factor. The faster knowledge is disseminated through society, the higher the total integrated value becomes. The higher the number of people using knowledge as a production factor, the higher the total production becomes.

Unless people are convinced that benefits accrue from sharing, knowledge (in this case) will be distributed in accordance with values and ethics; they will be reluctant to share. The key to sharing is trust, combined with privacy, and the key to trust is building social capital inside and between groups. Social capital depends on people adopting common values and ethics. Individuals network with others and groups build interaction inside the community with one another. This constitutes a break with existing (economic) distribution theory controlled by economic factors, which rules out values, frequently leading to inequality, or even worse, rising inequality, thus giving a part, and sometimes a majority of the population, the impression that they are not part of society.

Therefore the plinth of the production theory in future societies becomes, as was seen for consumption, not economic rationale, but values, ethics, and norms steering people's behaviour and opening the door for working more in groups and less individually.

An individualistic mindset pushes people towards doing what is in their interest instead of sharing, and in some cases this may sponsor breakthroughs as has been seen in many cases, for example, in the United States. But the price for this — as is also seen in the United States — is a compartmentalized society where social capital is low between groups, thus barring the way for a nationwide social capital while opening the door for strong social capital within groups. This results in a segmented society displaying high inequality and low social mobility.

Social capital and mutual trust among individuals and between individuals and institutions and enterprises will, in itself, enhance competitiveness and stimulate economic growth, but it may be even more important as the flywheel for reaping the benefits from ICT and knowledge as "new" production factors.

## Wealth[106]

The concentration of wealth signifies a break with three fundamental elements of the economic model over the last 200 years. *First*, private ownership of property, etc. is gradually being replaced by some kind of leasing. *Second*, the main idea of capitalism that production was owned by the citizens, with transparency of ownership, is disappearing. *Third*, so is the clear link between owners and workers who both operate inside the same model, fighting about distribution of wealth produced in common, but not separated from each others' interests.

In 1944, Austrian-British economist Friedrich Hayek published *The Road to Serfdom*, which argues that any form of collectivism — he targeted communism and fascism — would lead to the destruction of all individual economic and personal freedom. It is one of history's strange paradoxes that unwillingly the individual may find himself/herself in exactly the situation against which Hayek warned so eloquently and convincingly.

A leasing economy has taken the place of the market economy. Financial institutions provide money to the consumer conditioned to de facto ownership until the loan is paid back. The operation of the debt market is based on revolving credit facilities that serve to perpetuate themselves and protect financial institutions rather than truly serve borrowers and consumers.

Large outstanding loans indicate that paying back the principal increasingly fills the role as an exception to the rule relegating individuals to leasing property and goods. Looked at in terms of capitalism and communism, this is much more communism than capitalism, albeit with the difference that large funds instead of state-owned assets control economic activity. A labyrinth of faceless intermediaries has replaced the age-old direct link between debtor and creditor.

The stock market shows a similar pattern. In 1965, individuals owned the majority of U.S. stocks, with 84 per cent, and only 16 per cent was in the hands of institutions/funds. In 2005, institutions owned 67 per cent and individuals 33 per cent. Ordinary common sense tells that control over a large proportion of corporations in the United States has changed from individual stockholders to institutional ones with the inescapable observation that the whole panoply of measures to ensure corporate governance geared to the old model had to be changed. In Asia institutional investors in various forms far outnumber the individual investor.

The world is entering an era of institutionalized economics with capital, money, ownership, and power steering the economy according to the wishes and preferences of institutions. The problem is not funds or institutional investors, but why the new owners think they can do better than previous owners. Many of these operations are purely financial and opaque, opting for status as a fund because that status allows them to operate differently and "economize" on transparency, compared with what would be the case if they operated as normal, private limited companies. The funds step in as purchasers and owners of enterprises, not because of their better management know-how, but because they see opportunities for a financial gain, frequently by splitting the enterprise up into independent units, each to be sold separately, or waiting for mergers and acquisitions to progress and take part in that game. All this takes a considerable amount of time and resources and is done without creating any real value.

For the public and the authorities, the problem is that this new kind of "capitalism" and obscure ownership makes rules, regulations, and supervision less effective because the institutions do not need to comply with regulations to the same degree as "normal" companies. An increasing amount of market capitalization is amassed and controlled by funds and/or institutional investors trying to avoid supervision.

Fund ownership deviates in its outlook from the traditional form of capitalism where owners and workers fought for the distribution of the profits. They were, so to speak, two sides of the same coin, with both of them taking part in the physical production of goods and involved in the production process. The owners had responsibility for the workers and the workers could not do without the owners/capitalists. They knew each other and knew the repercussions of actions undertaken on the part of the other. This acted as a brake on belligerency, but also constituted some kind of social network, irrespective of the sometimes acrimonious battles for distribution with strikes and lock-outs. It was calculable what the results would be, and what actually happened was transparent. The market served as the clutch pedal allowing the two parties to interact with each other.[107]

As recent experience suggests, concentration of capital and opaque ownership tend to override signals from the market, opening the door to the accumulation of capital value and making a virtue of short-term profits, irrespective of long-term consequences. The potential for the individual to pursue his/her preferences and safeguard economic interests will be limited, very limited indeed. That is why Hayek's prophetic words may come true more than sixty years after he wrote them and inside the kind of society he thought would prevent this from happening.[108]

The individual is helpless to safeguard his/her interests faced with this juggernaut of economic power. The political system also finds it increasingly difficult to do so because the distinction between goals pursued by the political system and business interests has become blurred and the regulatory system is constantly bypassed by ingenuity on the part of economic operators. Thus the individual feels tempted to fall back on social capital, adhering even more strongly to a group of people having congruous values.

## Reactions to Shortcomings of the Market Mechanism

The market mechanism was coined by the classic economists such as Adam Smith and David Ricardo. In the twentieth century John Maynard Keynes, during the depression in the 1930s, disclosed imperfections of the market mechanism, while Milton Friedman a quarter of a century later came to its rescue. Over the last twenty-five years, the market mechanism has grown, and been allowed to grow, into a sacrosanct principle under the supposition that the market will get it right. But such a supposition rests upon a number of assumptions that rarely exit.

The national economy has been replaced by economic globalization.

The feedback between consumers and producers and between the public and policymakers does not operate as it used to do. It is gradually becoming clear that the market mechanism in its current form transfers short-term economic rationales into the price structure, neglecting long-term consequences.

The distinction between public services not aiming for economic profit, and the business sector quite legitimately doing so, is blurred or even disappearing very fast. Public services are gradually being steered by economic motives meaning that only services that can be measured and frequently shown to be profitable using business methods, will be offered. This cuts out a large number of public services that would probably benefit the economy in the long term by stimulating social coherence.

The fundamental problem is not that the market mechanism does not work. It works completely as expected and foreseen. The problem is that the relative price structure serving as the control panel for economic decisions has, over the years, been distorted or, even worse, does not work effectively anymore (no price elasticities, no substitution effects, no shadow price effects due to capacity or resource constraints).

Disregarding the international repercussions and the long-term effects, there was nothing the market mechanisms could not correct, albeit according to the models, it might take time. This is, however, not the world of 2010, and even less the world of tomorrow, where precisely, these two factors, international repercussions and long-term effects, become of crucial importance.

The market mechanism is nothing more than an instrument — a channel — for communication between producers and consumers. It is an interactive channel allowing both parties to evaluate feedback. Therefore it was a suitable instrument in the national economies where all the ingredients fitted together. Production was for national consumption, national consumers responded via the market mechanism, and the national governments stepped in to ensure that the result of this process was in conformity with political goals approved by a majority of the population at general elections.

The problem now is that a part, and sometimes and for some nation states a large part, of the effects are felt abroad, with no suitable channels for feedback as the market mechanism for various reasons is prevented from working like it does in national economies.

In the traditional model, overconsumption in the United States would lead to overheating of the economy, followed by wage and price increases which undermine real incomes, bringing supply and demand back into balance. With open economies, overconsumption is transformed into increased demand for goods and services produced abroad, which keeps consumption and production at a high level, but shifts a part of production to other countries and leads to credit build up with a large number of insolvent clients. The overall and global balance between supply and demand is maintained, but consumers are primarily in one country using feedback and political signals inside that country, while production takes place in another country. Suppliers (owners and workers) are left with little or no influence on policymaking in the country buying the goods and services they produce, and are exposed to the sometimes huge overhang of financial liabilities.

As seen over the last decades, the result of this dichotomy is that imbalances are not addressed, or if they are, only at a much later date when they have grown out of hand and produced an economic crisis.

A similar picture emerges when looking at the short term versus the long term. Those who feel the consequences of economic policy decisions or other economic phenomena use the market mechanism to provide feedback, and suppliers/producers take those signals into consideration when planning production (sometimes called economic signaling). If consumers deem a product to be too expensive or not delivering what it promises, demand will fall, communicating that there is something "wrong" with the product. The basic assumption is that those feeling the consequences are able to give feedback.

The discussion about global warming demonstrates all too clearly the gaping hole in this assumption. Global warming is the result of the economic activities of several billions of people, thousands of powerful multinational companies and nation states manoeuvring for power and influence. Their economic activities may lead to a rise of sea levels which will obliterate societies and nation states such as the Maldives. The Maldives is giving feedback, but balanced against powerful economic interests, the fate of a tiny society is not really taken into account.

$CO_2$ emissions balances (as opposed to quotas) may also build up in the wrong hands with insolvent emitters, who become incapable of tuning down their emissions, ending in disasters.

The market mechanism works as it is supposed to work, saying that the strongest economic interests weigh more than smaller ones even if the consequences for the smaller group of people are fatal, while the consequences for the stronger interests are measurable and a question of trimming living standards.

From a long-term perspective we see that economic consequences (such as credit overhangs, budget deficits, and $CO_2$ emissions balances) that will be felt several decades or longer ahead are simply not taken into account because they are not heard of, and as such, do not exist inside the principles of the market mechanism. Who is feeding back into the economic system that with current levels of exploitation of several commodities, topsoil, and water, the world may run out of these essential and fundamental conditions for sustaining life? It is only because groups and, at first, non-governmental organizations and scientists raised these issues that they are being taken seriously.[109]

The conceptual problem or shortcoming of the market mechanism is — like so many other concepts — that it rests on the assumption of it being an infallible instrument for delivering answers and solutions.

But the reality is much more common, ordinary, and simple. Inside the market mechanism sit people, ordinary people, who take economic decisions which are later represented and seen as taken by "the market mechanism".[110] People act in accordance with their own economic interest or in accordance with the interest of the organization or enterprise they serve without taking the interests and repercussions of their actions and decisions outside that box into consideration. The only way to tackle those problems is to change the foundations for economic decisions.

Economic decisions are mainly steered by prices or rather relative prices set by the market in accordance with the ruling market philosophy. The effectiveness of relative prices is demonstrated by a recent analysis of the birth of the industrial revolution.[111] The revelation is that relative prices of production factors were the main reason the industrial revolution happened in Britain and not elsewhere. In Britain, for historical reason, labour was expensive and coal was cheap. Steam power as the plinth for the inventions which paved the way for the industrial revolution worked to save labour and use more coal. Relative prices in Britain encouraged entrepreneurs to do that — and they did it — while in countries on the European continent relative prices worked as an obstacle. At the end of the eighteenth century France was the most populous country in Europe, with no or little coal, so why should French entrepreneurs introduce technology saving the use of the cheap production factor?

Over the last two hundred years relative prices have reflected the low prices of commodities, the human use of resources without thinking of long-term consequences, the human use of nature as storage for waste without looking at nature's own philosophy which is 100 per cent recycling, and high prices for manpower, that is, the use of the human being's time.

Using economic theory we should not find it difficult to change this behavioural pattern. The way to do it is by changing relative prices and making the use of labour cheaper, increasing the price for resources, and putting an explicit price on the environment and related elements now largely kept outside the price mechanism. This requires ruling out the market mechanism which is currently the sole determining factor for relative prices.

It also requires defining if and how obligations can still be deferred by credit and for how long.

To do that a much improved understanding of the manufacturing process is necessary, which points to a dissection of the product and its components.[112] Recently suggestions and ideas telling us how to do that have been forthcoming. A team of researchers from the Massachusetts Institute of Technology (MIT)[113] has analysed twenty modern manufacturing processes and come to the conclusion "that the intensity of materials and energy used per unit of mass of material processed has increased by at least six orders of magnitude over the past several decades".

This has come about not by inefficiencies or negligence in using production technology, but by introducing new manufacturing processes primarily in the form of precise, small-scale devices and product features, and enabled by stable and declining material and energy prices. In other words the relative price structure and the market mechanism based on short-term considerations have maintained low prices for high intensity use of energy and materials measured per unit of material processed. The interpretation for this finding is enormously significant, auguring that without our really knowing it, new manufacturing processes are being introduced all over the world which are assumed to be more energy efficient, but in reality, are alarmingly less so. The "wrong" conclusion is drawn because we do not look at the whole manufacturing process for the new devices, but only at the energy and material use at the end of the line.

The study points out that a manufacturing process is to transform materials into useful products. By doing so energy is consumed along the whole line of transformation of materials and the usefulness of the materials is altered. Manufacturing processes are made up of a number of steps. When we look at the actual machining, the electrical energy used may be small compared with the accumulated use of electrical energy over the range of functions integrated in the process. The study mentions as an example that for an automated machining line, the maximum energy requirement for the actual machining in terms of electricity is only 14.8 per cent of the total. It may be even worse if the automated machining line is not running at full capacity as some of the processes use energy not much dependent on total production (cooling, stand by, etc.).

New technology such as nanotechnology and solar panels, just to mention a few, may look more energy efficient, but the reality may be the opposite because the higher use of energy along the road is spread out on many subcontracting processes and not easily linked to the end product. The image of progress towards more energy efficiency through high-tech manufacturing process may not only be wrong, but may also hide the fact that the application of new technology for a large number of people moving into higher income brackets around the world will make energy and material scarcity much worse than the already worrying forecasts tell.

The market mechanism and relative prices disclose a partial analysis where only some of the implications are included, and the effects downstream as new technology is being introduced over the globe is not taken into account.

The interpretation to draw from this is not to stop new, more energy-efficient technologies than existing technology per unit of weight, but to incorporate their total effects in the price system, which would certainly change relative prices.

Economics have, in fact, entered this field of work with an adaptation of the original input-output theory,[114] introducing the idea of life cycle assessment.[115] What needs to be done is to incorporate the notion of units of weight as put forward by the MIT study, and broaden the scope to include emissions and energy intensity, and then draw consequences for the price mechanism.

The philosophies labelled "cradle to cradle" or C2C[116] reflect a holistic approach which says that in principle any product, whatever it is, must be composed of materials opening the door for 100 per cent recycling, exactly as nature is working. It has not been done so far because it was not profitable, and it was not profitable because relative prices made it cheaper to throw things away as waste or garbage instead of recycling.[117]

With the current price structure such shifts in behaviour cannot be counted upon. People may to a certain degree be willing to switch from a less expensive to a more expensive solution motivated by moral, ethics, etc., but only to a degree. For a global and significant shift, prices must be changed to make the recycling process more profitable than waste disposal.

Economists may have to do some intellectual wrestling to find out how to incorporate long-term perspectives and cost of the recycling process into the price structure and thereafter to suggest how relative prices can be adjusted — by incentives or taxes. The principle is not difficult to grasp at any rate.

It seems a foregone conclusion that with the relative price structure now reigning the global economy and, in particular, the Asian economies facing falling production resources, rising pollution, rising consumption, and rising production, that we are heading towards a cataclysmic show down.

The market mechanism and relative prices have also failed to respond to the impact of information and communication technology. Apparently we have entered an era where much information seems to be free as the individual or organization does not pay any visible price to access it on the Internet.

This is, however, untrue. Nothing is free. The information delivered on the Internet has a price. *Firstly*, it costs something to produce and that cost may actually be high as highly-skilled labour and valuable information are employed, and *secondly*, it has transaction costs even if they may be small, at least compared with transaction costs for information (books, newspapers, that is, printed media) in the industrialized age.

What is happening is that the price does not follow the goods or services we purchase (information), but is passed on to the consumer in other ways, which may imply that it is not the consumer accessing the information who pays, but other consumers. The significance of delinking the price and cost from the consumer must inevitably have repercussions on behaviour and production patterns. If information looks free, but is passed on to the overall mass of consumers instead of the targeted end-user, demand for information will go up, and it may be used in a non-optimal way until these other users rebel by rejecting these unsustainable business models.

Examples of this can be found when looking at how search engines such as Google are financed. The user does not pay, but the price for providing information is passed on to the companies posting advertising and/or websites, which pay the search engine. These companies of course, need to cover their costs and that is done by increasing prices for products and services offered in other contexts. Not only is the cost shifted among consumers, but the search engines and companies may be tempted to guide the consumer to websites capable of suggesting the highest price via the search machine. The business model combines the bidding mechanisms, exemplified by eBay, with Internet search. Advertisers bid for keywords. Based on their bid, they will get priority in their display. Google also has a large inventory of indexed content which means that the chance of giving someone the right answers is high — hence it has a better reach. With a better reach, it can charge more. So it is a virtuous cycle where, because of Google's size, it can expect advertisers to bid at even higher prices.

A whole new industry — SEO (search engine optimization) — is growing up, which derives its income from tailoring websites to respond to the way search engines work. The more "friendly" it is, the higher up the list it goes, with the aim being to be on page one as analyses indicate that not very many users bother to go on to page 2, 3, 4, etc. This industry, of course, has to be financed, and this is again being done by the owner of the website shifting the costs afterwards to consumers by higher prices. It is not difficult to spot some kind of "unholy" alliance between website owners, search engines, and SEOs to make the consumer pay.[118]

Current economic and social policies have not adapted to channelling the burden to what may be termed the end-user of resources. What is needed is a similar method to the polluter pays principle (PPP), which aims to transfer the cost of anti-pollution measures to persons and/or enterprises responsible for the pollution, even if a superficial analysis points to other persons and/or enterprises. By using the input-output and MIT method, a much more sophisticated instrument could be brought into play.

More than fifty years ago the idea of value added taxation (VAT)[119] was promoted. The principle is simple enough. At every layer of production the value added is taxed, making the tax neutral vis-à-vis the production structure. Since then, VAT has been introduced in a large number of countries. The same principle could be applied to taxing products by focusing on use of resources, especially scarce resources, at every layer of the production chain, thus penalizing (by taxing use of resources in every layer of the production process) the use of resources and rewarding less resource-intensive products and/or production methods. While the VAT is neutral, an adapted version would be deliberately biased towards resource-intensive production.

Even more important may be another social context that changes the nomenclature "rich" from a reference to material wealth, to a reference to contributing to society, and use "money" wealth for non-material consumption. In modern linguistic terms it is about making it "cool" to behave in a way that preserves resources instead of using resources. In a more value-based society/community with social capital, and which may perhaps incorporate parts of religious beliefs that point to the harmonious coexistence of man and nature, such a change of preferential structure may not be impossible.

When performing such a mental shift it is crucial that individuals — also in their capacity as voters — feel that burden sharing can be justified and fair. The present economic theory and economic policies applied based on this theory cannot deliver in that respect.

The philosophy of privatization, deregulation, and free market has "compartmentalized" economic models, making it difficult, not to say impossible, to evaluate public policy initiatives for the whole economy, and not just a particular item or activity. The idea is then to link this to a general equilibrium analysis for the economy as a whole.

Some of the efforts channelled into finding an alternative way of calculating GDP should instead be directed at quantifying societal cost/benefits of policies pursued by enterprises delivering public services, whether these have public or private ownership, to find out whether the policies are beneficial or not for society as a whole. The problem showing up in almost all studies is how objectively to quantifying intangible costs and benefits.

The philosophy behind this way of thinking is twofold. *First*, to put flesh on the idea of calculating GDP, taking into account how much of the growth needs to be "recycled" to address negative repercussions on the standard of living accumulated during the growth process (external diseconomies interpreted in a wide way). *Second*, to replace the idea that economic activities serving the public are economic or rather business transactions that should be measured by profitability, with the idea that they should be assessed by a cost-benefit analysis for society as a whole, taking into account economic and social consequences. Over the last years economic theory and philosophy have been guided by partial analysis instead of an overall or general analysis. This world view has contributed substantially to the many imbalances impeding economic and social development.

Privatization of an airport, road, bridge, or public utility means that the public service is run as a private enterprise. The implication of this is that policies increasing the profit for the public service will be implemented, irrespective of whether they increase or reduce the GDP of the city, region, or nation state in question. A city may spend a large amount of money to improve roads leading to its airport to increase the number of passengers using it and attract flights from other cities, thus increasing its market share and establishing itself as a hub. All this will be wasted if the privately run airport then raises parking fees making it profitable for it, but preventing the public investment from working as intended.[120]

When we look at health care reform in the United States or social welfare in China, it is comparatively easy to calculate the costs for the public budget or private enterprises or individuals and whoever else is saddled with the bill. The benefits such as higher productivity, less sick leave, etc., are, however, much more difficult to quantify. It becomes even more challenging if, as will often be the case, it is not the same person who pays the bill and gets the benefit.

For a railway company, a station with a low number of passengers may not be profitable. If the station is closed passengers will either go to another station, thus increasing their commuting time, or use other kinds of transport facilities, or switch to private means of transportation, such as cars. This would possibly have detrimental effects such as higher pollution, and may result in higher costs and lower GDP for the society as a whole, although the railway company can post a better operating profit.

The best illustration of how uncontrolled market forces, combined with disregard for environmental consequences and lack of understanding, or lack of the will to understand the negative repercussions on the national economy of policies favouring big businesses, dates back to the United States in the 1930s.

A holding company bought the private electric streetcar system in forty-five U.S. cities and then closed them down. It was owned by interests from the oil, tyre, and car industries. In 1949 a grand jury convicted General Motors, Standard Oil of California, Mac Trucks, Philips Petroleum, and Firestone Tires on a criminal indictment of antitrust conspiracy, but meanwhile 280 million passengers had been chased from streetcars onto buses and cars. These big companies earned a fortune while the U.S. economy suffered badly and the United States was left with a transport infrastructure in cities wholly reliant on the auto industry.[121]

## Measuring Production and Wealth

In the free market, capitalist model, wealth was perceived and measured according to the capacity for physical production — how much could be produced and its monetary value. It changed somewhat when manufacturing gave way to services as services are non-material and not measurable in the same way as manufacturing. However, the MIT study shows that a large step can be taken towards measuring services by looking at the underlying production process of the physical "hardware", for example, chips underpinning the service sector. The hard fact is that irrespective of whether it looks like that or not, all consumption, be it of goods or services, means the use of "hardware" — perceived in a broad sense of that word — to produce the goods and services. It is only a question of breaking down how the consumption goods were produced through an input-output model or whatever instrument is available.

Even if the global economy switches and fast towards a service economy in most countries — probably the service sector will move towards and beyond the 70 per cent mark of total GDP before 2020[122] — the intensity of resources will increase, pointing to a shortage (manifesting itself through physical shortages or price increases) of many, perhaps most, commodities as well as shortages in skills and even of labour willing to do not very attractive jobs, such as rubbish removal.

The challenge for a future society is *first*, to cope with increasing shortages and understand what that means for economic theory, economic policy, and, in particular, the perception of wealth. *Second*, it has to work out how to incorporate burden sharing instead of distribution of benefits in society via an economic mechanism.

Many observers have grappled with an alternative definition of GDP and tried to combine growth, welfare, standard of living, social balance, happiness, or whatever other term can be used for this, and, not least, incorporate how much resources and skills economic activity gobble up, giving high points to those economies not using many resources.[123] This is useful as a step towards thinking differently, but the more important thing is to analyse how these new concepts can be incorporated in economic policy, such as tax policies, industrial policies, social policies, labour laws, etc. If some kind of consensus is achieved that the existing and established GDP concept is misleading, and operate on a short-term, materialistic, and individual-focused platform, the question then is how business, government, and society can be steered into a different behavioural pattern. The first and indispensable step is to change, for example, tax systems, and tax the use of resources instead of income, financial profits more than labour or results from research, and also penalize material consumption and reward social behaviour. It may be achievable to a certain degree, but only if it is based on a holistic concept that breaks products and services down and takes into account the whole production chain rather than be taken with how the final product or service may look like.

The steady state economy means an economy where the use of resources over time corresponds to what is available.[124] According to the theory a society moves towards a state of equilibrium where the use of resources can be maintained even if production, income per head, and consumption go up.

The word "steady society" or "steady state" may be misleading because such a society actually requires far more changes than an ordinary society growing in the conventional sense of "economic growth". Getting more out of the resource and skills base calls for greater, better, and more efficient technology. Even more important, the mindset of citizens has to change from physical consumption and service consumption dependent on resources usage (for example, car transport) to, let us call it, more non-material consumption. In a way it could be labelled the non-material society.

On top of that comes the drive for social stability. With a growing population in Asia as a whole, albeit not in all Asian countries, rising living standards, migration from rural to urban areas, social stability will come under stress. In these circumstances it is highly unlikely that things will go right unless policies are put in place promoting social stability. Over the last decades figures show how inequality of income is growing in China and India primarily as a result of urban migration.[125] Economic theory over recent years has developed the notion of social capital that says that social coherence contributes to economic growth by freeing up the human and financial resources otherwise needed to ensure compliance and enforce the law, for productive life. When people know through upbringing, family life, and education how to act in society, there is little need for enforcement. When people do not know this, enforcement is mobilized, gobbling up resources.

Even more important is another factor which has yet to be incorporated in economic theory: the ability to change. We could talk about this as a production factor under the heading of adaptability.

The more smoothly and effectively a society adapts to new circumstances and a new environment, the higher production will be and the less societal confrontation will arise.

## General Equilibrium

Economic theory has always operated with various notions describing how and why the economic system is adjusting all the time, and whether it is moving away from or towards some state of equilibrium or is permanently in a state of disequilibrium, thus triggering adjustment.

The classic theory of general equilibrium is based on the aggregation of many markets into some kind of macroeconomic state. This perspective is based on the premise that the economic behaviour of the individual coalesces into a general state of equilibrium when aggregated (the sum of economic decisions at a lower level leads to an overall economy state in conformity with individual components). For Adam Smith, the wealth of a society or a state is the sum of the wealth of individuals pursuing economic interests for themselves. Theories about general equilibrium suppose that equilibrium for each individual market leads fully to general equilibrium for the overall economy.

A normative element was integrated into the theory about general equilibrium which says that a step is Pareto efficient if it increases welfare for one person without reducing it for anybody else. A Pareto optimal situation is at hand when economic resources and output have been allocated in such a way that no one can be made better off without sacrificing the well-being of at least one person.[126]

Other concepts such as dynamic, stationary, stable, and steady state economics have been introduced into the debate and analysis.

The plain fact is, however, that the problem with economics is not found inside the discipline itself, but in its lack of understanding human behaviour as a mixture of emotions and rationality, and in the lack of accounting for social needs and balance. Human beings are only *homo economicus* to a certain extent. Their attitudes and behavioural patterns depend on whether they act alone, in a family context or in groups, or in groups defending or attacking other groups. Much behaviour is rooted in psychology and sociology calling for an interdisciplinary analysis.

It is of little use for everybody else that economists direct their intellectual efforts towards complex mathematical models that make sense in theory, but not in practice. These models reveal part of trends in behaviour, but only parts. To use terminology from economics itself, it is a partial analysis. Many of the models depict behavioural patterns with regard to the handling of financial assets aimed at economic optimization and calculation of risks/opportunities. If the models work, those who did not subscribe to them previously will switch to them. However, if everybody follows the same model, it is almost inevitable that this will lead to unexpected results. If the model dictates "sell" when certain criteria are met and everybody obeys, of course the price will fall dramatically, which influences future behaviour. It is not possible to separate the model from the impact of the model on future behaviour which sees individuals starting to behave differently to what was assumed when the model was invented. Policymakers may in the future be tempted to listen more to sociological, cultural, and scientific forces.

Economics needs to incorporate or maybe even integrate disciplines such as psychology and sociology in its foundation. Studies[127] indicate that the human brain is susceptible to images such as money, or more money, which then lead us to decisions that in many ways could be irrational. Incorporating behavioural ideas indicates that humans do not act economically rationally — albeit they may well be rational in their decision making viewed in the context of other sciences. Even more crucially, it also indicates that prices do not incorporate all past and current information relevant for economic decisions. Prices actually swing up and down repudiating the economic thesis that they reflect everything necessary to know for buying or selling. What is not incorporated is human behaviour and constraints on resources and skills. People buy and sell based on trust among one another, but that leaves the main question unanswered, namely, what trust is it based on? Economists would say rational behaviour, but experience indicates that emotion-driven decisions may weigh more heavily — an element in behaviour already mentioned by John Maynard Keynes called "animal spirit". People are more willing to buy something, irrespective of the price, when they see happy faces around them and, in particular, if they associate these happy faces with other people having bought it. Having learnt from hard won experiences, the science of economics is gradually crawling out of its box and admitting that people are not *homo economicus* and do not — at least not solely — take decisions inscribed in rational behaviour. There is also an equally sour acknowledgement from economics that markets and prices do not reflect the reality because they are influenced by economically irrational behaviour.

This is especially true as economics turns to deal with burden sharing instead of the distribution of benefits because work over many years clearly suggests people behave differently according to whether they face a loss or a gain. Experiments routinely show that people see a loss as more important for them than a gain even if the money involved is precisely the same.[128] Applying analogous models for societies facing burden sharing, as was the case when the predominant question was the distribution of benefits, can easily lead to a political disaster as people lose confidence in the political system. Recent work[129] analysing how the individual may be nudged away from "poor" decisions towards "good" decisions based on behaviour may help to produce economic models incorporating elements from non-economic sciences that are much more receptive to how people react in reality instead of supposing that they react as *homo economicus*, which they clearly do not. This new branch of economics is called "libertarian paternalism".[130]

Changes will take place at a stronger pace and be packed into a much shorter time interval, but even more critical is the fact that changes will take place inside societies with stagnant or falling populations, and probably declining availability of resources. Psychologically people need to adjust from behaving as selfish individuals to working in networks and groups that exploit ICT as an instrument for human interactions and for finding out how human relations will fare in such a changed environment. The fixed organizational structures will be outmanoeuvred by networks and similar frameworks easily adjustable to new circumstances, opening the door for the individual to change allegiance, loyalty, and identity, according to value preferences instead of nationality or economic preferences.

Social groups building or embedded with social capital and shared and common values will be instrumental for distribution policies, thus shifting governance from the nation state to organizations or networks neglecting boundaries drawn on the map.

Consumer policy will change fundamentally as scarce resources and skills make it uncertain what material consumption will be available in the future, at what prices, if at all, and whether restrictions will be imposed on consumption using resources. One of the imponderables is whether the human mindset can switch from material consumption to non-material consumption, and whether humanity will look at the degradation of the environment as something taken away from us and consequently make it more and more expensive to pollute.

## Summing Up

Adam Smith's philosophy about the free market and competition with the invisible hand augured more than 200 years of a political and economic model where liberal democracy went hand in hand with the free market economy.

The plinth for this model to emerge and develop was that Adam Smith basically got it right when he said that the pursuance by the individual for wealth would coalesce into higher wealth for society as a whole because society's wealth is the accumulation of individuals' wealth. It worked because the world operated in an extremely propitious environment where access to commodities was regarded as unlimited even if prices could reflect temporary swings, and where productivity was measured through the performance of the individual and dependent on the performance of the individual, and competition among individuals and/or enterprises augmented production capacity of society as a whole without jeopardizing future production prospects. All in all, the model was coherent and its various elements — consumption, production, the individual, enterprises, the state — supplemented one another in a win-win interaction. Adam Smith's world view was and is not universal, but linked to the prevailing circumstances when he coined it. At the start of the twenty-first century hardly any of the premises for the model are valid anymore.

Individuals may pursue wealth, but the assumption that the sum of wealth coalesces into societal wealth has been perforated. The wealth of individuals may be achieved by depleting resources society needs for the future, thus actually impoverishing society, not enriching it. Individual wealth may still be measured in money terms, but this luxury is no longer at the disposal of societies facing scarcities, and whose growth demands non-productive activities in the form of social welfare. Even if the wealth of individuals adds up to higher societal wealth, the question of distribution invalidates the philosophy of accumulating individual wealth to get societal wealth. The growing importance of values as a steering instrument for individuals and for their adherence to groups makes social capital instead of economic capital decisive for economic development and political control. Also processes may emerge allowing science and culture/arts to help create another kind of growth than the one we have seen so far.

The nation state as the frame for economic activity and consequently for a political system capable of organizing society for that, is surrendering to economic globalization. When economic activity is global or international, economic policy cannot be national, and when it is moved from the national level to the international/global level, the nation state loses its grip as a provider of human security and economic welfare on citizens.

The nation state world view embodies symmetry between politicians and citizens/voters benefiting or suffering from decisions by the politicians who are accountable at the next election. Until the last decades of the twentieth century, the economy in the nation state was still predominantly national. In the era of globalization, politicians in one country make decisions, which by the openness of the economies, transcend to citizens in other countries, who cannot react to the decision makers, but only to their domestic politicians who are possibly not involved, but trying through international meetings to transfer the heat to those responsible, with limited success. Political systems cannot be national when the economy is international. And international political systems require an amount of transfer of sovereignty that so far only the Europeans have been willing to enter into.

Instead groups or societies or communities forged by values and ethics take over as the provider of human security, identity, and economic welfare. It weighs more to be a member of such societies/communities than to belong to a nation state and/or be in possession of wealth measured in money.

Sharing of knowledge will replace division of labour as the predominant factor determining productivity. Workers will no longer only do the one thing they are best at, but be partners in a team where their skill is linked to the skills of their partners. The composition of the team overshadows the capabilities and competences of the individual. A number of individuals, each surpassing individuals in other teams, may still form a team with lower productivity if wrongly put together.

Productivity will not be measured in output related to input of production factors, but to efficiency in the use of resources and skills.

Wealth will be seen as the potential for continued growth over a long term future on the basis of available resources. A rich society will be a society capable of sustaining its growth per capita, without depleting the mass of available resources.

Consumption theory will evolve to incorporate the fact that people are willing to pay a higher price with rising income (high income elasticity) to prevent a clean environment and their culture being taken away from them. In more general terms, consumption will be less focused on material consumption as preferences change.

Groups and working together will constitute the plinth of economic performance and societal coherence, crowding out the drive of the individual to enrich him-/herself. This has consequences for consumption, with consumption that reduces the potential for others being penalized.

Interdisciplinary methods of thinking, analysis, and working will get the upper hand compared with specialization and individualization, thus diminishing the role of systematic learning that focuses on a single discipline and probably raising doubts about the future of fundamental research. The time when economics served as an arbitrator or judge of progress in other disciplines may well be over.

Values will serve as the framework for social capital keeping societies together and auguring a less important role for the nation state. This brings into question whether the age of objectivity rooted in pure science can continue to rule the mindsets and methods of governance.

Transparency via the Internet and more relaxed social human interaction will replace many of the regulatory functions that are currently necessary for a strong state. Instead values transmitted via the Internet will take over much of the control function now exercised through laws.

Fundamental freedoms for the individual, but inside some kind of self-discipline defined by tolerance and respect — perceived as caring for others, even when disagreeing with them — will emerge out of the new technology.

The sketch above of the coming world view is based on future forecasting found in Chapter 2. Most of what we are going to live with over the next twenty-five years are known today, but what we do not know is which ones of the many opportunities will be transformed into realities framing everyday life for the citizens, business conditions, and also for government policies. There are so many alternatives available that this grows into something more like guesswork than forecasting. We may know about technology, but we do not know how human beings respond and react to new technology.

One of the themes running through this book as a connecting thread is the focus on groups, social networks — which, through the virtusphere and social capital are transformed into coherence — replacing that on individuals. For 200 years economic philosophy has basically analysed the behaviour of the individual and assumed that the wealth of a nation or a society is synonymous with the individuals' accumulated wealth. If the individual pursued what looked beneficial for him, the result would also be beneficial for society as a whole. This does not look so obvious anymore and we see instead a number of societal issues that are difficult, maybe impossible, to overcome unless a much stronger focus on groups and social capital emerges. This will be instrumental to manoeuvre in the coming era of burden sharing replacing distribution of benefits as the main issue for economic theory and policymaking.

The elements framing Asia's development, which we will look at subsequently, can be classified the following way: The *first* group consists of elements that are overwhelmingly favourable for development and will support continuous high economic growth. They are examined in Chapter 3. The *second* group is made up of elements that may support development or raise barriers depending mainly on which government policies are applied. They can turn into boosters or act as brakes and they are sufficiently strong to wreck Asia's future. They are examined in Chapter 4. The *third* group discussed in Chapter 5 reveals elements that will make growth in the traditional sense difficult and call for resources and policymaking problems to be overcome. The external circumstances are dealt with in Chapter 6.

With this as the background we look at how these forces, some of which reinforce while others contradict one another, will work together to shape the future — stimulating or blocking progress. This forms the stepping stone to outlining benchmarks and indicators showing policymakers in which direction Asia is moving. Future forecasting and scenario planning are all very interesting, but of little use unless accompanied by indicators making it possible for policymakers to monitor the course of events and form an opinion on which scenarios or directions are unfolding. A tool will thus be available that allows policymakers to step in to reinforce, weaken, or adjust the course revealed by the indicators.

The purpose is to jump out of the purely academic box and present something policymakers may find useful when faced with an undoubtedly strong and, at times, almost tumultuous development in Asia over the next twenty-five years.

The three substantive chapters on favourable, doubtful, and blocking elements are written with this in mind and discuss policy options and ideas. They are not just purely analytical chapters, but deviate from time to time to turn to normative arguments and point to courses of action that may help solve problems expected to arise in the future. By doing this, the door opens up to criticisms of this book abandoning a strict analytical and/or academic approach, but the virtue is to move the book beyond pure academic research. By stating that this is the case readers are warned, thus allowing them to exercise due scepticism and/or voice criticism about the ideas put forward. As no one knows the future — as is so rightly stated in almost all future forecasting — the objective is not to claim monopoly on the truth, but to forward ideas that may start readers forming their own opinions.

## Notes

1 The spirit, attitude, or general outlook of a specific time or period, especially as it is reflected in literature, philosophy, etc.

2 It can be discussed whether economics is a science as it is not based on unquestionable laws of nature, but a way to structure observations, paradigms and to justify political decisions. Here, however, the word science is used nonetheless even if some may contest this notion.

3 Strictly speaking Darwin-Wallace.

4 Thomas Malthus, *An Essay on the Principles of Population*, 1798.

5 The same fate befell the reports by The Club of Rome in the 1970s.

6 See my essay "Møller, Jørgen Ørstrøm, The Return of Malthus", *The American Interest*, July/August 2008.

7 See, for example, Eileen Hunt Botting. "Introduction, The End of Enlightenment", *American Behavioural Scientist* 49, no. 5 (2006): 643–46.

8 The world is not yet there, but the trend is moving in the direction of legitimizing the same approach that in the pre-science age, when people discussed, say, the universe, without any kind of observation and validation by others. A scientist once said to me "It is nowadays depressing for teachers to see that garbage found on the Internet is more true for the younger generations than science or data built over centuries."

9 See Chapter 4.

10 "To meet the needs of the present without compromising the ability of future generations to meet their own needs." This definition is not universally accepted and sustainability can be looked at in normative, instrumental, or descriptive ways. The UN definition serves our purpose irrespective of the intellectual and/or political discussion.

11 See, for example, Harold Underwood Faulkner, *American Economic History*, eighth edition (New York: Harper, 1964), pp. 64–66.

12 Walt W. Rostow, *The World Economy, History and Prospect* (Austin, University of Texas Press, 1978). Preceded by *The Process of Economic Growth*, Oxford, 1953.

13 He was not, far from it, the first to put forward theories about economic development and offer explanations setting out how to achieve economic development. Suffice to mention the works of W. Arthur Lewis, who in 1979, was awarded the Nobel Prize in Economics and whose thinking on the U-shaped cycle of economic development is still inspiring. To this can be added Kondratieff's theory about long cycles.

14 More manpower may be achieved by higher quality/productivity and does not necessarily mean larger manpower.

15 This amounts to an adapted version of *produit net*; no longer what can be squeezed out of agriculture, but what can be squeezed out of the commodity sector.

16 Laurence J. Kotlikoff, and Scott Burns, *The Coming Generational Storm: What You Need to Know About America's Economic Future* (Cambridge, Massachusetts: the MIT Press, 2005); Philip, Longman, *The Empty Cradle: How Falling Birthrates Threaten World Prosperity and What to Do About It* (Basic Books, 2004); George Magnus, *The Age of Aging* (Singapore: Wiley, 2008); Ben J. Wattenberg, *Fewer: How the New Demography of Depopulation Will Shape Our Future* (Chicago: Ivan R. Dee, 2005).

17 In December 2003 the U.S. Congressional Budget Office published "The Long-Term Budget Outlook", that predicted that the federal government's spending

for Medicare and for its share of the joint federal/state Medicaid programme together, could, in a worst case scenario, exceed 21 per cent of GDP by 2050, compared with 3.9 per cent in 2003 and 5.3 per cent in 2010 and in a best case scenario be capped at 12.5 per cent. Social security expenditure would rise from 4.2 per cent to 6.3 per cent of GDP. Taken together these figures would account for more than 27 per cent of GDP compared with less than 10 per cent in 2010. When we bear in mind that this projection was made in 2003, that is, before the economic crisis in 2008, it seems unavoidable that unless dramatic changes in policies are introduced a fiscal meltdown is bound to happen <http://www.cbo.gov/doc.cfm?index=4916&type=0/> and/or <http://www.cbo.gov/doc.cfm?index=4916&type=0&sequence=2>.

18 The European Central Bank system (ECB) may be the only exception.

19 See, for example, works by Cigdem Akin and M. Ayhan Kose, in particular, IMF Working Paper WP/07/280, December 2007; and M. Ayhan Kose, Christopher Otrok, and Eswar Prasad, "How Much Decoupling? How Much Converging?" *Finance and Development*, IMF 45, no. 2 (June 2008).

20 Ibid.

21 Denmark's national bank, *Monetary Review* 1st quarter 2009, pp. 10–11.

22 Malaysia after the outbreak of the Asian financial crisis in 1997 is one of them.

23 Jørgen Ørstrøm, Møller, "The Return of Malthus and International Order", *The American Interest*, July/August 2008.

24 The following paragraphs are sourced from my article "Protectionism Goes into Reverse", *Asia Times* online, 24 July 2008.

25 This is in fact how the repeal of the Corn Laws worked for Britain from 1846.

26 Information provided by Maersk Line.

27 See, for example, Alan S. Blinder, "Offshoring: The Next Industrial Revolution", *Foreign Affairs*, March/April 2006.

28 Carl Von Clausewitz, *On War*, edited and translated by Michael Howard and Peter Paret (Princeton: Princeton University Press, 1976, revised 1984).

29 Economic globalization has punctured Adam Smith's saying that the sum of a nation's wealth is the aggregation of its citizens wealth, meaning that if everybody pursues his own wealth, the nation will be better off.

30 In a philosophical/intellectual way it can phrased this way: In the former nation state model, the interests of the state subjugated the rights of its individual citizens, but internationally, the sovereignty of the state could not be set aside in the interest of the international community, and nation states should not work against groups of its own citizens. The constellation was not symmetrical. What is happening now is that the international order has been adjusted to work on the same principles as inside the nation state: the interests of the community are more important than the rights of the individual.

31 LTCM is a perfect illustration of how badly the science of economics has lost

contact with reality, entering as it does into overly sophisticated mathematical models that work in theory, but not in practice. It was set up by two economists who won the Nobel Prize in Economics for option pricing. Apparently the model set up allowed LTCM to win, regardless of whether stock prices fell or rose. What happened, of course, was that as soon as the fund started to show profit, behaviour changed, and even if in theory it could be said that markets move towards equilibrium in the long run, this can be pretty useless if the long run is really a long run. All in all LTCM may have lost approximately US$3.6 billion.

32 I have dealt with these problems in a number of articles published by *OpinionAsia* and *Asia Times* online in 2007 and 2008.

33 Central banks thought they had found the Holy Grail in inflation targeting and exercised self-congratulation, not realizing that the success in keeping inflation low had nothing to do with their monetary policies, but was, in fact, due to cheap labour in China. See Joergen Oerstroem Moeller, "The Holy Grail of Central Banking", in *The National Interest*, 6 June 2007.

34 Joergen Oerstroem Moeller, "Unconventional Wisdom on Exchange Rates", *Asia Times* online, 7 August 2007.

35 Andrew K. Rose and Mark M. Spiegel, "Non-Economic Engagement and International Exchange: The Case of Environmental Treaties", NBER working paper series, working paper 13988, April 2008.

36 James Martin, "Great Challenges of the Twenty-First Century", *The Futurist*, January–February 2007.

37 See, for example, <http://www.smallbrewers.com/members.htm>.

38 I picked these thoughts up by listening to Professor Jack Knetsch who has been so kind as to help me in formulating these two paragraphs.

39 The core of this thinking, as pointed out by Professor Jack Knetsch, is that the price people are willing to pay to buy a good is lower than the price they ask to sell the same good. Behaviour differs in the sense that what we have commands a higher value than something new we are getting. This is highly relevant when assuming behavioural patterns in the context of restructuring society.

40 Nicholas Stern, *The Economics of Climate Change: the Stern Review* (Cambridge, Cambridge University Press, 2007).

41 A report commissioned by the Australian Government (Garnaut climate change review), available at <http://www.garnautreview.org.au/CA25734E0016A131/ WebObj/GarnautClimateChangeReview-DraftReport-Ch1andPrelim/$File/ Garnaut%20Climate%20Change%20Review%20-%20Draft%20Report%20- %20Ch%201%20and%20Prelim.pdf>.

42 In a working paper from 2008, "Consumption Tradeoffs vs. Catastrophes Avoidance: Implications of some recent results in Happiness studies on the Economics of Climate Change", Professor Ng Yew Kwang discusses some of these aspects.

43 Charles Tilly, *Democracy* (Cambridge, Cambridge University Press, 2007),

pp. 13–14. See also by the same author, *Contention and Democracy in Europe 1650–2000* (Cambridge: Cambridge University Press, 2004), and *Trust and Rule* (Cambridge: Cambridge University Press, 2005).

44 In my own country, Denmark, most people associate democracy with three elements: free elections, fundamental rights of freedoms, and a fairly equitable distribution of wealth and income. It is inconceivable to separate these three elements — together they constitute what a Dane would classify as democracy.

45 The Asia-Europe Foundation (ASEF) published in 2006 a collection of essays under the title of "Democracy in Asia, Europe and the World", Chung-Si Ahn and Bertrand Fort, eds. According to the introduction, the objective was to examine and evaluate whether there is any ground for suggesting that the world is moving towards a universally accepted "definition" of democracy. It is admitted that beneath the surface of what seems to be a universal consensus, at least a part of the past controversies about what democracy means, what it entails, what the consequences are, to mention a few, continue to be voiced.

46 Hitler and the Nazi party assumed power in Germany in 1933, formally respecting all rules of the Weimar Republic. The Nazis lied and bullied, but on paper, the rules were followed. Was that democracy?

47 It should be noted, however, that the treatment of Maori people in New Zealand and the Aborigines in Australia differs widely.

48 This may admittedly also be the case in mature democracies.

49 1) David Madland and Ruy Teixeira, "New Progressive America: The Millennial Generation" (Washington D.C., Center for American Progress, May 2009) available at <http://www.americanprogress.org/issues/2009/05/pdf/millennial_generation_execsumm.pdf> and 2) John Halpin and Karl Agne, "The Political Ideology of the Millennial Generation, A National Study of Political Values and Beliefs Among 18- to 29-year Old Adults" (Washington D.C., Center for American Values, May 2009) available at <http://www.americanprogress.org/issues/2009/05/pdf/political_ideology_youth.pdf>.

50 These studies supplement the work by Don Tapscott on the Digital Generation. Reference is made to this in Chapter 4.

51 "Media Boss Eye's Clinton", 10 May 2006, *Sydney Morning Herald* <http://www.smh.com.au/articles/2006/05/09/1146940550729.html>.

52 This explains why member states of the European Union have transferred sovereignty to exercise it in common with adjacent nation states in pursuing analogous goals in many areas, but not concerning social welfare, which is still kept under national sovereignty.

53 I am grateful to Sudhir Devare for discussing this with me.

54 Don Tapscott, *Grown Up Digital* (New York: McGraw-Hill, 2009).

55 See Chapter 4.

56 With the exception of the European Union, where citizens can vote in local elections and the European Parliament, regardless of where in the Union they live, and what citizenship they enjoy.

57 This does not amount to saying that this continues to be the case as the materialistic lifestyle obviously attracts people around the globe.

58 <http://en.wikipedia.org/wiki/Four_occupations>.

59 <http://en.wikipedia.org/wiki/Tang_Dynasty>.

60 A valuable contribution to such analyses has been provided by "Religions of the World and Ecology", a series published by the Center for the Study of World Religions, Harvard University.

61 Series foreword by Mary Evelyn Tucker and John Grim to "Religions of the World and Ecology", a series published by the Center for the Study of World Religions, Harvard University. See, for example, p. xxvi in the volume on "Confucianism and Ecology" (Cambridge: Massachusetts, Harvard University Press, 1998). Same source used for the description of Hinduism, Buddhism, Confucianism, and Taoism.

62 Even at the risking of oversimplifying, argument is made to the words of God recorded in Genesis, the First Book of the Old Testament (1:26): "and God said, let us make man in our image, after our likeness, and let them have dominion over the fish of the sea, and over the fowl of the air, and over the cattle and over all the earth, and over every creeping thing that creepeth upon the earth" and (1:28) "and God blessed them, and God said unto them, Be fruitful, and multiply, and replenish the earth, and subdue it: and have dominion over the fish of the sea, and over the fowl of the air, and over every living thing that moveth upon the earth."

63 Lynn Townsend White, Jr, "The Historical Roots of Our Ecologic Crisis", *Science* 155, no. 3767 (10 March 1967): 1203–07.

64 See, for example, "Revue Ecologie", *L'Ecologiste* no. 9, February 2003 <http://www.inxl6.org/article945.php> and René Dubos, *So Human an Animal* (New York: Scribner, 1968).

65 O.P. Dwivedi, "Dharmic Ecology", in *Hinduism and Ecology*, edited by Mary Evelyn Tucker and Christopher Key Chapple (Harvard: Harvard University Press, 2000), part of a series edited by Mary Evelyn Tucker and John Grim "Religions of the World and Ecology".

66 In the Western world the loss of biodiversity discussed by recent books (e.g. *Sustaining Life*, see Chapter 5 for full references) may have initiated a world view more like the one embodied in Asian religions and philosophies, but a closer look reveals that it focuses more on respect for life than on a changed attitude towards the symbiosis between man and nature.

67 J. Baird Callicott, *Earth's Insights, a Survey of Ecological Ethics from the Mediterranean Basin to the Australian Outback* (Berkeley: University of California Press, 1994).

68 *Journal of Oriental Studies* 11 (2001), pp. 19–20 with a "Dialogue on Eastern Wisdom" among Ji Xianlin, Jiang Zhongxin, and Daisaku Ikeda. Available at <http://www.iop.or.jp/0111/special.pdf>.

69 I am grateful to Michael Yap for drawing my attention to the dialogue in *Journal of Oriental Studies*.

70 Sun Tzu uses water as an illustration that recalls Vandana Shiva's statement about water having its own spirit.

71 Sun Tzu, *The Art of War* (Oxford: Oxford University Press, 1971), Chapter 6.

72 Theodore Roszak, "The Making of a Counter Culture" (Garden City, New York: Anchor Books, 1969).

73 Quoted form Roszak (1969) who refers to Dorothy Lee, *Freedom and Culture* (Englewood Cliffs, N.J.: Prentice-Hall, 1959), p. 163.

74 The Whites she met were probably former urban poor Europeans.

75 Primarily about India.

76 Vandana Shiva, *Water Wars: Privatization, Pollution, and Profit* (Cambridge M.A.: South End Press, 2002).

77 These fall into the category with some justification of the normative versus behavioural debate, going back to the Age of Enlightenment with philosophers such as Rousseau, Diderot and Locke.

78 See, for example, Henry C.K. Liu, "Rule of Law versus Confucianism", *Asia Times* online, 23 July 2003, available at <http://www.atimes.com/atimes/china/eg24ad01.html>.

79 <http://science.jrank.org/pages/11387/Syncretism-Syncretism-in-Japanese-Shinto.html>.

80 Jonathan K. Ocko and David Gilman, "State, Sovereignty and the People: A Comparison of the 'Rule of Law' in China and India", *Journal of Asian Studies* 68, no. 1 (February 2009); Randall Peerenboom's comment on this article published in *Journal of Asian Studies*, and Randall Peerenboom, *China's Long March toward Rule of Law* (Cambridge, Cambridge University Press, 2002).

81 The rule of law is different from rule by law. Rule of law is linked to the state's actions and its sovereignty competing with the rule of men, while rule by law exists under both rule of law and rule of men as the instrument for compliance, enforcement, and punishment.

82 Jonathan. K. Ocko and David Gilman, op. cit.

83 The historian Arnold Toynbee reached this conclusion in a dialogue with Daisaku Ikeda published in 1989 by Oxford University Press called "Choose Life" and mentioned eight reasons for this prediction among which was "instead of dominating nonhuman nature, man's aim should be to live in harmony with it" (p. 249).

84 Callicott, *Earth's Insights*, p. 11.

85 Some observers may refer to Montaigne who spoke of nature and the Orient and that European missionaries brought back lessons about an Asian world view, but these thoughts remained peripheral at best in a European context.

86 It is more doubtful, however, whether it has worked with regard to human security. In many Western societies the crime rate has been relatively high.

87 Unfortunately that also means work in a distorted way (corruption, nepotism, etc.).

88 See, for example, Kishore Mahbubani, *Beyond the Age of Innocence* (New York: Public Affairs, 2005).

89 Samuel P. Huntington, *Public Order in Changing Societies* (New Haven: Yale University Press, 1968).

90 It seems difficult to contest that the European nation state finds it increasingly difficult to secure a satisfactory economic life for its citizens, offering suitable solutions to social life such as education, health, and care for the disabled and elderly, plus human security in its broad sense. All three show a low score. It is also legitimate to start with an analysis of the European nation state as it was born there.

91 Huang Yasheng and Tarun Khanna, "Can India Overtake China", *Foreign Policy*, July–August 2003.

92 *"Liberté, Égalité, Fraternité"* — Liberty, Equality, Fraternity.

93 The ugly form of this has already surfaced with terrorism and organized international crime where the "citizens" do not feel any loyalty vis-à-vis the nation state, but has shifted loyalty completely to these networks operating internationally and in some cases, globally.

94 I picked up some of this reasoning while listening to Bertel Heurlin.

95 Not to speak of private enterprises buying public utilities to run them on a business model, instead of seeing them as public *services*.

96 Arguments for and against private ownership can be found in, for example, Tim Jenkinson, "Private Financing", *Oxford Review of Economic Policy* 19, no. 2, 2003, available at <http://oxrep.oxfordjournals.org/cgi/reprint/19/2/323?ijkey=66JEvazZvBeJo&keytype=ref>. In a book from 1997, edited by Patrick M. Mallan and Joni E. Finney (*Public and Private Financing of Private Education*, American Council of Education, Oryx press) the point is made that a fundamental change in financing of higher education has taken place, drastically reducing public financing almost without any political debate.

97 <http://www.virgingreenfund.com/index.php?option=com_content&task=view&id=26&Itemid=121>.

98 <http://www.gatesfoundation.org/Pages/home.aspx>.

99 <http://www.soros.org/>.

100 See Chapter 3.

101 Hsieh Tsun Yan, "Building Global Champions in A Turbulent Economy", *Singapore Institute of International Affairs Reader* 2, no. 2, July 2002.

102 Kathy Fogel, Randall Morck, and Bernhard Yeung, "Big Business Stability and Economic Growth: Is What's Good for General Motors Good for America?" National Bureau of Economic Research, Working Paper 12394, July 2006, available at <http://www.online.mba.net/rmorck/Research%20Papers/Stability%20NBER%20w12394.pdf>.

103 Joseph Schumpeter, *The Theory of Economic Development* (Cambridge, MA: Harvard University Press, 1934).

104 See, for example, <http://en.wikipedia.org/wiki/Maslow's_hierarchy_of_needs>.

105 Branding is an example of how individuals express identity by signalling who they are, where they belong, and how they want to distinguish themselves from other people.

106 The following paragraphs draw partly on my essay "Asia to Follow Serfin' USA?" *Asia Times* online, 10 January 2008.

107 Not only is the link between owners and workers belonging to two groups, albeit the same social network, cut, but contrary to what economics predicts, real wage compensation as share of gross domestic income is falling in the group of major industrial economies; from 56 per cent in 2001 to 53.75 in 2006. Source: Morgan Stanley, Global Economic Forum, 23 October 2006, available online at <http://www.morganstanley.com/views/gef/archive/2006/20061023-Mon.html>.

108 It is interesting to draw a parallel to biodiversity — see Chapter 5. It looks like higher biodiversity confers a higher degree of stability for the system. Diversity means that species support one another, substitute for one another, step in to do one another's function and, of course, competes with one another. This creates a more stable system than with a loss of biodiversity. It is a tantalizing thought that the same may be true in economics and business, which explains why the global economy and the economic models fail to deliver: "economic biodiversity" suffers from a loss with deep consequences for the economy seen as an ecosystem.

109 Some of the first books were John Kenneth Galbraith with *The Affluent Society* and Rachel Carson in 1962 with *The Silent Spring*.

110 This observation is also valid for institutions, which are not god-given instruments, but actually serve as a framework for decision making among human beings.

111 Robert C. Allen, *The British Industrial Revolution in a Global Perspective* (Cambridge: Cambridge University Press, 2009).

112 As is the case for so many other topics, there is a need for interdisciplinary analysis, which is kept at bay by professionals of all sorts defending their turf.

113 Timothy G. Gutowski et al., "Thermodynamic Analysis of Resources used in Manufacturing Processes", *Environmental Science and Technology* 43, no. 5 (February 2009): 1584–90.

114 A matrix predicting the effects on other sectors in the economy of a change in one sector. If, for example, car production goes up, what does that mean for steel, plastic, ball bearings, etc?

115 See, for example, Carnegie Mellon <http://www.eiolca.net/Method/index.html>.

116 The main work is William McDonough and Michael Braunhart, *Cradle to Cradle: Remaking the Way We Make Things* (New York: North Point Press, 2002).

117 The Dutch city of Venlo has adopted this concept and has formulated the objective of zero waste by 2015, see <http://www.treehugger.com/files/2008/03/venlo-cradle-to-cradle.php>.

118 As this is an extremely interesting case of how economics and competition work in the information and communication technology age, it warrants a bit more clarification. If you search on say, "restaurants", the screen will show three different groups: yellow on top, sponsored links to the right, and the rest below the yellow links called organic links. The two first groups are organized via so-called adwords, specifying which search words the website owner wants to lead to the link. Every time somebody clicks on the website a fee is paid and not surprisingly the fee is rated according to how many clicks come in every day. The third group is where the SEOs come in. By tailoring the website it is possible to move it upwards. This seems straightforward and is, but opens the door to manipulation. If a company wants to crowd out competitors, it puts more efforts into tailoring its website. If some bad news concerning the company surfaces on the Internet, the company pays SEOs to tailor a number of hits better suited to the search engine pushing the websites with the bad news down the ladder to page 2, 3 or 4.

119 <http://en.wikipedia.org/wiki/Value_added_tax>.

120 The objectives pursued by the airport to get a maximum profit and by the public authorities as part of an overall investment in access roads and parking may lead to different fee structures.

121 Peter Newman and Jeffrey Kenwork, *Sustainability and Cities: Overcoming Automobile Dependence* (Washington, D.C.: Island Press, 1999).

122 As of 2006 the share of services in global GDP was about two-thirds, with the United States at about 75 per cent, Europe 70 per cent, and the Asia-Pacific just below 60 per cent. Japan's share is around 70 per cent, India is around 50 per cent, and China around 35 per cent. Source: <http://www.globalinsight.com/Perspective/PerspectiveDetail7319.htm>.

123 See, for example, 1) "The Commission on Measurement of Economic Performance and Social Progress", <http://www.stiglitz-sen-fitoussi.fr/en/index.htm> and M. Fleurbaey, M. "Beyond GDP: Is There Progress in the Measurement of Individual Well-Being and Social Welfare", available at <http://www.stiglitz-sen-fitoussi.fr/documents/Beyond_GDP.pdf>; 2) NEF (The New Economics Foundation, <www.happyplanet.org>), "the unhappy planet 0.2", University of Maryland, July 2009, available at <http://www.greennewdealgroup.org/wp-content/uploads/2009/07/HPI-EMB.pdf>.

124 Herman Daly, "Steady-State Economics: Second Edition with New Essays", by Herman E. Daly (Washington, D.C.: Island Press, 1991) and "Steady-State Economics", available at <http://www.dieoff.org/page88.htm>.

125 See Chapter 5 for specific figures and references.

126 For a brief discussion with references see <http://en.wikipedia.org/wiki/Walrasian_equilibrium>.

127 Source for this paragraph: Gary Stix, "The Science of Bubbles & Bursts", *Scientific American*, July 2009.

128 A pioneer in this work is Emeritus Professor Jack Knetsch, Simon Fraser University, Vancouver. See also Gary Stix, "Bubbles and Bursts", *Scientific American*.

129 Richard. H. Thaler and Cass R. Sunstein, *Nudge: Improving Decisions About Health, Wealth, and Happiness* (Yale: Yale University Press, 2008).

130 <http://www.jstor.org/pss/3132220>.

# 2

---

# FUTURE FORECASTING

## CHANGE, ASIA CERTAINLY WILL[1]

Change, Asia certainly will. The big question is how these changes, likely to be disruptive to economies and societies, will affect behaviour. The surrounding environment, developments inside nation states, and global trends such as technology and human interaction (values, norms, and ethics) are undergoing an almost dramatic change, which is why the starting point must be to form an idea of how the framework for Asia's future development will look. On that basis we can try to form an opinion of what will happen. The burning question, so difficult to grapple with, is how changes will affect behavioural patterns of people.

There is no reason to hide the fact that any analysis must start with *economic* growth, because growing financial resources over the next twenty-five years is a must. But how do we achieve this, what kind of growth is in the pipeline, and is it the kind of growth we want?

From 1979[2] until about 2007 Asia benefited from high global growth, low prices for energy and commodities, including food, no real water problems, a rising available and elastic labour force all over the region except in Japan and Korea, and little focus on pollution, the environment, and climate change. *Asia's political job was to manage economic growth.*

Over the next twenty-five years all this will change and for the worse. Global growth will almost certainly be lower, taking demographic trends and the economic outlook for the United States and Europe into account. Commodity prices including those of energy and food will go up. The environment will need much more attention that calls for financial resources.

In Asia demographic trends will split the continent into three groups of nation states: falling population, stagnant population, and rising population. A number of problems that could be, and were disregarded, will surface, calling for political solutions that require financial resources. *Asia's political job turns into establishing conditions for the preferred economic growth.*

Growth and stability support each other. No growth or low growth endangers social stability; social instability dents growth prospects. If Asia and its political leaders strike the right balance between changes and opportunities, Asia can look forward to an era of stable growth; if not the prospect of social unrest framing the life of three billion people jumps from theoretical to a policy perspective to be reckoned with. Also, if no such stability is engineered by proper changes, there is the danger of social differences leading to regional wars.

A futuristic study is a strange and intricate combination of certainty, probability, and guesswork. We actually know a lot about the future as long as the horizon chosen is in the range of twenty-five years. A shorter horizon turns an analysis into fairly safe prediction and a longer one pushes the analysis increasingly into guesswork. What we have learnt, certainly from the current global economic crisis, is that unexpected and sudden shifts in growth trajectories will happen.

We know for certain that there will be changes, but the challenge is to come as close as possible to telling what these changes will be, or at least sketch some possibilities.

Deng Xiaoping's coming to power in China and his reforms in 1979 could not have been foreseen, but a good analysis would surely have told the observer that the Maoist model was unlikely to persist. Something was going to give, but precisely what, in what context, and in which direction would have been more guesswork than analysis. China might have moved deeper into revolution had the Gang of Four prevailed, some more prudent reforms might have been chosen if a coalition inside the communist party had won the struggle for power.

The Soviet Union and its "empire" fell quite unexpectedly apart in 1989–91. It was, however, not completely unforeseen. A few observers did predict severe difficulties for the Soviet Union and got fairly close to unveiling some of the underlying tendencies threatening the coherence of that artificial state. Helene Carrere d'Encausse[3] pointed to the higher birth rate of the non-Russian peoples and the fiscal burden for the central government and centralistic economic planning (Gosplan) in running the empire as likely elements undermining its viability. Her analysis did actually reveal that something was "wrong" with the Soviet Union and warned that something might or would happen, albeit it could not and did not foretell exactly what was going to take place in 1989–91.[4]

Looking forward to 2035, we are on relatively safe ground when forecasting changes in technological, transport, and logistics infrastructure[5] because these elements take a considerable number of years to work their way through the system. Breakthroughs in science do not happen with a snap of the fingers; many investment projects take a long time from being conceived to being integrated in society. Some may disagree and say that new technology comes on stream so fast that even with a time horizon of ten or fifteen years we do not know what technology will be available. This is true, but the main interest in this context is not whether the technology is available and known, but whether it has given rise to new products and services that are actually used by a large majority of citizens and corporations. Technology and inventions are only part of the story; what is important in affecting change is the speed of diffusion and this speed is never known in advance. Mobile phones and the Internet are good examples.

There are two immeasurable factors known from experience to be difficult to predict:

- not so much new technology itself, but how it is applied in society and its impact on societal and economic fabric — it is quite simply impossible to predict the impact of new technology on societal development until it is deployed
- the reaction of people to new technology, new cultural patterns, and new trends

The Internet has completely changed the way young people interact, learn, and collect information. There is no comparison to how it was done one or two decades ago when the book was the main vehicle for learning and disseminating of knowledge, more or less just like it was for generations before that. We know with certainty today that young people are breaking away from that pattern.[6] They do not read books in the same way as their parents, if at all; they look to the Internet as the source for informing themselves about what is going on, and for deepening their knowledge. We can tell with certainty that this is going to change the education system and influence the skills of young people coming out from universities to work in business, society, and government institutions, but we do not know exactly how this will take shape.

An intriguing question illustrating this is the impact of electronic books[7] offering the option for reading books on screen as if they were genuine books.

As of 2009 more than 130,000 books are available[8] from digital bookstores, with about ten main suppliers of book reader devices, the best known of which are Amazon and Sony. The unanswered question is, however, what does it mean for people's ability to digest the contents of a book? Will it increase the number of books being read in this or another form? Will children start to read at an earlier age, etc? The list is almost endless as soon as we realize that the main question is not the technology, but the impact of technology on people's mindsets.

We can look at some of the new trends and draw projections, assuming they will persist, but quite often trends shift fairly quickly after the first phase of new patterns so we cannot be sure that what we see today will also dominate tomorrow.

Scientific breakthroughs are often slow in maturing, and yield several (competing or supplementing) technologies, the adoption of which may be turned upside down by users rather than their technical performance.

As we move from let us say, hardware or "building blocks" such as technology, demographics, etc., to societal fabric and human behaviour — what might be called software, or "the glue" — we come to realize that the real uncertainty, the imponderable, is the ability of the human mind to explore, adapt, amend, and find new ways to exploit opportunities and respond to challenges.

Scientific developments are steered by budgets for science and availabilities and windows of opportunities for talents to express themselves — to a large degree determined by the "supply" side. Technologies are frequently steered by user exposure (how it can be used, irrespective of whether that was the original purpose). The impact on society is also dependent on regulations opening up or closing down possibilities — to a large degree determined by the "demand" side. So all in all, the "glue" gets encouraged or disrupted by power structures and processes.

The great British historian, Arnold Toynbee, coined the phrase "response to challenge"[9] as the keyword to explain the rise of civilizations. When faced with challenges, civilizations would find answers not to perish. Those answers belonged to the unknown before human ingenuity dug them up. Many analyses and theories have been put forward to explain why civilizations have managed to do this, but without anyone giving a really convincingly better answer than the others.

When groping for answers and/or solutions, people tend to get together in groups defined by a fundamentally common mindset, meaning those with whom they have an analogous cultural background, who can help them approach problems in a similar way. In 2004 James Surowiecki published

*The Wisdom of Crowds: Why the Many Are Smarter Than the Few and How Collective Wisdom Shapes Business, Economies, Societies and Nations*, which sketched how people coming together actually tend to reach better and wiser conclusions than individual persons.

The next question is whether individuals can work together without a strict rule-based framework, and this has intrigued economists for a long time. Originally most economists took the view that selfishness would prevail, making what is labelled "commons" unworkable or, alternatively, that they might work until deprived of value. Newer work[10] shows not only that "commons" can work, but also how to make them work. In this context the crucial factor is that scientific analysis demonstrates that the human mindset adapts to working together when conditions are right.

That helps us one step further in the search for cognition of why, how, and where new breakthroughs happen, which indicate that the determining factor is a large number of people sharing some basic instincts/values and mode of reaction, plus challenges to established communities from inside or outside.

Communities emcompassing a large population are obviously better placed in principle to uncover talents, but as long as they are gripped by poverty, no infrastructure exists to search for and find talented people, and then offer them opportunities to turn into human assets. It is actually the other way round. A large population combined with poverty acts as a brake for development.

To flourish, mindsets must be tuned to a kind of common wavelength, so they mean the same thing when speaking the same language and using the same words, and act in an analogous way to similar challenges. If this is so, the wisdom of the crowd will work, if not the large population will split into several, possibly many, groups embedding what is called *Gruppenanarchie* (anarchy among groups fighting one another for influence and power, and impoverishing all).

Still, if everything looks fine and in place, there is very little incentive to do anything. Most human beings know about complacency, and communities/ societies free from challenges slip easily into complacency, ignoring change, innovation, and development.

We keep evoking the human mindset as the decisive element not only when speaking about development, but also in making future forecasting. Many societies/communities have had congruous technology, etc., but only a few of them have actually used these technologies to move ahead. Arun Bala,[11] looking into the background of influences that shaped the rise of modern science, comes to the conclusion that most of the established theories explaining how and why modern science developed in Western societies are, strictly speaking, not correct. Modern science did not emerge simply by drawing on intellectual and technological resources within Europe, but also depended on large reservoirs of knowledge and techniques already developed by Asian cultures and the Arab world. However, although the scientific base for modern science was available to many cultures outside Europe, his study also argues that Western societies acted differently by exploiting opportunities to develop modern science in a fashion that others did not.

Future forecasting is not like most scientific disciplines calling for deeper and deeper analysis. It is much more of an interdisciplinary analysis with the impact on the human mindset as its flywheel. The well known saying about the risk of not seeing the wood for the trees applies. Economics, technological forecasting, political science, psychology, sociology, to name a few disciplines, have to be put in the melting pot, which produces the magic image of how things might not necessarily look twenty-five years later.

Futurists have found a way out of their dilemma by falling back on scenario planning or scenario unveiling.[12] Almost every future forecasting comes to the point where the reader is offered three scenarios. It is like a thriller with the good guy, the bad guy, and the sweetheart they both covet. This is, of course, understandable, but not very informative for the reader who is normally able to guess which scenario will be presented, albeit not necessarily under what title, and of little help to policymakers. To make such work useful, it needs to be accompanied by two items: some indicators disclosing which one is unfolding before our eyes, and tools/suggestions about how to influence scenarios if policymakers want to steer them in another direction.

Two of the most recent futuristic studies offering scenarios are those published by Shell in 2005[13] and by Forum for the Future in 2008.[14]

Shell sees three possible global scenarios:

- **Low trust globalization** with absence of market solutions to the crisis of security and trust, rapid regulatory change, overlapping jurisdictions, and conflicting laws leading to intrusive checks and controls, encouraging short/term portfolio optimization, and vertical integration.
- **Open doors** where a number of factors encourage cross-border integration and virtual value chains.
- **Flags**, meaning some kind of zero-sum games with dogmatic approaches, regulatory fragmentation, and national preferences, conflicts over values and religion, giving insiders an advantage and putting a brake on globalization.

Key to these three scenarios are the legal environment, the market culture, the global forces of integration and fragmentation and, more generally, the complex interplay between these three forces.

The main objective in Shells scenario-building is to sketch guidelines for business management.

Forum for the Futures analyses the political, economic, and psychological consequences of climate change and puts forward five possible scenarios:

- An economy putting **efficiency first** with rapid innovation in energy efficiency and novel technologies. Innovation will revolutionize the economy. A high-tech, low-carbon transformation will deliver dramatic cuts in greenhouse gas emissions. High global growth will continue. Consumption will be more individualistic, but will not deviate fundamentally from what we know.
- An economy showing **service transformation** where a high price of carbon ushers in a revolution in how people's needs are satisfied. Companies will rewrite their business models and consumers will shy away from energy-using devices, such as washing machines and cars.
- An economy **redefining progress** where new priorities are of "well-being" and "quality of life". Low-impact lifestyles with more time for family and friends, better health outcomes, creative educational experiences, and a stronger sense of community will gain the upper hand.
- An **environmental war economy** which signifies a belated awareness and response to the problem of climate change, forcing the market mechanism to its limits with the ultimate consequence of individual freedom being sacrificed to catch up with the need to reduce greenhouse emissions.
- A **protectionist world** points to globalization in retreat and governments pursuing a game of everyone for him-/herself and hoarding whatever assets are necessary. Scrambling for whatever your hands can get hold of as resources gradually become *scarcer.*

The Shell analysis and the scenarios put forward by Forum for the Futures offer invaluable insights into possible, yes, likely, future trends. They are especially valuable in mixing various trends and telling how they might interact.

They choose their starting point, prioritize topics, and select target groups according to their own preferences. The Shell study is not aimed exclusively at the business world — far from it — but not surprisingly, writes with an eye to what is useful and relevant for business. Forum for the Future defines its task as looking at climate change and the repercussions of this admittedly looming threat, imposing crucial choices on mankind. They are global in the sense that they look on the world as a whole and consequently do not try to analyse what is special or unique for Asia.

Some futurists work with the great trend shifts or waves. That was the case for Alvin Toffler[15] who foresaw the coming trend of information and communication technology with his book, *Future Shock*, which itself caused a shock with its outline of how deeply changes would go. Toffler's insight was less to forecast the future technology, but more to shed insights on societal structure and social fabric. He used new technology as the player for far reaching changes in human behaviour, and relations between human beings and economic entities. This made his books and analysis about the third wave unique and distinguishes him from many others who also forecast and wrote about ICT.

Peter Drucker, who may be classified more as a management guru than a futurist, but actually predicted a good deal of trends and new developments, hit the nail on the head with his book about discontinuity.[16] Do we live, or rather, are we going to live in a society where change follows a steady curve and thus becomes more predictable, or are we entering an era of discontinuity? As we all know now, Drucker was perfectly right in opting for the age of discontinuity.[17] Mankind is seeing and entering a jump in technological performances and consequently changes in human behaviour. Drucker, like Toffler, distinguishes himself from many other by analysing changes in mindset instead of just how new technology will improve productivity.

Another school of thought is based on the Russian economist Kondratieff who put forward the theory that economic development is controlled by long cycles of about fifty years' duration. These cycles are formed by new technology. When new technology arrives — in a way a new wave to borrow Alvin Toffler's words — investment takes off and drives economic growth higher. The interaction between investment and consumption continues until the new technology withers away or loses its power as it has been fully integrated into society.

The twentieth century was shaped by two waves. The *first* one spanning the first half was based on electricity, chemical industry, oil, the car, and similar technologies improving the performance of the industrial economy. Electronics, aircraft, communication, and the audio-visual instruments drove the *second* one covering the second half of the century.[18]

John Montgomery[19] sees the first wave in the twenty-first century around biotechnology, pharmaceuticals, waste recycling and alternative forms of energy generation, software, mobile broadband communications, and digital technology.

John Petersen and Nassim Nicholas Taleb write and think about high impact — wild cards or black swan — and the process of surprise anticipation.[20] By elaborating on tools for forecasting surprises that are not normally on the radar screen, they improve a government's capability to take policy steps to avoid them if possible and, if not, to prepare for their onslaught, thus diminishing the negative impact on society.

A futuristic study can basically be made in two ways. One is to start with existing trends, what we know, and extrapolate from there. The other is to start in the future itself by projecting technology into the future and feeling your way forward to what kind of societal changes that will mean.

The approach chosen here is to start with what we know and from there extrapolate and guess if, or when, we can expect trend shift and what that will signify.

These reflections indicate the limits of future forecasting, but also the scope for qualified guessing. Forecasting from today can paint a fairly accurate picture of what is likely to be the framework for human communities around year 2040. What it cannot do and where we have to guess is which of the possibilities and opportunities will be used and in what way.

"Because social effects lag behind technological ones by decades, real revolutions don't involve an orderly transition from point A to point B" is how Clark Shirky, one of the leading web thinkers or digital gurus[21] put it. It was obvious that Gutenberg's printing technology would facilitate the spreading of knowledge and information, but not that it would open the door for Luther to break away from the Catholic Church and rally Northern Europe around The Lutheran Church. It was equally obvious that the mobile phone would lead to much more communication, but not that it would initiate text messages and implicitly promote a string of abbreviations, which in themselves have possibly introduced a new language, or at least a language of communication. No one foresaw that the Internet may spell the doom for the printed mass media in the form of the traditional newspaper. It has come as a surprise, posing the educational system with an unheard of challenge: that the Internet changes the way the new generation acquires knowledge and handles information.

## DEMOGRAPHY

Demographics are the natural and unavoidable starting point. *First of all*, population size, composition, and changes in composition, constitute some of the fundamental elements in depicting future trends for a nation. *Secondly*, demographics paint a picture of how things will look twenty-five years down the road, with a high degree of certainty.

Economic history shows very few, if any, examples of high growth over a number of years unless accompanied by a rising population. There are several reasons for that. A higher population means higher demand which stimulates supply. The share and absolute number of people in the working age bracket go up, keeping wage costs down, enhancing competitiveness, and thus boosting exports.

The accepted paradigm in emerging market economies in the second half of the twentieth century runs like this: Demand from external sources increases, there is a rising number of people in the working age bracket, exports go up, higher income leads to higher savings and investment, plus foreign direct investment follows, and domestic demand starts timidly to pull production upwards. For a while the combination of low wage costs and low cost on capital keeps competitiveness strong. After some decades the composition of the population changes, with a decreasing share of the population and reduced absolute numbers of people in the working age bracket; the country loses its competitive edge in low cost, labour-intensive manufacturing, facing the challenge to move up the value-added production scale.

This is in short what happened in Asia from 1950 to 2008. Japan initiated this pattern in 1960, followed by Korea, Taiwan, Hong Kong, and some parts of Southeast Asia, with China emerging in the 1980s. Now this is going to take place in India and perhaps also in Pakistan, Indonesia, Vietnam, and Bangladesh.

The tilting point is when the composition of the population no longer favours the working age group. Demography tells us that Japan and Korea reached that point about the year 2000. China will get there in 2025, Southeast Asia in 2045, India in 2050, Pakistan and Bangladesh in 2060. We know with certainty that the existing economic model will not suffice anymore. Those in doubt only need to cast a glance at Japan after the early 1990s. This is not the same as saying that economic growth will stop, but it is saying that only if the country in question is capable of changing tracks will growth persist. It has to find a competitive parameter other than low labour costs. Whether it can do that and how successful it will be are questions that do not fall into the category of certainty with a higher or lower degree, but belong more to guesswork, where the ability to predict future trends and the reaction of policymakers and the population will be decisive.

The social fabric of a community/society is very much, albeit not exclusively, defined by the composition of the population. In the first stages, a growing population may hold a country back as a larger proportion is to be found in the bracket below fifteen years of age and need to be fed by their parents. There is no *produit net.*[22] This may well constitute poverty for many countries. With a low income per capita, a high and growing population impedes economic take-off. However, it looks like there is a threshold beyond which this is no longer true, when income per capita moves beyond a certain level, it turns a high and rising population from being a barrier, to a boost for economic growth. China probably moved through that phase sometime in the early 1980s. India may have done so sometime in the 1990s.

Even more interesting may be the question of how the composition of a population influences social fabric when a larger share and increasing number of people move above the upper limit of working age, which will normally take place when they are in the 60–65 age bracket for most countries.

The implication is that a larger number of people will need care because the marvels of modern medicine keep people alive even if their body and/or mind start to fail them.

With some, but disquieting uncertainty, we can calculate how many people will need care. Disabled persons and people needing care for other reasons should be added to this calculation. With a fairly high degree of certainty it can be calculated how much it will cost community/society to provide that care if it is being referred to the shoulders of the public sector. An economic simulation can paint the whole economic, family wealth, and fiscal canvas for us.

What we do not know is how the younger generation in the working age bracket will react. In the United States and Europe, the tradition is not to ask younger people to take care of the elderly, but to pass this responsibility on to the public sector. A change in the composition of a population therefore solely affects economics, fiscal burden, and investment in social infrastructure — in brief, it is calculable, as it does not touch the social fabric. In Asia, however, for a variety of reasons, the tradition is the exact opposite. Children take care of their parents in their old age. That has worked relatively well in the past because, among other things, the composition of the population placed a high share of people in the working-age group, and a low share in the group needing care. But we do not know how those being asked to shoulder the burden will react in the future. A couple has four parents. To look after one set of them may be affordable (economically and family-wise), even if it is not exactly what they want to do, but what happens if there are two? And if the burden is passed on to the public, it does not mean a free lunch, but that the bill is paid through taxes, raising a distribution problem, because those not having elderly relatives needing care are being forced to pay higher taxes to pay for care of relatives of other people.

In more general terms, a changing demographic picture may also influence Asian values. It seems fair to ask the question whether Asian values, as they are commonly perceived and described (see Chapter 1), follow from the well known demographic structure, and if so, will they change as demographics change or are they anchored in culture, thus less likely to respond to demographics?

When trying to answer these questions and predict how community/society will react, we have to guess, weigh up various and, sometimes, contradictory social trends, to plot our way through and sketch a likely outcome.

The one-child policy in China falls in the same category. When that policy was introduced, it could with great certainty be calculated how the size of the population would develop. It could also be expected, without much guesswork that many parents would prefer a boy instead of a girl, eschewing the normal approximately 50–50 gender picture. All this could be put on paper. Authorities could plan investment in schools, universities, etc., without much risk of being caught making the wrong forecast.

The crucial point for how China will look for the remaining part of the first half of the twenty-first century is, however, something completely different. How will the behaviour of children change when they have grown up in families where they were the only child instead of one among many others, and it can be added that some of whom died in early ages. That generation of Chinese had virtually to fight for survival. The whole fabric of society is framed by this pattern. But what happens when it is turned upside down and spoilt children come out from the nest and meet other children who also feel they are the best and only ace in town?

The fertility and thus composition of the population in different countries vary. Even more intriguing may be how divergent, or at least different, fertility rates among ethnicities and religions may influence relationships between ethnicities and religions in Asia. With, generally speaking, similar fertility rates, the proportions of ethnicities and religious groups were, broadly speaking, unchanged. But this will not be the case between 2008 and 2035. We can calculate with certainty how different fertility will change composition, but we do not know how it will impact the minds of ethnicities and religious groups. They may remain the same or attitudes may change in a manageable way, or unpleasant repercussions may appear on the political agenda.

The number of cases where we jump from certainty to guesswork are legio. Even when we start with demographics, feeling on safe ground, we soon discover that the ground is shifting under our feet and what really matters

— the reaction of the human mind — is much more unpredictable than we thought and hoped for.

## TECHNOLOGY[23]

Research, development, inventions and innovations are, rightly, regarded as drivers for new waves in societal development. For the futurists there are at least three challenges.

*First*, new scientific breakthroughs do not lend themselves to easy prediction and consequently cannot be planned for.

*Second*, that contrary to common beliefs, it takes a long time for new technology to work its way into society even if developing new technology on the basis of scientific breakthroughs is not so time-consuming.

*Third*, that it is not so much new technology as the way it is used which creates the new waves.

We may not know what new technology will put its mark on societal development twenty-five years down the road, but the technology itself is known today. The challenge is to find out which of the available new technologies will make a breakthrough, how fast it will be, and how deep it will penetrate society and challenge behaviour and attitudes of human beings, business, and institutions.

History is full of evidence of misguided perceptions, frequently in anecdotal shape, of technologies; some of them have never been verified, but this illustrates how difficult even the first step — to predict which new technologies will move from the design stage into reality — is.

"Heavier-than-air flying machines are impossible" from 1895, "Radio has no future", and "There is nothing new to be discovered in physics now. All that remains is more and more precise measurement" from 1900, are all statements attributed to Lord Kelvin of the Royal Society who also allegedly discarded X-rays as a hoax. Apparently scientists do not always understand technologies and their development patterns.

"Everything that can be invented has been invented" is a statement attributed to Charles H. Duell, Commissioner, U.S. Office of Patents, 1899.

Thomas Watson (IBM) is well known for his alleged 1943 statement: "I think there is a world market for maybe five computers."

Even if it is doubtful whether those to whom they are attributed ever made these statements, they at least illustrate that many people thought so and did not really include new technology in their forecasting of the future.

Some of the innovations having the greatest impact on our daily life may not contain new technology at all, but are simply existing technology put together in a new way. Sony's Walkman did not market new technology, but a new way of using existing technology.

The definition used in this book goes back to Emmanuel G. Mesthene[24] who said that technology is tools in the broad sense of that word. Mesthene goes a step further by looking at new technology as a two-sided issue. It brings along new opportunities, but also new problems. It is no wonder that he made his contribution exactly at the moment in the late 1960s when awareness of the degradation of the environment was gaining traction in industrialized countries.

The crucial point, however, is revealing that new technology changes or, alternatively, has the ability to change our mindset. People start to behave differently with technological changes and that spills over into societal attitudes and behaviour, sometimes creating feedback effect. A futuristic study confronts technological change firstly, to look at how technology reverberates through society, and secondly, to form an assessment of how societal values have begun to oscillate.

New technology normally transits six stages.[25]

*Stage one* is when the scientific breakthrough is achieved. At this stage few people except a limited number of scientists and perhaps business leaders/ heads of research institutions will be aware of the breakthrough, very few of those will be sure about its applicability, and even fewer will have the slightest clue about its impact on future societal values. The efforts in this phase will be devoted to getting it from embryonic stage to finding out whether it can be used. Journals are full of news about such breakthroughs accompanied by warnings/reservations that it will now take X number of years before it is turned into a marketable product. Often it never happens.

There are several barriers to turning a scientific breakthrough into a useful product. It may quite simply be impossible because of the need for new technology in other areas, for example, strength of materials, to sustain use for a longer time. In that case it has to wait for new technology in other sectors. If there is a scientific breakthrough, normally there is no way to manufacture it beyond the laboratory. There may be economic constraints in the sense that the product may look good, but would be too costly for consumers, or would not bring a profit. Infrastructure (regulatory, technical, or administrative) may not be available or allow it, forcing the new product to wait.

*Stage two* is when a manufacturing process has been invented or adapted, and a product or service is available and bought by a small minority of the population. The product has proved its viability, but still suffers from teething troubles making it unreliable. On top of that it will often be costly compared with what it offers. Not many people will feel a need for what the product or service offers as behaviour changes slowly and under impact from trendsetters. Technologically the product is tested in normal circumstances to see whether it lives up to its promises.

*Stage three* is when it becomes a normal consumption good used by, let us say, 20–30 per cent of the population. The teething troubles are over and society is adapting to the product or service, which has been fine-tuned to work in society. It approaches the stage where it is an everyday product bought and used by a large number of the population and which is not giving rise (yet) to any particular surprise wherever it appears. In this phase it starts to lose its attractiveness as a trendsetting product and is replaced by the label of normal product.

*Stage four* is when it becomes a product of mass consumption. The new technology is no longer new; it has become part of society and may be one of the workhorses ensuring the well functioning of society. It is no longer classified as technology, but as a consumption product.

*Stage five* is when it dictates development such as political and technical infrastructure. Society no longer benefits, but adapts to the technology. What used to be new technology has now become such an integral part of society that infrastructure and development of society are planned taking technology into consideration and sometimes are even being planned and designed to accommodate the technology. Society cannot, or at least will find it difficult to, function without it.

*Stage six* is the decline. The technology has run its course and has become obsolete or is not accepted anymore due to its societal implications. The demand for what it offered is still there, but fulfilled by other products based on new technology. Gradually it is phased out. New infrastructure is planned and designed without taking it into consideration. Behaviourally people turn their back on this technology, to convey the impression that they are not backward.

The next question is how long it takes for new technology to jump from one country to another. The World Bank has looked into this and come to the following conclusion:[26] Over the last hundred years — from the early 1900s to the early 2000s — the number of years for a new scientific breakthrough to become global has fallen from approximately fifty to approximately sixteen years. But, and this is interesting and in this context important, the number of years it takes to reach 25 per cent penetration has almost remained unchanged at twenty years, implying that globalization does not make the six-stage process outmoded. The world has not improved its ability to bring new science across to a majority of the people.

The interesting stages for a futuristic study is the transition from stage three to four or from four to five and five to six. The first three stages are like an anteroom, where we wait to see whether the technology actually manages to transit into the last three stages. The time span for moving from stage one to stage four spans several decades — and actually this has not changed much over the last half century. Facebook and similar networks may seem to contradict the observation that new technology takes time to work its way into society, but in this context, Facebook is not really a new technology, but a new application of existing technologies. Consequently we know with certainty that the science that is going to dominate economic and social life in Asia (indeed globally) is here today, but we cannot know with certainty which of the derived technologies will be able to jump from stage three to stages four, five, and six.

Information and communication technology (ICT) looks like it is somewhere between stages four and five, but is still being renewed and updated; business, government, and the public are still adjusting to new opportunities and openings for use of basic discoveries in physics, mathematics, and semiconductor processing. It is a safe guess that ICT will still be here in 2035 as a workhorse of society, and some extrapolations and forecasting predicting increased communication with implications for productivity, interaction between business and its customers, impact on the education system, can be made with relative certainty. It is, however, an even safer bet that ICT would be used in a way that we cannot foresee today. We only need to think back to the early 1980s and search for words such as the Internet and the handphone to know how difficult this is.[27]

Over recent years a conceptual change in the perception of ICT has taken place. Formerly it was regarded as an integral part of the various segments of the economy — the primary sector delivering raw materials, the secondary sector producing manufactured goods, and the tertiary sector offering services. Now the tendency is more to look at it as an economic sector in its own right, coexisting with the three conventional sectors and dependent on scientific breakthroughs in all of them.

A study from 2007[28] analysing what makes those in the 12–24 years age bracket happy augurs fundamental changes in behaviour and values, primarily around the use of virtual networks/virtual communities. The demand driver is not technology, but social, human, and specific business needs. The following two excerpts are the key elements in this context:

"Technology will be important for staying in touch and for the pleasure of the moment. *37% of youths polled say they play videogames to stop unhappiness. 61% say technology helps them make new friends. In the 24 hours before the survey, half of the respondents said, they sent a text message; 71% said they received one.*"

"Youth will make little distinction between face-to-face and virtual friendships. They will have many friends they may never meet in person. *62% of youths polled have used social networking sites like MySpace and FaceBook; 53% have created their own profiles on such sites; 33% say they have friends online they've never met in person.*"

The study also says that *80 per cent of the youth polled say that having lots of close friends is very or somewhat important.*

In an article published in 2008[29] it was further revealed that one of the youngsters interviewed stated, "I've never met my best friend." Well, one swallow does not a summer make and it is always hazardous to jump to conclusions on scant evidence, but this quote falls in line with what many parents are hearing from their offspring about the use of the Internet. It gives rise to reflections on the role of human relationships in the future. If young people feel that people they have never met can be their best friends, how will that influence their behaviour vis-à-vis other human beings? And — as has been seen — what opportunities will it offer for disruptive activities, possibly in the form of crime, to steer young people's minds in a particular direction. If young people tend to rely increasingly on the Internet and non-personal relationships, they abandon human contact as a guide to behaviour vis-à-vis other human beings. There is no precedent, no paradigm to tell us how that will work out.

People, and especially young people, undoubtedly use the Internet as an instrument to get into contact, maintain relations and create new ones, exchange information and gossip, talk about themselves and others. The unanswered question, however, is how deep that goes and to what extent it crowds out human contact or replaces human contact. This is where we need to tread softly.

The impact of the Internet on social networks and social capital has for some time been a contentious issue, with one group saying that the Internet allows people from different backgrounds and different interests to "meet" one another, while the opposite view is that the Internet alienates people from one another. A recent study from Japan[30] concludes that participation in online communities enhances diversity of social networks, while email does not have the same effect. Online activities may thus — provided that these findings are universally applicable — play an important role, not only in establishing contacts and nourish communications, but also in breaking down social barriers.

The virtual world means a blurring of the distinction between reality and perception, what is real and what is imagined. Technology becomes a tool for replacing images from reality with perception/imagination. You do not know exactly with whom you talk in the virtual world; let us call it "virtusphere". Voice can be interposed on an image to give the image another voice than that of the real person, or the image can be maintained and another voice interposed. It is also possible to do both.

In virtusphere, a person can communicate with a friend without really knowing how much of what is said comes from the friend and how much from the virtusphere. We may jump into history and/or fantasyland and communicate with historic persons whose views are programmed according to what is known about them.

Thinking far ahead, we can go one step further. Two persons may communicate with each other via PCs or whatever form the network may have in the future. Gradually the power of the network may become so overwhelming that combined networks crowd out human intelligence. Without either of the two persons communicating realizing it, the network may use the image and voice of the other person so he/she, in fact, speaks with the network, instead of a person. Some observers would take the view that combined networks may create their own artificial intelligence that competes with human intelligence.

Researchers at Karolinska Institute in Stockholm[31] have conducted research into the scenario where the mind can be tricked into believing that the body is in a different place. This version or edition of virtual reality can make a person feel as if he/she is driving a car or riding a roller coaster when simply sitting in front of a computer or movie screen. It can also make the person perceive that he/she has the body of somebody else such as a sports star, a movie star, or any other person he/she admires.

These observations tend to focus on the worrying or unsettling side of ICT. Another study[32] takes a positive and optimistic view almost praising the new generation that has been born with access to the Internet, and that has never known a world or life without it.

According to this study the net generation is active, focused on improving society and how it works and, unlike the TV generation that was inactive, very interactive. They are not content to sit and receive information, they want to participate, contribute, make their views known, and engage in dialogue with other people.[33]

Eight characteristics are defined for this generation:

- They look for freedom and choice in everything they do
- They customize and personalize
- They scrutinize everything
- They have integrity and openness
- They want entertainment and the opportunity to play incorporated in all other actions
- They want collaboration with others
- Everything must take place fast for them
- They seek constant innovation

The fact that this generation wants to combine work and play means that they are more creative and able, even love, to engage in interdisciplinary and/or multitasking operations.

Emphasis on impersonal contact gives rise to two worries: loss of respect and sense of privacy, and technology piracy. The Internet apparently breaks down barriers that existed in earlier generations for privacy by offering opportunities to upload pictures, images, and/or information about other persons. Proliferation of technology piracy puts a question mark on the accepted definition of property rights — what is yours, and can I use it if it is not mine? Both issues have the power to stop further development.

The year 2008 also heralded a change in job seeking methods, at least for those in higher paid professions — financial services, education, and media that are already heavily shaped by ICT.

People who lost their jobs stopped looking for another job through traditional media such as newspapers and turned instead to ICT, in particular, the networks.[34] LinkedIn reported an increase in membership from eighteen to thirty-one million in the course of 2008 and a large part of the increased traffic seems to have been generated by people who had either lost or were afraid to lose their jobs, using the Internet to search for another job or job opportunities. The more popular networks such as FaceBook are not really suited to this purpose,[35] which explains why people turned to the more professional ones.[36]

Not only does ICT shape another culture, but it is also evident that this other culture — virtual relationships — will itself shape norms, values, and ethics differently from the ones reigning in society and societal norms before ICT entered the stage.

Alternative sources of energy are attracting investment and providing a larger share of energy consumption. The question is how large is this share and what will be its impact on societal norms. For the energy sector the time horizon for changes is fairly long because the investments are so big and normally take several years to implement, so changes will only work their way through the system at slow speed. Technologically, alternative energy sources may not be as important twenty-five years from now as some observers think. But the underlying reasons — climate change and global warming — may substantially change people's attitudes to a more sustainable economy and, if that is the case, the consumption pattern will also change. If the consumer swings away from one-time use products to longer lasting products and looks more closely at the impact on the environment of consumption goods, permanent shifts in the economy will take place, triggered by global warming and climate change. Such changes may affect the economy and may be more substantial than climate change itself.

Biotech[37] and nanoscience/nanotechnology[38] may well constitute the next batch of new technologies. We are still somewhere between phases one or two, where we know with certainty that these technologies "work" (except semiconductor physics and technologies, which are already widely adopted and renew themselves with new scientific discoveries), but are uncertain if they, or a part of them, will make it into phase three, and subsequently the three higher stages, and if so, how long it will take. Compared with ICT we may be where ICT was in the 1970s, that is a technology that can be used and is used, but so far with limits and not yet applicable for a large number of businesses, institutions, and individuals. Carbon nanotubes[39] are in phase one or two.

If we work on the assumption, which looks reasonable, that the two technologies (areas in genetics and, for example, carbon nanotubes) will transit into the later phases, we find that they pose more crucial questions about societal norms than has been the case for ICT.

ICT changed everyday life for business, institutions, and individuals, but did not move pickets regarding ethics, except for privacy. Whether we worked with a mechanical calculator or a PC mattered for productivity and capabilities, but not at all for our ethics. The same was the case for fixed-line versus mobile communication technology.

Biotechnology and nanotechnology do change both everyday life and ethics. The technical infrastructure may not need the same degree of adjustment, as was the case for ICT, but the political repercussions on administrative infrastructure calls for fundamental examination. Opportunities and possibilities never seen before will offer themselves to serve humanity, but will touch on what used to be exclusively under Mother Nature's control.

It is possible, with some uncertainty, to forecast some of the changes biotechnology and nanotechnology will bring, but it is extremely difficult to evaluate how these technologies and their opportunities will influence the human mind and the way we treat other human beings.

It may be useful to sketch briefly how the automobile and ICT as new technologies were incorporated in society.

Automobile technology took about twenty-five years to pass from phase one into phase two, knocking on the door to phase three. It is however doubtful whether its transition would have followed the same pattern without World War I. In the interwar years, it passed gradually into phase three in the 1930s in the United States and in the post-war period in Europe. So it took approximately fifty years for this technology to pass through the three first phases before becoming a normal consumer good and entering mass consumption.

It is now somewhere in phase five or six, unless it rebuilds itself on new scientific bases and may, depending on oil price versus possible new technology, enter phase six in the next twenty-five years.

Its life span will then be more than a hundred years. It first brought enormous changes in traffic infrastructure to the industrialized world, remodelling the relationship of urban versus rural districts, and opening the door for new kinds of consumption. The spin-off of new technology in other sectors has, however, been limited.

As a technology its most important impact on society has been the need to design cities to allow automobiles to flourish and to allow countryside living. Without the automobile the geographical distance covered by an individual on horseback in one day was limited, which favoured medium-size cities drawing on the economic resources of people living within a radius of perhaps fifty kilometres. With the advent of the automobile, the radius of this circle was extended, favouring big regional centres.

Semiconductors, computing, and computer science got their technological breakthrough in the immediate post-war period, but it took until the 1960s before they moved from a curiosity, or something only suitable for limited scientific and/or military purposes, to an applicable technology. They moved gradually from phase two to phase three during the 1970s and 1980s. Now they are in stage four for most developed countries and emerging economies such as China. We know with a high degree of certainty that ICT will be in stage four for most of the next twenty-five years and will probably start to move into stage five, and, in fact, may already be on its way there.

When we are analysing spin-off technologies, it is interesting for us to compare the automobile with ICT. New technology triggered off by the automobile had its origin in external diseconomies,[40] forcing society to develop new technology to reduce or prevent them. A shift in values turning against pollution was the background for these new technologies. ICT has so far not given rise to much pollution, albeit the disposal of PCs, etc., may emerge as an unwanted polluter. Another possible external diseconomy is ICT's role as a "gas-guzzler" with regard to energy consumption even if it does not look so. Concepts such as green ICT may be on the agenda in the next twenty-five years, triggering the same kind of technological response to ICT as was the case for the automobile.

## WISDOM OF THE CROWD

So far the world has seen two genuine breakthroughs — dubbed by Alvin Toffler as waves.

The *first* one (the industrial revolution) took place in Britain starting at the end of the eighteenth century and gaining speed at the beginning of the nineteenth century.

The *second* one started in the United States and got a firm foothold in the Western part of the country in the 1950s, gaining pace and breadth over the second half of the twentieth century. I prefer the label "the audio-visual revolution" (a more correct, but longer label is the convergence of computing, communications, and content) as it combines sound and picture/images as instruments for communication, but it is also known as the information age.

It looks like we are on the threshold of a *third* wave. In fact it has already been announced and given labels. Some call it the non-material age as production shifts from manufacturing to services. Others dub it the dream society because fantasy and imagination become the determining elements.[41] And yet others again focus on biotechnology and nanotechnology without a label that clearly indicates what it is about as was the case for the first two waves.

Not surprisingly most futurists see the next wave as an extrapolation and/or improved version of the second wave, and elaborate on the opportunities that will arise in the area of information and communication services. This is also my own preferred outcome for the technology of mobile communication.

The decisive element is, however, whether we are going to see the same depth of changing structures for such a wave as was the case for the first two.

The flywheel for seminal shifts of the magnitude deserving the label "wave" is an interaction between technology, culture, and organization, and sometimes also regulations and thus policies. For example, had a few European states not agreed on one common standard for digital wireless communications, that part of the wave would never have taken off, and the world would only have seen the fragmentation the United States and Japan are still subject to.

New technology takes root where culture and organization constitute a propitious foundation. There are many examples of new technology not making it beyond marginal interest and use for peripheral purposes. Steam power was not invented at the outbreak of the industrial revolution. The first device run by steam power goes back to the Roman Empire during the reign of Emperor Augustus.[42] There was no interest and no investments, however, to use such an engine in the Roman Empire. Slaves were used as manpower and they were cheaper! This underlines the fact that new technology is only turned into products if it is profitable, irrespective of its potential. Another example, this time of how an organization can stop new technology, is the offer of a telegraph in 1816 to the British Admiralty. The Admiralty delivered the following frosty answer "Telegraphs of any kind are now wholly unnecessary; and no other than the one now in use will be adopted."[43]

It is, therefore, not sufficient to look for new technologies, but instead to look for the interplay and combination of the three, or perhaps four of the above-mentioned elements: technology as tools, culture in the broad context of how we behave in our daily life,[44] and organization as the technical and administrative framework for societal and business life.

Such an interplay arose with steam power during the Industrial Revolution in Britain, a society open to new technology because the English society had undergone its own political revolution a hundred years earlier, and a reorganization, which, among other things, saw a financial system being recast after scandals in overseas trading companies introduced the idea of stockholder.

The same interplay was seen in the United States in the second half of the twentieth century. The audio-visual technology happened in a society already on its way to using images in the film industry, and the absence of regulations, national monopolies, etc., as seen in Europe, made the use of the new technology profitable, not the least because the market was big.

In these cases a virtuous interaction took place. New technology is introduced and starts to feel its way into society. On this basis a new culture, in the sense of new behaviour based on new consumption patterns, is born. This stimulates demand and asks for more new technology, influencing culture, the arts, and stimulating further demand and so on. This interaction was clearly seen in Britain during the Industrial Revolution and in the United States during the audio-visual revolution.

If the cultural framework and organization are not welcoming of new technology, it turns into, as was seen in the example of steam power and the Roman Empire, something funny, which can be discussed and used by a few for strange purposes, but it never finds its way into society. In a futuristic study of what's in store twenty-five years ahead, it may, therefore, be more rewarding and more to the point to analyse where the conditions for such interplay look promising and where bottlenecks exist, instead of trying to pinpoint which new technologies may emerge.

Although there is no scientific proof of this, it looks like such interplay can and will take place where you have a large number of people thinking in the same way. The theory about wisdom of the crowds[45] supports the theory that when a large number of people get together they tend to reach wise and good decisions. A recent article[46] analyses a similar situation with the intriguing sentence "one ant is not intelligent, but an ant colony is". Another study focusing on how ants react if their nest is threatened forcing them to find a new one, concludes by mapping out a rather sophisticated decision-making process, highlighting the interplay between the individual ant and the colony.[47]

A study about honeybees[48] and the group decisions to find nesting sites brings out how rational group thinking among animals can actually be. The core of the finding is the interaction among individuals, according to common rules or guidelines for thinking, to verify and check what individual honeybees come up with. Decision making is neither left to individuals nor group thinking, but to what in human terms would be called a complicated check and balance system when new information is brought to the attention of the group. It is subjugated to verification and analysis weighed up against an alternative by other members of the group before the group as such takes the decision.

What this amounts to is an embryonic theory saying that the human brain works like a computer — or vice versa — and that the phenomenon seen in computer networks can also be applied to the human brain: when brains link together, a network is born and the combined capacity leads to a higher performance level than if only one brain tackles the question to be solved. Human beings are apparently programmed by nature to call meetings when faced with intricate decisions. Implicitly they must know that when put together their brains will communicate with one another constituting a network producing a better solution than in isolation. It is irrelevant whether the brains create a network without human beings realizing it (subconsciously), or whether the persons present can actually switch off or on. Maybe the brains are capable of linking without asking the "owner" of the brain for permission!

Philosophers may have got there first. There are traces of collective intelligence in the works of Henri Bergson,[49] and Emile Durkheim[50] regards society as a whole — in today's terminology, holistic entity — as the sole source of logical thought. According to Durkheim, society — in reality collective intelligence — is intelligence at a higher level because it transcends the individual over space and time. In modern times these ideas have been followed up and deepened by philosophers such as Pierre Levy, who sees collective intelligence as an interdisciplinary question and linked to interactive communication sponsored by the computer networks.[51]

Wisdom of the crowd and a behaviour similar to animals working together to explore and find the best possible way to proceed is the driving force behind Wikipedia,[52] which combines open access to the Internet with information inside the caucus of ICT as an instrument of communication. Wikepedia itself is mostly knowledge with tagged text, extensive markup language (XML).

One or several persons write an explanation or definition of a certain phenomenon and the door is open for everybody else to intervene and correct, amend, or ask for sources or verification. This is human beings working together like the ants and the honeybees do, trying to distil the best possible result out of the wisdom of a larger number of individuals to transform it into collective wisdom. Like the ants or the honeybees we do not fully understand the process. Nor do we know the actual decision-making process, but what is on Wikipedia reflects what the larger majority of participating human brains have brought together and analysed in common.

The problem with this kind of wisdom of the crowd for human beings is that it works fine and without risk of abuse as long as we confine it to objective questions, with science and factual knowledge being the most obvious examples. If or when we move into normative questions where there is no — let us call it accepted wisdom — the floor is open to all kinds of views. Religious issues[53] are an example; opinions differ and arguments for and against are offered without any firm conclusion.

It is an open question how wisdom of the crowd will develop with access to, and use of, ICT, offering not only a new perspective of this behaviour, but also a range of new opportunities, some of which may be abused.

Such a theory would point to China and perhaps India as the most likely places for a third wave or breakthrough coming with potential new applications for ICT because this is where we find the largest numbers of people tuned in to the same way of using ICT. If so we will still operate with genuine geographic centres for the birth of new waves.

Another, perhaps heretical, thinking is to link this to virtual networks and ask whether virtual networks can do the same. If that is the case, new centres will be transnational, born out of a large number of people coming together via the Internet and thinking in the same way.

## THE TRIUMVIRATE OF MORAL VALUES, MUTUAL TRUST, AND SOCIAL CAPITAL

### East and West Compared

Moral values, mutual trust, and social capital play a crucial role in making the individual receptive or reluctant to adapt to discontinuities, disruptive processes, the likelihood that curves break, and tilting points.

The American researcher David Hitchcock[54] was among the first to go beyond intuitive statements and look into differences in values between East Asia and the West. He offers the following observations although he points out that the foundation for his survey was "thin":

> The largest gap between Americans and East Asians in the personal values/qualities list was in how each group scored "respect for learning" and "obedience to parents" (although the latter was not high with either group). The largest gap between East Asian and American replies on the list of societal values/practices was over the importance each attributed to an "orderly society" (71 per cent of the East Asians versus 11 per cent of the Americans); "personal freedom" (82 per cent of the Americans versus 32 per cent of the East Asians); and "individual rights" (78 per cent of the Americans versus 29 per cent of the East Asians). The percentage of East Asians indicating as "critically important", "decision by majority" or "decision by consensus" was, however, approximately the same as in the United States. And the percentage supporting "resolve conflicting political views through open debate" or "through private consultation" was identical — an interestingly high total for "majority" and "open decisions".

> In the 1996 study, I [Hitchcock] asked one hundred experts and opinion leaders — some of the same persons — to study a list of certain practices governing society, twelve practices in all, and identify those which were

in their judgment "most important" and "least important" to people in their country. The closest scoring by both Americans and East Asians was on the importance of "a speedy trial"; "humane working conditions"; and "to be paid a fair wage". The widest gap between East Asian and American respondents was over the importance of "can say and write what you think" and "can refuse to testify against oneself". But generally, there was considerable convergence between East Asian and American replies on the relative importance of practices governing society. The highest scores of "most important" practices by the East Asian respondents were "to be paid a fair wage", then "open elections" and "humane working conditions". The highest "most important" scores for Americans were "can say and write what you think"; "open elections" and "cannot be discriminated against because of race, religion, gender, age or physical handicap" (also high among East Asians).

The study supports, even if the foundation is thin and the number of people selective and small, the general view that there are differences in how people in East Asia and the West see the relations between the individual, the family, and society, with East Asians giving higher priority to society as a whole. The difficulty appears in interpreting what this actually means in practice.

The main Asian countries differ with respect to history, traditions, religions, and ethnicity, but there are some general trends among Asian countries that merit attention and may give a clue to moral values, mutual trust, and social capital.

The *first* trend is that people brought up in Asian societies tend to prioritize society — the collective caucus — ahead of concern for individuals. This should work in favour of strong social capital, but there are several snags in drawing such a conclusion.

The priority for an orderly society or whatever label may be given to this attitude does not mean that society is looked at in the context of a country or a nation state. The society or community may be much smaller and be defined by village connections, local communities, large families etc. If this is the case, and there is some evidence, including a lot of anecdotal evidence, strong local and confined — even narrow — social capital may work against the build-up of a strong national social capital.

This may be even more the case with the emphasis on the family, especially in an economic and industrial perspective. If the hiring of workers, promotions, etc., follow family ties, or narrow community ties, meritocracy may be crowded out and the end result may be lower productivity.

The fact that many of the nations in Asia are recent nation states warrants this observation. In these nation states social capital may be strong, even very strong and even stronger than that found in many established European nation states, but it may not be a nationwide social capital. As the nation states seek to forge a national economy, tapping into human resources from various regions, social capital born out of non-nationwide networks may obstruct such policies.

The *second* trend concerns religion — always a sensitive issue to bring up — but it harbours some lasting and powerful moral guidelines and cannot be separated from a discussion of social capital. Some religions, for example Christianity, are secular in the strict sense that religion is separated from the state. Other religions such as Islam look at it in the opposite way, seeing religion as a societal structure also.

Europe is, with few exceptions, dominated by Christianity albeit in various forms, but basically societal values in Europe have grown out of Christianity and do not differ very much among European nation states and/or regions/local communities. This is undoubtedly one of the reasons that mutual trust is normally comparatively strong inside European nation states and on a nationwide basis. The United States does not content itself with one religion; it opens the door for all religions, with the result that religion is not the source from which comparable societal values flow — sometimes quite the opposite. Nor has the public sector, which is weak, been asked, or invited, or wanted, to take a hand in forging nationwide societal values that lead to social capital, with the result that mutual trust may be strong inside societies and communities, but weak on a nationwide basis.

Asia is neither like Europe nor the United States, but harbours many religions with different histories and influence on nation building, and present nation states take a divergent view on the role of religion. No comparable societal values are to be found in Asia reflecting a common religious foundation. Some of the nation states see themselves as nation states based on a religion (Islamic nations) and even use religion to hold the nation state together, while others may not be based on religion; they may tolerate it, but keep it at a distance and they definitely rule religious values out of the context of forging nationwide values (China). Yet others fall in between.

This is not a question of whether there are Asian values or not, but a simple observation that several factors stand in the way not only for mutual trust to be perceived in an analogous way for Asian nation states, but also that even inside Asian nation states, a nationwide mutual trust/societal capital is not an easy task.

The Asian countries do indeed differ with regard to history, tradition, religion, and ethnicities, and a working assumption that the social capital for each differs seems warranted.

This is borne out by the work of Professor Takashi Inoguchi.[55] Ten Asian societies are analysed on the basis of three fundamental questions: (1) general trust in interpersonal relations, (2) trust in merit-based utility, and (3) trust in social systems.

With regard to general trust, Confucian heritage societies such as China, Vietnam, Korea, and Japan come up at the top, and Hindu/Buddhist/Islamic heritage countries such as Thailand, Malaysia, and Sri Lanka, are found at the bottom.

For trust in merit-based utility, another picture emerges. The top scorers are English-speaking or former British colonies such as India and Sri Lanka, with Korea, Thailand, and Japan at the bottom.

The *third* category — trust in social systems — gives a ranking with communist or former communist countries such as Vietnam and China at the top, and Korea and Japan at the bottom.

On this basis, Inoguchi draws the conclusion that the ten Asian countries studied can be divided into three groups with regard to social capital. The first one is composed of countries with a Confucian heritage, the second one comprises English-speaking countries, and the third are communist or former communist countries.

In a later analysis published with Zen-U Lucian Hotta,[56] twenty-nine Asian societies are quantifiably compared by one of the four dimensional components — altruism, utilitarianism, communitarianism, and concordance with the prevailing regime (trust in social system).

The twenty-nine societies are found to fall into seven clusters.

Group one: Japan, Korea, and Taiwan. This group of societies are geographically close to one another and actually at the perimeter of Asia, constituting some kind of tip or fringe of the continent as peninsular or islands, and sharing history and cultural heritage. It ranks high in terms of altruism, but low in terms of both communitarianism and utilitarianism.

Group two: Pakistan, Afghanistan, and the Maldives. The group ranks high with regard to altruism and communitarianism, but low in the level of concordance with prevailing regimes. Islam seems to play a major role in defining social capital among these three countries.

Group three: China and Turkmenistan. Both strongly emphasize altruistic values and differ from group one in that they are not too low in terms of communitarianism.

Group four: Singapore, India, Sri Lanka, and Nepal, with Bangladesh close to qualifying to be in the group. These countries reflect the British colonial influence, with low marks for communitarianism and concordance with prevailing regime.

Group five: Brunei, Malaysia, Indonesia, Vietnam, Bhutan, Mongolia. Mainly composed of Southeast Asian countries, this group is more oriented towards utilitarianism.

Group six: Hong Kong and the Philippines. Both are influenced by the Anglo-Saxon tradition, but nevertheless differs from group four, ranking high in terms of concordance with the prevailing regime despite a similarly low level of communitarianism. The two authors (Inoguchi and Hotta) offer the explanation for the low level of communitarianism in groups four and six as possibly the Protestant work ethic, Western individualism, focus on self-achievement, and emphasis on retirement and insurance systems.

Group seven: Thailand, Kazakhstan, Uzbekistan, Tajikistan, Cambodia, Bangladesh, Kyrgyzstan, Laos, Myanmar. This grouping looks a bit puzzling, but the common denominator between the four Southeast Asian countries, four Central Asian countries, and Bangladesh, is that they are more oriented towards reliance on the community.

The authors readily admit that the analysis has its limits and should be seen in combination with other social factors and indicators. It also states explicitly that an analysis of social capital and related issues should not be confined to the country level, but broken down into smaller segments such as societies and local communities.

In the context of this study the following seems the most interesting:

- The two strong drivers for social capital are Confucianism and the influence of English (Western or American) culture perceived as behavioural patterns
- Countries steered by these trends fall mainly into groups that are relatively homogenous
- China is in a group of its own (only joined by Turkmenistan)
- The Islamic influence on social capital judged by this analysis does not seem strong and uniform as Islamic countries (countries with Muslims as a clear majority of the population) are spread over three groups, perhaps even four, depending on the classification of Turkmenistan
- Southeast Asian countries are spread over four groups

This tells us that it will be difficult to establish some kind of common denominator encompassing Asia as a whole for social capital, but it does not preclude either creation of nationwide social capital or social capital for groups of nation states.

Like the rest of the world, Asia is caught by the cross influences of globalization on societal values and social capital inside nation states and among groups inside nation states.

## Social Capital: Nationwide versus Inside Groups

Parallel societies as seen in the United States and, to a certain extent, also in Europe may arise as a consequence of these cross influences. There is nothing wrong with having parallel societies, but the risk is that such societies may not only define social values contrary to the ones that the nation state likes to see, but may also cast the nation state and its values in the role of the enemy. The implication of this is nepotism, corruption, and other practices creating not only parallel societies, but parallel economies, parallel judicial systems, etc., thus posing a danger to the nation state.

The paradox could be that inside these parallel societies, good governance may be found as defined by them, but these may be classified as bad or even dangerous governance by the nation state in which they are found. It is not only a question of perception, but also of communication, in the sense that if the issue were to be raised about good governance, they might reply that they are exercising perfectly good governance.

A study about Italy may shed light on several issues of social capital related to the comments above. Italy is interesting because the country was not unified until 1861, and is still socially and economically divided primarily between the richer northern part and the poorer southern part.[57] Despite a common legal, administrative, judiciary, regulatory, and tax system, Italy is ruled by wide divergence with regard to societal values.[58] In some respects it can be used as a useful indicator for social capital and its development in Asian nation states, most of which are recent ones just as Italy is a recent European nation state. The study observes that social capital is stronger when the legal effect is weaker. It is also more pronounced among less-educated people who often prefer social capital in the form of trust in people they know instead of a legal system run by people they do not know and institutions they do not trust.

The interpretation is that social capital may crowd out or constitute a barrier to a nationwide social capital if the nation state is not fairly homogenous from the outset. The more heterogeneous, the more likely it is that parts of the population will fall back on regional or local social capital, leaving nationwide social capital or the national legal system as a torso. The difficulty is that regional or local social capital cannot easily be turned into nationwide social capital, so even if it is known that nationwide social capital can be used in nation building or as an instrument for holding the nation together, it is not obvious how this can be done. The key to change this is a much more coherent and elaborate social and cultural policy encompassing education, and probably touching religion and other foundations for values and ethics. In Europe the normal pattern was to let the majority's values constitute the basis of social capital. It has worked reasonable well so far, but only in nation states where the majority is large and homogenous (Great Britain, France, Spain, Portugal, and the Scandinavian countries), but even here immigration has exposed how difficult it is to shape multicultural social capital.[59] In the United States, the abbreviation WASP (White Anglo-Saxon Protestants) was used for many years as synonymous with the plinth of American values, but not many would say that today as the ethnic composition of the nation undergoes tremendous change.

In a world becoming more global and more susceptible to culture emanating from abroad, we need to distinguish between family culture, work culture, and leisure culture.

*First*, family culture or basic culture consists primarily of norms for how people interact inside a closely knit group such as the family: what is permissible and what is not, what is right and wrong, whom do they marry, how do they organize the upbringing of children, how do they treat their elders, etc. — all of these are fundamental questions for a society and the relations between individuals. These norms are also less malleable and, if at all, only over a long-term time horizon and very gradually. They are anchored in religion, ethnicity, and language — all elements that are again rooted in history and traditions. Family culture is, despite globalization, still very much local or regional and still separates individuals and families from other people. It is difficult for an outsider to penetrate these groups and those who try may end up by being neither fully accepted by the group, nor forgiven by his/her original group for having left it.

*Second*, work culture is how people behave in the workplace, teaching/learning from colleagues, analysing work to build up a relationship with people they meet when they work, but do not associate with outside work. This kind of culture is certainly influenced by globalization, and although it is an overstatement to say this, there is a considerable degree of harmonization, not least sponsored by multinational companies, which enter a market and adapt their marketing culture, but much less their work culture — how they do things in their company.

*Third,* Leisure culture is how people spend their leisure, what kind of entertainment they opt for, movies, for example, music etc. — distractions. This is much more a mass culture with broad characteristics attracting people all over the globe and having very little to do what is regarded as right or wrong. A high degree of harmonization is emerging perhaps not for deep cultural activities, but for the overwhelming part of mass cultures. The American entertainment industry has succeeded in putting its mark on a large part of the world and is resisted only by religious groups and some other groups maintaining a rigorous attitude to what its members can do.

The first category, family culture, is not susceptible to influences from modern instruments such as cyber networks and ICT, but the other two are.

Mutual trust, however, depends and rests on family culture much more than on work culture and leisure culture.

For Asia the challenge may well be whether it proves possible to maintain a large part of family culture as the glue keeping ties inside groups strong, and at the same time, loosening up to the outside influences from work culture and leisure culture, and moving towards a nationwide social capital and even entering into the game of accepting some global values, however difficult that may be.

Hitherto Asia's social capital predominantly safeguarded societies, communities, families, local communities, against too strong an influence from the outside. Although a superficial look at many Asian societies find them resembling what is found in the West they seem to have attained social capital with reasonable success. Asian values, perceived as the norms inside families and groups, not congruous from community to community across borders and not even inside the same nation state, have survived the onslaught of globalization from outside.

The next step is to see whether that picture can be maintained when Asia moves from being emerging economies to being dominant economies over the next twenty-five years. With the rise of Asian multinationals and, presumably as a consequence, consumer patterns, brands, and tastes starting to be shaped in Asia, the question is how that will affect social capital and the three components of culture.

Much will depend on governments and governance. Europe was helped towards nationwide social capital by Christianity and a fairly homogenous population that did not really need governments to step in to shape social capital. In Asia it is the other way around. Asia is much more diversified than Europe with many ethnicities, religions, and other particularities inside nation states. Asian governments play the role of a guarantor for minorities whereas the European governments have for a long time been the vehicle for imposing the majority's cultural patterns on the minorities.

These circumstances set out why nationwide social capital cannot be created in Asia without strong and decisive government. There may be exceptions, but they are few. Even where governments look weak they are determined to safeguard the rights of the minorities — otherwise the much more complex Asian nation states would fall apart.

Strong government and strong governance would be able to help nationwide social capital thus increasing productivity which helps to keep economic growth at a sustainable high level thus legitimizing the government's role and making more room for the government to further social capital, and thus the cycle starts again. This is a possible virtuous cycle. The opposite will be the case with weak governments not able or wishing to defend the rights of the minorities. This pushes a large part of the population back into group-based social capital and tears the nation state apart as the groups will depict other groups as villains to legitimize strong group social capital.

An understanding of the impact on social capital of achieved status versus ascribed status[60] underlines the importance of equitable distribution of income and wealth. Societies such as the United States or other migrant societies tend to focus on achieved status and, especially, wealth — not totally, but largely — irrespective of how it was earned, thus downgrading the value of societal work. Old fashioned societies such as the British society allow ascribed status to influence careers, making the economy work less efficiently. The way ahead for using status to promote social capital and, preferably, nationwide social capital, is to endorse achieved status, but let it be accompanied by ascribed status defined not by heritage etc., but by what has been done for society.[61] In this context, the inequality of income and wealth supplemented by family-owned enterprises in many Asian countries gives rise to anxiety about future prospects for building strong nationwide social capital.

Social capital is sometimes used as a label for mutual trust and identity among individuals. Social capital[62] can be defined in many ways, but in this context the focus is on whether society is governed by values so that the large majority of citizens trust one another, trust business corporations and institutions because they share the same basic values. It is believed to have appeared for the first time in 1916 when L.J. Hanifan (state supervisor of rural schools in West Virginia) said *inter alia* "The individual is helpless socially, if left to himself. If he comes into contact with his neighbor, and they with other neighbors, there will be an accumulation of social capital."[63] Trust constitutes the plinth of social capital. In the context of this study the definition of trust and trust networks is as put forward by Charles Tilly.[64] Trust consists "of placing valued outcomes at risk to other's malfeasance mistakes or failures. Trust relationships include those in which people regularly take such risks.... Trust networks consist of *ramified interpersonal connections, consisting of strong ties, within which people set valued, consequential, long-term resources and enterprises at risk to the malfeasance, mistakes or failures of others.*"

A value-based society needs fewer institutions and resources of a human and fiscal nature to ensure compliance with the rules from individuals and corporations as these know where to draw the line between what is right and wrong, what is good and bad.

Most value-driven societies with high social capital are embedded in genuine nation states comprising one predominant ethnicity and one predominant religion. Or they are found within nation states as regions or administrative units that have succeeded in resisting the blurring of the above-mentioned characteristics.

Globalization has led to multicultural nations and/or multicultural societies covering several nation states. With growing globalization accompanied by a higher degree of personal mobility, the question arises whether social capital anchored in common ethnicity and common religions will be eroded.

## GOVERNANCE

Governance is a tough challenge when a government has to try amalgamating several identities into not necessarily one identity, but a high degree of trust and confidence among people not used to trusting people from other ethnicities and religions.

This is especially true if policies move towards not only securing the fundamental right of freedom, but also representative democracy. The well functioning of representative democracy rests basically on one single factor: that voters are ready and actually do exercise this right to change voting patterns. In the United States, they choose between the Democratic Party and the Republican Party; in Europe, between traditional parties to the left of centre, to the right of centre, and in the centre. This can only happen when voters have as much trust in politicians from one political party as in those from another. Trust spans over the political spectrum and is not confined to people with a specific background.

If on the other hand voters tend to cast their vote according to ethnicity and/or religion, political parties will represent such groups and the voting pattern resists changes. Voters will not look at the record of politicians, but at their ethnicity or religion.

With the fast developing Asian nation states, we instinctively expect higher social capital since people should get more trust and confidence in each other with a higher income per head. On second look, however, we realize that the growing multiculturalism, socio-economic inequality/injustice, and shift in demographics inside, as well as between, nation states mean that this cannot be taken for granted.

## Incremental Development

The period from 1980 to 2008 brought an end to the rivalry between capitalism and socialism/communism which advocates a centrally-planned economic system and an authoritarian system. The American style of capitalism won the duel and is now more or less accepted as the global model even if some suspect it will undergo considerable changes over the next twenty-five years.

It also brought an end to communism as a political system. To digest why it happened it might be rewarding to look at China instead of the Soviet Union.[65] Communism heralded and implemented what some observers call "utopian engineering", which defines some kind of ideal society according to a political philosophy — in this case socialism. But it did not work as expected. Central planning takes away initiative and independence from the individual citizen and, by doing so, kills economic and personal incentives. Not only that; instead of a feeling of commonality, animosity among citizens, dislike of one another, indifference to how others fare, take over as societal norms.

China's reform from 1979 onwards offered "piecemeal engineering" where steps were taken one after another after careful testing of what worked and what did not. Philosophy and political theories were pushed to the background and a system rooted in meritocracy and applicability pulled to the foreground. Karl Popper[66] who wrote at the same time (1944) as Friederich Hayek[67] coined this particular political philosophy. Both were seeking a showdown with authoritarian political philosophies pointing to their flaws, shortcomings, and weaknesses.

Piecemeal engineering or incremental progress or whichever other term seems appropriate, has stood the test of seminal changes in China and it is likely that this political course will be followed over the next twenty-five years. Things may change and events may put their stamp on the development, but so far no incentives to change that model are visible.

Basically a political system is a mechanism for selecting leaders of the nation. The main difference between various systems is of course how this selection takes place and, in particular, to what extent ordinary people are involved. Almost all political systems have established channels for feedback, allowing leaders to know how the population feels, what the problems are, and how the government is rated. At the end of the day, the legitimacy of a government or a system depends on how good the system is in delivering what the large majority of the population wants.

It cannot be taken for granted that autocracy works more efficiently than democracy or that democracy ensures human rights better than other kinds of political systems.[68] It is more complicated than that. The decisive point is the readiness of political leaders to listen to the population and ensure basic freedoms. Another decisive point is whether political leaders are prepared to give up power, and here democracy offers a better guarantee than almost all other political systems.

All political systems are shaped by history, tradition, experience, and challenges. The way of selecting leaders may not be item number one on the wish list of the populations in Asia. Item number one will unquestionably be how good the political systems are in delivering what the population wants.

It therefore seems reasonable to assume that the incremental and/or piecemeal engineering of political system will continue, and to rule out a new kind of utopian engineering or political big bang. The piecemeal approach has not yet started in several Asian countries. The question is how political leaders respond to challenges arising and how the population responds to changes and policies put forward. Can the social (and political) contract between populations and political leaders survive, and if so, what are the main unknowns and uncertainties?

All political systems (and governance) work through institutions that in theory convey a sense of permanence, authority, and equality before the law, as main elements. There is however a fundamental difference in the way institutions operate.

Some political systems' institutions breed future political leaders. Even if it sounds strange, institutions are some kind of grass roots movement as they are not dependent on a particular person or organization. If the chosen political leaders do not perform as expected, they are removed and the institutional machinery produces a new set of leaders. The leaders assume the role of figureheads so to speak and are elected because their views conform to the institutions.

In other political systems the institutions function blamelessly, but they are in fact the instruments for a select or limited group of people using the institutions as a vehicle for governing the nation state. If the leading group fails in one way or another, the institutions crack because they have no foundation in society. The leaders are not figureheads, but helmsmen, and the ship obeys the rudder.[69]

## Pivotal Elements

There are three pivotal elements for the future of governance till about 2040.

The *first* element is the continued ability to deliver what the population wants and this is probably rising living standard, some degree of welfare, and human security. These preferences may change over time, but it is fair to assume that they will be the top three for most people in the foreseeable future.

The systems in Asian countries do not work in an analogous way as indeed the systems themselves differ markedly, but it is fair, again, to say that from 1980 to 2008, the various systems have delivered — albeit not necessarily optimally — sufficiently to maintain the image of a legitimate political system working in conformity with the wishes of the population (with a few exception such as *inter alia* North Korea and Myanmar). There have been examples where this was not the case as in Indonesia in 1997/98 and the result was fundamental changes. The Indonesian example underlines the point above that legitimacy rests on ability to deliver and it is even more interesting to note that otherwise, changes may take place.

Complacency constitutes one of the risk factors. Political leaders who have been in power for a long time and worked successfully may feel that they can take it for granted that power is in their hands regardless of policies and performance. In Western democracies, experience indicates that ten years in power is the limit after which leaders lose contact with realities. Very few political leaders have survived the ten-year mark. The way to avoid this trap is to create change from within. In some political systems no assistance is needed for this as political parties having legal or de facto monopoly of power are not the monoliths seen from outside, but composed of factions fighting one another. This, for example, seems to be the case for the Chinese Communist Party. Although these factional fights are not comparable to free elections, after some years another faction may win power in the party and install its members in leading positions. The likelihood of such changes constitutes a barrier to abuse of power as somebody else from another, and, in some cases, less friendly faction will assume power and get insights on what policies were pursued, how, and why. The ten-year bar for the president of China works the same way.

Nepotism and corruption fall in the same category. There is no doubt that these phenomena distort the economy, leading to lower growth than in a "clean" economy. The problem is how to get rid of such misbehaviour.

Superficial measures will not work. Corruption and nepotism reflect that official prices and income are out of step with reality. In economic terms the economy is not controlled by official prices and income, but by artificial prices and incomes set by forces steered by a market, yes, but not the visible one. These market prices and incomes reflect what services really are worth and corruption and nepotism operate according to these "real" prices and incomes. If a licence is put on public tender for US$10,000, but its genuine value is US$100,000, corruption and/or nepotism will ensure that it is sold for that price even if the published price is US$10,000.

The only way ahead is to bring official prices in conformity with real prices, but this can only be done if accompanied by a whole string of political and societal measures. Suffice to mention that salaries must be increased to reflect a decent standard of living and the higher cost for the government, financed by the revenue coming in from selling licences. Such steps take time and meet with many kinds of obstacles. The existence of strong social capital inside groups, but not across society and/or on a nationwide basis, may block transparency and open the door for corruption/nepotism driven by groups.

The *second* element is much more creativity in the Asian economies, lifting them to the stage of being genuine innovators and inventors, capable of entrepreneurship. So far Asia has done extremely well in catching up with the ability to produce effectively and use new technology, but has, with some exceptions but not many, not developed new science, only a few technologies and new production methods.

Over a twenty-five year horizon Asia may well continue to have high economic growth rates without changing track, but genuine creativity leading to new technology and new products must not be too far away if its ambition is to maintain high growth rates.

There is a large international discussion going on about whether creativity in technology, economics, and industry, can be separated from political changes towards more democracy. So far no conclusion has been reached.[70]

Creativity seems to be linked[71] to the individual's perception of the ability to express ideas, personal preferences, lifestyle, and behaviour in a broad sense. The more uniform societal values look being imposed from above, the less likely it is that creativity thrives.

Art has not played a large role on the scene of resurgent Asia contrary to the case in Europe. Maybe the explanation is found in the necessity for Asia to concentrate on technical skills in the first phase of economic development that normally revolves around manufacturing. Now as Asia approaches the next phase — the service economy or the knowledge economy or perhaps the term "skills economy" could be used — art will start to play a much more important role in honing skills for creativity by conveying a taste for art. As art rests on an acceptance of expression choosing its own ways, creativity may get a boost through a greater role for arts. Maybe art can be a litmus test: the higher the preference for engaging in art, the more likely it is that the mindset is shifting towards creativity.[72]

The question is, therefore, whether Asian societies and political systems can move towards a constellation where the political systems open the door for societies to steer towards frameworks perceived as suitable for fostering creativity, and do this without abandoning the preferred political system, especially the preferred method of selecting political leaders.

Admittedly it is easier to pinpoint decisive issues than offer a prediction of whether it can be done or not. The perception among potentially creative people of the room for personal freedom matters more than the exact political system. Doubt about how this is going to play out can be seen in the uncertainty about seeking creativity by encouraging nationals who have gone abroad to study and work to come home, and/or by attracting foreign talents who may bring along their own political views.

The *third* element when considering the future of governance is that it can come to function in accordance with, and influence, the fundamental shift from the industrial society which is characterized by large societal groups, segmentation according to groups and work, and limits to what the individual could or should do. The new society operates with people stressing individuality, no barriers between tasks, and open doors for testing abilities and opportunities.

Large societal groups — farmers, workers, clerks, craftsmen, intellectuals, and a few others — dominated the industrial society. They lived separate lives and distinguished themselves from other groups by politics (political party), the media (newspaper), how they dressed, and type of housing. Walking down the main street of a European or North American city in those days, the observer found it quite easy to classify passers-by according to these groups. Nowadays all this has become blurred. Occupations can no longer be categorized by a limited number of jobs; media and politics reach across societal borders, and people's homes no longer give a clear indicator of their identity. Walking down the main street an observer needs to look for logos on a shirt or other small signs giving hints about identity and informing other individuals adhering to a similar identity that they have shared values. Not only do different identities cross well-known societal borders, but they also are exploding in numbers and breaking away from politics, thus complicating governance. People no longer vote according to theories about income distribution, but according to values concerning schools, health, environment, and relations with people from other cultures, including immigrants.[73]

French sociologist Bourdieu[74] looking at the industrial society comes to the conclusion that social class determines tastes (what a person likes and dislikes) and that the distinction in tastes among social classes is aggravated or deepened through daily life. Tastes, preferences, etc., classify the individual and immediately indicate which social class — worker, middle class, etc. — the person belongs to. This is a perception based on Marxist philosophy. Viewed today, with hindsight, it may be — perhaps already when it was written — out of tune with society, which is steered as much, possibly even more, by microtrends as by macrotrends. Bourdieu's main observation is, however, still valid and of interest, namely, that persons distinguish themselves by their tastes and finding an identity with other individuals through shared tastes and they signal this by their behaviour and sense of fashion. While Bourdieu looks at distinctions governed by classes, the present study sees tastes used to signal identity linked to much smaller groups, with each of these groups being steered by values and norms. Society or community is formed by common values/norms constituting social capital/social coherence and their members distinguish themselves by choosing taste characteristics of various groups without breaking with the values/norms.

Politically the pendulum has swung away from the pure welfare society where the government felt — and the citizens encouraged this concept — that it was the responsibility of the government to ensure the welfare of each individual. Now the thinking has turned around to the idea that it is the responsibility of the government to guarantee that all citizens have opportunities according to their abilities and competences.[75] If the citizen or individual cannot manage or use these opportunities, it is not the fault or responsibility of the government, but the citizen. Criticisms against governments now are not so much directed at their welfare politics in the orthodox definition, but have more to do with education policy, universities, job training — all topics associated with opportunities.

The industrial society's work ethic, still prevailing in Asia, is the key to understanding why that has happened. In that society a job was defined as a singular function where the worker performed specified tasks in a specified time. The worker did so during working hours and went home afterwards, separating work time from leisure, family life from time at the factory/in the office. No one dreamed of a world beyond the well-defined tasks. Piecework contracts epitomize this — workers are motivated to work faster and more, but they do not do something better or different.

The future world is completely different. People are not going to perform jobs, but solve tasks or problems given to them, and it does not matter how they do it and how much or how little they need to work/think across boundaries and disregard job definitions. They do not work in jobs, but in groups designed to solve problems. When the group has solved one, it will be assigned a new one and each individual may or may not continue to work in that particular group. The walls, barriers, and boundaries disappear in the workplace, as they do between work, leisure, and home activities.

Governance must provide a societal framework and reorient the education system, social policy, and similar policies, to facilitate the transition.

## Uncertainties

The uncertainties concerning governance seem to concentrate on the following five elements: the risk of populism, the weakened role of the traditional form of government, ideologies offered to the individual of "identity shelter", the role of the mass media, and the future of social capital.

## *Populism*

Populism is often defined as a policy defending the interests of the common people against the elite. Academic and scholarly definitions go deeper and further.[76] In this context, populism will be defined as the tendency by political leaders to offer and/or implement measures, which, in the short term, benefit the common people, but erode a nation state's and/or society's longer-term capability.

Asia's political systems have over the preceding twenty-five years done well resisting tendencies for populist measures. Working in an environment of high economic growth and few, if any shortages of commodities, has facilitated this task.

As Asia turns to a new environment less conducive to high growth, it cannot be taken for granted that populism will continue to be rejected by the large majority of political systems and political leaders.

Experience from countries falling into the trap of populism indicates that populism thrives in an environment of burden sharing, and falls on barren ground in an environment of distribution of benefits. Lower growth, combined with shortages — even scarcities — of some commodities, which reduces purchasing power, presents political leaders with the awkward and unenviable task of offering less to a population asking for more. A high and rising inequality aggravates the risks as the lower social strata left behind reacts, thus identifying them as easy targets for politicians flirting with populism.

The temptation will be there to pass on the burden, or rather, try to pass on the burden to others and blame them for the problems. In the short term, a nation state can use reserves accumulated in good times to tide it over difficulties for a limited number of years, but not for long. This may even aggravate the problems as political leaders having promised too much may be dragged into, or drag themselves into, accusing selected groups of society of opposing measures, thus creating tensions and undermining social coherence. In the era of globalization an easy victim is the outside world, non-dominant ethnicities, foreigners, foreign countries, or foreign companies. Such an attitude increases the risk for semi-protectionism or outright protectionist steps taken in a bid to shift the burden to other countries which, of course, will respond by retaliatory measures, putting globalization at risk.

## The Weakened Role of Traditional Forms of Governance

Formerly the individual saw his/her link to government in economic terms. Before the nation state age, the individual in a farming society looked to the prince or feudal lord as the guarantor of welfare, in the sense of providing economic activity, access to markets, and a sort of legal framework. With the industrial age the link shifted to the nation state, but is still fundamentally of an economic character.

There was and still is a kind of social contract. The individual sees the government as the provider of welfare in the broad sense of this word, and the government still derives its legitimacy from its ability to deliver economic and social welfare.

The combination of rising welfare (economic living standard), ICT, and globalization changes the setting for governance and the link between the individual and the government. The government is increasingly losing out as the sole provider or guarantor of economic welfare, and the individual gets increasingly interested in seeking an identity inside an economic framework, but steered by other elements.

The higher living standard means that people take economic welfare for granted. Globalization means that the significance of governments as providers of welfare becomes less and less visible. The scope for domestic economic policies narrows and the domestic business cycle gets increasingly controlled by the global business cycle,[77] so the individual asks the simple question of what the government can do for him or her. This happens at the same time as governments find it increasingly difficult to shoulder the burden of expensive welfare systems, and switch their role away from securing the welfare of the individual — it becomes simply unaffordable — to securing opportunities for the individual. The responsibility for using these opportunities rests with the individual, not with the government. The world is moving towards societies where governments strive to create opportunities, but do not assume responsibilities for individuals unable to use them.

Individuals/citizens react by moving away from identifying with governments to identifying with other institutions or networks. This explains the growing role of organizations, non-governmental organizations, and networks of various characters, all of which are mushrooming, because of the growing adherence of citizens looking for participation in communities constituted by individuals sharing the same interests, ideals, ideas, values, norms, and behavioural attitudes.

The leverage of governments for governance gets more difficult in such circumstances whereas other institutions benefit and move into this gradually emerging vacuum. There are no strong economic links binding citizens to governments any longer, and on top of that, their sense of identity draws many citizens, if not most, away from governments and/or the nation state.

ICT and globalization aggravate this problem. Formerly citizens were referred to the immediate neighbourhood to find people sharing their particular interests. Nowadays they can use the Internet to take part in global virtual communities and find that they actually have more in common with a person in another geographical place than with the citizens they live next door to and meet every day.[78]

The emergence of ethnic, religious, or other value-anchored minorities around the globe exacerbates this development. In the industrial society, such minorities were small and they had to toe the line with regard to behavioural attitudes if they wished to live in a community or nation state away from where they were born and where their basic behavioural pattern was forged. Now they can use the Internet to communicate across borders and, by so doing, mobilize opinion around the world and, in some cases, from a large number of persons to support their drive for an identity not analogous with the predominant one in the society where they live, but do not feel a part of. They are able to distinguish between economic participation in the activities of a nation state where they live, and their sense of identity which deviates from that nation state, to link up, not necessarily with other nation states, but with communities living in other nation states.

This leads to one simple observation: individuals anchoring their identity according to values instead of economics are hollowing out the room for governance inside a nation state.

## *Identity*

The most visible and tangible evidence of this development is the drive for individuals to anchor identities in ideologies — not the old-fashioned, big and cumbersome ideologies such as socialism or communism, but ideologies catering to the individual or small groups of individuals. There isn't just one, two, or three ideologies tabling their bids all around the world for people to identify with, but hundreds or even thousands, fishing for individuals or citizens who feel that the nation state or society or community in which they live does not epitomize the values they cherish. Globalization and ICT offer the window to join up with other individuals around the globe. Both kinds of ideologies are global. The difference is that the old-fashioned ideologies tried to ensnare people with a simple ideology appealing to the masses — one idea, one ideology — suitable for a political movement. The new global ideologies reach out to segments of people living in nation states or communities, but not necessarily wanting to turn this ideology into a political system or other forms of governance.[79]

This is not dangerous for governance as long as the individuals continue to keep their economic life inside society and do not find themselves so alienated that disruptive even destructive ideologies are attractive — and this is the case for the large majority.

There is, however, a small minority who accuses society of having denied them opportunities. Most of these are actually social losers not able to find a place in society and refusing to recognize any shortcomings of their own. Ideologies telling them that the society is at fault for not appreciating their abilities pick these people up and are able to shape powerful global networks, so loyalty to the nation versus the group becomes a real issue.

A less visible challenge for governance is that as society does not meet the quest for identity, individuals lose interest and engagement in societal development, in particular, the political system. They do not look on it as "theirs" and leave it to "others" to run it. Not surprisingly this aggravates the gap between those feeling they belong to society and those who feel they are outside. The latter group chooses to abstain from the political process. In many countries the percentage of the electorate that actually vote is approaching the 50 per cent mark, which means those feeling they are outside also comprise about 50 per cent.

This growing apathy conveying a sense of frustration and the feeling of being outside may, in the longer run, constitute the most potent risk to governance in Asia and other parts of the world. People looking at the political system as their own are much more likely to understand political decisions even if they are painful ones.

Even if economics may no longer be decisive for individuals searching for their identity, one economic element may aggravate the apathy from part of the population vis-à-vis the political system and its governance: rising inequality. Worse than this would be a combination of inequality telling a part of the population that current governance does not take care of them much; globalization reducing the room for governance and thus conveying the feeling that the system is impotent; and insecurity, raising the fear of not holding on to jobs. This cocktail can already be spotted in North America and Europe — but not yet in Asia — and may be one reason for the low turnout at elections. As Asia's income per capita goes up, it is possible that this cocktail will spread, bringing along the same growing apathy as seen in parts of the industrialized world.

## The Role of Mass Media

The mass media is fostering this apathy and, to a certain degree, acting as spoiler for the link between populations and governments, thus eroding the scope for governance.[80] It is paradoxical because, at the same time, a kind of symbiosis between the mass media and politicians is emerging. Politicians see the mass media as a potential tool in the power game against political rivals, and mass media moguls seek the help of politicians competing among themselves for licences and other rights for dissemination of information and entertainment. This is becoming an interactive game with high stakes for both parties. It reflects the growing role of money in politics and the mass media.

Formerly there was a clear distinction between those creating the news, politicians, those disseminating the news, the mass media, and those controlling the mass media. This is no longer the case. Politicians are increasingly dependent on those in control of the mass media who determine which news to run, who is given air time, and the content and style of news coverage. Who is getting into the news at prime time and who is not? How is it presented? Favourable or unfavourable? This is in principle not new, but what is new is the limited scope for alternatives. A politician being rejected by one of the big news channels does not have many opportunities. Deregulation has not brought about more competition, but less competition as licences and other rights have been offered to the highest bidder putting the rich and well-established mass media in pole position to expand their domination. Those who determine who gets the licences are the politicians who are dependent on the mass media for outlets to air their views. An unholy alliance emerges between politicians and mass media moguls, both groups of whom are looking to the potential winner in an attempt to consolidate their own positions: the politician, to get air time, the mass media moguls, to get licences.

Modern technology offers the possibility of monitoring preferences of individuals. This is already a common activity for many supermarket chains that know to the smallest detail what the individual customer is buying, taking us into the kingdom of "targeted marketing". The same is seen in "political marketing". The preferences of the individual citizen and political wishes can be detected from the Internet. Political campaigns will move from the open media aimed at large audiences, to segmented media aimed at individuals or groups of individuals. Politicians can and wish to use the Internet and the media for this kind of political messaging, which gives mass media moguls a tremendous influence. Again there is very little scope for alternatives to be used by the politician falling out with those in control of the dissemination of news.

The contest between Senator Hilary Clinton and Senator Barack Obama for the Democratic nomination in the first half of 2008 showed how important the use of the Internet is in mobilizing supporters, getting funding and putting the message across.[81] Some observers take the view that Senator Obama won the nomination because of his handling of this tool. Even if he did not link up with the mass media moguls, the point is the same, that is the Internet is taking over as the controlling factor in winning the attention and, subsequently, the support of the people. It is also fair to suspect that the mass media moguls sided with Senator Obama because he was a new face that could "sell" whereas Senator Clinton was less likely to get the cash rolling into the coffers of the mass media.

Governance plays a double role in forecasting the future. On the one hand, it is the channel for introducing changes and incorporating changes into society without disrupting already well-functioning mechanisms too much. On the other hand, it is itself the "target" of changes, in the sense that governance may facilitate or constitute a barrier for changes. Good governance signifies that there are good relations based on trust between political leaders and the population, allowing society to adjust without too much friction. It operates on three levels: between political leaders and the population, among individuals, and between individuals and business corporations/societal organizations.

This is a sensitive process where mistakes, even if made with the best of intentions, may do harm to social fabric, societal coherence, and social capital. Insight into the willingness of citizens to absorb change is the essential ingredient; this is extremely hard to assess beforehand and even more so over a longer time horizon.

## Non-governmental Governance

The power of governance as exercised by the government is eroded by the emergence of at least two other strong segments of society exercising their own form of governance, sometimes in contradiction to the government: corporate governance and non-governmental organization's governance.

Corporate governance gradually muscles its way onto the playing ground as a crucial factor for the economy and, in particular, its competitiveness. The reason is that competitiveness may look like it is a question of economics — costs — but it is far more than that. The ability of a society to deliver an environment friendly to business attracts corporations in conformity with the cluster theory. If the corporate sector is able to build on corporate governance by itself or in tandem with the government, the performance level of the business sector is enhanced and competitiveness improves.

Over recent years the existence or lack of corporate governance inside the financial sector operating out of the leading financial centres such as New York and London has illustrated how corporate governance can make or break an economy.

Those countries understanding this and building or perhaps creating the conditions for good corporate governance gain a competitive edge. However, at the same time, corporate governance may arise as an alternative or even a competitor to the government, offering employees several of the services hitherto the prerogative of the government. In such an environment the identity and loyalty of the individual do not necessarily go to the nation state or the government, but may flow to corporations.

Non-governmental organizations play at the same pitch offering to the individual some of the same services as the government. The better organized they are, the more they may attract individuals looking for the particular kind of strong governance exercised by them.

These organizations enjoy the advantage that they can concentrate on some selected issues of governance while governments, for obvious reasons, need to offer services of all kinds to all citizens.

If individuals come to the conclusion that non-governmental organizations do better in the segments of governance vital for them than the government does, they may switch to identifying with and being loyal to them.

More generally citizens compare the efficiency and effectiveness in governance exercised by the government, corporations, and non-governmental organizations. They pick winners, and if the government is losing out to the other players, citizens may question how far their loyalty stretches.

The key factor is that government is no longer the exclusive provider of services. The better other players do in segments chosen by people, the more likely it is that they will attract parts of the population questioning whether it can succeed in its efforts to keep citizens attached to the nation state.

## CONCEPTUALIZE CHANGE

The main challenge for futurism is to conceptualize change, which means to systematize and organize information into a new framework, according to people's behaviour in the future instead of in the past.

With a twenty-five year horizon all the information about technology, economics, logistics, etc. are available. They are known. When analysing them and systematizing them, analysts tend to think like they used to think, that is, apply a mindset framed by the past. How can they be blamed for doing that? That is the only thing they know.

Subsequent analysis showed that before the Japanese attack on Pearl Harbor on 7 December 1941, American intelligence and the military establishment had all the information indicating that such an attack would take place. What they did not do, however, was to put the jigsaw together because the American military did not think Japan intended to attack Pearl Harbor. Expecting Japan to attack the Philippines, if it did attack, the military did not heed information pointing to Pearl Harbor.

Before 11 September, all the information necessary to predict such an attack was available, but the American intelligence system, not expecting such a kind of attack, did not see the arrows pointing them to the hijacking of a number of commercial aircraft and flying them in suicide missions into selected buildings in the United States.

These examples picked from foreign and security policies reveal that it is necessary to transform yourself and think like the enemy to make use of intelligence.

Exactly the same goes for futurism. To make use of available information we need to jump into the future and adopt the mindset of future citizens — what do they want, how will they behave, what will be their ethics and behavioural patterns?

This is to a certain extent guesswork, but only to a certain extent. There are a number of tools that can be applied. Horizon scan is the most well-known instrument.[82] It originated, however, in the scientific area and is most frequently used to spot future threats, while the focus of this study is somewhat different, as we are trying to gather a picture of many trends and tendencies, whether or not they constitute a threat.

The two most important rules for getting an idea of changing mindsets are:

*First*, reject extrapolations of past and present trends.[83] Irrespective of whether these depict a genuine picture of the future or not, this method is not really interesting for one reason: people and institutions would already have adapted to the behavioural pattern behind these trends.

*Second*, map out a landscape of what, in military language, is called normal pattern, that is, what happens every day and is in conformity with established norms, and on that basis, look out for changes.

The interesting thing is to predict if or when the trends will change because that, almost always, is accompanied by behavioural changes.

A number of social indicators may signal that change is under way and sometimes also give an inkling of which kind of change. Factors such as fertility, marriages, divorce rates, children born to single mothers, crime rates, age for leaving university, the number of the poor and homeless, analphabets, people denied their religion, and many others, are examples of new norms and attitudes.

A source readily available is the mass media and various kinds of websites such as Facebook, Youtube, etc. By reading and analysing what they focus on, the observer gets a fairly good idea if and what changes are brewing and waiting to happen. These media catch at an early date what people are interested in. Some of them are actually controlled by people themselves and what they write about and how they see things indicate their interests, preferences, and shifting societal norms.

## Notes

1   A word of caution about vocabulary is necessary to avoid misunderstandings or misrepresentations. "Change" signifies that we operate with extrapolation although "change" of course indicates that something new is happening. The interesting thing, however, is to look for discontinuities, disruptive processes, likelihood that curves break, and tilting points where events may force an evolution, other than that expected or foreseen. In this study we look for the factors telling us that something new and having repercussions outside its own narrow environment is taking place. It is the rate of "change" perceived in this way that controls most of societal restructuring and reorientation.

2   Chosen because that was when China changed course.

3   Hélène C. d'Encausse, *L'Empire Eclate, La Revolte des Nations en U.R.S.S.* (Paris: Flammarion, 1978).

4   In an article, "Global Tides, the Atlantic Alliance and the European Imperative", published in the Spring 1987 edition of the *Strategic Review*, I made the following observation: "the Soviet economy faces the choice between continuing with the present system, and at a snail's pace of economic growth, or changing the system

by introducing economic incentives which will trigger far-reaching political repercussions".

5   Even if not all areas are eligible for forecasting, e.g. genetics.

6   See, for example, "Twilight of the books" by Caleb Grain, *The New Yorker*, 24 December 2007 <http://www.newyorker.com/arts/critics/atlarge/2007/12/24/071224crat_atlarge_crain>; John Naisbiit, Michael Rogers, Christian Rosen et al., "The New Media Age", *The Futurist*, March–April 2007; Tucker, Patrick, "The 21st-Century Writer", *The Futurist*, July–August 2008.

7   See, for example, <http://en.wikipedia.org/wiki/E-book>.

8   <http://www.ebooks.com/>.

9   Arnold  Toynbee, *A Study of History* (Oxford: Oxford University Press, 1946).

10  Ostrom Elinor, *The Evolution of Institutions for Collective Actions* (Cambridge: Cambridge University Press, 1991).

11  Arun Bala, *Dialogue of Civilizations in the Birth of Modern Science* (London: Palgrave MacMillan, 2006).

12  An explanation of scenarios, what it is, and how it works can be found in Kees van der Heijden, *Scenarios, The Art of Strategic Conversation* (Chichester: John Wiley, 2005).

13  Shell Global Scenarios to 2025, "The Future Business Environment: Trends, Trade-offs and Choices", Shell International Limited, 2005.

14  Forum for the Future, "Climate Futures, Responses to Climate Change in 2030" <http://www.forumforthefuture.org/files/Climate%20Futures_WEB.pdf>.

15  Alvin Toffler, *Future Shock* (New York: Bantam Books, 1971).

16  Peter Drucker, *The Age of Discintinuity* (New York: Harper & Row, 1968).

17  Drucker operates with four discontinuities: new industries borne out of new technology; world economy instead of international economy; pluralistic institutions; knowledge and its impact on education, work, life, leisure, and leadership.

18  This is a simplification and many would say oversimplification. However, it stands for my interpretation of the basic elements of Kondratieffs theory. For an overview with references to sources see, for example, <http://en.wikipedia.org/wiki/Kondratiev_wave>.

19  John Montgomery, *The New Wealth of Cities: City Dynamics and Fifth Wave* (London: Ashagte, 2007).

20  John Petersen, *Out of the Blue: How to Anticipate Wild Cards and Big Future Surprises* (Arlington: Arlington Institute, 1997) and "How 'Wild' Cards May Reshape Our Future", *The Futurist* 43, no. 3 (May/June 2009). Nassim Nicholas Taleb, *The Black Swan: The Impact of the Highly Improbable* (New York: Random House, 2007).

21  Clay Shirky, *Here Comes Everybody, The Power of Organizing Without Organization* (London: The Pengion Press, 2008).

22  *Produit net* was defined by a school of economists in eighteenth-century France

and thus relevant for developing countries. It is quite simply what is left of agricultural production to sustain the non-agricultural sectors of the economy. A high *produit net* means that we can squeeze production out of the agricultural sector to support other sectors. A low *produit net* means that after having supported itself there is nothing left of agricultural production to support other sectors. The school is called the Physiocrats, with Quesnay (*Tableau Economique* published in 1759) as its foremost thinker, see, for example, <http://cepa.newschool.edu/het/schools/physioc.htm>.

23   The importance of technology is underlined by Peter Schwartz (one of the pioneers in scenario building) who stated that, "the single most frequent failure in the history of forecasting has been grossly underestimating the impact of technology", Peter Schwartz, *The Art of the Long View* (New York: Currency Doubleday, 1996), p. 173.

24   Emmanuel G. Mesthene, "How Technology Will Shape the Future", *Science* 161, no. 3837, 12 July 1968; and "The Role of Technology in Society" from 1969, reprinted in *Technology and Man's Future*, edited by Albert H. Teich (New York: St. Martin's Press, 1977).

25   Another presentation of this is to talk about an S-curve depicting the gradual rise of technology, followed by a speedy and phenomenal introduction, fading out in its last phases. It can also be summarized in four phases or stages. Inventions, innovations, commercialization, and diffusion. See, for example, David Smith, *Exploring Innovation* (Maidenhead: McGraw-Hill Education, 2006). Innovation and invention can be used as an example of Massachusetts Institute of Technology's opencourseware (<http://ocw.mit.edu/OcwWeb/web/about/about/index.htm>) that will be discussed in Chapter 3. The readings for "The Innovation Process" is available at <http://ocw.mit.edu/OcwWeb/Sloan-School-of-Management/15-351Managing-the-Innovation-ProcessFall2002/Readings/>.

26   *Global Economic Prospects 2008* (Washington: The World Bank, 2008), <http://econ.worldbank.org/WBSITE/EXTERNAL/EXTDEC/EXTDECPROSPECTS/GEPEXT/EXTGEP2008/0,contentMDK:21603882~menuPK:4503397~pagePK:64167689~piPK:64167673~theSitePK:4503324,00.html>; a summary can be found in "Bridging the Technology Divide", *Finance & Development* 45, no. 2 (June 2008): 44.

27   The theoretical underpinning for the Internet (the mathematical theory of packet networks) was developed by Professor Leonard Kleinrock in the period 1960–62, in parallel with similar developments on X25 networks at INRIA, France. The first internets in the true sense of that word were up and running in 1969 (DARPANET, Réseau Cyclades). The first web browser usage started at CERN in November 1990. This observation validates the saying that the technologies dominating life in year 2035 are known (somewhere), but we do not yet know how they will be applied.

28   "The Future of happiness, MTV/Social Technologies/AP Study finds

Today's Youth Pragmatic in Their Pursuit of happiness". Short version available at <http://209.85.175.104/search?q=cache:k1fs15W8mMQJ:www.socialtechnologies.com/FileView.aspx%3Ffilename%3DPressRelease08202007.pdf+mtv+future+of+happiness&hl=en&ct=clnk&cd=2&gl=sg>. Version with references to articles, <http://www.socialtechnologies.com/mtv.aspx>.

29  Andy Hines, "Global Trends in Culture, Infrastructure, and Values", *The Futurist*, September–October 2008.

30  Kakuko Miyata, Ken'ichi Ikeda, and Tetsuro Kobayashi, "The Internet, Social Capital, Civic Engineering, and Gender in Japan", in *Social Capital: An International Research Program*, edited by Nan Lin and Bonnie H. Erickson (Oxford: Oxford University Press, 2008), pp. 206–34.

31  <http://www.sciam.com/blog/60-second-science/post.cfm?id=mind-games-researchers-trick-people-2008-12-04>.

32  Don Tapscott, *Grown Up Digital: How the Net Generation is Changing Your World* (New York: McGraw-Hill, 2008).

33  But they do not mind and may even prefer this interaction to take place via the Internet (impersonal) instead of by personal contact as discussed above.

34  LinkedIn, Xing, Viadeo, and the largest address-book site Plaxo, are the most well known.

35  One factor may be the difference between these various networks in securing privacy.

36  Reuters, 26 November 2008 <http://www.reuters.com/article/technologyNews/idUSTRE4AP07T20081126?feedType=RSS&feedName=technologyNews>.

37  Any technological application that uses biological systems, living organisms, or derivatives thereof, to make or modify products or processes for specific use.

38  The study of objects one-billionth of a metre in size. Potential use in biotechnology, food and agriculture, materials, and energy.

39  Nanotubes' structure favours controlling other nanoscale structures, opening up the possibility of using them in nanotechnology engineering. See, for example, <http://en.wikipedia.org/wiki/Carbon_nanotube>.

40  Economic activity that benefits the company, but implies negative effects for other companies and/or the public. Pollution is a typical example of external diseconomies.

41  Jensen, Rolf, *The Dream Society* (New York, McGraw-Hill, 1999).

42  Hero of Alexandria (*C*. 10–70 AD) is normally credited with having invented the first steam engine. See, for example, <http://en.wikipedia.org/wiki/Hero_of_Alexandria>.

43  It was invented by Sir Francis Ronald. The one in use was the cumbersome semaphor system, which was a mechanical device showing signboards visible from tower to tower in a long line. See, for example, <http://www.theiet.org/about/libarc/archives/featured/francis-ronalds.cfm>.

44  The notion of culture has been discussed by, among others, Raymond Williams (*Keywords*, London: Fontana, 1983) who offers three definitions: (i) intellectual,

spiritual, and aesthetic development; (ii) a particular way of life, whether of a people, a period, or a group; (iii) intellectual and especially artistic activity. Edward B. Taylor is often referred to and Yahoo chooses the following as the best quote: "Culture is the product of human civilization. It is 'the complex whole which includes knowledge, belief, art, moral, law, custom and any other capabilities and habits acquired by man as a member of society' " (<http://answers. yahoo.com/question/index?qid=20070623124605AAHB7Vy>). Professor Jiang Zhongxin defines culture as "representing the sum total of the mental and material assets produced by human society. These assets have been created and stored up through the unremitting labour and intellectual activity of the human race", see *Journal of Oriental Studies* 11, 2001, with a "Dialogue on Eastern Wisdom" among Ji Xianlin, Jiang Zhongxin, and Daisaku Ikeda, p. 22 <http://www.iop. or.jp/0111/special.pdf>. For the purpose of this book, definition (iii) has been chosen. It is analogous to one offered by Danish philosopher Hartvig Frisch, stating (*Europas Kulturhistorie*, 1928) that culture is habits/practices governing our daily life. This definition focuses on what is of interest for the present study, namely how people and societies form opinions of what is good-bad, right-wrong and let it govern their daily activities, with anchoring in local communities, language, religion, and family as essential points.

45   James Surowiecki, *The Wisdom of Crowds: Why the Many Are Smarter Than the Few and How Collective Wisdom Shapes Business, Economies, Societies and Nations* (London: Anchor, 2005).

46   Peter Miller, "Swarm Theory", *National Geographic*, July 2007.

47   E. Sahin and N.R. Franks, "Simulation of Nest Assessment Behaviour by Ant Scouts", *Lecture Notes in Computer Science* 2463 (2002), preview available at <http://www.springerlink.com/content/rt35ylewg733lpy3/>.

48   Larissa Conradt and Christian List, "Group Decisions in Humans and Animals: A Survey, Philosophical Transactions", *The Royal Society B*, 364, no. 1518 (27 March 2009) <http://journals.royalsociety.org/content/7m28j15tp874l4n3/fulltext. pdf>.

49   His main work was *L'Evolution Creatrice* published in 1907 and translated into English as *Creative Evolution* in 1911.

50   Emile Durkheim, *The Elementary Forms of Religious Life*, 1912.

51   See, for example, Pierre Levy, "le Jeu de L'Intelligence Collective", *Cairn.info* 1 no. 79 (2003), <http://www.cairn.info/article.php?ID_ REVUE=SOC&ID_NUMPUBLIE=SOC_079&ID_ARTICLE=SOC_079_ 0105>.

52   <http://www.wikipedia.org/>.

53   Wikipedia in describing God (<http://en.wikipedia.org/wiki/Existence_of_God>) starts by saying "Arguments for and against the existence of God have been proposed by scientists, philosophers, theologians, and others." In philosophical terminology, "existence-of-God" arguments concern schools of thought on the epistemology of the ontology of God. The debate concerning the existence

of God raises many philosophical issues. A basic problem is that there is no universally accepted definition of God. Some definitions of God's existence are so non-specific that it is certain that *something* exists that meets the definition; in stark contrast, there are suggestions that other definitions are self-contradictory. A wide variety of arguments exist which can be categorized as metaphysical, logical, empirical, or subjective. Although often regarded as a non-issue in western academia given the generally held belief of religion and science as non-overlapping magisteria, the question of the existence of God is now subject to lively debate both in philosophy and in popular culture.

54 David Hitchcock, "The United States and East Asia: New Commonality, and then all those differences", proceedings of a conference held on 28 March 1997 in Hamamatsu, Shizuoka, Japan, as part of the first Shizuoka Asia-Pacific Forum: The Future of the Asia-Pacific Region, available at <http://www.unu.edu/unupress/asian-values.html>.

55 Takashi Inoguchi, "Social Capital in Ten Asian Societies", *Japanese Journal of Political Science*, 5, pt 1 (May 2004).

56 Zen-U Lucian Hotta and Takashi Inoguchi, "Psychometric Approach to Social Capital: Using AsiaBarometer Survey Data in 29 Asian Societies". *Japanese Journal of Political Science* (2009).

57 Luigi Guiso, Paola Sapienza, and Luigi Zingales, "The Role of Social Capital in Financial Development", University of Chicago, NBER and CEPR, 2001 available at <http://faculty.chicagogsb.edu/finance/papers/trust.pdf>.

58 Sometimes it is said that the distance between Roma and Napoli is greater than between Roma and Hamburg.

59 See, for example, Jørgen Ørstrøm Møller, *The Future European Model — Economic Internationalization and Cultural Decentralization* (Westport, Praeger, 1995).

60 For these Notions see Charles Hampden-Turner and Fons Trompenaars, *Building Cross-Cultural Competence* (New Haven: Yale University Press, 2000), pp. 189–233.

61 This is more or less the case for the Nordic countries and may explain why these countries, year after year, top international lists comparing social capital. At a lecture in Singapore organized by the Lee Kuan Yew School of Public Policy (22 August 2009) I heard Professor Jagdish Bhagwati saying that wealthy families in his home state of Gujarat in India took pleasure in helping poor families, reflecting a consumption pattern where "doing good" for society as a whole has a high value for the individual.

62 This is the way social capital is perceived in this study and it may not correspond to what a more rigid analysis would use. For a scholarly definition, see, for example, <http://www.gnudung.com/literature/definition.html> and the references in Chapter 5.

63 <http://en.citizendium.org/wiki/L.J._(Lyda_Judson)_Hanifan>.

64 Charles Tilly, *Trust and Rule* (Cambridge: Cambridge University Press, 2005), pp. 11–12.

65 Partly inspired by a paper (Norwegian text) by Arne Jon Isachsen "Deng Xiaoping og Karl R. Popper — to stykker af samme alen", July 2008.

66 Karl R. Popper, *The Open Society and its Enemies* (London: Routledge, 1945).

67 Friedrich Hayek, *The Road to Serfdom* (London: Routledge, 1944).

68 It is illuminating to recall that during World War II, the United Kingdom went into total mobilization of its production for war purposes faster and earlier than Germany. Hitler was afraid of his own population, fearing that if he could not deliver a high material living standard, he would lose, not power, but loyalty. Winston Churchill harboured no such fear knowing that an overwhelming majority of the British population stood solidly behind him.

69 The same distinction can be found for enterprises where some show an uncanny ability to produce great leaders time after time (sometimes throughout well managed, but low key companies like Johnson & Johnson and well anchored companies like Shell) while others face almost insurmountable difficulties to change from one leader to another (mostly family dominated companies of which there are many in Asia and some in Europe like Peugeot).

70 Robert Kagan, for example, says "growing national wealth and autocracy proven, compatible, after all. Autocrats learn and adjust" in *The Return of History and the End of Dreams* (New York: Alfred A. Knopf, 2008).

71 <http://www.thefreelibrary.com/Self-perception+of+gifts+and+talents+among+adults+in+a+longitudinal...-a0166696356>.

72 Not to be mixed up with art as an objective for economic speculation.

73 See, *inter alia*, *Microtrends: The Small Forces Behind Tomorrow's Big Changes* by Mark Penn with E. Kinney Zalesne (New York: Twelve, 2007).

74 Pierre Bourdieu, *La Distinction, Critique Sociale du Jugement* (Paris: les Editions de Minuits, 1979).

75 Note: Not necessarily equal opportunities! In the welfare society everyone was equal — albeit with some modifications — but in the future society there will be a much higher degree of understanding that actually everybody is not equal.

76 See, for example, <http://www.businessdictionary.com/definition/populism.html> and <http://en.wikipedia.org/wiki/Populism>.

77 To be more precise, by the business cycle among main trading partners.

78 An example is the Welsh language, which as the twentieth century was ebbing out, was threatened, but has staged a comeback by, among other things, people using the Internet to make contact with Welsh speaking communities around the globe. See, for example, the Welsh Community in Wellington, New Zealand, at <http://welsh.wellington.net.nz/>; and Patagonia, Argentina at <http://www.bbc.co.uk/cymru/tramor/straeon/pata-x.shtml>.

79 Socialism/Communism highlighted ownership of means of production, class distinction, and an economic deterministic conception of history. Nazism focused on distinction according to race. All this had global "appeal" to the masses and could turn — and indeed was turned — into governance. Even the current big

"ideologies" such as climate change or the ideology behind Al-Qaeda have not
— at least not yet — seen political systems or governance as a mirror image.

80   See, for example, my article co-authored with Terence Chong, "The New Media,
Inc.", *The National Interest* online, 27 October 2006.

81   See, for example, BBC, 12 June 2008, "Internet Key to Obama Victories"
<http://news.bbc.co.uk/2/hi/technology/7412045.stm>.

82   It is defined (British Chief Scientific Adviser's Committee, 2004) as the systematic
examination of potential threats, opportunities, and likely future developments,
including (but not restricted to) those at the margins of current thinking and
planning. Horizon scanning may explore novel and unexpected issues as well as
persistent problems or trends. This means that a horizon scan can see past usual
(policy) terms and beyond the boundaries of disciplines and departments. It
entails a rapid, systematic process of pattern recognition that apprehends both
positive and negative signals. All signals that can have a future impact, including
weak signals, are noticed, whereby possible interactions between signals can also
be researched.

83   Most predictions are basically an extrapolation of past and present trends. This
is understandable as it is what we know, but futurism is interesting by predicting
when the curve bends and analysing this phenomenon. Past and present trends
are not only useless, but counterproductive as they encapsulate our mind in past
behaviour.

# 3

# THE ASSETS

After several decades Asia now seems anchored in economic globalization while at the same time moving into higher technology and using its savings to cement further economic progress. For Asia's policymakers a number of assets are available to assist economic growth that do not call for fundamental new policies, but competent management.

Economic integration is regarded as the first asset because it follows on from one of the main observations looking at individual behaviour, namely, that in the future, groups, social capital, and the ability to work together (share!) may be more important as a driver of growth than individual behaviour. Not only are the economic benefits considerable and visible — even the United States is moving towards a stronger commitment to integration with other countries — but the impact on the mindset is decisive. Integration pushes nation states towards trust among one another, first in a regional setting and an economic framework, developing into politics, and then, it is hoped, at a global level. Through regionalization the world moves optimistically towards global governance — so obviously imperative and yet so embryonic if it exists at all.

Asia is still in the catch-up phase with regard to technology, innovation, invention, and science. For a time that will be good enough, but the moment will approach when not only Asia's future, but global evolution, will depend on Asia's ability to turn from playing catch-up to showing leadership channelling funds into basic research. While there are many reasons for optimism with regard to continued technological development as manifested through patents and by students at home and abroad, as well as several other indicators, the verdict on science is much more blurred.

162

In this game one of Asia's most important assets can be brought into play: savings. All signs speak the same language and say that global savings will continue to take place in Asia, offering it the pleasant policy dilemma of how to use the money available, rather than pondering where to get the money from. Not only will Asia be the world's creditor, but Asia will take over a large part of global economic activity.

Multinational companies will increase in importance not only as a kind of harbour for economic and industrial activities, but as a global pacesetter, giving rise to what may be termed the political enterprise. Most of the new multinationals entering the list of the world's largest and most important enterprises will grow out of Asia.

Consumption has many faces, but one of them is its role as trendsetter, signalling change in tastes and preferences. The luxury market is important in this respect and Asia is where we will see the luxury market in the next twenty-five years to come. New brands, new consumer behaviour, and new preferences will emerge here and gradually it will have the role of being the place where new things emerge and many of the benefits associated with this role will be transferred from the West to Asia.

## ECONOMIC INTEGRATION

### Economic Integration in Asia

The lesson from the large U.S. market and the European Single Market is unequivocal: Economic integration promotes growth. The large market engineers increasing returns to scale and opens the door for research and development, technology, innovation, cross border mergers and acquisitions, and large distributional networks as drivers for growth, competitiveness, and productivity. Large countries do not need integration for economic reasons, but may see the advantages also for them in a political context. Small and medium sized countries, however, will be dwarfed by the giants unless they manage to get into some kind of economic integration.

The alternative becomes the all too easy competition on costs: a blind alley in every respect and unfortunately one also that seeds mistrust among societal groups starting to focus on distribution of income and jobs instead of economic growth, which, for many, may be an evasive and distant concept. Economic integration transcends into a policy contributing to peace among adjacent nation states and domestic social stability.

ASEAN was established more than forty years ago as the first Asian attempt at economic integration. Since then economic integration has slowly, but steadily, gained ground. ASEAN has not only promoted economic growth but, as I have argued elsewhere,[1] successfully framed a three dimensional stability to Southeast Asia without which growth, unquestionably, would have been lower. In 2003 it was decided to establish an ASEAN Community "comprising three pillars, namely political and security cooperation, economic cooperation, and socio-cultural cooperation that are closely intertwined and mutually reinforcing for the purpose of ensuring durable peace, stability and shared prosperity in the region".[2] In 2008 the ASEAN Charter[3] came into force.

The countries in South Asia agreed in 2004 to establish their own free trade area (SAFTA) inside the South Asia Association for Regional Cooperation.[4] There are a large number of FTAs (Free Trade Agreements) in force or being negotiated and multilateral forums such as ASEAN meet regularly. Recently The East Asia Summit[5] has been added to the list.

It is no coincidence that the political and economic agendas are full of initiatives and endeavours to introduce economic integration among Asian countries. The consequence of economic globalization is a strong current of economic activities taking place across borders, with nation states at risk of losing control over economic development unless they manage to raise political control and economic regulatory frameworks onto the same level. To do this in an orderly way, a legal framework defining rules, rights, and obligations must be implemented. There are many ways to do this — from the European model based on the pooling of sovereignty to be exercised in common with adjacent nation states sharing the same political goals, to loose intergovernmental cooperation. The point, however, is that irrespective of which model is chosen, it is being done and is one of the fundamental parameters underpinning economic development in Asia for the next decades.[6]

There was and is a third and efficient model: the industrial and trading conglomerate model from Japan (*keiretsu*) and Korea, with satellites across Asia, which in 1960–90 were basically managed as "outposts" in all senses of the word. This also secured access to raw materials and built up logistics. It was later copied by Chinese state enterprises and Indian family conglomerates (often inspired by Japanese advisors). For many years the likes of Mitsubishi, Mitsui, Samsung had sales larger than many Asian nations. This model entails really tight integration at the corporate level, while recent political initiatives are more to do with coordination and integration. It is, to a certain extent, integration by the market, a concept also seen as a driver in the European integration process.[7]

Economic integration among Asian countries may open the door to economies of scale, crucial not only for growth, but also for transforming the economies from focusing on manufacturing to concentrating on higher value added production.

Only by using economic integration to remove barriers to trade, capital movements, services, and skills, will the comparative advantages among Asian countries be allowed to unfold their full potential. Institutions focusing on a rules-based framework should be supplemented by better infrastructure in logistics, communication networks, and transport. This batch of mutually reinforcing policies opens the door for freedom of localization. The view of many Western observers is that the present factor endowment favours labour intensive production in China; services and business, plus knowledge processing prefer India; and financial institutions and other business activities dependent on good governance may look to Singapore. This analysis looks good in Western-oriented economic models, but it cannot be taken for given that Asia follows that model.

Asia has managed to profit visibly from building up intratrade over the last forty-five years. Two economists in the World Bank summarize the significance of intratrade and how it works this way:[8]

> The key driver, and a major determinant of growth, in developing regions is intra-industry trade, mostly of parts and components. This type of trade is more sensitive to transportation costs than trade in primary goods and final products. In the world's largest markets — North America, Western Europe, and East Asia — intra-industry trade represents a high and increasing share of total trade... Increasingly sophisticated buyer-supplier networks in leading world regions have been a major feature of globalization. Customers for final products may be anywhere, but suppliers of inputs tend to be nearby. Increased specialization generates more trade, providing opportunities even to some small economies. For example, Cambodia may not be able to build computers or cars, but it can produce the cables or wires that will be used in assembly lines in China. Through this "vertical disaggregation" of production — made possible by falling transportation costs — growth and prosperity have spread within developing regions.

The architects behind this are rarely nation states (the nation states support it though), but business and, in Asia, almost always big business. The ability of Asian countries to enable integration policies as discussed here still depends on industry and, in particular, Asian industry conglomerates. It is interesting to observe how this rivalry or competition at the top to exploit buyer-supplier networks will work in Asia. At the start of the European integration it was often American enterprises which turned the integration to their advantage, with European industry much more reluctant.[9] In Asia the signs are that

Asian-based industry may be more ready and willing to step in and reap the benefits, but — and this is a very important *but* — in competition with American and European business enterprises.

There have been various attempts to analyse and quantify the advantages of economic integration for Asia or parts of Asia.

A study from 2008[10] comes to the conclusion that the welfare gains for integration among Japan, ASEAN, China, India, and Korea amount to US$147 billion if it is confined to trade liberalization, to US$153 billion if investment liberalization is included, and US$210 billion if labour mobility is implemented. The study also points out that the welfare benefits for the rest of the world in all three scenarios will be even bigger, driving home the argument that economic integration does not bring economic benefits for one group of countries at the expense of other groups.

An analysis by the Asian Development Bank[11] (ADB) concludes that regional integration is the way forward for rapid and sustainable growth in Asia. Developing Asia can leverage superior domestic growth rates, accelerate economic diversification, and broaden the basis for regional development. The analysis also finds that economic integration promotes the convergence of economic development among Asian countries.

A third study[12] comes to similar conclusions, saying that the creation of an Asian Economic Community (AEC) brings welfare gains of between US$40 billion and US$176.1 billion, depending on the formation of the integration (membership and depth of integration).

## Basic Elements to Make Integration Work

The economic landscape for Asia will change over the next twenty-five years. It cannot be taken for granted that the high share of intratrade will continue unless some kind of economic integration is introduced to constitute a framework for the equitable distribution of benefits and burdens. Five basic elements seem to interact to create favourable conditions for growth around economic integration as a flywheel.

- Freedom of localization offers the opportunity to exploit comparative advantage wherever it is, without regard to obstacles of various kinds
- Specialization through intratrade opens the window for supply chains to produce for domestic demand as well as export
- Low transport costs make it possible to combine the other advantages preventing obstacles for specialization
- Closeness to economic growth centres includes increasing returns to scale in the equation, and

- Rule-based integration stimulates long-term planning as economic parameters are known.

The food processing industry is an example of what may happen in Asia in the coming years and decades. With an excellent supply it should be possible for Asia and, in particular, Southeast Asia to build up world-class enterprises. The same can be said about tourism both in the form of mass tourism and high-end tourism with more sophisticated offers responding to the growing demand for adventure among consumers.

Politically the divergence between the strongest and largest countries such as China and India, and the smaller and weaker ones such as Laos and Cambodia, to mention a few, will exacerbate. Some Asian countries will emerge as global powers having the clout to be among the few to shape global policies, while other Asian countries may struggle to ensure a rising standard of living for their populations. In such circumstances economic integration, even combined with — if conditions prove favourable — some kind of framework for political cooperation, may be needed to open channels for smaller countries to voice their opinion and to allow them to receive a fair share of the benefits. The alternative is that Asia splits into the "haves" and the "have-nots" with possible severe repercussions in the form of a soured climate between the strong and the weak countries.

Business may play an important role in this respect, building trust among its employees, irrespective of which countries they come from, and with some luck, contributing to bridging gaps between the haves and the have-nots. Japanese multinationals have a fairly good record. Chinese conglomerates are newcomers and so far their impact has been limited and not spectacularly successful in bridging economic gaps. Indian conglomerates have been tempted more by Western markets than Asia. It remains to be seen whether Asian medium-sized, but fast growing companies can step into this role.

Security policies may work in the same way. The prospect of failed states looms ahead if small and weak countries are left to themselves, and if so, they develop into a destabilizing factor unsettling not only themselves, but also adjacent countries and/or regions. The likelihood of increased cooperation to keep various threats under control does not allow for loopholes in the form of safe haven for those who seek to jeopardize the global system. The likelier Asian nation states perceive threats as coming from non-conventional sources, the likelier they are to build up Asian cooperation in the defence area.[13]

Economically Asia will definitely change fundamentally over the next decades. Competitive advantages among Asian countries will not be the same, production will be reallocated, and adjustments called for. It is an open question whether there will be the same rivalry between nation states as history has shaped in Europe. Perhaps Asia will see a rivalry between industrial/business conglomerates, each wearing the flag of a community, region, or ethnic group inside the group's value systems.[14]

The demographic trend points to a transfer of labour-intensive, low-cost manufacturing from China to countries such as India, Pakistan, Bangladesh, Vietnam, and maybe Indonesia and the Philippines, which have continued growing labour supply. It cannot be said that such a transition is only manageable inside economic integration, but the odds are strong that if it happens inside economic integration, it will be smoother than if it were to take place without this framework. The point is to bring about a gradual transition and compensation for the countries losing jobs by encouraging alternative growing industries. Corporations may be better placed to manage this than Asian nation states.

The main advantage is, however, what the European integration has so clearly disclosed: that a stronger economic integration makes national business cycles work more in synchronization. A high share of trade and goods and services[15] plus investment[16] (integration of the market for goods, services, and capital) among members of the integration produces such an outcome.[17] When that is the case, the ground becomes more propitious for a common economic policy, and gradually the countries move towards a situation where some kind of monetary cooperation turns from plans and ideas to realistic possibilities. The economic and political advantages flowing from such a scenario of stability are obvious.

Asia is in possession of the world's savings and it looks likely that this will continue to be the case. Asia, however, lacks an economic and financial infrastructure to channel the savings back into Asian projects, with the consequence that much of Asia's savings flow into the global capital market. For various reasons, including domestic influence on banks in some nation states, an Asianwide corporation may feel more comfortable not depending too much on an Asian bank.

The initiative to create an Asian Bond Market[18] is an interesting attempt to build an Asian financial infrastructure and its development serves as a litmus test for whether the Asian countries are able to establish a framework for an Asian capital market.

In the same way, three grand schemes for infrastructure in Asia will play a role in determining whether Asia will integrate.

The idea of a Trans-Asian railway system[19] linking Europe to East Asia, including Southeast Asia, was born in 1960, but little has been achieved so far. One of the technical difficulties is the existence of at least four different major rail gauges across Eurasia. This obstacle can be solved, however, by mechanized facilities allowing continued use of existing tracks.

The Trans Siberian Railway takes the route to China and with plans for high speed railways the onward part to South China seems in order, but from there to Singapore, several important links are missing. Some of the missing links are explained by the absence of the need for heavy transport of sources such as oil and iron ore because of easy access to sea transport. With help from the Asian Development Bank some progress has been achieved and the project seems to have moved out of the doldrums. With the focus on less energy-consuming traffic links and emphasis on less emission of carbon dioxide, it is likely that railways will see a renaissance in Asia, as is the case for Europe, although it is difficult to lure goods and passengers away from road to railways especially in parts of Asia where geography favours sea transport.

There is little doubt that without a first class railway system offering both passengers and goods cost-effective and fast connections, Asia will face major impediments in building its integration. To rely on shipping for a large part of goods is possible, but two questions emerge.

*First*, shipping is more cost effective than railroad, but in future, costs will not be the only factor to be taken into account. Greenhouse emissions and consequently the impact on climate through $CO_2$ will have to be addressed. An OECD discussion paper[20] concludes that $CO_2$ intensity is less for large container ships than for rail transport, but about the same for smaller container ships. Road transport is more $CO_2$ intensive than both forms of container ships and rail transport.

*Second*, behind the logistics and cost-effectiveness of transport systems lie a rivalry between land states and maritime states where land states, or rather, inland areas, have been the loser so far.

The Asian Highway[21] is a network of 141,000 kilometres criss-crossing thirty-two Asian countries. The Intergovernmental Agreement on the Asian Highway Network was adopted on 18 November 2003 and a total of US$26 billion has already been invested in the improvement and upgrading of the network.

There is political agreement among the ten ASEAN countries to establish a power grid.[22] A memorandum of understanding covering the formation of the ASEAN power grid was signed in August 2007.[23] The project aims to interconnect the ten member nations that form ASEAN and is one of the key building blocks of the ASEAN Economic Community (AEC).

Energy is one of the areas that would benefit most from open trading within ASEAN. An electricity market, which would deliver tremendous benefits, depends on the state and compatibility of national electricity markets and efficient networks. This is not the case today, but in a longer-term perspective the ASEAN countries may be able to forge commonality and improve on power transmission, thus paving the way for a common market to exploit the possibilities for a power grid. Judged by the European experience, it may take longer than expected especially since Southeast Asia and, even more so, East Asia, suffer from the same problem that is harassing the Europeans, namely, that the member states encompass exporters, as well as importers, besides traders of energy, making a common policy difficult.

It is difficult — almost impossible — to see a strong and viable Asian integration arise without major progress being made to build transport, energy, and communication infrastructure. This challenge is enhanced by the increasing emphasis on climate change and global warming, which call for energy efficiency. As it is known that transport is a heavy consumer of energy this sector will definitely be in the forefront of attention. Asia's problem is that infrastructure is hampered by geography and the existing networks were all designed and built in an era where energy cost was much less important than it is today. Asia's advantage is that the funds are there; sitting on the world's savings, Asia can easily afford to build a first class infrastructure if that is what Asia's political leaders want.

In a political context one of the most "promising" and imperative areas for integration is working on measures to mitigate the negative effects on the environment of high economic growth, and even better, trying to forge another, more ecological growth model. If only one country tries to do that, the risk is obvious that its competitive position will be affected because of higher costs. Only by taking such measures in common can the respective pre-policy competitive positions be maintained. It is possible, perhaps even thinkable, that most Asian countries are ready and willing to channel funds into improving the environment, but only if adjacent countries walk in step.

Market driven integration favours the country/countries offering business corporations the most beneficial rules. So far Asia has benefited from tycoons being able to work their way around restrictions and regulations, but it cannot be taken for granted that this will continue, and if it does, costs for "dodging" may go up. Domestic deregulation and market economics, combined with the dismantling of barriers for not only trade, but also for the free movement of capital and labour, gives corporations freedom of localization. They can choose to go where they can make the most money. As an illustration, companies tend to locate production units, research facilities, financial headquarters, etc., based on the most favourable opportunities. As a consequence the other

Asian countries are forced to either adopt similar rules or set up economic integration instituting common rules. The most beneficial rules crowd out less beneficial ones.

This is actually what has been seen in Europe over the last decades where the European Commission is putting forward proposals, in particular, concerning company law to ensure that the playing field is level. It remains to be seen whether Asia can and will do something similar over the next twenty-five years.

This whole mechanism hinges on the assumption that the market continues to prevail, as it is the logical follow-up to deregulation and the dismantling of barriers to trade and investment among countries. The emphasis may be on dismantling barriers.

Irrespective of present question marks, in the slipstream of the 2008 global financial crisis this assumption seems realistic.

## Benchmarks

The result compared with the European integration points towards an integration steered by:

- Higher concentration on business issues. Topics such as social policy, education policy, etc., that play an increasingly important role in the European integration may be less attractive in an Asian environment.
- A rule-based integration, but with less emphasis on strong institutions and not based on the pooling of sovereignty, or if it happens, then only for a few, selected topics driven by necessity inside certain areas of economics and trade.
- The Asian integration may be less focused on common policies and more geared towards ensuring that the original agreed distribution of benefits/burdens is preserved even if the environment changes.
- Asia is more heterogeneous than Europe and the noble European goal that all member states subscribe to all common goals does not look suitable for Asia. Instead, integration driven by the market and corporations, with participation according to variable geometry is the more likely outcome. Some member states take part in particular types of integration, while others reserve their positions, although there will be some core policies encompassing all that are focused on trade in goods and services and possibly free movement for investment, but labour mobility cannot be expected to be anything like it is in Europe.

This model raises at least four crucial questions: Will Asia be able to:

- Avoid an economic and industrial structure leading to specialization, thus jeopardizing the endeavours to shape a synchronized business cycle and reap the benefits flowing thereof?
- Guarantee exchange rate stability?[24]
- Be ready to shape a common attitude towards global economic and environmental issues, such as trade and currency questions to safeguard Asian interests, or will the countries fall back on pursuing their own individual interests even if these are harmful to other Asian countries?
- Recognize that the drivers in Asia are primarily conglomerates and corporations and use this to promote integration so as to avoid seeing business competition spill over into national rivalries as big corporations are seen and perceived as "flag carriers"?

The answers depend to a large extent on which domestic policies are adopted and implemented. Economic integration is an extension of domestic policies pursued at the international level. Integration cannot shape common policies unless they are congruous with domestic policies, and very few domestic policies can be successful in today's global world if they are not incorporated in an international framework and are without champions to implement them.

As of 2009 it seems a reasonable bet that economic policies will converge and the business cycles become more synchronized. Sectors and businesses trading internationally will see this first, while this is less certain for non-exportable food, local transport, textiles, building, and handicraft catering to the large local populations. If the Asian countries pursue their hitherto acknowledged economic policy goal of low inflation, a platform for currency cooperation will emerge. If on the other hand economic policy goals start to diverge, with some countries accepting high inflation and others not, even a high share of intratrade cannot be counted on to be sufficient to bring about currency rate cooperation.

The pressure from partners will work in the direction of converging macroeconomic policy goals as economic difficulties in one country spill over, creating problems for other countries. The mechanism seen working in other geographical areas is that a low-inflation policy followed by the leading countries is sustainable only if adopted by competitors. Alternatively these countries' inflation policy requiring currency rate depreciation erodes the competitiveness of the low-inflation countries, putting the burden on them to make adjustments to keep the balance of payments in order and necessitate a demand-restrictive policy reducing growth. They are not willing to accept that. The only way to avoid it is to force the other countries into the same low inflation policy.

With such a policy adopted, the next step almost takes itself, that is, safeguarding interests in an international context. Repercussions for economic policies in non-Asian countries will not be welcome as it may destabilize the picture: to avoid that, a common macroeconomic, including monetary, policy vis-à-vis trade, economic, and monetary global issues is required.

The system is self-reinforcing, with one step leading to the next one, gradually building up an Asian sphere of economic and monetary zone approaching the stage where, in reality, much the same situation reigns as if an economic and monetary union had been put in place. The real actors (citizens and corporations) must see tangible benefits; they are the judges more than the nation states.

The assumption underlying this line of thinking is the adoption of low inflation and a stable macroeconomic policy by the leading country/countries. This assumption may be questioned, but presumably it is what the Chinese leadership wants as inflation threatens to undermine not only its economic, but also social stability, thus jeopardizing its whole social fabric.

The conclusion is then that the continued drive for social stability in China turns into a flywheel not only for the macroeconomic policy in that country, but also for the rest of Asia, thus preparing the ground for conditions leading to cooperation among these countries on a macroeconomic policy and monetary questions, including a common attitude to global trade and economic issues.

## TECHNOLOGY AND KNOWLEDGE

### The Catch-up Factor

Asia faces the task of catching up with the innovation advantage of Western countries' better global management and weight given to innovation. It underlines that research, technology, and innovation are not, strictly speaking, confined to "technical" matters, but related to societal structure. There are, however, two fundamental observations showing that technology will continue to boost productivity in Asia more than in the case for Western countries.

*First*, technology does not improve productivity much in itself, what matters is the application of new technology in society as a whole. Asia has entered the new age of technology at a comparatively late date, which offers it the advantage of access to experience gathered by others and opens the window for it to leapfrog. And this has been tapped — for example, Korea is ahead of the United States in broadband services.

*Second*, the well-known law of scarcity, saying that prices go up for scarce goods, does not apply for technology which is governed instead by the law of abundance that says that one more gadget improves user value not only for the newcomer, but for all those already having such a gadget (networking). The law of abundance explains a good deal of what has been puzzling economists — high growth, low inflation, and high productivity, and over a long period.[25]

The good use of a technology only postpones disruptive needs to be identified, and thus new disruptive solutions to appear. This is the innovation speed and depth law, hitherto rarely discussed in an Asian context, except in Japan where the MITI (Ministry of International Trade and Industry) in the late 1980s realized that the above two laws only apply over the medium term, and moved all its efforts back to basic disruptive R&D and, to a certain extent, also the humanities.

Consider the following example. A city has one million cars. The next car to be purchased may increase productivity somewhat for the owner, but reduce productivity for all others, and on top of that, bring along external diseconomies in the form of environmental damage, which augment anti-pollution costs. So all in all, the cost-benefit analysis shows it leads to a negative result for society as a whole. The same city has one million mobile phones, one million PCs, and several hundreds of thousands of people on broadband, and thousands on skype. What happens when one more user makes his/her entrance? Productivity goes up for that user, but productivity/user value also goes up for all the other users of mobile phones, PCs, broadband registrants and skype users. The effect is the reverse of the case of the car in an industrial society, and there will be little, if any, external diseconomies.

Recalling the words "disruptive solutions", we see there is a *but*. If in that city, one far-sighted user sees the potential of, for example, electrical cars (or for that matter, any other new transportation technology meeting the demand and at the same time shifting the paradigm and resulting from disruptive science in electrochemistry of batteries), a technology generation shift will happen. For that to happen, Asia must get rid of the tendency to follow, although not ubiquitously, because there is a real danger to the quality of growth from abundance only.

The value of ICT (information, communication, and technology) gadgets increases with the numbers already in use (networking effect). The larger the number, the higher the overall productivity for the economy as a whole. The smaller the number, the less attractive they are. Many of the gadgets we talk about here are products for both consumption and investment, but they are now also items for creation of content, if not of new usages.

The numbers game will be decisive. China, including Taiwan, and India will for a long time broaden and deepen the use of ICT, thus reaping increasing returns to scale. The fundamental long-term question is whether they will create new and native technologies or fail because of barriers of various kinds for creators/innovators perceived to be disruptive or just continue adopting imported technology.

It cannot be proved, but common sense supports the view that it is more likely that innovations and inventions will take place where the largest number of users is found. China and India, indeed Asia, are already filling that slot for adaptation of technology and waiting to move one step further into the area of creation. Japan and Taiwan are operating inside the creativity box, at least for segments of their economy, and may pull the rest of Asia along. Spending on research and technology in China is forecasted by the European Commission to surpass EU spending in 2009.[26] China intends to increase its R&D spending to 2.5 per cent of its gross domestic product in 2020.[27]

It looks, and is, good, but a relevant question is what the budget allocation is between research and development. For most Asian conglomerates research takes a low share, raising doubts about results blossoming into innovations in the future. It is hard to resist the impression that Asian business leaders, many of them tycoons, find it difficult to muster the patience to wait for research to yield results at a later stage, preferring instead to go straight for the end product by focusing on development. This can be seen by the difficulties with software specified and designed in East Asia. Despite huge investments in programmers, East Asia today, many years after the first instances of operating system software were obtained in the West, still fails to develop new systems and has problems even to add incremental changes to existing ones.

This applies not only to China and its public sector, but is equally and maybe even more valid for Asia's private sector. According to OECD[28] corporate spending on research and technology grew 23 per cent from 2001 to 2006 in China, compared with 1–2 per cent in the United States and Europe. One of the interesting revelations of this study is the divergence within Asia, where the established technology players such as Japan, Korea and Taiwan are challenged by China and India. An interesting case revealing a strong corporate sector is Korea, with the report mentioning that Samsung in 2007 spent more on research and technology than IBM did. Korean firms are spending 6.5 per cent of GDP on research and technology while the corresponding figure for European and Japanese firms is about 5 per cent, and for the United States, 8 per cent.

Without money nothing can be achieved, but two other factors determine whether the money spent will lead to results. *First*, whether it is spent wisely and channelled into long-term activities, which, in this context, calls for a better balance between research and development. *Second*, money is not sufficient and does not in itself "create creativity" and breakthroughs. That depends more on the broader environment to support and stimulate innovation and creativity, something yet to be introduced over a broad area in most of Asia. There must be the ability to identify and respect independent creative talent. The key problem for managers is to find those who contradict them constructively, keep all employees motivated and focused, and get consensus at decision thresholds to change to the newer, better thing. Because of the culture of respect for their elders who, fearing a loss of face, may not be very open to identifying and appreciating independent creative talent, this looks more difficult in Asia than in the Western world.

## Patents

### Overview

The more patents a country or region or group of enterprises registers the likelier it is that some years down the road new products will be forthcoming. The numbers game applies here. Asia's Achilles heel also works in this respect as the road from a patent to a new product may be less a question of research, technology, and innovation, than of societal structure and the ability of management and corporate governance to turn inventions into products. This is a process, which, judging from the experience in the United States and Europe, is more difficult and cumbersome than initially perceived. The following figures augur a buoyant Asia with regard to new products, but they should be read in context with other factors.

In the course of the 1990s new technologies such as nanotechnology, energy-related technologies, and space-related technologies, gobbled up an increasing share of patents. The proportion of nanotechnology patents has more than doubled from the mid-1990s to the mid 2000s.[29]

### The Figures

When we look at total numbers, statistics by WIPO (World Intellectual Property Organization)[30] confirm that Japan is still holding on to its number one position. Recent figures, however, disclose an almost explosive rise in patents fielded by other Asian countries, in particular China (this is the case even if most Chinese companies do not need, or are granted a patent, the exceptions being Huawei and a few others). The total number of filings for patents (2005) in China rose 32.9 per cent, and 1.3 per cent in India. If we only look at the number of patents filed by residents in the country in question (as opposed to also including those by foreigners), the figures show 42.1 per cent and 8.0 per cent respectively.

Over the 2001–07 period China surpassed Korea and Europe to take the number three slot.[31] Analysing priority country information for inventions,[32] which gives the closest link to the country of origin, we find that Japan is still number one, but with a decreasing volume, while the volume for the United States rose at the beginning of the period, but did not sustain the rise, while figures for Asia went up, and significantly so for China (and Korea). A projection of 2006–10 figures for priority country information for inventions shows that China surpassed Korea in 2007, Japan at the end of 2009, and the United States at the beginning of 2010, to become number one.[33]

Japan is also number one in Asia with regard to Nobel Prizes, with seven won so far, of which three were in physics, one in chemistry, one in physiology/ medicine, and two in literature. India has three with one in physics, one in literature, and one in economics. Pakistan has one in physics.[34]

In 2007 alone, China's State Intellectual Property Office (SIPO) received approximately 700,000 applications, bringing the total number of applications to the four million mark since its inauguration in 1985. Of these, 450,000 were for utility and design while 250,000 were invention patents. The share of applications from China rose from 58 per cent in 2006 to 63 per cent in 2007. In December 2007, China's science and technology laws were amended to allow scientists, institutions, and universities to own patents resulting from publicly-funded research.[35] The jury is still out with regard to the quality of Chinese patents, with some suspicion having been voiced that the number is deliberately inflated and that some patents actually cover new designs or new models not requiring much technological knowledge.[36]

The number of patents fielded in India is small compared with other major countries. One reason is that the institutional structure is weak, with legislation only recently introduced and with there only being a small administrative staff. About 80 per cent of the 30,000 applications come from foreign entities. The potential is there, however, as statistics show that the number of applications filed at USPTO (U.S. Patent and Trade Mark Office) that originated in India is growing rapidly.[37]

The number of applications fielded in Japan fell slightly in 2006 and 2007, bringing the total to about 400,000. JPO (the Japanese Patent Office) explains this fall by an increasing tendency of Japanese companies to keep their inventions confidential, fearing theft of technology.[38] In parts of Asia where research staff are more tightly linked to the company, there is less need to file for patents and incur the costs and time lags connected with that process because the stronger research staff is integrated in the company the less likely it is that research results will be passed on to other companies. This may be the case for Japan, while job hopping, motivated by higher salaries, may push the need for filing patents in China.

Over the 2002–04 period more than 80 per cent of all patent applications were fielded by companies globally. Governments, universities, private non-profit institutions, and individuals fielded the rest. The shares have remained stable except in China where company share has risen from 22 per cent in 1996–98 to over 50 per cent in 2002–04. The government accounts for 23 per cent of patent applications in India. The proportion of patents owned by universities has gone up sharply in Japan.[39]

There is a strong trend towards internationalization and international collaboration on inventive activities. It is interesting that the exception to this trend is to be found in Asia, with Japan and Korea much less internationalized in their innovative activities and China, except for Chinese labs of foreign companies, even less so. Globally 16.7 per cent of all inventions filed at the EPO (European Patent Office) were owned or co-owned by a foreign resident in 2001–03, compared with only 11.6 per cent a decade earlier. Of the Asian nations, China showed a decrease of 16.7 per cent from almost 60 per cent to 45 per cent; India registered a share of 38 per cent (no figures for a decade earlier). When we include patents filed by Chinese and Indian labs of foreign companies the decline becomes much steeper, while Japan and Korea both had shares below 10 per cent, which can be explained by the existence of relatively few research labs of foreign companies in these two countries.[40]

These figures tell us that Asia and especially China are going to play a major role in the filing of patents in the coming years and consequently can be expected to produce and market an increasing number of new technological gadgets and goods. To conclude from this that technology is shifting to Asia and China is a long way off. As the Japanese example illustrates, a country can actually lead in several areas of technology and occupy the top slot in patents without breaking through as a world leader and major producer of new technology. There is very little evidence to judge which way China will go, whether the patents signify a breakthrough, whether it will emulate Japan, or whether it will perhaps fall in a third category. Domestic patents in China are still relatively few, but growing, and technology transfer may be seen as less risky to China if done by Chinese. It is, however, a safe guess that the explosive rise in patents opens the door for some Chinese corporations to gamble and trade globally.[41]

## Economic Integration

One element playing a role might be Asian economic integration. The OECD study[42] goes one step further in its geographical analysis and groups patents according to regions instead of countries. This reveals that the twenty top research regions in OECD accounts for 35 per cent of all filings for patents. Of these twenty regions, nine are found in the United States, four in Japan, four in Europe, and one in Korea.

Outside Japan — and Korea — only Shenzhen in China comes close to the top twenty, ranked at number 21, but it is dominated by one company, Huawei. Bangalore, which has the Indian powerhouses in software, is number 121.

In this context, an interesting factor is that patents seem to cluster, so to speak, in the sense that an energetic effort draws research, technology, and innovation into a region once the momentum is there. The difficulty is to get started, as this requires not only finance, but also a broad spectrum of societal policies to attract top researchers.[43] Economic integration could help to promote policies to that effect and broaden the potential number of talents. The competition to attract talents among Asian countries is raging, with the Western world exercising a strong pull, but China and India are catching up.[44]

## Role of Foreign Nationals

A hidden asset for Asia in R&D — rarely quantified — is the contribution to U.S. patents of foreign nationals residing in the United States. A study[45] published in 2007 came to the following conclusion:

> Foreign nationals residing in the United States were named as inventors or co-inventors in 24.2% of the patent applications filed from the United States in 2006, up from 7.3% in 1998 and even more in some key strategic areas. This number does not include foreign nationals who became citizens before filing a patent. The Chinese were the largest group, followed by Indians, Canadians, and British. Immigrant filers contributed more theoretical, computational, and practical patents than patents in mechanical, structural, or traditional engineering. Overall, the results show that immigrants are increasingly fueling the growth of U.S.

engineering and technology businesses. Of these immigrants groups, Indians are leading the charge in starting new businesses, and Chinese create the most intellectual property.

This not only touches on the future competitiveness of the U.S. high-tech sector in itself, but also raises the question of the potential for China and India (and some other countries) if or when the pattern for foreign nationals staying in the United States or going home, changes. This is supported by combining the findings of two recent studies.[46] A little more than 20 per cent of U.S. patents are fielded by researchers not born in the United States, with those from China at number one accounting for 8 per cent (China surpassed Europe to enter the top slot in 1999), followed by those from Europe, 6 per cent, and those from India at number three, 4.5 per cent. Many of the patents are fielded in high-tech sectors such as computers and pharmaceuticals. Based on data from India, it seems that a scientific diaspora is built up in the sense that researchers in India are more likely to interact with researchers of Indian origin working in the United States.

The size of the potential is enhanced when looking at who are behind new companies in the United States. A study looking at 2,054 companies selected randomly reveals that one in four companies has a chief executive or chief technological officer who is foreign-born.[47] The top scorer was the semiconductor industry with 35.2 per cent, followed by computers/communications with 31.7 per cent, and software with 27.9 per cent. Immigrants from India accounted for 26 per cent of immigrant-founded companies, which equals the total for the next four groups of nationals — British, Chinese, Taiwanese, and Japanese.

## Future Development of the Patent System and Intellectual Property Rights

Over the preceding decades a global system has emerged based on various agencies. This system and its international organizations such as WIPO, or national ones such as EPO, USPTO, or SIPO, can hardly be expected to survive unchanged or unscathed by the strong technological and societal evolution on the cards.

In 2007 EPO published an attempt to build scenarios for the future of patents and IP (Internet Protocol).[48]

The time horizon is up to 2025 and EPO put forward four scenarios:

- One with *Market Rules* in which business dominates and other interests are brushed aside. Legal, commercial, managerial expertise will rule the game and IP becomes a financial asset.

- One asking *"Whose game?"* in which geopolitics is the key and several partners compete with business setting the agenda, but they are not as dominant as under market rules. Diplomacy and bargaining will be the skills sought after and IP becomes a tool for national competitiveness.
- One with *Trees of Knowledge* in which society is in the driver's seat, and negotiation and communication are imperative factors where IP becomes a moral issue.
- One of *Blue Skies*, with technology as the steering element, and legal, interdisciplinary, and negotiation expertise having high premiums, and where IP becomes an instrument for rapidly sharing technological solutions to complex problems.

## The Economic and Financial Crisis

A fourth element and uncertainty is the impact of the global economic recession that started in 2008. It primarily hit the United States, Europe, and Japan, but in most of the rest of Asia, in particular, China and India, there was lower, but positive growth rates, not contraction. The lesson from the Great Depression in the 1930s is that patent filings followed the same cycle as growth with a time lag of one year.[49] The number of patents filed fell the year following contraction and rose the year after growth. There is no law — economic or otherwise — saying that it will be the same this time, but logic tells us that corporations will be inclined to cut R&D spending during recession/depression as the benefit from these outlays will appear only several years later. The large corporations may not cut overall R&D so much, but shift the distribution or maybe speed up development, while small- and medium-sized companies may cut R&D. Public expenditure for R&D may be cut in endeavours to balance the budget.

If this happens to be the case again, the next question is whether a fall in the growth rate in Asia will influence R&D, and consequently the number of patents in the same way as contraction did in the developed economies.

There is no foundation for assuming one or the other result, but the fact that the Asian economies are less indebted than the U.S. economy may contribute to a further twist, closing the gap in number of patents between countries such as China and India on the one hand, and the United States on the other hand.

## Ownership of Patents

According to OECD, in 2005 82 per cent of all patents were owned by companies. Among the Asian countries covered by the study, Japan is top with almost 95 per cent of all patents owned by companies and the share is unchanged from the mid 1990s to 2002–04. The number of company-owned patents in India was below 80 per cent, and those in China below 60 per cent, but with a strongly rising trend. The ownership of patents is important for conversion into new products in the sense that a patent filed by a company, but not used, is a "dead" patent. There may be other persons or other companies that might have been able to convert it into a product, but they are denied the opportunity.

## Patent Revenue — Royalties

Patents are one factor showing future prospects. Another factor is how much countries already gain now from patents filed in the past. It also illuminates a potential future revenue source if the share of global patents develops in accordance with the above. Table 3.1 shows credits and debits for use of patents, indicating what a country receives for patents from other countries, and what it pays to other countries for using patents.

The Asian countries may see their share of patents filed by companies going up, but if that trend is not accompanied by a similar or more adventurous policy than that adopted by Japanese companies, or measures to make patents not used available to other companies, R&D may not turn into innovations and new products corresponding to the effort invested. A simple policy to boost R&D without follow-up measures to ensure that a channel is open to convert inventions into innovations and new products, can prove not only fruitless, but costly. The number of patents, as well as the sum of money going into R&D opens possibilities, but unless societal structure is accommodating, they may not lead to new products and, even less, a new economic and political philosophy based on innovations.

# Other Indicators of Future Technology

## Scientific Publications

According to OECD,[50] four Asian countries — Japan, China, Korea, and India — accounted for 18.1 per cent of global scientific articles in 2005, with Japan having the second largest number worldwide, China taking the number four position, Korea number eight, and India number nine. The potential of Asia is striking when we look at scientific articles in relation to population size, where China and India come far below almost all other comparable countries, and Singapore emerges as the highest ranking Asian country at number seven.

TABLE 3.1

Patent Credits and Debits for China, India, Japan, and Korea (2000–07)

|  | 2000 | 2001 | 2002 | 2003 | 2004 | 2005 | 2006 | 2007 |
|---|---|---|---|---|---|---|---|---|
| China |  |  |  |  |  |  |  |  |
| *Credits* | 80 | 110 | 133 | 107 | 236 | 157 | 205 | 343 |
| *Debits* | 1,281 | 1,938 | 3,114 | 3,548 | 4,497 | 5,321 | 6,634 | 8,192 |
| India |  |  |  |  |  |  |  |  |
| *Credits* | 83 | 37 | 20 | 25 | 53 | 131 | 112 | na |
| *Debits* | 282 | 317 | 345 | 550 | 611 | 767 | 949 | na |
| Japan |  |  |  |  |  |  |  |  |
| *Credits* | 10.23 | 10.46 | 10.42 | 12.27 | 15.70 | 17.66 | 20.10 | 23.32 |
| *Debits* | 11.01 | 11.10 | 11.02 | 11.00 | 13.64 | 14.65 | 15.50 | 16.68 |
| Korea |  |  |  |  |  |  |  |  |
| *Credits* | 688 | 924 | 835 | 1,311 | 1,861 | 1,827 | 2,046 | 1,920 |
| *Debits* | 3,221 | 3,053 | 3,002 | 3,570 | 4,466 | 4,398 | 4,650 | 5,075 |

*Note*: Millions of U.S. dollars (for Japan billions of U.S. dollars).
*Source*: IMF, *Balance of Payments Statistics Yearbook 2006* and *2008* (Washington D.C., International Monetary Fund, 2006). Country tables.

Asia's future strength in R&D is also borne out when analysing the *growth* of scientific articles from 1995 to 2005.[51] The overall growth rate for OECD is 20 per cent, but Asia, excluding Japan and Korea,[52] tables a growth of almost 200 per cent over the ten-year period. This is indicative of the growth and competition in the research-oriented, educational infrastructure, which may ultimately lead in twenty years' time to unique talent in science, but except in Japan, there are few industrial authors. Unless research leaders in industry emerge visibly, this financial effort may not bear fruit.

## Human Resources

From 1996 to 2006 the R&D personnel grew in China at a little more than 6 per cent per year, and in Korea at a little less than 6 per cent, putting these two countries among the top five to six countries in the OECD study encompassing most OECD countries, plus a few other countries. Growth has been focused on development of technology and engineering, with much less interest in science outside strategic fields. Japan is near the bottom with an annual increase of barely 1 per cent. It is noteworthy that comparing the number of science and engineering degrees out of the total new degrees shows that China and Korea actually top the list with almost 40 per cent, while Japan is in the middle with about 25 per cent.[53]

## Intellectual Property Rights

Until recently Asia has been able to take a relaxed attitude towards intellectual property rights as the overwhelming part of new technology materialized in the United States, Europe, and Japan. With the increasing share of global R&D taking place in Asia, and China plus India emerging as major players, Asia has been forced to change its attitude and contemplate what kind of R&D system/model and IP it prefers and deems suitable to safeguard Asia's interests. In 2007 China's Prime Minister, Wen Jiabao, stated that[54] "Core technology cannot be bought. Only by strong capacity of science and technological innovation, and by obtaining our own IP rights, can we promote [China's] competitiveness and ... win respect in the international society."

## Standards[55]

Standards play a crucial role for benefits accruing to industries and companies. In general it can be said that the country, region, and/or company setting an industry standard gets paid by others (royalties, etc.) using the technology and, even more important, forces others to comply with the standard, while enjoying a time advantage in the market (more important than royalties). The consumer market adjusts to the standard very fast and it is virtually impossible to get in later, even if a company offers a much better standard, as the costs of replacing terminals and infrastructure are prohibitive and have to be borne by the consumer, especially for ICT. As the inventor of the standard began sooner than competitors, it will of course reap first-mover benefits as suppliers.

How crucial standards can be is illustrated by the battle more than twenty-five years ago between VHS and Betamax for videotape standards, with Matsushita facing Sony. It was repeated ten years ago when Sony and Philips agreed to back down in favour of Toshiba/Warner Brothers for first-generation DVD players, being compensated instead by getting a share of the royalties.[56] At the beginning of 2008[57] it was Toshiba's turn to back out of a race, this time about developing high-definition DVD formatting, abandoning its own HD DVD and leaving the market to Sony's Blue Ray. It looks likely that Toshiba achieved some financial compensation as its share price immediately rose while the share price of the winner,

Sony, fell, probably reflecting investors' anticipation of market shares. These cases were all won as much by marketing and networking skill, as by technological prowess. The Japanese PDC (Personal or Pacific Digital Cellular) domestic wireless standard[58] and China's foray into 3G standard[59] underline the crucial importance of sharing and co-designing with global partners. China has also for the first time entered the fray with network operations (cernet, IPv4/IPv6[60]). Internet Protocol version 6 (IPv6) is going to replace version 4 (IPv4) because the existing version 4, with about 1.4 billion addresses, will run out of capacity in, at most, a couple of years' time, perhaps even sooner. The United States has for obvious reasons taken the majority of the addresses on version 4, but China is going to take the majority of addresses in the future; hence the strong Chinese interest not only in launching a new version with larger capacity, but also having a hand in its development.

The basic problem for a country floating its own standard is that it may well gather initial support inside that country, but unless it manages to catch a foothold outside the country, it is simply not viable. It will then also die inside the country because customers switch to a standard globally applicable and used in other countries instead of a national standard. As subscriptions come up for renewal and terminals cost more, customers leave, gradually suffocating the national standard. Some degree of technological independence may be obtained, but the question is whether China will be successful in avoiding past mistakes and rally other countries around the proposed standard, transforming it from a national standard into one of several international, even global, standards.

It is difficult to calculate the advantages for a country or companies of controlling/setting the standards, but it is quite simply enormous. Not only is it financially rewarding, but it also puts the company in an enviable position to determine the successor because standards must be looked upon as families with upgrades and evolutions, thus cementing a technological lead.

European and American companies such as Nokia, Alcatel, and Qualcomm were very successful in spreading their standards, GSM and CDMA, and the Asian companies tried to follow suit. Japan failed with PDC largely due to cultural issues as the global sales and marketing network wasn't there and, more importantly, you need device manufacturers who are on the same page in terms of product development for foreign markets (Nokia, Alcatel, Ericsson were all making equipment *and* devices to export and hence technical specifications could be synchronized), whereas the Japanese mobile phone manufacturers have only been focused on the Japanese market, due to huge subsidies from domestic carriers. In China, the TD-SCDMA standard was simply too little, too late, and the deployment of the technology was influenced by politics (worrying about sunk costs and "losing face"). The largest carrier was forced to use the Chinese standard to create scale, but the vast majority of countries had already made their decision on which 3G technology to use years earlier. China has two other mobile phone operators who are using the international standards and now they have a large competitive advantage as they can use devices such as the iPhone etc.

South Korea's two largest carriers (SK Telecom and Korea Telecom) were forced to use two 3G standards at the same time, the only operators in the world to do so. Obviously replicating their infrastructure was financially harmful to the operators, but using both UMTS[61] and EVDO[62] allowed the country's largest handset vendors, Samsung and LG, to develop products and gain scale in both technologies, and export across the world. Samsung is now number two in the world in shipments and LG is number three. Therefore there is some precedence for the argument that governments can enforce standards in order to foster an export-driven economy, but the timing and attention to target markets have to be there, which was not the case for China or Japan.

## Robotics

Robotics is a segment of new technology where Asia and, in particular, Japan currently has the edge. The world has known robots in manufacturing processes for many years. What is new is the development of robots to assist human beings, elderly and/or disabled people, in their daily lives. In a real long-term perspective, this opens up opportunities for embedding devices in human beings to help them or enhance their daily performance, or even by implanting devices in the brain.

With reference to the research fooling a person into believing he/she has the body of somebody else,[63] the implications or opportunities are immense for robotics, or perhaps rather, appendages that can be more easily controlled by the person in question. If the brain can be manipulated, so to speak, into believing either it is controlling another body or controlling artificial limbs, a new horizon opens up for robotics in the area of helping disabled people or people suffering from difficulties in controlling their body.[64]

## Space

Space programmes have often been seen primarily in a military or political context, and not as tightly linked to scientific discoveries, although scientific space programmes, with a 20 per cent share of all programmes, are the key vectors of progress. The endeavours to put humans in orbit are not always perceived in their economic perspective, namely that being capable of doing so means that a country is able to maintain and repair satellites and/or space stations, and by doing so keep them in orbit.[65] The economic cost-benefit analysis of such scientific capabilities may be questioned in the short run, but in a longer-term horizon, few will dispute that the benefits far outweigh the costs, besides having important spin-offs for technology.

In Asia it looks like the capability to operate in space and reap the benefits hereof is becoming the prerogative for China, India, and Japan; all of them are running space programmes that differ to a large degree. So far, Japan has favoured developing a large part of its own space performance, which explains setbacks. India seems to buy a large part of key technology. China has emulated or borrowed some Russian designs, but also tries to develop its own. A comparison of financial resources poured into space programmes point at the United States using more than 4 per cent of GDP, between 0.5 per cent and 4 per cent for Europe, and less than 0.5 per cent[66] for Japan, Russia, China, India, Brazil, and Canada.

Japan ventured into space much earlier than China and India. From a modest start in 1969 it looked in the mid-1990s to be a potential power capable of carving out a competitive position for itself in the global market for launching satellites. It had a dependable launcher (H-2) and the prospects looked bright. In the following ten years, disappointing or outright failures cast doubt on Japan's future as a space power despite the obvious strong Japanese interest in space capability and the unquestionable backup of industrial performances and R&D devoted to space.[67]

Since 2005 the Japanese programme has got back on track in that it looks much better organized and with clear objectives. Also the failures harassing it until 2004 have apparently been overcome. Japanese observers, however, admit that Japan is lagging behind the United States, Russia, and China. Two reasons for this are put forward: the problem that much space activity is linked to military purposes, ruling out Japanese efforts (no spin-off and difficulties every time a dual-purpose question arises) and the lack of comprehensive legislation until the Diet passed a basic law in 2008 setting out the purposes for Japan's space programme.[68]

China's space programmes follow a double path. The *first* is an attempt to use space for practical purposes such as launchers and satellites for telecommunication and observation of the earth. The *second* is to gain prestige and nourish pride among the population.[69]

An illustration of the national security context[70] is the objective of having a global satellite navigation system based on thirty satellites operating by 2015.[71] This is at the same time a tremendous financial and technological effort with strong foreign and security policy overtones. China quite simply does not want to depend on the United States or, for that matter, other foreign-controlled systems[72] that can be activated in a crisis situation to maim Chinese military operations. The existing system (Beidou) is only regional, and in April 2007, after the fifth orbiter launch, China embarked on the second generation programme, code named Compass.

Irrespective of the military thinking supporting the space programmes, China is keenly aware of the research, technological, and innovative perspectives of space operations, which is borne out by the following quote: "Chinese officials believe that it is a technology driver that can propel China's economy and facilitate innovation in pharmaceuticals and metallurgy. It can also provide other economic benefits, like increases in quality control testing and improving standards for selecting and training management personnel."[73]

India tries to see economic development as an objective for the country's space programme. By linking space activities to economic activities on the ground, tremendous gains in productivity and competitiveness are within reach. A study performed in 2003[74] showed that the Indian space programme has generated a return of US$2 for every US$1 spent. A description of India's space programme[75] reveals "India to be a world leader in practical applications of space technology which can improve the quality of life on Earth, such as assisting in communications, agriculture, weather forecasting, rural development and telecasting". The challenge for India is to turn this ambition into practical programmes and stay focused on that course.

The precise orientation of space programmes may be less transparent than it looks, but it demonstrates how space programmes such as ICT can be used to leapfrog by linking cutting edge technology to the real economy, opening the door for farmers, fishermen, and merchants, who are not yet used to scanning the horizon for opportunities, to do so and compare offers and opportunities. In India's case, attention has been drawn to the advantages for telemedicine and agricultural forecasting. "98% of the people from rural areas who become doctors leave those areas, resulting in a small number of doctors with the required training to serve a large number of people. The dream is to bring some of the medical resources of India's thriving urban areas to remote villages by telemedicine. Also important is remote sensing for agricultural assessment. India can now predict with 90% accuracy the national crop output one month before harvest. For a country that in its past frequently faced starvation and malnutrition, this is a vital resource."[76]

The opportunity is there for China and India to escape some of the more adventurous and costly space odysseys and opt instead for a lower cost and more down to earth approach, turning these investments into vehicles for economic growth and productivity. The caveat is that the more they start to see space as linked to defence and/or prestige, the more expensive space programmes become. It looks like they are both keenly aware of the vast economic opportunities, but India is more focused on how space may actually help productivity in a more low-cost way, while China is interested in the potential technological gains from space programmes.

In one area both countries will benefit. They will unquestionably enter the game as suppliers of rocket systems to lift heavy payloads into space and consequently attract customers, especially from developing nations. China is closer to that stage than India, which is still lagging behind with launchers.

Korea (South) is managing an embryonic programme to develop a space launcher vehicle called KSLV-1, based partly on a Russian design. There is little doubt that Korea has ambitions of not leaving the space and market for launchers to Japan, China, and India, but it is equally certain that it is a long way behind these, albeit the only Asian country outside the group of three with a space programme within a twenty-five year horizon.[77]

## New Breakthroughs

### Communication

A look at the industrial revolution in Britain almost 250 years ago and the audio-visual breakthrough in the United States almost fifty years ago reveals one determining factor: new waves happen where new science, technology, regulations, culture perceived as behaviour, and organization/institutionalization favour a disruptive vision.

A good guess is that the next breakthrough will revolve around two aspects: mobile communication as already seen, opening communication with anybody, anytime, about anything and allowing machine-to-machine and man-to-machine communication; and the conversion of the virtual world into something more tangible, useful, and commercially viable than just games. The evidence for making this prediction is available for the first aspect, where Japan is leading the M2M (machine to machine) communication vision, but scant for the second aspect despite visible trends pointing in that directions. If the law of abundance and the allegation that numbers tip the scale are accepted, China including Taiwan, plus maybe India, with the largest number of users, are obvious as the places where it will take place,[78] provided producers sense the opportunity. This would be a repetition of what happened with the Industrial Revolution more than 200 years ago. An analysis of how and why the Industrial Revolution took place in Britain and not elsewhere enumerates a number of reasons; one of them is the relative factor prices as discussed in Chapter 1; another driver is market demand for innovation[79] and that means the number of people with purchasing power. They were at hand in Britain in the second half of the eighteenth century and they may emerge in China followed by India, at the dawn of the twenty-first century. It is not a sufficient condition, but it is a necessary one that can, though not automatically, be exploited by entrepreneurs or whichever other drivers are controlling the game.

Some conceptual framework for the revolution around portable communication is already available. Although precise predictions are not possible, there is no doubt about the direction of what will happen.[80] The crucial messages are:

*First*, in future, mobile phones and computers will amalgamate into one unit providing the services we now fetch from two, and in many cases, cumbersome instruments. Mobile communication within transport, shops, M2M, may be even more important.

*Second*, Facebook and YouTube instruments will flourish in native Asian versions, sponsoring a new wave of interaction and thus also creativity around use of the Internet.

It is likely, but not certain, that the new technology available will force through open spectrum.[81] Hitherto the use of the spectrum for electronic messages (radio, etc.) has been controlled by licences for wavelengths. This was technically necessary when the technology was less advanced, imposing some kind of discipline on users of wavelength as they could not be used by more than one user at a time. Gradually technology has removed the need for regulation which, however, is still administered by governments for reasons other than technology. In reality open spectrum provides the technological opportunity for almost everybody to use or exploit communications and give access to the Internet obliterating the old-fashioned focus on wavelength. Even more important in terms of usage is the capability to craft and implement "personalized tariffs": each user states what is wanted and what he or she is willing to pay, and gets providers to compete around this request. It turns out that, as the number of charging operators then goes down, the overall sustainable profits and benefits for users and operators are higher than with the current prepaid or postpaid models. As has been seen so many times before in human history, when the technology is there, it is likely that it will be used.

A study by McKinsey published in February 2007[82] totals up the value added to the domestic economy from the gains for wireless operators, auxiliary players, and end-users. The figures confirm the intuitive belief that the value for end-users is much higher than for wireless operators, but also that for these gains to materialize, subscription prices and other economic and technical conditions must be tuned in to these objectives. Translated into policy terms, the message is that regulations and rules, or lack thereof, have a strong impact on productivity gains for the economy of mobile phone penetration.

Comparing India with a low penetration rate of mobile phones — but which since 2005, the year forming the statistical basis for the study, has risen exponentially — with China that has a much higher penetration rate, the study concludes that the positive impact of the penetration of mobile phones on GDP is 0.7 per cent for India and 3.2 per cent for China. Of these percentages, the direct impact from wireless operators is 0.4 per cent in India and 1.1 per cent in China, while the indirect impact from auxiliary players is 0.3 per cent and 2.1 per cent respectively. The study adds that the estimates are probably conservative and do not take into account the advances in the coverage and quality of network services. Doubts can be raised about the exact figures, but the message is unquestionable.

The World Bank[83] concludes in a study from 2009 that information and communication technology is a vehicle for growth. It underlines that mobile communication is important already and becoming increasingly so in rural areas with little or no existing infrastructure thus opening up markets for a huge mass of people. This is particularly relevant for Asia. The decreasing cost of mobile communication makes this vehicle accessible to people hitherto kept inside the local economy and outside the market economy.

A statistically thin but nevertheless interesting case study shows that mobile phones offer time savings of nearly 6 per cent for 600 workers in China who commute for their jobs (taxi drivers, salespeople, etc.). Translated into productivity gains for the Chinese economy, this amounts to US$33 billion in 2005, corresponding to 1.8 per cent of GDP.

The present technology imposes several sets of terminals for the end-user such as the PC, the handphone, and, to a certain extent, the TV and the fixed line phone. It is likely that these terminals will gradually be amalgamated into one offering a much more user-friendly environment. This is actually already taking place, not so much with terminals, but with in-house connection points to backbone(s), for example, in France with Freebox and Neuf Box.

What is termed open source and often called the open source revolution changes the playing field. In reality we have at least five types of open source.[84]

- Open source systems such as Apache, PHP, Mozilla, Firebird, and the Linux operating system.

- Open Science with free collaboration and rapid public disclosure of results with e-post peer review instead of prior peer review.
- Open access where users are free to download, copy and distribute, print, search, or link to the full texts, but not to edit or merge due to intellectual property rights.
- Open Innovation that prioritizes partnering, licensing, and venturing, to combine internal and external sources of ideas and technologies and share the benefits.
- Open standards such as XML and HTML that provide a common method of achieving a particular goal.

To exploit these options, a network for dissemination of knowledge must be built. Technically that requires networks such as the Internet or similar infrastructure, but even more important, socially knitting people together by virtue of some kind of common understanding about how to use the knowledge.

## A Road Map

Beginning in 2008 eighteen leading thinkers who served on a U.S. National Academy of Engineering (NAE) met to identify the greatest technological challenges facing society in this century.[85] The list looks like this:

- Engineering better medicines
- Advancing health informatics
- Providing access to clean water
- Providing energy from fusion
- Making solar energy economical
- Restoring and improving urban infrastructure
- Enhancing virtual reality
- Reverse engineering the brain
- Exploring natural frontiers
- Advancing personalized learning
- Developing carbon sequestration methods
- Managing the nitrogen cycle
- Securing cyberspace
- Preventing nuclear terrorism

This is a tall order and it catches the eye that environmental issues are not well covered. What is striking is that most, if not all, are out-of-box and several are interdisciplinary activities.

The global economic crisis starting in 2008 leads to thoughts about how the global economy may look after the crisis, with a particular eye to how opportunities might be snapped up. How many of the dominating global multinationals would actually have been born now and what kind of technology would be embedded in them?[86]

An analysis published by Bloomberg in December 2008 says this about what technologies could emerge out of the economic recession:[87]

> In recessions, ground-breaking technologies tend to get going. Perhaps that is because they don't usually require big upfront investments or entrepreneurs have to focus on essential, breakthrough products when times are tough.
>
> So where will the cutting edge be? Bio-technology has promised more than it has delivered so far, but put it together with computing, and dozens of new products and industries might blossom, as they did in the electrical industry in the 1930s.
>
> Books will go digital. Printed, bound books have been around for more than 500 years and have overcome predictions of their demise for at least a few centuries. Somehow they have survived. They aren't about to go away, but they may be about to evolve.
>
> Electronic books are set to take off in a big way. Alternatively, books can be downloaded in bite-size chunks onto mobile phones. As the technology becomes universal, new types of story-telling will emerge to take advantage of it: more episodic, more concise, and probably more communal. The publishers who get that right will create a whole new industry, but the whole copyright model will change.
>
> History suggests that in the next three or four years (2009–13) we will see the birth of the new companies and industries that will dominate the next few decades. Recessions wipe old slates clean. They create space and resources for new entrepreneurs.
>
> So, while the economic news as of 2009 are gloomy, it is worth remembering that beneath the hard frost the first buds of the next spring are germinating. Spotting them is the tricky bit. But catch them early enough, and you will make a fortune.

If Asia wants to have a say in breakthroughs in segments of science and technology such as these or others more relevant to Asia — and that is necessary for Asia to move from importing and adapting technology focusing on use of technology to creating new technology — hierarchical group structures will have to give way to the freedom of flatter information structures and organizations, and it is not clear this will be tolerated. The two go hand in hand: only if political hierarchical information and power structures allow for a significant spread of flat networked structures and social fabrics, will inventions blossom.

## A Holistic Approach

The holistic approach for turning R&D efforts into useful results for the economy and the difficulties embedded in this venture is analysed for China in two papers from the China Policy Institute, University of Nottingham. Both of them underline the massive effort China has put into developing an R&D base over the last few years, but uncover weak elements in the strategy. It is also a common thread that the focus on economic growth, regardless of how it is delivered, is simply not sustainable. A much more diversified and sophisticated approach, bringing not only R&D but also its use into the picture, is a pressing need for China.

The *first* paper[88] says that Chinese enterprises lack innovative ability and points out a number of impediments for building such ability into the enterprise system. The most important ones are inadequate investment, too much reliance or trust on imported technology, strong policy support for domestic products, and ineffective management of scientific talent, plus irrational allocation of scientific research resources. The steering mechanisms do not favour R&D in enterprises and in many cases work instead as barriers favouring the use of enterprises funds for purposes other than R&D.

The *second* paper[89] points out that China is far behind the leading industrial and technological nations in the world. The reasons are lack of investment in R&D, absence of an effective incentive system for R&D, and shortage of talent and innovative capacity.

The Chinese State Council issued in February 2006 the guidelines on national medium- and long-term programmes for science and technology development (2006–20),[90] which sets the proportion of research and development expenditure in the GDP at 2.5 per cent. By 2020, the progress of science and technology will contribute at least 60 per cent to the country's development. Meanwhile, the country's reliance on foreign technology must decline to 30 per cent and below. Such science protectionism, or rather, infant industry policy, is risky as it may bar China from access to technologies from abroad, and even more to science. China must also rank among the top five in the world in terms of the number of patents granted to Chinese nationals and the introduction of their academic essays.

These are ambitious targets. It is not certain that they can be fulfilled, but they serve as an illustration of how determined China is to move ahead with research, technology, and science, and the financial resources it has at its disposal to carry out the plans.

INSEAD and CII (Confederation of Indian industry) published in January 2009 a Global Innovation Index ranking nations according to their excellence in innovation.[91] The study outlines the main ingredients a country needs to possess to innovate. They are: ability to garner the best from leading-edge technologies, expanded human capacities, better organizational and operational capabilities, and improved institutional performances. The value of the report lies not only in its coverage of the overall capacity of nations to innovate, but also in the breakdown of innovation criteria into a number of sub-segments that allow for the diagnosis of the strengths and weaknesses of individual countries. The weakness of the study is that large swings for some countries' positions are difficult to accept and even more difficult to explain, thus raising some questions about the validity and method of the study.[92] There is, however, no doubt that it gives a clue about how the Asian countries are ranked in the future race to excel in innovation.

The top twenty includes Singapore (5), Korea (6), Japan (9), Hong Kong (12), and Taiwan (16). China is ranked 37 and India 41. For several Asian countries, in particular the two large ones, the current ranking is promising, provided that it serves as a platform for moving upwards. But it is not good enough — far from it — in a long-term perspective. The ranking for Japan is puzzling. Both with regard to its R&D share of GDP and the number of patents filed, Japan is among the top countries. The study supplements the strong position of Japan by ranking it at number 9. Japan has a wise technology management policy in companies, which is to start small and test selected usages before broadening while the productivity of these niche innovations grows to enable a real benefit for users in big markets, make more new products thereafter, and finally clinch revenues and market share.

The statistics indicate a much stronger potential ranking for China than 37, with reference to expenditure on R&D, numbers of researchers, and the positive impact of foreign direct investment on innovation. India already has strongholds, but these have not so far initiated higher innovation in the Indian economy as a whole. India's best score was for the pillar of human resources, and China's highest score was for competitiveness — neither of which comes as a surprise. Where they severely lag behind is in regulatory performance, governance, and similar vectors making innovation and the economy work smoothly, without disruptions from neglected infrastructure, corruption, and other distortions left inside society to block progress.

It is dangerous to attempt to draw common lessons, but a couple offer themselves:

- The main big Asian countries in R&D (except Japan and maybe Korea) have not really managed to integrate their R&D and subsequent innovations in the global economy.
- Much of the R&D flows top-down either through the government or in large enterprises, leaving the large numbers of small and medium-sized enterprises in a non-innovative role.
- There are many cultural, talent selection, and "governance" barriers for R&D and innovation to filter through the system.
- Short-term development, engineering, and goals are favoured by business and political systems, with negative consequences for the long term and science.
- The basic philosophy still seems to be that money is the main catalyst, ignoring the more tedious efforts in science and humanities, and the restructuring of societal norms, rules, regulations, and legislation.
- The potential is enormous when we keep the large populations in mind, but this will not be realized by itself. Besides, the quantity of unique creative talent to emerge from a population is far from proportional to its size.
- Asia's problem in turning out new products as the end result of R&D and innovation seems to be more societal than a question of economics and technology.
- Apart from China, Japan, and India, no Asian companies have significant strategic R&D in aerospace, nuclear, and biology.
- It is of paramount importance to ensure an open Chinese science and technological policy to prevent protectionism in R&D.

## SAVINGS

### Asia is the World's Financier

Asia is where the world's savings take place and that will continue to be the case in a twenty-five year time horizon.[93] From 2000 to 2006 China's savings rate rose from 38 per cent of GDP to 47.3 per cent, India's from 23.7 per cent to 32.4 per cent and, to pick another country, Vietnam's, from 27.1 per cent to 30.2 per cent.[94]

This has turned one of the well-known economic laws upside down. Normally countries undertaking industrialization borrow from abroad, but Asia is lending. In fact, Asia is financing U.S. consumption and public deficits while at the same time financing its own industrialization. One of the problems of the global financial system is that it is designed to channel funds from the developed countries to developing countries, but it is doing the exact opposite.

One of the lasting consequences of the sub-prime crisis is that it woke Asia up to take a stronger interest in how its own savings are used, instead of letting Western financial institutions shuffle these around. Over the last months of 2007, Asia took important stakes in well-known Western financial institutions such as Merrill Lynch, UBS, Morgan Stanley, and Citigroup, just to mention a few. Assuming that Asia's savings and the U.S. dissavings continue — which looks like a fairly reasonable assumption — Asia will over the next decade gradually, but surely, get control of how the global financial system is run. Economic history shows that economic power leads to control over global investment patterns. That was seen with the British Empire and later with the United States. It is likely to repeat itself for the rising Asian economic power houses.

Until the global financial/economic crisis, Asia's capital export primarily took the form of passive investments, for example, large purchases of U.S. treasury bonds judged to be 100 per cent safe assets, with a low, but predictable yield. In the decades to come, Asia's capital export will favour direct investment by purchasing foreign companies and building their own corporations in the form of multinational corporations. The new owners may see things differently from Western investors and even if all statements say the opposite, political preferences and corporate governance will play a role. Asian nation states may wish to secure natural resources according to strategies far more decisive than those of U.S. and Western interests. Some of these strategies have backfired in Australia and even in Africa and South America, but this does not augur a shift in strategy.

Until 2008 funds were transferred from one market to another, savings in one country were used to finance investments in other countries. This was not the same as a genuine global capital market with common rules and regulations, and even more important, common financial corporate governance stipulating what is good behaviour and what is not. The lesson learned is that it is not enough to link national markets together.[95] And it will be up to a re-engineered financial system, probably under stronger Asian influence, to turn that lesson into practice.

## Savings — Demographics and Social Welfare

Around 2015, when the number of people in the working age bracket in China peaks, the savings rate may and will probably be affected and most likely fall — at least from current high levels.

A recent study of Japan supports the view that an ageing population means a lower savings rate. The conclusion is that the Japanese savings rate will fall from 30 per cent at the end of the 1990s, to 19 per cent in 2040. The investment ratio will follow the same trend, declining from 28 per cent to 22 per cent.[96]

There is no law saying that China will tread in the footsteps of Japan. Forecasting savings rates is generally an economic issue involving analysing income trends, etc. In China's case societal and sociological issues might, with benefit, be brought into the picture. Almost all studies of the correlation between the savings rate and rising income are made in industrialized countries for the very reason that they are the ones that have gone into such income brackets. They are, however, also the countries with a social welfare system either set up or run by the state, or linking social welfare to corporations, with the implication that the individual knows social welfare (old age, pensions, health care) are under the aegis of society in one way or another. This is not the case in China and several other rising Asian economic powers. In these countries social welfare, mainly health expenses, and at least part of the education expenditure for children, have to be financed by the family.

The unanswered question is how this influences the savings rate. Not many would disagree with the deduction that it leads to a higher, much higher, savings rate than in the existing industrialized countries. The next unanswered question is whether Asian countries in the years to come will build up a social welfare system, and if so, what the impact will be on the savings rate. The sensitive political question of redistribution of income and wealth will certainly play a role in this context.

Hints coming from Chinese think tanks in public statements indicate that China is on its way to developing a social welfare system, albeit it will take a long time and be embryonic in the initial phases.[97] There is little doubt that pressure and encouragement are growing to build some kind of welfare system. The arguments in favour are strong and find increasing support. It will shift the burden, or at least some of the burden, from individuals to the public sector.[98] This may not change the picture for continued high savings in absolute terms, but will affect consumption (lower savings rate equals higher consumption rate), thus changing the whole structure of the Chinese economy. In fact, as long as China does not have even an embryonic welfare system, it is kept in the grips of the societal structure from 1979, even if the economy and society look completely different today. The risk is resistance to change when the economy looks set for an overhaul to embark on a course for the next twenty-five years.[99]

An analysis[100] published in 2009 estimates the cost of a total welfare system in 2020 to be 5.74 trillion yuan, equal to US$839 billion. The basic idea is to create an overall social welfare system covering pensions, education, health care, housing, employment, and other services across the nation, and encompassing urban and rural districts. If the plan is carried out it will mean that the share of social welfare in the public budget goes up from 27 per cent to 35 per cent. One of the interesting things is that the plan opts for social welfare financed with the public budget and not via private schemes or corporations.

It seems fair to assume that China, under pressure from growing social problems (employment, the elderly and pensions, and inequality), is contemplating a social welfare system as a kind of safety net. If such policies take root in China and develop into a safety net enjoying the confidence of the population, the repercussions on the savings rate will be tangible, pushing it lower.[101]

In India and Indonesia the welfare system is largely private with a stable structure, but very limited coverage of the population. In Japan the welfare system is in place, cannot change for political and demographic reasons, and has a large coverage of the population, although it runs with deficits and low yields.

## Future Savings Rate and Capital Markets

A reasonable assumption is that in the decades to come, the savings rate in China will stay higher than is the case seen in industrial countries with similar income brackets, but will not be as high as was seen before the trend for the workforce changed.

For Asia as a whole the change in outlook for China may be compensated by a rising labour force in countries such as India, Indonesia, Vietnam, and the Philippines keeping savings high. India as the biggest economy may be decisive. Sanjeev Sanyal[102] ventures the forecast that India will operate with a savings rate of 45 per cent of GDP in 2020. He adds that such a savings rate means that scarcity of capital will no longer — as used to be the case — constitute a barrier for continued high economic growth.

If this assumption proves right and this is likely to be the case, judging from performance over the last twenty-five years, total savings in Asia will be at a high level, keeping global costs on capital low, as was also seen from 1979 to 2008. However, a large part of Asian savings are in risky investments (family businesses, housing, and shares), betraying a systemic risk from the coexistence of big and, in some cases, growing savings, and the absence in effect of risk managed receptacles for these savings, which points to the role of the capital markets.

This scoreboard is less unequivocal. As was seen before 2008, the Asian capital markets did not live up to the ambition of having efficient, effective, and smooth-running linkages between savings and investments. The high surplus on China's balance of payments clearly indicates that savings were kept, or even neutralized in the Chinese economy, instead of being channelled abroad. The large number of domestic investment projects sometimes gave rise to the question of whether they were subject to a proper investment calculus investigating their profitability and societal relevance, or simply carried out because capital was plentiful and available through a Chinese banking system that is not really operating under market economy conditions.

While there is little doubt, if any, that global savings will continue to take place primarily in Asia, there are some doubts about where, under what conditions, and how they can or will be used. One aspect is the role of capital markets in financing the domestic economy and this is where Asia faces two basic challenges: the financing of social welfare, in particular, pensions for the growing number of elderly people and building a financial system able to take on the task of furthering Asia's private consumption. Another aspect is the global capital market where Asia definitely continues to finance the world, but has to adjust because foreign direct investments are changing from coming into Asia to going out of Asia.

## MULTINATIONAL COMPANIES[103]

### Foreign Direct Investment

So far Western and Japanese multinational companies have dominated the picture with their market share, drawn the lines between technology to be transferred or kept in the drawer, and also defined corporate governance. All this is going to change although the picture right now is the same in terms of share of global GDP. An X-ray shows the West in command, but trends will reveal Asian companies to be the breeding ground for new patterns.

The figures for China and India speak a clear language outlining differences between the two countries. From 2002 to 2006 China's outgoing foreign direct investment (FDI) rose from US$2.7 billion to US$16.1 billion, corresponding to a change from 0.50 per cent to 1.57 per cent of global FDI. Based on a linear model the forecast says it will be US$67 billion in 2020, but if the

Japanese and Korean experiences apply to China, the figure rises almost astronomically to US$227 billion.[104] Official figures estimate outward FDI in 2007 of US$20 billion — a sevenfold rise from 2002.[105] China's inward FDI amounted to US$74.7 billion.

India's inward FDI came up to US$15.7 billion for the first three quarters of 2007, which when converted to an annual basis would result in US$20 billion for the whole of 2007.[106] Outward FDI for 2007–08 is estimated at US$15 billion on an annual basis.[107]

Comparable statistics and forecasts for the two countries by the Economist Intelligence Unit[108] are available for up to 2011. They show outward FDI in China rising from US$2.5 billion in 2002 to US$17.8 billion in 2006, and US$72 billion in 2011. For India the corresponding figures are US$1.7 billion, US$9 billion, and US$16 billion. Measured as a percentage of GDP, the figure for China rises from 0.2 per cent in 2002 to 1.2 per cent in 2011, and for India from 0.3 per cent to 0.8 per cent. In 2011 China will account for approximately 4.5 per cent of global FDI, up from approximately 1.5 per cent in 2006, and approximately 0.4 per cent in 2002, with the corresponding figures for India being about 1 per cent, about 0.6 per cent, and about 0.3 per cent. It may not look like much, but keep in mind that the Chinese economy in 2011 will be roughly the same size as, and the Indian economy about 25 per cent of, the U.S. economy (in terms of purchasing power parities),[109] and you will see that the figures signify a big jump. It is noteworthy to mention that the U.S. figure for 2011 is estimated at 1.6 per cent (2002: 1.3 per cent). The figures for China are higher, especially for inward FDI, and while India has almost balanced inward and outward FDI, China's outward FDI lags far behind, albeit rising fast.

The European Union has for several years been the largest investor in Asia (excluding Near and Middle East countries), with a total sum of about EUR 30–40 billion annually in the years 2004–06, corresponding to 10–12 per cent of total outflows from the European Union. The flows in the opposite direction amounted to less than half, of which the overwhelming part was from one country: Japan.[110] It is interesting to note, however, that over the last five to ten years, much of the surge of FDI into East Asia has been intraregional, with Japan being one of the main drivers, supplemented by other Asian newly industrialized countries, and with China, and to a certain degree, Southeast Asia, being the recipient.[111] If we look at Asia, excluding Japan, it is clear that Japanese investments have played a crucial role with a part of inflow FDI to East Asia fluctuating around 15 per cent of all inflows over the fifteen years from 1990 to 2004.[112] Japanese FDI into Asia has been going on since the

1960s, is increasingly sophisticated, and is organized around the key notions of supply chains and market share sustainability.

## Chinese Multinational Corporations

Most Chinese activities have the characteristics of minority shareholders in well-established companies and aim at investing in emerging countries. A significant share of the Chinese outflow of FDI is in resource exploration and, sometimes, distribution networks, and these are not always via stock markets. Illustrations are China's biggest bank (ICBC) buying 20 per cent of South Africa's biggest bank, Standard Bank, which also operates in eighteen other African countries; Lenovo buying IBM's PC division; and attempts at buying car companies in the West. The background of Chinese enterprises can explain this tactic. The majority grew up either as state-owned companies or under the umbrella of a centralized economy. They are not used to operating in an international environment and especially not one combined with global market economy rules of the game, and they want two things: *first*, to gain experience in how to manage companies outside China without risking too much, *second*, to acquire knowledge about management, technology, staff, etc. The government is also pumping up selected companies as champions, and steers FDI towards key sectors (resources, technology, banking, telecoms). This is contrary to the case for most Western multinationals, which are looking for increasing market share when entering into mergers and acquisitions (M&As).

The Chinese computer company, Legend, which changed its name to Lenovo, is the company best known for its endeavours to turn itself into a multinational company. It took over IBM's computer division and moved the new company's headquarters to the United States as a visible sign of its intention to be multinational, and not Chinese or American for that matter. What it wanted was to acquire a brand name, but most of all, know-how. Since then, like all other multinationals, it has expanded its production units across the globe and set up manufacturing in India and Mexico.[113] Late 2008 rumours told that Lenovo wanted to acquire Brazil's Positovo Informatica.[114] This seems to reflect a conscious strategy for getting a foothold in developing and/or newly industrialized countries and, from there, expand. The basic thinking is apparently that dynamic markets are no longer to be found in North America or Europe, but in other parts of the world. With Positovo Informatica included, Lenovo would come close to being the number three in this market — currently held by Acer behind Dell and Hewlett Packard — with a global market share of 7.9 per cent.

Since the merger with IBM, Lenovo has tried to penetrate other and new markets with some, but limited, success. The problem is to understand and have the willingness to understand other markets than the one the company originally prospered in. This shift into the mindset of a multinational company has apparently been more difficult than expected for Lenovo and the same can be expected for Chinese corporations dealing with a large consumer mass abroad.

Another Chinese company, Huawei (infrastructure equipment for telecommunications network), has found it easier to grow by choosing organic growth, but has also been helped by a crucial factor in dealing with international customers. Lenovo's millions of customers are consumers, many of whom do not have much knowledge of the world outside their daily life. Huawei delivers equipment to a few companies in other countries. The customer base is much more limited and it has a much better understanding of the globalized world, putting less stress on Huawei to integrate into its policies, new and, for Huawei, strange cultures, and new sets of behaviour in the marketplace. The strategy has been accused of being one that dumps prices and siphons off talent from competitors when they are in trouble, by setting up labs in their backyards.

An analysis of Chinese foreign direct investment and establishment of multinationals point to a policy — deliberate or otherwise — of prioritizing having a foothold, especially in the commodity sector, followed by the financial sector, with technology as number three.

Manufacturing is absent from this strategy. This was already visible in the mid-2000s with Chinese acquisitions or taking stakes in major commodity companies' operations, especially those in Africa, but also in other geographical areas. Security of supply of commodities is a major Chinese strategic goal and the building of multinational companies to that effect is a logical next step. China started to gain influence and, in some cases, control over financial companies with the global financial crisis in 2008. Some of these investments were channelled through its new investment arm, CIC (China Investment Corporation), one of the rising sovereign wealth funds.

Chinese companies are acutely aware of their own shortcomings and tread carefully and cautiously. They follow one of the sayings of Deng Xiaoping, "Crossing river by feeling stones." When reaching the other bank (having acquired the knowledge and management skill), Chinese enterprises are ready to enter the big game and establish themselves as full-scale multinationals. "Crossing the river by feeling the stones" is a process where you are in control of your own speed, which gives you the option of stretching the time horizon. In analysing the rise of Chinese multinationals, confusion between financial power and management skills should be avoided. The Chinese may be quite ready to draw out the learning process if they deem it necessary, instead of jumping into the water only to discover it is cold.

## Indian Multinational Corporations

India and its companies have a completely different background. Most of India's successful enterprises are entrepreneurial (personal or family owned) and have grown up under conditions of a market economy. They do not feel impeded in taking the jump from the domestic market to the international one. And they have the management skill the Chinese often lack. In their eyes, minority shareholders may be an unnecessary deviation, while the direct route towards M&As commends itself, especially for M&As in Western markets, the culture of which they understand better than Asian markets which often give rise to problems. This approach was seen by the operations of Mittal Steel in 2005 when buying European steelmaker Arcelor for US$33.1 billion and making it the world's largest steel maker; and in Tata Steel's US$7.6 billion takeover of Anglo-Dutch Corus Group[115] in 2006 putting it into the number five slot for this market. Both these cases illustrate the intrepid business philosophy displayed by several Indian companies. In 2006 Indian companies announced 125 acquisitions totaling about US$10 billion in all kinds of fields. Even more important are the forays of medium-sized Indian companies abroad, helped by the Indian diasporas.

Multinationals from Korea, Thailand, Indonesia, and from Taiwan seem to have models closer to the Indian one than the Chinese model for multinational companies.

## Asian Multinational Corporations in the Global Picture

Working on the assumption that the world's savings will continue to take place in Asia and that Asia's financial system/capital market will develop into a world class system geared to scrutinizing investment projects, we find it is likely that a large number of Asian multinationals will emerge — backed by the largest home markets in the world, exploiting new technology (applications as well as inventions), and supported by financial power. As is the case for all newcomers, there will be mistakes and costly ones, but Asia can afford to make such mistakes to learn from them and gain experience. An intriguing question though, is whether these Asian multinationals, especially the Chinese ones, will actually "forget" the home market, and, over time, distance themselves from domestic links, including relationships with their governments, as they will have to move the manufacturing out of the home country to cater to non-Asian customers' imperatives.

The size of the home market and the shift in favour of emerging economies and multinationals originating there is remarkable. The World Bank[116] states "multinational enterprises will be able to market their products to a much larger audience in 2030 than they do today. Furthermore, the rules of this new global marketplace will be increasingly determined by the tastes and preferences of the developing world, particularly the desires of consumers in China and, to a lesser extent, India." If we look at economic growth, it is debatable where the biggest market for products from Asian multinationals in 2030 will be, but there is no doubt dynamic and growing markets will be found where the growing middle class emerges, and that is, as stated by the World Bank, in China and India, as well as other developing markets.

The adjustment process to bring the U.S. economy in line with realities has so far produced a decline in the U.S. dollar. It is likely that the U.S. dollar will continue to be weak over the next decades as all omens point to a shift in economic power from the United States to other regions. A weak U.S. dollar could make it slightly cheaper for Asian multinationals to invest abroad and empower them with more purchasing power in the M&A game, depending on how large a share of currency reserves are held in U.S. dollars. The United States now accounts for nine out of the twenty-five largest corporations, compared with eighteen in 1998. There were in 2008, four Chinese corporations on the list (so far no Indian corporation); indeed the biggest global corporation is now Chinese: PetroChina.[117] The dependence on the U.S. market forces many Chinese corporations to diversify and look for other markets to avoid being dragged down with the recession harassing the American economy and the U.S. dollar in 2008–09. This may contribute to the drive and interest in China to create multinationals although this started well before the downturn, as well as the drive to other emerging countries (Russia, Brazil, India) to diminish the role of the U.S. dollar in the international monetary system.

In 2003, the Fortune Global 500 list included thirty-one corporations from developing or emerging countries. In 2008 the corresponding figure was more than seventy.

The Boston Consulting Group[118] analyses 100 challengers from fourteen rapidly developing economies (RDEs), of which forty-two come from China, twenty from India, thirteen from Brazil, seven from Mexico, and six from

Russia.[119] Classified according to industry, thirty-four deal in industrial goods, with automotive equipment as the most important sector with twelve corporations; seventeen are in resource extraction with fossil fuel as top scorer; fourteen are to do with consumer durables, with household appliances and consumer electronics both registering six corporations; and food and beverages accounting for fourteen.

The picture is fairly predictable showing that China is the clear front-runner among those classified as emerging market countries, and industries in the labour-intensive brackets take the lion's share, while advanced technology and service industries are not spectacular on the list. Nevertheless it depicts a picture of rising multinationals in large numbers and with sufficient strength to take on the existing multinationals.

Boston Consulting Group discloses the following reasons for these corporations' wish to be multinationals: access to growth and profit pools as the home market is not deemed sufficient enough to sustain continued growth; developing complementary skills, such as R&D expertise; acquiring intangible assets such as brands; and experimenting with new business models.

The challengers use six globalization models listed by Boston Consulting Group.

- Model 1 takes brands built up in the home market global. Twenty-nine corporations including eleven from China and seven from India have chosen this approach. India's Bajaj Auto, the country's largest exporter of two- and three-wheeled vehicles, falls into this category.
- Model 2 turns domestic based engineering into global innovation. Twenty challengers pursue this approach. An example is Embraer (aviation) from Brazil and China Aviation.
- Model 3 is a drive for global leadership, and China's largest producer of rechargeable batteries, BDY, is mentioned as an example.
- Model 4 focuses on monetarizing natural resources, for example, Gazprom, Petronas, Hindustan Petroleum.
- Model 5 consists of rolling out new business models to multiple markets, which primarily takes the form of mergers and acquisitions.
- Model 6 involves acquiring natural resources abroad, an area where several Chinese corporations have been very active.

## New Multinational Corporations

In the coming decades managerial and technological talent may not be the preserve of Western multinationals. Patterns of FDI will be influenced by Japanese, Chinese, and Indian multinationals, and transfer of technology may no longer be a predominantly one-way traffic from Western countries, via their multinational companies, to developing or newly industrialized countries. Japan is already earning more from industrial licences in the United States than vice versa.[120] For industrial property rights, Japan is building up a solid overall surplus vis-à-vis the rest of Asia, the United States, and Europe. Including fees for copyrights, the surplus first appeared in 2003–04, but has grown since. The balance with the rest of Asia reveals a strong surplus for industrial property rights and a deficit for copyrights where the figures are much smaller.[121] The exchange with the United States shows a surplus for industrial property rights from 2002 which is growing, but not enough to wipe out a deficit on copyrights (mostly for media and software). For Europe the figures are smaller than for the United States, but taken together, are bigger than for the rest of Asia, giving Japan a surplus for industrial property rights in 2004, and for copyrights in 2007.[122]

Everything has its price and the Chinese and Indian multinationals, with dynamic domestic markets, are moving into a position where they — and not Western multinationals — will determine the bidding wars, primarily in commodity products, to be seen as global businesses move towards a higher degree of concentration. Japanese multinationals have the time advantage of playing these bidding wars with localized Asian assets in lower-cost countries.

That will also mean that the future of corporate governance will lie in the hands of Asian multinationals. The fundamental *first* difference so far between Asian business values and American (to a certain extent, also European) values is that American companies live under constant pressure to show higher profits every quarter, which exercises a heavy drain on management resources, while Asian companies are not yet under the same sway.

A *second* difference is ownership and the role of the stock market. The stock market finances American and European companies. Shareholders own American and European companies, and ownership has over the last decades moved from private investors to institutional investors.[123] Asian companies are primarily owned and financed by governments, government-controlled funds, or families not seeking much funding from stock markets.

A study from 1999[124] looking at 2,980 corporations concluded that more than half were controlled by a single shareholder. There are wide differences across East Asia, but generally this concentration of ownership in very few hands diminishes with higher economic and institutional development. At the time more than 50 per cent of market capitalization in Indonesia and the Philippines was controlled by ten families and a high concentration was also visible in Thailand, Malaysia, and Hong Kong. Japan was found at the other end with only 2.4 per cent of market capitalization in the hands of ten families. This raises a number of questions with regard to the interaction between business and politics, competition, the financing of corporations, and the management of companies. Asian governance may be less transparent and less disconnected from specific family or government interests than in the West and Japan.

If this continues to be the case the global stock markets will be left to finance multinationals in relative decline, while the profitable part of financing takes place outside stock markets. If Asian multinationals turn away from the existing model of relying on stock markets, ownership of and financing for these companies will undergo fundamental changes and so will the role of the global capital market. Not only will global savings originate in Asia, but also a majority of multinational companies seeking financing from there will be Asian. It is difficult to escape the conclusion that such a course will put Asia in control of the global capital market.[125]

A *third* difference may exist with regard to global trade issues such as intellectual property rights where the industrialized countries have asked for stricter rules. With Asian multinationals moving into more value-added production, they will gradually bring out new products, and shift their interest to support stricter rules about intellectual property rights. Nation states negotiate on behalf of their big corporations. What is likely when Asian multinationals start to market high-tech goods is that they ask their governments to ensure that property rights are not eroded by piracy and other methods of copying. It is no revelation, but it is sometimes overlooked that the interest in intellectual property rights lies with those having the technological edge and information control discipline.

A *fourth* difference is that Asia's strong domestic economic growth and dynamic markets have still not fully come to terms with how to nurture leaders, scientists, technologists, innovators and inventors, artists, and other creative people to serve as a pool for future innovative growth. Many people in Asia are definitely in the forefront of science, technology, and creativity, but many of them choose to ply their skills abroad. In the section about technology above, the difference between new applications of new technology and inventing new science leading to technology was discussed. Asia faces the same problem with regard to future leaders of its multinationals.

## A New Way of Doing Business

### *An Asian Model?*

Asian and some European multinationals will influence the future trend of business practices, paradigms, and corporate governance in the coming decades. Will the world see an Asian capitalism in whatever form it may take, or will Asian multinational companies choose to adopt American capitalism, albeit with some adjustment? The global financial crisis transforming into a global economic crisis may have given China's leaders second thoughts if they ever contemplated shifting the burden of welfare onto the corporate sector. The absence of a genuine social welfare system run and financed by the public sector is one of the reasons for the calamities hitting the American economy. Putting their savings into corporation-organized welfare systems for several reasons attracted employees. One of them was that it looked like a promising investment. By doing that they actually bought a share of future production and their welfare payments could be expected to follow economic growth. This was a correct assumption, but suffered from two snags. The *first* is that economic growth was not linked to specific corporations. A shift in competitiveness and industrial structure meant that what seemed to be impregnable economic fortresses for growth turned into sunset corporations and in some cases faced bankruptcy. The *second* is that public welfare services were not offered, making private funds the only alternative to corporations, and for many this was just too risky.

From a prudent perspective — and to all accounts the Chinese Government and Communist Party have proved to be prudent operators for more than thirty years — the American corporation model does not recommend itself.

The question is relevant because multinational enterprises are multinational with regard to business activities, social obligations, and responsibilities, but mono-national, so to speak, about where the strategic thinking takes place and where they find the main research and technology laboratories, and financial headquarters. In short: the brain. If we assume that Asian multinationals will grow in economic size, it is likely, almost certain, that a considerable part of multinationals' management "brain" will move to Asia.

The jury is still out on whether China and India will be able to foster an entrepreneurial class of their own and, if so, how strong and dynamic it will be and whether there will be any differences between the two countries.

A recent study takes a buoyant look at the emergence of an entrepreneurial class in both countries.[126] The study concludes that both societies "have woken up" and the result could reshape business, politics, and society worldwide.

The key sentences formulating what is happening run like this: "In some sense people in these societies are running faster than their rules and laws can keep up. So they are creating the rules as they go along. And entrepreneurship is, after all, doing things in new ways, ahead of social norms and customs, and establishing the rules and laws. In both countries, these processes are unfolding not just in the mainstream business sector but in society writ large and even in politics and civil society." Rules, regulations, and laws are quite simply bypassed — left as dead letters. It brings out clearly that entrepreneurship has much more to do with societal structure as a whole than pure economics, and relates to happiness/creativity.[127]

## *Networks*

The future business organization looks increasingly to be framed by the velcro concept.[128] This concept gives corporations the flexibility to cobble together teams to solve particular problems, thereafter dissolving them to form new teams to solve new problems. It is also called in academic/business spheres, "smart business networks", with quick connect and disconnect options. The virtue of this kind of organization is its ability to fit into the evolution of the marketplace, changing its nature with the growing digitalization.

The core of the concept is that personal consumption not only becomes increasingly steered by digitalization, but ever more personalized as digitalization opens up the possibility that the consumer can influence the product he/she is going to buy. In other words, the consumer does not look into a catalogue or go to a showroom, but logs onto a digital Internet to interact with the producer to determine the kind of product or service he/she is going to buy. In the academic/business world, this is called mass customization.[129] In a way the tables are turned because corporations exploiting this mobilize customer-created values for the firm. The consumers and customers are not only buying its products, but also becoming assets for the firm and contributing to its development.[130]

The Internet gives consumers the possibility to interact with one another about the products they buy, and to get from there to interacting with the company is not a long way to go, provided the company senses the opportunity to tap into consumer preferences and tastes. Indeed many consumers, especially those in the segment of the market where brands play a significant role, are more than happy to get into contact with the company. The company Threadless[131] apparel, engages its consumers in interaction to gain access to ideas among those buying its product.

Feedback 3.0[132] is an omen for what to expect. Feedback 1.0 opened the door for consumers to utter their grievances and protests about products, but companies did no really pay attention. Feedback 2.0 — where we are now — has seen the use of these instruments among consumers skyrocket and companies realizing that they cannot ignore them. Feedback 3.0 — to which we are moving — signifies first, that companies seriously begin to follow and gather information useful for them from consumer postings on the Internet and, second, that they slowly wake up to the fact that the interaction with the consumers can be turned into an asset pool, a catalogue of ideas, for the company to use.

The emergence of this new business model is likely to take place in new marketplaces where consumers are not weighed down with practices linked to conventional behaviour and those with a high and growing degree of digitalization. These markets will probably be found more in Asia than elsewhere and thus provide a propitious ground for this evolution to take root[133] even if traditions of whom you buy from with confidence are strong across all of Asia, forcing mass customization to adapt to this Asian twist.

The same basic concept will govern business-to-business activities. In the industrial age a machine was delivered and that was that. The spread of technology and its availability mean that even if there are differences with regard to price and performance levels, most machinery and, especially investment goods, cannot easily be distinguished from what competitors offer by comparing cost and effectiveness.[134]

Therefore the competitive parameter shifts to accompanying services. The most competitive bid will be from the company offering services or software, in the interpretation of the word to service the machine, upgrade it, guarantee repair within $x$ hours in case of a breakdown, train, and upgrade skills for staff.

We move into what could be termed the product concept for machinery in the sense that what is offered is a total concept of machinery, performance, services, and maintenance (sometimes called product/service-systems, PSS).[135] The buyer actually does not buy the machine, but the machine plus what it offers — a total concept where services is not an add-on to the machine, but the machine and the service are integrated in PSS. Very few buy the machine only.

In my book from 1995[136] I used signal equipment for railroads as an example. The railway does not buy a number of signal posts and miles of electrical wire, but a total concept guaranteeing that the trains run safely.

When offering its 787 aircraft, Boeing moved into this kind of marketing by putting a total service concept called GoldCare at the disposal of airlines, meaning that airlines not only buy the aircraft, but the aircraft plus accompanying services over a broad front. It can even be said that airlines do not really buy the aircraft at all, but its performance, with Boeing guaranteeing performance level, and the airline providing pilots and cabin crew.[137]

Xerox started more than twenty-five years ago to lease photocopiers instead of selling them and managed this policy so adroitly that it gained a near monopoly in segments of the market for photocopiers. One of the advantages for the customer was the ability to upgrade to new technology without much investment outlay. That experience underlines that this particular kind of competition may be best suited to a market where the product is constantly changing, for example, high-tech products. Xerox was later attacked by Canon, which managed to encroach on its market share, especially for smaller machines.[138]

Emerson Climate Technologies[139] has grasped that customers do not buy refrigerators or cooling systems, but a total solution delivering conservation of food while securing its quality. For the time being the relevant technology is cooling, but it is not cooling in itself that is relevant, but what cooling means for conservation of the food. If or when another technology emerges customers will move to that. The philosophy of Emerson Climate Technologies runs like this: "to move beyond stand-alone products and create solutions that provide competitive advantages for our customers. This shift is made possible through advanced electronics, software, and networkable products." Emerson offers solutions that provide "energy reduction services, maintenance management and food quality monitoring". Comparable solutions or services are offered by Danfoss Retail Care[140] and now many others. Japanese multinationals have been agile in adapting to this, capitalizing on their sense of quality as a dogma, and winning respect.

## The Political Enterprise

A long shot is to talk about a political enterprise. The first multinational companies followed the flag and were in that respect political enterprises.

In a later phase they grew so big and powerful that they were able and willing to assume a political role, playing their own game, irrespective of whether it synchronized with the political goals pursued by the nation state they were linked to or associated with.

Economic globalization has introduced multinationals of a size that often decouples them from a particular nation state. With their size, values emerging as a steering factor for politics, and the awakening of minority groups inside nation states supplemented by migration, many multinationals feel uncomfortable being linked to a particular nation state with which they may or may not share basic values and, even more crucially, political actions.

Looking for similarities between terrorist organizations and multinationals is far from being an ideal comparison, but the two have several things in common: they place headquarters and training facilities inside one nation state, they operate internationally, and in many cases globally, and they switch to values as the most important factor in "marketing" themselves. It is likely that this trend will continue, with multinational enterprises turning away from nation states and nationality to focus on global values.

The question is what this means for multinational enterprises growing out of Asia. The initial observation is that Asian multinationals in the decades to come will differ from established, Western multinationals. Purchasing power and probably also trends will emerge in Asia, that is, their home market, and not in the United States or Europe any more. They will get increasing returns to scale operating in their home markets, while Western multinationals must penetrate the competitors' home market to get increasing returns to scale. The picture differs from company to company, however. It is true of China Petroleum, but not of Huawei. It was initially true of Honda, Nissan, Toyota, Indian steel companies, but may not be anymore.

The Asian business model — still closely linked to family hierarchies without much prospect of changing — will continue to favour a more closely-knit owner and capital structure. Presumably this will mean Asian multinationals will see their actions and role inside the home market and the nation state — at least for the large Asian companies — as determining their vision and mission.

As is already seen with some Chinese and Indian multinationals, the implication is also a stronger interest and awareness of the growing potential in emerging markets outside Asia: in Latin America, the Middle East, and Africa. The West is losing some of its lure simply because it cannot deliver growing markets and because Asian multinationals may find it easier to adjust to the kind of products demanded in these other countries. One of the growing markets in the world is the emerging middle class in developing countries, and multinationals originating in Asia are better tuned to catering for their demand pattern than Western multinationals. Asian multinationals are welcomed by the governments of these emerging countries, for their ideology and their "more flexible" business arrangements, which do not depend much on abiding by policies as required by Western governments.

An illustration of this is Lenovo's "panic" button. It recovers a computer system within 60 seconds of a crash and is developed primarily for the Chinese, and in a longer term perspective, Indian rural districts, where power supply is frequently disrupted.[141] This technology is now being incorporated in its computers everywhere. From there to developing this into a system incorporated in all its computers, thus improving their performance, will not be a long step.[142]

The increasing investment in R&D, plus branding, etc., in their home markets, makes them capable of delivering new products, and following up on new products while at the same time having an eye for special effects because of lower and less quality supply of public services such as electricity, infrastructure, etc.

Taken together, all these factors point to Asian multinationals being more Asian in their way of thinking and choice of business model, probably losing exclusive or dominant links to their home market (Asia), albeit not losing their markets there, and being more interested in emerging markets than their American and European counterparts. The competition among multinationals for the top spots looks set to move away from the United States, and sometimes Europe, to take place in Asia, where Asian multinationals have a comparative advantage, and emerging markets, where they will presumably also fare better.

It will however take time for them to develop into genuine multinationals and even more time for them to change the business model for multinationals. What they need are capital and the ability to tap markets where purchasing power is strong. The Asian multinationals have that. Another requirement is to master all the intricacies of running a genuine multinational enterprise — understanding how to accommodate various groups of staff, taking into account their cultural differences; dealing with nasty surprises from judging foreign markets wrongly, etc. Such know-how and experience take time to gain and this will keep the rise of big Asian multinationals at a slow pace at least for some decades to come, except in niche markets.

## CHINDIA

### Comparative Advantages

MasterCard[143] has analysed the two countries' comparative advantages in labour and respective capital productivity, and concludes that in 2004 China's GDP per worker was 55 per cent higher than India's, while India's capital efficiency was 45 per cent higher than China's. That opens the door for allocating production according to these comparative advantages. MasterCard illustrates this with the following sentence, "the US industrial machinery company integrates Indian engineers and Chinese factories seamlessly into a single team. The world-class expertise and low cost Indian software engineers allow the company to run ten or twenty times more the number of computer simulations than they could have done in the US, for instance. Results of these simulations are fed directly to the operations of the Chinese factories for instant feedback and quality improvement." The illustration uses a U.S. company, but Chinese and Indian companies can do the same with any other company and in this context will become even more important when they discover the opportunities for this and learn to cooperate.

In a ten-year horizon this growth machine will drive the global economy by improving productivity, thus counteracting other trends pushing inflation upwards. It will also shift more and more economic activities to Asia.

Not surprisingly MasterCard's prognosis for the two countries' production of manufacturing exports and IT and service exports reveals a growing Chinese specialization in manufacturing and, correspondingly, Indian specialization in services. China's manufacturing exports will grow from 2004 to 2014 by 570 per cent and India's by 600 per cent. For services, India's exports are projected to rise by 1375 per cent and China's by 430 per cent.[144]

In the longer term, things do not look exactly the same. The two countries' comparative advantages may converge, blurring the clear distinction shown above.

The International Monetary Fund (IMF) has analysed China's capital productivity.[145] The analysis discloses that state-owned companies account for one third of manufacturing assets, but their marginal revenue product of capital is approximately 35 per cent of that of domestic private firms. If we work on the assumption that privatization will continue and former state-owned companies in their new role as fully or partly private owned companies converge towards the same capital productivity as existing private firms, the result should be a strong rise in China's overall capital productivity over the next decade.

As for India, the increase in labour supply will continue for several decades, whereas it stops for China in 2015, with the likely outcome that India will start to reap the benefits of abundant labour. The shift in comparative advantages must trigger off another production pattern (interaction) between the two countries. If they manage to integrate economically, which looks likely, they may follow in the footsteps of Europe after integration, that is, specialization inside segments of industry and not between industries. In other words comparative advantages may no longer be decided by factor endowment, but by the fact that the most efficient producer inside a segment will squeeze out the less efficient ones and conquer the market. If so the gains in overall productivity may be even stronger.

The World Bank[146] predicts a slight convergence between China and India towards 2030 with China's share of services in GDP rising from 38 per cent in 2005 to 47 per cent in 2030; India's going up from 50 per cent to 57 per cent. Manufacturing sees a small relative decline in China from 49 per cent to 46 per cent while the share for India is practically constant — 29 per cent in 2005 and 28 per cent in 2030. Firm conclusions are hard to draw, but these figures point in the direction sketched above.

One of the uncertainties with regard to India's prospects is the lack of sufficient infrastructure and political will to build high-class infrastructure capable of supporting India's move into industrialization. PricewaterhouseCoopers (PcW) has analysed the need for investment in infrastructure to facilitate India's growth over the coming decades.[147] There is a need for investment of more than US$500 billion in a short-term horizon from 2007 to 2012. It is not only the construction of new roads, ports, railway lines, and airports that is pressing, but also the upgrading of existing ones no longer serviceable, at least not with current and expected use. A breakdown (in U.S. dollars) discloses the following costs for selected sectors: electricity $167 billion, railways $65 billion, road and highways $92 billion, ports $22 billion, airports $8 billion.

India's public finances are not in a healthy state and PwC suggests public-private partnerships, including domestic and foreign investors, as a way to fund the projects.

## Outsourcing

Outsourcing has always been a part of international economics and international business albeit for many years under another name, that is, international division of labour. It is sometimes forgotten in the debate that outsourcing is part of international trade and investment and takes place because it increases global welfare through higher production. It is not some kind of moonlighting scheme where somebody under obscure conditions moves jobs around from country to country. McKinsey[148] calculated the *benefits* for the United States of outsourcing and came to the conclusions that:

- For every dollar of corporate spending outsourced to India, the U.S. economy captures more than three quarters of the benefit and gains as much as $1.14 in return
- far from being a zero-sum game, offshoring creates mutual benefits
- the Bureau of Labor Statistics at the beginning of the decade predicted a job gain of 22 million in the United States from 2000 to 2010, mainly in business services, health care, social services, transportation, and communications

What is new over the last decades is the sheer volume and speed of outsourcing, not the idea and/or principle itself. On top of that comes outsourcing, not only controlled and initiated because of cost advantages, but because of performance level comparisons. This is, in fact, a sort of cost-benefit applied to outsourcing and not only has economic, but also political repercussions. When sectors previously sheltered against international division of labour suddenly become a target, many white-collar workers, used to looking at outsourcing as something that does not affect them, suddenly realized that international division of labour encircles all kinds of jobs, including theirs. Economic globalization means that not only jobs in a classical or conventional sense are global. Performances have joined this category because skilled people are found all over the world.[149]

Economist Alan Blinder wrote in 2007[150] that "offshoring may be the biggest political issue in economics for a generation" and "In some recent research, I estimated that 30 million to 40 million U.S. jobs are potentially offshorable. These include scientists, mathematicians and editors on the high end and telephone operators, clerks and typists on the low end."

This shift away from outsourcing dominated by cost savings and instead focusing more on comparing performances is also illustrated in an analysis by McKinsey.[151] The conclusion is that developments in respective wage levels have narrowed the wage differences even if they are still substantial, but when differences in productivity and transport costs — with oil prices expected to continue being at a much higher level than they were over preceding decades — are brought in, the cost advantages are eroded. Outsourcing leads to overhead considerations for management and coordination. This aspect is often forgotten although it may make or break outsourcing.

With the rise of China and India, two questions present themselves that press for answers: what is the future of these two countries in attracting outsourcing, and/or will they start to outsource to developing countries as they gain weight in the global economy, possibly influencing their labour costs and overheads in an upward direction? This debate is a revamp of the one around Japan's Asian operations, which no one questions today, but which capitalized on better work organization than in Chinese or Indian companies.

An analysis of the Indian IT sector gives an idea of what has happened and also a clue about what may happen in the next decade, laying the foundation for future industries. Evalueserve[152] concludes that India in 2016 will have the second largest IT services labour pool in the world after the United States, employing 1.25 and 1.33 times more professionals during that same period. The U.S. IT industry is likely to generate US$810 billion in annual revenue in 2016, with the figure for India at 20 per cent that size. Even more interesting is the observation that the two countries will become inextricably linked with each other and the rest of the world, underlining the implications and strengths of globalization.

Evalueserve[153] estimates the global market for KPO (knowledge processing outsourcing) to be US$17 billion in 2010, rising from only US$1.29 billion in 2003. Seventy-one per cent of this will go to India. The important subsectors are banking, securities, and industry research services; contract research organizations and bio-pharmaceutical services; and data management, mining, searching, and analytics. In general KPO outsourcing seems to follow the IT-sector, with a time lag of ten years, and instrumental in the future growth for outsourcing in KPO may be the Western small- and medium-sized companies where 10 per cent of ten million companies might benefit even in the short run from outsourcing of KPO.[154]

China is sporting a high growth rate as receiver of outsourcing in IT and software services, but from a low level, and Chinese industry seems to suffer from certain weaknesses, in particular, too high a fragmentation, depriving corporations of size and expertise to appear as a real threat to established receivers such as India. The impediments for China, however, can be overcome, and the Indian software industry is keenly aware of the potential from rising Chinese competition.[155]

It is likely that outsourcing of labour-intensive production will start to take place and on a considerable scale among developing countries, instead of from developed to developing countries. The first wave, already visible, shifts low cost manufacturers to Asian countries other than China.[156] In a second wave, outsourcing to countries in Africa with rising populations, such as Morocco and Nigeria, may emerge as one of many new trends in global trade and investment. Towards 2040–50 Africa will be the only continent with a rising population and it is difficult to escape the observation that this will shift at least some of the competitive parameters, driving outsourcing away from Asia to Africa.[157] India and maybe China will continue to be the powerhouses and no African country will have economic clout and population size to match these two countries, but there will certainly be a window for labour-intensive production and services shifting to Africa[158] — and elsewhere, perhaps some of it even back to Europe and the United States.

Preliminary answers to the two questions point towards China with Taiwan and India as establishing themselves more firmly in the coming decades in the higher end of IT outsourcing, in particular, KPO, and China shedding some of its labour-intensive production to other countries.

## China-India — Differences

In discussing the main differences between the two countries, this study concentrates on three major points.

- In China the government or provincial governments often assume the role of showing entrepreneurship, taking initiatives, launching projects, and, in fact, standing behind many investments down to the level of villages and local communities. In India it is the private sector, individuals, and civil society showing entrepreneurship while the government is inefficient and frequently constitutes a barrier for entrepreneurship. Entrepreneurship in India is almost always started as a bottom-up process; in China it is the other way round.

- China has traditionally been less open to outside influence than India, which explains why foreign stimulus and impact on China's development have come in a more organized way via foreign direct investment, whereas India holding back on foreign direct investment relies instead on the private sector to channel new ideas from abroad into the Indian society.

- China has embraced its diasporas that can be estimated at approximately 50 million people or even more, and allowed them to exercise a role in promoting entrepreneurship inside China. Until recently India took a much more reluctant attitude towards its diasporas, shunning the large positive repercussions a closer relationship would bring to the economy. But this is changing very rapidly in that Indian diasporas in the United States and elsewhere have a fundamental role in creating companies with operations back in India.

## PRIVATE CONSUMPTION

### Role of Private Consumption

Over the last two decades the share of private consumption in GDP has been declining for China, India, and most Southeast Asian countries. Measured in absolute terms, however, private consumption has actually gone up as their strong growth translates even a smaller share into higher absolute figures.[159]

From 2015 the picture starts to get more uncertain. A number of factors (less abundant production factors, lower growth in the United States, Europe, and Japan, and higher prices for energy and raw materials) will influence growth in a downward direction, albeit still at a high level. In China demographics will shift to favour a lower savings rate (higher consumption), while India will probably stay for one or two decades more on a high savings rate, as will be the case for some Southeast Asian countries, in particular, Vietnam. Taken together, these factors warrant a preliminary, albeit somewhat uncertain, conclusion that total consumption in absolute figures will continue to grow at a high level even if its share of GDP may be uncertain.

Both before and after 2015, the composition of consumption will change and change quite dramatically. There are three determining factors: the emergence of a much larger middle class,[160] the composition of consumption, including goods versus services, and the ageing population.

The World Bank[161] has calculated that the global middle class' share of global income in 2000 was 13.8 per cent and will be 14 per cent in 2030 — no increase, the same! But its distribution is completely different. In 2000, the middle class in developing countries sat on 7 per cent of total global income while the corresponding figure in 2030 will be 12.9 per cent, an increase in share of 84 per cent. In 2000 only 13 per cent of the global middle class was Chinese and the figures for India and Southeast Asia are even smaller. China in 2030 will account for 38 per cent, equal to 361 million people in the global middle class, while India will account for 6 per cent, equal to around 55 million people.[162]

Similarly the share of services reflecting higher purchasing power and living standard will go up in China from 36 per cent in 2000 to 55 per cent in 2030, and in India from 46 per cent to 58 per cent. These figures confirm that China is catching up with India in the services sector as both countries will show a share of services in private consumption in 2030 in the mid-fifties range.

A special consumption pattern will emerge in Asia, driven by the large number of people above sixty-five years of age, demanding health care, personal care, and facilities specially designed for people in that age group.

It still remains to be seen how the "new" generation of "old" people in Asia will act in the consumer market, but it may well be one of the strongest growing markets after 2015, imposing structural changes on the industrial sector which is not yet geared to this market and not at all to its size. The caveat is that the numbers are staggering, but it is uncertain how large the purchasing power of the old generation will be actually.

## Brands

China and India are predicted to be the most important markets for luxury goods by around 2020, with approximately 100 million consumers asking for luxury goods in China, India, and Southeast Asia. Sixty-five per cent of the global demand for luxury goods will be from Asia, of which 30 per cent points to China.[163]

It is therefore no wonder that a number of studies[164] have looked into the possibility of Asia developing its own brands, thereby becoming a trendsetter in global consumption. The sheer size of its purchasing power and the number of people in Asia point in that direction, even if many, maybe most of them, are still attracted by the "Western" consumption style. Nevertheless Asian brands have emerged globally and in Asia: Toyota, Sony, Samsung, Honda, LG, Acer, Oriental, Daikin, Singapore Airlines, etc, but very few are from China (Haier maybe) or India.

The decisive element may well be the ability of Asia to link multinationals with a new pattern of consumption. Japan, Korea, and Singapore understood this a while back, while China, India, and Indonesia are still searching.

Western multinationals are already shifting their outlook on Asian countries away from seeing them primarily as places for outsourcing and cheap manufacturing, to viewing them as growing and dynamic markets. Asian multinationals will realize the potential of the home market — not always obvious when expanding abroad. In 2008 China was already the world's largest market for television sets and cellphones and the second largest for automobiles and personal computers.[165]

A recent indicator of a new trend shifting the role of trendsetter or initiator of new products and/or new marketing ideas from established industrial countries to emerging economies or even developing countries, is the so-called trickle-up effect.[166] It means that some new technologies or market ideas are either invented or tried first on the market there before being transposed to the market in rich countries. Nokia is reportedly trying a new cellphone technology in Kenya, Western banks are looking at technology used by the Indian bank ICICI in India, Infosys is marketing some new technology first in India, and Danone is developing a new kind of yoghurt in Bangladesh. Renault is selling millions worldwide of the Romania designed and produced Dacia car, and repeating the trick in Maroc with a revamped Russian Lada. The main point is that these inventions are not geared for use in developing countries — full stop, but used there first for later use in developed economies.

There are several reasons for this. Lower costs is definitely one of them. Another is the opportunity to try a new technology in circumstances where a failure will not be a catastrophe for the company. The basic explanation is, however, to be found in the fact that developing countries and/or emerging economies have narrowed the gap in consumer patterns, and in some cases, started to offer themselves as a test bed for new ideas. Not only do they offer realistic market conditions for products to be tested, but they may also eventually emerge as important markets themselves.

If Asia manages such a positive interaction it is likely that Asian brands will emerge as competitors and, eventually, even winners in the global battle for brands, luxury goods, and trendsetters. It is, however, unlikely that this can be done without a strong Asian presence among the leading multinational companies. As discussed above, the growing domestic markets put an asset in the hands of Asia's rising multinational companies, which is up to them to use or lose.

## Segments of Market

Young singles especially in China will constitute a special market.[167] The size of the Chinese urban population in the age group of twenty to thirty-four years and never married will rise from 49.4 million in 2007 to 61.7 million in 2017, corresponding to an annual growth rate of 2.7 per cent. However, the number of young singles, properly speaking, will go up from 5.3 million to 11.7 million with an annual growth rate of 12 per cent. The young, urban singles have grown up in an economic environment where money has rarely been sparse and they have learned to value personal freedom and opportunities to shape their own lifestyle. This is borne out by "self-respect" as the most important thing in their life, followed by "have fun and enjoy life". They can be regarded as the path-breakers or storm troopers in opening new consumption patterns based on lifestyle, identity, education, and thereby in tracing a new course of consumption in China and Asia. Their upbringing makes it possible that it is here that the world will see a combination of Asian and Western lifestyles forging new trends in consumption, be it money oriented or steered by other factors. They are single because they want to be in control of their own lives and that will also be the case for consumption.

Modern women, defined as well educated, professionally employed, and urban based — married or single — constitute likewise a social category of leading consumers.[168] The number of women in China falling into this category will rise from 17.4 million in 2006 to 31.5 million in 2016. This market has for several years been researched in Japan.[169]

The number of DINKs (double-income couple with no kids) is still small in China, but growing from 0.6 million in 2006 to 0.75 million in 2016. Nonetheless they belong to a group of individual-minded persons with purchasing power who are determined to define and choose their own lifestyle.

Online shopping is one of the parameters where few will deny its growing importance, but still fewer are able to predict exactly how and when it will jump from something of a curiosity to a real market mover.

In 2006 online sales in the United States rose 29 per cent to US$146.4 billion, representing 6 per cent of overall retail sales.[170] E-commerce sales in Asia[171] are expected to grow at an annual rate of 23.3 per cent, reaching US$168.7 billion in 2011. As of 2008 Japan is the largest market, followed by

Korea, Taiwan and Hong Kong, but China and India are forecast to move into that position if for no other reason than the sheer size of their populations. Even if their penetration of the Internet may for several years lag behind that of more developed Asian countries such as Japan, the numbers mean that every hike of one percentage point enrols a large number of people, opening the door for e-commerce.

The Chinese search engine, Baidu, regarded by many as the "Chinese Google", serves as an example of how fast new technology enters the market.

A list of what is frequently shopped for online in Asia/Pacific shows books and art, electronic products, CDs/DVDs/VCDs, ladies fashion, airline tickets, and toys and gifts in the top positions. This is not surprising. Online shopping is most attractive where the consumer buys a well defined product without having to make many choices and decisions with regard to tastes and preferences which require seeing or feeling the product. Not only in Asia, but worldwide, this still constitutes one of the most important limits for online shopping. Another limit is the wish of acquiring fresh products such as food and beverages, so a pizza, but not beef, may be bought online. As long as the consumer reacts in this way and so far the penetration into other market segments is not scoring telling points, online shopping will be important, but limited. It will especially not be an active player in the big game of shaping new trends for consumer preferences and tastes.

Another factor apparently limiting online shopping is security, particularly in connection with payments. A large part of online shopping is made because it is convenient, but the full benefit of this convenience is only obtained if payments are made via credit card and a considerable number of shoppers are holding back for fear of security. On average 74 per cent of online shoppers in Asia/Pacific feel that payment security can be improved. For China this percentage is 84 per cent.

These findings underline that social capital and, in the same vein, confidence in the financial system, are decisive elements in furthering online shopping. Irrespective of convenience and savings there are limits to how many people will shop and how much of it they will do unless they are convinced that no greater risk is run than with normal shopping.

## Future Consumption in China and India

McKinsey has analysed the characteristics of the future consumer in China[172] and India[173] and the findings can be summarized thus:

On average, Chinese consumers are willing to pay a premium of 2.5 per cent for a branded product. The premium can be as high as 20 per cent for a product from developed markets. A majority — actually 63 per cent — enter the shop with a shortlist of preferred or known brands. A decreasing share of Chinese consumers is willing to try unfamiliar products. One of the reasons may be lower quality or, rather, fear of lower quality, in particular, for food products that can have dramatic effects as has been seen over recent years with several scandals making the consumer aware of the risk of trying new and unknown products.

Chinese consumers do not favour trendy products, but are more likely to look for functionality such as quality and taste. Value for money in a functional and practical sense seems to be high on the list of characteristics the Chinese consumer is looking for. They are for now still less demanding than Japanese consumers.

Nationalistic feelings do not influence consumer choices very much. In fact the findings show that a majority of consumers do not really know the nationality of the product they purchase, and faced with a choice, they rarely give priority to a product because it is made in China.

The most effective way of catching the attention of the Chinese consumer is by word-of-mouth, that is, recommendations from friends and relatives. Hearing that a particular product has done well and that other people are happy with the way it functions is the number one factor on the list. Television is good at catching the attention and a large majority of consumers say that they had to see a new product advertised on television before they would consider buying it.

This survey confirms that the Chinese market may not be unique, but differs from many other markets, especially those in developed countries, and to enter it, a company needs to take these particularities into account. With time and as the purchasing power of the Chinese consumer rises, it may well be that the characteristics of the market will tend to be like those seen in developed countries.

For a future perspective, these findings underline the fact that for some time the large majority of Chinese consumers will not be adventurous, but will prefer to stick to what is known and what is known to work. The implication for future trends is that the hypothesis of Chinese consumers becoming trendsetters is valid, but this will take time and is not to be expected in the near future.

The Indian consumer market will be steered by a strong upward trend, moving millions out of poverty and favouring the growth of the middle class as well as the segment at the very top end.

In 1985 93 per cent of the population was found in the household income bracket of below US$1,970.[174] These are labelled *deprived*. By 2005 the figure had dropped to 54 per cent and is forecast to account for only 22 per cent in 2025. The middle class is composed of two segments labelled *seekers* (US$4,380–US$10,940) and *strivers* (US$10,940–US$21,820), plus the top end labelled *global* (more than US$21,820).

The total number of those classified as middle class is for 2005 still relatively small, at 5 per cent of the total population, or thirteen million households comprising fifty million people.

In 2025 the number of households in the different categories compared with 2005 is forecast to rise from 1.5 million to 9.5 million for the *global* group, who will be in possession of almost 25 per cent of the nation's total income, and 21 per cent of India's total consumption. *Strivers* will rise in numbers from 2.4 million households to 33.1 million and account for 25 per cent of total consumption. *Seekers* will go up from 10.9 million households to 94.9 million and account for 38 per cent of total consumption, while *aspirers* (a group between *seekers* and *deprived*) will see a modest rise in numbers from 91.3 million to 93.1 million, with a share of consumption equal to 18 per cent. *Deprived* households will fall remarkably in number from 101.1 million to 49.9 million and their share of total consumption will be as small as 3.6 per cent.

The combined result shows a concentration of purchasing power at the top end with the rich and upper end of the middle class managing almost half the consumption, but constituting only 43 million out of 280 million households in India.

It is no wonder then that the structure of consumption is changing very fast: falling for necessities and favouring discretionary spending. Spending on food and beverages and apparel will fall from 61 per cent of total consumption in 1995 to 30 per cent in 2025, whereas spending on health care, entertainment, recreation, etc. will see a strong increase in their share in cities, but not in rural areas.

Taken together these trends for the Chinese and Indian consumer market point towards:

- A strong increase in purchasing power
- A concentration of purchasing power at the upper end of the scale, opening the door for discretionary spending
- A significant reduction of spending on necessities in cities, but not in rural areas

The key message is not surprisingly transformation for both the Chinese and Indian markets and very little trace of the structures we know today will be left. Purchasing power will generate new consumption; technology and changing social structure will change the retail market; and these changes will be boosted by a further integration of China and India into economic globalization.

The middle class will be the driver.[175] Asia's share of the global middle class will almost double, and its share of population in this category, more than triple. Measured in national definitions, this means a phenomenal rise of the Asian middle class is in store. This raises an intriguing question, however, namely, whether the rising middle class in Asia and, in particular, in China and India, will adopt the same values as the existing global middle class predominatly in Western countries. This cannot be taken for granted for several reasons. Cultural and family influence on values and consumption patterns are not the same all over the globe. On top of that comes the fact that the composition of the nationally defined middle class in Asia may not be the same as the case in the Western world.

This may open up competition between China and India about who is going to be the trendsetter and define new tastes and preferences, giving rise to multinationals marketing brands originating in Asia, born out of Asian tastes and consumer patterns. Culturally and traditionally the two countries diverge and it is far from certain — actually the opposite is more likely — that they will adopt the same kind of lifestyle, identity, and consumption pattern seen in the perspective of a trendsetter.

## Distribution Networks

The market and consumer behaviour are, of course, the determining factors, but distribution networks for retailers have for many years had a strong impact, as these serve as the middlemen or, some would say, as barriers between the suppliers, retailers, and ultimate consumer.

For years efforts have been deployed to remove or reduce the number of Japanese middlemen, but to no avail, and with the consequence that distribution networks are inefficient and have negative effects on the economy. Japanese legislation opens the possibility for foreign retailers to establish themselves in Japan, and over the last decades many have entered the market, both in special sectors and in the supermarket/hypermarket segment. An analysis[176] concludes that failures — of which there have been many (the most notorious is Carrefour that entered the market in 2004 and left in 2010, closing eight stores) — are due to wrong strategic management and a lack of understanding of the Japanese market. It looks like domestic operators have been forced to streamline their mode of operation and the wholesale market has seen a consolidation. The analysis expects productivity — estimated at 50 per cent of the U.S. sector about twenty years ago — to have improved, but has no figures to substantiate this view. Even with the progress mentioned above, there are unquestionably large economic gains to be reaped if or when a real breakthrough takes place.

Japanese retailers started a deliberate policy of expanding overseas in the early 1980s in the wake of Japanese tourism, and after some consolidation in the 1990s when the slowdown of Japan's economy also hit tourism abroad, continued this expansion with China as the prime objective, with more than twenty Japanese retailers moving in there.[177] The biggest Japanese supermarket/hypermarket, Aeon Jusco, is focusing on the Japanese home market with 290 branches in Japan, fifteen in China, ten in Thailand, and nine in Malaysia.[178]

China seems to be less caught than Japan and India in terms of customs and traditions standing in the way of opening up the retail market and distribution system. The Chinese legislation opening the market to foreigners date to 2001 and 2004, and despite some tergiversation, the law actually ended up fairly straightforward, with few remaining obstacles. It is estimated that approximately 20 per cent of the retail market is Western-style, with supermarkets and hypermarkets. The "organized" retail market is also spreading into second- and third-tier cities. An illustration is Gome Electrical Appliances Holding, China's leading retailer of household appliances and consumer electronic products, with 305 outlets in 171 second-tier cities, representing more than one third of its total number of stores and generating more than 20 per cent of its total sales.[179] Chinese businesses have taken up the competition with foreign investors, for example, Wumart with 434 retail outlets at the end of 2008, a revenue for 2008 estimated at 9.749 billion yuan, an increase of 24 per cent over that of 2007, and profits of 1.76 billion yuan, up 37.2 per cent from 2007.[180] The biggest Western retailer is Carrefour that beat Walmart to the number-one spot with 116 stores (end of 2008) and a revenue of 39 billion yuan in 2007. Carrefour underlines the fact that one of the keys to its success is the shift from having international managers/staff to employing Chinese managers/staff and its adoption of a Chinese name Jia Le Fu ("happy and lucky family" in English).[181]

The retail business is still a young Chinese business sector and therefore concentrates on building a firm base at home and meeting competition from foreign companies entering the market. Even the biggest Chinese retailer, Bailian Group, is concentrating on the domestic market and consolidating its foothold there. Other Chinese retailers are testing the waters abroad though. The pioneer was Hualin which went to Singapore in 2005, and Suning and

Gome is cautiously starting to invest abroad.[182] There are even rumours about Chinese retailers entering the Japanese market.[183]

In India the policy about opening or not opening the market to foreign retailers has long been a hot potato, and even if some progress has been achieved, it is not unlikely to see fundamental restructuring leaving India more or less in the same category as Japan, with an inefficient distribution system. Only 5 per cent[184] (20 per cent for China) of the retail market is "organized" retailing comparable to Western-style retailing. Foreign investors have been allowed to set up stores, but not multibrand retailers, thus limiting the access to the Indian market. This changed at the beginning of 2009, but, as has been seen in Japan, the rules are one thing, the existing culture and business practices another, so even with a change in legislation there is no certainty that Western-style retailers will get the same share as is the case in the Chinese market.

One study projects nearly 315 hypermarkets in most of tier I and tier II cities by 2011. Organized retailers have percolated fifty to sixty cities/towns, however, not only business practices, but also India's larger rural dependence, constitute an obstacle to expansion.[185] The leading Indian stores are Big Bazaar with 158 retail outlet as of mid-2009,[186] and Reliance Fresh/Reliance Retail, with more than 800 stores.[187]

There can be little doubt that one of the largest political battles to be fought in the coming years will be about reform of the retail market and who is permitted to run distribution networks in the big Asian economies. The Asian corporations are players, but are still holding back with the exception of some big Japanese chains, while the Europeans are moving in, and the United States is not really entering the game.

What all these assets will not do, however, is help Asia find the answers to many of the problems associated with changing track from a conventional type of growth to a more societal type of growth, taking into account the fact that the crucial parameter may switch from economics for the individual, to what is good for the group. This is dealt with in the following chapter.

## Notes

1 Jørgen Ørstrøm Møller, "ASEAN's Relations with the European Union: Obstacles and Opportunities", *Contemporary Southeast Asia* 28, no. 3 (2007).

2 <http://www.aseansec.org/15159.htm>.

3 <http://www.aseansec.org/ASEAN-Charter.pdf>.

4 <http://www.saarc-sec.org/data/agenda/economic/safta/SAFTA%20 AGREEMENT.pdf>.

5 This involves ten ASEAN countries plus China, Korea, Japan, New Zealand, Australia, and India.

6 In my book *European Integration — Sharing of Experiences* from 2008 (Singapore: Institute of Southeast Asian Studies) I have analysed not only the European integration, but also many aspects of integration applicable in general.

7 See Jørgen Ørstrøm Møller, *European Integration — Sharing of Experiences* (Singapore: Institute of Southeast Asian Studies, 2008), pp. 440–41.

8 Uwe Deichmann and Indermit Gill, *The Economic Geography of Regional Integration, Finance and Development*, 45, no. 4, December 2008 <http://www.imf.org/external/pubs/ft/fandd/2008/12/deichmann.htm>.

9 Jacques Servan-Schreiber, *Le Défi Americain* (Paris: Editions Denoel, 1968).

10 Nagesh Kumar, *Relevance of Broader Regional Economic Integration in Asia and a Roadmap, Asia's New Regionalism and Global Role*, edited by Kumar Nagesh, K. Kesavapany, and Yao Chaocheng (RIS and ASEF, 2008).

11 Douglas Brooks, David Roland-Holst, and Fan Zhia, "Growth, Trade and Integration: Long-term Scenarios of Developing Asia", ERD Policy Briefs no. 38 (Manila: Asian Development Bank, 2005) <http://are.berkeley.edu/~dwrh/Docs/PB38-for-upload%20(3).pdf>.

12 S.K. Mohanty and Sanjib Pohit, "Welfare Gains from Regional Economic Integration in Asia: ASEAN+ 3 or EAS", in *Asia's New Regionalism and Global Role*, edited by Kumar Nagesh, K. Kesavapany, and Yao Chaocheng (RIS and ASEF, 2008).

13 Neither Asians nor Europeans should fool themselves: regional security cooperation has only been possible because of U.S. commitment.

14 Banks and telecommunications carriers in Asia will still propagate rivalry between nations.

15 M. Baxter and M.A. Kouparitas, "Determinants of Business Cycles Co-movement: A Robustness Analysis", *Journal of Monetary Economics* 81, no. 1 (2005).

16 The International Monetary Fund, *World Economic Outlook* (October 2001) <http://www.imf.org/external/Pubs/FT/weo/2001/02/pdf/chapter2.pdf>.

17 It is assumed that integration does not lead to specialization among member countries, which makes it less likely that business cycles move in synchronization as international repercussions hit randomly. This is one of the reasons that the United Kingdom (specializing in oil and financial services) had never really been attracted by the single currency and that economists generally speak of a core EURO-zone comprising Germany, France, The Netherlands, Belgium, and Luxembourg, plus sometimes Austria — all of them more manufacturing economies competing with one another.

18 ABMI, see chairman's press release published by ASEAN in August 2003, available at <http://www.aseansec.org/15030.htm>, plus an online review available at <http://asianbondsonline.adb.org/regional/asean_plus_three_asian_bond_market_initiatives/overview.php>.

19 <http://en.wikipedia.org/wiki/Trans-Asian_Railway>; <http://www.unescap. org/ttdw/common/TIS/TAR/annex1_corrected_e_14nov06.pdf>; <http://news. bbc.co.uk/2/hi/asia-pacific/7719404.stm>.

20 Philippe Crist, "Greenhouse Gas Emissions Reduction Potential from International Shipping", Discussion Paper no. 2009–11 (OECD Joint Transport Research Center, May 2009) <http://www.internationaltransportforum.org/jtrc/ DiscussionPapers/DP200911.pdf>.

21 <http://www.unescap.org/TTDW/index.asp?MenuName=AsianHighway>.

22 Paul Breeze, "ASEAN Region Powers Toward Interconnection", *Power Engineering International* (October 2008) <http://pepei.pennnet.com/display_ article/344418/17/ARTCL/none/none/1/ASEAN-region-powers-toward- interconnection/>.

23 <http://www.aseansec.org/20918.htm>.

24 A single currency, meaning that at least for some Asian countries there is only one currency, looks a long shot, while a common currency circulating alongside national currencies seems a better bet.

25 In manufacturing equipment the same phenomenon applies, although less visibly. The Japanese, Korean, and Taiwanese, with their incremental improvements on European or American processes were among the first to benefit from science embedded in returnee scientists to those countries. This led to their having a global competitive edge, magnified by a larger base in Asia.

26 <http://en.ce.cn/Business/Macro-economic/200706/12/t20070612_11713604. shtml>.

27 "Patented in China, the Present and Future State of Innovation in China" (Thomson Reuters, 2008).

28 "Rising in the East", *The Economist*, January 2009 <http://www.economist. com/business/displaystory.cfm?story_id=12863581>.

29 OECD, *Compendium of Patent Statistics* (Paris, 2007).

30 <http://www.wipo.int/ipstats/en/statistics/patents/patent_report_2007.html>.

31 On 28 January 2009 WIPO reported that China's telecommunication company, Huawei, was the top patent seeker for 2008; *South China Morning Post*, "Huawei is Top International Patent Seeker" <http://www.scmp. com/portal/site/SCMP/menuitem.2af62ecb329d3d7733492d9253a0a0a0/ ?vgnextoid=a9194c59f781f110VgnVCM100000360a0a0aRCRD&ss=Tec hnology&s=Business>.

32 Patent applications are published eighteen months after priority filing, which means that these figures are only available with a time lag of two years.

33 Bob Stembridge, "Made in China — A Glimpse into the Future of Patent Information" (Thomson Reuters, July 2008) <http://scientific.thomsonreuters. com/news/2008-07/8464838/>.

34 <http://www.iqcomparisonsite.com/Nobels.aspx>.

35 Joff Wild, "Ever Increasing Circles: Thomson Scientific Patent Focus Report, 2008" <http://scientific.thomsonreuters.com/news/2008-01/8430053/>.

36 *Thomson Reuters*, "Patented in China, the Present and Future State of Innovation in China", 2008.

37 Ibid.

38 Ibid.

39 OECD, *Compendium of Patent Statistics*.

40 Ibid.

41 Another source looking into the link between patents and future R&D and innovation is OECD, *Science, Technology and Industry Outlook* (Paris: OECD, 2008).

42 OECD, *Compendium of Patent Statistics*. Also summarized and discussed in *L'Expanison*, no. 732, July–August 2008.

43 Many of these studies and analyses are difficult to compare because they look at patents and inventions in different contexts and do not always specify precisely what they look at. It is, however, noteworthy that *L'Expansion* (Ibid.) in analysing the figures come to the same conclusion as OECD, namely that the strong rise in applications from China and India will see these two countries surging ahead. *L'Expansion* concludes that China will surpass Europe in 2020 and India will do so in 2030.

44 See figures later in this chapter revealing shifting preferences among Chinese and Indian students on whether to stay on in the United States or go home.

45 Vivek Wadwha et al., "Seeing Through Preconceptions: A Deeper Look at China and India", *Issues in Science and Technology* (Spring 2007) <http://www.issues.org/23.3/wadhwa.html>.

46 William R. Kerr and William T. Lincoln, "The Supply Side of Innovation: H1-B Visa Reforms and Ethnic Invention", Harvard Business School Working Paper 09-005, December 2008 <http://casi.ssc.upenn.edu/system/files/NBER_WP_14592.pdf>; and Ajay Agrawal, Devesh Kapur, and John McHale, "Brain Drain or Brain Bank? The Impact of Skilled Emigration on Poor-Country Innovation", NBER Working Paper Series no. 14592, December 2008 <http://casi.ssc.upenn.edu/system/files/NBER_WP_14592.pdf>.

47 Vivek Wadhwa, "A Reverse Brain Drain", *Issues in Science and Technology* 25, no. 3 (Spring 2009).

48 European Patent Office, "Scenarios for the Future: How might IP regimes evolve by 2025? What global legitimacy might such regimes have?" (Muenchen, 2007) <http://documents.epo.org/projects/babylon/eponet.nsf/0/63A726D28B589B5BC12572DB00597683/$File/EPO_scenarios_bookmarked.pdf>.

49 Tom Nicholas, "Innovation Lessons from the 1930s", *McKinsey Quarterly* (December 2008) <http://www.mckinseyquarterly.com/Innovation_lessons_from_the_1930s_2266>.

50 OECD, *Science, Technology and Industry Outlook* (Paris: OECD, 2008).

51 Ibid.

52 Japan follows the OECD average.

53 OECD, *Science, Technology and Industry.*

54 *Wipo Magazine*, 4/2007, "National Strategies and Policies for Innovation: A View from China and India" <http://www.wipo.int/wipo_magazine/en/2007/04/article_0007.html>.

55 Marc Einstein from Frost and Sullivan helped in formulating this paragraph.

56 <http://www.nytimes.com/2006/02/26/business/26disks.html>.

57 *Yahoo News*, 19 February 2008 <http://news.yahoo.com/s/ap/20080219/ap_on_bi_ge/japan_toshiba>.

58 Personal or Pacific Digital Cellular. A Japanese standard for digital mobile telephony in the 800 MHz and 1500 MHz bands. To avoid the previous problem of lack of compatibility between the differing types of earlier analogue mobile phones in Japan (i.e. NTT type and U.S. developed TACS type), digital mobile phones have been standardized under PDC. In the case of the PDC standard, primarily six-channel TDMA (Time Division Multiple Access) technology is applied. PDC, however, is a standard unique to Japan, which renders such phone units incompatible with devices which adopt the more worldwide prevalent GSM standard. Nevertheless, digitalization under the standard enables ever smaller and lighter mobile phones, which in turn has spurred market expansion. As a result, over 93 per cent of all mobile phones in Japan are now digital; Agilent Technologies <http://wireless.agilent.com/dictionary/p.shtml>.

59 <http://www.networkworld.com/news/2007/102607-arguments-cdma-gsm.html?nwwpkg=50arguments>.

60 <http://www.edu.cn/20060111/3170189.shtml>; <http://www.technewsworld.com/story/39233.html>.

61 Universal Mobile Telecommunications System.

62 Evolution, Data Optimized.

63 Chapter 2.

64 Unfortunately there is also a sinister side to this research, opening possibilities for terrorists and criminals to exercise some kind of remote control of other persons.

65 It is forecast that China will have the capability to operate a manned space station in 2020; Dwayne A. Day, "The New Path to Space: India and China Enter the Game", *Space Review*, 13 October 2008 <http://www.thespacereview.com/article/1231/1>.

66 Isabelle Sourbès-Verger and Denis Borel, *Un empire très céleste: la Chine à la conquête de l'espace* (Paris: Dunod, 2008).

67 Steven Berner, "Japan's Space Program, A Fork in the Road", *RAND Technical Report* <http://www.rand.org/pubs/technical_reports/2005/RAND_TR184.pdf>.

68 Setsuko Kamiya, "Japan A Low-key Player in Space Race", *Japan Times*, 30 June 2009 <http://search.japantimes.co.jp/cgi-bin/nn20090630i1.html>.

69 Sourbès-Verger and Borel, *Un empire très céleste.*

70 For a short description, see Day, "The New Path to Space".

71  <http://news.xinhuanet.com/english/2009-01/19/content_10684404.htm>.

72  The other three systems operating or near full operational activity are the United States' Global Positioning System (GPS), the European Union's Galileo Positioning System, and Russia's Global Navigation Satellite System (GLONASS).

73  Day, "The New Path to Space".

74  U. Sankar, et al., "Economic Analysis of Indian Space Program: An Exploratory Study" (Chennai: Madras School of Economics, November 2003).

75  The K.R. Narayanan Orations 1994 to 2006 <http://epress.anu.edu.au/narayanan/mobile_devices/pt01.html>; contains one chapter (10) by K. Kasturirangan on India's Space Enterprise — A Case Study, in "Strategic Thinking and Planning" <http://epress.anu.edu.au/narayanan/mobile_devices/ch10.html>. Other short sources are *Newsweek*, 27 October 2008, "Space You Can Use"; and *Asia Times* online, "It's All Go for Moon-struck India", 22 October 2008 <http://www.atimes.com/atimes/South_Asia/JJ22Df02.html>.

76  Day, "The New Path to Space".

77  Stratfor, "South Korea: The Korea Space Launch Vehicle", 16 August 2009.

78  Two recent studies have analysed the impact of mobile phones on productivity (1) UNCTAD information economy report 2007/08 <http://r0.unctad.org/ecommerce/ecommerce_en/ier07_en.htm> (2) a study on Africa by the Centre for Economic Policy Research, the Department for International Development, and Vodafone Group <http://www.vodafone.com/start/media_relations/news/group_press_releases/2005/press_release09_03.html>.

79  Robert C. Allen, *The British Industrial Revolution in Global Perspective* (Cambridge: Cambridge University Press, 2009).

80  See, for example, Clay Shirky, *Here Comes Everybody. The Power of Organizing Without Organizations* (London: Penguin, 2008); and Charles Leadbeater, *We-think: Mass Innovation, Not Mass Production, The Power of Mass Creativity* (London: Portal Books, 2008).

81  <http://www.openspectrum.info/>.

82  Luis Enriquez, Stefan Schmitgen, and George Sun, "The True Value of Mobile Phones to Developing Markets", *The McKinsey Quarterly* (February 2007) <http://www.mckinseyquarterly.com/article_print.aspx?L2=22&L3=78&ar=1917>.

83  World Bank, Information and Communication for Development, "Extending Research and Increasing Impact" (Washington DC, 2009) <http://web.worldbank.org/WBSITE/EXTERNAL/TOPICS/EXTINFORMATIONANDCOMMUNICATIONANDTECHNOLOGIES/EXTIC4D/0,,contentMDK:22229759~menuPK:5870649~pagePK:64168445~piPK:64168309~theSitePK:5870636,00.html>.

84  European Patent Office, "Scenarios for the Future", p. 28.

85  Princeton University, "News at Princeton, Science and Technology", 15 February 2008 <http://www.princeton.edu/main/news/archive/S20/31/01G52/index.xml?section=science>.

86  The December 2008 issue of *McKinsey Quarterly* contains an article by Tom

Nicholas ("Innovation Lessons from the 1930s") saying that an economic recession opens up tremendous opportunities for companies with cash and strategic outlook. The prime example is DuPont's discovery of neoprene (synthetic rubber), one of the twentieth century's major innovations. Hewlett-Packard and Polaroid were born during the depression; <http://www.mckinseyquarterly. com/Innovation_lessons_from_the_1930s_2266>.

87  Matthhew Lynn, "Five Opportunities to Help Beat World Recession", *Bloomberg*, 16 December 2008 <http://www.bloomberg.com/apps/news?pid=20601039&s id=aS98ereBggE8&refer=home#>.

88  Yongnian Zhen and Minjia Chen, "China Plans to Build an Innovative State", Briefing Series, issue no. 9, China House, University of Nottingham, China Policy Institute, June 2006 <http://www.nottingham.ac.uk/shared/shared_cpi/ documents/policy_papers/Briefing_9_China_Innovative_State.pdf>.

89  Shujie Yao, "Building a Strong Nation: How does China Perform in Science and Technology?" Briefing Series, issue no. 15, China House, University of Nottingham, China Policy Institute, June 2006, ibid.

90  Available at <http://english.gov.cn/2006-02/09/content_183426.htm>.

91  INSEAD and CII, Global Innovation Index 2008–2009, INSEAD <http://www. nottingham.ac.uk/shared/shared_cpi/documents/policy_papers/Briefing_15_ China_Sci_Tech.pdf  http://www.insead.edu/facultyresearch/centres/elab/gii/ GII%20Final%200809.pdf>.

92  It is difficult to understand the following large changes in the course of one year: Korea from 19th to 6th position, France from 5th to 19th position, and Sweden from 12th to 3rd. As most elements steering innovation should, by intuition, be long-term factors, changes should be small or even incremental and not large. The explanation may be that they interviewed or surveyed key people, so the output depends on surveyed population.

93  Barring the Middle East, regarded as a petroeconomy.

94  *Key Indicators: Inequality in Asia* (Asian Development Bank, 2007) <http://www. adb.org/Documents/Books/Key_Indicators/2007/pdf/rt15.pdf>.

95  Asia is on its way, but prudently so, with the value of equity and debt markets rising from 50 per cent in 2003 to 140 per cent of GDP in 2008; "Asia's Future and the Financial Crisis", *McKinsey Quarterly* (December 2008) <http:// e.mckinseyquarterly.com/W0RH00122B4E3B6C606092E5D935B0>.

96  Robert Dekle, "Understanding Japanese Savings, Does Ageing Matter?" 2004 <http://books.google.com/books?id=pIR-m6pwj_IC&pg=PA6-IA2&lpg=PA6- IA2&dq=japan+savings+rate&source=web&ots=0TP6qfjiFI&sig=YgPuxSdvY HJS2mVCQcFhQMrVVsg#PPA6-IA3,M1>.

97  See, for example, *The Chinese Academy of Social Sciences* (Cass) *Yearbook*, December 2008, on social development (blue book) reviewed at <http://www. scmp.com/portal/site/SCMP/menuitem.2af62ecb329d3d7733492d9253a0a0a0/ ?vgnextoid=fc00a60d88b3e110VgnVCM100000360a0a0aRCRD&ss=Chi na&s=News>.

98 See also the discussion in Chapter 5 on pensions.

99 Li Peilin and Chen Guangjin, "China's Social Development Meeting New Challenges", in *Blue Book of China's Society*, edited by Rui Xin, Lu Xueyi and Li Peilin (Beijing: Social Sciences Academic Press, 2009), pp. 1–15; Zhang Shifei and Tang Jun, "Urban and Rural Subsistence Security System: New Steps and New Leaps", ibid., pp. 143–60; Wang Fayun and Li Yu, "New Progress on Old-Age Insurance", ibid., pp. 161–71; Edward Gu, "The Direction and Choice of China's New Health Care Reforms", ibid., pp. 185–98.

100 China Development Research Foundation, quoted in "China Needs $839b for Social Welfare by 2020", 26 February 2009 <http://www2.chinadaily.com.cn/china/2009-02/26/content_7517265.htm>.

101 According to the Chinese government (official website posted 11 June 2009), <http://english.gov.cn/2009-06/11/content_1337978.htm>, the statistics for social welfare in China at the end of 2008 look like this: About 218.91 million Chinese (an increase of 17.54 million over a year) were covered by an urban basic pension insurance system. Urban basic medical insurance covered 318.22 million people in 2008, up 95.11 million from the previous year. The urban basic medical insurance and pension systems are part of China's preliminary social security system, which also includes work injury insurance, unemployment insurance, and maternity insurance. The unemployment insurance system covered 124 million people in 2008, up 7.55 million from 2007. The work injury insurance system covered 137.87 million people in 2008, up 16.14 million year-on-year. Maternity insurance covered 92.54 million people, up 14.79 million from 2007. The sums paid to each individual may be small, however. All rural citizens should by 2020 have access to health care on the basis of a system starting as a pilot project in 2009; Xinhua, "China to Set Up Health Care for All Rural Residents", 6 August 2009 <http://news.xinhuanet.com/english/2009-08/06/content_11838555.htm>.

102 Sanjeev Sanyal, *The Indian Renaissance* (Singapore: World Scientific, 2008), p. 150.

103 Figures may not be totally comparable, but I have chosen to live with that in view of the obvious advantage of getting the newest data albeit from different sources, instead of relying on one source with the drawback that figures would go back several years.

104 Leonard K. Cheng and Zihui Ma, "China's Outwards FDI: Past and Future" <http://www.nber.org/books_in_progress/china07/cwt07/cheng.pdf>.

105 <http://bh2.mofcom.gov.cn/aarticle/chinanews/200801/20080105344904.html>.

106 <http://dipp.nic.in/fdi_statistics/india_fdi_Oct2007.pdf>.

107 <http://www.indiaprwire.com/businessnews/20070316/21445.htm>.

108 The Economist Intelligence Unit, "World Prospects for Investment to 2011" <http://www.cpii.columbia.edu/pubs/documents/WorldInvestmentProspectsto2011.pdf>.

109 Ibid.

110 Eurostat Pocketbooks, *European Union Foreign Direct Investment Yearbook 2008* (Luxembourg: Office for the Official Publications of the European Communities, 2008), Tables 1.1 and 2.1 <http://epp.eurostat.ec.europa.eu/cache/ITY_OFFPUB/KS-BK-08-001/EN/KS-BK-08-001-EN.PDF>.

111 Masahiro Kawai, "Overview of FDIs: The US, Europe, Japan, and Emerging Asia", 13 November 2009 <http://www.tcf.or.jp/data/20071113-14_Masahiro_Kawai-PPT.pdf>.

112 Rabin Hattari and Ramkishen S. Rajan, "Sources of FDI flows to Developing Asia", ADBI Working Paper 117, Tokyo, Asian Development Bank Institute, September 2008 <http://www.adbi.org/files/2008.10.wp117.fdi.flows.developing.asia.pdf>.

113 <http://news.softpedia.com/news/Lenovo-Goes-to-India-And-Mexico-61196.shtml>.

114 "Lenovo's Shares Post 26.6 pc Jump on Talks of Major Brazilian Acquisition", *South China Morning Post*, 11 December 2008 <http://www.scmp.com/portal/site/SCMP/menuitem.2af62ecb329d3d7733492d9253a0a0a0/?vgnextoid=4e0c155c2912e110VgnVCM100000360a0a0aRCRD&ss=Technology&s=Business>.

115 <http://www.rediff.com/money/2006/oct/20tata.htm>.

116 The World Bank, Development Economics Prospects Group, "Global Growth and Distribution: Are China and India Reshaping the World?", Policy Research Working Paper 4392, November 2007 <http://www-wds.worldbank.org/external/default/WDSContentServer/IW3P/IB/2007/11/12/000158349_20071112111936/Rendered/PDF/wps4392.pdf>.

117 Elvis Picardo, "Dollar Decline Reshuffles Deck of Titans", Reuters, 13 March 2008 <http://www.reuters.com/article/reutersEdge/idUSDIS3594112008 0313>.

118 The Boston Consulting Group, "The 2008 BCG 100 New Global Challengers, How Top Companies from Rapidly Developing Economies are Changing the World", December 2007 <http://www.bcg.com/impact_expertise/publications/files/New_Global_Challengers_Feb_2008.pdf>.

119 The thirteen are composed of one each from Chile, Egypt, Hungary, and Poland, two from Malaysia and Thailand respectively, and three from Turkey. Due to classification of countries, Korea is not included.

120 The first major study was made by Eika Yamaguchi, "Recent Characteristics of Royalties and License Fees in Japan's Balance of Payments", Bank of Japan Working Paper Series, No. 04-E5, March 2004.

121 It is interesting that Japan's only deficit is with the rest of Asia for copyrights and it is growing.

122 "Japan's Balance of Payments for 2007", BOJ Reports and Research Papers, Tokyo, International Department of Bank of Japan, July 2008.

123 In 1965, individuals owned the majority of U.S. stocks, with 84 per cent; only

16 per cent was in the hands of institutions/funds. In 2005, institutions owned 67 per cent and individuals 33 per cent; Lawrence and Weber, *Business & Society*, 12th ed. (2008), Figure 15.1.

124 Stjin Claessens, Simeon Djankov, and Larry Lang, "Who Controls East Asian Corporations?" The World Bank, Policy Research Paper 2054, February 1999 <http://www-wds.worldbank.org/external/default/WDSContentServer/IW3P/IB/2000/02/24/000094946_99031911113874/Rendered/PDF/multi_page.pdf>. Also Stjin Claessens, Simeon Djankov, and Larry H.P. Lang, "The Separation of Ownership and Control in East Asian Corporations", *Journal of Financial Economics*, October 2000.

125 In particular recalling the paragraph about savings on p. 196.

126 Tarun Khana, *Billions of Entrepreneurs: How China and India Are Reshaping Their Future and Yours* (Boston: Harvard Business Press, 2008). Summary available at <http://hbswk.hbs.edu/item/5766.html>.

127 See Chapter 4.

128 To be flexible, decidedly an asset in today's global environment of business, a company's infrastructure needs be like Velcro, cohesive and workable when in place, but capable of being easily rearranged when circumstances and strategy call for it. But developing a Velcro-like infrastructure requires formidable mastery of the basics; Joseph L. Bower, "Building the Velcro-Organization", Ivey Management Services, November/December 2003 <http://www.iveybusinessjournal.com/view_article.asp?intArticle_ID=451>.

129 See, for example, Frank T. Piller and Michael M. Tseng, eds., *Handbook of Research in Mass Customization and Personalization: Strategies and Concepts/Applications and Cases* (Singapore: World Scientific, 2009).

130 See, for example, C.K. Prahalad and V. Ramaswany, *The Future of Competition: Co-Creating Unique Value with Consumers* (Boston: Harvard Business Press, 2004).

131 <http://www.threadless.com/catalog>.

132 <http://trendwatching.com/briefing/>.

133 Prahalad, C.K. and M.S. Krishnan, *The New Age of Innovation: Driving Co-Created Value Through Global Networks* (New York: McGraw Hill Books, 2008); and Prahalad, C.K. and V. Ramaswany, *The Future of Competition*.

134 See Jørgen Ørstrøm Møller, *The Future European Model: Economic Internationalization and Cultural Decentralization* (Westport: Praeger, 1995), pp. 17–23.

135 Coined by two researchers in 1999, see <http://en.wikipedia.org/wiki/Product_service_system>. For a short overview, in Danish, see "Det faste forhold som forretningsmdoel", *Mandag Morgen*, 29 January 2007.

136 Møller, *The Future European*.

137 <http://www.boeing.com/commercial/goldcare/index.html>.

138 <http://www.unitedbit.com/strategic-innovation-how-canon-radically-refined-the-customer-base/>.

139 <http://www.ecopeland.com/literature/eCopeland/Companyportrait_0108_E_0.pdf>.
140 <http://www.danfoss.com/North_America/BusinessAreas/Refrigeration+and+Air+Conditioning/Retail+Care.htm>.
141 *The Economist*, "A Bigger World", 18 September 2008 <http://www.economist.com/surveys/displaystory.cfm?story_id=12080751>.
142 <http://www.pc.ibm.com/us/think/thinkvantagetech/rescuerecovery.html>.
143 MasterCard "Insights", third quarter 2005.
144 These projections may not be fulfilled as shifts in the market make the picture less rosy than when they were originally made.
145 "Underutilized Capital", *Finance & Development*, June 2007.
146 The World Bank, Development Economics Prospects Group, "Global Growth and Distribution: Are China and India Reshaping the World?" Policy Research Working Paper 4392, November 2007 <http://www-wds.worldbank.org/external/default/WDSContentServer/IW3P/IB/2007/11/12/000158349_20071112111936/Rendered/PDF/wps4392.pdf>.
147 PricewaterhouseCoopers, "Infrastructure in India, A Vast Land of Construction Opportunity", November 2008 <http://www.pwc.co.uk/pdf/india_infrastructure_construction_opportunity.pdf>.
148 *Indiatimes*, "Infotech", 10 January 2004 <http://infotech.indiatimes.com/articleshow/478100.cms>; and "Exploding the Myths of Offshoring", *McKinsey Quarterly*, July 2004 <http://www.mckinseyquarterly.com/Exploding_the_myths_of_offshoring_1453>.
149 Some may recall the scene from *The Simpson's*, where the boss explains to the worried workers that "your job is safe, only it will be done by somebody else".
150 *Washington Post*, 6 May 2007 <http://www.washingtonpost.com/wp-dyn/content/article/2007/05/04/AR2007050402555_pf.html>.
151 "Time to Rethink Offshoring", *McKinsey Quarterly*, September 2008 <http://www.mckinseyquarterly.com/Operations/Outsourcing/Time_to_rethink_offshoring_2190>.
152 Evalueserve, "India's Role in the Globalization of the IT Industry", July 2008.
153 Evalueserve, "India's Knowledge Process Outsourcing (KPO) Sector: Origin, Current State, and Future Directions", 5 July 2007; and <http://www.evalueserve.com/Media-And-Reports/HTML-Press-Releases/Recent/India_to_Account_for_Global_KPO_Revenues.aspx>.
154 Ibid. See also Evalueserve, "The Future of Knowledge Process Outsourcing", 18 April 2007.
155 "Can China Compete in IT Services", *McKinsey Quarterly*, February 2005 <http://www.mckinseyquarterly.com/High_Tech/Software/Can_China_compete_in_IT_services_1556?gp=1> and <http://news.cnet.com/Will-China-dominate-outsourcings-future/2008-1022_3-5668199.html>.
156 This is the case for Vietnam seeing Chinese investment — outsourcing

— take place. See, for example, <http://www.taipeitimes.com/News/worldbiz/archives/2007/10/09/2003382393>.

157 Africa will see its population rise from about 700 million people in 1995 to a little above two billion in 2050; <http://www.iiasa.ac.at/Research/LUC/Papers/gkh1/chap1.htm>. This book is not about Africa, but such an explosion in population totally disrupts existing social and national structures. It is possible that Africa will plug into the same development path as Asia started in the last decades of the twentieth century and, in 2050, present itself as another economic miracle. For the opposite, pessimistic view, see, for example, Philip Bobbitt <http://www.theglobalist.com/StoryId.aspx?StoryId=3681>.

158 Otherwise, that would contradict what the world has seen from 1945 until now with labour-intensive production shifting from country to country, steered by rising population and, in particular, rising numbers of workers keeping wage levels down.

159 Asian Development Bank, "Key indicators: Inequality in Asia", 2007 <http://www.adb.org/Documents/Books/Key_Indicators/2007/pdf/rt14.pdf>.

160 For a definition of middle class, see The World Bank, Development Economics Prospects Group, "Global Growth and Distribution: Are China and India Reshaping the World?", Policy Research Working Paper 4392, November 2007 <http://www-wds.worldbank.org/external/default/WDSContentServer/IW3P/IB/2007/11/12/000158349_20071112111936/Rendered/PDF/wps4392.pdf>.

161 Ibid.

162 The figures may be confusing when comparing statistics for the global middle class with statistics for the national middle class as the definition for global versus national middle is not the same. In year 2000 most of the Chinese in the upper end of the national income scale belonged, not to the global upper end, but to the global middle class. McKinsey has calculated that the middle class in China and India, defined in national terms in 2025, will number more than 900 million people in China and more than 550 million people in India — much higher than the World Bank's calculation; <http://knowledge.wharton.upenn.edu/article.cfm?articleid=2011#>.

163 <http://www.thegff.com/Publisher/Article.aspx?id=52439>; <http://www.ibef.org/artdisplay.aspx?cat_id=60&art_id=16727&refer=n42>; and <http://www.aplgasia.com/The_Region.html>.

164 See, for example, Martin Roll, *Asian Brand Strategy: How Asia Builds Strong Brands* (London); and <http://www.kpmg.de/library/pdf/070719_Luxury_Brands_in_China.pdf>.

165 <http://knowledge.wharton.upenn.edu/article.cfm?articleid=2011#>.

166 Michael Fitzgerald, "How Innovations from Developing Nations Trickle-up to the West", *Fast Company* 133, March 2009 <http://www.fastcompany.com/magazine/133/as-the-world-turns.html?page=0%2C0>.

167 Mastercard and HSBC, "China's Dynamic Consumers — the Young Singles", MasterCard Worldwide Insights, 1Q 2008.

168 Mastercard and HSBC, "Dynamic Drivers of China's Consumer Market — the Middle Class, Modern Women and DINKs", MasterCard Worldwide Insights, 4Q 2007.

169 See, for example, JMNR Insights Briefing, "Japan's Changing Consumer", October 2007 <http://www.ecotechjapan.com/qualia/UserFiles/File/InsightsBriefing_JMRN(1).pdf>.

170 MasterCard, "Online Shopping in Asia/Pacific — Patterns, Trends and Future Growth", MasterCard Worldwide Insights, 3Q 2008.

171 Ibid.

172 "What's New with the Chinese Consumer", *McKinsey Quarterly*, September 2008 <http://www.mckinseyquarterly.com/Retail_Consumer_Goods/Whats_new_with_the_Chinese_consumer_2218>.

173 McKinsey Global Institute, "The 'Bird of Gold': The Rise of India's Consumer Market", May 2007 <http://www.asiaing.com/the-bird-of-gold-the-rise-of-indias-consumer-market.html>.

174 Calculated from rupees at the official exchange rate. Purchasing power parity calculation would have led to a much higher figure measured in U.S. dollars, but would not change the relative proportions of the respective groups.

175 Reference is sometimes made to the convergence into consumers of people with lower incomes. They constitute a significant share of total population at the beginning of the century and absolute numbers are staggering, but the plain fact is that over the next twenty-five years, both their share of total population and absolute numbers will fall dramatically. Even if we will still have a large number of people in what has been termed the "deprived class", their purchasing power will be small. If we look for a sociological change it may be found in the lower tier of the middle class, composed of people who have worked themselves into this category from being close to the poverty level. They are the ones who will have the car, the fridge, the TV, the air-conditioning, etc., for the first time. Their cultural behaviour may change and because of their large numbers that may cause social changes.

176 Ralph Paprzycki and Kyoji Fukao, *Foreign Direct Investment in Japan: Multinationals' Role in Growth and Globalization* (Cambridge: Cambridge University Press, 2008).

177 Roy Larke, "Expansion of Japanese Retailers Overseas", *International Retailing Plans and Strategies in Asia*, edited by Erdener Kaynak, John Dawson, and Junghee Lee (Bingham, New York: Routledge, 2005).

178 <http://www.jref.com/society/supermarket_industry_japan.shtml>.

179 <http://www.marketresearch.com/product/display.asp?productid=2294242&xs=r>.

180 <http://www.chinaretailnews.com/2009/04/15/2520-wumart-net-profit-up-63-in-2008/>.

181 *China Daily*, "Carrefour's Expansion in China", 12 August 2009 <http://www.chinadaily.com.cn/bizchina/2008-08/12/content_6928230.htm> and <http://

www.icmrindia.org/casestudies/catalogue/Business%20Strategy/BSTR246.
htm>.

182 <http://seekingalpha.com/instablog/419344-china-market-research-group-
cmr/6622-chinese-companies-go-abroad-part-10-the-retail-sector>.

183 Summer 2009 brought the news that Suning Appliance Co. (Chinese retail
chain) and Laox (Japanese electronics retailer) were discussing a deal for Laox
to be an affiliate of Suning <http://www.marketwatch.com/story/china-retailer-
to-buy-part-of-japans-laox-report.

184 <http://www.marketresearch.com/product/display.asp?productid=2294242&xs
=r>.

185 KPMG and the Association of Chambers of Commerce and Industry of India
(ASSOCHAM) <http://www.assocham.org/prels/shownews.php?id=2081>.

186 <http://www.pantaloon.com/jun09.pdf>.

187 <http://www.retailduniya.com/index.php?module=Users&task=retailnews#031
201>.

# 4

# ACES OR DUDS

This chapter analyses elements and policies primarily directed at people's mindsets, that is, how they act and react to challenges and how we enhance human capital/intelligence to serve not only the economy, but society as a whole. Topics such as education, creativity, social capital, gender, and megacities/megaregions stand in the foreground. They have as common denominators group behaviour, how people react when working together and asked to trust one another.

Their role is much more equivocal than the first group analysed in the preceding chapter. They can point in many directions and it is not clear which one will emerge. Much depends on government policies. If governments get it wrong they may turn from potential drivers to potential shoals, wrecking Asia's future.

No sector illustrates this dilemma and challenge more clearly than education, which must make itself relevant to society as a whole by serving as a stakeholder. The skills embodied in new generations are honed over the years inside the education system. The task is to sense future needs for skills so that the supply of skills matches the demand for skills. If this is not the case, economic growth suffers and, even more important, inequalities grow making it much more difficult to build social capital. The problem is to foresee what kind of jobs will dominate twenty-five years from now and what kind of skills they will require.

Furthermore the information and communication technology (ICT) revolution means that many of the well-established teaching/learning methods are no longer applicable, and yet applied. Young children wish to learn differently from those who are employed to teach them and this threatens to turn into a generational gap.

With new tools it is at hand to switch the education system from the assembly line — mass consumption model — to a more tailor-made system offering students individual training and building blocks to form a set of skills. As it is, students "purchase" education modules available on the shelf. In the future students may "compose" their own education, asking the education system to deliver according to specifications they set.

If education gets it right, using new tools and instruments to influence the mindset, a higher degree of creativity may be one of the main benefits. Creativity is the driver for society to turn out new products. It is more a societal competitive parameter than an economic one considering that traditional economic instruments and economic policies will not do much to enhance creativity. Most creative people are happy and the key to happiness seems to lie in the opportunity to express themselves without the kind of societal barriers that put pressure on them to strike the right balance between discipline and freedom.

Creativity embodies risks in the form of willingness to run political risks and accept higher volatility to stimulate people to think differently — otherwise they are not creative. Therefore a high degree of social capital — and at the nationwide or community-wide level at that — is preferable as a kind of bulwark keeping society together through common and shared values while at the same time allowing for "thinking differently or thinking out of box".

The financial system is necessary to finance society and the economy, but also serves as a weathervane for trust as people in a society with high social capital are more likely to deposit savings in banks, while societies with a low degree of trust see savings in the form of gold or accumulation of foreign currencies. Social capital and trust turn a financial system into a vehicle for the smooth development of society as a whole.

The gender question is obvious as a rise in discrimination that may often appear in a hidden way actually stops a large part of the population from stepping forward and using their skills for the good of society.

Megacities and megaregions are going to dominate Asia. The mere fact that millions of people are put together in such big agglomerations makes it of preponderant importance to build up social capital and trust. These agglomerations cannot be governed by rules and regulations solely. If social capital is not available, the situation may give rise to social capital being within groups based on animosity towards other groups. This then breaks up the agglomerations which are replaced by enclaves interested in fighting one another instead of working together.

## EDUCATION AND THE ECONOMY

## Why Look at Education?

The main reason for looking at education is its potential contribution to economic growth and the development of the societal model.

Previously focus used to be directed at the impact of education on economic growth (productivity, etc.), but gradually an observation strikes root that an education system shapes social coherence, social capital, inequality, and related issues for a number of decades to come.

Economists have generally agreed on two things and disagreed on a third element.[1] The *first* point of agreement is that education pays off for the individual, even if some doubts exist for overeducated people, especially those having a high and expensive education out of tune with demand. The *second* point of agreement is that education benefits society.

The disagreement arises when trying to quantify these benefits. There are several reasons for this. Benefits of education are incremental and work their way through the economic system with a time lag; benefits today may be the result of educational efforts decades ago. Furthermore it is difficult to distinguish between education and other societal policies when analysing origins of growth, innovation, and new products.

Asian education systems have over the last decades basically been seen and used as a supportive element in tuning society to high growth rates by focusing on those educational sectors turning out those capable of entering the economy straight away and contributing to growth. This tandem has been successful. Gopinathan[2] formulates it the following way:

> the implementation of policies in education and training designed to boost stocks of human capital. The enhancement of labour productivity was seen, in the earlier context of low innovative capacity, to lie in expansion of education. In addition to expansion of secondary and post-secondary institutions, a greater emphasis on science and technology in the curriculum and expansion of vocational and polytechnic education these states[3] were able to achieve a tight coupling of education and training systems with state-determined economic policies.

The problem is that it may no longer provide the answer as Asia faces a diversity of challenges focusing on growth, but a different kind of growth, and at the same time is confronted with a whole string of societal challenges. The starting point therefore seems to be that the current structure of Asia's educational sector is plugged into current or maybe even past problems and not really switched on to future demands.

Over the coming years Asia's educational systems and their role in societal development will run into many of the problems the Western education systems have encountered, and this warrants our taking a look at some of the analyses — often critical ones — which have been published primarily about the American education system. Admittedly the findings are only partially relevant for Asia. They can, however, normally, give us some pointers.

The *first* analysis studies the effect of increases in educational attainment in the U.S. labour force from 1915 to 1999. The direct gains estimated resulted in at least 23 per cent of the 1.62 per cent annual increase in labour productivity. The most important policy step was the move to universal high school education from 1910 to 1940 which extended economic benefits for the United States into the rest of the century.[4] This corresponds to what Korea, Taiwan, and Singapore experienced in the 1960s and 1970s.

The *second* analysis[5] treads carefully, even cautiously, but ventures anyway into the open by comparing how fifteen-year-olds score on the PISA (Programme for International Students Assessment from OECD) science scale and the current number of full-time equivalent researchers. The result is a positive correlation which leads to the cautious conclusion supporting intuitive impressions that the better the education system is preparing future personnel in science and technology, the higher the number entering this occupation will be. The same tendency can also be spotted in professional education. This is not the same as saying either that future R&D is determined by the present school system, or that it promotes economic growth, but it points in that direction. Besides, with the present instruments in economics, there is not much else for us to go on.

In the *third* analysis, J. Barro[6] concludes that the years of schooling at the secondary and higher level have a significantly positive effect on growth for men aged twenty-five and over. He also draws the conclusion that the study supports the observation that education has a positive effect on an economy's ability to absorb new technologies.

The *fourth* analysis[7] looks at the PISA ranking produced from the American education system compared with those of a number of other countries also taking part in the PISA and classifies what is termed "educational gaps" as the economic equivalent of "permanent national recession". If the United States had closed the achievement gap in education visible at the beginning of the 1980s and raised its performance level to the top level on a par with countries such as Finland and Korea, U.S.

gross domestic product (GDP) in 2008 would have been between US$1.3 trillion and US$2.3 trillion higher, corresponding to 9 per cent to 16 per cent respectively of total U.S. GDP.

A comparative analysis of human capital and economic performance for three Asian countries — India, Indonesia, and Japan — comes to the following main conclusions:[8] the impact on GDP of education is strongest in periods when growth of secondary education was strongest, which coincided with the substitution of private for public education. This happened in Japan in the 1920s and 1930s, in Indonesia in the 1930s and 1940s, and in India in 1970s and 1980s. Japan surged ahead because its education sector was more efficient, favoured early adoption of technology, and was large enough to support rapid industrialization, turning Japan into a manufacturing economy, pushing it towards the status of a country capable of competing in high technology.

Economists also disagree on the impact of education on economic growth when it comes to, among other things, whether it is an income or productivity determinant, and whether its impact depends on the stage of development of societies. This is analysed by Risti Permani[9] who, looking at East Asia, offers two crucial observations.

The *first* is that when analysing from 1965 to 2000, education becomes more important as a factor promoting economic growth and reaches a significant size at the end of the period. The significance of education outperforms (physical) capital as measured by investment shares of GDP.

The *second* observation is on the importance of education as a factor in facilitating societies to reach the level of a steady state economy.[10] Without incorporating human capital, the length of time for the East Asian states achieving halfway the GDP per capita of steady state economies from the present GDP per capita is sixty-four years. Incorporating human capital reduces the time span to about twenty years. Such findings are not only significant in this particular context, but bring out how important education is as a factor in marshalling societal resources and human beings (human capital) behind the preferred societal model.

It is further pointed out[11] that "the idea that education is the key to the success of an economy as a whole is a relatively new concept and the evidence for it is not especially compelling". Conventional economic wisdom has been that a nation's economic strength, that is production capacity, is linked to its physical capital and not its human capital. A U.S. engineer is seen as much more productive than an engineer in India with an equivalent education and training because the United States has built up a technical and management infrastructure opening the door for higher productivity. This assumption may have been rocked over the last decade by the arrival on the scene of Indian software companies, albeit it is still debatable how to distribute the enhanced competitiveness of Indian software companies between skills and lower costs.

The interesting point in this analysis may not necessarily be the question mark over education for its role in promoting economic growth, but its link to societal structure as a necessary condition for higher education to fulfil its potential. It may not so much be about whether higher education is enhancing growth patterns and production capacity, but whether the surroundings allow it to do so. In other words, unless society is organized, structured, and supplied with infrastructure of various kinds, higher educated people will not make much difference to growth trends.

This line of thinking was in fact floated in the 1970s by Gintis and Bowles.[12] Many of their observations were linked to a critique of the capitalist society, but they disputed the conventional wisdom that society, through the impact of education on human capital, makes a profitable investment or, at least, contended that it does not get the profitability expected and sought. They found the explanation for their contention in the fact that students often select the kind of education out of tune with what society needs and that was due to the fact that education often lags behind societal and technological developments. Education is nonetheless a profitable investment, but the profit is found outside the strict linear analysis linked to economic theory. Instead it improves the overall quality of society to adapt and perhaps also generates positive effects on social capital. A higher educated society would, in principle, be a society acting more in conformity with common and shared values, thus enhancing its capacity to withstand shocks, disturbances, and disruptions, as well as exploit windows of opportunity.[13]

## Demand for and Supply of Skills

The starting point for an analysis of education is therefore its connection to and place in the society it is built to serve.[14] And the number one thing to do is to compare the skills the education system delivers and offers to the students with the skills in demand. Do the higher educated people leave the education system with the skills required by the economy and industry?

A number of analyses in the United States and other countries come to the conclusion that the answer is *no*.

Cappelli[15] recalls that the General Social Survey of the United States reports that 30 per cent of adult workers have education levels that exceed the requirements for their current jobs, a figure that has actually gone up over time. He comes to the conclusion that if the United States could produce graduates with more occupationally-specific requirements, the benefits would be clear.

Robert I. Lerman[16] says that the skills of workers in the United States are critical to their own economic performance as well as that of society at large. To his mind policymakers should pay more attention to what skills workers really need to succeed (and skills change as the economy changes), rather than focusing on an assumed set of skills that may not be so critical after all. A debate is going on about the quality of education systems, including the U.S. system, but for the United States it is much worse: over half of its manufacturing firms report that the shortage of workers with the right skills is affecting their ability to serve customers and 84 per cent say that the U.S. school system is not doing a good job preparing students for the workplace.

Lerman continues setting out in no uncertain terms that the present U.S. system does not generate feedback to policymakers telling them what kind of skills are currently in demand, and even more crucially, will rise in demand in the coming years, so as to allow the system to produce graduates in segments of the workforce where the demand may be growing, but still account for only half the workforce.[17]

Lerman's prediction referring to U.S. Bureau of Labor statistics discloses that 47 per cent of all job openings will be in heterogeneous, middle-skill positions. They will basically require a varied array of skills generally gained through community colleges, occupational training, and work experience. This has severe implications for the funds put at the disposal of precisely this kind of education/training. Lerman adopts the definition of general skills as capabilities that increase a worker's productivity in a range of firms, and specific skills as capabilities that increase productivity within one firm. The growing demand is for general skills, but private firms are not ready to pay for such training as workers may use their enhanced skills to move to another firm, while the public sector in the United States is not making (enough) money available. The result is that, precisely in this area of skills actually needed in the United States, money is not forthcoming to increase the productivity of the workforce. This has foreseeable implications such as falling competitiveness and outsourcing.

Similar statements are heard from China. At the end of 2008[18] the *People's Daily* published comments on the employment situation in China which also questioned how well the education system matches the skills required. The comment makes the same point as that for the United States.

"Many college graduates now lack the skills needed to compete for jobs in a fast-changing economy but are unwilling to take less respected jobs...

Our graduates need to use their brains and hands together. But instead, they come out aiming high but their actual skill level is low…. This leads to disappointed expectations" Chen Guangqing[19] said.

Chen's quasi-government organization, the National Association of Vocational Education, which has 1,000 offices nationwide, plans skills training through university networks to reach college students. It also offers locally-organized training to harness skills of migrant workers returning home.

University graduates and the vast numbers of migrant workers were particularly vulnerable in the job market due to oversupply, the survey found.

The Chinese Academy of Social Sciences, CASS, had stated a few days earlier that about 5.6 million college students graduated that year, but 1.5 million failed to land jobs. The prospects for college graduates could be even bleaker next year, as a record 6.1 million students would graduate from universities.[20]

The signals coming out from both the American and Chinese economies and education systems paint a worrying picture that suggests that already at this juncture the education systems are not geared towards educating and training graduates in what society and industry need. If this is the case, it does not portend well for the coming decades because even though jobs may have changed over the last decades, what we have seen is nothing compared with what we are going to see in the coming twenty-five years.

The trend in outsourcing away from low-cost, labour-intensive manufacturing to jobs defined by a higher degree of science, technology, or management that make automation profitable, in particular, in the services sector, poses an immediate challenge to the Asian education system. To respond to these opportunities and challenges, the labour force needs to have a higher skills level than is the case today.

The main risks to Asia's economic growth is that this incapacity of the education system to deliver an increased number of persons with such higher skills will enhance competition for such persons and drive wages up. While this may benefit multinational companies outsourcing to Asia, it may constitute a barrier for the up-and-coming national Asian companies in this future-oriented sector. The Asian economies themselves are vastly different ranging from highly diversified countries such as Japan, Korea, and Singapore, to rapidly emerging economies with high populations such as China and India, to countries rich in commodities and agriculture such as the Philippines, Thailand, and Vietnam, and to developing countries such as Bangladesh. This entails the need to think of the complex and differentiated nature of each economy and its significance for the education sector, and calls for diversified and differentiated answers/solutions.

This dilemma is analysed by Jacob Kirkegaard[21] who concludes:

> Developing Asia therefore faces a double educational challenge in the
> coming years. Not only must a large group of the population in several
> countries be provided with more than simply the most basic numeracy
> and literacy in order to be employable outside the agricultural sector,
> many more workers must also acquire the advanced skills needed to staff
> domestic services companies hoping to challenge incumbent services
> sector multinationals.

Goldin and Katz[22] point out that technological developments may also have
a "dark" side in the form of adverse distributional consequences that may
foment social tension. Technological advances could lead to the earnings of
some groups increasing more than those for other groups. The conditions
necessary for an equitable distribution of rising income/wealth are flexible
skills and an educational infrastructure that expands sufficiently to match
demand for skills with supply of those skills. Growth and the premium for
skills should be balanced. If on the other hand the education system does not
follow this recipe, imbalances will arise, unsettling not only the education
sector, but also the social fabric.

Goldin and Katz divide the wage structure and education in the United
States in the twentieth century into three phases. The *first* phase was from
1920 to around 1940 when wage differentials narrowed and earnings of the
more educated were reduced relative to earnings of the less educated. The
*second* phase was from the 1940s to the beginning of the 1970s when wage
differentials widened only slightly and income distribution was fairly stable.
The *third* phase was from the 1970s to the end of the century when inequality
rose steeply, but productivity only slightly (later productivity rose sharply, but
not in those twenty and more years). The wage/income premium for college
education went up. The interpretation of this development is a mismatch
between demand for skills from industry, and the education system's ability
to deliver students having these skills.[23]

McKinsey Global Institute comes to the same conclusion in a June 2009
report saying that "in light of the growing demand for skills, appropriate
education and training play a critical role in giving workers access to more
attractive jobs" and "unless the mass of America's workers can develop new
skills over the next ten years, the nation risks another period in which
growth resumes, but income dispersion persists, with Americans in the
bottom and middle-earning income clusters never really benefiting from
the recovery".[24]

These observations about the impact of "wrong" educational systems on
the whole complexity of social structure and coherence threatening social

capital and the sense of belonging to one society is possibly the most hair-raising issue when looking at the future role of the education system. It is not just about education or productivity, but also about what kind of society is at hand in twenty-five years time.

## New Kind of Skills

In a twenty-five year perspective, a safe assumption points to a large part, maybe even a majority, of citizens holding jobs not existing today. But adaptation may be slow in Asia, where family values often weigh more than societal needs. Those who hold the same type of jobs will work in a different way. Already workers function as human resources using new technology as a tool to extend and enlarge performance levels. And the new technology is itself dependent on instructions given by the "worker". Ability to change, adjust and adapt, search for new ways to solve problems, accept frequent changes in job definition, and perform in a multicultural context, will be decisive elements when judging the competence level of the citizen. This focus will diminish the risk of turning out a large number of students with competences for which there is little or no use, thus turning them into a dissatisfied mass of people that constitute a serious threat to social coherence and social capital.

The impact of knowledge on the job and skill market is staggering. It has been pointed out that from 2000 to 2006 the number of American jobs requiring "tacit interaction" has grown two and a half times as much as transactional jobs, and three times as much as traditional jobs. These kind of jobs accounts for 40 per cent of all American jobs, and 70 per cent of all jobs created from 1998 to 2006.[25]

A futurist enumerates the following top jobs from 2015 to 2030[26] and even though the prognosis is made for the United States, the same trend will be visible in Asia (in an Asian context jobs inside the food and beverage sector may weigh more heavily than in the United States).

2015[27]
Neuro-medical techs, person protectors: personal security techs, organ cloners, biofuture therapists, quantum scientist, realtime business executives, online consumer marketing wizards, health enhancement therapists, cancer enablers.

2020
Knowledge management advisors, nanobio entrepreneurs, artists, writers, poets, on demand supply chain designers, global headhunters.

2025
Reality interactive TV producers, gene engineers, robotic psychotherapists, cyjacks: antihackers, personal privacy advisors, personal identity finders.

2030
Space market planners, climate change forecasters, solar fuel developers, holographic game developers, poets, customer knowledge mining specialists, antiterrorism techs, neuro marketing managers, hydrogen marketing managers, renewable energy entrepreneurs, real time supply chain designers, nano manufacturing agents, health performance enhancers.

The point in giving this enumeration is not whether the lists are right or wrong, but that most, if not all, of these jobs are totally unknown to us today. We do not know what they mean and even worse when seen in the context of education, we do not know what skills they require.

The U.S. Department of Labor[28] gives the following prediction for spectacular job growth in 2006–16, looking at information and communication:

| | |
|---|---|
| Computer scientists and database administrators | 37 per cent |
| Computer and information scientists, research | 22 per cent |
| Database administrators | 29 per cent |
| Network systems and data communications analysts | 53 per cent |
| Computer specialists, all other | 15 per cent |

Goldin and Katz try their hand in defining the future challenge by focusing on the role of education.[29] Changing technology entails changing the demand for skills. If the workforce is trained and educated to adjust, economic growth means ensuring that equality of income is favoured — and a stable path of evolution. If not, the lack of skills slows down economic growth and the mismatch between demand for skills and available skills leads to a premium for the relevant skills, exacerbating inequality and destabilizing society.

In their analysis, jobs requiring in-person skills are less susceptible to be threatened by outsourcing and surpassed by new and other skills; in short, they are difficult to replace or replicate. People who can think abstractly and who understand finance, nanotechnology, and cellular biology in a deep, non-routine manner, meet these requirements. Another skill set gaining in value are interpersonal skills, the ability to interact with other people inside a group.

The findings underline the ability to look at skills outside the narrow framework of being able to do something, focusing instead on "the other side of the hill" and understanding how to combine skills from various disciplines and/or other persons. Interpersonal and interdisciplinary skills — creativity across disciplines — which are not really being rated today are crucial elements.

The potential put on the table by new technology can only be fully realized if the mindset of citizens is geared towards creative and ingenious thinking. The genuine virtue of new technology is to perform existing tasks differently and spot new and unknown opportunities. But technology only thrives inside a societal caucus accommodating new technology. It is the linkage between science, technology, and societal structure that determines which direction a society chooses to go. Science and arts may sometimes be overlooked, but they are drivers of change. The role of education is to sense this and adjust to the trends set out by technology, societal structure, and these two in tandem.

An illustration of this is seen in the way seekers are moving away from traditional methods to the Internet.[30] Individuals realize the significance of the Internet and online activities in getting across to corporations offering job openings. They do not rely on official systems. The same method can be used in sensing where job opportunities are going to be in the future. The need is not only for adjusting the education system, but doing this fast and on a permanent basis, and making the system flexible or, rather, adaptable to meet new demand. This applies not only to job seeking or the economic sector as education must acknowledge this shift away from traditional methods to the Internet as a changing paradigm across the spectrum.

Institutions find it difficult to offer new job opportunities and adjust the education system because institutional virtue is the ability to lay down rules applicable to everybody. Asia is no exception as educational institutions are rigid and, sometimes, an extended arm of existing power structures. This was good for guiding the education system in the industrial age where most work activities were characterized by repeating certain well-established operations. The opposite is becoming synonymous with the future society or whatever we choose to call it. Instead of performing some well-defined work task, the worker as an individual is expected to participate in solving a problem, a challenge, or a task on a temporary basis, using skills which may not be useful or required in the preceding or subsequent job.

In his PhD thesis titled, "The Project Society", Anders Fogh Jensen has elaborated on this point.[31] His central idea is "that we have moved from plan to project. As such a great deal of the management literature using the word 'project' is not really part of the society of projects since it is still a plan. The society of projects functions without outer shells like guarantees and contracts in the old sense of the term. When contracts are used, they are used as instruments to test and build up motivation, not as a sign of reciprocal agreement as it was the case in the disciplinary society. The project is *limited in time*. It is not oriented towards repetition. For example, the one night stand is for the society of projects, what the marriage is for the disciplinary society. Limited in time means: Every person must be oriented towards the next project, even when in one project. One must ask oneself before committing to a project: Does this project optimize my chances of passing on to another project? And one must structure the activity within the project so as to make remarkable and visible results optimizing his connectability".

The role of education in this society is perceived this way: "The idea of *education* and upbringing is not so much about teaching people to desist from doing what they want or feel like, as it was before. Rather it is a question of facilitating the auto-evolvement of the so-called competences that lie within everyone. The grown-up and the teacher now become coach-like figures that help children as consultants. The authority has moved from the position to the person, and — as is the case in the companies — it becomes more important to expose the personal preferences, than the rules."

Irrespective of whether it is or should be an institutionalized system or not, education is organized as a system and as such it is gradually being subjugated to benchmark analysis. Norms are being set and some systems — whether deliberately or otherwise — have been nominated as the best ones with the consequence that the rest try to catch up. This is not bad in itself as it spurs lower-quality institutions to enhance their efforts. The problem in this context is that it rests on the assumption that the results of the education system can be measured. The implicit disadvantage of measuring performance levels is that it focuses on elements that can be measured, which tends to twist the system in this direction, so non-measurable elements receive less attention even if they may be more important. In the well-known industrial society most performance could indeed be measured[32] and this method worked. The education system delivered cohort after cohort of students educated and trained to do the repetitive tasks required of the industrial system and those could be measured without too much effort. The difficulty now is that we want adaptability, creativity, etc. and these cannot be measured. In such cases benchmark analyses and comparative analyses may not help much. In fact they run the risk of being counterproductive, initiating a race among education systems to produce students with the same kind of skills and who focus on doing these skills best, regardless of whether it is those skills that are in demand especially in the future. Moving from one education system to another asks for experimentation and indeed requires acceptance of failures — otherwise we will not know what works and what does not.[33]

The alternative approach to wait and see how students perform and their contribution to economic growth by enhancing human capital delivered by the education system suffers from the drawback that it can only be done with a considerable time-lag.

This overview of education and its role leads to four preliminary conclusions:

- The important thing is not the level of education, but whether the education system turns out students with the required skills. If not, three things happen. *First*, students cannot find jobs, irrespective of their education level, and industry is left with unfulfilled jobs even if a large number of graduates are unemployed. This is social waste and, on top of that, augurs trouble. *Second*, the money invested in the education system does not give the yield it should. A wrong investment — to use economic vocabulary — has taken place. Even with a large amount of money, measured in absolute terms and as a percentage of GDP, society does not reap the benefit such investments warrant. *Third*, unwelcome distributional, potentially socially disruptive, results may take place.
- No education system can deliver if it is perceived to be outside and disconnected from the society it thrives or rather not thrives in. Society forges young people entering the education system, and society is the ultimate user of what the education system produces. To look at an education system as a self-sustaining sector of society is a deadly sin.
- Financing must be linked to those who benefit from it. If as may often be the case, society as a whole benefits from general skills embodied in the workforce, it is imperative that the government step forward to make the money available. Firms will not do so because they know that productivity gain may not accrue to them, but go to other firms.
- Education should, at all levels, foster creativity, especially in science, arts, philosophy. Otherwise the education system risks becoming a copy machine or adapter.

## Basic Education

### *Literacy*

A large number of Asians have never gone to primary school and thus fall into the category of illiteracy. Based on UN statistics[34] the adult literacy rate[35] in China is 90.9, in India 61, Indonesia 90.4, Vietnam 90.3, Thailand 92.6, Malaysia 88.7, the Philippines 92.6, and Myanmar 89.9. The other major countries in South Asia — excluding India mentioned above — are Pakistan with 49.9 and Bangladesh 47.7. The interpretation of the picture is thus fairly easy. Southeast Asia has a literacy rate a little above 90 per cent and so has China, while the three South Asian countries have a much lower literacy rate, with India doing better than Pakistan and Bangladesh.[36]

Looking at the net primary enrolment rate, we see the following picture (percentages): China 97, India 89, Indonesia 96, Vietnam 88, Thailand 90, Malaysia 95, Myanmar 90, Pakistan 68, and Bangladesh 94.[37]

Sanjeev Sanyal[38] has looked at illiteracy and enrolment in primary schools in India and concludes that primary school enrolment is now close to 100 per cent even in the poor states. The gender gap is also narrowing, with the enrolment for girls having increased from 64 per cent to 96 per cent from 1990 to 2003. He estimates that the literacy rate will be over 90 per cent in 2020. The implication for the economy is a large number of people joining the labour market with basic skills which qualify them to take up jobs in manufacturing and to "run simple machinery".

In absolute numbers this means that approximately 450 million people in India and 150 million in China cannot read and are thus deprived of the option to master skills necessary for active participation in the society that is being shaped over the next twenty-five years. Viewed over the last decade (1985–94 to 1995–2005) the literacy rate has gone up in both China and India by twelve percentage points, which is good, especially for China which is operating at a level of 90 per cent or more, but it points to a long march ahead for India and its two neighbours on the subcontinent.

There is no way around the conclusion that resources that could have been used to further economic growth need to be diverted to this effort. Present growth rates suggest that resources will be forthcoming, but raise the question of how to train the teachers to educate adult illiterate people and children in societies where there is no tradition and sometimes no understanding of the need and virtues of education. Unless this can be done, these countries will lag behind in their endeavours to grow and create the resources to solve the many challenges and problems their societies face. On top of that, dichotomized societies may emerge in which a large number of people are left behind in a modern communication society, posing enormous social and political problems.

## *Emergent Technologies — ICT and Education*

The next step in basic education, that is, primary school, is to realize the potential of ICT, but there is also the need to adapt to the system. ICT answers the wishes and preferences of children much better than former education methods. But every system was born out of and forged by the society existing at the time and the technology embedded in that society.

The education system in the industrial society was based on the factory as a model. Children arrived at the school (factory) in the morning and stayed there until the afternoon. They faced a teacher (worker versus supervisor model from the factory) conveying one-way communication and were required to learn skills most of which were repetitive and/or encyclopaedic. They were not so much asked to think and reflect on their own as to gather already existing knowledge and learn how to apply that knowledge in a production process. The skeleton of all learning and teaching was to confront children with questions — to which there was only one correct answer — and verify whether the children knew that answer. There was neither much group work, nor focus on the individual. The concept was to shape a worker in the mould of the industrial society. It was an admirable system when judged on objectives and its link to society and its technology — and it worked. The problem now is that we no longer live in an industrial society.

When we watch the behaviour of children, especially young children, it is perfectly clear that this education system violates fundamental instincts guiding the child. Any child wants to learn by doing and experimenting. This is why a child touches and tastes everything. Nature's teaching model is learning by doing. And children step forward to learn by playing if they are allowed to do so. ICT opens this window — not by games — but by offering the children the possibility of trying, experimenting, and learning via the discovery of what happens if they do this or that.

In such an environment a school perceived as a factory is a mistake holding the children back. No child is encouraged to use his or her instinct when sitting on a bench receiving instructions. The factory concept must be got rid of and replaced by a more "equitable" relationship between teacher and pupil, based on the understanding that the child needs to go on with his or her experiments even if the teacher knows very well that it will fail. But by failing, the child gains the knowledge that this was not the way to do things and tries another method next time. This view of the teacher-student relationship is not one currently supported around the world and probably not widely held in Asia, so the transformation of the learning environment will take time, be uneven, and probably spark some sociological and social problems as age old structures are contested.

The basics for all teaching/learning should be to let children ask questions which the ICT instruments can answer and encourage them to seek several options from which they can choose or make a list of priorities. By doing so they comprehend that the responsibility for choosing by posing the right questions on the table is theirs, and even more, the responsibility for getting the options enumerated is theirs. A stronger form of a mix of individualism, creativity, and teamwork should be one of the main targets of the education system. In an Asian context, where the emphasis is on age-linked maturity, the willingness to see children as competent and independent individuals might be an issue — at least in some Asian cultures.

From this foundation children can move on to other aspects of the education system whether it be tertiary or another segment that prepares them for life in a society where much of adult life may be like what is described by the Project Society, even if not all flywheels will be exactly like that, in fact, far from it.

No discussion of basic education can ignore two fundamental factors: the role of ICT, or rather the impact of ICT, on the minds of children, and their ability to learn; and the role of parents in this changed education system.

## ICT and Education

Marc Prensky's work on Digital Natives versus Digital Immigrants is regarded as one of the pioneer works setting out the difference between those (the young people of today) growing up with digital media at their disposal, and those (immigrants) trying hard to get the feel of how these new instruments or tools can be used.[39] In fact, you sometimes hear people talking about mobile versus non-mobile technology.

Prensky starts by laying down in no uncertain terms that "today's students are no longer the people our educational system was designed to teach". From that platform he makes pertinent observations about how young people learn, and their ability to handle several sources of information and communication at the same time, which unfortunately is not the case for the teachers. Today's student thinks, absorbs processes, and handles information in a completely different way to that of preceding generations. We may be jumping to a conclusion saying that this has fundamentally changed their brains, but it is not premature to say that this has completely changed their way of thinking compared with that of those who teach them. This development has not taken place because technology has speeded up, but because technology is an enabler.

Below are Prensky's major observations and statements in the context of this study:

- Digital Natives receive their information fast. They like to parallel process and multitask. They prefer graphics more than text. They thrive on random access (hypertext).
- Digital Natives can absorb learning while watching TV or listening to music; in fact, for many of them, this is what they have been doing for most of their lives. They cannot or find it difficult to concentrate or focus attention on one task only.
- They expect learning to be fun as everything else they do using digital instruments is fun or entertaining, and have little patience or understanding for step-by-step lectures or other forms of education or teaching taking place outside the frame of the digital world — their world.

Rose Luckin[40] has studied the impact of the Internet on a pupil's critical and meta-cognitive skills and says that "The worrying view coming through is that students are lacking in reflective awareness. Technology makes it easy for them to collate information, but not to analyse and understand it. Much of the evidence suggests that what is going on out there is quite superficial."

It looks like what the digital age set — the Digital Natives — are good at is collate information, browse, and combine this in a quick way. What they are losing out on is the conventional way of acquiring knowledge by concentrating on a textbook or another form of learning material that systematically sets out what they need to learn about a particular subject and nothing else.

So far no method has been formulated to combine the two, which leads Prensky to ask the rhetorical question, "Should the Digital Natives student learn the old way or should the Digital Immigrants instructors learn to teach according to the new way?"

Sometimes the way out of a dilemma is to avoid choosing, but if the paradigm has permanently and irrevocably changed, which seems likely, the education system can only survive by adapting to accommodate the Digital Natives and the way they think. It has the advantage of opening the door for an interdisciplinary and multitasking world, which may be the key to controlling and extracting from the flow of information what we need.[41]

There will always be a need for specialized people and the industrial society invested the education system with the ability to turn out specialists. The new challenge is interdisciplinary training and perception, opening the eyes of people to what is going on outside their jobs, but is not irrelevant for their job definition. The knack to discover and put various trends together and take sociocultural constraints and enablers into account in a new coherent framework suitable to what is needed here and now defines a strong competitive edge. It does not come by itself; it comes by training, education, access to a full picture of trends and tendencies, and tearing down intellectual and cultural barriers between disciplines.

Anders Fogh Jensen[42] tries to square the circle this way: "Development from the disciplinary society to the society of projects has taken place in different fields. This development consists in a double movement: The movement from the disciplinary society to the society of projects and the persistence and returning of disciplinary structures, which exist within the society of projects as orders, as point of return or as borders to transcend."

Don Tapscott has analysed the net generation. His analysis discloses basically what the works by Marc Prensky and Rose Luckin do, but in his conclusion he chooses to adopt an almost watertight, positive view of how the digital generation will affect and influence societal development.[43]

Tapscott perceives the net generation as bringing a seminal shift in values to the world. This generation is ready to choose, assume responsibility, search for personal freedom, and care for others. Thanks to the digital generation growing up, these values crowd out older and less virtuous values, changing the world into a better place. Here, a bit of scepticism may be in order as this is an extremely rosy picture. Tapscott underlines how the net makes it possible to interact in a criss-cross way without being hindered by borders or other artificial barriers. Formerly, people belonging to a small minority in a geographical place held on to values even if they were not the same as those adopted by the majority, but were under pressure. Thanks to the net they now have the possibility of finding supporters and like-minded people spread over the globe, changing their perception of themselves from a small and frequently powerless and isolated minority to a much bigger group.

Tapscott's work may be less relevant for education than some of the other studies, but his two main points about other values and global connectedness giving minorities more clout are of significance to the education system, and make it clear that it cannot neglect these trends.[44]

The University of Sussex[45] has developed a prototype of what is termed the "Homework Project". The idea is to activate parents and give them an opportunity to see and follow what their children are learning and doing in school by way of ICT instruments. This may work in the Western world and some parts of Asia, but not in Asia as a whole as many parents will not be able to step into that role because they missed out on basic education.

According to the university the system works like this:

> The teacher uses a whiteboard — a kind of giant touch-screen PC — for class lessons, while pupils can work on their own using the tablets. The teacher can then monitor every child, even sending messages offering help or fresh instructions. All this information is stored on the tablet, which the children can take home to show their parents. The tablet, which is run off batteries or the mains, can be viewed by the parents without the need for the internet. There's no need to plug it into a TV or computer either.
>
> By clicking on an interactive picture screen, parents can view: Activities that the child has completed at school that day and previously, along with lesson plans, photos, film, music, worksheets and fun items, sent direct to each tablet; homework activities set by the teacher; tips for parents about the class and homework activities; fun activities that relate to learning, but are not specific pieces of homework; a messaging system that allows messages to be sent/received to/from the teacher.

This way of teaching does away with the factory model and mobilizes teachers, pupils, and parents in an interactive way. No one is really the boss, but all of them can step in and work by taking initiatives and/or forward proposals. It fits into the child's picture of the world and how to learn which is by doing, trying, playing, and basically using audio-visual instruments instead of just sitting there and listening.

We do not know yet if this system will prove workable, and there is certainly a need for much more research, but the basic idea to accept and open the door for interaction using digital instruments will, in some way or another, do away with the old factory model as the paradigm for the educational system. It is also noteworthy that the parents are drawn in. That may help to close the generational gap between children using ICT as an integral part of their daily lives and parents using ICT in the same way they used pen and paper. It is thought-provoking that in the end this model may actually do more for the parents than for the children!

## Reform of Basic Education

Charles Leadbeater has put forward a thought-provoking synthesis of how to reform the education system in many ways, advocating lines similar to those set out above,[46] but which are more specific and have been tried in several schools. His views are that participation will become the central organizational basis of society and that an education system that does not understand and interpret the changed relationship between the pupil and their communities will not be able to deliver the kind of education pupils expect and perceive as conforming to their daily lives.

A school needs strong leadership with a vision making it clear to pupils/students where they are going, how, and why, and this leadership must — again — be in conformity with the pattern of society as it is now, and not as it was in the industrial age based on the factory concept. Adopting participation means a say for the student in what the school is teaching. Furthermore it spells the end of the old regimented way of dividing the school day into five or six lessons all of which are forty-five minutes long. Instead a lesson is scheduled to take whatever length of time is estimated for pupils to digest what they are supposed to learn, whether this be thirty minutes, half a day, or a whole school day.

The pupils/students are also being exposed to something new in the school system, namely, learning how to learn and use the instruments available.

Two researchers combine cognitive and non-cognitive skills when putting forward the argument for investing in disadvantaged young children in the United States.[47] According to the study, "a large body of empirical work at the neuroscience and social sciences has established that fundamental cognitive and noncognitive skills are produced in the early years of childhood, long before children start kindergarten. The technology of skill formation developed by economists shows that learning and motivation are dynamic, cumulative processes".[48] Schooling comes too late in the life cycle to be the main locus of remediation for the disadvantaged.

The main argument is that children's ability to acquire knowledge and learn not only depends on their intellectual capacity, but also their background, that is, the social fabric and societal norms. Neglecting this makes no sense. The implication for basic education is that schools should be in much closer cooperation and coordination with the local communities and the parents. The study says explicitly that "schools work with what parents give them" and this sentence or observation can be enlarged to say that schools work with what local communities and social structures give them.

The core argument or point brought forward by the study supports other evidence given above for the school and education system to adjust to society, and realize their place as being incorporated in and an integral part of society working on the basis of social norms, values, and structures.

# Higher Education (Tertiary)

## *Quantity versus Quality*

Asia's higher education system will turn out an increasing number of graduates in the next decades.[49] The question is whether the graduates will have gone through an education and the kind of training preparing them for economic life and business as it will look twenty-five years from now. The risk of rapidly mobilizing a sector such as education is not difficult to spot: quantity takes precedence over quality. It is also tempting to opt for good encyclopaedic knowledge instead of constructive criticism, which requires much more intellectual input and is more time-consuming, but which promises creativity, perhaps at a later stage, whereas fast rising societies look for results now. Universities simply do not have the time and resources to accommodate many more students and restructure at the same time. Many instructors are conservative. It is easier for them to continue in the same mode that they have been doing for many years, even decades.

The statistics on engineers, etc. graduating from Asian universities seem overwhelming, but do not reveal much about their competencies and, in particular, whether the education system is running on the old track or adapating to future demands. The yardstick often used is whether Asian graduates look capable of assuming job functions with multinational enterprises and particularly whether the education system provides not skills needed, but skills in demand. Another problem is that the increasing introduction of a market-driven system (financed partly by tuition fees and partly by fund raising) drive universities towards a money-biased development which prioritizes what students and sponsors are willing to pay for, irrespective of whether the demand for such skills is forecast to exist ten or twenty years down the road.

Higher education may underpin Asia's rise by detecting these trends and adjusting, thereby turning out students capable of working in a new technological environment, taking on new jobs, and fitting into an interdisciplinary and multicultural world. But it may also go the other way if the system fails to adapt. If so it will be a drain on Asia's development, turning out students who do not understand why they were let down and consequently start to question not only the universities, but society for allowing this to happen.

Two researchers at the East Asian Institute in Singapore[50] disclose that the Chinese Government in 2006 decided to slow down the growth in tertiary education to focus instead on quality. They also say that the teacher-student ratio is deteriorating and a growing tendency among universities to choose programmes that favour revenues instead of education and research can be spotted.

In the 1980s China introduced a review system for universities and colleges[51] to help promote the quality of higher education. In 2005, 1,778 institutions were on the list of qualified institutions signalling that the quality of education offered by an institution not on the list was unacceptably low. Sixty institutions received warnings asking them to step up efforts to improve on quality.[52] In October 2008 it was rumoured — but subsequently denied by the authorities — that an official from China's Ministry of Education had admitted that the decision in 1999 to expand higher education was made in haste and had resulted in the lower quality of higher education.[53] Xinhua reported in 2007 that the government had allocated US$320 million for improving the teaching quality at the universities aimed at undergraduate students.[54]

Fundamentally universities have to realize that their integration in societies means having the same exposure to change and need for adaptation as all other institutions. For China that means a change away from the socialist/communist mindset towards the market economy combined with globalization. The state of Chinese universities and their transformation process is provided by Mohrman[55] who points out that there are 23 million students in Chinese universities and that a new relationship between the state and the university is emerging at the same time that institutions are adapting to international norms. China is unique in educational history with its rapid enrolment rate growth, new governance structures being instituted, and efforts to build world-class universities — all happening at the same time.

Access to higher education is meanwhile suffering from the rising inequality in Chinese society. Hitherto it was the norm that children who pass the tests, which are often rigorous, would enter the education system, and even higher education. The shift to a market-driven system, at least partly financed and steered by money inflows, pushes the universities to increase fees, crowding out students from poorer families. The consequence is that the recruitment basis narrows when, in fact, it should broaden in view of the changing age composition diminishing the number of children coming into the relevant age bracket.

It is also pointed out that Chinese universities do not enjoy the same degree of self-governance and academic freedom that Western universities commonly do, thus raising barriers for building creative intellectual environments. Sometimes the criticism is voiced that Chinese and Indian professors spend most of their time teaching crowds of students and some administrative work on top of that, which leaves them with little or no time for research.

The same gap between quantity and quality can be found in India. McKinsey[56] comes to the conclusion that less than 25 per cent of Indian educated and trained engineers were qualified to work for multinational enterprises.[57] For finance and accounting officials the percentage was even lower. Sanjeev Sanyal[58] finds it worrying that India produces only 6,000 doctorates per year compared with 25,000 in the United States. He adds that about 4 per cent of U.S. science-engineering graduates and 7 per cent of those from Europe finish their doctorates while the percentage for India is 0.4 per cent. China produced barely 1,000 doctorates in 1990, but the figure is now more than 9,000 per year.

The quality gap is also spelled out by Shashi Nanjundaiah[59] who calls for a qualitative assessment system such as the ones operating in several Western countries. Only 25 per cent of all professionals holding degrees can find a job working for multinational companies. It may be lower for the kind of engineering where a high degree of technical skills is required.

Like the case in China, one of the acute problems in India is that institutions are driven towards money-steered activities because of the change in financing of universities. India, however, is somewhat different from China in that its universities were more Western-oriented to begin with, making the problem more one of having an old system which the universities themselves and the government cannot, will not, or is not, capable of changing. The basic problem for India's higher education, according to Shashi Nanjundaiah, is "that higher education has not kept pace with changes in the economy and the marketplace".

Duke University[60] researchers found in 2006 that when comparing the number of students earning degrees from accredited four-year programmes in engineering, computer science, and information technology, the United States remained in a strong position, with about 137,000 in 2004. India had 112,000. China saw about 352,000 graduates, but that figure, based on less directly comparable data, could well include "the equivalent of motor mechanics and industrial technicians", the study said.

Only a year later another study from Duke University[61] painted a much more nuanced picture, actually pointing towards China taking the lead and India catching up, even if the study still says that comparing degrees from the United States, China, and India is comparing something that cannot really be compared.[62]

The figures often mentioned in public debates say that each year the United States is turning out 70,000 undergraduate engineers, China, 600,000, and

India 350,000. These figures are not correct according to the Duke University study. A more realistic estimate is 133,854 for the United States, 517,225 for China, and 170,000 for India and even these figures seem to overestimate the number from China. Interviews with representatives of multinational and local technology companies revealed that they felt comfortable hiring graduates from only ten to fifteen Chinese universities. At the same time, China's National Development and Reform Commission reported in 2006 that 60 per cent of that year's university graduates were not able to find work. The quality of education being too low was not given as a reason, but keeping in mind the above-mentioned analysis, one suspects that this might have been one of the reasons.

Private enterprise has been India's salvation, says the study. In 2004, India had 974 private engineering colleges, compared with only 291 public and government institutions. New training centres have sprung up to address skill gaps between companies' needs and the capabilities of college graduates. The Indian Institutes of Technology (IIT) are best known and reputed to provide excellent education, but they produce only a small percentage of India's engineers. For example, in the 2002–03 academic year, the institutes granted a total of 2,274 bachelor degrees. The quality of other universities varies greatly, but representatives of local companies and multinationals told the authors of the study that they felt comfortable hiring the top graduates from most universities in India — unlike the situation in China. Anecdotal evidence suggests that it is easier to "buy" a diploma in China than in India. Even though the quality of graduates across all universities was inconsistent, corporate officials felt that with additional training, most graduates could become productive in a reasonable period.

Although the statistical data are not so good in China and India, the study ventures to forward estimates over the ten year period 1994–95 to 2004–05 for the United States, China, and India of Engineering and Technology Master's degrees and Engineering and Technology PhDs.

The results reveal that for master's degrees China overtook the United States in 2003–04 and India is fast closing the gap. For PhDs, China overtook the United States in 2002–03, while India is still lagging far behind. The figures are impressive, but as mentioned above, do not say much unless accompanied by verification of the quality and scrutiny that plagiarism has not taken place.

## Overseas Students' Role in Quality

A study looking into how many researchers return home and how many of the foreign nationals currently enrolled in U.S. universities intend to return home, confirmed that the lure of the United States is fading and homelands are becoming more attractive.[63] Such a flow of researchers educated in high-performance universities in the United States will not only boost the economy and high-tech industries, but also provide a pool of potential researchers and university professors for improving the quality of universities in the homelands.

Based on the LinkedIn network of professionals surveyed — the study admits it is not a flawless scientific approach, but good enough to form an idea of the trend — the findings say that for 1,203 researchers in their early thirties of whom 85 per cent had advanced degrees, career opportunities and quality-of-life were the main reasons for leaving the United States and going home. This contradicts much off-hand discussions and conventional wisdom focusing on difficulties with visa status (75 per cent said that this did not really influence their decision). Opportunities for career advancement into better jobs and/or getting higher responsibilities were mentioned by 61 per cent of the Indians and 70 per cent of the Chinese in the survey. Interpreted in the context of the present study, this simply means that the United States is losing out as the place to be for young, ambitious high-tech personnel looking for advancement, and a place where their talent can flourish, with India and China taking over.

This interpretation is reinforced when we switch to the findings in the part of the study asking foreign nationals currently in U.S. universities whether they intended to stay temporarily, or for a longer time, or permanently in the United States. The study recalls that past patterns for a five-year stay show a rate of 92 per cent for Chinese PhD holders and 85 per cent for Indian PhD holders from the science, technology, engineering, and mathematics disciplines.

Currently the scoreboard indicates that most students intend to stay in the United States, but for a short period. Fifty-eight per cent of Indians, 64 per cent of Chinese, and 40 per cent of European students intend to stay for at least a few years, but only 6 per cent of Indians, 10 per cent of Chinese, and 15 per cent of European students envisage staying permanently. When asked where they thought the best prospects lay — the United States or their home country — 86 per cent of the Indian students and 74 per cent of the Chinese students opted for their home country. These findings do not distinguish between scientists and other groups of students, otherwise, one suspects from anecdotal evidence, that the figures would tilt much more in favour of the United States. Sixty per cent of PhDs in engineering in the United States are awarded to foreigners, of whom Chinese and Indians dominate. Approximately 30 per cent of these return home after their education and this trend is going up — as the findings of the Duke University study confirm.

These figures and trends are encouraging for the future of quality education, but leave little doubt that Asia faces the challenge not only of taking in an increasing number of students, which is difficult enough and requires resources, but at the same time also of improving and enhancing the quality of education from primary school level to doctorates — a tall order by any account.

## *Reform of Universities*

Whether Asia can do that or will stumble depends — at least partly — on its ability to sense the way universities are going in the coming years, or even decades. The signs are that the university of today will not survive unscathed, but will undergo a deep and probably agonizing adaptation to the new age.

Higher education is going through a total recasting, resulting in the introduction of a new kind of university.

The individual must be able to find his/her bearings in a complicated, sophisticated, and ever changing society. There is a need for enhanced capability and boldness to navigate and assume responsibility for decisions and actions while at the same time keeping in mind, knowing, and giving due consideration to, repercussions on society as a whole. Political systems turn from securing welfare to offering opportunities. The responsibility for using these opportunities rests with the individual. The education sector becomes a cornerstone for this policy shift, and is entrusted with the task of providing the individual with the necessary skills.

Anders Fogh Jensen[64] defines this new paradigm linking it to *The Projective Society*:

> The passage to the society of projects has developed ways of organising where control is delegated to the employees or freelancers. The head of the company cannot control everything. The *company*, the *factory*, the *organisation* outsource the control to the individual. You are given [a] free hand, but if you do not perform and deliver a profitable result, you are not asked for the next project. Furthermore, in various lines of business, you are not expected to follow rules and fulfil duties, you are expected to anticipate changes and problems and you're expected to get ideas and throw out new suggestions, if you will pass on to the next project. This is the case even though it is rarely said.

Keywords in the new paradigm also framing the development of universities are creativity and independence, followed by multicultural behavior, interdisciplinary activities, and ability to adjust.

In a more complex and holistic society no sector or institution can operate on its own. There will emerge some kind of social contract encompassing citizens, enterprises, universities, and the public sector, about how to meet the need for constant change by developing knowledge, offering tools for a smooth transition process, sharpening competitiveness, and distributing benefits as well as burdens. If not the society may crack under the strain. Social coherence that deepens mutual trust and confidence making social capital a competitive parameter moves to the forefront.

Universities must:

- Undergo a fundamental transformation towards *enterprises* in that they need to produce something that somebody is willing to pay for, and become profitable over the medium term. The time when they knocked on the door of the government to get a big bag of money belongs to the past.

- Emerge as *intellectual enterprises* producing knowledge, skills, and abilities that are useful for society and communities. They deepen and sharpen knowledge as a competitive parameter and combine research and education to deserve the label of knowledge centres. Knowledge is different from traditional production factors (land, labour, and capital) because it can be used again and again and by many persons at the same time.

- Turn into *intellectual, multinational enterprises* competing in the global environment to produce students which the business sector deems competent enough to employ. Those from successful universities get a higher salary thus enhancing the reputation of the university which will then attract the best students. Competition among the leading universities follows the same pattern as competition among luxury brands. You produce a brand, you market it, you defend it, you enhance it, you communicate why your brand meets a demand better than other brands, and you charge a high price for what is regarded as a unique product. Universities out of this game are relegated to competing on price at the lower end of the spectrum, instead of competing on performance and brand — and in this spectrum there are hundreds, if not thousands, of other universities/enterprises and each one is anonymous.

The *financing* of universities is changing dramatically from public financing to private financing, which is a mixture of grants from private enterprises supplemented by an increasing share of expenditure met by tuition fees.[65] The role of private financing is growing with public financing reduced to 63 per cent in 2002 for fifty-three countries,[66] which raises the question of who is governing the direction/development of higher education? Is the aim to serve the public — the state — or is it to further economic development in the way seen by private enterprises taking over the financing? The significance of tuition fees raises another question, namely social and financial barriers for students who do not have access to money, despite having the ability to qualify for universities.

There are globally accepted benchmarks which are an indicator of how the university rates itself and how it is rated by customers (those that offer jobs to its undergraduates with examinations). These ratings are often controversial. It does not matter because they are decisive for how the three groups mentioned above rate the university and, therefore, its standing.

Asian universities are well placed to improve their standing in the years to come. According to the latest *Times* rating[67] the following picture emerges for ranking (all fields) in 2008, with ranking for 2007 in parenthesis:

| | |
|---|---|
| University of Tokyo | 19 (17) |
| Kyoto University | 25 (25) |
| University of Hong Kong | 26 (18) |
| National University of Singapore | 30 (33) |
| Hong Kong University of Science and Technology | 39 (53) |
| The Chinese University of Hong Kong | 42 (38) |
| Osaka University | 44 (46) |
| Peking University | 50 (36) |
| Seoul National University | 50 (51) |

All in all, nine Japanese universities, nine Chinese, three Korean, two Indian, two Singaporean, and one from Thailand are on the list of global 200 universities.[68]

Alliances between universities start to play the same role as business alliances. A couple of years ago, IARU (International Alliance of Research Universities), was created as probably the first of its kind stretching out to Asia. There will be many others. Fundamentally these alliances work towards a uniform quality and validity of education, regardless of how the education is spread among the partners in the alliance. It will promote mobility of students and faculty staff, thus opening up opportunities for universities to learn from one another, which is essential for improving research and education.

We will see mergers and acquisitions among universities. So far they have not emerged, but it will come. Rich and well-established universities would buy weaker and poorer-performing universities to get a foothold in new markets.

Large conglomerates will not be viable. Instead universities will tend to focus more and more on segments where they already have a competitive advantage.

That may and probably will lead to stronger links among institutes in the same research area from different universities, instead of strong links among institutes and faculties in different segments, but inside the same university.

Perhaps the future pattern is that Asian universities will be tempted to pursue the track of virtual universities and will be even more likely to accept link-ups between similar institutes, regardless of which university they belong to. To illustrate: nanotechnological institute A in university X may not find much common ground with the faculty of law in university X, but a lot of common interest with nanotechnological institute B in university Y. It is only a matter of time before the new breed of universities, based on the virtual world, break away from the traditional university structure and take the form of, say, nanotechnological university Z, comprising a number of nanotechnological institutes across the world.

Research and development will tend to be outsourced, by adopting the Battelle model. Batelle, headquartered in Ohio, is the world's largest non-profit independent research and development organization. It employs 20,000 people in more than 120 locations worldwide and conducts $4 billion in R&D annually through contract research, laboratory management, and technology commercialization. Its scoreboard is impressive as it has developed, in collaboration with its clients, commercial products, ranging from those to fight diabetes, cancer, and heart disease, to the office copier machine (Xerox).[69]

Large companies such as Boeing, Dupont, and Procter & Gamble, gradually manage R&D through the outsourcing or off-shoring of R&D.[70] The basic idea is that these companies, instead of using the conventional way of asking their own R&D department to solve a problem, put it on the Internet for auctioning to the best bidder, taking into consideration cost, benefits, and quality. There are several implications for this. One is that the window opens up on to a much larger mass of talent, thus increasing the chances of a better solution as the company's own R&D department may be inclined to think in "company ways". There is nothing wrong in that, but other ways may remain unexplored. Another implication is that R&D is spread around the globe, giving even remote places an equal opportunity to bid.

In this context the third implication is the most interesting. University institutes may bid. If they get the contract they earn money and, in some cases, a lot of money. They do not want to share these earnings with other non-earning institutes inside the same university. Indeed, they need the money to sharpen their edge and defend their competitive position. So the growing trend among businesses to outsource/offshore R&D may turn out to be the most powerful instrument for breaking up universities and pushing institutes in the same field to cooperate with one another, instead of cooperating with institutes outside that field but within the same university.[71] One of the stumbling blocks is the American universities' fascination with publications as a hallmark of academic excellence. They work by publishing or perish, so researchers who do not get their works published see their academic career blown away. The problem is that publishing does not bring in money, at least not very much, while universities need money. To unleash the R&D potential in universities, the publish or perish principle must be removed.

## Weaving Aspects of Education Together

If we accept the premise that the education system is an integral part of society, the main steering factors for the education sector in an Asian perspective over the next twenty-five years might be summarized in six points. We will start by quoting D.H. Hargreaves[72] about what universities teach: "the ability to learn how to learn and other metacognitive or thinking skills, the ability to learn on the job and in teams, the ability to cope with ambiguous situations and unpredictable problems".[73]

*First*, education is becoming an industry and may well grow into one of the largest and perhaps even the largest worldwide industry in the decades to come. The transformation of universities into multinational, intellectual enterprises stimulates this evolution. So does the trend towards a cost-benefit analysis of education and the gradual adoption of business models in running universities. Not many universities are left in the yesteryear mould of serving society, irrespective of cost versus benefits, and financed by a gracious government that does not ask questions about what it is getting for the money poured into the university.

Globalization means that it is becoming an international global industry. Students go where they get the best education for the money they can afford to spend.[74]

In 2005, 22 per cent of the tertiary students who went to overseas universities instead of universities in their home countries went to the United States and about 40 per cent to the European Union (Britain, 12 per cent; Germany, 10 per cent; France, 9 per cent; Spain, Belgium, and Italy, each 2 per cent; and Sweden plus Austria, 1 per cent). Australia accounted for 6 per cent and the Russian Federation, Canada, and New Zealand 3 per cent each.[75]

Of these foreign students, 48.9 per cent come from Asia. Looking at students from OECD partner economies, China was in the lead with 16.7 per cent, followed by India accounting for 6.2 per cent. Of the Chinese students 22.8 per cent went to the United States and 20.6 per cent to Japan.[76]

In the United States, the number of foreign students was just below 600,000. In 2008 Korea filled the number one slot for foreign students in the United States with 110,083, India came second with approximately 100,000, and China third with about 90,000. There is then a large fall in number to the next country, Japan, with about 40,000 students. Taiwan took the number six slot, Vietnam was number eight, and Nepal number ten.[77] This is encouraging as it suggests that Asian students have seen the writing on the wall auguring an international education system. These students and the best of the domestic crop will, however, only be tempted to work in Asia if Asian universities make it to the top tier.[78] It is a self-reinforcing process as quality enhancement is a function of resources, depending on economic growth itself stimulated by high quality universities. The best students and faculty staff will go abroad unless Asia's top universities join the league of global top universities. Also, it is not enough just to look at the number of Asian students. There are economic implications.

Foreign students in the United States spend almost US$14 billion in tuition fees, living costs, and related expenses amounting to more than one per thousand of the U.S. GDP.[79] Australia earns US$13.7 billion from the education sector, which corresponds to about 2 per cent of its GDP,[80] and New Zealand gets US$2.3 billion, equal to a little over 2 per cent of its GDP.[81]

When we look at the evolution in a longer-term perspective, we find that nothing prevents Asia from turning this situation around and over that time span emerge as an exporter of education. It depends to a large extent on its ability to take over the leadership in R&D, combined with a grasp of the new learning methods. In a foreseeable future the growing market will continue to be Asian students, but further down the road, the large increase in cohorts asking for education and higher education without finding this in their home country might be Africans due to demographic trends. It is not a foregone conclusion that they will follow in the footsteps of Asian students and seek their higher education in the United States, Europe, and Australia plus New Zealand.

Emerging Asian countries with high economic growth have begun to receive students from poorer Asian countries and the flow of students has started to go the other way — from Western countries to Asian countries, even if the figures still are modest.

According to the *China Daily*[82] 190,000 overseas students went to China in 2008 compared with less than 50,000 in 1997. They came from 188 countries, with the largest share from Korea (South), Japan, the United States, Vietnam, and Thailand. The target is 500,000 foreign students by 2020. Indian universities attracted 14,456 students from abroad in 2005–06. The majority came from West Asia, followed by South and Central Asian countries. The UAE had the lead accounting for 2,034. Nepal followed with 1,411 students, while 1,264 students from Iran went to India.[83] Several years ago Singapore set a target to attract 150,000 students from abroad in 2015 and the trend is encouraging, showing that the number rose from 50,000 in 2002 to 80,000 in 2006.[84]

*Second*, education becomes life-long, spanning from kindergarten almost to the end of life. We all need to enhance our skills and acquire new skills, regardless of our age and role in society.

Society needs to allocate more resources to education outside the conventional sphere of education, which means for people not necessarily in the productive part of society, and the skills of teachers must be diversified and adjusted to those they are teaching. Teaching methods must be enhanced and made to fit into the frame provided by society and technology.

*Third*, the world is becoming a combination of a learning and teaching society. It is no longer possible to dichotomize learning and teaching. In fact the relationship between teacher and students turns into some kind of interactive play where both gain from mutual contact. The teacher has lost the role of the person who speaks to a number of students listening.

Rose Luckin[85] puts it this way: "We now face a situation in which the teachers and experts, who know more than the learners about the 'stuff' we want people to learn, may well not know as much as the learners about the technologies that could act as learning tools. There is now a real opportunity for reciprocal teaching and learning. Learners need to know enough about these tools to learn more about a particular subject or skill, and teachers and experts need to know enough about these tools to scaffold learning."

This statement underlines succinctly how the new instruments of teaching, based on ICT and/or digital instruments, have completely changed the setting for teaching/learning, and the relationship between the teacher and the learner, and have done away with a distinction that for most of us looked ingrained in the system as a natural element, but has now come to block adaptation and adjustment.

*Fourth*, the main future pedagogic principles are known under the label of "from sage-on-the-stage to guide-by-the-side"[86] and is closely connected with PBL (problem based learning).[87]

The basic idea is to focus on the method to solve problems, instead of directly approaching a particular problem. By honing the skills for interaction between tutor and student, this kind of learning aims at problem solving, encourages asking questions, facilitates acquiring methods for understanding, and improves the reasoning of students, and, therefore, a higher level of understanding.

The students not only get to master the subject and some technical learning methods, but are also guided to look at the reasons behind the problems and how they can be solved. The horizon of students is broadened and their curiosity stimulated.

They are steered towards interdisciplinary approaches and the ability to apply their skills to problem solving, irrespective of what subject is on the plate. They have enhanced capacity to enter the challenging field of combining working alone, with working in teams, as well as knowing how and when to switch from one to another.

Correctly applied, this pedagogic principle becomes a stepping stone towards creativity by sharpening the skills of students to ask the simple question "why" every time they encounter a problem.

*Fifth*, in the digital future learning methods may well be more important than the curriculum. Put in another way, learning methods, rather than curricula, may distinguish universities from one another in their role as multinational, intellectual enterprises. This may be the new competitive parameter.

Open CourseWare (OCW)[88] is revolutionizing education. Nowadays each student has access to course material used for all courses taught at the Massachusetts Institute of Technology (MIT).

It is risky to jump to conclusions, but it is difficult to see OCW stopping with MIT. Other initiatives of a similar kind are Open Knowledge Initiative (OKI)[89] and Sakai.[90] Digital instruments open the door for access through open educational resources to the best possible curriculum, meaning that other curricula will be crowded out. Curricula are posted on the Internet and are accessible and available to all universities and for all courses and all students around the world. As a result, course material converges, because the best material wins the biggest number of students.[91] Why would anyone use a lower quality courseware than what is available on the Internet?

This does not mean, however, the uniformization of universities, but that universities will differ with regard to teaching methods — implying a shift in competitiveness from curriculum to teaching methods.

Universities putting effort into developing curricula risk losing out in the race as the best curriculum worldwide will almost automatically, gradually be applied, and those who employ graduates when they leave university will pay attention to whether they acquired their knowledge on the basis of this well-known curriculum or standard acknowledged as the "best".

This is foreseen and stated explicitly with great lucidity by three researchers[92] who say that "the university may need to reorganize itself quite differently, stressing forms of pedagogy and extracurricular experience to nurture and teach the art and skill of creativity and innovation. This would probably imply a shift away from highly specialized disciplines and degree programs placing more emphasis on integrating knowledge. To this need, perhaps it is time to integrate the educational mission of the university with the research and service activities of the faculty by ripping instruction out of the classroom — or at least the lecture hall — and placing it instead in the discovery environment of the laboratory or studio or the experimental environment for professional practice."

The shift to the focus on learning methods will be combined with improved capability to access information and use information — that is, store it, classify it, sift through it to make new combinations that open the door to using the information better than others. As information such as curricula is available to everybody, those who gain the competitive edge are those who are best in applying knowledge. Some kind of new skill to be acquired as a teaching/learning tool will develop around this parameter.

The first step for universities is to focus more on improving teaching/learning skills for the faculty. The digital age opens up the opportunity for a renewal and renaissance of individualization in teaching/learning, rather than doing this using the old tutorial system, but possibly embedded with some of its advantages. Teachers can interact with students via ICT and by so doing tailor learning and judge the capability of students to access step by step what they need to learn and are mature enough to digest.

The tendency to individualize and personalize products is already seen in consumption, with retailers analysing the preferences of consumers and trying to guess what they want when they enter a store, or contacting them without even luring them to the store. Many consumers have, in fact, a profile with retailers — most of them without being aware of this.[93] Dissemination of news is being more and more customized. So why should this not apply to education and higher education where the opportunities are so obvious?

The second step for universities is to realize that they cannot survive if they downgrade teaching and learning to beef up R&D, or disregard R&D to beef up teaching and learning. Universities need to be in the forefront doing both.

It is not possible to attract good faculty unless there is access and possibilities for R&D as this is the driver for the ambition of many, if not most, high ranking professors. But students do not go to a university to be left more or less in the cold without receiving good learning/teaching equipping them with the competences they look for. And unless good students come to the university, the interaction between teachers and learners is stalled before it has even taken off.

Students bring not only talent with them, but money. Competition among universities is growing increasingly harsher and they need an inflow of money to attract a good faculty that lures students. The same concentration of money and knowledge that can be seen in the business sector is making its way into the university world. There is a need for a growing number of students to contribute financially to the university and students grade universities according to what salaries graduation qualifies them for.

Universities need to be not only multinational, intellectual enterprises, but also knowledge centres accumulating competences — knowledge — that business, government, and society look for. They become some kind of bank storing knowledge and competences for society while at the same time producing a flow of students, ready to enter productive life to increase growth and prosperity. Ultimately universities are servicing the nation state/society/community with business, the government, and the public sector as the three main stakeholders, as they are the ones using the results coming out of the knowledge centres. Consequently they must be included in the steering process to ensure that universities are capable of delivering the output society wants and needs. In a review of Singapore's education system Gopinathan makes the point that "education is central to the ways in which the state makes itself relevant to its citizens".[94]

These knowledge centres must be in possession of competences and knowledge and also be ready, willing, and able to perform the R&D business demands and is willing to pay for. Therefore the third vector to integrate in the university model is knowledge someone (mostly the business sector) will be willing to pay for. A much higher integration of business and knowledge centres will take place in the decades to come, based on the simple observation that otherwise, money to finance the universities will not be forthcoming.[95]

*Sixth*, Asia cannot escape the choice between public and private financing, and concomitantly, the political question of who is controlling and governing higher education in the next twenty-five years: the nation state, the regions and/or local communities, or private enterprises. As funding is shifting away from the public sector and relying more and more on private enterprises, a crucial political decision awaits Asia's political leaders. If they want universities to be integrated in the public sector services available to the population, financing needs to be bolstered, increasing the share coming from the public sector. The alternative is to continue to rely on private funding, accompanied by the inevitable consequence of less public direction and more private control of higher education, underlining the transformation of universities into multinational, intellectual enterprises.

A synthesis of how Asia is placed in 2008, inspired by Professor S. Gopinathan,[96] might look like this:

Japan, Korea, Taiwan, Hong Kong, and Singapore can be classified as early modernizers, with expanded access to education, promoting gender equality, modernizing curricula, introducing relevant skills training via technological/vocational education, and investing in teacher training — actually going towards an education system suited to technology and society. They have been successful in coupling education outcomes (skill creation) with labour market needs. Their success in meeting the changes for education posed by the modern industrial society does not, however, mean that they are automatically on their way to meet the challenges of the future technology and societal structure.

This has led them to positive education results for the economy and social fabric. A considerable part of the population has got an education that helps them adjust to a modern society using modern technology. Economically the benefits have been there for everybody to see. But perhaps even more important is the contribution to social stability.

Significant technological/research and development capacity have been built up in Japan, India, China, and Korea in selected sectors such as IT for India, and microelectronics for China,[97] but none of these countries has managed to move into the category of an overall technological power, albeit Japan by numbers of patent filings, is actually a technological power. The contribution to the CERN collider[98] by Asian countries, in particular Japan, conveys the message of an understanding of basic research and its role in economic and technological development.

R&D in China is concentrated in universities, with two thirds of key national laboratories and one third of academicians of the Chinese Academy of Sciences and of Engineering, all working in universities. China, like many Western universities, tries to combine teaching, research, and enterprise as a concept of a university. There are over forty-four parks with almost US$4 billion private sector investment, over 5,000 enterprises that created 1,860 industrial products from research findings, and China attracted 1,300 Chinese students from abroad to create 100,000 jobs.

Indian companies account for more than US$25 billion in software exports. New areas such as Bangalore and others (Hyderabad, Chennai) are linking software and medical imaging and biotechnology in a forward-looking cluster of advanced techno-industry. The Indian Institutes of Technology are a major source of indigenous talent and workers, and are viewed as world-class centres.

## CREATIVITY[99]

### Happiness as Driver

Assuming that the societal model influences and maybe even forges creativity, different societal models and different educational systems produce different kinds of creativity. A crude interpretation is that some models enhance creativity and other models constitute an obstacle or at least make it more difficult to be creative. But, in fact, the distinction can be much more subtle when it comes to levels of creativity, segments, layers or variations/editions of creativity. The link to economic performance becomes obvious in that if the societal structure fits the economic and technological global trend, productivity and competitiveness increase. The next step is to open the door for discussion of whether societal structure or social fabric can be changed; in other words, enter into play as an economic instrument or competitive parameter, and if so, what time lags we are operating with. If the thesis is that societal structure is not very malleable in the short run while creativity is one of the determinants of competitiveness, then countries are caught in a competitive respective non-competitive position, based on their societal evolution, and economic policies lose much of their potency. If, on the other hand, the thesis is that societal structure is malleable also in the short run, another, and maybe crucial, policy instrument is at our disposal.

When we look back over the last thirty years, we will find it striking that around 1975, Japan, Germany, Switzerland, and Sweden were at the top of the economic league. All four had specialized in high quality — and expensive — investment goods. This was marvellous at the crest of the industrial age. Their societal structure supported this economic positioning. When the industrial age was replaced by the information society or whatever other term may be used to describe this, they all ran into difficulties. Economic policies did not suffice to turn them around. It is fair to say that these countries actually benefited from a particular societal structure in the era of industrialization, but were hit when the trend changed, forcing them into — not an economic adjustment — but a social restructuring requiring much more time and effort.

It is thus reasonable to assume that an economy's creativity, lack of creativity, and form of creativity, will at least partly be determined by societal structure.[100] Creativity thus becomes a competitive parameter influencing comparative advantages in economic globalization and creativity grows at least partly out of societal structures that are synonymous with institutions of society.

There is already evidence of such analyses in the work of the International Monetary Fund (IMF) and the World Bank. They apply a rather narrow definition of institutions looking only at governance, intellectual property rights, and so on. What is needed is a much broader definition of institutions, perceived as the social framework for citizens and enterprises, and forged by social evolution, for example, how the existence of a welfare society affects competitiveness, and the education system's role as "creator" of a creative mindset.

Societal organization via institutions is one of the most effective elements, if not the most effective element, behind economic success. Institutions promote innovation through education in the broad sense of the word — not confined to the school system — but encouraging and preparing people to try something new, and removing their various kinds of inhibitions. Institutions promote trust, making people less nervous when trying something new because they know that the underlying structure will help them through if they fail.

In this respect, trust and institutions are two sides of the same coin. The common perception of values growing out of societal structure means that people trust decisions taken by institutions even if they do not know the persons or the background of those deciding on issues of vital importance for their economic life. Without a common perception of values as the plinth of societal structures there would be no trust in institutions because decisions would depend on the individuals in charge.

Professor Teresa Amabile from Harvard has used twenty years to study the interaction between creativity and business and her findings are summed up in this way:[101]

Money, it turns out, does not foster creativity; Amabile found that people doing creative, innovative work do not focus daily on salary or a potential bonus. The same goes for severe deadlines, which despite common perceptions, generally stifle creativity. Competition and fear of retribution also hinder employees from doing their most creative work, she found. While these findings might chafe against popular management wisdom, they support Amabile's core hypothesis, formulated in social-psychological laboratory experiments, that creativity is a product of intrinsic motivation. "That's being motivated to do the work because it's interesting, it's positively challenging, it's captivating", she says. On the flip side, extrinsic motivators — expected evaluation, competition, and anticipated reward — tend to decrease creativity. Apparently people are much more likely to be creative when they are allowed to make progress, and even more so, when allowed to register their progress.

Mihaly Csikszentmihalyi[102] ventures the following:

> My hunch is — and, of course, there is no proof of this — that if an organism, a species, learns to find a positive experience in doing something that stretches its ability; in other words, if you enjoy sticking your neck out and trying to operate at your best or even beyond your best, if you're lucky enough to get that combination, then you're more likely to learn new things, to become better at what you're doing, to invent new things, to discover new things. We seem to be a species that has been blessed by this kind of thirst for pushing the envelope. Most other species seem to be very content when their basic needs are taken care of and their homeostatic level has been restored. They have eaten; they can rest now. That's it. But in our nervous system, maybe by chance or at random, an association has been made between pleasure and challenge, or looking for new challenges.[103]

What Csikszentmihalyi says is basically two things: happiness is the foundation for creativity, and individuals become happy/creative when living in surroundings allowing them to express themselves.

If this approach is accepted, the challenge of society is to shape an environment where people become happy by self-expression. That will lead them to try new ideas — stick their necks out — whereas a society holding back will confine individuals to be, let us say, less creative.

One could add to this observation the importance of pride in the company, in its performance, the staff, and history, and indeed in the performance of each staff member. Pride is the result of having achieved something and realizing that it was done because of a high performance level and making progress, and this must be acknowledged by top management as one of the most important drivers of creativity.

Turning to the question of what makes people happy, we see a growing number of research and studies being published, indicating that whereas such topics were judged a bit "non-academic" some years ago, this is definitely not the case anymore. It also reflects that researchers are increasingly coming to the conclusion that economic growth models which do not incorporate the human factor and people's state of mind are less accurate than those acknowledging the significance of a fluid element such as happiness.

Ruut Veenhofen[104] points to the same factor for happiness as Mihaly Csikszentmihalyi, but phrases it a bit differently, saying that the more freedom of choice an individual has, the more he/she can live the life they want and the happier he/she becomes. Security and wealth may have been decisive factors for economic growth in the past, but now human happiness and well-being become more important. Professor Veerhoven underlines that happy people show a lot of personal initiative. They know what they want, are independent and active, tackle problems head on, can handle stress. They know how to approach other people and nurture contact with them.

Richard Layard in his monograph from 2005[105] takes the view that there is actually a possibility for measuring happiness and that money and wealth do not make people happy or, let us say, happier; happiness depends on family relationships, financial situation, work, community and friends, health, personal freedom, and personal values.

Layard is an economist and analyses happiness, and, more importantly, what government can do and which government policies can make people happy/happier. The foundation for his analysis is the philosopher Jeremy Bentham,[106] who more than 200 years ago, was instrumental in sketching the ideas of utilitarian thinking.

Adrian White[107] has collected data from 80,000 people worldwide in 178 countries to map out what makes people happy and to rank nations.[108] His findings can be summarized the following way:

Temporary swings in mood have only a marginal effect on subjective well-being (SWB) whilst long-term changes and situational factors do have an important impact on SWB.

A nation's level of happiness seems to be associated with health levels, wealth, and the provision of education. The three-predictor variables of health, wealth, and education were also very closely associated with one another, illustrating the interdependence of these factors. People in countries with good health care, a higher GDP per capita, and access to education, were much more likely to report being happy.

The large Asian countries come in the happiness ranking with China at 82nd, Japan 90th, and India 125th. Adrian White notes this with surprise as these are countries that are thought to have a strong sense of collective identity which other researchers have associated with well-being.

Michael Norton[109] forwards the observation that even if people use a lot of time and effort earning money and amassing a big fortune it does not in itself bring happiness — a conclusion also reached by Amabile. Money, however, can do so if it is spent in a prosocial way. Even if the money spent is quite small it can bring happiness to the person spending it to help or assist others. If we assume this to be correct, it casts another angle on understanding altruism and fund-raising.

Denmark occupies pole position as the happiest country in a number of studies.[110] Justina Fischer[111] has analysed the reason for Denmark's position and the results are interesting for looking at happiness, creativity, and economic activity in a general context.[112] The main point is that mutual trust is the key. Fischer explains the importance of trust for economic growth this way: "If you trust someone in a market transaction you have lower transaction costs. You do not even have to have a contract because you trust his or her words. So you have no contract costs, you have no enforcement cost." Christian Bjørnskov, researcher at the University of Aarhus, goes one step further by adding, "It means that the judicial system functions better in Denmark, education works better than in a lot of other countries. The trust contributes to the happiness, but it also contributes to concrete economic results."[113]

A study by the University of Cambridge about happiness among Europeans[114] points in the same direction by coming to the conclusion that happiness has little to do with wealth. Peoples' jobs gave them a sense of self-respect and the most important factors influencing happiness appear to be the quality of our social interaction with others and the confidence we have in our country's institutions.

The importance of social networks and, consequently, societal structure for happiness is the core of a study by two researchers (Fowler and Christakis)[115] called "Dynamic spread of happiness in a large social network".[116]

The main points of the study are:

- Happiness is a network phenomenon clustering in groups of people
- Happiness spreads across diverse arrays of social ties
- Network characteristics independently predict which individuals will be happy years into the future

Happiness is thus primarily neither a question of economics nor of individual behaviour and/or choice, but the property of groups of people. Changes in individual happiness ripple through a social network and generate large-scale structure in the network, giving rise to clusters of happy and unhappy people — but not mixing with each other.

The findings support and enhance the fact that basic characteristics, such as trust and a common set of values which draw people together, strengthen happiness and particularly generate a framework where the feeling of happiness spreads among individuals.

## Creative Organizations

If there is a link between happiness and creativity, and we assume that this is the case, the next step is to analyse how to forge a frame for creativity inside organizations, institutions, and enterprises. What makes an organization creative? Can a non-creative organization be turned into one that is creative? Is it good/necessary that the whole organization becomes creative?

These questions find some answers in a paper by Austin and Nolan.[117] Their findings[118] conclude that it is very difficult, albeit not impossible, to turn an enterprise from being non-creative to being creative, and that the most propitious model is to ensure that some segments of an organization are creative while other segments are not.

The core to most management in enterprises are predictability, planning and a well-known organizational structure with a hierarchical set-up as a kind of backbone. The worst thing, dreaded by all well-managed enterprises, is surprise. Therefore almost all management techniques focus on avoiding surprises and building a structure with that purpose in mind.

This is the death warrant for creativity. The creative organization must, per definition, aim at producing something new, something not expected, and/or something not known. Otherwise it is not creative. For that to flourish, the structure must be loose, open, and allow for people to operate according to their own preferences. If they are squeezed into firmly established structures their creativity is stifled.

That explains why an organization cannot easily be changed because it means that the whole organization and its work culture must be turned upside down. It can be done, but at a high cost. It is better to lay the foundation for a creative organization from the start and let it grow. The industrial model, rooted in hierarchy, rule following, and control mechanisms, fits unfortunately this description, which explains why several industrial countries (Japan, Germany) have found it difficult to become more creative.

Traditional incentives and methods to motivate and encourage staff, such as promotions and high bonuses, do not really work to bring about a creative organization. Other factors such as a creative environment which leaves doors open for independent thinking, easy contact with other people, and activities mixing work and leisure, are more promising.[119] Young people like challenges and may be demotivated by what is traditionally classified as motivation.

The snag in this is the temptation to make parts of the enterprise running normal business activities creative also, when there is no need to do so. If the operational parts of an enterprise are engulfed in a loose, creative, stimulating environment, it can go very wrong as these departments' strict business models are based on predictability and planning is called for.

The follow-up question is whether creativity is embedded in the genes of some human beings to be unveiled by circumstances and opportunities, or whether it can be learned. Can we learn to be creative?

Amabile tackles this question[120] and says that "creativity does depend to some extent on the intelligence, expertise, talent, and experience of an individual.… But it also depends on creativity thinking as a skill that involves qualities such as the propensity to take risks and to turn a problem on its head to get a new perspective. That can be learned." It also follows from Amabile's perception of the background for creativity that management must take an interest in the daily life of staff and employees to ensure that they feel motivated and nourish a dedication to their work and the company. Only if they feel able to progress and are motivated can creativity be expected. The lesson to draw is that creativity is not an isolated phenomenon, but is integrated in the corporate policy, and particularly in the conditions of work and life offered to employees.

Shaping conditions for creativity also reaches beyond a narrow environment.

The Medici Effect[121] coined by Frans Johansson[122] says that the interaction of fields, disciplines, or cultures, constitutes the most propitious background for creativity because confrontation with another way of thinking forces people to think differently and out of the box, thus giving birth to new ideas. A deliberate policy of matching people from various cultures, etc. in a working environment might lead to benefits from such interactions. It goes without saying that low tolerance and a low inclination to interact outside one's own cultural circle makes such a policy a genuine management challenge. Only by ensuring that staff are motivated can it work; otherwise it may easily backfire.

Tripsas[123] adds that the introduction of a new product or innovation immediately has a spin-off effect on suppliers, competitors, distributors, and, of course, consumers. They need to adjust, and by forcing them to do so, a new wave of creativity arises. Companies may not pay much heed to this spin-off effect, but it is important for societies because, handled correctly, it can spread creativity to other sectors.

The triumvirate of the quest for happiness, creativity, entrepreneurship means that people inside these groups introduce new societal behaviour and consequently new social rules framing how to do business among people and companies, and breaking out of the established patterns. In many societies and certainly in stagnant or stationary societies, people and companies conform to rules and regulations. That kind of attitude stifles creativity. Societies undergoing creative changes allow creators to shape the rules and subsequently transpose informal rules into laws, rules, and regulations. Khanna[124] formulates it this way:

> People in these societies are running faster than their rules and laws can keep up. So they are creating the rules as they go along.… these processes

are unfolding not just in the mainstream business sector but in society writ large and even in politics and civil society.

Tapscott[125] synthesizes the impact of the new generation — in his terminology, the grown up digitals, and their norms — in eight points.

- Number one. They want freedom in everything they do, from freedom of choice to freedom of expression. They use new technology to escape from traditional constraints on their private and work lives.
- Number two. They love to customize, personalize. They want to customize the use of the World Wide Web and what it brings them, and they particularly want to take part in the process of shaping things and developments.
- Number three. They are the new scrutinizers. They are critical about what is offered and expect suppliers to deliver according to what is promised.
- Number four. They look for corporate integrity and openness when deciding what to buy and where to work. Basically ethics and values take on a more preponderant role in steering their choices.
- Number five. They want entertainment and play in their work, education, and social life. They do not suffer dullness gladly, but expect life to deliver entertainment and distractions — all the time.
- Number six. They are the collaboration and relationship generation. They use the Internet to shape networks and do not see themselves in isolation, but look for people sharing the same identity and values.
- Number seven. They want speed. Things must be done and must happen now.
- Number eight. They are innovators, always looking for ways to personalize and do things differently, with a view to improving themselves and being entertained, and working and learning — all the time.

Every one of these eight norms points in one direction. The new generation — grown up digitals — wants more happiness and more ways to self-fulfilment and is much more creative than preceding generations. And they see the Internet or the World Wide Web as an instrument to support their endeavours to achieve that.

Two American studies[126] of attitudes among the young generation, labelled the millennial generation, come to analogous conclusions. This generation seeks adventure, change and challenges, entertainment, shies away from boring jobs based on routine, is flexible and ready to adapt, provided they see and understand the purpose, and looks constantly for new jobs, which they feel offer them opportunities to fulfil and develop their potential and enlarge their competences. They are loyal to the corporations if the corporations match their ambitions and offer them opportunities to grow their skills. Otherwise they are not loyal.

The results of various academic works on happiness and creativity are not fully congruous. Some surveys associate wealth with happiness; others reject that as an important determinant. Even if there are discrepancies among studies, a preliminary conclusion, based on the literature mentioned above and the observations in the prelude of happiness as a driver for creativity and growth, might contain the following elements:

- Happiness is basically interesting because it improves productivity and enhances competitiveness.
- The main ingredients seem to be trust and reasonable equality of income, and quality of life such as health and education, but not so much wealth and income.
- Without happiness creativity falls and an important, probably crucial, factor in the happiness-creativity equation is the freedom of choice to live the life preferred.[127]
- Creativity cannot be confined to a narrow analysis or to policies looking at one sector or segment of society; it is interdisciplinary in nature.
- Creativity must be seen in the broader context of sociological, even psychological, circumstances, drawing in its repercussions on other sectors of economic life.
- Studies and analyses confirm that happiness, and particularly happiness as the plinth for creativity, has much more to do with societal structure than economic variables.

## SOCIAL CAPITAL[128]

### What is Social Capital and How Does it Work?

Before starting on the theme itself, it may be useful to draw the link to education discussed above. Education may play a crucial role in shaping social capital especially in new nation states. It did so in European countries such as France, where the school enjoyed unanimous respect, and the teacher — *l'instituteur* — prestige. Nationwide social capital was promoted by the school system with some success. It can be seen from many other countries how schools and the education system grapple with the problem of whether to bring about nationwide social capital, and, if so, how to do it. In many countries with a pluralistic school system — private versus public schools, non-religious versus religious schools, to mention a few examples — the education system may form an obstacle for nationwide social capital and instead foster group-based social capital. The education system faces the same kind of problem in countries with several languages and races confronted with the question of whether to disregard their cultural particularities, or accept them with the inevitable consequences for nationwide social capital, irrespective of what decision is made.

Economic theory operated originally with three production factors: land, labour, and capital. This has been reviewed, and one new perception is that of human capital, perceived as the technological knowledge and skills embedded in human beings, so that more knowledge leads to higher productivity. Human capital relates the performance of one individual to education, training, and knowledge enhancing the ability of the individual to produce. Social capital is the latest "discovery" to interest economists because it is generally accepted that higher social capital is synonymous with higher economic growth.[129] Social capital relates the performance of many individuals to the societal environment and the ability to work together in such a way that their relationship enhances or impedes the combined performance level.[130]

This seems to be verified by various studies and analyses. Robert J. Barro[131] concludes that greater maintenance of what he terms "the rule of the law" is favourable to growth. A similar conclusion is reached by a business forum (the Caux Round Table) with its chairman in 2001 stating that higher social capital serves as a basis for economic growth, and social capital should precede policies for growth.[132]

The concept of social capital fundamentally rests upon the works of three researchers[133] who started their work twenty to thirty years ago — and which have been refined and elaborated by many researchers since. And the heart of the matter is that social networks are important for behaviour and incorporate values which is why social relations constitute some kind of capital, making it advantageous for human beings to enter into social relations and build a social network.[134] We can generalize this by saying that social capital is the supplementary advantages/enhanced capabilities accruing to individuals who enter into relations with other individuals without an institutional framework, such as rules and legislation, forcing them to do so. The intriguing question is, however, why people are willing to put resources at the disposal of others?

Sociologists[135] point to two motivations. The *first* is that they sense an obligation to do so. Norms and values and behavioural patterns are so strongly embedded in society that breaking them implies such high costs that very few individuals contemplate it and even fewer actually do it. The *second* one is that individuals have come to the conclusion that this is mutually beneficial, and saves them costs and time in effecting economic transactions, as well as a mixture of normative (value based) and instrumental behaviour (efficiency based).

Interestingly enough, these explanations do not include one of the observations from the study of happiness — that people's happiness increase by spending money to make other people better off. If we generalize the observation about happiness, we get a third explanation telling us that people enter into social relations and put advantages at the disposal of others not only because it adds to their own advantages, but because the action of spreading happiness to others increases their own happiness.[136]

Political scientists[137] extend the concept of social capital from individuals to larger communities, even nations, saying that inside large communities social capital by following common values and putting advantages at the disposal of one another enhance the economic performance of the community/nation they live in. Social capital becomes a competitive parameter or economic policy instrument.

The snag in this perspective is that in a larger community, social capital may emerge inside various groups, but may not encompass the whole community/nation. If so, social capital develops into a potential factor for breaking the community/nation up into subcommunities, viewing one another with distrust, even enmity. This is seen in the United States, where various groups based on ethnicity and/or religion, create strong social capital within their own groups, but this takes place at the cost of the country missing national social capital. This underscores the fact that social capital, if allowed to exist or even be promoted within subgroups, may turn into a deleterious factor having potential damaging effects for the development of the community/nation.[138]

## Significance for the Economy

The crucial importance of trust and confidence for any economic system is highlighted by the economist Kenneth Arrow: "Virtually every commercial transaction has within itself an element of trust, certainly any transaction conducted over a period of time."[139] Good governance promotes social capital (mutual trust and a feeling of common destiny among citizens and between citizens, business, and governments) that encourages citizens to put in an extra effort and run higher risks. Knowing that it has earned the trust of the citizens, the government will be bolder and not shy away from introducing legislation deemed necessary to cope with globalization and change.

Adam Smith, normally credited with laying down the intellectual framework for economics, also stressed trust and confidence for example by saying:

> When the people of any particular country have such confidence in the fortune, probity, and prudence of a particular banker, as to believe that he is always ready to pay upon demand such of his promissory notes as are likely to be at any time presented to him; these notes come to have the same currency as gold and silver money, from the confidence that such money can at any time be had for them.

This is stated in connection with the virtue of paper money in what Adam Smith called "the great wheel of circulation".[140]

According to Charles Darwin, those who survive are those best at adapting to changing circumstances. A society where citizens act only by command and control will find adaptation more cumbersome, time consuming, and costly, compared with a society where citizens act on their own initiative, are rooted in mutual trust, and have an understanding of the long-term goals. The ability to adapt with speed and no loss of time are essential factors in a game where the first to adapt reaps a rich reward and latecomers are punished.

On top of that, resources are freed for productive purposes as consensus diminishes conflict within society, thus reducing the necessity for rules and dispute settlements to be enforced.

Trust, coherence, and social capital enhance the competitiveness of a society through its shorter and speedier adaptation, and free its resources for productive purposes. It has one more asset to its advantage.

New technology is wonderful for productivity, but its effectiveness depends on how smoothly it is incorporated in the production processes. In itself it does not matter much. What matters is its application across a wide spectrum of society — not only in industry and business, but also in public service. The key is willingness of people to change from one technology to another. The barrier is uncertainty about what it will mean for remuneration, performance, wage levels, and, most important of all, employment opportunities. The mindset of citizens must be geared to adaptation, reinforced by the message that change and adaptation are the key to job security and economic wealth. Trust embedded in social capital makes this message credible and legitimate. Even if it sounds strange, it is nevertheless true that change and transition enhance stability and social security, whereas clinging on to existing structures imposes brutal burden-sharing on societal groups. To get this message across is the art of true statesmanship, but if done successfully, the distribution of benefits replaces burden sharing. Social capital and trust form a propitious ground for the acceptance of this sometimes unwelcome truth.

Job security depends on mobility. In June 2009 the European Commission[141] put forward an ambitious plan for the European labour market. The basic idea is to lay the foundation for adaptability, change, and mobility. It rests on the conceptual thinking of how *flexicurity* (flexibility and security) and *mobication* (mobility and education) can combine to form a smooth functioning labour market, opening up the possibility of workers having new competences in the future, precisely to meet the challenge of new jobs, irrespective of changing circumstances.

Job mobility is a well-known concept, meaning that the worker changes job within the same scope of competences, e.g. an IT worker shifts from one IT company to another one. Geographic mobility is also well known and calls for the readiness to move geographically to take up a job — again with the same competences — in another geographical place.

The new ideas focus on a combination of mobility and education. One vector is functional mobility, meaning that a person over a lifetime shifts from one job function to another. In the first phase he/she can be teacher, in the second phase, a researcher, and in the third phase, perhaps move into coaching other persons, or consulting. The other vector is transitional mobility, meaning that a person can shift between working, studying, going on sabbatical, taking care of the family, working again — in short, is going in and out of completely different functions. The main point in this is to instil in the person the ability to change and adapt as one of his/her competences, perhaps the most important one.[142]

## Group-based Social Capital

Unavoidably the debate about social capital and trust has been captured by its links to religion and form of government.[143] The point in this context is that figures revealing individual trust in other people say a good deal about social capital. In an international comparison, answers to the question "Can most people be trusted?" China with 53 per cent and India with 39 per cent do not fare badly. They are well above the United States with 36 per cent and so is the largest Southeast Asian country, Indonesia, with 46 per cent, but far below the frontrunners — the three Nordic countries showing around 60 per cent.[144] If these figures are correct and some scepticism is warranted for an international comparison like this one, Asia is not badly placed to play the card of social capital in the future.

The study about happiness in Europe[145] has as one of its conclusions that trust in society is very important. The countries that scored highest for happiness also reported the highest levels of trust in their governments, laws, and one another. Seen in a broader context, this implies that higher social capital increases people's happiness and in light of the thesis about the link between happiness and creativity, this means it promotes creativity.

The challenge for governments is to build bridges among and between groups often having very little common ground with respect to values and norms. Social capital based on trust exists in all societies and communities. An illustration of how strong subcommunities' social capital can grow is given in the book *Freakoconomics*[146] which tells how a criminal gang in Chicago developed social capital by keeping its members together, irrespective of the high risk of being murdered by other gangs or arrested by the police. The gang members are born and brought up in communities not linked to the rest of society and do not know of any other kind of life and so find themselves completely lost outside their gang (community). The authorities and society as a whole do not in reality exist for them — actually these constitute a threat to the community they have built for themselves.

This threat may be accentuated by a distorted version of wisdom of the crowds,[147] where the crowd uses ICT to shape knowledge, intelligence, and wisdom. If social capital breaks up, each group will have its own social capital and constitute a "crowd", and perhaps shape its own and separate "wisdom of the crowd". In that case a conflicting mass of information and knowledge would dominate the Internet and aggravate tensions and differences between groups.

Further light on the risk that segmentation of social capital may affect society and the economy in a negative way is provided by an Australian study[148] that analyses social inclusion and social exclusion in Northern Adelaide. The study looks at elements leading to social capital inside groups which constitutes barriers for these groups to join economic life and take part in social activities of a broader character outside the groups in which they find themselves comfortable.

The study selects three sub-locations: a disadvantaged area, a more affluent area, and a relatively affluent town.

The conclusion is that people living in the disadvantaged area were more likely to have inward-focused relationships based upon neighbours and friends than outward relationships involving taking part in economic and social life. In other words, these subgroups tended to live their own lives and keep a distance from the rest of society, while the two other subgroups had lower social capital of the inward-looking type, but showed a stronger degree of reaching outside their groups to society as a whole.[149]

In the vocabulary of social capital, the inward-looking subgroups were strong in bonding that focuses on social relationships where people share basic values of a non-economic character to help and assist one another because they trust one another, but not outsiders. It is difficult to leave the subgroup and equally difficult to enter the subgroup. It also tends to freeze relationships, preventing adaptations and adjustments to what is going on in society as a whole, and constitutes a barrier — or at least potentially — to building nationwide social capital. The other two groups were weaker in bonding within their own groups, but displayed stronger social capital that reaches beyond the subgroup, which serves as a tool for relations among people without common ethnicity and religion, and helps people to interact with authorities, thus boosting economic growth and nationwide social capital.

A recent study[150] throws some light on how narrow or broad or diversified the network is for people, and why the network of some people is broad, while for others, narrow.[151] The broader it is and the more diversified it is with regard to occupations of the contacts in the network, the more likely it is that the person can move from one subgroup to another.

Several economic studies have disclosed the costs of subcommunities running separate economic systems inside a nation state, preventing the emergence of a nationwide economic system.

Amartya Sen[152] observes that in the absence of a market economy for the economy or nation as a whole, the economic system degenerates into segments of markets, each having its own characteristics and price structure, and not developing into a national market with common prices and a common price structure. The segmentation of the market prevents transparency so separate markets with separate market conditions can exist almost next to one another. Sen does not use the word social capital in this particular context, but it is clear that what allows separate markets to function, each according to specific economic characteristics, is social capital inside the groups running these economic systems, whereas social capital shared by the groups would break down the barriers.

Avinash K. Dixit[153] analyses the creation of groups in the absence of national social capital and concludes that in a society without an efficient and trustworthy legal system, citizens and enterprises fall back on establishing groups in which they can trust the behaviour of others on the basis of values and norms nurtured inside the group, which have little to do with norms and values being flagged for the nation state. As there is no national social capital and no effective legal system, citizens and enterprises do business with those they trust, and they are to be found inside a congruous value system based on social capital inside a group.

The result of lacking social capital is a non-optimal allocation of production factors because these will be steered by the economic structures inside the groups and are not effective for society or the nation state as a whole. The groups and/or members of the groups can be better off compared with other groups by maintaining their own closely knit operative economic system instead of taking part in a national economic system that would actually make the GDP higher. They do not trust the national authorities — or national governance — to ensure an equitable distribution of the higher income, so they prefer a lower income over which they have control and can distribute within the group according to the group's values.

## Institutions

The importance of institutions as a link between the government, the citizens, and the most important groups in society was pointed out in 1968 by Samuel Huntington.[154]

The main function of the institutions is their ability to absorb conflicts between groups with different, and sometimes contradicting, values/social capital. In the absence of institutions such conflicts just roll on making it even more difficult to shape national social capital. The stronger the institutions, and the better they function, the more likely it is that conflicts can be avoided or stopped, thus opening up space for efforts to shape nationwide social capital.

Before looking into what makes institutions strong, it is worthwhile to cast a glance on why institutions and common norms/social capital go hand in hand. Institutions look faceless, but are, in fact, composed of human beings. It is a person or several persons who take decisions effective for citizens and/or enterprises.

Let us suppose there are many variants of social capital and consequently norms in a society. Citizens or enterprises referring a matter to the institutions will then not know the norms of the person(s) making decisions that may be of vital importance for their lives. If so they will harbour a good deal of scepticism towards the institutions and will likely not trust or confide in the institutions at all. They may fear that the person(s) in charge of the matter belong to the same group as their opponents so they could not possibly expect a neutral judgment. If, on the other hand, some nationwide social capital is emerging or already exists, they know that the person(s) in charge will have the same values as they and their opponents have, so the decision will be made on a neutral basis, factoring in pros and cons.[155]

The decisive question is then whether institutions frame already existing social capital/norms/values, or whether institutions have been given the awesome task of imposing common behaviour on a nation state and its citizens where this does not exist.

In the *first* case, institutions serve as a final resort in cases of which there will be few where citizens and/or enterprises interpret the common values in a different way — not different values, but interpretations of the same values. The overwhelming part of economic transactions run smoothly and institutions do not gobble up many resources from society. This can also be stated in the way that institutions codify norms or already existing behavioural patterns normally through legislation.

In the *second* case, the role of institutions becomes much more difficult and cumbersome as groups adhering to diverging social capital/norms go to institutions asking them to decide which one is the correct rule for the nation. The role of institutions here is not to codify already existing behavioural patterns, but to lay down what behavioural pattern is valid. The institutions establish norms/values and social capital. The resources channelled into the institutional framework, as can be seen for example in the U.S. legal system, become large and weigh down the economy.

Citizens/enterprises also have different perceptions on social capital and how to behave. In the first case, citizens/enterprises make up their mind on what they think is the right behaviour and move on without actually checking with legislation. They know their rights and obligations by instinct and upbringing. In the second case, citizens/enterprises start by studying legislation to find out what are their rights and obligations, and afterwards decide what to do and often find out that somebody else contests whether that is the warranted action and whether it is in accordance with the legislation.

The same pattern is visible with regard to enforcement. When institutions have made a decision, those who took a matter to court or applied whatever procedure, will, in the first case, be much more likely to abide by the judgment than those in the second case. Even if the institutions' decision did not favour them, they trust the decision to be "fair". In the second case, those who lose do not trust the institution either before or after the decision and will consequently continue trying to reverse its decision and sometimes not abide by it.

Not all societies are lucky enough to have strong social capital anchored in common values. For those that do not, governance becomes extremely important. In the first place they have to establish institutions to hold society together, and in the second place, disseminate from above a common rule set, combined with common values that can form the basis for nationwide social capital.

Francis Fukuyama[156] takes up the challenge to analyse how the stock of social capital can be increased. He outlines the following possible instruments or policies.

- Nation states do not have many obvious levers for creating many forms of social capital, which are fundamentally a by-product of factors outside the control of the government, such as religion, tradition, shared historical experience.
- Governments probably have the greatest direct ability to generate social capital in the education sector. Educational institutions do not simply transmit human capital, they also pass on social capital in the form of social rules and norms.
- Nation states indirectly foster the creation of social capital by efficiently providing necessary public goods, particularly property rights and public safety.
- Nation states can have a serious negative impact on social capital when they start to undertake activities that are better left to the private sector or to civil society.

The conclusion is that social capital is a long-haul process calling for patience and mobilization of societal policies. In the short term, there is very little, if anything, the government or nation state can do. Another conclusion is that social capital may have strong repercussions for the economy that affect its competitiveness, but is itself not susceptible to influences from economic policy.

## Financial System[157]

The financial system is a weathervane indicating the strength of social capital. If people trust one another and the government, they put their savings into the banks. If not, they keep them at home as gold, jewellery, and invest in property.

A study mentioned above that takes Italy as a case with characteristics that make it worthwhile as an indicator for other countries also[158] includes the link between social capital and the financial system. The conclusions confirm the intuitive belief that high social capital increases the tendency to use financial instruments and make deposits with banks while a smaller proportion of wealth is invested in cash, jewellery, or gold. Higher social capital makes it less likely that financial transactions are confined to groups or subgroups such as families where people automatically trust one another, but instead take place among individuals who do not know one another, and involve financial institutions as intermediaries. Higher social capital also makes it more likely that cheques are used and credit is easier to obtain.

It is still a widespread practice in Asia to keep part or all of one's wealth in gold, etc., but confidence in financial systems, evidenced by fast rising deposits, is growing. Bank deposits in China and India[159] reveal a growth rate far outstripping the growth in the total amount of savings. It may be too hasty to draw the conclusion that trust in financial institutions lies behind this development, but it seems obvious that people do not shy away from banks now.

An important element for building trust in the financial system, which at the same time enhances the efficiency of the system, will be the performance of Asian pension funds in the coming years and decades. With the growing number of elderly people to be catered for, investment policies chosen will have far reaching economic and social impact on society.

A study by the Association for Sustainable and Responsible Investment in Asia, sponsored by the Asian Development Bank, predicts a strong rise in funds available for pension funds to invest in and recognizes the trend towards more diversification, including in equities. The study advocates that Asian pension funds take steps to promote ESG investment (taking environmental, social, and governance factors into consideration), thus contributing not only to growth, but also leading the way in channelling Asia's savings into a new kind of growth that is much more in conformity with sustainability.[160]

In a more orthodox context it is difficult to see an Asian financial system emerging and functioning smoothly as a vehicle for channelling savings into investment unless substantial progress is made towards building an Asian bond market. The Asian Development Bank has consistently advocated this step.[161]

A comparison of growth between China and India discloses that the Chinese financial system/capital market is not working as it should. With a savings rate much higher than India's and an inflow of foreign direct investment four times as high as India, Chinese growth is only approximately two percentage points higher than India's. There may be several reasons for this, but one of them is certainly the inefficiency of the Chinese financial system.

Compared with stock markets in developed countries such as the United States and measured as a share of GDP, the Chinese and Indian stock markets are small, depriving these countries of what is generally regarded as a financial institution that channels savings into profitable investments. The U.S. stock market measured by capitalization is thirty times bigger than either the Chinese or Indian market. In Asia, excluding Japan, the Korean stock market is the largest, followed by India's and China's, which are approximately the same size as Hong Kong's, all of them with a capitalization of about US$600 billion.[162]

It also looks like the abundance of savings allows non-profitable investments to be carried out. As corporate governance in the financial sector is still weak, many investment decisions will be approved without "normal" scrutinizing. Some of these may be politically motivated in that reasons other than economic profitability led to approval. One example often mentioned is the maglev train from Pudong airport to Shanghai. Other examples include investment to keep state-owned enterprises going despite their clear inefficiency, because politics dictate keeping workers employed at least until other job opportunities can be found for them.

A comparison of financial markets in 1995 and 2003 shows that non-Japan Asia bank loans and stock market capitalization were both about 80 per cent of GDP in 1995, but rose to almost 100 per cent and 120 per cent respectively in 2003. The corresponding figures for China were a little below 10 per cent in 1995, rising to approximately 15 per cent and about 40 per cent respectively in 2003.[163] The marginal size of the bond market serves as an illustration of the imperfections in Asian capital markets outside Japan.

There can be little doubt that one of the most important tasks to maintain high growth in Asia until 2015 and even more important after that date, is the reform of the financial markets that is under way, but is still far from having produced an efficient system based on market economy considerations. The advantages are double as a better financial system will improve social capital and increase economic efficiency. If the efforts are unsuccessful, Asia will find it extremely difficult to stay on a high growth pattern.

## GENDER

Demographies clearly show that the number of people in the working age bracket will start to fall in China in 2015 if the share of women joining the labour force remains unchanged. If economic and social trends in China encourage more women to join the labour force, its working population may continue to grow for some years, also after 2015.

In fact women constitute a hidden reserve in Asia with regard to workforce and education.[164]

Both for China and India the percentage of women joining the non-agricultural workforce has risen slightly over the last fifteen years from 37.7 per cent in 1990, to 40.9 per cent in 2004 for China, and from 12.7 per cent to 17.3 per cent for India. The figures are not clear-cut for Southeast Asia where some countries see a fall, others, a constant share, and yet others, a rise. Most Southeast Asian countries show a figure in 2004 of between 40 and 50 per cent.[165]

The conclusion to draw from this is that China, but in particular India, has an unused potential for increasing its workforce. If anything, it strengthens the prediction that after 2015, the number of people in the working age group favours India.

Analysing tertiary education shows a similar picture. In 2005 the ratio of girls to boys in tertiary education was 0.95 for China, 0.70 for India, and a blurred picture for Southeast Asia.

Barro in his work from 1996 looks at the question of whether female education is related to economic growth. Intuitively one should expect this to be the case, especially because most countries in Asia have a lopsided education system with a higher percentage of boys getting into higher education than girls.

It comes as a bit of a surprise that the analysis does not show such a relationship. Studies and analyses of this kind are always subject to dispute and sometimes controversy about methods, particularly when the findings do not support intuitive expectations.

The question about women in the workforce cannot stop there, however. A higher percentage of women working will have social consequences. It is likely that fertility will go down, and social functions, such as caring for children and elderly people normally undertaken by women, need to be picked up by "somebody else". Consequently it is something of an illusion to look at a higher share of women in the workforce without contemplating the repercussions for social welfare and how the care functions will be solved. Otherwise steps in one direction thought to have a positive effect may turn out to be harmful in other sectors of society, resulting in disruptive and unexpected side effects.

If the percentage of women who join the labour force goes up, which is likely albeit not certain, society needs to divert resources into social welfare. As is known from many European countries, the result is higher production, but also a change in the social fabric now seen in Asia or at least hitherto seen in Asia.

This is actually supported by Barro's findings, which add that even if the results for education are not significant, higher education is important for other factors of economic and social development, such as fertility, infant mortality, and political freedom. Female education may not show up in growth figures, but it certainly shows up in social indicators.

There is no doubt that women's perception of their own roles, the size of their families, and the social norms to be passed on to children, are some of the most crucial factors in determining how the next generation will behave and integrate, or opt out and seek to change society and social fabrics.

As shown by an American study,[166] abortion is decisive for societal stability or instability. With no abortion rights many children are born to young, uneducated women not really wishing to have children, and not married. They are simply speaking not capable of raising a child, with the result that children easily glide into a social environment characterized by violence and antisocial norms. They may join groups with high social capital, but are confined to the group which has an adversarial perception of the rest of society. This leads to a higher crime rate. With abortion rights, a larger proportion of children born get an upbringing integrating them into society and are raised in well-functioning families.

The one-child policy in China has provided ammunition for a large debate on the attitude of children raised in a family as the only child, especially against the background of a tradition for large families. This makes the child the centre of the family, who is used to seeing every wish fulfilled in a way and to an extent incompatible with how a society/community works. It also carries the risk of seeing a large number of spoilt children entering the social system who are unable to participate in teamwork and adjust to one another. It remains to be seen whether this is going to be the case or not.[167]

In Asia which has a less-developed school system, the role of the family in raising children and forming values may be more important than in say, Europe. The children look for a role model. The first place to look is the family and the second is the school. If neither of these delivers on this, the children may go outside this framework and find their role model in gangs or other groups offering security, respect, and norms.

The attention to the issue of a higher share of women in the workforce and a higher percentage of women in tertiary education may thus be less relevant for economic growth than for repercussions on the social fabric. It also raises the question of whether this will produce a result more or less in conformity with political objectives. The link to economic growth is indirect. A more stable social structure will increase social capital thus augmenting economic growth, while a less stable society constitutes a barrier for economic growth.

A second hidden reserve is retirement age, which can be raised if need be. The retirement age is now sixty years for men and fifty-five years for women in China, and fifty-five years for both men and women in India. For most other countries in East Asia and Southeast Asia it is about sixty years.[168] Experience from Europe indicates that it is difficult to raise the retirement age as it is regarded as a well-earned right. On top of that are changes in the social fabric as mentioned for the increased participation of women in the labour market. Statistically this reserve is available, if governments want to use it, but it is doubtful how much of an impact a higher retirement age will have on total labour supply. It may, however, have some, albeit limited, impact for professionals and highly-skilled workers who may choose to do part-time work after retirement.

Another aspect of gender[169] is the difference between men and women from the perspective of social capital, trust, sharing, and competition analysed respectively for individuals and groups. A study from 2007[170] concludes that although there are no gender differences in performance that involves solving a real task, first working for a non-competitive piece rate and then in a competitive tournament for individuals, twice as many men as women select the tournament. The conclusion of this study is that women shy away from competition while men embrace it. A subsequent study[171] concludes that if we look at men and women working in teams in tournaments, there are no gender differences to be found. There may be several reasons for this outcome. Women might have a high expectation of the partner's skill while men tend to be overconfident about themselves and do not trust their partner's ability. Women might enjoy competing when they have partners, while men lose interest when they have a partner.

If an overall conclusion can be drawn, and it looks possible, then it is that there is no gender difference with regard to performance level, but that women are more attracted than men to team tournament, an interesting perspective that opens up the possibility for a society/community steered by social capital and groups, especially when building in knowledge as a new and important production factor requiring a high willingness to share. We are skating on thin ice here, but it seems justified anyway to draw a preliminary conclusion that the movement towards such a new setting will favour women more than men and, in the long term, may bring along a a stronger role in societal structure for women.

# MEGACITIES/MEGAREGIONS

## Urbanization

Big agglomerations such as megacities and megaregions pose visible and often colossal problems with regard to infrastructure, sanitation, and social fabric, thus sucking resources out of society.

The other side of the coin is the theory about megacities/megaregions being a magnet for the global elite with talent, purchasing power, lifestyle, and identity. This theory rejects the thesis that the world is flat,[172] saying instead that the world is spiky.[173] The megacities/megaregions become richer and more powerful, while the rest of the world is relegated to second-rate economic areas out of the loop with regard to technology, innovation, services, higher education, and a whole string of activities that are going to dominate the world in the next twenty-five to fifty years.

The decisive factor for assuming the role of megacity/megaregion in this respect, is not the conventional criteria of economic activities and population, but a critical mass in the segments determining creativity and shaping new trends.

The thesis that new technology makes it irrelevant where people live because they can communicate irrespective of where they are is wrong, according to this school of thought. The correct interpretation is that high technology makes it possible for people to choose where they live and the geographical place becomes increasingly important because people want to live together with other people having the same lifestyle, and while communicating via high-tech means with people not having this lifestyle. In other words, megacities/megaregions intertwine people with an identical lifestyle and the virtual networks are brought in to communicate with other people not having this lifestyle.

Using this way of looking at megacities/megeregions as a yardstick for potential development in Asia places Asia in a good position to use the new form of critical mass to turn its megacities/megaregions into spiky areas attracting the global elite. Mumbai, Shanghai, Hong Kong, and Singapore are cases in point.

A study by the World Bank looks at China and its urbanization.[174] Although China cannot *ex definitione* be representative[175] of all of Asia, many of the opportunities, challenges, and problems encountered, or to be encountered in the course of urbanizing China, are analogous to what the rest of Asia will meet.

The study strikes a balanced view, but concludes[176] that:

> China is generating the resources to finance an urban big-push and to date has been able to channel these resources into urban industry and infrastructure, through the fiscal system, the banks, and new financial instruments.

> Because China is a relatively late starter and much building and renewal of urban physical capital lies in the future, there is unparalleled scope for designing efficient and livable cities.

Chinese municipalities have the autonomy and the authority to introduce and implement regulation governing land use, the transport system, and the urban environment.

The hukou system[177] enables municipalities to exercise some control over the flow of permanent migrants. Industrial growth virtually throughout China is such that manufacturing, construction, and services are already able to absorb inflows of migrants.

Although many Chinese cities must cope with a backlog of air and water pollution, the slums and endemic poverty that have taken root in other countries are largely absent from Chinese cities thus far.

As a late starter, China can draw on the experience of other countries with respect to urban design, the effects of private vehicle use, and pollution. At the same time, it can exploit advances in a host of technologies that will conserve energy and water and curtail harmful emissions.

The study also says,[178] "The potential gains to China from urbanization are substantial. So, too, are the costs. Striking the right balance between the two will be the greatest challenge for Chinese policy makers over the next quarter century and more."

In a more general analysis, the World Bank[179] stresses the importance of cities for economic growth and development.

To avoid misunderstandings it is clarified[180] that "several important aspects of the spatial transformation do not get the attention they would in a fuller study. The main aspects not considered — except when emphasizing or qualifying the most important messages — are *the social and environmental effects* of a changing economic geography." In the same paragraph a reference is made to Adna Weber[181] who say that "The cities have always been the cradles of liberty, just as they are today the centres of radicalism. Every man of the world knows that isolation and solitude are found in a much greater degree in a crowded city than in a country village, where one's individual concerns are the concern of everybody."

The World Bank detects a common thread in economic development in Europe, North America, and Northeast Asia around cities and their role. Even more crucial, the study includes how policymakers have handled the issue of growing cities — turning them into a driver or succumbing to infrastructure or social problems and allowing them to grow into non-productive economic spaces. This pattern is likely to repeat itself in other parts of the world, including the rest of Asia, and put its mark on development distinguishing those nation states which get it right, from those which cannot handle it or bow to pressure for policies constituting barriers to the role of cities.

Three key words emerge from the study: density, distance, and division.

Density is the most important dimension locally with short distances and few challenging political and cultural issues. The problem is to handle density in the right way to boost markets and create a pattern for development at various levels, instead of letting density be drowned by congestion and other external diseconomies standing in the way of the full potential of density's advantages being unveiled.

Distance to density is basically a problem of diminishing the distance to density for production units and production factors such as labour. Distance is, however, not only measured in kilometres or miles, but also in terms of the divisions of a cultural, behavioural, or political nature, making it more troublesome and time-consuming to get in contact with density. The policy implication is that if obstacles for material or non-material character are allowed to persist, the potential of density will be neutralized.

Division can be found both domestically and internationally as differences in economic infrastructures (rules, regulations, and acknowledged behavioural patterns) such as different currencies,[182] labour regulations, environmental standards, or rights of establishment, to mention a few, augment costs or even prevent linking up with density outright.

The World Bank highlights three new insights in theory in examining economic growth and development.

*First*, plants have to be big to exploit economies of scale, but places do not have to be big to generate them. The point in this revelation is that what matters is less the absolute size of cities than how they function. Medium-sized cities can actually perform better than megacities.

*Second*, human capital moves to where work is abundant. The point here is that skilled people are looking to work and communicate with other skilled people, instead of revelling in being the solo performer of accomplished skills.

*Third*, falling transport costs made possible by computerized container transport and other technological innovations have accelerated trade almost exponentially, but also, and perhaps more important, changed the pattern of trade. What is now visible is that trade is driven less by conventional theory focusing on factor endowment and more by specialization, encouraging each country or locality to specialize in product variants of the same goods, and by specializing, gain comparative advantage and crowd out goods under the same label, but not of the same variant (another car, another shoe, another shirt, etc.). The implication is that trade is growing more among countries close to one another with broadly speaking the same tastes and on the same level of economic activity/wealth than among countries differing from one another.

Jacques Attali took up some aspects of this study of economic space in 1990.[183] He tried to predict how the global economic space would look ten years after his work, that is year 2000, and looked into the European, North American, and Asian economic space. He also defined the following concepts: the core, hinterland, and periphery. The main thesis[184] is that economic activity takes place and is concentrated in core areas that determine the tastes, preferences, and direction of the development, drawing in talented people and capital (financial and human) — in fact assuming the role of not only driver, but also leader in its geographical area. The hinterland supports the core with a pool of talented people and subsidiary market, giving the core more economic clout. The periphery supplies commodities and labour and in many other ways acts as a pool of resources to be drawn upon by the core or centre if or when needed.

Asia will take the world into uncharted waters with not only a larger share of urbanized people than ever seen before, but also a concept of megacities new to civilization. Cities as drivers for culture and commerce and, in some cases, without much hinterland and/or periphery, are not, in principle, unknown to civilization,[185] but the scale and magnitude to which these emerge in Asia certainly is.

## Ability of Megacities/Megaregions to Adapt

John Montgomery[186] sees each city as an individual entity created in a unique place with a particular environment and individual topographical and fertility characteristics. However, there are also common characteristics for the development of cities. Over time a balance of commerce, culture, and built form will emerge and shape the cities, at the same time making them adapt to new conditions and challenges.

He points to two other fundamental factors influencing the evolution of cities: technology and governance. New technology stimulates new products, new distribution channels, a new labour force with new skills, etc., forcing the city to change or wither away. Governance is a question of how well cities respond to new challenges. Are they capable of changing track or will they stay tuned in to the preceding technology and gradually lose out to other and more vibrant cities?

The main thesis is that the future of cities and the selection of which ones will make it and which will not is determined by the fifth wave and the abilities of cities to grasp that and adapt. The fifth wave is seen in the

Kondratief perspective as adapted by Joseph Schumpeter.[187] Each wave lasts about fifty years and is dominated by new technology and its integration in society.[188] The first wave — 1789 — was dominated by industries rising from the industrial revolution which focused on how to generate power instead of relying on muscle power only. The second one — 1840s — was based on steam, steel, railroads, and ships. The third one took off in 1896 with electricity and the automobile ("Fordism"). The fourth one — 1940s — brought electronics, consumer household goods, radio, and commercial aviation. The fifth one, about to take off with power to support high growth and profits until 2030 or thereabout, has as its flywheels software, the Internet, biotechnology, and digital methods. Personalized consumption will enter the picture. Arbiters of taste play a pivotal role and typical goods and services will be dominated and steered by design objects and arts. There will be a strong link to creativity in a broad sense and Montgomery underlines how the new technologies will correspond with artistic expression and entertainment.

This is why he stresses the interplay between technology and cultural creativity as a decisive parameter for the evolution of cities and their adaptation to the fifth wave. The key sentence[189] is "Successful cities will need to be creative milieu, and such creativity must be applied dynamically. For this to happen, cities will need a repository of advanced technological, artistic and craft skills, or they will need to import and/or educate to provide these."

It is a reasonable assumption that these megacities will create energy and power drive not yet seen in the history of civilization. The interaction between so many people living so close to one another can be expected to produce synergies. Mass may prove critical. With megacities of up to thirty, forty, or fifty million people, political and technical infrastructure grows into major challenges, but the impact on the human mind of so many people living in a limited space is unknown. Intuition combined with the theory of normal distribution or Gaussian distribution[190] indicates that there is some kind of proportion between the number of people living close together and extremist behaviour, probably with a rising degree of violence. Normally the word "extremism" is associated with fanaticism in its violent form, and true enough, the moderating influence from familiar neighbours, the family structure, and next-of-kin living nearby, seen in agricultural districts and village societies, is absent in megacities.

It is, however, not a foregone conclusion that the energies from megacities cannot or will not be channelled into a more benevolent development that leads to better societies with opportunities for the overwhelming part of the population. The theory about wisdom of the crowd, and experience from biology of how animals organize themselves in colonies, give some basis for optimism. So does the evidence from various studies, including those mentioned above, that financial resources necessary to ensure a better quality of living are more plentiful in urban societies than in village societies. Village societies may provide a more "social" environment with a banister for every citizen, but they also hold back on initiatives and new endeavours if for no other reason than because of their limited size. There is also support for the theory that village societies tend to be conservative, or prone to praising life as it used to be rather than advocating change.

The heart of the matter seems to be the ability of Asia to build megacities as societies or clusters of societies (or communities) offering citizens a high degree of human security and economic well-being.

If megacities are perceived to be economic powerhouses only serving as a resource base for human beings entering economic activity, a significant number of people will probably fall out of the social networks that keep human behaviour within agreed frames, and instead be tempted by extremists luring them to have an aggressive attitude towards megacities and their other inhabitants.

The alternative is to build up a social network reaching out to individuals and families that offers interaction with others, thus using the same basic instruments as the village — the social network. That might make it possible for the energy of megacities to be controlled and steered into relatively stable societies with high economic growth. Combined with policies that encourage the creativity likely to flourish in such large societies megacities could turn into drivers of economic prosperity and vehicles for social stability.

The conventional industrial age model that accepts the heavy use of resources and relies on the car as seen in North America will simply not work. The concept of cities in Asia needs to swing to a much more ecologically productive mode, where people live and work with a much lower use of resources. This requires them to live together and near to their workplace, or alternatively change the concept of the workplace from the factory/office to the home or, at least, to the idea of not having to commute long distances — which makes a car indispensable — and using ICT instead.

If we accept that happiness is a prerequisite for creativity and we wish to see creativity in Asia's new cities, such a closer agglomeration may not be bad, provided that privacy and human security can be delivered. Human interaction as a counterweight to the "negative impersonal or non-human" side of ICT that calls for people to sit, work, and reflect alone, can be better achieved if people live close to one another.

A kind of "village in cities" concept might emerge, making it possible to shape local communities inside megacities. This should not reflect the ghetto concept of dividing megacities into segments, where only those sharing the same values and lifestyle dare enter, but should nevertheless serve as a base for people having comparable lifestyles and identities. The challenge is to combine the advantages of the village serving as a banister for people with those of megacities, which open up to many different values and attract different people who communicate with one another nonetheless. In such megacities various groups may mix, even if they do not combine. A concept coined in a completely different context called "separable but not separate"[191] may illustrate this kind of thinking.

Megacities as drivers of cultural behaviour, economic power, and new technology may be more important than nation states. For the nation state, economic and social relations between the megacities and the countryside may be one of its crucial policy issues. It seems easier to create a reasonable equality inside the megacities, and use that as the basis for megacities as the hub in a centre, periphery, and hinterland construction.

This will constitute megaregions inside a nation state, politically part of nation states, but economically, technologically, and culturally not really integrated in the nation states, and not seeing the nation states as contributing very much to their development.

The megaregion does not need the national market as its horizon is defined by the global market and it is therefore more interested in the conditions for selling there than in the national market. If its expansion is limited, it is more likely to be by cultural factors outlining competitive parameters in terms of trends in tastes and behaviour.

The analysis mentioned above of trends in Asia determining elements for social capital does not include nationality, but focuses on other factors rooted in values, norms, and perceptions.

## Megacities as Driver in Asia

The incentive for megaregions to decouple from nation states becomes more visible and understandable when we recall that in most cases, the nation states actually want the megaregions — the most dynamic parts of the nation state — to contribute to the development of other, and often poorer, parts of the nation state. The nation state sees national solidarity as a high priority; the megacities/megaregions do not necessarily share that view.

It will happen as has been seen in Europe that when nationwide social capital has been built up, it will instil not necessarily a feeling of common nationality, but a feeling of common norms and values in citizens — the feeling that an individual or groups of individuals share basic norms with individuals and/or groups elsewhere in the nation state. If this commonality does not exist the transfer of resources becomes a sensitive political problem as people earning more will ask whether they have to contribute to people earning less with whom they have very little in common, except a passport.

Megacities cannot survive as drivers of growth, providers of human security, and as reasonable socially stable environments, unless they manage to build up social capital enticing the population to share knowledge, capabilities, and money to keep the megacities going.

Megaregions will emerge if the megacities look more promising and attractive as anchors for the periphery and hinterland than the nation state. If, which is likely, dynamic economic development takes place inside megacities and not in the framework of the nation states, megaregions may emerge as a robust — not only cultural, but also political — framework, contesting the privileges of the nation state.

Megaregions and the nation state may continue to coexist and even supplement each other depending on the political constellation and the need or wish for centralization versus decentralization.

Social capital defined in this context as a feeling of common identity is more likely to take root in megacities/megaregions in Asia as cultural trends based on religions/philosophies are rarely defined by nationality or nation states, but often transcend national borders.

The challenge is then whether Asia can manage to create a new economic and political infrastructure to frame stronger megacities/megaregeions, some of which will be trans-border ones, with weaker nation states, increased economic globalization, and a communication flow often steered by cultural patterns that will not respect political borders, but tune in to cultural patterns.

A contest between megacities/megaregions and nation states will jeopardize the future, while a smooth adjustment to a new order will stimulate growth and economic prosperity. One of the crucial cards in this game is Asia's willingness and capability to establish an Asian economic integration which may be followed up by stronger efforts of political cooperation.

Investment flows and movement of persons (primarily skilled labour) may be more important between megacities/megaregions and their respective peripheries and hinterlands than inside nation states. The question is whether a national identity sufficiently strong to steer investments and/or movements of persons according to national identity will emerge, or whether the social capital and identity linked to megacities/megaregions will overshadow loyalty based on nationality.

The historically weaker Asian nation states when compared with the historically stronger European ones give rise to the speculation that megacities/

megaregions, in fact, may be able to overshadow nation states. This does not mean that nation states will disappear or be wiped from the slate. They will still be there and serve useful purposes of various kinds, but the scales will be tipped in favour of megacities/megaregions.

In Europe, the nation states there today are much less potent than they were sixty years ago when European integration started, but they are still a player exercising power in competition with the European Union and the national regions, plus new players such as multinational companies, transborder regions, and various groups. Europe has not really seen megacities/megaregions because the European population is smaller and the European cities well established historically, but in Asia it can be expected that these new agglomerations will emerge as one of the parameters for future development.

The prospect for a modus vivendi between megacities/megaregions and nation states is good, but the threat to the creation of social capital comes from group anarchy and the risk of segmentation under pressure from a dense population living in close quarters. This is what has been seen in certain major cities of the United States and also lies behind organized crime in big Asian cities.

The magnitude of this threat is proportional to the inequality in megacities/megaregions; the degree of commonality of values and norms for the inhabitants in the area, making it possible to build upon such norms instead of creating them; and the role of the family in the upbringing of children. In all three areas, Asia stands a reasonable chance of success, judged from past experience and historical traditions, provided that the authorities are able to convey the impression of good governance, meaning that corruption and nepotism are not allowed to influence legal and moral guidelines, but it is being steered instead by meritocracy, respect for rules, and ability to join in groups.

## The "Cool" City

So far the analysis has focused on growth of cities, megacities and/or megaregions. It is, however, not a foregone conclusion that cities will continue to grow, or indeed, continue to be a seedbed for innovation, creativity, new ideas, etc. In 1938 Lewis Mumford[192] ventured the prediction that the "megalopolis" would eventually strangle itself.

With increasing pollution, congestion, density, etc., the concept of sustainability for cities and, even more, for the development of cities, has been brought to the forefront by, among others, Peter Newman.[193] The challenge is how cities can avoid the fate of societies unconsciously moving towards a certain death by their own — misguided — development which highlights material consumption and individualism.[194]

Newman defines sustainability this way:[195] "reducing Ecological Footprint (energy, water, land, and materials, waste) while simultaneously improving quality of life (health, housing, employment, community...) within the capacity of the city".

The point is that unless cities are capable of acting in this way, the growing pressure for creating wealth, combined with the increasing scarcities of resources, may bring an abrupt end to urbanization and turn cities into hotbeds of conflict and confrontation, with individuals and groups veritably fighting for access to resources, and the authorities being unable to control this development.

If we assume that cities will be able to avoid such a fate, the next step is to recognize that cities or, rather, megacities, will compete on ability to turn themselves into sustainable entities, translate their wealth into cultural and artistic activities attracting talents from abroad, and deliver "cool" societies[196] where people can enjoy life without congestion and density.

This requires a completely different approach to a development of cities steered by future criteria and Peter Newman offers the sustainability criteria to be followed in planning urbanization. In his book of 2009[197] Peter Newman and his co-authors see four possible scenarios for the development of cities. The first is a collapse of cities; the second, ruralized cities; the third, divided cities; and the fourth something called resilient cities. There are examples of the first three possibilities, but here we concentrate on the prospects of resilient cities in Asia.

Broadly speaking, the authors perceive a resilient city as a city where every step of development and redevelopment makes the city more sustainable. It is seen as part of the sixth wave of innovation[198] where the first one was dominated by simple mechanization often using water power, the second by steam power, the third by electricity, the fourth by pharmaceuticals and electronics, the fifth by digital networks and biotechnology, and the sixth, which the world is moving into, by sustainability, radical resource productivity, whole system design, green chemistry, industrial ecology, renewable energy, and green nanotechnology.

When Peter Newman et al. rank global cities according to how resilient they are perceived to be, the observation is that U.S. cities are at the bottom, especially with regard to public transportation which accounts for less than 10 per cent of all motorized transport in the United States.[199] Many European cities are found in the bracket above 20 per cent and the wealthy Asian cities display figures above 40 per cent, with Hong Kong showing a figure as high as 73 per cent.

Asian cities seem to be well placed to transform themselves into resilient cities on the basis of present structures. New policies being introduced in China support this observation. Lee Schipper[200] points out that "if Chinese cities continue the momentum they have gained in the past few years, transport will serve city development, the strangulation by smaller vehicles seen elsewhere will be avoided and Chinese cities will move a large step towards sustainability".

S. Talukder has outlined ten principles for the governance of megacities in Asia to transform the problems which have for so many years dominated Asian megacities.[201] This illustrates that sustainability is not only for cities in developed countries/regions, but is indeed a relevant, even pressing, problem for cities/megacities in developing countries which have the possibility of avoiding many of the mistakes committed by cities in industrialized countries.

The political and social problem of sustainability is that it is not always obvious for the cities and those in power that sustainable policies are preferable for long-term development. Social capital generating such awareness is a condition for success in that there must be acceptance of new policies from an egalitarian point of view that convinces the large majority that the burdens and benefits will be distributed in an equitable way.

The main reason for highlighting social capital and social coherence in this respect is that sustainability is difficult to fathom, without giving individual interests less priority than, say, public transport and other facilities aimed at the public. Individuals may be very much aware of the apparent sacrifices they are going to suffer and are only ready to do so if benefits accrue to a group they belong to. Then they know who will share some of the benefits, and some of the burdens they shoulder will translate into benefits for other persons with whom they have shared values. If that is not the case and they fear that the burdens they suffer will give rise to benefits for other people with whom they do not share values and norms, the whole operation becomes extremely difficult and hazardous, and risks aggravating social tensions.

That may lead to the observation that sustainable megacities may best be undertaken by steps starting in districts and/or areas populated by people having common values and thereafter spreading it to the other parts of the city.

If we assume that the technological, administrative, political, and sociological considerations can be woven together in a coherent picture, megacities/megaregions may take off towards sustainability, and at the same time blaze the trail for a new kind of city and ensure lasting and tangible benefits for themselves by cutting down on use of resources and building up social capital.

The understanding of group behaviour, social capital, creativity, and how education fits into the picture constitutes the platform for moving to the next stage, which is to take a hard look at a number of elements that threaten future economic growth and societal development. They can all be overcome with the right policies, but the philosophy coming out of the preceding chapters constitute the plinth for a mind in search of solutions.

## Notes

1 For an overview see "What's the Return on Education?" *New York Times*, 11 December 2005, <http://www.nytimes.com/2005/12/11/business/yourmoney/11view.html>.

2 S. Gopinathan, "Globalisation, the Singapore Development State and Education Policy: A Thesis Revisited", *Globalisation, Societies, and Education* 5, no. 1 (March 2007): 53–70.

3 Primarily East Asian fast industrialization states inter alia Japan, Korea, and Singapore.

4 J. Bradford deLong, Claudia Goldin, and Lawrence F. Katz, "Sustaining U.S. Economic Growth", July 2002 <http://www.j-bradford-delong.net/Econ_Articles/GKD_final3.pdf>; Claudia Goldin and Lawrence F. Katz, "The Race between Education and Technology" (Cambridge, Massachusetts: Belknap, 2008); Claudia Goldin and Lawrence F. Katz, "The Returns in Skill in the United States across the Twentieth Century", NBER Working Paper, No w/7126, May 1999 <http://papers.ssrn.com/sol3/papers.cfm?abstract_id=165170> and "What's the Return".

5 *OECD Science, Technology and Industry Outlook* (Paris: OECD, 2008).

6 Robert J. Barro, "Determinants of Economic Growth: A Cross-Country Empirical Study", NBER Working Paper 5698, August 1996 <http://www.nber.org/papers/w5698.pdf>.

7 McKinsey, "The Economic Impact of the Achievement Gap in American Schools", Summary of Findings, April 2009 <http://mckinsey.com/clientservice/socialsector/achievement_gap_report.pdf> and "The Economic Cost of the US Education Gap", *McKinsey Quarterly*, July 2009.

8 Bas van Leeuwen, *Human Capital and Economic Growth in India, Indonesia, and Japan, A Quantitative Analysis 1890–2000* (Box Press Shop, 2007), pp. 206–16 <http://books.google.com/books?id=JAxpCWzpDuQC&pg=PA106&lpg=PA106&dq=japan+education+system+economic+growth&source=bl&ots=3vESudR1Ay&sig=U69C1ct9ZexwJ-MRkJv6f0Nd8kw&hl=en&ei=GGa

CSsPHFIeA7QPv8eDGCQ&sa=X&oi=book_result&ct=result&resnum=3#v=onepage&q=japan%20education%20system%20economic%20growth&f=false>.

9 Risti Permani, "Education as a Determinant of Economic Growth in East Asia", 15 January 2008 <http://www.uow.edu.au/commerce/econ/ehsanz/pdfs/Permani%202008.pdf>. See also his references to other works in the bibliography.

10 For a definition of a steady state economy see Chapter 1.

11 Peter Cappelli, "Schools of Dreams, More Education is Not an Economic Elixir", *Issues in Science and Technology* (Summer 2008).

12 Samuel Bowles and Herbert Gintis, "The Problem with Human Capital Theory — A Marxian Critique", *The American Economic Review* 65, no. 2; Papers and Proceedings of the Eighty-seventh Annual Meeting of the American Economic Association (May 1975), pp. 74–82; and *Schooling in Capitalist America: Educational Reforms and the Contradictions of Economic Life* (New York: Basic Books, 1976).

13 Jørn Skovgaard drew my attention to this point.

14 Much of the literature is biased, focusing on the United States and/or OECD countries, and looking at unitary economies i.e. similar across countries and/or historical periods.

15 Peter Cappelli, "School of Dreams".

16 Robert I. Lerman, "Building a Wider Skills Net for Workers", *Issues in Science and Technology*, Summer 2008.

17 According to Lerman middle-skill occupations account for nearly half of all jobs.

18 <http://news.yahoo.com/s/nm/20081217/wl_nm/us_china_unemployment>.

19 Chen Guangqing, of the National Association of Vocational Education.

20 "China's Grads Face Tougher Jobs Picture as Financial Crisis Deepens", *People's Daily*, 16 December 2008 <http://english.people.com.cn/90001/90776/90882/6554682.html>.

21 Jacob F. Kirkegaard, "Offshoring, Outsourcing and Production Relocations — Labor Market Effects in the OECD and Developing Asia", *The Singapore Economic Review* 53, no. 3 (2008).

22 Goldin and Katz, "The Race between".

23 The work by Goldin and Katz analyses the U.S. education over the last hundred years and touches on several aspects not relevant for Asia. Its basic message is, however, of crucial importance for Asia, spelling out that the education system is contributing to growth according to how well it is geared to society, but at the same time, is embedded with the seeds of disruptive forces if policies are out of tune with societal and technological developments.

24 McKinsey Global Institute, "Changing the Fortunes of America's Workforce: A Human Challenge, June 2009 <http://www.mckinsey.com/mgi/reports/pdfs/changing_fortunes/Changing_fortunes_of_Americas_workforce.pdf>.

25 *The Economist*, 7 October 2006.

26 James Canton, *The Extreme Future, The Top Trends That Will Reshape the World in The Next 20 Years* (London, Penguin, 2006).

27 Evalueserve has analysed the number of jobs in the IT sector in the United States and India to 2015–16. For the United States the number of IT professionals employed rises 25 per cent from 2006 to 2016, with an absolute figure of 4,010,000. For India there is almost a tenfold increase from 2001–02 to 2015–16, with an absolute figure in 2015–16 of 3,750,000: Evalueserve, "India's Role in the Globalization of the IT Industry", July 2008.

28 U.S. Department of Labor, *Occupational Outlook Handbook*, 2008–09 <http://www.bls.gov/oco/ocos042.htm>.

29 Goldin and Katz (2008) "The Race between", pp. 352–53.

30 "Global Downturn a Boon for Professional Web Networks", ABC news, 26 November 2008 <http://www.abc.net.au/news/stories/2008/11/26/2430389.htm?section=world>.

31 A summary in English is available at <http://www.filosoffen.net/tekst/projektsamfundet/phdthesis-thesocietyofprojects%20(0609).htm>.

32 Industrial production like agricultural production can easily be measured in performance level (for example, horsepower) or weight (tonnes), while the performances of the ICT society is much more difficult to quantify.

33 An example of measuring knowns in the educations sector is the OECD programme for international student assessment, PISA <http://www.pisa.oecd.org/pages/0,2987,en_32252351_32235731_1_1_1_1_1,00.html>. The reference to this programme does not imply any judgment on its validity, but serves to illustrate how benchmarking is finding its way into the education sector.

34 *Human Development Report*, 2007–08 (New York: UNDP, 2007), Table 12.

35 Percentage aged fifteen and older. Latest published figures.

36 The statistics give official figures without entering into a qualitative judgment of how much or how little is actually learned.

37 Recently religious schools, in particular in Islamic countries (madrasa and *pesantren*), have attracted considerable attention. The number of students enrolled in the Islamic religious schools is estimated to be about two million in each of the Asian countries with a large majority of Muslims; Indonesia, Pakistan, and Bangladesh. Source: Uzma Anzar, "Draft on Islamic Education, A Brief History of Madrassas with Comments on Curricula and Pedagogical Practices", March 2003 <http://209.85.175.132/search?q=cache:TvNlcVOSr7wJ:www.uvm.edu/~envprog/madrassah/madrassah-history.pdf+madrassahs+indonesia+number+students&hl=en&ct=clnk&cd=11&gl=sg>. The number of Madrasas in India, with a large Muslim minority, is estimated at 30,000, which would correspond to about one million students. Source: <http://en.wikipedia.org/wiki/Madrasah>. The question, to which answers vary — and probably is not uniform for all religious schools — is whether religious schools provide students with the necessary knowledge to prepare them for the modern society.

38 Sanjeev Sanyal, *The Indian Renaissance, Singapore* (World Scientific, 2008), pp. 150–54.

39 Marc Prensky, "Digital Natives, Digital Immigrants", *On the Horizon* 9, no. 5 (2001) <http://www.marcprensky.com/writing/Prensky%20-%20Digital%20N atives,%20Digital%20Immigrants%20-%20Part1.pdf>.

40 "How the Google Generation Thinks Differently", *The Times*, 9 July 2008 <http://women.timesonline.co.uk/tol/life_and_style/women/families/article4295414.ece>.

41 To avoid any misunderstandings, here we speak about the education system and not science or research and development, where the picture may look different.

42 <http://www.filosoffen.net/tekst/projektsamfundet/phdthesis-thesociety ofprojects%20(0609).htm>.

43 Don Tapscott, *Growing up Digital* (New York: McGraw-Hill, 1999) and *Grown up Digital* (New York: McGraw-Hill, 2008).

44 Tapscott makes the valid point that those evaluating the performance of the new generation are the old generation — so a clash of approaches is evident. When someone from the old generation characterizes a young one as "dumb" this person may be right, but the point is that the person's yardstick is no longer the correct one or at least, not the only one. The young generation could with as much justification label the old generation "dumb", judging them from criteria essential for mastering the net and the possibilities brought to us by the Internet.

45 " 'Tablet' Gives Parents a Pupil's Eye View of the Classroom", University of Sussex, Press Release, 26 February 2006 <http://www.sussex.ac.uk/press_office/media/media539.shtml>.

46 Charles Leadbeater, "What's Next: 21 Ideas for 21ˢᵗ Century Learning", 10 July 2008 <http://www.innovation-unit.co.uk/about-us/publications/whats-next.html> and <http://www.innovation-unit.co.uk/images/stories/whats_next_-_21_ideas_final.pdf>. See also reviews in *The Guardian* for 8 July 2008, "Blue Skies Learning" <http://www.innovation-unit.co.uk/images/stories/blue_skies_learning_-_edu_guardian_08_07_2008.pdf> and *TES* for 11 July 2008, "They Learn More Working in Tandem" <http://www.innovation-unit.co.uk/images/stories/leadbeater_article_in_tes.pdf>.

47 James J. Heckman and Dimitriy V. Masterov, "The Productivity Argument for Investing in Young Children". Paper based on the lecture given as the T.W. Schultz Award Lecture at the Allied Social Sciences Association Annual Meeting, Chicago, 5–7 January 2007 <http://jenni.uchicago.edu/human-inequality/papers/Heckman_final_all_wp_2007-03-22c_jsb.pdf>. See also <http://jenni.uchichagho.edu/human-inequality/>.

48 For references see the study with a list of literature.

49 The latest statistics from the Asian Development Bank shows the percentages for gross tertiary enrolment to be 20.5 for China and 11 for India. See <http://www.adb.org/Documents/Books/Key_Indicators/2007/pdf/rt02.pdf>.

50 Zhao Litau and Sheng Sixin, "Fast and Furious, Problem's of China's Higher Education Explosion", EAI background brief no. 395, 28 July 2008 <http://www.eai.nus.edu.sg/BB395.pdf>.

51 An official overview of China's higher education provided by its Ministry of Education is available at <http://www.moe.edu.cn/english/higher_h.htm>.

52 <http://www.timeshighereducation.co.uk/story.asp?storyCode=196312&section code=26>.

53 <http://www.timeshighereducation.co.uk/story.asp?storyCode=404023&section code=26

54 "China Emphasizes Quality of Higher Education", Xinhua, 27 January 2007 <http://www.china.org.cn/english/education/197946.htm>.

55 Kathryn Mohrman, "The Emerging Global Model with Chinese Characteristics", *Higher Education* 21 (2008): 29–48 <http://www.palgrave-journals.com/hep/journal/v21/n1/full/8300174a.html>.

56 Diana Farrel, Noshir Kaka, and Sascha Sturze, "Ensuring India's Offshoring Future", *McKinsey Quarterly*, September 2005 <http://www.mckinseyquarterly.com/Operations/Outsourcing/Ensuring_Indias_offshoring_future_1660?gp=1>.

57 For China the figure is estimated to be about 10 per cent. The question can be raised as to why working for a multinational company is a valid benchmark. The answer may be that such a company can compare work performance among staff across geographical areas and have often laid down performance criteria.

58 Sanyal, 2008, *The Indian Renaissance*, p. 130.

59 <http://highereducationmanagement.wordpress.com/2008/10/21/449/>.

60 Henry Chu, "India's Looming Talent Shortage", *Los Angeles Times*, 23 September 2006 <http://articles.latimes.com/2006/sep/23/business/fi-engineer23>.

61 Vivek Wadwha et al., "Seeing Through Preconceptions: A Deeper Look at China and India", *Issues in Science and Technology* (Spring 2007) <http://www.issues.org/23.3/wadhwa.html> and <http://www.soc.duke.edu/GlobalEngineering/pdfs/media/WhereEngineersAre/Investors_ChinaLeaps.pdf>.

62 What we learned was that no one was comparing apples with apples, says the study.

63 Vivek Wadhwa, "A Reverse Brain Drain", *Issues in Science and Technology* 15, no. 3 (Spring 2009).

64 An English summary of his work and thinking is available at <http://www.filosoffen.net/tekst/projektsamfundet/phdthesis-thesocietyofprojects%20(0609).htm>.

65 Patrick M. Mallan and Joni E. Finney, *Public and Private Financing of Private Education* (American Council of Education, Oryx, 1997).

66 IHEP, "The Global State of Higher Education and the Rise of Private Finance", 2007 <http://www.ihep.org/assets/files/publications/g-l/GlobalStatePrivateFinancing.pdf> and <http://www.ihep.org/press-room/news_release-detail.cfm?id=57>.

67 Times Higher Education, World University Ranking 2008 <http://www.

timeshighereducation.co.uk/hybrid.asp?typeCode=243&pubCode=1&navcode
=137>.

68 Nine from Australia and three from New Zealand.

69 <http://www.battelle.org/spotlight/7-29-08NREL.aspx>.

70 The main pioneering work by Henry Chesbrough, *Open Innovation: The New Imperative forCreating and Profiting from Technology* (Boston: Harvard Business School Press, 2003). See also, for example, "Outsourcing Innovation", *Business Week*, 21 March 2005 <http://www.businessweek.com/magazine/content/05_12/b3925601.htm, <http://ieeexplore.ieee.org/Xplore/login.jsp?url=/iel5/416123 1/4144550/04161715.pdf?arnumber=4161715>; <http://www.thedeal.com/corporatedealmaker/2005/02/rewriting_the_rules_in_rd.php>.

71 To facilitate the contact between companies and potential bidders, websites have emerged that specialize in linking companies and institutes. One of them is Innocentive, with a global network of 160,000 of "the world's sharpest minds". See <http://www.innocentive.com/>.

72 Brought to my attention by Professor S. Gopinathan, Associate Dean, Office of Education Research, National Institute of Education, Singapore.

73 David H. Hargreaves, *Education Epidemic, Transforming Secondary Schools through Innovation Networks* (London, Demos, 2003).

74 OECD estimates the number of foreign students (tertiary) in 2005 to be 2,725,966 of which 2,296,016 (84 per cent) studied in OECD countries. Source: OECD, *Education at a Glance*, 2007, Table C3, 6 (Paris, OECD, 2007). According to the Institute of International Education, demand for international education will rise from 1.8 million students in 2002 to 7.2 million by 2025. Source: <http://www.iienetwork.org/page/116259/>.

75 OECD, *Education at a Glance*, Chart C3.2, Paris, OECD. 2007.

76 Ibid.

77 U.S. Immigration and Customs Enforcement (ICE), "Student and Visitor Exchange and Information System, General Summary, Quarterly Review", 5 January 2009 <http://www.ice.gov/doclib/sevis/pdf/quarterly_report_january09.pdf>.

78 Figures showing how many of them return are not consistent. The latest information is about Chinese students in the United Kingdom which says that three-quarters return, see <http://www.chinese-embassy.org.uk/eng/sghd/t388706.htm> and <http://www.indiaenews.com/america/20071113/80271.htm>. A Danish report referring to the *China Statistical Yearbook 2006* says that 90 per cent of all Chinese students having achieved a PhD were still in the United States five years later.

79 <http://www.iie.org/Content/NavigationMenu/Pressroom/PressReleases/U_S__SEES_SLOWING_DECLINE_IN_INTERNATIONAL_STUDENT_ENROLLMENT_IN_2004_05.htm> and <http://www.iht.com/articles/2007/11/11/america/students.php>.

80 <http://www.idp.com/research/statistics/education_export_statistics.aspx>.

81 <http://www.educationnz.org.nz/comm/Mediarealeases/Punching%20Above%20Weight-26-11-08.pdf>.

82 Wang Ying, "Foreign Student Quota to Expand", *China Daily*, 29 July 2008 <http://www.chinadaily.com.cn/china/2008-07/29/content_6884445.htm>.

83 <http://www.siliconindia.com/shownews/Indian_Universities_rope_in_more_foreign_students-nid-45439.html>.

84 <http://www.iienetwork.org/page/116259/>.

85 Rosemary Luckin, "The Learner Centric Ecology of Resources: A Framework for Using Technology to Scaffold Learning", *Computers & Education* 50 (2008): 449–62 <www.sciencedirect.com>.

86 Drawn to my attention by Hans Peter Jensen.

87 See, for example, Matthews Sim Heng Chye, Matthews Wee Keng Neo, and Megan Kek Yih Chyn, "From Sage-on-the-Stage to Guide-by-the-side: Effective Tutor Skills in Problem-based Learning", Temasek Business School <http://pbl.tp.edu.sg/Facilitation/Articles/SimWee.pdf> with a bibliography referring inter alia to the works of Professor Howard S. Barrows.

88 <http://ocw.mit.edu/OcwWeb/web/home/home/index.htm>.

89 <http://www.okiproject.org/>.

90 <http://sakaiproject.org/portal>.

91 In arts, humanities, and social sciences, the local curriculum could still be valuable, possibly in combination with an international one.

92 James J. Duderstadt, W.M.A Wulf, and Robert Zemsky, "Envisioning a Transformed University", *Issues in Science and Technology* (Fall 2005).

93 You cannot try to buy a book, for example, on Amazon without immediately being bombarded with the information that those who bought this book also bought…

94 S. Gopinathan, "Globalisation, the Singapore Development State and Education Policy: A Thesis Revisited", *Globalisation, Societies, and Education* 5, no. 1 (March 2007): 53–70.

95 Politically another trend works in the same direction. The weakening of the nation state means less financial resources available and most of them will be allocated to social needs, leaving less money to be channelled to universities. Primary and possibly also secondary schools may continue to enjoy financing from the nation state as they are less likely to be globalized than the universities, but the universities glide away and fast from their anchoring in a national setting, depriving them of governmental financial support as the governments see them less and less as national institutions.

96 S. Gopinathan, presentation to symposium on 15 October 2008 on "Asia's Future", Institute of Southeast Asian Studies, Singapore.

97 Singapore's biopolis is an attempt to build a base for R&D in biotechnology.

98 A particle accelerator used by physicists to study and discover the smallest known particles — the fundamental building blocks of all things. It will revolutionize

our understanding of matters ranging from the minuscule world deep within atoms, to the vastness of the universe, see <http://public.web.cern.ch/public/en/LHC/LHC-en.html>.

99 The following paragraphs draw partly upon my essay "Happiness as a Driver for Creativity and Growth: The Example of Denmark", submitted to the "Interdisciplinary Studies on Happiness Workshop II", 20–21 November 2008, organized by the Centre for Liberal Arts and Social Sciences (CLASS) at Nanyang Technological University (NTU).

100 Science may, somewhat like societal structure, influence creativity. The rise of ICT as a tool means that the choice between a rule-based, a control-based, or a value-steered organization may tilt our mentality towards rule-based or control-based systems. ICT provides the tools for subordinates to consult upwards, and managers to keep in touch with what is happening in the organization. Formerly, e.g. in the Roman Empire, the British Empire, and the Chinese dynasties, not to speak of the great religions, distances and time between the "headquarters" and the "branches" constituted an impediment for contact with "headquarters" when a problem surfaced. These institutions were forced to rely on the ability of the person on the spot to make decisions reflecting its interests. To ensure this, a value-steered organization was necessary, and knowing they were alone not only encouraged managers to be creative in solving problems, but forced them to be so — inside a support system of common and shared values.

101 *Harvard Science* <http://harvardscience.harvard.edu/medicine-health/articles/hbss-teresa-amabile-tracks-creativity-wild>. A recent article is "Affect and Creativity at Work", *Administrative Science Quarterly* 50 (March 2005) and a complete list of works can be found at <http://www.getcited.org/mbrx/PT/99/MBR/11058741>.

102 Mihaly Csíkszentmihályi, *Flow: The Psychology of Optimal Experience* (New York: Harper and Row, 1990); Mihaly Csíkszentmihályi, *Creativity: Flow and the Psychology of Discovery and Invention* (New York: Harper Perennial, 1996); Mihaly Csíkszentmihályi, *Finding Flow: The Psychology of Engagement with Everyday Life* (Basic Books, 1998); Howard Gardner, Mihaly Csíkszentmihályi, and William Damon, *Good Work: When Excellence and Ethics Meet* (New York, Basic Books 2002).

103 Interview in *What is Enlightenment* magazine <http://www.wie.org/j21/csiksz.asp?page=3>.

104 Professor Ruut Veenhoven, Erasmus University of Rotterdam, interview <http://www2.eur.nl/fsw/research/veenhoven/>. General website for Professor Veenhovens work <http://www2.eur.nl/fsw/research/veenhoven/>.

105 Richard Layard, *Happiness, Lessons from a New Science* (London, Penguin, 2005).

106 Jeremy Bentham (1748–1832 ) advocated political and social life to be so organized that it brought about "the greatest happiness of the greatest number".

107 Adrian G. White, social psychologist at the School of Psychology, University of Leicester <http://www.le.ac.uk/users/aw57/world/sample.html> and <http://www.eurekalert.org/pub_releases/2006-07/uol-uol072706.php>.

108 Denmark shares the number one spot with Switzerland; Burundi is at the bottom.

109 <http://hbswk.hbs.edu/item/5944.html>.

110 <http://abcnews.go.com/2020/story?id=4086092&page=1> and <http://www.articlesbase.com/destinations-articles/a-most-happy-countrydenmark-1048376.html>.

111 Justina Fischer, economist at the OECD, see data at <http://ideas.repec.org/e/pfi55.html>.

112 Summarized by Reuters on 17 October 2008, "Happy Danes Find Trust is Key".

113 Ibid.

114 See a synthesis at <http://www.admin.cam.ac.uk/news/dp/2007041701>.

115 4,700 people followed over twenty years.

116 James H. Fowler and Nicholas A. Christakis, "Dynamic Spread of Happiness in a Large Social Network", bmj.com, December 2008 <http://www.bmj.com/cgi/reprint/337/dec04_2/a2338?maxtoshow=&HITS=10&hits=10&RESULTFORMAT=&fulltext=happiness&searchid=1&FIRSTINDEX=0&volume=337&resourcetype=HWCIT>.

117 Richard D. Austin and Richard L. Nolan, "Bridging the Gap Between Stewards and Creators", *MIT Sloan Management Review* 48, no. 2 (Winter 2007): 29–36.

118 Based on a large number of enterprises such as those involved in movies, music, and furniture in various countries such as the United States and Scandinavian nations.

119 Some years ago the research chief of a leading pharmaceutical enterprise told the author that a new laboratory had been set up in Paris. I asked why since Paris was known for the Pasteur Institute, but not as a centre for R&D in pharmaceuticals. The answer ran something like this: We do not aim at seeing our researchers mix with other researchers in pharmaceuticals. Instead we want them to go to the opera. That will stimulate them to combine various impressions and input out of the box helping to improve their ability to see how discoveries in the laboratory can be used in combination with other discoveries. We need, of course, people to make in-depth research, but they are not so difficult to find. What is scarce are researchers also having the horizon to scan possible uses for their work, including outside the narrow path. In 1996 I visited Seattle and noted that this city attracted high technology by underlining, not research and development, but a creative and good environment in general, such as entertainment, schools, and leisure. Sophia Antipolis (30,000 researchers, close to Nice) is built on this principle: sun, snow, and science.

120 <http://hbswk.hbs.edu/item/5902.html>.

121 The Medici family became known when living in Firenze during the Renaissance period and attracted talents from various segments of society such as those focusing on literature, political science, the arts and, not least, finance, to constitute a melting pot for ideas and creativity.

122 Frans Johansson, *The Medici Effect* (Boston: Harvard Business School Press, 2006) <http://www.themedicieffect.com/downloads/MediciEffect.pdf>.

123 <http://hbswk.hbs.edu/item/5902.html>.

124 <http://hbswk.hbs.edu/item/5766.html>.

125 Tapscott, *Grown Up Digital*, 2009, pp. 34–35.

126 (1) David Madland and Ruy Teixeira, *New Progressive America: The Millennial Generation* (Washington D.C.: Center for American Progress, 2009) <http://www. americanprogress.org/issues/2009/05/pdf/millennial_generation_execsumm. pdf>; and (2) John Halpin and Karl Agne, "The Political Ideology of the Millennial Generation, A National Study of Political Values and Beliefs Among 18- to 29-year Old Adults", Washington D.C.: Center for American Values, May 2009, available at <http://www.americanprogress.org/issues/2009/05/pdf/ political_ideology_youth.pdf>.

127 An interesting and some would say weird attempt to measure the environment for creativity is the Bohemian-Gay Index invented by Charlotte Mellander and Richard Florida. They take the view that no barriers — legal or cultural — to gays and lesbians through tolerance and open culture attract people on the fringes who frequently happen to be those harbouring new and unconventional ideas. The index has sometimes been misunderstood to mean that gays and lesbians are supposed to be more creative, but that is not the point. Any other so-called marginal group could have been chosen. The point is that opening up to one marginal group conveys openness and tolerance saying that cultural innovation and, by implication, other forms of innovation are welcome. Richard Florida, *Who's is Your City* (New York: Basic Books, 2008), pp. 136–43.

128 The pioneering works about social capital as a production factor such as human capital, are two contributions by James S. Coleman, both from 1988: (1) "Social Capital in the Creation of Human Capital", in *American Journal of Sociology* 94: 95–121, and (2) "The Creation and Destruction of Social Capital", in *Notre Dame Journal of Law, Ethics & Public Policy* 3: 375–405. An interesting more up to date work is Nan Lin, *Social Capital, A Theory of Social Structure and Action* (Cambridge: Cambridge University Press, 2001) and Nan Lin and Bonnie H. Erickson, *Social Capital: An International Research Program* (Oxford: Oxford University Press, 2008). See also Pierre Bourdieu, *la Distinction, Critique Sociale du Jugement* (Paris, Les Editions de Minuit, 1979); Robert D. Putnam, *Making Democracy Work: Civic Traditions in Modern Italy* (Princeton: Princeton University Press, 1993); and *Bowling Alone: The Collapse and Revival of American Community* (New York, Simon and Schuster, 2000).

129 There are several definitions of social capital. The World Bank puts it this way: "The social capital of a society includes the institutions, the relationships, the attitudes and values that govern interactions among people and contribute to economic and social development. Social capital, however, is not simply the sum of institutions which underpin society; it is also the glue that holds them together. It includes the shared values and rules for social conduct expressed in personal relationships, trust, and a common sense of 'civic' responsibility that makes society more than just a collection of individuals." Source: The World Bank, "The Initiative on Defining, Monitoring and Measuring Social Capital: Overview and Program Description", Social Capital Initiative Working Paper No. 1. Washington, The World Bank, 1998. See also Chapter 1.

130 An individual is not afraid of sharing some common activity with others because he/she does not fear that others will take advantage of this. It saves costs. An individual does not keep an idea about how to improve productivity to himself/herself because they are convinced that the fruits of higher productivity will be distributed in a relatively equitable way.

131 Robert J. Barro, "Determinants of Economic Growth: A Cross-Country Empirical Study", NBER Working Paper 5698, August 1996 <http://www.nber.org/papers/w5698.pdf>.

132 Winston R. Wallin, former chairman of the Caux Round Table, chairman emeritus of Medtronics, "Making It Possible for Poor Nations to Share in Global Prosperity" <http://www.uas.mx/cegc/Winston%20Wallin%20-%20Poverty%20Paper.pdf>.

133 Pierre Bourdieu, "The Forms of Capital", in J.G. Richardson, *Handbook of Theory and Practice for the Sociology of Education* (Connecticut, Greenwood Press, 1986); James S. Coleman, "Social Capital in the Creation of Human Capital", *American Journal of Sociology* 94 (1988); and Robert D. Putnam, *Making Democracy Work: Civic Traditions in Modern Italy* (Princeton: Princeton University Press, 1993).

134 A good summary is found in Sara Lea Rosenmeier, "Den Sociale Kapitals Fædre" in *Social Kapital*, edited by Poul Hegedahl and Sara Lea Rosenmeier (København:Forlaget Samfundslitteratur, 2007). For a reference to main works, see, for example, <http://www.socialcapitalgateway.org/NV-eng-growthempirical.htm>.

135 For the following two paragraphs see Luigi Guiso, Paola Sapienza, and Luigi Zingales, "The Role of Social Capital in Financial Development". University of Chicago, NBER and CEPR, 2001 <http://faculty.chicagogsb.edu/finance/papers/trust.pdf>.

136 Reference is made to intuitive and anecdotal findings in the Nordic countries and areas of India referred to in Chapter 1.

137 See, for example, Francis Fukuyama, *Trust: The Social Virtues and the Creation of Prosperity* (London, Hamish Hamilton, 1995).

138 Jørgen Ørstrøm Møller, "Social Kapital — I et Globalt Perspektiv", in *Social Kapital*, edited by Poul Hegedahl and Sara Lea Rosenmeier (København, Forlaget Samfundslitteratur, 2007).

139 Kenneth Arrow, "Gifts and Exchanges", *Philosophy and Public Affairs* 1, no. 4 (1974): 357.

140 Adam Smith, "An Inquiry into the Nature and Causes of the Wealth of Nations", first published in 1776.

141 Commission of the European Communities, Communication from the Commission to the European Parliament, the Council, the European Economic and Social Committee, and the Committee of Regions, "A Shared Commitment for Employment", Com (2009) 257 Final, Brussels, 3 June 2009.

142 Ove Kaj Pedersen, "Næste skridt i den europæiske vækstmodel: mobication", *Mandag Morgen*, no. 24, 22 June 2009.

143 See, for example, a paper by Fares al-Braizat, "Muslims and Democracy" <http://209.85.175.104/search?q=cache:5jebabErHDQJ:www.worldvaluessurvey. org/Upload/5_Islamdem_2.pdf+world+values+survey+trust+denmark+sweden+ norway&hl=en&ct=clnk&cd=1&gl=sg>. UNDP has included personal trust in its works on the Human Development Index. See also World Values Survey at <http://www.worldvaluessurvey.org/>.

144 Ibid.

145 <http://www.admin.cam.ac.uk/news/dp/2007041701>.

146 Steven D. Levitt and Stephen J. Dubner, *Freakonomics* (New York: HarperTorch, 2005).

147 See Chapter 2.

148 John Spoehr et al., "Measuring Social Inclusion and Exclusion in Northern Adelaide". A Report for the Department of Health, The University of Adelaide, February 2007 <http://72.14.235.132/search?q=cache:24ogC2ynWBoJ:www. sapo.org.au/binary/binary6522/Social.pdf+Measuring+Social+Inclusion+And+ Exclusion+In+Northern+Adelaide&hl=en&ct=clnk&cd=2>.

149 The study outlines a model for measuring social inclusion and social exclusion based on a number of economic, social, and educational characteristics.

150 Nan Lin and Bonnie H. Erickson, *Social Capital: An International Research Program* (Oxford, Oxford University Press, 2008), in particular, Section I, "The Position Generator, Methodology: Its Reliability, Validity, and Variation".

151 The instrument used is "positional generators", which broadly speaking means seeking links with other persons in positions in which they generate power, influence, or are masters over resources. In short, help other persons in their careers.

152 <http://nobelprize.org/nobel_prizes/economics/laureates/1998/sen-autobio. html>.

153 Avinash. K. Dixit, *Lawlessness and Economics. Alternative Modes of Governance* (Princeton: Princeton University Press, 2004).

154 Samuel Huntington, *Political Order in Changing Societies* (London: Yale University Press, 1968).

155 This observation is valid for rule-based international economic integration, especially in the European format, with transfer of sovereignty to exercise it in common. A nation state will know that the person(s) in the institution having power over its economic life comes from another nation state and will only trust the institution if the member states subscribe to common values.

156 Francis Fukuyama, "Social Capital and Civil Society". Paper to IMF Conference on "Second Generation Reforms", October 1999 <http://www.imf.org/external/pubs/ft/seminar/1999/reforms/fukuyama.htm>.

157 Source for this chapter, unless otherwise stated, is a paper by Franklin Allen, Jun Qian, and Meijun Qian, "China's Financial System: Past, Present, and Future", 2005 <http://fic.wharton.upenn.edu/fic/papers/05/0517.pdf>.

158 When the people of any particular country have such confidence in the fortune, probity, and prudence of a particular banker, as to believe that he is always ready to pay upon demand such of his promissory notes as are likely to be at any time presented to him, these notes come to have the same currency as gold and silver money, from the confidence that such money can at any time be had for them, Luigi Guiso, et al., "The Role of Social Capital".

159 Table 2-A in Allen, Qian, and Qian, "China's Financial System".

160 Association for Sustainable and Responsible Investment in Asia, "The Time to Lead is Now", July 2009 <http://www.asria.org/publications/lib/ASrIA_The%20Time_to_Lead_is_Now.pdf>.

161 See, for example, <http://news.xinhuanet.com/english/2009-05/03/content_11304013.htm>.

162 <http://futurist.typepad.com/my_weblog/2006/07/stock_market_ca.html>.

163 Table 5A and 5B in Allen, Qian, and Qian, "China's Financial System".

164 <http://www.adb.org/Documents/Books/Key_Indicators/2007/pdf/MDG03.pdf>.

165 *Newsweek*, 24 March 2008, puts the percentage of women working outside the home at 67.1 per cent in East Asia and 62.6 per cent in South Asia, but these figures include the agricultural sector, while the most interesting aspect for the future are figures for urban districts and economic activities there.

166 Steven D. Levitt and Stephen J. Dubner, *Freakonomics* (New York: HarperTorch, 2005).

167 <http://en.wikipedia.org/wiki/Little_Emperor_Syndrome>.

168 *The Future of Population in Asia* (Honolulu: East-West Centre, 2002), p. 89, Table 2.

169 Brought to my attention by Fang Zheng.

170 Muriel Niederle and Lise Vesterlund, "Do Women Shy Away from Competition? Do Men Compete Too Much?" *Quarterly Journal of Economics* (August 2007).

171 Marie-Pierre Dargnies, "Does Team Competition Eliminate the Gender Gap in Entry in Competitive Environments?" Documents from Travail du Centre d'Economie de la Sorbonne, June 2009.

172 Coined by Thomas Friedman in *The World is Flat* (New York: Farrar, Strauss and Giroux, 2005).

173 Florida Richard, *The Rise of the Creative Class* (New York: Perseus, 2002) and *Who is Your City* (Perseus, 2008).

174 Yusuf Shahid and Tony Saich, *China Urbanizes* (Washington D.C.: The World Bank, 2008).

175 The study thus says that "China's urban development is better placed than counterparts in other countries".

176 Shahid and Saich, "China Urbanizes", p. 27.

177 Basically it means that every Chinese citizen is assigned a Hukou location, specifying where the citizen belongs.

178 Shahid and Saich, "China Urbanizes", p. 32.

179 The World Bank, *World Development Report 2009: Reshaping Economic Geography* (Washington: The World Bank, 2008).

180 Ibid.

181 Adna Weber, *The Growth of Cities in the Nineteenth Century: A Study in Statistics* (New York: MacMillan, 1899).

182 Economists have long wondered whether a common currency boosts trade or not. In 2000 Andrew K. Rose, using the gravity model, put such quantification of positive effects on trade forward. Based on a comprehensive study he draws the conclusion that two countries which use the same currency trade much more than comparable countries with their own currencies. Rose's analysis separated common currency from other and related effects, but he admits that even if common currencies increase trade flows, he does not know why; Andrew K. Rose, "One Money, One Market: The Effect of Common Currencies on Trade", *Economic Policy* 30 (2000).

183 Jacques Attali, *Lignes d'Horizon* (Paris, Fayard, 1990).

184 See also Jørgen Ørstrøm Møller, *The Future European Model, Economic Internationalization and Cultural Decentralization* (Westport: Praeger, 1995).

185 Venice and some other Italian city states from the renaissance can be mentioned in this context.

186 John Montgomery, *The Wealth of Cities, City Dynamics and the Fifth Wave* (Aldershot: Ashgate, 2007).

187 For references, see Montgomery, *The Wealth of Cities*, pp. 7 and 8.

188 There is a certain resemblance to the six-stage approach for integration of new technology in society as outlined in Chapter 1.

189 Montgomery, *The Wealth of Cities*, p. 370.

190 <http://en.wikipedia.org/wiki/Normal_distribution>.

191 In NATO during the 1990s in a discussion on a European military vector inside the alliance. The velcro concept discussed in connection with multinational companies may also be relevant.

192 L. Mumford, *The Culture of Cities* (New York: Harcourt, Brace, 1938).

193 See list of references in Peter Newman, "The Environmental Impact of Cities", *Environment and Urbanization* 18, no. 2 (2006): 275–95.

194 The works of Jared Diamond show how difficult it sometimes is for societies/

communities to adjust to change and new challenges different from those present when the society/community was created. This is actually the case for cities facing the question of sustainability. Jared Diamond, *Guns, Germs, and Steel* (New York: Norton, 1998) and *Collapse, How Societies Choose to Fail or Survive* (London: Allen Lane, 2005).

195 Newman, *The Culture of Cities*, p. 286.

196 Expression used by Peter Newman.

197 Peter Newman, Timothy Beatley, and Heather Boyer, *Resilient Cities, Responding to Peak Oil and Climate Change* (Washington, Island, 2009).

198 The classification is not exactly the same as mentioned earlier for the sixth wave.

199 Transportation accounts for 15 per cent of carbon emissions worldwide.

200 Quoted in Peter Newman et al., *Resilient Cities*, p. 93, note 197.

201 S. Talukder, "Managing Megacities: A Case Study of Dhakka". PhD dissertation, ISTP, Murdoch University, Perth, 2006 <http://wwwlib.murdoch.edu.au/adt/pubfiles/adt-MU20070508.145238/02Whole.pdf>.

# 5

# BARRIERS TO GROWTH

The following elements all augur a society with less — at least relatively — to distribute among citizens, irrespective of the expectation that has been built up over the preceding twenty-five years that says every year should deliver more to distribute. We thus move gradually into circumstances which see society moving from distributing benefits to burden sharing.

This explains the emphasis in this book upon social capital. Burden sharing among citizens with no or little trust in one another is almost an insurmountable political task, while burden sharing among citizens held together by common values inside the framework of social capital may be manageable, especially when we recall that adroit policymaking may turn this situation into one of distributing fewer benefits rather than outright cutting down on what is at the disposal of each citizen.

Demographics has favoured Asia for the preceding twenty-five years, but has now turned into a major policy issue affecting the competitiveness among Asian countries, changing the composition of the various populations, calling for more care functions, asking for more resources, and shifting, albeit moderately, the proportions of people adhering to main religions.

This in itself makes future economic life and, in particular, future consumption more uncertain for the individual. Given the embryonic structure of welfare benefits, the consumer is pushed towards weighing up consumption here and now, against future pensions without any certainty about their size which depends on economic growth and societal development.

With high economic growth, resources are available for building a welfare system, but policymakers need to make up their minds and rally the population behind the course they choose, from the many options available, both with regard to the size of benefits, including pensions, and the way they are financed (private savings, through corporations, or using the public budget via taxes).

At the same time Asia, like the rest of the world, must face the coming era of scarcities and shortages in at least five sectors: food, commodities, energy, water, and a clean environment factoring in climate change. They all call for more money that has to be diverted from other economic activities of which private consumption is an obvious candidate.

There are many ways to address these problems and some of those will succeed while others may fail. The overriding priority is, however, to keep societies together and avoid the situation where individuals or selected groups of individuals benefit at the expense of the rest of society, which again brings us to the issue of social capital.

# DEMOGRAPHICS[1]

## Fundamental Trends

### Overview

Demographic trends look unfavourable for Asia in a twenty-five year horizon.

*First*, the demographic window (the period of time when the proportion of its population in the working age group is particularly prominent — normally a duration of approximately forty years) comes to a stop for Asia in 2040, after which (2045 to 2080) it shifts to Africa as the only geographic region with a prominent part of its population in the working age group.[2]

*Second*, the demographic trends of the three largest economies — China, India, and Japan — diverge, with India still on an upward trend, China starting to decline,[3] and Japan being locked in a situation of a falling population since 2005 and forecast to decline a further 20 per cent by 2050.

*Third*, the population in the working age group will mirror that trend. Japan will for many years now have lived with a decreasing number of people in this age bracket and will probably have come up with and tried ways to cope with a falling population. If it has been successful, the world will be eager to learn from it. This is also a reason productivity-enhancing technologies are so high on the Japanese agenda. For China it will be a new challenge after decades of relatively successful policies to trim population growth. India still has a number of years left before the size of its working age population starts to shrink.

*Fourth*, inter-Asian (country-to-country) migration is still limited by tight immigration laws, although illegal immigrants are plentiful. This poses two problems. The *first* is whether Asian countries do or do not accept immigration. The *second* is that currently there is a schism between formality posing obstacles, and realities making immigration possible.

*Fifth*, the number of elderly people will eventually rise in all Asian countries, both in absolute numbers, and as a share of the population. The number of young people will grow slower and, even if it takes some time before it happens in countries such as India, Indonesia and Vietnam, the share of young people will decline. That puts an awkward problem squarely on the agenda: how to care for an increasing number of people needing care with a decreasing number of people available to do so? On top of that comes the next issue, which is that although the traditional Asian family structure with three generations under one roof may survive, it is unlikely to be the norm for the large majority of families. The dilemma is enhanced as growing income and adaptation of other consumer preferences make it less likely that young people and their families will offer care for their parents.

To a certain degree it is an economic problem in the sense that countries may build up facilities to take care of the elderly, but that requires a shift in preferences and there is by far no guarantee that the political system will be ready to make the money available. Investment in infrastructure for the elderly will have to be financed from funds otherwise available for productive investment and thus reduce future growth potential. Some of the younger generation may be ready to pay for their parents, but even if this is the case, the question cannot be avoided as to how many young Asians twenty-five years from now will take on jobs in the care sector.

## The Figures

Demographic figures expose the problem Asia faces in the next twenty-five to fifty years.

The demographic window for Asia is almost congruous with the global one, which cannot cause any surprise in view of Asia's large share of the global population. For the world, this window is between 2005 and 2045, and for Asia, 2005–40.

There are, however, large discrepancies between countries. China's demographic window lasts from 1990 to 2025, India's from 2010 to 2050, and Southeast Asia's from 2010 to 2045. China peaks before the rest of Asia, excluding Japan and Korea. Southeast Asia, regarded as an entity, follows the same track as India, peaking in 2045–50, but the pattern is slightly different for individual countries: Singapore entered the demographic window just like Hong Kong in 1980, Thailand in 1995, Brunei Darussalam, Indonesia, and Vietnam in 2005, Malaysia and Myanmar (like India) in 2010, the Philippines in 2015, Laos in 2030. Bangladesh enters this in 2020. Pakistan and Cambodia in 2035 will be the last Asian countries to enter the demographic window.

The next interesting figure is the dependency ratio (the ratio of the economically dependent to the working-age population).

The World Bank[4] has calculated that the youth dependency ratio (those 0–15 years compared with those 15–64 years) for Asia as a whole falls from a peak of 0.8 in the 1970s and 1980s, to under 0.4 in 2050. The number of potential active people supported by people actually working declines almost dramatically. In the short term, this alleviates the burden for people in the working age group, but it augurs a much higher future social burden for these children. The picture is worse when we look at the old age dependency ratio (those above 65 years compared with those 15–64 years), which goes up from about 1 at present for Asia, to 2–3 in 2050. Every ten persons working have to support two to three older persons, against only one older person at present.

A summary of the demographic window[5] and overall dependency ratio for Asian countries can be seen in Table 5.1.[6]

From a high dependency ratio due to a young population promising to boost the workforce and the economy at a later stage, the dependency ratio dips as the children grow up while fertility goes down. The dependency ratio then climbs again with an ageing population increasing the actual and future burden of the population in the working age bracket.

The growing population in Asia is not so much due to high fertility (defined here as the number of children per woman) as statistics show that

### TABLE 5.1
### Demographic Window and Dependency Ratio in Asia

| Country | Demographic Window | Dependency Ratio | | | |
|---|---|---|---|---|---|
| | | *1975* | *2000* | *2025* | *2050* |
| China | 1990–2025 | 0.78 | 0.46 | 0.46 | 0.64 |
| India | 2010–50 | 0.77 | 0.62 | 0.46 | 0.53 |
| Indonesia | 2005–40 | 0.81 | 0.55 | 0.46 | 0.57 |
| The Philippines | 2015–50 | 0.90 | 0.70 | 0.47 | 0.52 |
| Vietnam | 2005–40 | 0.92 | 0.63 | 0.47 | 0.59 |
| Thailand | 1995–2030 | 0.84 | 0.47 | 0.45 | 0.62 |
| Malaysia | 2010–45 | 0.85 | 0.62 | 0.48 | 0.54 |
| Japan | 1965–95 | 0.47 | 0.47 | 0.70 | 0.96 |

*Source*: United Nations, *World Population to 2300* (United Nations, 2004) <http://www.un.org/esa/population/publications/longrange2/WorldPop2300final.pdf>.

the fertility ratio in Asia from 1950 to 2010 is below that of Africa, with the gap widening over the period, while being more or less at the same level as for Latin America and the Caribbean. The improving health system may influence not only the size, but also the composition of the population. If the development is lopsided so that better health care is primarily directed at the elderly population while child death levels are fairly stable, the population grows, but with the prospect of an increasing proportion of elderly people.

UNICEF[7] points out that while Asia was doing very well in the 1960s and 1970s in reducing child mortality, the annual reduction rate has been halved from 1980 to 2000, while Latin America and the Caribbean have managed to keep the reduction rate more or less unchanged.

We know the number of fragmented families continues to rise even if statistics are difficult to find, but developments in the labour market — with more women taking jobs, and divorce getting less unusual — point to that. This has repercussions on the fertility and child mortality rate because the possibility of family care for children — still overwhelmingly used — can be taken less for granted.

## The Pension Problem[8]

### The Pension Burden

A study by OECD and the World Bank[9] points out that Asia's ageing process will be at its most rapid between 2010 and 2030, especially because of the demographic development in China. The study also says that there are four reasons present pension systems will prove inadequate:

- Coverage of formal pension systems is relatively low.
- Withdrawal of savings before retirement is very common.
- Pension savings are often taken out as lump sums with the risk that people outlive their resources.
- Pension payments are not automatically adjusted to reflect changes in the current costs of living.

Transforming these into three main questions/observations gives a picture that explains why present pension plans look inadequate.

The *first* question is how good the population coverage of the pension is.

Coverage is defined as the proportion of the population, or alternatively, of the labour force, covered by mandatory pension schemes. The OECD average is 60.4 per cent of the population between fifteen and sixty-five years of age, and 83.3 per cent of the labour force. The corresponding figures (Table 5.2) for Asia reveal the looming pension problem.

As more and more people are moving into the age bracket where they need a pension, these figures augur difficulties for a large number of people in Asia to maintain a living when they reach the end of their working age.

The *second* question is how good the pension and/or social benefits are compared with the standard of living enjoyed by the pensioner before retirement. There are two indicators.

The *first* indicator is the gross replacement rate, which is the pension benefit as a share of the individual's lifetime average earning (for an average earner, the gross pension income is $x$ per cent of the previous earnings level per year).[10] The OECD average is 60.2 (for men) and 52.6 per cent for women meaning that a pensioner will, broadly speaking, get paid every year 60.2 and 60.3 per cent respectively of his/her average lifetime annual income.

For Asian countries there are wide variations, with some countries coming close to 70 per cent, and others below 20 per cent. The picture also differs according to whether we look at low, middle, or high-income individuals, and men or women. China's gross rate is 67.6 per cent and India's 40.4 per cent.

Refining this further, we can look at the net replacement rate, which takes into account personal income taxes and social security contributions paid by workers and pensioners. In principle, the net rate should be higher than the gross rate, which is also the case for the OECD average (71.6 per cent).

TABLE 5.2
Coverage of Mandatory Pension Schemes

|  | *Percentage of population aged 15 to 65* | *Percentage of labour force* |
|---|---|---|
| China | 17.2 | 20.5 |
| Indonesia | 11.3 | 15.5 |
| Philippines | 18.7 | 27.1 |
| Thailand | 18.0 | 22.5 |
| Vietnam | 10.8 | 13.2 |
| India | 5.7 | 9.1 |
| Pakistan | 4.0 | 6.4 |
| Sri Lanka | 22.2 | 35.6 |

*Source*: OECD, *Pensions at a Glance*, Special Edition Asia/Pacific (Paris: OECD, 2009) <http://www.oecd.org/dataoecd/33/53/41966940.pdf>. Table on p. 41.

For Asia the net rate improves the situation for the pensioners somewhat, with several countries above the 70 per cent mark, while the floor for this rate is also lifted. China shows a net rate of 73.5 per cent and India 48.4 per cent. The increase by changing the calculation from gross to net rates is certainly much higher than for OECD as a whole.

The *second* indicator analysed by the OECD and the World Bank is gross pension wealth which shows how many times the pre-retirement earnings level the pension promise constitutes (a figure of ten means that the pension promise equals ten times the pre-retirement earnings level, or ten years of pension, if the level of the annual pension is fixed at pre-retirement earnings level). The OECD average is 9.6, meaning that the pension promise of a person who retires at the normal pension age, is on average 9.6 times the pre-retirement earnings level. Most Asian countries have a figure near this, with Singapore, Indonesia, India (6.2), and Malaysia below, and China and Vietnam — 15.0 — for both countries — far above. A calculation of the net pension wealth does not change this picture.

These figures taken together reveal an almost alarming picture. Asian countries fall into several groups. There are those with almost no universal pension schemes and those who rely on personal or employer-managed optional pension schemes. For those with mandatory pension schemes, the coverage is limited in the case of countries with large populations even if the sums to be expected do not look bad compared with the OECD average.

China's coverage of around 20 per cent is relatively low by OECD comparisons while not too bad compared with other Asian countries.[11] In spring 2009 the Chinese authorities took the first step towards introducing a pension scheme for the 800 million people living in rural districts that have been left out of the urban pension system. The main idea is to start cautiously with a pilot scheme covering 10 per cent of the population in rural districts to form a basis for evaluating the scheme, in particular, how it will be received by the rural population. The scheme will be voluntary and financed by contributions from the people and the central and regional governments.[12]

Other countries in Asia have low pension levels, low pension wealth, and low coverage of workers enrolled in the system, which give rise to the observation that not very many will get paid a pension and most of those who do can barely survive on it.

With demographic projections announcing an increasing proportion of people above sixty-five years in almost all non-OECD Asian countries, the pension problem takes on unpleasant proportions — politically, economically and financially, and socially.

The *third* question — for both public and private financed pension schemes — is how to finance them.

If we assume high economic growth — a reasonable assumption — the money may be there, but not the mechanism to distribute it, and the political question is whether the next generation will agree to a distribution of income and wealth that allows the economic burden to be financed by current production. If so, there is no problem, but it is unlikely that this will happen. The alternative is a distributional political fight between the current working-age population and the people above sixty-five years old, about how much of the current production can be sliced off to pay out present and, particularly, future pensions. To solve such a problem which, in view of the number of people involved, will be on a large scale, calls for a high degree of social solidarity and social capital. Perhaps this will be there, but perhaps not, and what then?

Another analysis covering eleven countries comes to similar conclusions and is relevant even if only three Asian countries (China, Japan, and Singapore) are included in it.[13] Singapore is rated highest among them and on a level with the United States while China falls in the category of having a pension system that has some good features, but also major risks and/or shortcomings that should be addressed. Without improvements, its efficacy and/or long-term sustainability can be questioned. China is rated somewhat higher than Japan, but both fall in the category of countries with a system that has some desirable features, but also major weaknesses and/or omissions that need to be addressed. Without these improvements, their efficacy and sustainability are also in doubt.[14]

The study uses three sub-indexes: Adequacy, looking at the income provided and the net replacement rate; Sustainability, defined as the ability to finance future claims; Integrity, perceived as the governance of private pension schemes. China scores well on adequacy where it is in line with developed countries such as Germany, Canada, and Sweden, and above Britain and the United States. Japan scores well in integrity, but is still below all other developed countries included in the study except Germany. Singapore scores well on sustainability, where it is number three out of all eleven countries.

A related aspect is how good pension managers across Asia are judged by performance. As most pension schemes are not transparent and supervision apparently weak, it is not known how well pension funds are managed. There is, however, a certain suspicion that they are not too well run. This risk then arises that the return on savings becomes negative, measured in real value, undermining confidence in the system and weakening the incentive to deposit savings in pension funds. For people choosing where to deposit their savings, it is a question of the right combination/balance of risk and remuneration, combined with confidence that the money will not lose its purchasing power in the long period before payout.

## Risk of Destabilization

Wrong handling can easily turn pension funds into a destabilizing social factor if the active population tries to get rid of the pension burden by breaking away from solidarity and this will inevitably pose challenges for the nation state as the political entity responsible for elderly people.

If social capital cannot be established on a nationwide basis, but instead grows inside megacities/megaregions or other frameworks, there is the fear that the elderly will be offloaded to the poorer parts of society with little or no care.

The Asian family tradition may play a role, but no one really knows how the future reactions of people in Asia will respond to the need for care of the elderly.

Presumably savings will be channelled into pension funds in Asia to provide the financing. Two fundamental economic and sociological problems arise.

The *first* is whether the savings are invested in stocks or bonds, and, prior to that, whether investments are in financial markets at all, or are used by governments as budget extenders (for example, the huge debate in Japan on the Postal Bank).

If the investment is placed in shares, future pensioners buy themselves a share of future production by ownership of enterprises that will generate production in the future. They will be on an equal footing with owners among the active population as they have a right to a share of production. If we work on a hypothesis of high growth, this will produce a high and rising level of pensions, and at the same time channel a part of production into their pockets. As they share the upside and downside risks with the active part of the population, this may work to strengthen social capital. They did forego consumption in the past to get their share of production now, accepting in the process the risks associated with buying into future production, which in turn means that in case of an economic downturn, their pension decreases as does the wage level of those in the workforce.

If, on the other hand, they invested in bonds, they forego consumption now by securing a fixed payment, irrespective of future levels of production. If the economy turns downwards they maintain their pension even if the active part of population is forced to accept lower incomes. The risk factor is associated with inflation, but bonds can be offered that incorporate indexing to future price increases. With such an investment pattern, a niche is carved out for pensioners who have the right to special treatment regardless of the current economic situation. If growth continues to be high this should not pose a social problem, but if trend growth falters, their claims will gobble up an increasing share of GDP, at the risk of social tensions because the active part of the population feels deprived of what they regard as their rightful share. The problem may be aggravated if the economy is caught by deflation which increases the real burden of their bonds.[15] The existence of a sufficiently developed bond market is in itself a problem. Japan and a few other countries may have one, but not India, Indonesia, and China.

The *second* problem concerns the institutional mechanisms for savings: in the public sector via taxes or contributions; corporations, the self-employed, and private financial institutions. It is a crucial question whether funds are independent or regulated.

What has happened in the United States demonstrates the risk of a system leaving this issue to corporations. As the money for pensions are not paid out now but later, while higher wages are eroding competitiveness now, corporations can be tempted to offer pensions that are simply not sustainable in the long term and will bring the corporation to its knees. This model amounts to asking corporations to assume a political responsibility, which they are not equipped to do. Financing via the public means via taxes and is somewhat similar to putting savings into shares as future governments will decide how to honour pledges and whether the money is there and, if not, how to find it — in other words, distributing present production among currently active people and people who were in the workforce some decades ago. The option of private, independent, and regulated financial institutions managing the savings for future pensioners becomes a question of shares or bonds, depending on which investment policy such institutions follow and whether such financial instruments are available at all, which is not the case in all Asian countries.[16]

For Asia it is of paramount importance to tackle these problems and map out a pension policy designed to solve the future problem of distribution of income in conformity with what is deemed to be acceptable (how high future growth will actually be) and to maintain social coherence (social capital) in a situation where a rising portion and absolute number of persons must be maintained even if they are past the working age and thus not participating in the creation of wealth.

The pension problem is only one of many challenges to social stability in Asia where, according to newspaper reports, growing inequality and protests against working conditions are becoming more frequent, signalling that the population is determined to stand up and voice dissent and demand that the political system step in to respond. As has been seen, the alternative to tackling these problems may well be riots of which there have been a number over the years and these may grow into serious challenges unless appropriate policies are applied.

## Migration

The divergent demographic and economic developments may trigger off migration between the Asian countries. This falls into two categories: migration of low-skilled labour to replace indigenous labour in the care, agricultural, and construction sectors (construction and agriculture are overwhelmingly the largest part of country-to-country migration), and high-skilled labour to where business opportunities are most promising. Both types of migration augur problems and opportunities.

The *first* type of migration usually sees a richer country with a fast growing group of elderly workers or those in the higher bracket receiving a large number of young people from a poorer country. It will be difficult to segregate these from the rest of society. The longer they stay, the more likely it is that they look for citizenship. If they do so, they may try to bring some of their family members to their new country.

In the agriculture, construction, and sometimes tourism, plus transportation, sectors, the immigrant workforce is usually poorly paid, but tend to stay long, although not always in the same location in the host country. They are the ones forming immigrant families, while skilled immigrants are more hesitant to do so apparently.

The *second* type of migration consists of highly-skilled younger people, primarily from India, the Philippines, Indonesia, and Vietnam supplementing a potential pool of educated young people probably needed in China and sometimes Japan, or other countries. What are the economic repercussions of this that can be expected? Will it require stronger economic integration in Asia? If not, will the countries seeing talent move abroad try to stop this and, if so, how will the young people who know they can earn a better living in another Asian country, but are denied the chance, react?

Some Asian countries have seen migration and, in some cases, on a grand scale, but in the past this has always been on a purely economic scale where the workers came for a limited period, could only stay as long as they had a job, were kept, and kept themselves, outside society, avoiding any kind of integration. They constituted a parallel society, but under conditions that prevented them from giving rise to any kind of risks. They could not be a disturbing or disruptive factor in society because they were not part of society and had no access to society. This has changed as these temporary immigrant flows have become almost permanent, not the least because the locals they have been replacing do not want to do the kind of jobs the immigrants do anymore.

This pattern may continue for some years, but not eternally. It is based on three conditions. *First*, the divergence in living standards makes it profitable for foreign workers to migrate temporarily to another country and accept what are considered low wages there, which are high, sometimes very high, compared with what they could earn, if a job was available at all, in their home country. *Second*, a social and political understanding between their home country, the country they work in, and themselves that they accept this special status even if it puts them outside society and alienates them from many "human" activities such as raising a family (this is changing very much as the home-based families want to share the better living). *Third*, that the home country stands ready and capable of receiving them after their temporary stay abroad.

Insofar as migrating persons with a higher educational standard have — and that will be the case to some extent — norms and values not analogous with the host country, social coherence and social capital may come under pressure. Even if they do not wish to do so their presence constitutes a kind of cultural diversity, which the host country is not used to dealing with. Many Asian countries are multicultural or whatever label is preferred, but composed of persons anchored in various cultures that are part of the cultural heritage in the nation state or political entity in which they grew up. They are integrated in the social fabric. This may not be the case for the persons coming in who adhere to the same religion or ethnicity as part of the population in the host country there, but who do not necessarily have the same cultural pattern. The Europeans have grappled with this problem for several decades without finding a solution. The Asian nation states/societies may, by tradition and history, be better placed to find a way out, but there is no certainty that this will be the case.

Some observers[17] take the view that robots can replace human staff in care functions. This remains to be seen, however. There is little doubt that robots can perform basic functions, but can we presume that elderly people will accept this form of care? If this takes place it will unquestionably not only influence the care sector, but also industry, because a phenomenal market for such robots will emerge in the next decades.

The point has been made that robots are spreading in Japan because the "Shinto religion often blurs boundaries between the animate and inanimate, experts say. To the Japanese psyche, the idea of a humanoid robot with feelings doesn't feel as creepy — or as threatening — as it might do in other cultures."[18] The robot industry in Japan, which in 2006 had a revenue of US$5.2 billion, could amount to US$25 billion in 2025.[19]

## Religious Groups

An unknown factor not often discussed is that while we may speak about divergent demographic trends among China, India, Japan and Southeast Asia, these national or geographic terms in fact hide a shift in races and religions. Measured in shares of total population, Asia will, twenty-five years from now, have fewer ethnic Chinese, more ethnic Indians, more ethnic Malays (and Indonesians). There will be more Muslims, more Hindus, and a smaller share of religions rooted among ethnic Chinese. No one knows what the impact of this will be on relations, not so much between Asian nations, but between ethnic and religious groups.

The most significant change is that the percentage of Muslims around the globe is forecast to rise from 16.5 per cent in 1980 to 19.2 per cent in 2000, and 30 per cent in 2025.[20] As 69 per cent[21] of the world's Muslims live in Asia it is a certain conclusion that the proportion of Muslims among Asia's population will rise visibly.

Muslims today constitute 13.4 per cent of India's population,[22] and with a concentration in the north, not only is it possible/likely that some Indian states will have a Muslim-dominated government, but also that Muslims will be a force in the Indian Congress. After years of difficulties in Japanese society, the mostly Korean Christians (explicit or in disguise) are gaining local influence. In the Philippines, the Muslim communities have feuds, but are collectively not without influence in Parliament. In Thailand, one of the underlying tensions in the south of the country are comparisons between communities governed by Muslims and communities in other parts of the country dominated by Thais.

The U.S. National Intelligence Council[23] stated in 2004 that "Over the next 15 years, religious identity is likely to become an increasingly important factor in how people define themselves. The trend toward identity politics is linked to increased mobility, growing diversity of hostile groups within states, and the diffusion of modern communications technologies."

Of particular importance for Asia the report says:

- Christianity, Buddhism, and other religions and practices are spreading in countries such as China as Marxism declines.
- By 2020, China and Nigeria will have some of the largest Christian communities in the world, a shift that will reshape the traditionally Western-based Christian institutions, giving them more of an African or Asian or, more broadly, a developing-world face.
- The spread of radical Islam will have a significant global impact leading to 2020, rallying disparate ethnic and national groups and perhaps even creating an authority that transcends national boundaries and continues to appeal to many Muslim migrants who are attracted to the more prosperous West for employment opportunities, but do not feel at home in what they perceive as an alien culture.

According to the report, figures about adherents to major religions and projected numbers look like this:

Christians will continue to be the largest group — globally — rising from about 2,000 million people in 2002 to approximately 2,500 million in 2025, followed by Islam rising from 1,200 million in 2002, to approximately 1,700 in 2025. Hinduism comes in at third place, with 800 million increasing to a little over 1,000 million people.

Looking at growth rates, we see Muslims come in as a clear number one, followed by Sikhs and Hindus in the number three slot.

It is not a foregone conclusion that these changes will create problems for Asian societies, but it is possible, perhaps, even likely. It would be hazardous to discount religion and growing religious feelings among the population. Much depends to a large degree on whether:

- Religion, as assumed in the report, takes on a more important role as a factor for people's identity or not. The prognoses are not unanimous, but the trends seem to indicate a revival for religions as a framework for people's identity or, at least, part of their identity,[24] especially as poor people get bewildered by consumerism and megacities.
- The trend moves towards more secularization, especially for Islam, or whether this religion and others advocating theocracies maintain the position that religion is not only a question of belief, but also sets the rules for societal behaviour.
- The big world religions can continue to attract the overwhelming part of populations seeking refuge in religion, or whether smaller and, in some cases, segregationist religious groups, including sects, inside the

FIGURE 5.1
Number of Religious Adherents, 1900–2025

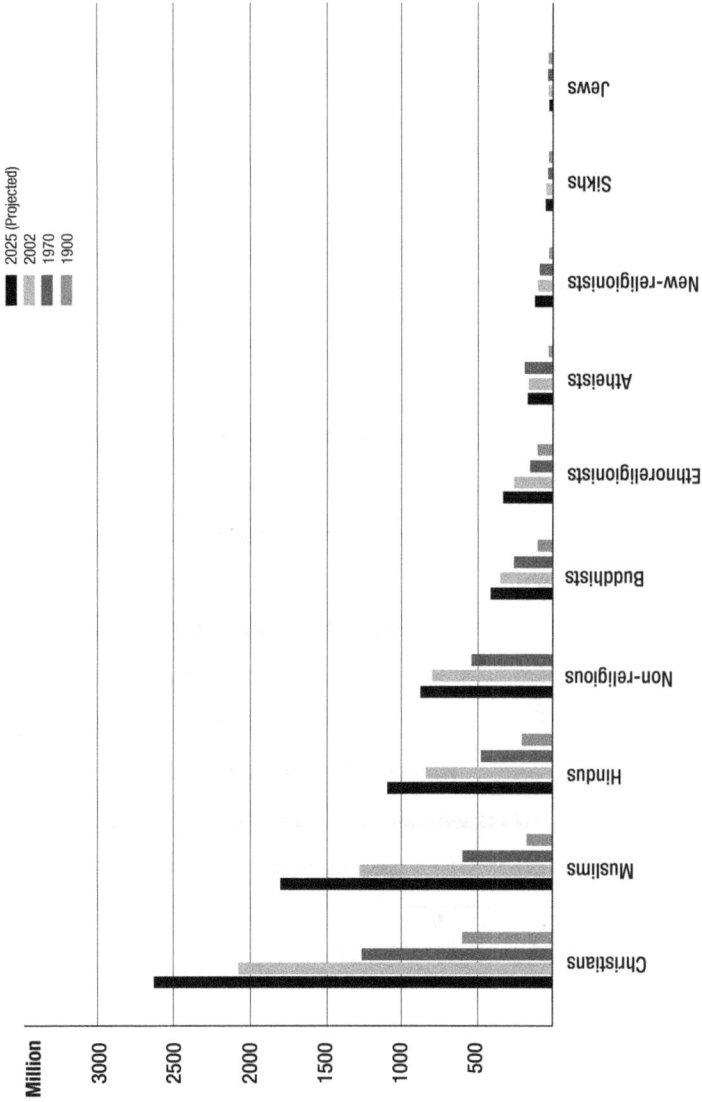

*Source:* U.S. National Intelligence Council, *Mapping the Global Future* (Washington, 2004) <http://www.dni.gov/nic/NIC_globaltrend2020.html#contents>.

FIGURE 5.2
Projected Percentage Growth of Religions, 2002–2025

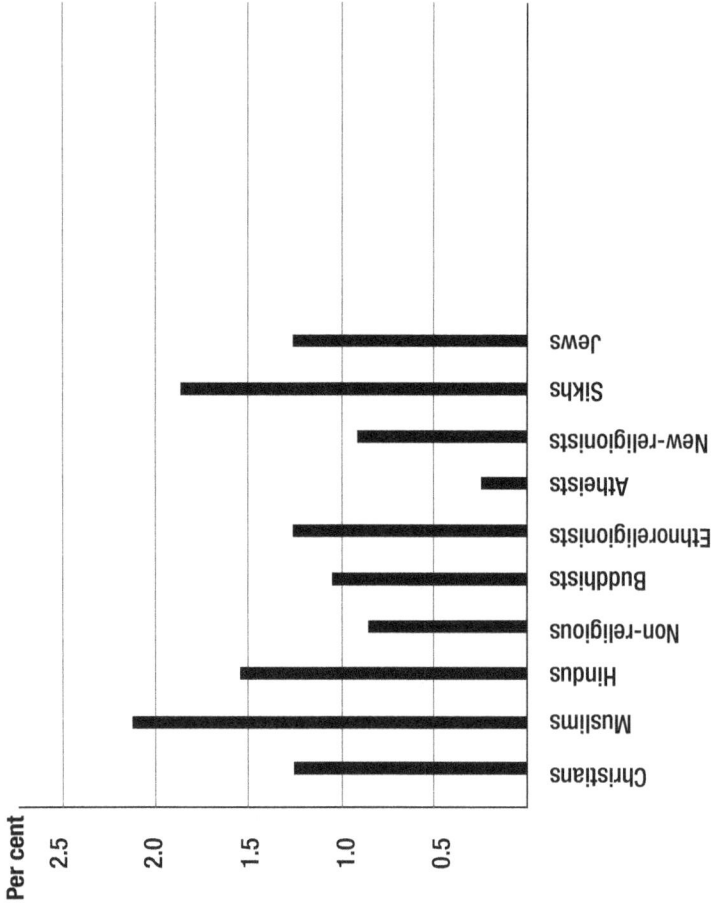

*Source*: U.S. National Intelligence Council, *Mapping the Global Future* (Washington, 2004) <http://www.dni.gov/nic/NIC_globaltrend2020. html#contents>.

well known religions, manage to find followers to erode the position of the main religions.

• Religion gets a stronger foothold in countries such as China, which hitherto offered its citizens philosophies such as Confucianism or Taoism rather than religions, and if so, will the religion go further in demanding identity and loyalty. If religion enhances its position in such countries the next question is how the political system intends to react, if not try to reshape religious institutions.

Of these uncertainties the possibility that the big religions break up from inside may be the most serious one as it may open the door for extremist views and fanaticism grounded in religious beliefs.

Extremist or uncompromising religious beliefs are rarely confined to religion alone. Frequently it brings along a certain lifestyle or social order as an inseparable "diktat". For many years Islamic banking has existed, but recently it has expanded into areas not yet embracing such financial systems. The same goes for food processing where Islamic rules call for special treatment on it which differs from what is regarded as common practice. At first glance this may not look like a problem, but after some thought it becomes clear that it actually breaks society up. If a large part of the population is no longer content or ready to operate inside the framework of the existing financial system and/or the existing system for processing and distributing food, societal consensus starts to crack with consequences for social capital. In economic terms, it inevitably leads to a loss of efficiency and productivity as different rules have to be implemented according to who is involved. This means two separate systems operating. The next observation that is again unavoidable is that economic and financial transactions between groups become more difficult and, ultimately, not possible. In a long-term perspective, this breaks up societal infrastructures along national lines and/or regional or megacities/megaregional lines, and replaces them with systems operating across borders on the basis of religious societal order.

This is not — as yet — a threat. It is estimated[25] that the world today has 10,000 distinct religions, of which 150 have one million or more followers. Within Christianity there are 33,830 denominations. Such religious *gruppenanarchie*, where people guided by religious fervour feel vindicated in breaking out of the social fabric and creating their own social capital for small groups anchored in the belief that they alone know the whole truth, spells deep problems for societies and communities trying to rally a large number of people around common values.

If the big religions can hold together, it is less likely that Asia will see a clash between nation states and religion. The large religions have hundreds of years or even more of experience in dealing with relations between religion and the state. They are not interested in a confrontation and mostly know where the borders are to be drawn. The nation states may be more uncertain and unsettled facing religions, especially a nation state such as China that has never really had strong religious forces inside, but their political systems look for stability, and provided that a reasonable compromise can be struck with religions, will probably opt for peaceful coexistence. For the nation state, the crucial issue is whether a religion understands that if it tries to draw people away from identifying with and being loyal to the nation state, trouble will brew. In other words, as long as a religion follows a clear secular line and refrains from interfering in societal matters, the risk for confrontation is not imminent. On their part, nation states must establish processes, and check on their fairness, to hold dialogue with the different religions and return favours with some concrete actions (building school systems, churches, etc.).

## INEQUALITY/URBANIZATION

In the early phases of economic development, economic inequality tends to increase as a part of the population reaps the benefits while another part is still caught in the former developing structure. Inequality is not in itself a bad thing in this phase as it increases savings, making capital available for investment; indeed it is difficult to see economic development without rising inequality.

The yardstick for inequality is the Gini coefficent, where a figure of zero indicates complete equality and 1 means one person possesses all wealth. According to the United Nations, at the beginning of the twenty-first century, Asia is the most equal region in the developing world with an urban Gini coefficient of 0.39. It is, however, also the region with the greatest variations in income distribution.[26]

Normally a figure of 0.40 is classified as the danger threshold, perceived as the moment when social tension can be expected to grow. Figures for 2004 from the Asian Development Bank (ADB) show that China and Hong Kong with 0.472 and 0.454 respectively are well above the 0.40 threshold. Most of Southeast Asia has a figure around 0.40, with the Philippines at the top end (0.444), and Indonesia plus Laos at the low end (0.34). India's Gini coefficient is 0.362.[27]

Compared with developed OECD countries[28] with an average Gini coefficient of 0.31 (e.g. Japan 0.314) Asia is actually showing an inequality at the high end of the scale. That may not, in itself, give rise to worries, but two factors attract attention.

*First,* inequality in most of Asia has been rising over the last two decades.[29] A large part of the population has seen their income and standard of living increase,[30] but relatively — compared with other groups of the population — they may not feel better off. Low and high incomes have both risen, but high incomes more than low incomes.

*Second,* especially for China, inequality has developed into a rural versus urban problem, with rural districts lagging behind.[31] The problem is that separate analyses of urban districts and rural districts taken on their own do not show inequality above what would be regarded as more or less normal, but urban districts compared with rural districts do show a high inequality, pushing the Gini coefficient above the 0.40 level.

This is elaborated in the 2008 report from UN Habitat[32] which says that urban incomes are 3.2 times those in rural areas, while at the same time, income disparities inside the urban areas are small compared with other cities in the world. Beijing is nominated in the report as the most egalitarian city in the world, with Jakarta as a close runner-up, giving further proof that the disparity in Asia is between cities and the countryside, and not within two social strata/geographical areas.

The observation that the problem is urban versus rural is borne out by classifying inequality in cities. Not only is Beijing Asia's and the world's most equal city, but out of fourteen Chinese major cities, only four surpass the 0.40 threshold and two of those come in at 0.42 and 0.45. Hong Kong and Shenzhen are the only ones showing a Gini coefficient of around 0.50. The highest Gini coefficients in urban Asia are found in Chiangmai (0.58), Udonthani (0.56), and Hong Kong and Ho Chi Minh City, both at 0.53.

China and India follow divergent paths when we are looking at inequality between urban and rural areas, and inside rural areas.

China compared with India has much higher inequality in terms of urban versus rural areas, and also inside rural areas. For various reasons, including migration to urban areas to find employment, inequality is higher in rural areas in China than in urban settings.

Inequalities in India's urban areas have risen faster than in rural areas because of the shift from labour-intensive to capital-intensive economic activities. In fact, rural inequality declined in the 1990s.

This turns inequality from an economic to a political and social problem. For China it is short term, for India it is long term.[33] For both of them the crucial question is whether to move a larger part of the population into the cities hoping that the lower inequality among urbanized people will also be true of the newcomers, or keep a large part of the population deliberately or inadvertently where they are, accompanied by measures to beef up their income, or a combination of both policies.

Going back to 1975 China had 17.4 per cent of its population in urban areas; India, 21.3 per cent. In 2005 the corresponding figures are 40.4 per cent and 28.7 per cent respectively. UNDP's forecast for 2015 is 49.2 per cent and 32 per cent.[34]

China has chosen primarily to move people into the cities by stimulating migration, increasing the urban workforce, and restricting upward pressures on wages, in the expectation that the lower inequality among the urban population will continue, and that by isolating the urban-rural inequality, turn it into a manageable problem. The migration will be on a scale the world has never seen before (between 300 and 500 million people) and increase the urban population from 500 million in 2000, to 800 million in 2020 (an urbanization ratio of 55–60 per cent).[35]

The Chinese Government seems determined to carry out a policy of better balance and equality, but the jury will be out for a long time on whether it can do so. The policy is known as *Xiaokang*, meaning all round and well-adjusted development aimed at quadrupling per capita incomes, balancing human centred development, care of the environment, support of individual empowerment, and commitment to improved governance accountability. The time span for obtaining these goals is year 2020.[36] This was confirmed by the "Resolution on Major Issues Regarding the Building of a Harmonious Socialist Society", adopted by the Sixth Plenary Session of the 16th Central Committee of the Communist Party of China (CPC) on 11 October 2006.[37]

Such a policy will put enormous pressure on investment in infrastructure, housing, etc., and may change the social fabric of Chinese society as the newcomers from the rural districts bring along another family structure other than the existing one of urbanized people. It is not an overstatement to say that this will strain resources and political stability. If the policy succeeds, China may well be stronger after such social engineering, but if it fails, the consequences may be disastrous. If there is no clear success nor failure, discontent will grow and centralized power control in the cities will become impossible — gangs, riots, socially dangerous "islands" will multiply as we have already seen in affluent Western agglomerations (e.g. Los Angeles, Sao Paulo) and in South Africa.

India looks like it has chosen the other alternative, meaning keeping a large part of its population where they are, albeit the less stable political environment in India cannot guarantee that this policy will actually be carried out. The official prognosis says that in 2020, out of a total population of 1.3 billion people, 540 million will be living in cities — an urbanization ratio of 41.5 per cent.[38] India's advantage is that the country currently has a significant lower inequality than China, but one suspects that this is partly due to less urbanization. India has taken off economically by using the service sector and not industrializing. To create jobs it must, however, move into industrialization fast, which will bring along urbanization and probably higher inequality. Looking at the growing population, the high level of rural population, the increasing numbers of people moving into the working-age bracket, we see that a policy of solving inequality by urbanization looks incredibly difficult.

This may explain why apparently the government is trying to ride on both horses. The national rural employment scheme[39] may have two purposes. *First*, to prevent growing inequality between rural districts and urban areas. *Second*, to motivate people to stay in rural districts, thus alleviating the strain on investment in the cities.[40] The risk is that this will turn into an income transfer without stimulating economic activity and, in fact, will become social welfare on a grand scale, freezing structures instead of promoting adjustments.

A concentration of wealth is a hidden time bomb in India's future development.[41] A report says that fifty people control 20 per cent of the country's GDP and 80 per cent of its stock market capitalization. To judge from the experience from other countries, such concentration does not need to stop economic development, provided that governance, institutions, and rules plus legislation, manage to channel the activities into not only economic growth, but growth of a societal nature, that spreads the benefits to a large number of citizens, thus reducing or, at least, holding back inequality in the long run. This is precisely where the fear emerges that India, with a weak governmental system, will not be able to build up such a framework and without it too much power may rest with a tiny group of people more interested in their own wealth than in developing the country.

For both China and India their future depends to a large degree on how they will tackle the urban-rural income gap and what the consequences will be for their economic and social policies and, at the end of the day, political stability.

Urbanization itself cuts both ways. The almost phenomenal rise in investment (infrastructure, housing, facilities) can be a booster for the economy and keep demand at a higher level. It may also promote new technology as megacities need to cope with problems of congestion, etc., on a scale not seen before. China may have many cities or agglomerations of more than twenty million inhabitants. India likewise. Judged on the basis of human history, it is unlikely that this will happen without any breakthrough in new technology, planning, sustainability etc.

The lack of global vision in actions on rural areas is often alarming. When trying to bridge the digital divide in Indian rural areas, the Indian authorities did not grant licences for technologies affordable to the rural population. On the contrary, licences have been awarded to high-cost, often unproven, technologies, and monopolistic rights granted to rich investors seeking short-term gains.[42]

One of the most obvious targets for new thinking will be the role of the car. It is predicted that China will have 140 million cars in 2020, eventually rising to 250 million.[43] The prognosis for India says 63 million cars in 2020.[44] India has already, with the Nano car, shown ingenuity, but it still represents thinking inside the box. Perhaps Asia with its megacities will be the place where virtual workstations — meaning where people do not move to go to a workplace, but work at home — will take off.

Another aspect of urbanization more difficult to grapple with is the repercussion on the family structure. So far mankind has basically lived in cultures forged by agricultural societies and contact with nature. Even if Europe and the United States went through urbanization in the twentieth century, the large majority of people had roots in the countryside as they were first or second generation to be in the cities. The urbanization in Europe was also slower and more gradual.

The picture for the United States is a bit more complicated as immigrants went straight to the cities, accounting for a considerable proportion of the rise in absolute numbers of people in cities. The picture emanating from various studies on the social fabric in big American cities is, in fact, not encouraging.

A UN study from 2008[45] looks at 120 cities worldwide and concludes that New York was the ninth most unequal city, with Atlanta, New Orleans, Washington, and Miami on similar levels of inequality. It is even more disturbing that in the big American cities, race is one of the most important factors determining levels of inequality. There is no "law" saying that Asia will follow the same track and there are, of course, many and large differences between Asian and American cities, but what has happened in the United States serves as a warning signal not only with regard to inequality, but also with regard to which social strata are likely to fall into this trap.

A group of sociologists[46] published a study in 2006 focusing on the United States and came to the conclusion that there had been large social changes over the past two decades. They conclude that:

- The number of people having someone to talk to about matters that are important to them has declined dramatically and the number of alternative discussion partners has shrunk.
- The share of the population being isolated from counselling has gone from a quarter to almost half.
- The American population has lost discussion partners from among both kin and outside the family. The largest losses, however, have come from the ties that bind us to the community and neighbourhood.
- The education level at which one is more connected through core discussion ties to the larger community than to one's family has shifted up to the graduate degree, a level of education only attained by a tiny majority.

American cities see subcultures emerging which are disconnected from "normal" connectivity, and which substitute family, local community, and neighborhood with "strangers" who happen to share the same lifestyle and identity. This phenomenon was detected in 1988.[47]

The social and cultural problem for Asia is that urbanization will take place in a very short time interval, leaving not much time for people to digest the differences between life in a village and life in a city of, for example, twenty million people. We simply do not know how people will react to such a change on such a scale. What has happened in the United States does not necessarily constitute a trend. It is too early to say so, and it may not necessarily happen in Asia. The only thing we know is that cultural and behavioural patterns will change.

## SCARCITIES

### Food[48]

### *Overview*

The Food and Agriculture Organization of the United Nations (FAO)[49] concludes on the basis of long-term population and income projections that global food production needs to increase more than 40 per cent by 2030, and 70 per cent by 2070, compared with average 2005–07 levels. Looking at whether and where arable land is available, the picture we see is comparatively reassuring: globally the current area of 1.4 billion hectares (ha) of cropland can be supplemented by 1.6 billion hectares.

Currently arable land in Asia amounts to a little above 500 million ha, placing it at the top spot, followed by the Americas with a little bit less than 400 million ha; Europe, with about 300 million ha; Africa, about 200 million ha, and Oceania, about 50 million ha. From the mid-twentieth century to 2007, the area has increased steadily in all regions except Europe.

The picture is, however, completely different and quite worrying for Asia when looking at where to find the 1.6 billion ha. More than half of this land is to be found in Africa and Latin America, and the same regions account for most of the available land with the highest sustainability class for rain-fed crop production. Asia's problems with finding new land suitable for agriculture are exacerbated when recalling that in South and East Asia, one third of arable land is irrigated.

Figures from the WTO[50] (World Trade Organization) bear out that Asia is already a net importer of agricultural products. Globally trade in agricultural products accounts for 8.3 per cent of total trade, with North America and South plus Central America as the biggest net exporters. Asia (2007) accounts for 5.6 per cent of global exports and 7.4 per cent of global imports of agricultural products, which means that Asia is moving into a substantial deficit, making it dependent on other regions in the world to feed its people, with little or no prospect for escaping consequential political, economic, and social problems in the decades to come.

While the global problem may be surmountable when looking at production, it is likely that turning out more food requires a significant economic effort that will translate into higher food prices. The signs for a changing trend are found in the figures. The *Economist*[51] food index was in 2008 at its highest level since it began to be recorded in 1845, after having risen in 2007 by one third, and this despite a global cereal crop at record level. According to ERS (Economic Research Service, U.S. Department of Agriculture)[52] worldwide agricultural commodity price increases were significant in 2004–06: corn prices rose 54 per cent; wheat, 34 per cent; soybean oil, 71 per cent; and sugar, 75 per cent. But this trend accelerated in 2007 due to continued demand for biofuels and drought in major producing countries. Wheat prices have risen more than 35 per cent since the 2006 harvest, while corn prices have increased nearly 28 per cent. The price of soybean oil has been particularly volatile, due to high demand growth in China, the United States, and the European Union (EU), as well as lower global stocks.

FAO estimated that the high food prices of 2006 increased the food import bill of developing countries by 10 per cent over 2005 levels. For 2007, the food import bill for these countries increased at a much higher rate — an estimated 25 per cent.[53]

The year 2008 gave a respite as all commodity prices fell. The overall index went down from a peak of 340 mid-2008 (100 for year 2000) to 220 at the beginning of 2009. Food prices displayed smaller fluctuations, falling from a peak of 220 in mid-2008, to150 beginning 2009.[54] There can be little doubt, however, that this fall is a blip on an upward rising curve, signalling a trend for the next decades. Food will be much more expensive and will call for a larger share of household incomes than has been the case for a long time. Indeed, the downward trend of foodstuff prices over the last two hundred years — accompanying industrialization — may well be over, to be replaced by what would historically be more normal conditions.

There is another disturbing phenomenon starting to characterize the demand-supply equation for food and that is the declining fallback on global offset through trade. In the half century since the end of World War II, the world got used to some regions facing temporary scarcities because of failed harvest or wrong policies (often the first a consequence of the second), which easily was off set by surplus from other regions.[55] There were national or regional food crises that for a time disturbed the markets, but trading between regions took the world back to "normal" conditions. This can no longer be expected as food surpluses are wound down almost everywhere, making food shortages in one place spill over to the global level without much prospect of any regional offsetting.

Over the last 200 years productivity helped feed increasing populations and some observers point to continued productivity as the way out. The figures tell another tale or rather they tell how colossal this task is. In 1960 one hectare produced food for 2.4 human beings, and in 2005 the figure was 4.5 human beings. In view of the known increase in population from 2009 to 2030, one hectare needs to feed 6.5 human beings.[56] No one says it cannot be done — we don't know — but few will dispute the difficulties and the uncertainties surrounding productivity increase of that size.

Even with such a tremendous increase in productivity, agriculture over the last fifty years did supply a relatively modest share of the human need for animal protein. It actually came from fisheries which recorded a fivefold growth in total catch. But that was achieved by depleting fishery stocks, making any increase in fishing over the coming years unlikely. Higher demand for animal protein must, therefore, come exclusively from agriculture, putting even harsher strains on that sector.[57]

The synthesis of the political, economic, and ethical problems posed by food shortage is found when looking at the number of undernourished people in the world and where they are found. The total number rose in seventy least-developed countries from 776 million in 1997 (30 per cent of the total population in these countries) to 1,200 million people (33 per cent) in 2007 — and those figures are from 2007, that is, before the price rises in 2008.

In coming years and decades the risk of not being able to feed a large part of the population threatens a number of nation states either already classified as failed states or on their way into this category, which poses a risk for regional or global stability and constitutes a genuine spectre of political and economical upheavals.[58]

The problems are exacerbated by investments by rich countries that are short of agricultural land (e.g. Saudi Arabia) around the world.[59] Objectively this is like any other investment, but if the consequence is to divert food production from domestic consumption into exports for the owners of the purchased land, it may turn into social and political problems.

A closer look at demand and supply paints a fairly pessimistic picture of the next twenty-five years.

Fundamentally this is due to:

• a strong rising demand for food (more people and more well-off people asking for processed foods requiring more input of corn, wheat, etc., than basic foodstuffs) and
• limited possibilities to increase food production as there is not much more virgin soil, actually reduced soil, to put under the plough and fewer farmers to do so.

## Demand

An analysis of the global food gap (the amount of food needed to raise the consumption of all income groups to the nutritional requirement of roughly 2,100 calories per person per day) by 2016, which assumes that food prices rise 1 per cent annually from 2007 to 2016, shows that there will be a food gap of 25.2 million tons by 2016.

Compared with other parts of the world, Asia is not doing so badly with a food gap of between 3.6 and 3.9 million tons. But Asia is doing comparatively well because it can afford to buy more foodstuff than other and less poorer regions.

Table 5.3 below compares the exports and imports of Asian countries that are among the fifteen leading global exporters/importers as a percentage of total global exports/imports from 2000–2007:[60]

TABLE 5.3

Share of Asia's Leading Importers/Exporters in Global Imports/Exports

| | 2000 | | | 2007 | | |
|---|---|---|---|---|---|---|
| | Exports(+) | Imports(−) | Net | Exports(+) | Imports(−) | Net |
| China | 3.0 | 3.3 | −0.3 | 3.4 | 5.5 | −2.1 |
| Thailand | 2.2 | | +2.2 | 2.2 | | +2.2 |
| Indonesia | 1.4 | 1.0 | +0.4 | 2.1 | 0.9 | +1.2 |
| Malaysia | 1.4 | 0.8 | +0.6 | 1.8 | 0.9 | +0.9 |
| India | 1.1 | | +1.1 | 1.4 | | +1.4 |
| Japan | | 10.4 | −10.4 | | 5.8 | −5.8 |
| Korea | | 2.1 | −2.1 | | 1.8 | −1.8 |
| Hong Kong, China | | 2.0 | −2.0 | | 1.1 | −1.1 |
| Taipei, Chinese | | 1.3 | −1.3 | | 0.9 | −0.9 |

*Source*: WTO, *International Trade Statistics 2008* (WTO, 2008), Table II.15 <http://www.wto.org/english/res_e/statis_e/its2008_e.pdf>.

The picture corresponds to expectations with China, plus Hong Kong and Taiwan, accounting for substantial net imports, which, taken together, are growing (from −3.6 to −4.1), Japan, a substantial net importer, with a decreasing share because total global trade is going up, and India, with slightly growing net exports.

In the years to come, China's demand for foodstuffs and, to a lesser extent, India's, will force a structural change in world production of agricultural produce and agricultural trade, with Latin America in particular benefiting. China has already become a net importer, with a net import of agricultural produce per year in 2003–05 of about US$15 billion, while India is a net exporter to the tune of US$2 billion. The share of agricultural products in total imports is approximately 2 per cent lower for India than for China.[61] The Chinese policy of moving people from the countryside into cities will unquestionably increase dependence on import of foodstuffs, thus increasing the gap between exports and imports, and pushing China's share of global imports of agricultural products upwards. The same may not necessarily happen in India, which may also experience a strong increase in demand for foodstuffs, but also a higher production, making it uncertain when the country will swing from being a net exporter to being a net importer.

If we assume high economic growth, the food problem may be more an economic problem than a supply problem. The implication of this will be structural changes in industrial and retail sales as the share of foodstuffs go up, making it more lucrative for people to operate in this sector and for the urban population to change to shopping in supermarkets, etc.

Lester R. Brown discovered what he has labelled the "Japan Syndrome" which says that if countries are densely populated when industrialization begins, they will soon move through three phases and end up being a net importer of grain: grain consumption climbs as income rises, grainland area shrinks, and grain production falls. This happened in Japan which was self-sufficient in grain in 1955, but within a couple of years became a net importer, and now imports 70 per cent of its grain needs.[62] China seems to follow a similar curve, increasing its grain production from 90 million tons in 1950 to 392 million in 1998, production is now declining and in 2008 the Chinese Ministry of Commerce announced that China would become a net grain importer.[63]

As people grow richer they tend to eat more meat, which requires more grain to be produced, so increasing the amount of grain required to provide the same amount of calories. Economic forecasting tells us that several hundreds of millions of people in emerging economies, not only China and India, but a large number of middle-sized countries, will see their income per family rise to a level where this switch will take place.

FAO[64] has looked at the situation for biofuels and the repercussions for agriculture, taking as a starting point the rising interest in, and production of, biofuel means that the market for agricultural products and biofuels gets more closely integrated as pointed out by Schmidhuber.[65] Not only will prices for food go up, but relative prices will change, making some crops more profitable than others, and consequently changing the composition of agricultural production and resulting in food supply being influenced by sectors other than the demand for food.

Most Asian countries run programmes to stimulate biofuel production according to FAO. China plans to produce about six million tons of ethanol by 2010, and fifteen million by 2020. It is, however, interesting to note that China steers the production of biofuels away from staple grains such as maize, sugarcane, sweet sorghum, cassava, and rapeseed. India intends to promote biofuel by ethanol derived from sugar molasses. The government wants to mobilize wasteland to this effect. Indonesia looks to palm oil, but ran into the problem that cooking oil prices have started to rise. Malaysia also intends to use palm oil. Thailand and the Philippines have programmes to increase ethanol production. It is clear that all Asian countries encounter the dilemma that increased production of biofuel will spill over into higher food prices and, in most cases, hit the poorer segment of the population.

In the analysis FAO depicts a number of countries according to their net balance for food and energy. The main Asian countries[66] fall in the following category: net importers of food and energy are Japan (in an extreme position), followed by Korea (South), and the following countries close to striking a balance, but not quite and show a deficit for both food and energy sectors — Pakistan, Bangladesh, and the Philippines. Australia is at the other extreme, with a strong positive/surplus balance for both fuel and food, followed by Malaysia, Indonesia, and Vietnam. The following countries are net importers of energy, but net exporters of food: Thailand, India, and China (the last country close to balance in the FAO statistics for food). There is only one net importer of food which is a net exporter of energy in the FAO statistics: Turkmenistan.

## Supply — Constraints

Production may be increased by using more land, achieving higher productivity, better irrigation or technology such as GMO (genetically modified organisms) — and possibly a combination. GMOs have found widespread use around the world, but according to FAO, less in Asia than in other regions. There has been some progress in particular with regard to cotton and promising experiments with rice and maize, but overall the scope for introducing GMOs seems large.

Around the globe more barren land may be turned into arable land, but this will almost inevitably constitute an enormous drain on resources, which are also in short supply. Irrigation may be used, but water is among the five scarcities, although this option may for a short while alleviate the situation, it may worsen the long-term shortage of water. The growing population limits land available for agriculture, and turning forests into agricultural land degrades the environment and may worsen global warming. Topsoil, the layer of soil harbouring nutrients for plants, is normally six inches deep and reports have been coming in for some time that this is eroding because of wind, the breakdown of surroundings, overreliance on fertilizers, and sheer neglect of how to treasure this vital foundation for agriculture. It cannot easily be regenerated if it is first allowed to be swept away.

Ukraine and Southern Russia, parts of South America, and Africa offer prospects of potentially fertile land. Before 1914 Ukraine and Southern Russia constituted a breadbasket, but collectivization followed by bureaucratized agriculture destroyed the basis of farming communities which know how to cultivate the land, and it will take some time to produce a new generation of farmers able to read and understand nature's signals.

Productivity gains seemed quite good for a time as grain yield per acre went up by more than 2 per cent a year from 1950 to 1990, but since then the growth rate has fallen to approximately 1 per cent. GMO delivered a substantial lift in productivity for wheat and rice, but efforts to do the same for other crops have not been met with success.[67]

Water is increasingly a scarce resource not only because there is a limit on how much more water humanity can find but also because there are severe doubts as to how long water will be available in sufficient quality and quantity to support growing populations and their food needs. Large parts of the globe are already threatened by either a physical or economic water shortage, making it unlikely, maybe impossible, to fall back on irrigation in the same way as over the last half century.

Rising temperature works in the same direction unfortunately. A model forecasting the probability of where on the globe summers are going to be warmer than the warmest on record[68] depicts an alarming picture. The trend towards global warming and its implications for food production are: over the twenty-first century, a large proportion of tropical and subtropical Asia and Africa, plus parts of South, Central, and North America, will experience unprecedented high temperatures. A large part of the globe will see growing seasonal temperatures in excess of the highest on record. The effect will first be felt in tropical countries and thereafter in temperate geographical zones.

There is little doubt that agriculture and food production will suffer, but doubts persist and will probably continue to do so on exactly how much. For some years crop ecologists operated with the general but never endorsed guideline that for every rise of one degree Celsius above the norm, wheat, rice, and corn yields fall by 10 per cent.[69] A study published by the U.S. National Academy of Sciences[70] is along the same lines, but is more cautious, and says that the impact of rising temperatures of the order normally assumed in climate projecting will be small on a global scale in the first half of the twenty-first century, but progressively negative after that.

It is always dangerous to jump to conclusions, but aside from technological progress, which is not visible at present, it is difficult to see how the curves of rising demand and falling supply can be twisted to avoid a shortage that invariably leads to higher prices, and maybe even physical shortages, manifested through undernourishment and famine in some parts of the world.

Another case in point is local sea fishing, which nourishes large Asian populations. Some fishing communities in Indonesia already report undernourishment, while many Indian coastal populations have almost abandoned this way of living.

## Commodities

Taken as a whole Japan, Korea, China and India are dependent on imports of raw industrial materials. That raises a string of problems of which supply, price, and foreign policy look like the most important ones.

Southeast Asia is less dependent on imports of raw materials as it exports some raw materials and has less heavy industry requiring large inputs of raw materials.

The supply problem is the less difficult one, as Asia in this forecast does not differ much from other industrialized parts of the world. The problem is that Asia emerges as the main buyer of several important raw materials such as iron ore, but also of raw materials that will be essential in the future, such as lithium and boron. The supply problem then turns into the unease of being dependent on sources deemed to be potentially unreliable.

The circle to square for Asia, in particular, China, is to secure supplies, prevent the rise of dominant suppliers, and avoid inter-Asian rivalry. It is likely that a visible part of China's U.S.-dollar assets will be used to secure supplies, but the snag is that every time China gets a stronger hand on production and supply of raw materials, some other nations will lose — this is not a win-win game, but a win-lose game where the likely winner is China and the likely loser may be the United States and, to a certain extent, Europe, Japan, and perhaps also India. Hidden intense rivalry is also emerging between China and Japan on raw materials, not to mention the control of sea lanes, with its attendant risks of confrontations leading to a battle for political influence across Asia, and visible in deals considered with Russia.

History is rife with examples and illustrations of problems triggered off by discrepancies between population size and production capacity on the one hand, and available commodities on the other. Currently the discrepancies are at the highest level ever seen, with the rise of Asian economies. Due to production costs steered mainly by low wage rates in China and India,[71] manufacturing becomes concentrated in countries having large and growing populations, but few indigenous sources of commodities. An analysis comparing availability of commodities puts the United States and Russia at one end of the spectrum, with reasonable balance,[72] and Japan at the other end, being extremely vulnerable. Europe, China, and India are closer to Japan than to the United States and Russia.

If it is assumed that China's GDP will continue to grow at about 10 per cent per year until 2015 and after that somewhat slower, and India at 8–9 per cent, with a gradually stronger industrialization, rising prices for raw materials seems almost certain. Two changes can influence prices in a downward direction: a shift towards a service economy which requires less input of raw materials per unit of end product, and higher efficiency in the use of raw materials.[73] Realistically these factors may hold back price increases somewhat, but not stop them.

With strong growth Asia may be able to pay for costlier raw materials, on the assumption that added value generated grows faster than the commodity prices — which is questionable, but possible — and that it diverts financial resources away from other activities, thus making the development of society more difficult.

This opens the door for the speculation that the big Asian importers of raw materials may use their U.S.-dollar assets to purchase large multinational corporations that trade in raw materials, and so this puts them in the situation where at least some of the price increases will flow back as higher profits of multinational companies owned by them. It is not a bad guess that world trade in raw materials will move towards some kind of semi-monopoly and semi-monopsony. The big sellers and buyers will fight it out between themselves and the smaller ones will be squeezed out of the game. An example was seen at the beginning of 2008 when BHPs intention to buy its rival Rio Tinto triggered off a Chinese reaction to prevent one company from sitting on one third of the world's seaborne trade in iron ore, and the biggest producer of aluminum and coal.[74]

The decisive factor will be whether the world and, in this context, the established Western powers and Western-domiciled multinationals, are ready to keep global trade in raw materials inside the economic box, that is, disregard who the owner is and let prices, costs, and capital determine ownership. And, not least, whether Asia (China) is willing to use the same yardstick. If so, there is a good chance that the need for raw materials will not develop into a global foreign and security policy problem.

However, if China and Japan (Japan in a remodeled structure) want to take over or create controlling processes for raw materials, including Asian resources, interrivalry may lead to instability and fights. Russia wants to establish this kind of control for gas/LNG (liquefied natural gas) with Asian, North African, and Central Asian powers. Thailand and Vietnam have embarked on a similar enterprise for rice.[75]

On top of the general question on raw materials comes the issue of rare, and not very well known, raw materials of strategic importance found in few geographic places around the world and of vital importance for the production of many high-tech products. In this category we find cobalt and magnesium, cadmium, mercury and molybdenum, antimony, ferrochrome, gallium, germanium, indium, manganese and tantalum, vanadium, and lithium.[76]

# Energy[77]

## Supply/Demand

Over the next twenty years — to 2030 — world consumption of energy will rise by about 50 per cent, going up from 283 quadrillion Etu[78] in 1980, to 508 quadrillion Etu in 2010, to 678 quadrillion Etu in 2030. Most of the rise will come from Asia, excluding Japan, with an annual increase of 3.2 per cent which is equal to a doubling of energy consumption. China and India are in the forefront with a share of total world energy consumption rising from 8 per cent in 1980, to 19 per cent in 2006, to 28 per cent in 2030[79] (if we recall an estimated annual economic growth rate of over 5 per cent for this part of the world, these figures do not come as a surprise). Not only is global demand rising fast, but the distribution among buyers is changing even faster. A swing in share of eleven percentage points over twenty-six years may not at first glance, look like much, but when we realize the amounts involved, it becomes clear we are talking of swings of almost seismic proportions that put strains on suppliers, buyers, infrastructure investment in buying countries, and the global distribution network for energy, in particular oil, and on the environment. The composition of supply will change with the share of oil/petroleum falling from 37 per cent in 2005 to 33 per cent in 2030, the share of natural gas rising from 20 per cent to 25 per cent, and the share of coal going up from 27 per cent to 28 per cent. There is not much change in the share of renewable sources plus nuclear power, although they take up a slightly higher proportion.[80]

The whole system has to change, albeit within the known paradigm, with repercussions on the global economy and the global strategic picture. The weight of countries spills over into their positioning in geopolitics — inevitably. So does the interest they attract from terrorist groups and/or countries in control of significant shares of global supply, wishing to use that card for their own game.

The fluctuations in oil price illustrate that oil is not only a commodity, but also an object of speculation. The official oil price is set at the margin; only a small amount of oil is involved in the day-to-day price setting. Suppliers cannot forecast future prices with certainty in their economic and investment/infrastructure planning, and buyers cannot know with certainty what the price and the "drain" on their economy will be. The impact of this uncertainty is more important for suppliers than for buyers, as investments in energy exploration and exploitation are long-term ventures requiring enormous amounts of money. A wrong guess about future oil (energy) prices may turn a profitable investment into a disaster. As oil equipment need to be maintained and upgraded before we even start to talk about new investment, it is clear that the oil suppliers face a difficult decision. Some of them are in the fortunate position that they can ride out a price fall without too much pain (Saudi Arabia, for example), while others immediately see the negative impact on their whole economy (Russia and the United Kingdom are examples).

A switch to other energy sources is possible, depending on price and demand structure, plus logistics, but this takes time, requires large investments, and will sometimes be under political scrutiny as in the case of nuclear energy. The future level of oil prices is hard to predict. Most likely demand and costs for diversifying will keep them on an upward trend.

A forecast by a U.S. government agency[81] with a reference case of US$130 (real 2007 U.S. Dollar) per barrel, and two scenarios for the oil price in 2030 — one at US$200 and another one at US$50 per barrel — concludes that total 2030 world energy consumption will not depend very much on the oil price. The difference between total demand in the high- and low-price scenarios respectively is about 8 per cent. The composition of energy sources is, however, influenced, and visibly so, by how the oil price develops.[82]

With low oil price, the incentive to switch from oil to other sources will be feeble. The world will continue to be heavily dependent on oil, which is a major source of emissions of greenhouse gases. If the oil price goes up, substitution will take place, but to a considerable extent into coal (coal will overtake oil as the most important energy source), which produces even more emissions of greenhouse gases. Looked at in the context of energy and the environment, this is discouraging. Even with a continued drive to switch to clean energy sources, the reduction of greenhouse gases must primarily come from higher energy efficiency and better anti-pollution technology.

A slightly different view[83] sees total energy consumption rising less, by 15 per cent from 1990 to 2010, but only by 6 per cent from 2010 to 2020. The main difference is, however, the composition of supply predicting a decrease of petroleum's share from 35 per cent in 1990 to 26 per cent in 2020, the share of gas going up from 23 per cent to 33 per cent, and coal accounting for 27 per cent and 22 per cent respectively. These three sources of energy supply account for 85 per cent in 1990 and 81 per cent in 2020, compared with almost unchanged percentages in the analysis quoted in the introduction to this topic.

It can be expected that energy efficiency will continue to improve until 2030 for both OECD and non-OECD countries.[84] New equipment will be much more energy efficient than existing ones, not the least because of the growing awareness of emission and climate change, opening the door for economic incentives and possibly regulatory measures to that effect. The efficiency of OECD countries will continue to improve steadily, but for non-OECD countries, there will be an almost dramatic increase, bringing the amount of Btu per US$2,000 down from about 14,000 in 2005 to about 7,000 in 2030.[85] The intriguing observation is that higher global growth enhances energy efficiency as more money is available for investment, R&D, etc., while lower growth depresses energy efficiency.

Energy efficiency can alleviate the problem somewhat; investment in alternative energy such as nuclear power,[86] wind, solar, etc., may do likewise, but in a twenty-five-year perspective, the conclusion is simple: Asia continues to be dependent on fossil fuels (oil, LNG, and coal). There is no way out of this "trap". In a way it is ironic that Asia has an energy problem. Both China and India have more than enough, but for other reasons they do not want to rely on what they have: coal. China sits on the third largest coal reserve in the world, India on the fourth largest, with the United States in number one position, followed by Russia. Despite all efforts to reduce consumption of coal, its share of global energy consumption will go up, not down.[87] Global coal consumption is expected to rise by 74 per cent from 2004 to 2030, accounting for 29 per cent of global energy demand compared with 26 per cent in 2004. Irrespective of policies to use energy sources other than coal, China plus India will account for almost three quarters of this increase.[88] In 2010 coal may surpass oil as the most important energy-related source of carbon dioxide emissions.[89]

A number of factors point to coal and maybe nuclear power as the most important energy sources for the next twenty-five years. They are where the demand is, and that is the United States, China, and India. There are reduced costs for transport and connected infrastructure, in particular, sea transport. At the same time, they reduce the risks of terrorist attacks to disrupt oil supplies. For China and India, they also make the fear of a U.S. naval blockade to stop their oil import less plausible. All in all, low transport and infrastructure costs, combined with security of supply and reduced fear of foreign and security policy complications, speak in favour of coal and possibly nuclear power.

The drive for clean energy is something of a wild card.[90] When we recall the role of coal now and projections of it to 2030, it is an illusion to see clean energy without a breakthrough for coal. The United States is running FutureGen,[91] aimed at building a coal-fired plant with near to zero emission. China has a similar project called GreenGen.[92] The technology that can provide a solution is liquefaction of coal.[93] The problem so far has been that the technology is not fully developed at a cost-effective level.[94] New technology is always tricky and no one can be sure of it, but it looks like this is nearing a stage where it can be used, even if large-scale investment is not yet on the agenda.[95] It is often heard that an oil price of US$30 per barrel makes liquefaction of coal profitable, but this seems too optimistic. There are still uncertainties as it has not really been tried yet on a big-scale commercial basis.[96] In 2007 a bill was introduced in the U.S. Congress to further liquefaction of coal. The arguments for this were analogous to those enumerated above.[97] Another more recent, but untried technology, is carbon sequestration, which means that carbon dioxide is permanently stored away from the atmosphere. This technology is getting attention in Japan.

Nuclear power is staging a comeback after several decades in the cold, where the anxiety associated with its use overshadowed its potential. The debate about global warming and pollution from oil and, in particular, coal power stations, acts as a booster for the renewed interest in nuclear power being a "clean" technology.

Worldwide there are (as of 2009) 436 nuclear power stations operable, with the largest number in the United States (104) followed by France (59) and Japan (53). There are fifty-two nuclear power stations under construction, with China in the lead with fifteen, followed by India, six, and Korea (South), five. One hundred and thirty-six are planned, with India at the top (23), followed by China (18) and Japan (13). Two hundred and seventy-seven stations are proposed — a very uncertain figure, but nevertheless indicating interest in nuclear power — with eighty in China and twenty-eight in India.[98]

The main Asian nations with nuclear power have the following share of energy production from nuclear power:[99] Korea (South), 35.9 per cent; Japan, 24.9 per cent; China, 2.2 per cent; India, 2 per cent; and Pakistan, 1.9 per cent. Of Asian countries not yet operating nuclear power stations, Vietnam is planning two and proposing eight; Indonesia and Thailand are both planning two and proposing four stations.

With China, India, Japan, and Korea channelling resources into nuclear power, there is little doubt about its significance for Asia's supply of energy in the twenty-five years to come. For the same countries, there is little doubt about their dependence on the supply of uranium from outside. Nuclear power may help to solve the pollution problem, but does not make them less dependent. There is uranium in about twenty countries, but two thirds of the total supply comes from just ten mines. Australia is the main supplier with 24 per cent of the global supply, followed by Kazakhstan (17 per cent), Canada (9 per cent), the United States (7 per cent), South Africa (7 per cent),

Namibia (6 per cent), Niger (6 per cent), and Brazil (5 per cent). China and India only possess 1 per cent each of the global supply.[100]

Unavoidably, nuclear power entails a number of sensitive issues, such as safeguards, security, and fear among neighbouring nations that nuclear power stations may ultimately lead to interest to produce nuclear weapons. Its big advantage is no greenhouse gas emissions, being a "clean" energy.

Normally energy efficiency is perceived solely as squeezing more output out of one unit of energy while taking process costs into account. There is, however, another aspect to consider: an energy grid. With strongly rising demand, the economies and efficiencies to be reaped by building a pan-Asia energy grid are simply too enormous to ignore.[101] It has two positive side effects: a large pan-Asian infrastructure project boosting demand, and an element in economic integration displaying trust and confidence among the Asian countries. The second element may be the more important one. If such a grid, despite the obvious advantages for all Asian countries, is not built, the main reason will be a lack of mutual trust, and that is a worrying omen for other aspects of economic integration in Asia.

The European Union and the United States are contemplating a so-called smart grid, based on digital technology, to coordinate supply and demand by a two-way communication between suppliers and consumers that incessantly steers supply to where demand is highest, and squeezes the most out of this technology instead of the conventional technology for grids — much of which is 100 years old — and incorporates a lot of waste as it cannot adjust to changes in demand. The snag is that it requires a retooling of the whole grid, including meters, transformers, and transmission lines.[102]

## Energy Security

Until the 1970s energy security was seen in the context of warfare, that is, a country tried to conquer oil sources or, alternatively, protect them against attack. The part of World War II fought in the Middle East, the German drive towards the Caucasus, and the Japanese invasion of Southeast Asia all illustrate this.

After 1973 energy security has primarily become a question of securing supply against terrorism or domestic upheavals in failed states possessing oil reserves or against political interference by third parties in oil production or distribution (for example, Russia interfering with the Central Asian gas supply to Europe which crosses the Ukraine). The first step was directed at protecting supply from events inside oil producing countries, but gradually the security challenge has spread to the whole supply chain for oil from the source, pipelines, ports, ships, or other kind of transport, to refineries and infrastructure in the oil consuming countries. Daniel Yergin has calculated that in the United States alone, there are more than 150 refineries, 4,000 offshore platforms, 160,000 miles of oil pipelines, facilities to handle 15 million barrels of oil a day of imports and exports, 10,400 power plants, 160,000 miles of electric power distribution wires, 410 underground gas storage fields, and 1.4 million miles of natural gas pipelines.[103]

From the terrorist point of view (including state terrorism) oil and gas supplies are an attractive target. Traditional and conventional enemies wanted to attack another nation state to conquer a slice of its territory. Oil was an instrument to keep the war machine running. Today's threat is completely different. Terrorists want to destabilize nation states pursuing political and/or religious goals contradictory to those chosen by them. They want the political systems and political leaders they oppose to lose legitimacy in the eyes of the population by undermining the well-functioning of society. Attacks against oil or installations in the supply chain fit the bill as no industrial country can function without oil. If successful, terrorists can point to the disruption of the economy as an illustration of the weakness of the political system.

This tactic is also attractive for terrorists for two reasons: (1) to defend oil, gas, and the supply chain countries are forced to divert resources into what, in an economic context, may be labelled the sterile use of resources. Instead of building schools, money is poured into antiterrorism measures or infrastructure investments, with resultant negative effects on the living standard and the risk of creating a police state; (2) the supply chain is so vast that an effective defence is difficult to establish, taking resources away from other military purposes and creating opportunities for the terrorists. Just by letting rumours float around that an attack on oil or gas installations is in the planning stage, terrorists can push the oil or gas importing countries into a state of nervousness.[104]

As the supply chain starts in the oil or gas exporting countries, security also starts there. From a terrorist point of view, the oil or gas importing countries can be tempted to press for rights to station troops, or have a say in domestic security of the exporting country, which in itself will antagonize a part of the population not wishing to have "foreigners" demand rights to exercise some kind of control or even sovereignty on their territory.

As no major destructive attack against oil or oil supply installations has taken place in Asia, it is tempting to draw the conclusion that terrorists have decided not to risk an attack against a high-profile and consequently well-defended target, and instead use the threat of this happening to force oil consuming countries to divert security forces into that sector, leaving other sectors more open to attack.

Oil accounts for 50 per cent of Japan's energy needs and 90 per cent comes from the Middle East, with Saudi Arabia and the UAE (United Arab Emirates) both delivering approximately 25 per cent of Japan's oil. The only major suppliers outside the Middle East are Brazil, Indonesia, and Nigeria each with 2–3 per cent.[105]

In 2006, 44 per cent of China's import of crude oil came from the Middle East with Saudi Arabia as the biggest supplier, followed by Africa with 32 per cent, of which Angola is the biggest supplier, Russia, 11 per cent, Latin America, 5 per cent, and Asia-Pacific, 4 per cent.[106] It is official policy to achieve a visible hike in the share of oil from Africa where more than US$30 billion has already been invested.[107] Compared with the United States, Europe and Japan, China stands out as being less dependent on only one or two sources, and with a high share of its imports from Africa. The corresponding figures for India are 67 per cent from the Middle East again with Saudi Arabia as the biggest supplier, 23 per cent from Africa with Nigeria as the biggest supplier, and 8 per cent from other sources.[108]

As could be expected, there is a race to diversify. There are two problems, however. The *first* is that it costs money as the importer substitutes a less expensive source with a more expensive one, taking the supply chain into consideration. Furthermore, countries can diversify, but it does not change the overall dependence on oil for all importing countries. The *second* problem is that the Middle East accounts for 50 per cent of undiscovered oil reserves and 30 per cent of gas,[109] basically meaning that even with all possible endeavours to diversify, the world is moving towards greater, and not less, dependence on the Middle East for oil. The situation is the same as for diversifying out of oil into other energy sources. It can be done, technically, but it is expensive, so it boils down to a strategic question: how much will a country pay to be less dependent on one energy source and one or two main suppliers?

Two thirds of all oil is transported by sea, with 40 per cent of all traded crude oil passing through the Strait of Hormuz. The Strait of Malacca is also used for the transport of oil. They are generally analysed in the context of a terrorist attack with the obvious potential of not only disrupting supply, but also disrupting it in a spectacular fashion. It is often overlooked that terrorists have their own constituencies. They need to demonstrate that "they are in business", which forces them to attack theatres with high publicity significance (New York, and not St. Louis, is an example). The threat has forced a number of nations to cooperate with regard to naval patrols and other efforts, which so far has proven successful. We find again a high profile target, but precisely because it is a high profile target, it is also heavily defended and countries have got together despite barriers to cooperate of a historical nature. Terrorist attacks in the Strait of Malacca is seen as terrorism only, while terrorist attacks in the Strait of Hormuz has the potential of being masterminded by states — state terrorism (by say, Iran), which calls for a more beefed-up defence.

Behind the veil is a completely different potential threat in the form of major powers blocking the supply of oil through choke points, in case of crisis or conflict with other powers. It is often mentioned that China fears a U.S. naval blockade in the Strait of Malacca in the event of a Chinese-American confrontation. It is difficult to assess how likely this will be, but without doubt it belongs to a list of potential threats in the drawer of strategic planners in the United States and China. Some observers see China's drive to diversify out of oil as stemming from the fear of such an American policy. According to the Institute for Strategic Studies,[110] roughly 72 per cent of China's imported oil passes through the Strait of Malacca. President Hu Jintao has referred to the potential vulnerability of energy supplies as China's "Malacca dilemma".

China has taken action. It is building or acquiring port facilities in Pakistan (Gwadar and Pasni), some facilities in Sri Lanka and Bangladesh, and has a strong build-up of infrastructure for oil supplies in Myanmar. The strategic implication of this is that, irrespective of whether these facilities are solely for securing China's oil supply, eyebrows are raised in India especially as the Myanmar coastal islands have the potential for ELINT (Electronic Intelligence Teams) facilities.

Pipelines constitute another sensitive part of the supply chain. It is most vulnerable where it crosses one or several countries and, in particular, where two of the countries do not trust each other. The idea of a gas pipeline from Iran to India crossing Pakistani territory is a case in point, another is Russia's attempts to build pipelines that evade the Central Asian countries, but these are far from the only ones.

The fear or risk of *first*, political pressure (blackmailing), and *second*, disruption, makes these pipelines a pawn in the strategic game. In the Middle East there are big construction works under way to lay pipelines from the Saudi oilfields near the Gulf to harbours in the Red Sea or the Arabian Sea to avoid the Strait of Hormuz. These pipelines, however, constitute a target themselves and may prove to be more difficult to defend than originally expected, depending on political developments in the Middle East and, in particular, Saudi Arabia.

Choke points cannot be avoided, but the risks may be diminished, for example, by switching from tankers through sea straits to pipelines. However, there is a price for this measure: the cost of transportation goes up and the pipelines require defence.

## The Role of Oil and Gas Exporting Countries in the Geopolitical Game (e.g. Sovereign Wealth Funds)

One perspective seldom raised is how the suppliers of oil and gas, primarily in the Middle East, can be expected to safeguard their position, bearing in mind that their natural resources will not last indefinitely. So far their game has been a relatively easy one, with Western powers (read the United States) in the driver's seat militarily, economically, and in terms of industrial power. They did not have to weigh different aspects against one another. But from now on the tracks will start to diverge. According to WTO,[111] the import of fuels for the following countries rose as shown:

### TABLE 5.4
### Rise of Fuel Imports

| Country | 1990–2005 | 2000–2005 |
|---------|-----------|-----------|
| China | 50 times | 3.1 times |
| United States | 4.3 times | 2.1 times |
| India | 7.8 times | 2.9 times |
| Japan | 2.3 times | 1.7 times |
| Korea | 6.1 times | 1.8 times |

Source: WTO.

Depending on growth and various other factors, it is only a matter of time before China and India emerge as such important customers that supplier countries will need to pay increasing attention to these two countries. The time horizon may be a bit long, but China is poised to take over from the United States as the biggest net importer of oil.

Obviously oil gives the oil exporting countries power. In principle there is nothing "wrong" with this; the problem arises if oil exporting countries or a group of oil exporting countries want to exercise that power in a way that upsets the existing political and economic system.

That may have been close to the case when the oil price was raised 300–400 per cent in 1973/74, but as it could be seen as a long-awaited realignment of the oil price to its historical trend, it was not perceived as a challenge to the system, but merely a redistribution of global wealth.

The Russian gas threats towards the Ukraine and several Central and Eastern European countries may come closer to oil being used in a strategic game. By threatening to cut off deliveries of gas, most of which did not even originate from Russian sources, Russia threw the dice on the table, sowing uncertainty whether the move was just a question of the price for energy, or an attempt to roll back political developments since 1990, and regain some or all of its lost supremacy in that theatre. The dependence of the European Union on gas from Russia and via Russia raised the fear that the Russian threats towards the Ukraine were actually meant as a reminder to the European Union of Russia's power.

Irrespective of what lay behind the Russian steps, they initiated a costly and ambitious European programme of diminishing dependence on supplies from Russia.

The Russian predicament about the pipeline (oil and gas) from the fields in Siberia to China or the Pacific coast illustrates how oil is not only an asset to be used, but how it can pose problems for the oil exporting country. If the pipeline runs to China, Russia becomes partly dependent on China as a buyer while if it runs to the Pacific coast, not only China, but also Japan and the United States become potential customers. The snag is that extending it to the Pacific coast costs money and currently Russia needs money. Recently it appears that Russia has chosen to make an oil/gas-for-money deal with China.[112] The details of the deal remain to be revealed, but it looks like Russia, out of the need for money having been hit by the global financial/economic crisis, has accepted to deliver oil to China on a long-term basis on terms favourable for China.[113] In fact it is a case where the oil exporter makes itself dependent on the oil importer!

Oil means money and money means power. For many years the oil exporting countries have accumulated large assets in U.S. dollars that gave rise to the sovereign wealth funds (SWF). Out of total assets amounting to US$2.1 billion held in 2006 by SWFs, approximately US$1.4 billion are found in oil exporting countries.[114] As with oil power, there is nothing wrong in this, but the fear is that such funds may be steered by non-economic considerations. There may not be evidence for such suspicions, but the fear is dominating the position of oil importing countries vis-à-vis SWFs.

The established industrialized countries worry about the rise of SWFs, the fact that they are government owned, and, in many cases, operate under opaque decision making, opening the possibility for politically-steered investment decisions. The SWF countries maintain that there is not much difference between their funds and industrialized countries' pension funds and, furthermore, that the disastrous policies pursued by many financial institutions originating in industrialized countries led the world to global financial chaos. The argument could also be put forward that in 1992 George Soros was credited with bringing the pound sterling down and out of the European exchange rate mechanism, with political consequences, even if that may not have been the purpose.

For the United States, the fact that other countries have accumulated sufficient U.S. dollar holdings to throw the dollar into turbulent waters is unquestionably a reason for anxiety. So far the United States apparently takes the view that there are limited alternatives as both the euro and the yen look somewhat fragile, but that is not really the point.

The point is that these funds may not necessarily continue to be used for U.S. treasury bonds. In fact, the tables can be turned by saying that the willingness of SWF-countries to hold U.S. treasury bonds illustrates their willingness to use their dollar assets in a non-economic way to help the United States to finance its deficits, based on purely political considerations that a strong United States is in their interests. They keep holding U.S. treasury bonds as long as they feel that the United States is stabilizing geopolitics in conformity with their interests. If the United States starts to pursue American interests only, they may not show the same willingness to finance American policies.

This shift will be exacerbated when we look at the currency mixes of reserves held by the major Asian Central Banks which have far larger amounts than SWFs whose moves to diversify gradually out of the U.S. dollar are clearly visible. These banks may not hold shares in foreign companies, leaving this task to SWFs that diversify and acquire company assets also serving strategic interests.

There may or may not be an alternative to U.S. dollars, but there is an alternative to treasury bonds and that is buying into American companies. Economic globalization has opened the door for such investments and U.S. resistance would amount to making the rules of the global economy invalid, while acquiescence would amount to seeing U.S. companies, including high-tech ones, coming under the control of foreigners and foreign governments.

## Asian Oil Companies

The analogy to the raw materials is striking when we look at the role of multinationals. Over the last decade Chinese and Indian, but also Thai (Thai Petroleum) and Malaysian (Petronas) oil companies have emerged as some of the biggest and most active in the world, eating into the established positions of Western oil companies. CNOOC,[115] Petrochina,[116] and Sinopec[117] from China, and the Indian Oil Corporation[118] plus ONGC[119] from India — are just a few examples. In fact, Sinopec and Petrochina have managed to break into the top fifty companies on Fortune's list of global 500 largest corporations.[120] It is unrealistic not to forecast a stronger role for Chinese and maybe Indian companies in the next twenty to twenty-five years. The question pops up again whether they will act as carrier of their country's flag, or base their activities solely or overwhelmingly on economic and industrial considerations.

The days of the so-called seven sisters — a group of Western oil companies dominating the oil industry — are definitely gone. Now the major companies will gradually be Chinese and other Asian ones, supplemented by, *inter alia*, Brazilian ones. Economically the effect will be that much of the windfall profits of operating in the oil business will accrue to these companies and consequently to their home countries. Management, know-how, financial strength, strategic planning, and contact to the oil exporting countries, will gradually, but surely, fall into the hands of companies other than the seven sisters. Politically this means corporate power, but also the ability to influence political decisions in oil exporting and oil importing countries.

## The Outlook

For the major emerging Asian economies there does not seem to be a fundamental problem of access to energy and/or oil supplies in a twenty-five year perspective, but energy may be more expensive, asking for resources to be channelled into protecting the whole supply chain, and the geopolitical picture may change somewhat.

This evolution will come about by the strategic commitment by some Asian countries to nuclear power and reducing the impact from environment/global warming. The motives may be different for the various countries: independence for the smaller resource-poor ones; diversification and expanded capacity for some of the larger growing ones; reducing emissions progressively and reducing geopolitical risks by some bigger, established ones.

If we assume that the world, despite strenuous efforts, cannot significantly reduce its dependence on fossil fuels, major changes to the basics of energy security are possible, but unlikely. There will be new suppliers and new major consumers, a new investment pattern, new multinational companies will see the day, and the global flow of money may be different, but the basic functioning of the market does not seem to be in jeopardy.

The threats to energy security by terrorism and other forces wanting to use power and influence to cut off supply will probably continue for the next few decades, but, so far, security measures have proven sufficient to prevent major disruptions.

The fundamental change in the great global game to secure supply in the coming decades will be that the major consumers, China and India, which do not have any significant oil reserves — or if they do, these are not easily accessible or are found in disputed areas — will probably make a strategy based on the following elements:

- Efforts to diminish the use of oil — diversification, bringing other energy sources such as nuclear energy and sustainable energy, but also coal, into the picture. The object will be to get as much as possible of their energy supply from domestic sources. The question is what price they will be ready to pay for higher energy security.
- A determining factor is whether the existing order in Asia will be maintained — in which case there is no incentive to pay a high price — or whether the emergence of China and India, combined with uncertainty about the U.S. attitude and Japan seeking a role in the new geopolitics, unsettles Asian stability — in which case there is a strong incentive to pay a high price.
- When buying energy, in particular, oil, from outside, they will try to find suppliers with a small risk for disruption. Supply through choke points or vulnerable pipelines will be the last resort.
- Oil supply will be distributed among as many suppliers as possible, taking costs into consideration.
- The assets these new large consumers posses will basically be money and they will use that to secure supply through owning multinational companies, combined with ownership, if possible, of oil fields.[121]
- A strong effort to buy or invest in oil and gas fields in other countries to diminish the economic and, possibly, also political risks.

That makes Central Asia and Russia interesting for China and India. These two countries need the oil and they have logistical but surmountable problems caused by geography and topography. Pipelines will run through foreign territories, which are likely to be more under the control of others than is the case with most other suppliers, which have more vulnerable pipelines and offer transport of oil through maritime choke points.

In a geopolitical context the major event will be a decline, even a significant one, of U.S. power and influence as the country's share of global imports fall, the strength of its multinational companies weaken, and doubts arise about the future of its economy and the U.S. dollar. This will trigger adjustments and adaptations in geopolitics among which energy security figures significantly. It seems reasonable to assume that this should not create upheavals for energy security as the United States will still be the strongest power, with a preponderant interest in supporting economic globalization, which requires a well-functioning energy and oil market.

The major risk for energy security is linked to political upheavals or armed conflicts, primarily in the big oil-supplying countries such as Saudi Arabia and other countries in the Middle East and maybe also Central Asia. Since 1973 strategists have pondered over the probability of such events, but so far the areas have managed their own brand of stability inside instability. The key decisive factor for future energy security may thus be the combination of domestic stability with adaptations to economic globalization, and the opening up of societies to outside influence. If this adjustment does not happen, unpleasant upheavals in Middle East countries and/or Central Asian countries cannot be ruled out, casting doubts over future oil supply, thus jeopardizing economic growth in Asia, but motivating increased interest in other energy sources such as nuclear energy.[122]

## Water[123]

Water shortage may be the most dangerous of the scarcity problems (the others being of energy, food, raw materials) as it touches on the very survival of human beings and hits in a short-term perspective, while the other scarcities may gradually build up. It is much more difficult to solve than the other scarcity problems as money will "do the trick" only to a limited extent. It spills over into agriculture thus aggravating food shortages, and has a strong impact on the possibilities for further urbanization.

The picture of global water shortage runs like this:[124] Water is physically scarce in South Africa, North Africa, the Middle East, Iran, Pakistan, the western part of India, the northern part of China, and Australia. Almost two billion people live in these areas. It is scarce, but not to a threatening degree yet in Latin America, Turkey, and the rest of India, the rest of China, and Southeast Asia, home to another two billion people. North America, Europe, the Asian part of Russia, Korea, and Japan face no water shortages.

China is the prime example of what water shortage or the threat thereof means.[125] In 2001 the Chinese Government acknowledged that in 2030 water shortage would reach danger levels. Most Chinese cities already now live with hidden or open restrictions on the use of water. Political problems arise much sooner as water is unevenly distributed. Eighty per cent of water resources are found in the southern part of the country, with just above half the population, and just above one third of the arable land. About 44 per cent of the population sitting on 59 per cent of arable land has to make do with 14 per cent of the water supply. No wonder then that the Chinese Government almost desperately works with grand designs to turn rivers around to redirect water from the southern part of the country to its northern provinces.

The policies hitherto applied are a catalogue of short-term measures. Some of them that are devastating in the long run involve the irresponsible use of aquifers and the unsustainable tapping of groundwater which creates new problems; others such as recycling, are useful, but do not explore new sources, and yet others include restrictions/levies to reduce water consumption.[126]

The global use of water from 2000 to 2050 has been estimated to almost triple,[127] going up from about 3,350 cubic kilometres in 2000, to about 9,250 cubic kilometres in 2050, assuming that the incomes of the poorest countries continue to climb to levels equivalent to middle-income countries at the beginning of the twenty-first century. When we take into consideration that water is already a scarce resource and that two billion people live in areas with physical scarcities, such an increase looks alarming and impossible to accommodate without disastrous consequences for the environment or social issues.

The main culprits are rising populations and rising income per capita influencing demand for food. About 70 per cent of global water use goes into irrigation.[128]

Scrutinizing the possible sources for augmenting water supply we will not find it difficult to see where and how the supply can be increased, but it is difficult to see how it can increase to meet such a hike in demand.

Water conservation, like energy conservation, is an obvious first target and a combination of persuasion, awareness of the problem, taxes, and regulations can certainly depress the demand, but they are unlikely to be of a magnitude required to bridge the gap to supply.

Some of the main rivers are not able to sustain the level of demand, and will dry up or be in danger of doing so. A prime example is Australia's Murray-Darling river basin that was actually presumed to be a model of water management, but where the planners got it wrong, resulting in the depletion of its water supply, which is difficult to regenerate.

The same is true of aquifers around the globe. Many aquifers are replenishable, but some are not, and when we look at the situation, we find that aquifers do not look in a satisfactory state that promises to deliver water in the foreseeable future.

The main option seems to be desalination where technological progress has been fast and holds promise for the future, but desalination is costly, requires money, and uses energy, thus aggravating the energy problem.

Ambitious plans or ideas are gradually being implemented in China to assuage the water shortage problem in the northern part of the country by linking the country's four main rivers — the Yangtze, Hwang Ho, Huaihe, and Haihe (South-to-North-Water Diversion Project[129]).[130] The Chinese Government is caught between alleviating the water shortage problem in the north with water from the south which has enough water, and risking social conflict between the haves and have nots in respect of water. It also has to find the money (total cost is estimated at US$62 billion), plus it runs the risk of a grand environmental disaster if the planners get it wrong when assessing the impact on the environment. As numerous examples from such big projects show — the Three Gorges dam in China being one of them — negative environmental effects tend to be underestimated.

The transport of water in ships or pipelines like for oil and gas will probably be a lucrative business over the next twenty-five years and, to a certain extent, it can alleviate the shortage of water in exposed areas. However, the fear is that after some time the new water sources will start to dry up or be more difficult to tap.

Asia is at the top of the list of threatened areas and the rising population in a number of countries, combined with rising incomes per capita, means that water shortage will be high on the list of issues calling for solutions. These will be costly and financial resources must be diverted from other policy objectives. In most Asian countries, water supply is dominated by private interests, so public interest is usually remote, and regulators/water boards weak.

There will be awkward choices between favouring agriculture or industry, rural areas and urban districts, and in some cases regions having plenty of water will be asked to put this at the disposal of other regions, raising the political question of compensation and/or readiness to show solidarity with other parts of the nation state that in some cases may not share the same basic values.

## Clean Environment

### *How to Pay for a Better Environment?*

The issue of a clean environment has worked its way up the list of priorities. Disregard of the environment creates several major problems, which the two most important ones are economic costs and social/health disruption. External diseconomies arise, gradually to the extent that production costs get prohibitively high. The classic example is the congestion of roads preventing normal flow of goods necessary for the supply chain. Perhaps a turning point in the Asian conscience was the huge constraints under which the Beijing Olympic games had to operate to meet environmental thresholds. Uncontrolled growth may in unfavourable circumstances be so strong that it chokes societal development and increases health costs. An indirect cost often overlooked are the negative consequences for building social capital. Pollution separates those directly responsible from those hit, and among those hit, the burden is unequally distributed. Pollution conveys a sentiment of an unfair and unjust societal structure and delegitimizes the government as many people take the view that it does not care or is not capable of caring for its citizens. Youth in particular are becoming very outspoken about the environment. There is a price for a clean environment and that price increases over the coming years/decades as it becomes a scarce "good".

The conceptual problem is who is going to pay for a clean environment. To a large degree it becomes a distributional problem within a country and between countries, rather than a matter of achieving it, which does not pose insurmountable technical or economic difficulties. Economic globalization means that this problem cannot be solved in a national context. For Asia the problem is that manufacturing and transport — the two most polluting activities — combined with toxic waste will shift to Asia even more than is currently the case. In 2006 China overtook the United States as the world's biggest emitter of carbon dioxide.[131] For a variety of reasons this necessitates an Asian effort to protect the environment and the trend clearly indicates a political and popular awareness of this without an accompanying acceptance of the costs as yet.

Pollution abatement costs money, a lot of money. The list of political objectives asking for money in Asia over the next twenty-five years is long. But unless high growth is accompanied by less, much less, pollution, the equation cannot be solved.

Internationally established industrialized countries take the stand that newly industrialized countries must bear the lion's share as they are responsible for the deterioration of the environment. The latter group counter-attacks, saying that established countries have been industrializing without any consideration for the environment so the time has come for them to pay up.

PPP (Polluter Pays Principle) has gained some ground among industrialized countries when formulating their domestic environmental policies. Even if it looks like factories, etc., are the polluters, the culprit is the ultimate consumer and accordingly the bill must be passed on to the main culprit. The best way to do this is through the price mechanism where relative prices are tinkered with through taxes or subsidies to punish the consumption of polluting products, and reward the consumption of less polluting or, even better, non-polluting products.

Seen from the perspective of the rich, climate change is no longer contested by Western countries, but classified as a genuine problem, threatening the future of the world. Reports by the International Panel on Climate Change (IPCC)[132] and the Stern Report[133] have taken the wind out of the sail of the few scientific doubters. Support for massive financial and technological measures is forthcoming. The European Union is at the forefront of this with its ambitious plan to reduce green house gas emissions by at least 20 per cent by 2020. Japan is on the same track with a target of a 14 per cent reduction, and envisages a 60–80 per cent cut in greenhouse gas emissions by 2050.

## Burden Sharing

The U.S. position for a number of years (during the Bush Administration) and the link to other countries' efforts give rise to the widespread suspicion in the world outside the club of rich Western countries that the issue of climate change is being hijacked to forestall emerging market economies overtaking established countries as leading economic, and subsequently political, global powers.

Many in the West will probably be taken aback on hearing this, as they see the rallying of troops to combat climate change as a seminal issue, something akin to a challenge for our generation, and a crusade not to be missed. The fact that many of the developing nations and emerging economies are heading towards grave environmental problems that threaten their future development, and therefore call for action, masks the underlying fear that the rich countries may have a hidden agenda. They are on board the endeavour to combat pollution and fight climate change, but they are adamant that these efforts must not be used as a vehicle to slow down the change in the balance of global economic power.

On 26 June 2008 the *Washington Post* reported[134] that climate change is linked to U.S. security saying that "U.S. intelligence agencies have concluded that global climate change will worsen food shortages and disease exposure in sub-Saharan Africa over the next two decades." The article went on enumerating various problems and threats to the United States: "Climate change and climate change policies could affect all of these — domestic stability in a number of key states, the opening of new sea lanes and access to raw materials, and the global economy more broadly — with significant geopolitical consequences."

In a U.S. context, this perspective seems natural. But developing countries and emerging economies do not have U.S. security at the top of their priorities. These countries are kept outside the inner core of global decision making by the United States and wonder why they are suddenly invited to the party. Their suspicion grows further on learning that it is a threat to U.S. security and not a global problem. They try to look behind the curtain to get a glimpse of what they fear might be the real U.S. objectives.

By making it a global problem that calls for action from all countries around the globe, the United States tries to get the rest of the world to pay for U.S. security. It is conspicuously absent from U.S. analyses that all the problems mentioned as potential threats emanate from the fact the United States is richer, which should point to the United States as the largest contributor. The U.S. analyses do not speak about future threats, for example, to Bangladesh, Indonesia, and China either. The size of immigration to the United States as a consequence of climate change and rising sea level in the Caribbean is nothing compared with what might happen in parts of Asia with populations many times larger than those found close to the United States.

The likely security problems pointed out are humanitarian disasters, water shortage, immigration, and the outright fight for resources, but they are, strictly speaking, global security threats. The question that looms in the background is whether the United States responds and reacts governed by its own interests, or in the interest of global security. In other words, is it the U.S. perspective that such crises, if they did not undermine U.S. security, could be allowed to continue without any action, but that it will respond to crisis posing dangers for commodity exports to the United States or raising the spectre of immigration to it or nourishing terrorists.

Even Al Gore, having established his credibility, uses language and arguments highlighting U.S. security when presenting his case to the American people. Suffice to mention his speech on 17 July 2008.[135] Try to imagine how the following phrases are perceived in developing nations and emerging economies:

> Just two days ago, 27 senior statesmen and retired military leaders
> warned of the national security threat from an "energy tsunami" that
> would be triggered by a loss of our access to foreign oil ... a strategic
> initiative designed to free us from the crises that are holding us down
> and to regain control of our own destiny.

Both sentences disclose access to oil and its crucial role not only to American
security, but also the American way of life, as the driving force behind efforts
to combat climate change, not how global warming affects millions of people
around the globe.

The United States, indeed the Western world needs to grasp this political
reality, but at the same time, emerging economies and developing countries
must resist the temptation to use such analyses as an excuse for backing away
from measures which are undoubtedly necessary to improve the environment
and combat global warming.

## Global Warming and Poverty

A decade or two ago the rich countries looked determined to do something
about global poverty. This no longer seems to be the case. Over the last years
development assistance has dwindled. The suspicion is that climate change
serves as a suitable dummy to divert attention from poverty, justifying the
fading engagement from rich countries. In July 2008 the president of the
World Bank laboured hard to catch the headlines with his appeal to help
poor countries hit by rising prices of food, raw materials, and energy by
stating:[136]

> For 41 countries, the combined impact of high food, fuel and other
> commodity prices since January 2007 represents a negative shock to
> GDP of between 3 and 10 percent. These numbers translate into broken
> lives, and stunted potential. For the most vulnerable, especially poor
> children, they mean malnutrition, reduced resistance to disease, and
> too often death.
>
> Record oil prices and high and rising food costs threaten a growing
> number of countries with rising poverty and social instability. Already
> we have seen food riots in over 30 countries, and unrest over high fuel
> prices is spreading. The urban poor are especially affected by the double
> hit of food and fuel.

At the same time as the G-8 meeting, a D-8 meeting[137] was taking place in
Kuala Lumpur. It did not devote much time to climate change, but deliberated

on food prices and the need for higher food production. Not only was its focus a different one, but also the emerging gap in perception between the G-8 nations with the United States at its head, and countries such as the D-8 group, became clear when looking at the coverage of the D-8 meeting in the Western dominated media. It was almost completely absent. You had to go to Al Jazeera[138] and Xinhua to learn about it.

Al Jazeera also drew attention to information from Oxfam that out of the promise at the G-8 summit three years ago in Gleneagles of US$25 billion to Africa before 2010, only US$3 billion had materialized so far.

The Western world congratulates itself and other countries adhering to the global model of capitalism for the fact that several hundred millions of people in Asia have been lifted out of poverty over the last decades. Admittedly this is, by any standard, phenomenal. But it is not the same as being able to say that poverty and problems linked to poverty have been dealt with. Contagious diseases, illiteracy, just to mention a few examples, are still with us. For those who do not know this, 1,600 million people worldwide are still without electricity (400 million in India alone). Just recall that without electricity, people are not connected to information and communication networks that are decisive nowadays for economic growth. One of the most pressing and efficient ways of improving health in poor countries is better sanitation, but 2.6 billion people or approximately 30 per cent of the global population lives without such facilities. It has been calculated that an investment of US$38 billion would yield US$347 billion worth of benefits.[139]

## Comparative Advantage

Over many years the rich countries have laboured to introduce environmental and labour standards in international trade policy. The emerging market countries have reluctantly agreed to be pulled along part of the way, albeit always flagging their suspicion that the real agenda was to hollow out their competitiveness, thus helping to stem the outflow of jobs from industrial countries.

Now they fear another — and similar — scheme under the guise of climate change. The rich countries have shifted a large part of manufacturing to emerging market economies with the accompanying — unwelcome but unavoidable — emission of greenhouse gasses. Global production and consumption of goods and services may not have changed, but the geographical locations of emissions have. Limits for emissions based on quotas distributed among countries will penalize receiving countries and alleviate the burden on outsourcing countries.

The newborn competitive edge will be eroded or possibly erased. It is even worse when rich countries float the idea of special duties on imports not produced according to Western emission standards.

Hitherto transport costs have been so low that their impact on the final price was negligible, opening the window for comparative advantages, regardless of geographical location. The rising oil price may not change the global supply chain, but it lifts transport costs from irrelevance to a visible cost factor. If, on top of this, a special levy determined by emissions is introduced, transport costs may move to a level where the effect on outsource production becomes relevant with the obvious consequence that emerging market economies are undermined. The plans to impose a special carbon levy on air traffic fall in the same category.

The common denominator is quite simply a distortion of the competitive advantages of outsourcing and favouring production near the source of raw materials and/or markets. In the longer term, this may not matter so much as markets are also moving to emerging market economies, but in the short term, some of the outsourcing may be rolled back.

Behind all this verbal fighting lies the risk that international division of labour and comparative advantages may suffer, or perhaps even be destroyed. If a mechanism is introduced to that effect, economic globalization may not continue in the form we know today.

The rich industrialized countries enmesh themselves and the rest of the world in complicated schemes about certificates and auctioning of certificates, etc., to combat global warming. The plain truth, however, is that the large majority of the polluters are to be found among the population living in these rich countries, and as long as some kind of PPP has not been endorsed by the rich countries, suspicions that, yes, they may want to do something about global warming, but they are also trying to shift as large a part of the burden as possible to other countries, are warranted.

## Societal Policies

The shift to the service economy will help somewhat as services may be less polluting than manufacturing, but green computing tops Gartner's list of the ten hottest technologies in 2008.[140] Long-term goals around server and infrastructure virtualization, data centre outsourcing, thin client computing, tough supplier benchmarking, and even building incentive schemes that reward IT for low energy consumption are expected to appear soon. International Data Corporation has also estimated that for every U.S. dollar spent on computer hardware at the moment, an additional U.S. 50 cents is spent on the power to run it and cool it down over its estimated lifetime. And this is expected to rise by 54 per cent to 71 cents for every U.S. dollar over the next four years. Studies indicate that greenhouse emissions in the United States can be cut to half of its existing levels by 2030 by use of available technology and technology in the pipeline.[141]

The United Nations Environmental Program estimates that every year fifty million metric tons of electronic waste is produced globally.[142] In the United States, the Environmental Protection Agency is aiming at a recycling rate of 90 per cent for mobile phones.[143] The situation with regard to computers looks much less promising. In 2008 the number of PCs globally passed the one billion mark, but it was also noted that about 35 million PCs were dumped into landfills instead of being recycled.[144] In the context of Asia the problem is not only technological, but political. Greenpeace has analysed where e-waste ends up and its findings confirm anecdotal evidence, which is that a large part of e-waste in developed countries are shipped to Asia, often in contradiction to international obligations or because — as is the case for the Basel Convention — obligations have not been undertaken by the United States, therefore transferring an enormous future burden to Asia while at the same time risking the health of millions of people living in Asia.[145]

Urbanization likewise aggravates the problem, explaining the strongly growing interest in sustainable cities. With an urbanization rate of 60 per cent for its total population in 2020, and 140 million cars, it is no wonder that the Chinese authorities are looking into sustainable cities — normally perceived as having low energy consumption that is as close to being carbon neutral as possible.[146] The first ecocity or sustainable city, Dongtan, near Shanghai, will house 80,000 inhabitants in 2020, and build up to 500,000 in 2050.[147] The Dongtan project is not the only one as similar cities around China are on the drawing board.[148]

Issues such as a clean environment illustrate how big the problems actually are for countries such as China and India with a high and, for India, rising population, strong economic growth, continued manufacturing and, for India, probably rising share of manufacturing in the economy, and how comparatively little help is coming by itself. Almost all trends point to a rising environmental problem. A shift to service industries, better technology, higher efficiency in the use of raw materials and energy, may all contribute, but on a scale that is far from tipping the balance towards a more ecologically sustainable economy.

The main contribution towards this goal has to come from deliberate and well-defined policies implemented by governments on the basis of a societal consensus. So far this has not been forthcoming irrespective of some encouraging signs. A whole panoply of measures is called for. Economic incentives have worked reasonably well in the United States and Europe and may also do so in most parts of Asia. One suspects, however, that Asia needs to do much more to drive home the point to the large majority of the population that degrading the environment is a threat not only to economic welfare and health, but in the long term may turn large parts of Asia into some kind of wasteland.

The societal costs of doing nothing are already high and mounting for every year inaction is allowed to continue. The ADB[149] has tried to estimate the costs of inaction for Southeast Asia, which the bank classifies as "likely to suffer more from climate change than the global average". If we assume that current policies are maintained, the mean cost of climate change alone could be equivalent to losing 6.7 per cent of combined GDP each year by 2100. This is an enormous amount of money and to this must be added other pollution costs and the spillover to very likely social discontent, possibly threatening political stability.

The issues are so serious and great that innovative thinking far removed from westernized models and references may be the best way out, with roots distant from economics and politics. Some have floated the idea, at research level, to turn each family core into its own energy and environmental cleaning unit, by rebuilding homes completely based on kits (that have a low lifespan anyway). Others, with demographic roots, have thought of starting to mandate environmental policies in coastal zones, first on the seashore and along rivers (with the incentive of making them more attractive), then progressively moving inland, following supply routes.

A societal policy supported strongly by politicians, enterprises, and incorporated in the education system is called for. The message must be drummed home that everybody and all organizations are stakeholders in the environment. Otherwise improving the environment will lose the battle for financial resources to health, education, and social welfare. Positive side effects such as new technologies, which may spread into other sectors, increase productivity and growth, thus augmenting GDP, must be brought into play much more visibly than they are now.

## Interaction among the Five Scarcities (Food, Industrial Commodities, Energy, Water, and Clean Environment)

Two crucial elements have to be factored into the equation when dealing with the five scarcities:

The *first* is that they may look like technical problems calling for technical solutions, but they have all arisen from a particular societal and technological structure. They cannot be changed, much less solved, unless social structure is also changed. The triumvirate of technology-culture-organization also applies in this context.

The car may be the best illustration. Over the last one hundred years, the car has dictated the structure of the Western cities and decidedly influenced the location of manufacturing plants and residential areas. Around the year 1900, a map of the United States would have shown a large number of medium-sized cities, each with a couple of hundred thousand inhabitants spread out along the railway system, and with a distance between them measured by how long it would take to drive from the perimeter to the city and back in one day by horse-drawn carriages. All of these cities had one or several department stores, a theatre, and what else a city is expected to offer its inhabitants and the people living in its surrounding areas. With the car, the constraints on transport disappeared, making it possible for people to travel much longer distances and these cities gradually withered away, to be replaced by larger metropolises. Asia had the opportunity to learn from the mistakes of the West in letting the car dictate the structure of cities, but so far it has been allowed to do to Asian cities what it did to Western cities.

In a way the car is synonymous with, and can even be taken as, the symbol for the era dominated by cheap resources. Cheap petrol paved the way for suburban districts where people could live while working in the city. Property was cheap because housing was built far away from the city centre. The car supplemented by the fridge killed the small local store which was replaced by large supermarkets where families went once or twice a week to fill the car with food to be put into the fridge at home. Long haul transport with trucks became feasible and cost efficient with the interstate highway system built in the United States in the 1950s.[150] Production of cars gave employment to hundred of thousands, even millions, of people, if subcontractors are included. It all formed a coherent whole with sub-systems supporting and dependent on one another. It was a new culture and a new infrastructure and societal structure — all dependent on cheap oil.

The congestion was the first whistleblower, showing that this way of organizing societies had its limits, and as petrol grows more expensive accompanied by increasing awareness of its harmful effects on the environment, the omens are that mankind is moving into another era and the car is being phased out. This will have strong repercussions on societal structure especially in the United States where many cities can only continue to function with a strong switch to public transport, which requires money that the American taxpayer is reluctant to provide because societal values dictate that the individual, through ownership of a car, and not the public, offering mass transport systems, is responsible for transport facilities.

Cities built on the assumption that people have a car at their disposal cannot function in a society that does not give high priority to infrastructure accommodating the car. To roll these political preferences and established values back is a long-term effort running into stiff opposition.

Although this looks like a technical or environmental or domestic political question, it has geopolitical consequences. American cities are built around the car. An increase in petrol prices affects competitiveness as workers need to be compensated for the higher cost of getting to work. Alternatively money has to be channelled into new transport infrastructure by trimming other investment programmes. For the American society the bill for stepping out of the era of the car will be horrendously high.[151] The cost for Asian cities would be much less as very few of them have been built to accommodate the car. Europe is probably somewhere between the United States and Asia in this regard. Phasing out the car will definitely shift competitive parameters in favour of Asia and, to a certain extent, Europe compared with the United States.

To broaden the analysis, it can be said that the last hundred years may possibly be recorded as the oil age. The point in this context is that the world exploited a cheap energy source to move to mass consumption based on large-scale manufacturing, transport, and logistics. It could not and would not have been done without a cheap energy source and, as this happened to be oil, societal structure adapted to oil, its opportunities, and its constraints. In short, not only the technical infrastructure, but the way society worked, was steered by cheap oil.

Addressing the environmental problems posed by this by recommending a sharp increase in the price of oil or outright restrictions on the use of oil is a non-starter because society has no alternative to oil in the short run. Only a wide range of policies starting with societal changes harbour any chance of success.

Another example can be found by looking at agriculture. Production of food has become dependent on the use of fertilizers, which, thanks to the abundant availability of the three essential elements — nitrogen, potassium, and phosphorus — have been cheap, like all other commodities.

The problem with fertilizers is not the continued availability of the three ingredients — there is enough for a long time — but that the current way of using fertilizers wash them out into the oceans where they create nutrients for the blue-green algae and algae. However, they starve other forms of marine life of oxygen, which is harmful to fisheries.[152]

Continuing the current use of fertilizers contributes to the depletion of fish stocks which are already entering a dangerous zone of depletion, but attempts to restrain their use will inevitably lead to a rise in food production costs which will in turn affect retail food prices and have repercussions for social structures all around the globe.

Societal structures reflect cheap food, among other things, brought about by the use of fertilizers. If the observation of negative side effects gives birth to the conclusion that the use of fertilizers must be reduced, the policymaker needs to know that food prices will go up. Unless that problem is factored into the equation — possibly by accepting that in the future a larger share of income must be allocated to the purchase of food — such measures will take us nowhere.

The lesson to register is that it is in our power to change relative prices by taxes or subsidies or other measures, and that such change will be effective in an economic sense. Higher prices for oil, for example, will reduce consumption of oil and vice versa, but only to the point where price elasticity no longer applies. This is, however, a partial analysis that does not take into account the fact that societal structure has conformed to existing prices, so a tangible change in relative prices will distort and disturb the function of society. Higher oil prices will mean higher petrol prices and that will influence real income for the workforce living in the suburbs, setting the ball rolling towards a whole string of political, economic, and societal reverberations. Only if these are foreseen and incorporated in the analysis, possibly in the way that includes measures to compensate for the effects (e.g. public transport in case of an oil price increase, or relocation of production closer to where the workers live, or encouraging workers to move closer to factories) will such policies stand any chance of success.

The *second* element to be factored into the scarcity equation is that the scarcities are interlinked so that changes for one of them immediately spill over, affecting one or several of the other ones, ruling out a one-by-one solution method.

The energy problem would be less urgent if biofuels are introduced on a big scale, but biofuels in their current form means that agricultural land is taken away from producing food, leading to the ethical question of whether it is right to divert land from food production to production of petrol for cars. This, if we can call it the first generation problem, may be over, and the second generation using human waste, plus third generation using natural waste, may change the picture in favour of biofuels.

The breakthrough for biofuels overcoming this ethical obstacle will come when agricultural leftovers, not usable for food and presently regarded as waste, can be turned into fuel. Technology is on its way to achieving this and the potential is tremendous. What is called cellulosic material or "grassoline" can be produced from a variety of sources, all of them classified now as waste, for example, sawdust. It is estimated that the United States can produce 1.3 billion dry tons of cellulosic biomass every year without any negative effects on food production. This corresponds to half the current annual consumption in the United States of gasoline and diesel.[153] This speaks in favour of protecting Asia's forests and seeing them as renewable resources, with its timber for the construction of houses, and its waste converted to biofuel, the opportunities of which slip away with present forest policies.

Food scarcities may be overcome, at least in the short run, by using more land for agricultural purposes, using more fertilizers, or going for more irrigation.

More irrigation automatically leads to the question of where the water is to come from. Large parts of the globe are already trying to cope with water shortages and further irrigation will make that problem even worse. Genetically modified products may shed some of the reservations and hesitations for them to be used more intensively, but it looks like the large jump in food production through this method has already been achieved, and what is left seems to be useful, but to a large extent, will lead to only incremental increases in food production.

The flow of commodities may be forced to rise, but how? A decline is more likely. More mining will have detrimental effects on the environment, and a resort to seabed mining also runs into that obstacle. More intensive use of existing mines requires more energy, which is itself becoming a scarce resource.

The production of energy is not difficult to increase as there are enormous reserves of coal, but it is difficult to do this without harming the environment even more than is already the case, and the prospect of uncontrollable global warming will then move one step nearer to reality. Ideally coal should be replaced by nuclear energy and renewable energies, but the impediments for a substantial shift are all too clear.

Water can be made available either by desalination or by new infrastructure to transport water from areas with sufficient supply to less fortunate areas, but the transportation of this will have negative environmental effects and require energy.

Many of the environmental problems can be reduced by various measures, but the majority requires more energy or water. In almost all cases, alternative sources are less cost effective — if not, they would already be in use.

These few thoughts serve to show that the five problems of scarcities are interrelated. A coherent plan is needed that looks for a solution for all the scarcities if it is to stand any chance of success.

This may not be profitable in the conventional and traditional short-term economic analysis, but the plan needs to be based on a different set of relative cost factors and relative prices reflecting long-term consequences. In other words, it cannot be done without bringing the price mechanism into play and the general public must have an understanding of how and why more expensive ways are preferred to less expensive ones.

This brings us back to the first point made above. That scarcities cannot be attacked inside a sectoral analysis, e.g., economics. An interdisciplinary analysis and a political plan elucidating burden sharing among countries, populations, and societal groups, must be put forward.

There are a few examples of attempts to apply an interdisciplinary approach which kills several birds with one stone. The American physicist Carl Hodges has proposed digging channels leading seawater (saltwater) inland and then converting this to water fit for irrigating desert land — or other land needing irrigation — thus turning large areas of hitherto unfertile land into agricultural areas. If his ideas can be turned into practical and applicable technology, water shortage is diminished, increase of food production takes place, and the inland channels help to alleviate the rise of sea levels as a result of global warming.[154]

An even better and more sophisticated example of interdisciplinary approach is offered by biodiversity. The plain fact that species are becoming extinct implies a long-term threat to humanity, which until recently, has gone remarkably unnoticed and not received the attention it deserves. In 2008 a study[155] focused on the long-term consequences on humans of the loss of biodiversity and disclosed a number of disturbing observations.

The relevance for interdisciplinary analysis is that it explains how complicated biodiversity actually is and how the many ecosystems interact and support one another and live off one another. If one of them comes under attack and finds it difficult to survive unscathed, many others, which apparently were not involved, find it difficult to maintain their rhythm, and this results in falling contribution from them also to the total mass of ecosystems.

Human beings through their activities, deliberately or otherwise, destroy many ecosystems without realizing the impact on those particular ecosystems, and even less the impact on many other ecosystems. Deforestation, for example, improves breeding opportunities for insects spreading infectious diseases, thus augmenting the risk of deteriorating health for humans living nearby.

The study shows, what actually seems to fall in line with common sense — that higher biodiversity makes the systems more resilient because there is a diversity of response to stressors, accompanied by an ability to put one species in to substitute for another in case the first can no longer perform and live up to its responsibility in the system.

The examples are numerous, but what matters here is the focus on interdisciplinary action and interaction calling for a holistic approach and not being content with looking at one effect of the consequences of human activity on the environment, but trying to understand the complete system that forms the basis for all life and, in particular, human life.

This also means that political powers in Asia, who have been driven by a mix of top-led ideologies and economic success fulfilment, will have to change their value systems to rely on rejuvenated Asian notions such as solidarity, patience in effort, nature driven spiritism, and local enterprise, to allow all initiatives to be harmonized to remove scarcities and risks mutually.

## Analytical and Synthetic Thinking

In conceptual and philosophical terms, interdisciplinary analysis and interaction among various elements can be looked upon as the difference between analytical and synthetic thinking, and the perspectives thereof for Eastern and Western culture open up a broader cultural analysis.[156]

Analytical thinking means that we approach a given substance and continuously break it down into smaller components, aiming at the smallest particle to reveal the design or origin. This leads to a narrow, but deep analysis, where the particularities of the object in question are disclosed, without considering the consequences for the object, and whether or not it interacts with other objects. Sometimes this is labelled as not being able to see the wood for the trees, but being able to know everything about every tree being analysed.

In an analysis of how to deal with a problem or seek a solution, the method is, strictly speaking, limited to the object in question. When it is solved, everything is fine and good, irrespective of what impact it may have had or will have on other objects. In connection with economic growth and the environment, it means that if we aim at higher growth, we measure whether the growth is higher, and do not include repercussions on other segments of nature and/or society. This is a kind of thinking very much embodied in pure science in trying to dig deeper and reach a perfect understanding of a particular object.

Synthetic thinking realizes that an object — any object — forms part of the aggregate or the entity as a whole and of the universal relationship. Religions operate more on such principles.

When dealing with a problem or seeking a solution, we do not solve any problem or reach any solution unless we are certain that the method applied to address one problem has not raised new ones, or damaged other objects hitherto untouched. All that matters is that we appear with a total solution to solve the matter in question without harming other objects or raising other problems.

It is what we may call a holistic approach or looking at each tree to get an idea of what the forest looks like.

These challenges are to a degree susceptible to policies. It can be expected that the five shortages will be addressed by international and global efforts taking some of the strain for policymaking off individual countries and shifting it to regional or international or global institutions. In the next chapter we turn to external circumstances, some of which and perhaps most of which evade control by national policymakers.

## Notes

1 Sources for demographics, unless otherwise stated are: *World Population to 2300* (United Nations, 2004) <http://www.un.org/esa/population/publications/ longrange2/WorldPop2300final.pdf>; Xiujian Peng and Dietrich Fausten, "Population Ageing and Labor Supply Prospects in China 2005 to 2050", *Asia-Pacific Journal* (December 2006); Wolfgang Lutz et al., eds., *The End of World Population Growth in the 21st Century* (London 2004); Wolfgang Lutz, *The Future Population of the World, What Can We Assume Today?* (London, 1996 [revised edition]).

2 United Nations, *World Population*. For the world as a whole, the demographic window closes/closed in 2045, for Asia in 2040, Latin America, 2040, Oceania, 2025, North America, 2015, Europe, 2000.

3 It is sometimes mentioned that China may reverse the one-child policy and such a step will alter the demographic outlook. First, a policy change may be discussed, but it is far from certain. Second, even if this step is taken, it cannot be assumed that the population will start to grow. We do not know how many

Chinese families actually want more children. Third, if so, the effect may be felt more in rural districts than in urban districts, posing another problem.

4 <http://info.worldbank.org/etools/docs/library/48377/dhakbkg.pdf>.

5 United Nations, *World Population.*

6 *The Future Population in Asia* (Honolulu: East-West Center, 1996), Appendix Table 2.

7 <http://www.unicef.org/progressforchildren/2004v1/eastAsiaPacific.php>.

8 The reader should bear in mind that countries' social systems cannot always be compared and in this case public versus private pension and the role of national schemes, e.g. Singapore's Central Provident Fund, may complicate comparisons.

9 OECD, *Pensions at a Glance*, Special Edition Asia/Pacific, 2009 (and earlier editions) (Paris, OECD) <http://www.oecd.org/dataoecd/33/53/41966940. pdf>.

10 As for the other indicators used in the study, several methodologies can be applied, giving some differences in absolute figures, but not skewing the picture. The figures are also somewhat different depending on whether they are calculated gross or net, which takes into account personal income taxes and social security contributions.

11 At the end of 2008, 218.01 million people, were covered by China's urban pension scheme.

12 "Pension Scheme Extended to Countryside", *South China Morning Post*, 25 June 2009 <http://www.scmp.com/portal/site/SCMP/menuitem. 2af62ecb329d3d7733492d9253a0a0a0/?vgnextoid=6c0a303e73312210Vgn VCM100000360a0a0aRCRD&ss=China&s=News> and <http://english.gov. cn/2009-06/25/content_1349783.htm>.

13 Melbourne Centre for Financial Studies and Mercer, "Melbourne Mercer Global Pension Index" <http://www.mercer.com/referencecontent. htm?idContent=1359260>.

14 The list looks like this, with the following countries having indices above the average index of 61.4: Netherlands, 76.1; Australia, 74.0; Sweden, 73.5; Canada, 73.2; the United Kingdom, 63.9; and the following countries having indices below, the United States, 59.8; Chile, 59.6; Singapore, 57.0; Germany, 48.2; China, 48.0; Japan, 41.5.

15 This is, to a certain extent, what was seen in Japan for part of the period after 1990, when deflation increased the wealth of the pensions, enhancing the burden of the active part of the population and thereby contributing to low trend growth.

16 The Chinese bond market is perhaps small because the Chinese Communist Party is hesitant to let the market have the freedom to raise funds independently of the state budget or public/political control.

17 <http://www.livescience.com/technology/071004-ap-elderly-robots.html>; <http://www.health24.com/news/General_health/1-915,44264.asp>.

18 <http://news.yahoo.com/s/ap/20080301/ap_on_re_as/japan_robot_nation;_ylt =AuNehaYB9WWbU5ocWyAHClEBxg8F>.

19 Ibid.

20 <http://muslim-canada.org/muslimstats.html>.

21 <http://islam.about.com/library/weekly/aa120298.htm>.

22 Central Intelligence Agency, *The World Factbook* <https://www.cia.gov/library/ publications/the-world-factbook/geos/in.html>.

23 US National Intelligence Council, *Mapping the Global Future* (Washington, 2004) <http://www.dni.gov/nic/NIC_globaltrend2020.html#contents> and specifically about religion at <http://www.dni.gov/nic/NIC_globaltrend2020_s3.html>.

24 The same theme is struck in a book published in 2009 by two writers from the *Economist*, which says, among other things, that religion is surging everywhere, it has proved possible for religion and modernity to live together; nowadays religion is driven by sentiments reminiscent of economic incentives such as "cluster-driven salvation", people do not adhere to a specific religion because of heritage, but choose it in a competitive framework; and the global rise of religion and faith will influence geopolitics significantly. Source: *God is Back: How the Global Revival of Faith is Changing the World* by John Micklethwait and Adrian Wooldridge (Penguin, 2009).

25 World Christian Encyclopedia (Oxford: Oxford University Press, 2001).

26 United Nations, *State of the World's Cities, 2008/2009, Harmonious Cities* (Nairobi: UN-HABITAT, 2008), p. 74.

27 *Key Indicators: Inequality in Asia* (Asian Development Bank, 2007) <http://www. adb.org/Documents/Books/Key_Indicators/2007/pdf/rt01.pdf>.

28 <http://fiordiliji.sourceoecd.org/pdf/fact2006pdf/10-03-02.pdf>.

29 The Gini coefficient was 0.288 for China in 1981. Source: *People's Daily* online, 20 July 2006 <http://english.peopledaily.com.cn/200607/20/eng20060720_ 285083.html>.

30 The Human Development Index has gone up from 1990 to 2004 for almost all countries reflecting, among other things, that the number of people below the poverty threshold has fallen dramatically. ADB, *Key Indicators* and UNDP, *Human Development Report 2007/2008* (New York: UNDP, 2007).

31 See, for example, *People's Daily* online, 20 July 2006 <http://english.peopledaily. com.cn/200607/20/eng20060720_285083.html>.

32 United Nations, *State of the World's Cities*.

33 The UN-HABITAT Report 2008 says that as urbanization gains pace in India, so does inequality, moving the country, formerly more egalitarian than most other Asian countries, towards higher inequality.

34 UNDP, *Human Development*.

35 *People's Daily*, 28 November 2003 <http://english.peopledaily.com.cn/200311/28/ eng20031128_129252.shtml>.

36 UNDAF (United Nations Development Assistance Framework 2006–2010), "The People's Republic of China", March 2005 <http://www.undg.org/archive_ docs/5988-China_UNDAF_-_UNDAF_China_Narrative.pdf>.

37 "China Publishes 'Harmonious Society' Resolution", Xinhua, 19 October 2006 <http://www.china.org.cn/english/2006/Oct/184810.htm>.

38 Committee on India Vision 2020, Planning Commission, Government of India, 2002 <http://planningcommission.nic.in/plans/planrel/pl_vsn2020.pdf>.

39 Strictly speaking, The National Rural Employment Act. See website of the Ministry of Rural Development at <http://www.nrega.nic.in/>.

40 BBC, 2 February 2006 <http://news.bbc.co.uk/2/hi/south_asia/4674560.stm>.

41 "India 2039 — An Affluent Society in One Generation", a Centennial Group report prepared for the Emerging Market Forum with the support of the Asian Development Bank (ADB) <http://www.emergingmarketsforum.org/papers/pdf/2009-EMF-India-Report_Overview.pdf>.

42 L.-F. Pau and J. Motivalla, "India: A Case of Fragile Wireless Service and Technology Adoption?", *International Journal of Mobile Communications* 6, no. 3 (2008): 376–89.

43 <http://www.busrep.co.za/index.php?fSectionId=565&fSetId=304&fArticleId=2211763>.

44 Committee on India Vision 2020.

45 United Nations, *State of the World's Cities*.

46 Miller McPherson, Lynn Smith-Lovin, and Matthew E. Brashear, "Social Isolation in America: Changes in Core Discussion Networks over Two Decades", *American Sociological Review* 71 (2006) <http://www.asanet.org/galleries/default-file/June06ASRFeature.pdf>.

47 Michel Maffesoli, *Le temps des tribus: le déclin de l'individualisme dans les sociétés postmodernes*, 1988. An American work appeared some year later by Ethan Watters with an article in the *New York Times Magazine* followed by the book, *Urban Tribes: Are friends the New Family?*, 2004.

48 Main sources for this chapter unless otherwise stated are: <http://www.ers.usda.gov/AmberWaves/February08/Features/CornPrices.htm>, <http://www.ers.usda.gov/AmberWaves/February08/Features/RisingFood.htm>.

49 OECD-FAO, *Agricultural Outlook 2009–2018*, OECD and FAO 2009 <http://books.google.com.sg/books?id=VoQjj2MNgJ8C&pg=PA96&lpg=PA96&dq=fao+agricultural+production+asia&source=bl&ots=EYitOsWDB8&sig=NCudvfHI8hWxL29UXzCQstQvXtE&hl=en&ei=IO-ZSsjROsefkQW_mIysAg&sa=X&oi=book_result&ct=result&resnum=6#v=onepage&q=fao%20agricultural%20production%20asia&f=false>.

50 WTO, "International Trade Statistics 2008, Merchandise Trade by Products" <http://www.wto.org/english/res_e/statis_e/its2008_e/its08_toc_e.htm> and <http://www.wto.org/english/res_e/statis_e/its2008_e/its08_merch_trade_product_e.pdf>.

51 <http://www.economist.com/displaystory.cfm?story_id=10250420>.

52 Stacey Rosen and Shahla Shapouri, "Rising Food Prices Intensify Food Insecurity in Developing Countries", *Amber Waves* (February 2008) <http://www.ers.usda.gov/AmberWaves/February08/Features/RisingFood.htm>.

53 Main source, note 40 above.

54 <http://www.imf.org/external/pubs/ft/survey/so/2008/NUM121008A.htm>.

55 In 1972, a catastrophic harvest in the Soviet Union, principally caused by abnormally high temperatures, was behind purchases of grain from the United States, leading to a stark increase of wheat (four times) and corn prices, engineering a hike in overall food prices, but this proved ephemeral <http://www.organicconsumers.org/articles/article_3953.cfm>.

56 *Mandag Morgen Elite* 26, 2 March 2009.

57 Lester R. Brown, "Pushing beyond the Earth's Limits", *The Futurist* (May–June 2005), pp. 18–24.

58 Lester R. Brown, "Could Food Shortages Bring Down Civilization?" *Scientific American* (May 2009), pp. 38–45.

59 See Joergen Oerstroem Moeller, "Protection Goes into Reverse", *Asia Times Online*, 24 July 2008.

60 WTO, *International Trade Statistics 2008* (WTO: 2008), Table II.15 <http://www.wto.org/english/res_e/statis_e/its2008_e/its2008_e.pdf>.

61 World Trade Organization, *International Trade Statistics 2006*, Table IV.10 <http://www.wto.org/english/res_e/statis_e/its2006_e/its2006_e.pdf>.

62 Japan, Korea (South), and Taiwan display a similar picture. Their self-sufficiency rate in major grain products, including feed grain, is about 30 per cent, while their self-sufficiency in rice is about 100 per cent. In all these countries the rice question is a very difficult item on the political agenda. Source: <http://www.agnet.org/situationer/stats/16.html>. China is moving towards self-sufficiency in rice through hybrid rice. Source: <http://www.tribune.net.ph/business/20090521bus9.html>.

63 Sources for this paragraph: Brown, "Pushing beyond the Earth's Limits", pp. 21–22 (note 57) and <http://www.resourceinvestor.com/News/2008/6/Pages/China-Will-Become-a-Net-Grain-Importer-in-the.aspx>.

64 FAO, "The State of Food and Agricultural Asia and the Pacific Region 2008" (RAP: 2008) <ftp://ftp.fao.org/docrep/fao/010/ai411e/ai411e00.pdf>.

65 J. Schmidhuber, "Biofuels: An Emerging Threat to Europe's Food Security". Policy paper. Paris: Notre-Europe, 2007 <www.notre-europe.eu>.

66 As the statistical basis and reference year differs from what WTO uses the figures above for net export/imports of food are not fully comparable with the FAO figures.

67 Brown, "Could Food Shortages".

68 David. S. Battisti and Rosamund L. Naylor, "Historical Warnings of Future Food Insecurity with Unprecedented Seasonal Heat", *Science* 323, 9 January 2009.

69 Brown, "Could Food Shortages".

70 Fransesco N. Tubiello, Jean Francois Soussana, and S. Mark Howden, "Crop and Pasture Response to Climate Change". Proceedings of the National Academy of Sciences of the United States of America (PNAS), 11 December 2007, 104, no. 50

<http://www.pnas.org/content/104/50/19686.full.pdf+html?sid=7830ab9c-f73a-469e-b02d-8cdc0eb6843b>.

71 In itself such low wages are an anomaly reflecting that relative prices of production factors, perceived as labour versus commodities, do not look beyond a short term horizon.

72 The United States is presumed to have access to commodities in North America.

73 That is not even certain if the analysis aims at use of resources per unit of weight. See Timothy G. Gutowski et al., "Thermodynamic Analysis of Resources used in Manufacturing Processes", *Environmental Science and Technology* 43, no. 5 (February 2009): 1584–90.

74 <http://www.news.com.au/business/story/0,23636,23155387-462,00.html>.

75 <http://deltafarmpress.com/mag/farming_vietnam_thailand_countries/>.

76 <http://afp.google.com/article/ALeqM5hf9GS9a2d2HPPDeh3BWvLs66 N2UA> and <http://www.scmp.com/portal/site/SCMP/menuitem. 2af62ecb329d3d7733492d9253a0a0a0/?vgnextoid=93c6a4d906b48110 VgnVCM100000360a0a0aRCRD&ss=Markets&s=Business>.

77 The following paragraphs draw partly on my paper submitted to the seminar on "Emerging Challenges to Energy Security in the Asia Pacific", 16–17 March 2009. Jointly organized by Centre for Security Analysis (CSA), Chennai, India, the Institute of Southeast Asian Studies (ISEAS), Singapore, and the Hanns Seidel Foundation, New Delhi, India. Paper on energy security: "The Global Scene".

78 Etu = Energy technical unit; Btu = British thermal unit.

79 *International Energy Outlook 2007*, Energy Information Administration, official energy statistics from the U.S. Government <http://www.eia.doe.gov/oiaf/ieo/world.html>, *International Energy Outlook 2008*, Energy Information Administration, official energy statistics from the U.S. Government <http://www.eia.doe.gov/oiaf/ieo/> (Chapter 1 on html) <http://www.eia.doe.gov/oiaf/ieo/world.html>), preliminary release 2009 <http://www.eia.doe.gov/oiaf/aeo/overview.html>.

80 Other studies come to another conclusion with regard to the share of renewable plus nuclear power. An EU study, <http://europa.eu/rapid/pressReleasesAction.do?reference=MEMO/07/2>, says that in 2050, fossil fuels provide 70 per cent of total energy consumption (coal and oil 26 per cent each, natural gas 18 per cent) and non-fossil sources 30 per cent; the non-fossil share is divided almost equally between renewable and nuclear energy.

81 Note 79.

82 The impact of global growth on world consumption of energy is much higher. Based on a reference case of 4.5 per cent growth per annum, the gap between an increase to 4.5 per cent and fall to 3.5 per cent is 113 quadrilllion Btu, equal to about 16.2 per cent (more than double the impact of high versus low oil price, compared with the reference scenario for oil price).

83 E. G. Frankel, *Oil and Security: A World Beyond Petroleum* (Dordrecht, Springer, 2007).

84 Same source as for note 79.

85 For the OECD countries the corresponding figures are 7,000 and 5,000 Btu respectively.

86 China is planning for thirty more nuclear reactors in 2020 and there are hints that before 2050, 200 new nuclear plants may be built; see <http://www.wired.com/wired/archive/12.09/china.html>. India envisions a tenfold increase in nuclear power until 2020 — from 3 gigawatts to 30 gigawatts; see <http://www.iht.com/articles/2006/03/16/opinion/edvictor.php>.

87 A certain degree of scepticism with regard to these forecasts is advisable as countries and/or industries may pursue their own interests, but the U.S. Energy Information Administration and International Energy Agency under OECD agree in predicting an increased role for coal. The role of coal may be influenced by how ambitious the nuclear power programmes in Asia turn out to be.

88 International Energy Agency, *World Energy Outlook, 2008* (Paris, OECD/IEA, 2008).

89 Ibid. See also International Energy Agency, *World Energy Outlook, China and India Insights* (Paris, 2007).

90 A wild card in futuristic terminology is defined as an event with little probability of happening, but with enormous impact if it did.

91 <http://www.futuregenalliance.org/about.stm>.

92 <http://www.greengen.com.cn/en/aboutus_02.htm>.

93 For a short explanation and up to date status, see, for example, <http://www.physorg.com/news9723.html>.

94 It was used in Germany during World War II and by South Africa under blockade, but in both cases it was a question of survival so the cost factor was largely irrelevant.

95 <https://www.zacks.com/research/get_news.php?id=324u0483&t=YZC>.

96 For a plan to rewrite US energy policy and include liquefaction of coal on a grand scale see Tsvi Bisk, "A Realistic Energy Strategy", *The Futurist*, March–April 2009.

97 S-115: Coal-to-Liquid Fuel Promotion Act of 110th Congress 2007 <http://www.govtrack.us/congress/bill.xpd?bill=s110-155>.

98 <http://en.wikipedia.org/wiki/Nuclear_power_by_country>.

99 <http://en.wikipedia.org/wiki/Nuclear_power_by_country>.

100 <http://www.world-nuclear.org/education/mining.htm>.

101 See, for example, Asia Times online for 1 December 2005, "The Foundations for an Asian Oil and Gas Grid" <http://www.atimes.com/atimes/south_asia/GL01Df02.html>.

102 Stratfor (Strategic Forecasting Inc.), "Obama's Energy Plan: Trying to Kill 3 Birds with 1 Stone", 18 February 2009.

103 Daniel Yergin, "Ensuring Energy Security", *Foreign Affairs* 85, no. 2.

104 There is a certain analogy to the concept of fleet in maritime strategy, meaning that as long as a nation state possesses a navy it forces potential enemies to take that into consideration when structuring and positioning armed forces. A weaker maritime power can impose strategic constraints on an enemy by letting rumours float that it is planning to use its fleet.

105 <http://www.enecho.meti.go.jp/topics/energy-in-japan/energy2006Epdf/p2122_energy2006E-9.pdf>.

106 International Energy Agency, *World Energy Outlook, China and India Insights* (Paris, 2007).

107 Stratfor, 17 March 2008.

108 International Energy Agency, 2007, as in note 89.

109 Secretary of State Condoleeza Rice, Testimony before the U.S Senate Foreign Relations Committee, 5 April 2006 <http://www.iags.org/luft_dependence_on_middle_east_energy.pdf>.

110 "The Military Balance", quoted in the *Wall Street Journal*, "As China Grows, So Does Its long-Neglected Navy", 18 July 2007 <http://www.iiss.org/whats-new/iiss-in-the-press/press-coverage-2007/july-2007/as-china-grows-so-does-its-navy/>.

111 WTO 2006, *International Trade Statistics*, available at <http://www.wto.org/english/res_e/statis_e/its2006_e/its2006_e.pdf>, Table IV.19.

112 From Skovorodino in the Amur region of Russia, to Daqing in China.

113 Stratfor, 18 February 2009.

114 Standard Chartered Bank.

115 Third largest oil company in China after CNPC and Sinopec, see <http://en.wikipedia.org/wiki/CNOOC_Ltd>.

116 Petrochina is the listed arm of CNPC, the state-owned and biggest oil company in China; <http://en.wikipedia.org/wiki/PetroChina>.

117 23rd on Fortune's global 500 list, <http://en.wikipedia.org/wiki/Sinopec>.

118 India's biggest enterprise and number 135 on Fortune's list of over 500 global largest enterprises, <http://en.wikipedia.org/wiki/Indian_Oil_Corporation>.

119 Number 369 on Fortune's global 500 list, <http://en.wikipedia.org/wiki/ONGC>.

120 <http://en.wikipedia.org/wiki/List_of_companies_by_revenue>.

121 As can be seen for commodities, where Chinalco's offer to buy a 919 per cent share of Rio Tinto is a case in point.

122 In an Asian context it is difficult to discuss energy demand/supply without looking at the infrastructure, which, for many countries, is simply not good enough, leading to a faltering supply of electricity and power failures. Unless this infrastructure is built up to serve the communities, the efforts so far to ensure supply do not suffice.

123 For a general source setting out the water problem, see Marq De Villiers, *Water: The Fate of Our Most Precious Resource* (Houghton Mifflin Harcourt, 2001). Reference is also made to Erik Orsenna, *L'avenir de l'eau* (Paris: Favard, 2008) and Petrella Riccardo, *le Manifeste de l'eau* (Paris: Fides Editions, 2009).

124 <http://whyfiles.org/131fresh_water/2.html>.

125 <http://english.peopledaily.com.cn/200111/16/eng20011116_84668.shtml>.

126 An investor's point of view can be found at Reuters ("Investors Warm to Water as Shortages Mount") on 18 March 2008. The article also contains interesting comments and information about where and how acute water shortage is <http://www.reuters.com/article/ousiv/idUSL1256474720080319>.

127 Peter Rogers, "Facing the Freshwater Crisis", *Scientific American* (August 2008) and International Water Management Institute (IWMI), "Water for Food, Water for Life", *Earthscan*, 2007, a 40-page summary is available at <http://www.iwmi. cgiar.org/Assessment/files_new/synthesis/Summary_SynthesisBook.pdf>.

128 Brown, "Could Food Shortages"; <http://www.iwmi.cgiar.org/assessment/files_ new/publications/Discussion%20Paper/InsightsBook_Stockholm2006.pdf>.)

129 <http://www.water-technology.net/projects/south_north/>.

130 The Soviet Union in the 1980s contemplated turning the main river in Siberia around, but these gigantic projects never got beyond the drawing board.

131 "China Overtakes US in Greenhouse Gas Emissions", *International Herald Tribune*, 20 June 2007 <http://www.iht.com/articles/2007/06/20/business/emit. php>.

132 <http://www.ipcc.ch/>.

133 Nicholas Stern, *The Economics of Climate Change: The Stern Review* (Cambridge: Cambridge University Press, 2007).

134 CAN Corporation, "The National Security Implications of Global Climate Change to 2030" <http://securityandclimate.cna.org/report/National%20Secu rity%20and%20the%20Threat%20of%20Climate%20Change.pdf>.

135 Available at <http://i.cdn.turner.com/cnn/2008/images/07/17/climate.speech. pdf>.

136 World Bank Press Release 2009/006/EXC, 2 July 2008 <http://web. worldbank.org/WBSITE/EXTERNAL/NEWS/0,,contentMDK:21827981~ menuPK:34463~pagePK:34370~piPK:34424~theSitePK:4607,00.html>.

137 Bangladesh, Egypt, Indonesia, Iran, Malaysia, Nigeria, Pakistan, and Turkey. Iran also attended the meeting.

138 <http://english.aljazeera.net/news/asia-pacific/2008/07/200878593529361. html>.

139 <http://www.eurekalert.org/pub_releases/2008-03/unu-sii031808.php>.

140 <http://www.infocommsingapore.sg/industry/index.php/web/events/29_feb_ seminar_on_green_computing_and_it_for_energy_efficiency>. The other nine can be seen at <http://www.itjungle.com/two/two101707-story05.html>.

141 "Green IT: Corporate Strategies", *Business Week*, 11 February 2008 <http://www. businessweek.com/innovate/content/feb2008/id20080211_204672.htm>.

142 <http://www.greenstudentu.com/encyclopedia/recycling/computer>.

143 "National Cell Phone Recycling Week Starts Monday", *Capital Times*, 4 March 2009 <http://www.madison.com/tct/news/stories/445664>.

144 "Computers in Use Pass One Billion Mark: Gartner", Reuters, 23 June 2008 <http://www.reuters.com/article/technologyNews/idUSL2324525420080623>.

145 <http://www.greenpeace.org/international/campaigns/toxics/electronics/where-does-e-waste-end-up>.

146 <http://www.arup.com/eastasia/project.cfm?pageid=7047>.

147 <http://edition.cnn.com/2007/TECH/08/14/dongtan.ecocity/>.

148 <http://news.bbc.co.uk/2/hi/asia-pacific/5084852.stm>.

149 *The Economics of Climate Change in Southeast Asia: A Regional Review* (Asian Development Bank, April 2009).

150 Under the Eisenhower administration and partly for military reasons.

151 This explains the strong interest in the United States for biofuel. If cost-effective the car will still be affordable and biofuel can use the existing infrastructure for petrol. The cost of a switch would be small.

152 David A. Vaccari, Phosporus: A Looming Crisis", *Scientific American*, June 2009, pp. 42–47.

153 George W. Huber and Bruce E. Dale, "Grassoline at the Pump", *Scientific American*, July 2009.

154 See the Seawater Foundation website at <http://www.seawaterfoundation.org/sea_gallart.html> and a short outline of the idea at <http://www.celsias.com/article/seawater-farming-solution-rising-sea-levels-food-a/>.

155 Eric Chivian and Aaron Bernstein, *Sustaining Life: How Human Health Depends on Biodiversity* (Oxford: Oxford University Press, 2008).

156 Reference is made to the *Journal of Oriental Studies*, 11, 2001, with a Dialogue on Eastern Wisdom among Ji Xianlin, Jiang Zhongxin, and Daisaku Ikeda. Available at <http://www.iop.or.jp/0111/special.pdf>.

# 6

# THREATS

Foreign and security policies have changed over the years and their main challenges in the years to come will be attempts to disrupt the well functioning of societies.

Many of the threats towards nation states and societies will come from within them through social unrest, possibly triggered by inequalities, repercussions on the social fabric of the coming era of scarcities, or perhaps natural or environmental disasters.

Globalization brings about some of these threats that warrant speaking of threats to and from globalization. Global developments penetrate the conventional cultural defence perimeters in the form of languages and cultural behaviour, and confronts individuals, groups, and society with new norms and ethics.

Failed states, of which there are a growing number, and can be expected to grow further, pose a threat to globalization and may destabilize adjacent nation states through emigration, pandemics, and other developments which may not have destabilization as their purpose, but actually end up having this effect.

Organized crime, which may soon be stronger than nation states and/or corporations, exploits the opportunities offered by globalization to run rings around national police efforts and undermine social capital by offering a life inside their caucus, which for some people, may look better than life inside the social fabric of the nation state.

Therefore the main defence is to build up strong social capital among citizens that constitutes a bulwark against such attacks. The stronger the social fabric is and the more people adhere to common and shared values, the more difficult it will be to break up society by various forms of attacks. Wars and/or armed conflicts move from being between nation states or between peoples, to being among people aiming to conquer hearts and minds. Societal policies become, by definition, a part of the defence effort, much more than conventional military policy, designed primarily to defend a nation state against an armed attack to possess territory.

The conventional and well-known threats emanating from foreign and security policies do not go away, but may be less of a threat in the future. One of the most prominent among these threats is the competition for water, with the Tibetan plateau, which is of vital importance for both China and India, probably emerging as the most difficult one to solve.

Another aspect that has to be considered is the role of the United States, which has for more than fifty years stabilized Asia. It is likely that it will continue to be the strongest and most powerful nation, but it is also likely that U.S. supremacy will be eroded, which leads to question marks about the continued willingness and ability of the United States to serve as stabilizing power in the Asian theatre.

## THREATS TO THE WELL FUNCTIONING OF SOCIETY

### Modern Warfare — Among the People

Warfare in the twenty-first century has changed from the possession of territory to the imposition of the will of the strongest on the weakest. Power means somebody is forcing somebody else to do something other than what they originally intended to do. In foreign and security policy it translates into adopting another attitude towards societal order or an international question than the one originally intended.

Established global powers wage war to defend globalization and extend political systems. This is what happened in Iraq. The United States and a number of other countries judged Iraq under President Saddam Hussein to be in possession of weapons of mass destruction (WMD) and having the will to use them, and, therefore, being a threat to the international community. It has become a cornerstone of U.S. foreign policy to promote democracy around the world[1] even if critics say that when U.S. strategic interests are at stake (e.g. in Central Asia), the picture is ambiguous, to say the least.

Terrorist organizations rooted in Islam, but not only those that are, want to reinstate societies based on religion and/or other traditional values. They have taken aim at globalization because they see this as the main barrier to their political goals. As they are not able to wage conventional war they aim to cripple the well functioning of societies that are committed to globalization.[2] In doing so, they may undermine the confidence of citizens in their governments, weaken the resolve of such societies, roll back their economic and technological capabilities, and tell their own followers that globalized countries are weak, not strong.[3]

Asian countries are particularly vulnerable because their current political systems are still young, with almost all of them being born not more than sixty years ago, and earning their legitimacy precisely by delivering well-functioning societies and high economic growth to their citizens.

The British General, Rupert Smith,[4] came to the conclusion that modern warfare is not waged between nation states, or between nation state and groups or organizations; but is, in reality, a war among individuals. He found this to be characterized by six major trends:

- The ends for which we are fighting are changing from the hard, absolute objectives of interstate industrial war, to more malleable objectives to do with the individual and societies that are not states.
- People fight with other people, a fact amplified literally and figuratively by the central role of the media: we fight in every living room in the world as well as in the streets and fields of a conflict zone.
- Our conflicts tend to be timeless since we are seeking a condition which then must be maintained until there is an agreement on a definite outcome, which may take years or decades.
- We fight so as not to lose force, rather than fight by using force at any cost to achieve the aim.
- On each occasion new uses are found for old weapons: those constructed specifically for use in a battlefield against soldiers and heavy armaments are now being adapted for our current conflicts since the tools of industrial war are often irrelevant to war amongst people.
- The sides are mostly non-state since we tend to conduct our conflicts and confrontations in some form of multinational grouping, whether it is an alliance or a coalition, and against some party or parties that are not states.

This analysis says one thing: wars are about maintaining societal cohesion and keeping people attached to societies. Those who can disrupt society and/or what links people to society and/or other members of the same society, win, regardless of how many tanks or artillery pieces can be mustered on the conventional battlefield. This is the battlefield chosen by terrorists, and the military in almost all nation states have been slow in, or totally incapable of, adapting to warfare aimed at people's minds.[5]

## The Soul of Terrorism

Looking ahead we find three basic questions to pose:[6] Will terrorist acts change from attacks on symbolic targets to attacks on people; Will global/ international cooperation among the authorities of nation states catch up with or even surpass terrorists' exploitation of globalization to slip out of the hands of police forces; And will Asian societies produce social coherence strong enough to reduce the recruiting base? Taken together, the answers to these questions determine whether it will be terrorists or Asian societies and governments that will win. The Western notion of terrorism has to be adapted, taking into consideration Asia's ethnicity and minorities who sometimes see terrorism as the only outlet for them to be heard against powerful political systems.

We must *first* note that so far the primary targets of terrorists have been symbolic structures, but terrorist organizations have not shied away from killing people, including those of their own religious belief accidentally at the spot for terrorist attacks. The World Trade Center, the White House, the Pentagon, and Capitol Hill in Washington were all on the list for the 11 September attacks, because they symbolized U.S. power and the way the United States exercised global power. By hitting these targets the terrorists could demonstrate that U.S. power was within their reach. And the photos of burning buildings hitherto regarded as impregnable were immediately digested round the world.

The main aim was not to kill U.S. citizens, even if the terrorists did not care how many they actually did kill. This tactic (symbolism) limits the number of potential targets and makes defence less difficult than if the terrorists were going to kill people indiscriminately, meaning if public utilities, housing areas, etc., were the targets. One only needs to ponder what an attack on the water supply of a city in Asia with ten million inhabitants would mean and how society can protect itself against this sort of attack.[7] The Western inclination is to focus on the large terrorist attacks on targets in the United States and Europe, while Asia and Asians are more occupied by the large number of terrorist attacks going on for decades which hit civilians and infrastructure such as the Mumbai attack, and attacks in Indonesia, primarily Bali and Jakarta, which are popular with tourists and/or foreign businessmen. Thailand has also recently seen such attacks and the subway system in Tokyo was attacked in 1995 with sarin gas.[8]

A *second* thing to note in answering these questions is that the choice of tactic depends on whether terrorist leaders continue to see terrorism as a vehicle for rallying their own followers by exposing weaknesses in globalized countries, or whether they may feel strong enough to move to instilling another level of fear among the population in globalized countries by hitting at growth and productivity. If, for example, water supply or mass transport networks are hit repeatedly, so people do not dare use these facilities, cities stop working and the social fabric starts unravelling. For terrorists, such an escalation requires a more solid base of support and knowledge than they have at present. If, however, global growth shifts into lower gear, creating an urban proletariat that does not have much to lose, the moment may come when such a tactic changes from being unlikely to being possible.

It is worthwhile to note that local terrorists seem to have a good grasp of symbolism and pick as their targets those that have commonalty with the local people, as evidenced by the attacks in India and Indonesia.

Strong urbanization over the next decades opens the window for this risk to grow substantially. Such terrorism would be less likely to follow in the footsteps of, for example, Al-Qaeda, which wants to substitute one societal order with another. It might take the shape of destructive terrorism or nihilism and attack the existing order without offering any alternative.[9] Authorities would find it more difficult to counter-attack, as the profile of potential terrorists would be much more hazy.

Recent experience suggests that as long as terrorists do not have a base — a safe haven — where they can train, regroup, exercise, and develop tactics, they are not capable of mounting large-scale attacks. Before the 11 September attacks, Al-Qaeda was based in Afghanistan, beyond the reach of forces from the countries they attacked. After 9/11 this safe haven has been denied them even if certain areas in Afghanistan and probably also Pakistan harbour elements of their "brain", making it possible for them to operate a network, but not to mount large-scale attacks.

A *third* observation indicates that failed states and/or nation states not able or willing to exercise authority over their territory, or unable/unwilling to cater for cultural/ethnic diversities, are at the largest risk for future threats. Consequently one of the most efficient counter-attack policies is preventing states from failing, and/or helping the governments of weak states to exercise control over all their territories, and/or to cater on a continuing basis for cultural/ethnic diversity. This lesson does not seem to have been fully learned because it is a difficult policy in many areas where national governments do not enjoy support and, even less, popularity. The periodically resurging Thai Muslim revolts offer an interesting case of a lasting political system, where bad temporary measures by time-limited mandates of governments limiting ethnic diversity, lead to flare-ups of revolt, although territorial control and respect for the King are still values held by the insurgents!

In a futuristic perspective the main question is whether terrorists will be found in Asia's coming megacities. The experience from the United States and, to a certain extent, also Europe and Asia (e.g. Mumbai) indicates that in big cities, gangs or other kinds of organized social networks are able to seal off parts of cities from the authorities and build their own "city state" or "parallel society". As long as they are content to do this inside their enclaves, do not challenge society as such, do not see society as a threat to their existence, and society retreats from them peacefully, "co-existence" is workable, irrespective of the misgivings one can have about it.

The signs for Asia are, however, worrying. Asian megacities will be much larger than the big cities in North America, and if organized groups revolting against terrorism try to set up "city states", they may well succeed in constituting a serious challenge to the well functioning of the rest of society outside. If this coincides with a jump to the next stage in terrorism — where terorists go for killing people instead of only attacking the well functioning of society — the situation could turn ugly indeed.

A more sanguine view is taken by an American study looking ahead to 2025[10] and coming to the conclusion that the large international and value-based terrorist networks such as Al-Qaeda and Jemaah Islamiya will lose some of their power while their offspring proliferate in the form of decentralized and deconcentrated groups with some kind of franchising. In short, this study sees a less organized terrorist threat, but raises the spectre that the terrorist networks existing in the future will posses weapons of mass destruction (WMD). Such a prediction may prove to be right, but leads to the observation that WMD in the hands of terrorists is a one-time-only threat. It will change the paradigm in the sense that such weapons cannot be used again and again to exercise pressure against the establishment. One wonders how terrorists can actually use WMD unless their aim is to destroy and kill a large part of civilization, and if that is the case, there is not much left for futuristic thinking or analysis.

Globalization has produced marvellous economic growth through the free movement of production factors across borders. These opportunities have not been lost on organized international crime and terrorist groups.

Terrorist groups such as Al-Qaeda work like a multinational corporation in the true sense of that word. The headquarters is virtual, dependent on where their leaders are maintaining communication with the various subsidiaries, markets, and wherever else the terrorist organizations have chosen to spread their activities; they have salesmen recruiting new adherents, workers placing bombs or whatever means are chosen for attacks, and the measure of success is output — destruction in this case. Modern marketing methods such as franchising is being used. They try to erode the support for their opposition — the authorities — by a combination of promises and threats, and address loyal customers, the adherents, to ensure them of the organizations success and solidity. They have realized long before most multinationals that the strongest parameter for attracting good staff is ethics, and giving staff a "feel good" sense.

It is plausible that urban-based terrorist organizations may build up a network among themselves, thereby turning them into really powerful global or international players. Whether the authorities will be able to deal with such networks depends on a number of things; one of them is the ability and will to establish a counter-attack on the same level and with the same means, that is, a truly global, international police force.

It becomes a paradox if, which is possible, one of globalizations strongest trademarks twenty-five years down the road is a truly global financial and power elite moving freely from megapolis to megapolis where they find analogous lifestyles and networks with urban terrorists equally ready and capable of moving from one urban slum to another.

The other strong parameter in the combat against terrorism is social coherence. A number of books[11] have been published that have tried dissecting terrorism trying to analyse where and how terrorism appears. There are many explanations. The most likely one is that terrorists are actually dichotomized into officers led by ideology, and soldiers socially motivated.

Officers are relatively few and highly educated, with many of them educated at top global universities, but for various reasons convinced that the globalized world needs to be destroyed. They are "religious" in their beliefs, thinking they have the right and duty to smash ways of life other than the one they are committed to, even if the religion they adhere to prescribes non-violence, which is the case for all world religions. They are not unlike the group of British communist spies in the post World War II period.[12] Nothing can convert them back to societal order. For them as for society it is a question of "them or us".

Soldiers are those who do most of the necessary groundwork and without their support terrorism cannot jump from a peripheral ideology to a menace. They harbour the activists and in some cases are activists themselves. Their numbers may be comparatively high because many of them are kept in reserve and only called to the "front" if or when needed.

Most, if not all of them, are social losers. They have not been able to find a place in society corresponding to their abilities as they see them. Like all human beings they find it difficult to admit their own faults so they succumb to the luring belief that they are social losers only because society does not recognize their abilities which terrorist organizations do. By converting to terrorism, they find a home.

They can be turned back, however, to societal order, if or when the appropriate social and educational means are used. It may take time and cost money and it requires patience and skills, but it can be done. The tactic to be applied is the same as the one that has proved itself in successful fights against guerillas: identify potential terrorists by drawing a profile of them and then put them under secret supervision. If they join a group, try to isolate this group from the rest of society so it cannot recruit, and at the appropriate time, arrest members. When they have been arrested, apply a whole string of measures to bring them back into society.

In a longer-run perspective, Asia's ability to keep terrorism at bay seems to depend on social coherence, its education strategy, and the reduction of inequality.

One of the challenges is distinguishing between terrorism aimed at attacking society and terrorism growing out of ethnic, religious, and cultural groups that are voicing their discontent with remote central political power which they see as denying them the right to shape their own destinies.

The second group (soldiers) can be negotiated with if a central government wants to do so, and unless discontent has become an almost insurmountable barrier, a political solution can be found. Attacks from this group do not reflect general dissatisfaction, but rather a minority group's discontent with conditions/restraints imposed upon them. An even bigger risk would be a central government's use of the fear of terrorism as a pretext to suppress minorities, thus aggravating animosities vis-à-vis the government.

The basic question is whether Asia can create societies where the overwhelming part of the population feels that it is their society and that they are better off within it than outside. If so, the terrorist officers may still be around, but will find it difficult to recruit soldiers, thus running into obstacles when trying to mount large-scale attacks on society.

The most fundamental break with the classical perception of threats as a conventional military phenomenon may have been taken by the so-called Hart-Rudman National Security Report published by the United States Commission on National Security/21st Century in 2001.[13]

The report states (on p. ix) "the inadequacies of our systems of research and education pose a greater threat to national security over the next quarter of century than any conventional war that we might imagine".

Of its five main recommendations, ensuring the security of the American homeland is number one, but recapitalizing America's strength in science and education is number two on the list. In other words, it is second only to the threat of terrorism in a broad sense and ranks above all other conventional military threats.

The commission defines six key objectives for U.S. foreign and national security policy, of which to defend and ensure that the United States is safe from dangers is number one, but number two (p. vii) says "maintain America's social cohesion, economic competitiveness, technological ingenuity and military strength".

What this amounts to is not only a new perception of threats in the framework of securing the well functioning of society, but a realization that in the decades to come, such threats will not primarily emanate from military actions undertaken by nation states, but from terrorism resulting from domestic problems such as threats to social cohesion, and the lack of capability to maintain a competitive edge in new technology.

The United States in the new age is forced out of its shell to realize that threats can emerge from inside nation states as a consequence of wrong policies, whether deliberate or otherwise, creating social problems that undermine cohesion and social capital. The lack of resources to sustain a strong military and perhaps even more important, the country's ability to finance its own development, rank as a crucial danger to U.S. society.

This analysis and the enumeration of objectives and actions flowing from it are not confined to the United States. The picture may be a bit different, depending on circumstances for other nation states, but the interpretation is difficult to escape that in today's world, war and conventional military actions are diminishing as threats, to be replaced by threats to the well functioning of society. And some of these threats may not come from outside, but from groups inside nation states, and the lack of national identity and loyalty. It may, in fact, come from domestic policies disabling society.

## THREATS TO AND FROM GLOBALIZATION[14]

### Organized Crime

Terrorists may try to disturb society's well functioning. Organized crime may want to create parallel societies to siphon off a part of the wealth generated by economic globalization. Various analyses[15] disclose that international crime has been as efficient and may be more so than multinational companies in exploiting opportunities offered by globalization. Criminal organizations want to preserve normal societal structures as a target for exploitation. They operate outside it and the authorities leave them in peace as long as they do not interfere with normal social life. This is the equation explaining why well-known criminal organizations such as the Mafia, the Triads, the Russian Mafia, the various drug cartels primarily in Latin America, and the Yakuza in Japan, have all been able to survive and thrive.

Crime still seems rooted in their home countries, but recent trends suggest that they are fast building up international networks and moving towards the shape of a multinational company.[16]

With growing wealth and increased economic integration in Asia, it is almost certain that organized crime will grow and be more international. That poses at least four problems.

The *first* problem is that criminal organizations will escape authorities by moving in and out of countries, transferring money etc. Here we come back to the point about terrorism, which is that only strong police activity at an Asian — international — level will constitute a bulwark against organized crime. If not, organized crime will cross the borders hitherto respected, and involve itself increasingly with parts of society it has not touched so far. As with terrorism, it may appeal to persons or groups of persons who feel left out of society and want to find an environment where they feel at ease.

The *second* problem is that competition for "market shares" may turn into gang wars of a violent nature. Wars among criminal groups have been known for a long time, but the future risk is that lured by growing wealth, megacities will lose touch with their citizens, resulting in a weakened societal structure, in which gang wars may escalate to an intolerable level for society.

The *third* problem is that organized crime grows almost exponentially and has, in some cases, reached a level where an alternative or parallel society is built, making the government powerless. This augurs a situation where organized crime may, perhaps, not formally, but in reality, take over a nation state and their leaders become the de facto rulers.[17]

The *fourth* problem is that cybercrime seems on the rise to becoming a major threat. At the beginning of 2009 it is estimated that theft via the Internet and related cyber instruments amounted to US$1 trillion and is strongly on the rise.[18] It is also clear that the world has moved from trivial crimes committed by individuals to cybercrime organized by global gangs — that is, multinational companies committing crime, cybercrime — which are in possession of knowledge, money, and power.

Potentially these gangs are becoming so powerful that a kind of blackmail vis-à-vis corporations and even nation states cannot be ruled out. The heart of the matter is that they may be capable — or at least this cannot be ruled out — of exerting denial of services to corporations or nation states.

For the world and the authorities, the security of their network of protective devices and programmes (networks security) is in the hands of private companies. There is nothing wrong with this per se, but these companies are actually performing a policing or protective duty which, in principle, should be the task of the authorities. There is no guarantee that they can or will perform to the satisfaction of users and the authorities. In fact, often the opposite is true: that is, it is in their interest not to design really good security protection or threat-tracking systems so as to ensure a continuous need for their products and services, with as many upgrades as possible.

The safety of the Internet is not in the hands of a global authority. Who is actually responsible for guaranteeing that the Internet continues to function and that any potential onslaught will be thwarted, or if it takes place, that the damage will be repaired?[19]

These are fundamental questions. They may not rest on the shoulders of Asia, but Asia, as the upcoming major player that is beefing up its use of the Internet, seen to be a cornerstone for economic growth, becomes one of, and, perhaps, the most, affected power if cybercrime continues to rise.

A new item for international crime are policies to reduce global warming. Trading in certificates for emissions of $CO_2$ is already a known and used instrument. Failed states or large, well-organized, international criminal groups may exploit the hunger for rights to pollute and/or access to scarce commodities to step in, under the guise of a respectable corporation, to trade in some of the coveted assets.

## Pandemics

The global supply chain, combined with business travel, which does not seem to decline in importance irrespective of the virtual world, makes the risk of global pandemics real.

Seen in the prism of globalization, contagious diseases appearing in one country may lead to international rules prohibiting travel and/or movements of goods out of the said country. The international community wishes to protect itself against pandemics. This is understandable, but the effect is the disruption of the global supply chain and/or business travel. Globalization can survive relatively unscathed if a limited number of countries are hit for a limited period, but not if several country partners in globalization are affected over a longer period.

Over the last decades most diseases with the potential of turning into a pandemic have arisen in South China (the most recent one, however, arose in Mexico). If one should spread from there to the rest of China and gets a foothold in large parts of Asia, it is obvious that a cutoff of supply from China and/or business travel would have strong negative consequences for globalization.

It is debatable how high and real the risk of such pandemics is. It looks like it is growing, however, because small-scale farms that did not always have the capability to secure health and safety standards of a high level are becoming more involved in economic life outside their local boundaries.

Another factor may, however, be even more important. The tendency to opt for higher economic efficiency leads to growing health risks. It is not so much because of falling standards, but of rising competition pushing farmers to exhaust land and animal husbandry to produce increasingly more in a shorter time. This sounds fine, but many crops may, in the process, become less resistant to various diseases. The same tendency occurs in animal husbandry, where we see a focus on a few types of animals, namely those producing more meat. Hitherto diversity gave a certain amount of protection as you could hope that not all animals were susceptible to the same disease, but with fewer types being bred the risk of a potentially disastrous disease jumping from animals to human beings becomes real.

## Biodiversity

Biodiversity, or rather the lack of biodiversity, may be the next aspect of environment and pollution to grab attention. So far some attention has been drawn to the fact that biodiversity is decreasing at an alarming rate, but it is only recently that researchers have started to analyse how this will affect our future.

One of the problems is the increasing risk of pandemics as mentioned above. In more general terms nature via biodiversity has wisely put many species on earth foreseeing that some of them may succumb to various threats and/or changes. Others will then be there to take over. Biodiversity is like a kind of life insurance. Keeping to this analogy, we see that if "income" falls because of the loss of a job, a lesser income, but one still adequate to survive on, may be available. Edward Wilson[20] points out that the world's food supplies now rest with merely twenty species. This is a most dramatic slimming down of the situation from fifty or a hundred years ago when countries, and continents, in particular, were kept apart.

Most people would agree that nature behaves sensibly, which leads us to the conclusion that there must be a reason there are so many species. If nature had thought that one species of frogs was enough, all the others would be superfluous. We may not know this yet, but many species and subspecies must be the foundation for life in the long run.

Recently medical science has discovered that many animals actually supply the raw materials for medicines and this may be even more important in the future.

Globalization undermines biodiversity as high economic growth destroys habitats, and this then improves the conditions for species to invade areas in which they have not hitherto been present and attack species already living there that have not built up a defence (invasion of non-native species) against them. Global warming is causing the destruction of habitats.[21]

## Corporate Power

As corporations grow bigger they adopt measures and policies hitherto reserved for nation states. Corporations use communication almost in the sense of propaganda against one another. They have started to spy on one another to reap the benefits of other corporations' breakthroughs in technology, marketing knowledge, and management skills.[22] The *Annual Report to Congress on Foreign Economic Collection and Industrial Espionage — 2004*[23] gives the following breakdown of collectors targeting U.S. technology:

Private companies, 36 per cent.
Foreign governments, 21 per cent.
Government affiliated organizations, 15 per cent.
Individuals, 12 per cent.
Those with unknown affiliation, 16 per cent.

Spying is also growing among Asian companies and among corporations inside Asian countries, such as Chinese-Chinese or Japanese-Japanese corporations, even if figures such as those for the United States are difficult to find. Some years ago, a case about Huawei against Fujitsu surfaced.[24] A compilation encompassing a large number of Asian companies presumed to spy against one another is also available on the Internet.[25] The perception that Asian countries, in particular, China, are spying against American corporations may be partly correct, but the analysis of this is wrong, because Western corporations also spy on Asian corporations, and Asian corporations on one another. The U.S. figures are indicative and interesting, auguring what may also be the case in Asia.

These figures show that foreign governments are less important than domestic or foreign companies and/or individuals. The days when the main part of industrial espionage was performed by nation states trying to steal precious knowledge from corporations in other countries are over. Now it is corporations against corporations, meaning that corporations in one country can spy on another corporation in the same country.

The report mentioned above discloses that almost 75 per cent of suspicious incidents in the defence sector were direct approaches to corporations. This is surprising because such activity must be based on the assumption that at least some of these direct approaches result in access to technology or other kinds of knowledge.

Even more astonishing is the revelation that although most private companies thought that their virtual private networks were invulnerable to hackers, the fact was that nine out of ten had exploitable weaknesses. When we think of how crucial networks have become to corporations, we have to wonder why corporations apparently take things so easy.

It is likely that this trend will strengthen in the years to come. It is even more likely that corporations will escalate these kinds of activities against one another. The risk to globalization is that measures to make the networks watertight may also make them more expensive, exclusive, and, in some cases, closed to corporations and/or countries deemed to be insecure or untrustworthy, thus undermining the global supply chain. Both the report mentioned above and several other sources[26] reveal that traditional spying methods are the exception to the rule. Industrial espionage (or business intelligence) uses open sources more than sophisticated spy measures.[27]

## Disinformation

The Internet has many virtues, but in this context a potential risk stands out: the opportunity to blur the distinction between reality and false information or disinformation. Those juggling with technology can make information look genuine when in fact it is made up.

The world has seen how the Internet could be used to disseminate information and disinformation during the presidential election campaign in the United States in 2008.[28]

As the large majority of people these days, and probably all some years down the road, get their information online, the risk of information "wars" grow substantially with companies trying to paint an image of their competitors that scare customers away.

The difference between disinformation via the traditional media and that via the Internet is that the Internet offers the opportunity for those disseminating it to hide. An example of the damage done by disinformation was the fall of about 75 per cent on Monday, 8 September 2008, of United Airlines' stock, when a link to an almost six-year-old *Chicago Tribune* news report circulated through the Bloomberg News Service.[29] This dissemination of wrong news was by accident, but it is obvious that similar wrong information could be made wilfully.

Such activities may provide one more stone in the security building erected, making the Internet more cumbersome and slower, thereby reducing its capacity to further effective and efficient globalization.

A common denomination for the threats mentioned above are the endeavours of the international community to protect globalization from events happening inside one country. This may lead to the isolation of the said country from the rest of the world, and if such isolation has a bearing on the global supply chain, or in other ways disrupts trade, services, or capital movements, globalization may suffer.

## Economic Growth versus Identity

Globalization as a model has legitimacy, despite its shortcomings and sometimes costs/disadvantages, because it brings with it a higher material living standard, higher economic growth, and higher employment, among other things. A number of people feel — either justifiably or otherwise — that they are giving up a part of their identity when they participate in economic globalization. For the equation to result in a solution favouring globalization, the increase in material living standards must be markedly higher than what other models would offer.[30]

Even economically, full-scale globalization may only be adopted in selected parts of the Asia-Pacific, such as Singapore, Hong Kong, and Australia. In most other parts of Asia, globalization is accepted, in effect, by necessity and logic, but not by conviction. For many Asian countries globalization equals exports — a one-sided "love affair" — but not imports of consumer goods, except for limited groups of and/or linked to brand names. The economic ratio to be followed is cost of imported consumer goods versus purchasing power; the ratio is growing almost everywhere in Asia, and it is no surprise that domestic production and consumption are favoured in many places, while many Asian countries still look to export-led growth as the economic policy to follow.

Conceptually the triumvirate of industrialization, the nation state, and economic globalization has been the cornerstone of global development for the last two hundred years. The interesting question is that as both industrialization and the nation state are losing weight, can economic globalization survive and perhaps even strengthen, or will it follow its two partners in decline?

An affirmative answer for the first possibility, meaning it will survive, rests on three assumptions.

*First*, that a majority of the population get their share of the cake and feel that they are better off with economic globalization than with any other model. This assumption has started to erode over the last decade. Globally a growing discrepancy between the rich and the poor becomes increasingly visible.

TABLE 6.1
Global Picture: Ratio of the Richest 20 per cent to
the Poorest 20 per cent

| | |
|---|---|
| 1820 | 3:1 |
| 1870 | 7:1 |
| 1913 | 11:1 |
| 1960 | 30:1 |
| 1991 | 61:1 |
| 1997 | 74:1 |
| 2005 | 103:1 |

*Source*: UNDP, *Human Development Reports* (New York, 1999 and 2005). See also Isabel Ortiz, "Distribution Analysis, Poverty and Social Assessment", presentation, 8 February 2008 <http://www.un.org/esa/socdev/csd/2008/events/OrtizPSIA.ppt#256,1,UN DESA>, United Nations Department of Economic and Social Affairs.

These figures illustrate not only that international inequality is growing, but also that it is accelerating, making the rich richer and the poor poorer. Inside nation states a similar picture is visible as was shown in Chapter 5.

The message is that economic globalization may deliver higher growth and higher wealth than other models, but allocates it to a diminishing share of the global population, sowing the idea among them that the model may be good, but not necessarily the best for them.

The *second* assumption is the ability of economic globalization to continue to deliver higher growth than any alternative. This may still be so, but the global economic crisis in 2008–09 has sown doubts in the minds of many over whether this is actually so.

The *third* assumption is that free trade is the best model, a belief that has political support anchored in scientific analysis. This was true, broadly speaking, until 2004, when the American economist Paul Samuelson[31] demonstrated that there are cases where free trade is not beneficial for all participants. The threat of outsourcing may exert downward pressure on American wage levels, forcing American workers to accept lower wages in order to keep their jobs, and these lower wages are not fully compensated for by lower prices resulting from outsourcing.

The point in this context is that Samuelson also concludes that the gains to poorer countries outweigh the losses to richer countries — in other words the overall conclusion is that some persons in the United States may be better off breaking with the principle of undisputed free trade, even if the theory says that free trade increases global wealth.

It is not difficult to see the discord inside richer nation states sown by academic views of this kind, which if they gain ground, erode the plinth for free trade.

Economic globalization is not the only model; there are alternatives. Only as long as the majority of a population is convinced that economic globalization is better than the alternatives can it survive. The main threat may thus come from inside the model.

The rising schism between the elite and the majority of the population illustrates this. The elite corresponds and interacts increasingly with other elite in other nations states and less and less with the majority of the population inside the nation state. They do not share very much in terms of lifestyle, identity, etc., with the majority of the population, but do this with the elite in other places. An international elite is emerging that does not care very much about the majority of the population inside nation states. The elite is thus abandoning one of its most important tasks, which is to lead. It creates social capital, but not among different groups of the population inside nation states or megacities/megaregions, but among the international elite, thus casting away its link to geographical places and, significantly, the people living there.

## FAILED NATION STATES

The Global Policy Forum puts forward the following definition of a failed state:

> failed states can no longer perform basic functions such as education, health, social welfare, security, or governance, usually due to fractious violence or extreme poverty. Within this power vacuum, people fall victim to competing factions and crime, and sometimes the United Nations or neighbouring states intervene to prevent a humanitarian disaster. However, states fail not only because of internal factors. Foreign governments can also knowingly destabilize a state by fueling ethnic warfare or supporting rebel forces, causing it to collapse.[32]

Claire Lockhart[33] traces the reason for failed states to the application of a world view from before 1980, to a world that has outlived this paradigm, resulting in between forty and sixty nation states in the category of failed states or those close to being so. She analyses how some of the failed states or nation states close to this category managed to extricate themselves from the abyss and offers a number of explanations among which good governance, a leadership team having a clear vision, and focus on human security and human resources such as basic education, figure prominently.

An analysis from RAND defines the threats failed states constitute the following way:

> Insecurity in the 21st century appears to come less from the collisions of powerful states than from the debris of imploding ones. Failed states present a variety of dangers: religious and ethnic violence; trafficking of drugs, weapons, blood diamonds, and humans; transnational crime and piracy; uncontrolled territory, borders, and waters; terrorist breeding grounds and sanctuaries; refugee overflows; communicable diseases; environmental degradation; and warlords and stateless armies. Regions with failed states are at risk of becoming failed regions, like the vast triangle from Sudan to the Congo to Sierra Leone. For security, material, and moral reasons, leading states cannot ignore failed ones. While no two failed states are alike, all typically suffer from cycles of violence, economic breakdown, and unfit government, rendering them unable to relieve the suffering of their people, much less empower them.[34]

This summary sketches the problems failed states constitute for themselves, for their neighbours, and for the international/global community. They form a destabilizing element often of a considerable dimension. The door is opened for terrorists to establish training bases. Waves of political, economic, and environmental refugees flow over to their neighbours, imposing strains on these countries most of which do not have the resources to deal with such problems, especially not problems coming from the outside.

The risk could even grow if or when failed states are taken over by others, and there are three, perhaps four, possible contenders.

*First*, terrorist organizations. So far there have been several cases of failed states harbouring terrorists, but not really cases of failed, terrorists' states where the official policy is to adopt terrorism — exception: Afghanistan under the Taliban. This might happen in the future, especially if the international community is unable or unwilling to assert its authority over such states.

The high risk is that failed states acquire WMD either on their own, or allow terrorists using their territory to have such weapons. They may do this for various purposes. One possibility is to get money, which would otherwise not flow into the country. They could blackmail the international community or sell technology to other "customers" of which there might not be many, but some. A second possibility is political blackmail, meaning they threaten to break out of established cooperation or exercising pressure on vulnerable nation states.

*Second*, international crime. By getting the clout and capital such organizations may buy themselves into a nation state and gradually usurp power from within. The advantage they gain is a safe haven from international pursuit and a "legal" government to protect them.

*Third*, other and richer nation states. They loan the failed states money until these collapse and they then assume de facto power turning the failed state into some kind of client state or surrogate nation state obeying whatever orders the "owner" gives. With the growing financial power in some parts of the world, especially the oil exporting countries, such an evolution is by no means impossible. It is already visible how many of the oil exporting countries are buying large chunks of agricultural land in other countries.[35]

*Fourth*, but less likely, big multinational companies. De Beers in Swaziland and perhaps Del Monte in some Central American countries are illustrations of corporate power coming close to that description.

*Foreign Policy* publishes an index every year on failed states or, to be more precise, "where the risk of failure is running high".[36] Among the top twenty-five, we find eight Asian countries: Afghanistan, Pakistan, North Korea, Myanmar, Bangladesh, Timor-Leste, Nepal, and Sri Lanka.

The list encompasses about 400 million people. Two countries — Pakistan and Bangladesh — have populations of over 100 million people each. And two of them — Pakistan and North Korea — possess nuclear weapons.

It is frightening that failed states present both a traditional threat, in the sense of armed conflict, because political leaders may succumb to military adventures against neighbours to divert attention from their internal problems, and new kinds of threats such as terrorism and the flow of refugees to adjacent countries.

It is also frightening to note that out of South Asia's major nation states, only India is not on *Foreign Policy*'s list.

For more than half a century world order has moved incessantly towards global rules that set limits for what the strong nation states can do, and that protect the weak, just as the rule of law does inside nation states.[37] Over the last decade this movement has been stopped and in some case even rolled back. In almost all cases, the reason lies with failed states and how they undermine international law.[38] They are not capable of enforcing national laws inside their own territory and even less capable of implementing international law. Instead they, willingly or unwillingly, offer safe havens for all those breaking international law and eroding its credibility.

For Asia this is worrisome or worse. *First*, Asia is feeling its way into an international system built since 1945 on respect for the law. *Second*, the relationship between Asian countries will suffer if authority and credibility for international law fade away. Politically Asia is a conglomerate of small nation states, medium-sized nation states, and large nation states. It is also starting to be a conglomerate of very powerful nation states, powerful nation states, and powerless nation states.

Unless the relationship among the Asian nation states is rooted in trust, it will become difficult to tackle and solve problems, existing and foreseeable (for example, resources in disputed areas), and this results in a state of affairs based on power and size, sowing discord between the less powerful and more powerful nation states and jeopardizing Asia's future development.

In such circumstances, a coalition of the willing may arise, but the question remains unanswered and uncertain as to what such coalitions will and can do. The United States has opened the door with the Proliferation Security Initiative (PSI),[39] that is a global initiative aimed at stopping shipments of WMD, their delivery systems, and related materials worldwide.[40] If coalitions of the willing operate inside international law they may fulfil an important mission. If not, questions arise about their purpose. The risk of international law lacking strength is to push the smaller and less powerful nation states towards a coalition of the willing under the tutelage of one of the very powerful nation states. If so, Asia will be divided into two or three groups of nation states.

## CYBERWARFARE

Cyberwarfare offers a unique possibility for crippling an opponent's capacity to wage armed conflict, conventional war, and economic war or cyberwar, without bloodshed and/or destruction of infrastructure.[41]

It is somewhat reminiscent of warfare in Europe in the late medieval period, where mercenary armies were manoeuvred around, and the general commanding the outmanoeuvred army withdrew, thus offering a bloodless victory to his opponent. Armies were simply too costly to risk in war.

Cyberwarfare means that an enemy's capacity to maintain communication — either between military units or, even worse, throughout society — is incapacitated while your own capacity is maintained[42] (denial of service or cyberattack aiming at destruction).

Cyberwarfare has been used for more than a decade as of 2008.[43] India and Pakistan have engaged themselves in this warfare and so have China and Taiwan. Until recently it was fairly innocent and involved website defacing and shutting down sites with massive amounts of junk traffic (Distributed Denial of Service, DDOS attacks) — the kind of attacks that are annoying, but not really threatening. In many cases the culprits looked like individuals even if one suspects they may have been encouraged or even mobilized by governments.

In 2007 a change took place, with Russian cyberwarfare against Estonia, and in 2008, against Georgia. Not only was it a nation state employing this kind of attack against another nation state, but it was also an act of deliberate aggression, taken on the calculated assumption that NATO, of which Estonia is a member, would not retaliate. This calculation proved to be partly right as NATO did not step in, but responded by setting up an anti-cyberwarfare centre in Estonia, which not only helps Estonia, but also enables NATO to get valuable knowledge in an area where it has had little experience. The centre was not yet operational as of 2009, but a knowledge centre is, but it is uncertain how NATO technology in this particular category compares with what Russia can mobilize.[44]

One episode in the Russian cyberwarfare against Georgia in August 2008 attracts attention in particular. CNN tried to interview President Saakashvili by phone. The first attempt was unsuccessful, but a second attempt shortly afterwards was successful. President Saakashvili blamed the problem on a "cyber attack" against the Georgian VoIP (Voice over Internet Protocol) phone system, which, in fact, is easy to do.

The Georgian Government relocated President Mikheil Saakashvili's website to a hosting service in the United States. The strategic thinking surrounding this move was that Russian cyber attackers, presumably under the control of the Russian Government, would think twice about attacking a website hosted on servers located in the United States because such attacks on U.S. soil might amount to a cyber attack not only on Georgia, but on the United States, and therefore escalate the conflict into a U.S.–Russian confrontation.[45]

In Asia there are constantly rumours about China, in particular, building up the capacity in cyberwarfare. One rumour says that China has developed a first strike capability based on computer viruses.[46] According to various analyses, 120 countries are engaged in building up a capability in cyberwarfare with China in the lead.[47] This view is supported by reports of potential cyberwarfare between China and India, and between China and Taiwan.[48]

The cyber attacks against Estonia and Georgia are verifiable, albeit still somewhat uncertain as to how many of these were controlled or orchestrated by the Russian Government. It is more uncertain what the rumours and reports about cyberwarfare capability in Asia signify. There is no doubt that such capabilities exist and are steadily being built up, but it is still unclear how effective they actually are and how much of the recent harassment in the form of attacks on government websites originate from individuals, and how much is controlled/orchestrated by governments. There may also be disinformation games involved. By creating rumours about a potential adversary, government funds may be made available for a country's own cyberwarfare programme. This game of disinformation is more difficult with conventional weapon systems that are definitely easier to verify.

What is not uncertain, however, is that cyberwarfare is going to be in the arsenal of conflicts in the coming decades. It fits neatly into the philosophy of the terrorists that modern warfare is meant to cripple the well functioning of the adversary's society, not to conquer territory, kill people, or destroy infrastructure.

It is also applicable as a weapon in crisis management. It allows an aggressor to step up threats of the attacks while maintaining strategic ambiguity. How much is coming from the government and how much from what the aggressor might label "irresponsible individuals"? How far will a potential aggressor go and how far can it go? Who is actually most capable in this kind of warfare and how do we measure gains or losses?

As the Russian-Georgian conflict demonstrates, it also entails the possibility of drawing a third party into a conflict, perhaps even without that party knowing or wanting it.

An analysis from 2008 uses the Estonian and Georgian cases as a starting point for a briefing on cyberwarfare. It discloses an almost exponential rise in what is termed new malicious code threats from the first half of 2006 to the second half of 2007 (seven times) and categorizes the threat from China and Russia as high, from Iran and North Korea as elevated, from Syria as moderate, and from Libya, almost zero. The defence capabilities of the United States are classified as high, United Kingdom,[49] as elevated, and Russia, Syria, Israel, and Iran, as moderate.[50]

At the end of 2008 the Center for Strategic and International Studies (CSIS)[51] published an alarming report about the state of U.S. defence against cyber threats, spelling out clearly that the lack of appropriate defence is one of America's most acute security problems.

It points to three major conclusions:

• Cybersecurity is one of the major national security problems the United States has to deal with and the threat is growing;
• Decisions and actions to meet these threats in various forms must respect privacy and civil liberties; and
• Only a comprehensive national security strategy embracing domestic and international aspects will improve the situation.

CSIS did not enter into legal or other means for retaliation or compensation or methods to estimate business and social impacts quantitatively. This is done, however, in a study by Louis-Francois Pau.[52]

Threats fall into two categories. The *first* consists of threats emanating from organized sources aiming to undermine or outright jeopardize the functioning of vital parts of society. They may be foreign countries seeking advantages by such actions, or terrorist organizations perceiving it as an attack on the United States or using cyberwarfare as a tactical instrument capable of maiming U.S. defences prior to a more conventional terrorist attack. The *second* category are threats from criminal organizations either based in the United States or abroad, seeking to reap profit by extracting data from the United States and using such data subsequently to pursue their own goals.

In its review of the report, *Business Week*[53] focuses on examples in the course of 2008 which set out how vulnerable the United States is and how much is needed to counteract this threat:

> The Secretary of Defense's unclassified e-mail was hacked and DOD officials told us that the department's computers are probed hundreds of thousands of times each day; a senior official at State told us the department has lost "terabytes" of information; Homeland Security suffered "break-ins" in several of its divisions, including the Transportation Security Agency; Commerce was forced to take the Bureau of Industry and Security offline for several months; NASA had to impose e-mail restrictions before shuttle launches and allegedly has seen designs for new launchers compromised. Recently, the White House itself had to deal with unidentifiable intrusions in its networks.[54]

Terrorists, nation states, and multinational corporations have got a terrifying weapon at their disposal. It does not have the potential to wipe out humanity as nuclear weapons can, but it can destroy globalization.

## WARFARE IN SPACE

Potentially war in space is cyberwarfare blown up to gigantic proportions, only within the reach of the really big boys. Essentially it consists of the ability to defend one's own satellites from being attacked by the enemy, while having the capability to shoot down or disable the enemy's satellites.

Almost all major military forces depend on space as the hub for their communication and navigation. The U.S. military uses GPS (Global Positioning System) operated from satellites, and an enemy which knows how to put the U.S. satellites out of action achieves more by doing so than meeting U.S. armed forces on the battlefield.[55]

The United States is the undisputed leader in potential warfare in space, with China, Europe, and Russia, and, to a lesser degree, India and Japan following. It is likely that only a handful or maybe even fewer countries around the world will be able to sustain the efforts — financial and technological — required. The costs are enormous.

It is, however, interesting to note that the United States has already earmarked China as the major challenger.[56] This indicates that among Asian powers, China is ahead of the pack. While this does not mean that China envisages using its presumed superiority in potential space warfare, it means that China can do so if it chooses, which inevitably influences strategic thinking and the power balance in Asia.

In January 2007 China used ground-based missiles to shoot down one of its own weather satellites.[57] This caused international alarm as it was taken as a demonstration of Chinese capabilities in this area. A number of academics[58] have started to analyse and ponder on China's space war capability and discuss whether China might win or lose a space war. This is speculation, but the point of interest in this analysis is that so far China, alone among all Asian countries, possesses space war capability. The question remains, however, how capable China is to locate targets in space. The United States is certainly capable, and Russia has the capability, but doubts persist over whether it is kept up to date and has global coverage. France may have global space tracking and mapping capabilities in service — it is highly doubtful whether any other countries really possess such capabilities which are among the most difficult and expensive to put in place.

## CONVENTIONAL FOREIGN AND SECURITY
## POLICY THREATS

### China, India, and Japan

Many observers analyse the prospect of war between China and Japan or between China and India to be rooted in the nineteenth-century European nation state philosophy, predicting China to be the most powerful nation state in Asia, and India and/or Japan not peacefully acquiescing with such a development. According to this philosophy it is possible/likely that rivalry among the rising powers in Asia will lead to war. A representative of this line of thinking is found in an essay from 2008, which marshals a number of arguments for predicting that China plans to "teach India a lesson" in the same way as it was done in 1962, with the short-lived armed conflict in the Himalayas.[59]

Such an analysis and conclusion are, however, based on the assumption that the Asian powers will act like the European nation states did more than a hundred years ago. There is no basis for such conclusions. In view of recognized domestic weaknesses and problems, it seems much more likely that the Asian powers will do whatever they can to avoid war, making such an outcome a remote one, and turning the power game into one involving economics, societal structures, and technology.

Similar statements saying that a grand-scale war is unlikely were made just before World War I.[60] War had become obsolete because both winners and losers would find themselves weighed down by tremendous losses, making it nonsense to speak of winners.

All the arguments put forward prior to World War I to prove that war was unthinkable are as valid today as then, but there are two major differences making it likely that they will prove to be right this time.

*First*, in those days politicians spoke openly of war as a legitimate policy instrument and nation states looked on war as a perfectly suitable means to achieve objectives. In many countries war was regarded as an element of civilization, an inevitable segment of development, and the prospect of hundreds, even millions, of dead in the battlefield did not look scary, even if that proved to be so when the shooting actually began. In the decades leading to World War I, nation states frequently threatened one another with war, and war was integrated in international law which laid down rules for how to act and how to wage war in conformity with civilization.[61] Today war is excluded from the agenda. That does not mean that war cannot take place, as the last decades have proved, but that the mentality is shifting away from wars, making it much less likely than was the case when the theory about the impossibility of war was formulated about a hundred years ago.

*Second*, irrespective of all the arguments that can be advanced for or against armed conflict or war between two or even three of the major countries in Asia over the next twenty-five years, the basic question remains: Is there a substantial segment of the political leadership now or on its way into power that actually wants war and preaches the virtues of war? The answer to that question seems quite clear: no. Of course there may be politicians who toy with irresponsible ideas, and/or military leaders who rattle the sabre, but there is precious little visible planning or preparation for grand-scale war. It may be the case for the Korean peninsula, between India and Pakistan, and some would add the Taiwan issue, but for all of them the observation applies that war is not being planned and will only erupt by a miscalculation by one or several of the actors on the scene. This may of course happen as history is full of miscalculations leading to war, but in a rational analysis, the thrust must be directed by policymakers' preferences and not what might happen by mistakes — history concentrates on cases where things went wrong and not on cases where things went according to plan and/or expectations.

To analyse the likelihood of war, the starting point, the crucial one, is to diagnose whether powers threaten one another's vital interests. Is the survival or development of a nation state, as laid down in political guidelines, at risk unless war is chosen as a policy instrument?

If we assume the main hypothesis that economics and societal elements are determinants for war instead of conventional power games, then the main Asian powers may only clash in securing access to resources. And there seems to be only one case where two of them threaten each other's vital interests: The shortage of water may drive the two major future Asian (and probably global) powers, China and India, to war.[62] China and India share the Tibetan plateau as source for a large part of their water supply, but politically, it belongs exclusively to China. In case of a real scarcity of water — and that is possible, even likely — the survival of these two countries' economies and living standards for the population are at stake.[63] Access to other resources, such as energy (e.g. the offshore fields contested by China, Japan, and Korea), commodities, food, and a clean environment are basically a question of money and, therefore, negotiable — burden sharing. These kinds of conflicts have been the basis of diplomacy and negotiations for centuries and can be handled if there is a political will. Not so with water. It can be acquired to a certain extent by investing (money again), but only to a certain extent.

Traditionally China and Japan have been rivals and gone to war. It is, however, difficult to find observers genuinely predicting full-scale war between these two Asian powers. There is a growing trend of nationalism in both countries, which appears worrying and needs to be kept under control. China may hold back to avoid raising fears and animosity towards its growing economic and accompanying political power that may destabilize its development. Nationalism may lead Japan towards a change of foreign policy, but economic interests point towards accommodation with China, however painful that may be psychologically for Japan. A synthesis of a sober view can be found in an edited work from 2007 that looks at the two countries from several levels of analysis including the domestic-state interface in both countries and the important role of historical perceptions. It is pointed out that China-Japan Relations in the twenty-first century should be perceived from an international relations-based perspective. The study set the existing relationship in the context of historical interaction, the influence of culture on mutual perceptions, and the role of ideologies — particularly nationalism.[64]

An omen of what is more likely to happen than war are the meetings among the three Northeast Asian powers (China, Japan, and Korea) and even more the initiative calling for an "East Asian Community" put forward by Japanese Prime Minister Yukio Hatoyama in early autumn 2009 after the change of government in that country.

It reveals that Japan is tinkering with the notion of wriggling out of the American straitjacket and replacing it with a much more even-handed foreign and security policy posture. The basic ideas in the initiative[65] may still be unclear, as are the full reactions of China and Korea, as well as the Southeast Asian nations.

The heart of the matter is nonetheless that Japan is trying to get leverage vis-à-vis the United States and a much stronger foothold in an Asian context. Economically it can be said to reflect the diminished role of the United States in Asia's economy. The implications, however, reach beyond economics. If some kind of East Asian community or Asian community emerges out of the number of initiatives floated in recent years, it will inevitably strengthen the trust among the Asian countries, making armed conflict even less likely.

As China is often presented as the potential aggressor, not the least in some American works, it is worthwhile to look at what the Chinese themselves are saying about their security/military policy:[66]

> China is still confronted with long-term, complicated, and diverse security threats and challenges. Issues of existence security and development security, traditional security threats and non-traditional security threats, and domestic security and international security are interwoven and interactive. China is faced with the superiority of the developed countries

in economy, science and technology, as well as military affairs. It also faces strategic maneuvers and containment from the outside while having to face disruption and sabotage by separatist and hostile forces from the inside. Being in a stage of economic and social transition, China is encountering many new circumstances and new issues in maintaining social stability. Separatist forces working for "Taiwan independence," "East Turkistan independence" and "Tibet independence" pose threats to China's unity and security. Damages caused by non-traditional security threats like terrorism, natural disasters, economic insecurity, and information insecurity are on the rise. Impact of uncertainties and destabilizing factors in China's outside security environment on national security and development is growing. In particular, the United States continues to sell arms to Taiwan in violation of the principles established in the three Sino-US joint communiqués, causing serious harm to Sino-US relations as well as peace and stability across the Taiwan Straits.

It is clear from this that China sees the threats against it as diversified, even incorporating economic and social transition. This is supported by the following statement. "China makes overall plans for the use of its national resources and strikes a balance between enriching the country and strengthening the military, so as to ensure that its strategy for national defense and armed forces building is compatible with its strategy for national development."

When outlining China's military vis-à-vis the outside world it is worth noting that the paper says that China cannot neglect global issues, but neither can the world ignore China's role. This looks like a clear message that China is ready to enter into collaborative efforts to stabilize the world, but at a clear price of being recognized as — not necessarily a stakeholder — a stabilizing power. China does not ask for changes in the global system, it wants to be among those powers upholding it. An omen of this design becomes visible when the paper talks about MOOTW (Military Operations Other Than War). The modernization of China's military away from the old concept of mass power and not very sophisticated weaponry towards a modern force capable of undertaking various tasks and challenges puts China in a position where it can begin to offer its participation in military, but non-war, global operations.

## Force Structure

Without going into detail the structure of the armed forces in all three countries looks incapable of launching an offensive. Due to geography, naval power is the best indicator of the composition of the armed forces and thus how strategy is perceived — offensive or defensive.[67] Japan is an island and a Japanese attack or an attack on Japan requires a large amphibious capability that no Asian power possesses. Japan has one of the largest navies in the world, but no capital ships such as aircraft carriers or nuclear powered submarines. It is a navy built to defend (keep the sea lanes open) and not attack. China's armed forces are said by the United States to have increased with "remarkable speed and scope".[68] Figures about military spending point to a strong hike, but when we bear in mind how much money, training, and experience are needed to turn a peasant army, broadly speaking, into a sophisticated twenty-first century military machine, it looks unlikely that China's armed forces are capable of much more than operations nearby and primarily of a defensive nature. China's naval build-up has to choose between a capability to harass or even more prevent the U.S. navy from entering the strait between China and Taiwan, or a force that can project power around Asia. One type of navy cannot do both. China cannot, within even a long-term horizon, build both kinds of navies and has apparently opted for the first one. India falls very much in the same category but with less expenditure than China, although it is difficult to compare defence spending between countries doing their best to hide how much they spend, but the Indian naval perspective is exactly the same as the Chinese one and for historical reasons: threats have in recent historical time come from the sea, not from the land, and therefore the job of the navy is to defend the nation.

It seems a fair guess to conclude that all three major Asian powers have some capability to defend themselves, but very little to project power outside their borders and near vicinity. As military history shows, it takes a long time to transit from one state of military capability to another, not the least because of training and experience. To jump from a defensive military structure to an offensive one is not just about building hardware, but even more about how to use it. The United States is the only power really able to manoeuvre groups of carriers that constitute the nucleus of projecting power around the world. The question can certainly be posed whether carrier groups are needed in the future. The answer seems to be *yes*. As an instrument for projecting power they are still unrivalled. The same goes for its signal of intent value, where such a group is visible, forcing opponents to choose between backing down or escalating the threat.

It takes somewhere between ten and fifteen years even for the United States to build a single carrier. An Asian nation would probably need more time, as it does not have the know-how, and to turn such a ship into operational status requires a long time. It is unlikely that any Asian power in the next twenty-five years will posses weapon platforms of that calibre albeit they may approach the stage where they can do so.[69]

China and India posses nuclear weapons and Japan may acquire such weapons over the next twenty-five years, but their actual use of nuclear weapons can be classified as such a remote possibility to warrant it being excluded from the analysis.

Almost all military analysts tend to see a military build-up as being steered by geopolitical or exclusively foreign and security policy considerations. This is not true. Military expenditure competes with other forms of expenditure in political preferences for public funding. For China and India, the challenges to restructure and modernize society are so awesome that few would dare think it likely that military expenditure will gain precedence for public funding over other contenders. In both countries priority number one are funds for housing, infrastructure, health, education, etc. To cut down on funding for these purposes so as to build up a strong military seems unlikely. Political leaders may rely on the top brass in the power struggle at the top, but they rely even more on the population to remain in power.

It is difficult to see which one of the major Asian powers could win from an armed conflict and what gains would make the population grateful to political leaders for going to war. It is easy on the other hand to see how more funding to the military can delay efforts to modernize the economy thus undermining the political system's legitimacy. Broadening the analysis from a strictly military one to one including societal aspects strengthens the belief that the risk for an armed conflict between the three major Asian powers is remote.

## Taiwan

Taiwan is a well-known and well-analysed security problem. The main players — the United States and China — have undoubtedly been through all thinkable scenarios to make sure that war does not break out by mistake. It is a classic problem where all the insights from conventional conflict theory can be applied, and certainly have been applied, for sixty years.

Taiwan is gradually being integrated economically into China. They have started to operate as a single economy. The figures speak for themselves. China is Taiwan's biggest trading partner with a total trade of more than US$40 billion, accounting for more than 10 per cent of Taiwan's gross domestic product (GDP). More than 50,000 Taiwanese companies operate in China, and Taiwanese companies own 60 to 70 per cent of the Chinese information technology market. Taiwanese investment in China is estimated to be over

US$160 billion and grows by more than US$4–US$6 billion every year. It is estimated that more than one million Taiwanese live in China, 300,000 in Shanghai alone.[70]

If a military confrontation occurs between the United States and China, Taiwan will be the flywheel for engineering the circumstances leading to such a conflict. The U.S. interest in Taiwan is political and strategic. Politically Taiwan yields considerable influence on U.S. politics as it is seen to be democratic as opposed to the reign of the Communist Party in China. Strategically Taiwan is the cornerstone in deciding where China's defence perimeter goes. At the moment Taiwan is outside confining China to a defence posture close to its coastline. If Taiwan falls under Chinese dominance in one or another way, China's sphere of interest and its perimeter will be pushed into the Pacific, thus necessitating strategic reconsideration on the part of the United States.

The United States has successfully applied strategic ambiguity for decades and China has no wish to be drawn into a costly military conflict that will derail its efforts to develop the domestic economy.

It is unlikely, but not totally unthinkable, that the United States can be tempted either to go directly to war, or provoke China into choosing between a war or a humiliating climb down. Strategic considerations could dictate such a course for policymakers if the United States chooses the option of stopping China when it is comparatively weak, instead of letting it grow into a full-fledged challenger to the U.S. global power position.

Another risk is that right wing nationalist forces in Japan may manage to get policies under control that will trap the United States and Taiwan, forcing them to adopt steps that they know are unacceptable to China, thus leading them down the path to war.

A third risk is a miscalculation, possibly in the form of brinkmanship or attempts to score cheap political points for use in domestic policies, as has been seen in Taiwan. If one of the players judges the other one to be too weak, or misreads political signals, such a course may open up.

The basics, however, point to the odds that none of these courses is likely. By far the most likely outcome is that the issue will still be open for settlement twenty-five years down the road, or that a peaceful and negotiated solution will have been found.

## The Korean Peninsula

The geopolitical situation on the Korean Peninsula has been frozen since 1953, but is likely to change over the next twenty-five years, if for no other reasons than that the North Korean leader, Kim Jong-il, cannot be expected to live that long, which opens the door for a succession that will probably lead to political changes.

The prospect of a unification of the "two Koreas" has often been discussed, but is not likely to happen in a foreseeable future. If it does happen, the economic repercussions will reverberate throughout East Asia, as it will impose a heavy burden on South Korea.

The cost of the German reunification has, for obvious reasons, been brought into the debate. There is no unanimous estimate of how much it cost, but most analyses operate with the assumption of an annual transfer from 1991 to the beginning of this century, from the former West Germany to the former East Germany of around four to five per cent of West Germany's GDP — in itself, an enormous amount of money. In spite of this financial effort, the former East Germany is still lagging behind the former West Germany in living standards, albeit the gap has been considerably narrowed.

When looking at these figures as some kind of basis for assessing a potential Korean reunification we should bear in mind that the GDP per capita in the former East Germany was estimated at about two thirds of that in West Germany.[71] The size of its population was approximately 25 per cent, and the total size of its economy, a little less than 10 per cent compared with West Germany. The corresponding figures for the Korean peninsula are difficult to quantify for GDP per capita, but undoubtedly the gap is much bigger than for Germany in 1990; some analysts set it at somewhere between 10 and 20 per cent of the level for the South. North Korea's population is about half of the South's and North Korea's economy is put at three to five per cent of South Korea's. It is not difficult to see that the task of lifting North Korea's economy just near the level of South Korea's will be many times more challenging and costly than was the case for Germany.[72] The lowest estimate from almost ten studies[73] points to a figure of about US$300 billion and the highest comes to a sum of more than US$3 trillion, compared with a total GDP for the Republic of Korea (2008) of about US$750 billion.

In reality the major powers operating in Northeast Asia are fairly content with the division of Korea. It legitimizes a U.S. military presence, which is stabilizing not only for the region, but also for the whole of Asia. If a reunification took place, the American military presence would be questioned, not necessarily by countries in the region (except in the case of a more self-assertive Japan), but at home in the United States, with its own people asking for justification for using money to keep military forces in or near the Korean Peninsula. China's policy vis-à-vis North Korea may seem opaque, but probably reflects a Chinese interest in keeping millions of poor people at bay, and an interpretation that the nuisance value of an independent North Korea is valuable vis-à-vis Japan.

If the United States chooses to maintain a military presence beyond a token force, it would be clear that they were there because of China and not to protect South Korea. This will make it more difficult for the United States and China to move in tandem as the Chinese perception will be to see the United States as a potential enemy. Without a U.S. presence the credibility of the American umbrella — nuclear at that — will be less robust and Japan may wonder whether the time has come to build its own deterrence, including nuclear weapons. China must have foreseen this, but even if that is the case, and even if many observers can and will put forward arguments for such a step, the consequence will be changed relations between China and Japan. Japan's industry (*keidanren*) is already worried that Japan's Asian multinationals will be dislodged by China's emerging multinationals, making the game complicated.

The Korean Peninsula poses little risk of a classical military conflict, although with the unpredictable North Koreans, one may never know. However, the North Koreans will know that a military conflict will inevitably end with North Korea's destruction and possibly the loss of life for the leadership. They want to survive and obtain advantages for themselves and North Korea — not to commit suicide. North Korea's foreign and security policy seems to be controlled by two factors that are not hidden: A genuine wish to obtain a guarantee that the United States will not attack the country,[14] and blackmail — politically and economically — exacting a price for not doing what adjacent countries and the United States do not wish North Korea to do. These basic elements will not change as long as the present leadership continues to hold the reins of power.

## Pakistan

Pakistan is a fragile nation state created in 1947 with independence from the British Empire. The background goes back to the religious feelings that make it difficult for Hindus and Muslims to live together. This explains why Islam and, to a certain extent, Islamic extremism are still very much present in Pakistan. It also explains why Pakistan has strong links with other Islamic countries such as Saudi Arabia, but does not explain why China and Pakistan have built up close relations over many decades.

It is likely that Chinese interests in Pakistan will wane over the years, as there is little fundamental Chinese strategic interest in supporting Pakistan, but the potential risk of undermining its far more important relations with India. China-Pakistan relations from 1955–2000 helped China to assert itself and annoy the United States and India in one go, but this has changed. China also has its own Muslim minority groups and may tilt towards improving relations with countries sharing such problems, instead of nurturing strategic relations with an Islamic country such as Pakistan.

The United States has for decades been a security guarantor and economic stabilization power, but after the terrorist attack in September 2001 and the subsequent wars in Afghanistan and Iraq, it has found it increasingly difficult to deal with Pakistan, as it does not really know whether that country shares its interests in fighting terrorist groups, given its roots in Islam, or whether behind the veil it sympathizes more or less with such groups. The United States is tempted to shift the balance in India's favour, seeing that country as more valuable in a potential power game with China. Furthermore the United States has never understood that for Pakistan's political leaders, the problem was survival in a domestic political setting unknown to the United States, and that Pakistan, like any other country, pursued its own strategic goals, which actually have rarely been the same as the ones pursued by the United States. For the United States, the game is about ideology — the enemy being communism or extremist Muslim terrorism — when for Pakistan it is about manoeuvring between India and China to secure its survival, and a reputation as a power to be reckoned with.

These considerations may leave Pakistan without many friends outside the traditional Islamic countries, thus making it more difficult to modernize and/or secularize the country. The accumulation of wealth among Middle Eastern oil exporting countries empowers them with the possibility of exercising "dollar diplomacy" with two objectives. *First*, to cement Islamic countries. *Second*, to buy assets which they need and they need agricultural land to protect themselves against forthcoming shortages and/or higher food prices. Pakistan is probably the most obvious example of a country where their influence will increase in the years to come, so in a geopolitical context, American and Chinese interests in Pakistan might be replaced by interest from the Middle Eastern oil exporting countries.

Over the next twenty-five years such a power shift will ask for a revised Indian foreign and security policy vis-à-vis Pakistan. Much will depend on the underlying foreign policy of the Middle Eastern oil exporting countries and whether they themselves are moving towards modernizing their countries and finding a place in globalization, or whether they continue to ride two horses: the acceptance of extremist Islamic groups, combined with the role of exporting oil, but basically not participating in globalization.

Pakistan[75] may not be a failed state, but one analysis indicates that it may become one. The country is divided ethnically, and tribal loyalty is strong and, as far as can be seen, outshines national loyalty. Its terrain, especially in the north-western part, is not easily accessible, which has made these areas tempting grounds for terrorist groups or groups wanting to escape authority.

Its possession of nuclear weapons makes a change in government a risky venture, in particular if a new government needs the support of segments of society allegedly having links to terrorist groups rooted in Islam.

In a short-term horizon, a coup or similar event bringing such extremists into power would constitute the most visible and largest danger to stability in Asia. It is difficult to see the United States and India acquiescing to extremist groups — directly or indirectly involved in Islamic terrorism — having access to nuclear weapons. A pre-emptive strike would, in such circumstances, be a definite possibility, and one that would trigger incalculable effects.

In a longer-term perspective, much will depend on whether the majority of Muslims in Pakistan will start to be attracted by the modernization of their country that will bring higher living standards to the population.

At the moment, large parts of Pakistan and its population are caught in a situation where being outside the globalization picture does not seem to be a big loss, irrespective of all the arguments for globalization, which improves the recruiting ground for terrorists groups.

Pakistani diasporas are powerful in playing Middle Eastern and sometimes Chinese economic interests, and are sitting on many financial flows, but, contrary to the Chinese and Indian diasporas, are not investing or building up economic capabilities in the country itself.

## Central Asia

Central Asia holds one of the largest reserves of oil and gas and is potentially unstable. Nation states here were born after the break-up of the Soviet Union in 1991. Their political systems are fragile and, in some cases, dependent on a "strong" man holding the reins of power, with uncertainty about who will succeed him. Many run a political system born out of self-assignment by some groups getting dividends from the rivalry of others. Kazakhstan and Kyrgyzstan have a large minority of ethnic Russians who can be used to destabilize them if the rulers in Moscow find this convenient. Russia has not forgotten that they used to be part of the Soviet Union and, before that, Czarist Russia.

Instability may invite outside intervention, starting a scramble between two or more powers to get influence. China wants to be certain of the supply of oil and gas, and so does India. Russia is wary of the possibility that China and/or India might get too strong a foothold in the region. Still, the mountain barrier poses difficulties for an Indian engagement, however tempted India may be.

A vehicle for cooperation in trying to pre-empt such a situation is the Shanghai Cooperation that goes back to 1996, with Russia, China, and the four nation states in Central Asia as full members, and four other Asian nation states, including India, as observers. The basic idea is/was to stabilize the region and so far this policy has been successful. It has, however, never really been tested by a crisis in the region, or in one of the member states bordering on one or several of the others.

Perhaps the greatest security risk is that one or more of the Central Asian nation states may develop a failed state situation, opening up the opportunity for, or even inviting, adjacent countries to intervene.

The Central Asian countries can in some ways be compared to Pakistan. They differ, however, in the sense that some of them have large oil and gas reserves, putting them in the category of oil exporting countries not in need of cash. For states without such reserves, it is difficult to see any future without a firm link to a larger and/or richer power, which makes them some kind of client state. It may be Russia, China, India, or the Middle Eastern oil exporting countries. The United States is also a candidate, but less likely to maintain its foothold in Central Asia twenty-five years from now. It seems a fair bet that the oil exporting Middle Eastern countries and China will build up a stronger influence in this part of the world, albeit it is difficult to define exactly how this will unfold and how deep their influence will run. Historically there are few links between Central Asia and the Middle East. Another candidate for stronger influence is Turkey. If Turkey becomes a member of the European Union, an interesting perspective emerges for European influence in this part of the world.

## Southeast Asia[76]

Security and stability among the Southeast Asian countries are based upon three dimensions:

The *first* is to protect the region from outside interference by major powers, be it the Soviet Union during the Cold War, the United States, and now China, and also Japan.

Instruments such as the ARF (ASEAN Regional Forum), TAC (Treaty on Amity and Cooperation in Southeast Asia), and the Treaty on Southeast Asia Nuclear Weapon-Free Zone have been adopted and implemented to this effect. They do not primarily aim at strengthening and deepening the cooperation among the Southeast Asian nations; their purpose is to hold outside partners at arm's length and define the limits for their potential and possible operation in Southeast Asia.

The *second* dimension is to promote economic growth offering their citizens an increase in living standard, thus cementing the existing social fabric and reducing the risks for not only insurgency, but also other forms of attempts to destabilize Southeast Asian societies.

In the early phases the risk was almost exclusively seen in the form of communist insurgency and the events in Indonesia in 1965 seemed to give proof that such a risk was real. The political events in Singapore in the 1950s, the insurgency in Malaya, and in the Philippines throughout most of the 1950s and even 1960s, and anti-Chinese riots in several countries offered further proof that the Southeast Asian nations faced a threat to be taken seriously. Reviewing the developments today, we notice how close some of the countries came to civil war.

In recent years the threat comes from Muslim extremists in Indonesia, the Philippines, Malaysia, Thailand, and Singapore. The 9/11 attacks and global organizations such as Al-Qaeda found a resonance in the region with organizations such as Jemaah Islamiyah, Abu Sayyaf, and MILF (Moro Islamic Liberation Front).

This kind of terrorism constitute a threat to the nation states' effective control over their territory and the well functioning of their societies. In both cases success for terrorism would undermine the legitimacy of the various political systems vis-à-vis their own citizens and start a destabilization process.

Insurgency and terrorism might have destabilized Southeast Asian countries, thereby jeopardizing the conditions for sustained economic growth. If so, political stability would have been endangered. Stability was the cornerstone in attracting foreign direct investments so vital for making an export oriented economic policy a success. High economic growth was instrumental in bringing about a "feel good" sentiment among the populations, thus cementing stability.

The *third* dimension of Southeast Asian stability is the right to forge its own political system without outside interference — a kind of pledge among member states not to interfere. Most of the member states are newborn nation states, which, not surprisingly, make them vigilant towards outside interference. On top of that almost all of them comprise several races, with a variety of religions, posing the risk of a spillover from groups in one member state to minority groups in another, with obvious risks for destabilization.

Growth and prosperity in Southeast Asia depends largely on whether China and India continue to have high growth. The countries in Southeast Asia constitute too small an economic base to establish self-sustaining growth. They can adjust to and exploit economic globalization, but are so heavily engaged in globalization that they can do very little to steer an economic policy out of sync with the main players in Asia. The second dimension of stability will consequently be decided by globalization and the large economies of Asia.

Of the three dimensions discussed it seems a fairly certain bet that the first and the third will come under pressure.

If the U.S. military presence in Southeast Asia is scaled down, the door opens for increased military presence by China, India, and Japan. A stronger military posture by the Southeast Asian countries individually is often perceived as a threat to stability, as it is presumed that such military forces will be used against adjacent countries. It could, however, turn out in another way. A stronger military posture may deter the big Asian powers from pushing their military parameters forward. A weak military offers a power vacuum. If, on the other hand, it is well known that each country can and is willing to defend its territory and keep terrorists and similar threats under control, it becomes much more difficult for Asian powers to do so. The defence build-up has been mostly for domestic political reasons, one of local armies, and only a few of the Southeast Asian nation states have built up powerful navies and air forces. This is well observed by the big Asian powers and may be one of the reasons that recently several Southeast Asian nation states have started to invest in higher-scale military hardware.

The third discussion, non-interference, is unlikely to continue unchanged over the next twenty-five years. A stronger interaction also means a stronger societal interlinkage, and even if the political systems will not necessarily converge, values will tend to do so, lowering the threshold for how populations react to political systems in neighbouring countries based on values other than the ones dominating the whole Southeast Asian area.

Non-interference may not last due to other essential issues, such as water, the environment, immigration, and nuclear energy. Such issues will touch a raw nerve among nation states and force them to move towards a stance where what happens in neighbouring countries cannot be disregarded.

The region has benefited from stability and security for the last twenty-five years. It is far from certain that it will be plain sailing to achieve the same degree of stability and security over the next twenty-five years. The outside world is changing fast, making it necessary for Southeast Asia to re-examine some of its traditional links with other countries inside and outside Asia. Internally, religious, ethnic, and social groups are more visible and more determined to manifest themselves. This does not in itself augur instability, but it calls for forward-looking policies to avoid cracks in the social fabric.

## Role of the United States

The United States is not an Asian power, but a power in Asia, a situation resulting from the outcome of World War II and, subsequently, economic interests. It has more or less been forgotten that the United States was absent from that space before World War II,[77] when the players were the United Kingdom, France, and the Netherlands. From 1945, the United States played the role of a stabilizing power and an implicit guarantor of borders and peaceful relationships between Asian countries, but this was mainly the side effect or mechanism of ensuring strategic interests vis-à-vis the Soviet Union, and China, combined with a degree of control over Japan. Without the United States' benevolent military presence, many Asian countries would have run higher military expenditure and the funds would have had to be taken from other purposes such as stimulating their development.

U.S. foreign policy has since the time of President Woodrow Wilson included a streak of idealism — which should not be overlooked when analysing why the United States takes this or that position — but basically the United States as a superpower is not different from other superpowers in world history: its actions are dictated by its interests.

The United States did not want to be involved in another war in Asia after the Korean War and the Vietnam War, and the best way to avoid this was to stimulate an Asian economic revival and keep a military presence to hold back military build-ups in Asia. It worked and it worked to the benefit of the United States and the Asian countries. Declaratory diplomacy may have criticized the United States, but fundamentally almost all Asian countries (possibly even China) saw the U.S. military presence as indispensable, benefited from it, and wanted it to continue.

The question is how the game will unravel in the next twenty-five years.

In the 1990s the United States watched the rise of China, but still saw a strong China many years away, and not a factor to be integrated in strategic analysis and, even less, policies. This has changed. Now U.S. strategy rates China as the major potential challenger in the course of the first half of this century.[78] U.S. absolute power looked impregnable and enormous, but inability to resolve historical problems (Taiwan, Korea) first, then the war against terrorism from 2001 onwards, disclosed fundamental flaws in U.S. strength.

When developing its major strategy from watching the rise of China to fighting global terrorism, the United States could basically choose between two policies.

The *first* was to seek allies and partners such as China, but not be confined to that country rallying around the United States in a grand global coalition. This might have been possible, although the effort to push Japan into that role in the 1970s and 1980s failed. It would have taken some of the burden off its shoulders, but the major partners in the alliance would have to be given stronger influence in the global power game. They probably shared a good deal of the U.S. strategic outlook on terrorism, but also knew that the United States was committed to a war against terror, regardless of their position. That led them to the view that unless the United States accommodated them in the global steering mechanism, there was no real incentive to join it. But the United States did not do so.

The *second* choice was to maintain the perception of the United States as the only superpower with the military capability and economic strength to fight the war against terrorism alone, and afterwards be even supreme *in extremis*. The risk of that policy was that if things went wrong, the United States would be militarily bogged down and sapped for economic strength, thus opening the door for rising powers such as China to move into the position as a challenger faster than envisaged.

The United States chose the second option and things went wrong. Instead of enhancing U.S. power, events have shown the limits of U.S. power. The United States could not win the war against terrorism alone, and the decision to fight alone was probably the main reason for the financial crisis in 2008, which cast doubts over the future of the U.S. economy. These lessons will not easily be forgotten and will be taken into account in the framing of U.S. strategy in the years to come and will also influence its policies vis-à-vis Asia.

Three a priori options offer themselves to U.S. policy planners.

The United States can hang on to the perception of being able to defend its position as the only superpower. This is what many of the previous superpowers have done, but none of them has escaped the inevitable decline.

The problem is that the United States no longer has the resources to do this, thus making its policy posture hollow, as this will soon be discovered by other powers, starting with China and Japan, which can read U.S. resolve and strength (or lack thereof) much better than the United States itself. A lot has been written about "imperial overstretch"[79] and it looks likely that the United States is moving into that phase of an imperial power's lifecycle. A weaker U.S. economy will force other powers to rethink their strategic priorities to match what the United States is trying to achieve with its means. Its role of stabilizer and implicit guarantor in much of Asia will be reconsidered. Already now it is hardly trusted in this role. It is not a foregone conclusion that a U.S. military withdrawal is going to take place, but it is probable that twenty-five years from now, U.S. military presence in Asia will be diminished and the United States will likely concentrate on its hard core interests, with Guam as the nearest and most obvious replacement for Japan, Korea, Australia, and other bases. Such a development would hardly underpin a genuine American military ability to project power in Asia.

This *first* possible development will disclose a gradually weakened and weakening United States with lower capabilities to safeguard its own interests. Its credibility as a partner and ally will wither. Asia will face a strange sort of power vacuum and Asian stability will very much depend on Asia's own will and ability to manage this transition as the United States fades away.

The United States can seek to prevent China's rise by containing it, just like it won the Cold War by containing the Soviet Union. This has been a recurrent theme in U.S. strategic thinking for a number of years. One of the most vocal statements advocating a policy of containment came from the Secretary of State in the second Bush administration, when, in 2000, she outlined what she thought should be U.S. foreign policy under a Republican administration. Dr Rice wrote:[80]

> China is not a "status quo" power but one that would like to alter Asia's balance of power in its own favor. That alone makes it a strategic competitor, not the "strategic partner" the Clinton administration once called it…. The United States must deepen its cooperation with Japan and South Korea and maintain its commitment to a robust military presence in the region. It should pay closer attention to India's role in the regional balance.

The United States has constantly encouraged two of its staunchest allies over the decades to enter into a stronger military cooperation and succeeded in its endeavours when Japan and Australia signed a joint declaration on security cooperation in March 2007,[81] but after the change in the political environment in Japan in autumn 2009 this may lose traction. Much of the rhetoric was about North Korea, but few observers doubted that the real target was China, and the agreement an element in U.S. efforts to build up a potential alliance against China.[82] It has tried to draw India into this framework by a number of policy measures labelled a strategic partnership, including an agreement on nuclear cooperation.[83] The United States and India have also started common naval exercises, which are, not surprisingly, watched by China.[84] There is no doubt that the United States and India are moving closer together after many decades of cool relations, but it is an open question how many strategic interests they actually share.[85] Apparently India is willing to move closer to the United States, but not be drawn into some kind of U.S. alliance system directed against China in the context of containment. The same hesitation can be seen in Australia after the change in government at the end of 2007.

The United States has tried to rally a number of Asian nation states in a more or less explicit containment of China or, at least, in keeping this policy option open, but it is doubtful whether the Asian countries share the United States' basic strategic outlook. It seems clear that only a few, at most, are willing to join such a policy around a military vector, while a large number of countries including some hitherto sceptical towards the United States and relying on the network of non-aligned states, are interested in improving ties.

This *second* possible development will therefore be played out primarily by economics and trade means with the United States putting spanners in the works for economic integration in Asia and calling on its partners (Japan and Australia) to do this job. The problem for it with this step is that a buoyant American economy hinges on an economically strong Asia and, in particular, China, so such a policy will slow down economic growth in the United States. It is possible, but unlikely, that it will lead to war. If a military conflict arises, it will be engineered with a political purpose and played out around the issue of Taiwan, or perhaps to fend off offensive Chinese capabilities in space or of a maritime character.

The United States can adjust to a new power balance by promoting Asian integration and adjusting the global steering system to reflect Asian interests more and American/European interests less, while at the same time changing the decision-making procedures.

Such a policy would ensure a smooth transition from the American dominance of global politics and economics to another system, whatever that may be. It still looks possible for the United States to frame such a system in conformity with basic American or rather Western values. The major Asian powers, indeed almost all of Asia, with the exception of some parts with extremist movements, have adopted the Western economic model and moved towards recognition of a large part of fundamental rights of freedom although this movement is stopped or rolled back from time to time.

In short, Asia is not distancing itself from the model put in place by the United States with the support of Western Europe in the immediate post–World War II period. Asia is adopting the model and looking forward to assuming leadership if/when the time is ripe, and that is not just around the corner.

This is a basic element for judging the possibilities for U.S.–Asia relations over the next twenty-five years. There is no alternative system on the plate. What we talk about is the power balance inside the system.

In a longer-term perspective, this *third* development would actually preserve more American influence and power than the two other developments, but it would not look like that in the initial phase when many people would point their fingers at the U.S. president accusing him/her and saying "You give up power and influence where you should have resisted such a change in the power balance."

This third development is the best for Asia, but the most difficult one for the United States as it requires the superpower to give away some of its power to other nation states voluntarily in the expectation and hope that they will show patience and magnanimity, which history does not offer much evidence of. The era of globalization may lead to that outcome, making it clear that all will benefit, but this is far from certain.

An unstated other route even in U.S. debate is that the United States hands the keys to China, with some defined boundaries and dividends, which China will gladly accept. The United States is getting very few natural resources from Asia, and cheap labour will not continue to have its role in political debate in the United States.

## Stronger Nationalism?

It is almost inevitable that almost all of Asia is going to see stronger nationalism. Decolonization made people proud of their own nation states. In many cases these nation states comprise different ethnic and religious groups, calling for the mobilization of a national identity to prevent society from fracturing into groups that do not want to have much to do with one another. Their economic performance showed Asia's population that they could compete with the strongest Western economies, stimulating pride. Large parts of Asia had well-established religions with a strong following among the people, but in other countries, such as China, religion was not the main factor, opening the door for nationalism to emerge as a common thread binding people together.

All this is understandable and good for the future development of Asia. The problem to be analysed is whether nationalism — in some case with the blessing of the authorities — can be contained, preventing the strengthening of societal cohesion and behaviour that may spill over to a national feeling directed against foreigners. If the first option materializes it will be good for Asia; if the second one wins the day, it may turn into a catastrophe.

## Japan

There is disagreement on how strong the growing nationalism in Japan is, what it signifies, and whether it actually means that Japan is reverting back to being a "normal" nation state after many decades of artificial existence under the American umbrella.[86]

Much of the debate rotates around symbols such as the Yasukuni shrine[87] and the choice of the then prime minister to visit the shrine or not, the status of the flag, schoolbooks, and the national anthem.[88] The question that may be seen more from the outside than the inside is whether it reflects a genuine reversal to nationalism or just a return to a Japanese ritual. From an optimistic perspective, a stronger, but moderate type of nationalism is taking over from the almost unquestioned link to the United States.

It is not unnatural that nationalism in Japan or Japanese nationalism has had a rough time. Japan was defeated in World War II and since then American troops have been stationed on Japanese soil. After the war Japan first suffered economically only to stage a phenomenal economic development later that took it to the point where many observers saw it replacing the United States as the world's strongest economy, but which has ended in a financial crisis keeping Japan in some kind of semi-recession since 1990.

With this background Japan may see a rise in nationalism, but most likely in the form of inward-looking pride and not aimed at expansion abroad. In other words, Japan may become more difficult to deal with, more assertive and conscious of its own values, and less inclined to act as the good boy in class who does not question the rules.

It is plausible, however, that younger Japanese see nationalism as an instrument for defensive purposes. One strategic vehicle is the joint ventures with Western powers with Japanese say and influence, indicating that Japan wants to align with European multilateralism rather than China. Another omen could be the Japanese initiatives to step up some kind of European system integration, with a looser role for the United States and Russia, but accompanied by an Asian security arrangement.

The main problem interpreting Japanese nationalism from the outside is the variety of signals and the lack of clear political leadership to show what Japan really wants vis-à-vis China (Japan cannot survive economically without strong links, but does not want to play second fiddle to it), India (too far away and not really a partner vis-à-vis China), Korea (a growing competitor and one disputing offshore areas with oil), the rest of Asia (being drawn more towards China as the upcoming economic giant than towards Japan as the existing one), the United States (Japan does not really want to continue its present role as the obedient partner, but is fearful of changes), and Russia (an unresolved question of high importance for Japan).

## China

Chinese nationalism may actually be a deeper problem, but there seems to be some confusion among observers of what it actually represents.[89] Chinese nationalism is growing and becoming increasingly visible. The outstanding question is how it will develop and whether it will put its mark on China's policy in the coming decades.

Over the last hundred years Chinese leaders have dithered in their assessment of nationalism and, in particular, the role of minorities. In the 1930s Mao Zedong promised China's minorities self-determination, but discarded that policy when he came into power. The Kuomintang took the opposite approach. Sun Yat-sen lauded Chinese nationalism in strong words — "if we want to save China and to preserve the Chinese race, we must certainly promote nationalism" — he argued in the 1920s. Consequently he opposed self-determination for China's minorities, a policy later to be adopted by Chiang Kai-shek.[90]

Internally nationalism may be said to have replaced communism or, rather, when speaking about China, Maoism. It starts to emerge as the common basis for the Chinese not only in China, but also abroad, assuming a strange role like some kind of semi-religion. That makes it easier for the political leaders to rally the people around their political goals, but carries the snag that the minorities are not allowed to express their nationality while watching Chinese nationalism taking shape. This may give rise to difficulties between ethnic Chinese and minorities down the road.

Externally nationalism conveys the message that the time when China was subject to the will of the Western world belongs to history and a part of history the Chinese know, but prefer not to remember. China is fast moving back onto the stage, reclaiming its "rightful" place. Japan is looked upon as the arch-enemy after the wars over the last 120 years, and the Japanese adoption in the interwar period of Western imperialism.

The basic question about Chinese nationalism is whether the political leaders can keep it under control. If so, they may even be able to exploit it to rally the people and the nation around common objectives and, even more important, a common identity, irrespective of vast differences between regions and peoples inside China. If not, it may force them into policies they know are against the long-term interests of China.

The other Asian nation states are keenly aware of the rising Chinese nationalism. While they may not fear it now (except for Vietnam), they may start to do so if it continues to rise. China's political leaders must then prevent a backlash from other Asian nation states in view of the colossal rise in China's power and expectations of even larger power twenty-five years down the road. The fundamental problem is not the combination of nationalism and the exercise of power now, but whether China will continue to act as a benevolent and benign power, and, in this equation, nationalism is not reassuring.

Apparently Chinese nationalism does not constitute a barrier for its change into a country accepting globalization. The Chinese openness — or maybe it is a belief that whatever happens, China and Chinese culture will not only survive, but prevail — makes it possible that nationalism can go hand in hand with a revival of Chinese society. In an optimistic view, nationalism may help open up Chinese society as a glue for keeping coherence (social capital).

## Generational Impact: China and Japan

The young generation growing up in China and Japan harbours completely different images of the outside world, including the perspective of their neighbours, to the ones of their parents. They have neither known the Cold War nor Japan as the rising economic power-to-be punctured in 1990. Their picture of the world and the main players are uncertainty about the United States, Japan as a stationary society, and China as the rising, almost unstoppable, power.

China's youth rules — not the waves as Britain was said to do — but the waves perceived as the Internet. They see it as an outlet for their feelings and, as far as can be judged, they are nationalistic, proud, and sensitive about any kind of insults to the motherland. The former perception among the Chinese to see China as the victim of colonialism or Japanese aggression or American imperialism may still be there, but gathers little traction in today's China.

Japanese youth are dominated by doubts about the society in which they grow up. They have heard how wonderful the Japanese economic machine used to be, but all they know are economic stagnation, difficulties in landing a good job, and doubts about where the political system, which they do not trust, takes them.

They may have mixed feelings about China as they correctly apprehend China as the main competitor, but this is not the same as seeing China as an enemy. They are certainly sceptical about the role Japan has played in the U.S. system and want much more room to manoeuvre to shape Japan's own destiny.

The problem in this equation is that Japanese youth, if disappointed or see their doubts confirmed, may turn against the ruling class, and externally start to see Japan surrounded by foes: the United States, which they do not really like; Korea, which they know does not like them; China, as the main competitor and country assuming the role of leader, which before 1990, could have been Japan's; Taiwan, as a former colony now being coveted by China.

## India

The fight against British colonization plays an important role in India's nationalism, with accounts of how the nation's leaders steered India through the obstacles to independence.[91] This pattern of nationalism is still visible in Indian society. Over the last half a century another characteristic has entered the play in the aftermath of the division of what was British India into India and Pakistan, based on religion. The large majority of Indians are Hindus, but many other religions thrive in the country and the dominating minority religion is Islam, which mobilizes 154 million people, corresponding to 13.4 per cent of the total population,[92] and more than 30 per cent in some states.

While nationalism in China and Japan are not linked with religion (except for Shintoism in Japan) it has been difficult to maintain the same separation in India, despite endeavours to do so. The two major parties, the Indian National Congress[93] and BJP[94] (Bharatiya Janata Party) both appeal to Indian nationalism. The BJP party is seen from the outside as being associated with Hinduism and clarifies its own position vis-à-vis nationalism and religion the following way: "Hindutva or Cultural Nationalism presents the BJP's conception of Indian nationhood, as explained in the following set of articles. It must be noted that Hindutva is a nationalists and not a religious or theocratic, concept."[95] That it is extremely difficult not to mix politics, nationalism, and religion in these circumstances becomes clear when reading Indian newspapers.[96] The example may not be representative and there may be many other newspaper comments and articles available to put these elements in their proper context, but the difficulty in view of India's past and religious, as well as ethnic, minorities are clearly visible.

In October 2008 Prime Minister Manmohan Singh stated, "There are clashes between Hindus, Christians, Muslims and tribal groups. An atmosphere of hatred and violence is being artificially generated. There are forces deliberately encouraging such tendencies." He also elaborated on the danger for India and social and cultural coherence by adding, "Perhaps the most disturbing and dangerous aspect today is the assault on our composite culture … we see fault-lines developing between, and among, communities."[97]

## Pakistan

Pakistan is today the western part of the Pakistan created at the dissolution of what was British India in 1947. The eastern part seceded in 1971 and became a sovereign state by the name of Bangladesh. The western part kept the name Pakistan.

In Pakistan there is unquestionably a strong trend of nationalism, but many observers discuss whether it is Pakistan nationalism or nationalism originated in and heralding ethnic and/or tribal or regional entities.[98]

## Southeast Asia

Southeast Asia has seen both tendencies to nationalism and successful efforts to curb such tendencies. Thailand and Cambodia confronted each other in the early summer of 2008 on a border issue involving a religious site, but managed to get their sentiments under control.[99] Indonesia and Malaysia have seen rising nationalism over the question of Indonesian workers in Malaysia, and disputes on sovereignty over certain islands.[100] They acquiesced in taking the case to the International Court of Justice (ICJ) and accepted its rulings, though they did not cover the entire complex of outstanding matters.[101] Singapore and Malaysia also went to the ICJ and also accepted the decision of the court on the question of a disputed territory.[102] This is good, but should not disguise the fact that neither the issue of the Spratly Islands nor the disputed maritime area of China-Japan-Korea have been taken to court.

There is no reason to hide the possibility that sentiments might have boiled over, and the political decision to go to the court was not undisputed by some segments of society which feel that pride and nationalism speak against such a course. Fortunately wisdom and restraint won this round, but there is no guarantee that it will be the case next time, especially for countries which lost the first case.

For Southeast Asian nation states, the concept of stability as outlined earlier will probably be decisive for whether nationalism will grow or be kept under control. Can nation states and their political systems maintain the three dimensions of stability? Nationalism may grow, but not to a worrying extent, and not threatening stability. If one or more of the three dimensions start to falter, the popular response may turn out to be stronger nationalism.

Asian nation states and/or their political leaders try to stem nationalism from gaining strength and run out of control. This is a laudable effort. The fact is, however, that nationalism is rising in most Asian nation states, and in some cases with an element of religion, making it a potentially inflammable cocktail. There is no guarantee that political leaders in the next twenty-five years will be able to keep their foot on the brake. As has been seen in other parts of the world some political leaders may be tempted to use nationalism in one form or another to get into power, and for their own purposes, thus initiating a development without any guarantee that it can be controlled.

This will be especially true if the economic climate sours, putting Asia on a lower growth pattern than seen from 1978 to 2008, and enhancing the battle for resources needed to create the conditions for growth while at the same time meeting expectations among the populations for a rising living standard. History tells us that in such circumstances the temptation to invoke populism or nationalism becomes strong and, in some cases, irresistible.

## Problems Related to Nationalism, Ethnicity, Religion or Competition for Resources

Asia at the end of the first decade of the twenty-first century is stable, but beneath the surface, a large number of potential conflicts between groups inside nation states, or between nation states, fuelled by one or more of the elements enumerated above, lurk. In a futuristic perspective these conflicts may never arise, or if they do, may find a peaceful solution. Other conflicts not known today may emerge and possibly influence events more markedly. They illustrate the kind of problem many Asian nation states struggle with diverting political attention and economic resources from the development of the nation state.

Many Asian nation states and, in particular, the large ones such as China and India, are extremely sensitive to the attention from outside on their domestic problems and this sensitivity is aggravated when Western sources try to interfere. Rightly or wrongly, they fear that established powers, mainly the United States or, at least, groups in the United States, see domestic discontent as an opening for destabilizing their development and/or derailing them, thus preventing them from rising fast and challenging established powers. This explains the sensitivity, often difficult to understand in many Western circles, when interest is shown in the conditions for minority groups. The following are some minority issues in Asia:

*First*, the position of the Han People, Falun Gong, the Uighur question, and Tibet, are some of the minority issues inside China. Anthropologist Dru Gladney[103] takes the view that China could become further divided along cultural and linguistic lines. China's threats will most likely come from civil unrest, and perhaps internal ethnic unrest from within the so-called Han majority. Gladney supports this thesis by underlining that the Han majority constituting 91 per cent of the population, with the remaining nine per cent split among fifty-five minorities, is more fragile than assumed. The fertility of the Han people is less than for most minorities. They speak eight mutually unintelligible languages (Mandarin, Wu, Yue, Xiang, Hakka, Gan, Southern Min, and Northern Min) and even within these groups, there is linguistic and cultural diversity. The minorities are certainly in the minority, but they live in resource-rich parts of China and often close to the borders.

Falun Gong is a spiritual movement that attracted attention in the 1990s and is apparently seen by the government as a potential destabilizing force, perhaps even aiming to play a political role. The Uighur people are found in the north-eastern part of China — Xinjiang province — and are predominantly Muslim. Tibet is constantly attracting headlines not the least because of the Dalai Lama, who in 1987 was awarded the Nobel Peace Prize.

These three problems, and there may be more and new ones in the future, have one characteristic. In the eyes of the Chinese Government they constitute a threat to the Communist Party and the stability and cohesiveness of China. Many Western observers tend to see them as manageable minority problems, or a question of extending to them certain political or cultural rights, but in the Chinese view, keeping the nation state together is a vital matter that does not leave space for accommodating such groups. It is difficult from the outside to judge their strengths and political goals, but actions taken by the government indicate that they are seen as a threat, and the government's attitude is seen as unconditionally setting the nation state above other interests. The risk in a security context is mainly connected to events that would force strong governmental action, leading to international reaction as was seen with Tiananmen in 1989.

*Second*, India and Indonesia may face analogous problems, albeit not attracting comparable attention. India with its many minorities (ethnic and religious) has gained a certain leverage in dealing with protests, also of violent character, by its political model (democracy) which opens up channels for dissent and for voicing discontent, which China does not offer and so far has not been willing to put in place. Indonesia, likewise, faces minorities, and has also opened channels like India for voicing discontent, even if there is some suspicion that some of the minority problems are hibernating and will raise their heads again. The Aceh problem was solved, but doubts persist on whether it is a permanent solution. These doubts are nourished by frequent rumours that Aceh wants to introduce Sharia legislation.

The Indian and Indonesian policies give rise to the debate on whether a more open political system serves as a safety valve, letting dissatisfied minorities voice their opinions, thus feeling that their grievances are more likely to be taken seriously. This would certainly be a Western view, but so far a large part of Asia does not feel tempted to follow this road, apparently fearing that the situation could run out of control.

Several other Asian nation states (Thailand in its southern provinces) face similar problems.

An illustration of how fragile at least some Asian nation states are is the Tamil conflict in Sri Lanka, which has been harassing the nation state for decades and threatening to break national unity

*Third*, Kashmir is a case where two nation states (India and Pakistan) both feel outside intervention is out of the question, and both regard it as their province, ruling out any say for the neighbour. So far the problem has been managed, irrespective of its potential explosive character, and the fact that it is an issue between two nation states both in possession of nuclear weapons — which actually may be one of the reasons that the lid has been kept on.

*Fourth*, the potentially unstable Myanmar with large minorities and ruled by a military government may, in case of real unrest, not be left to itself, but may trigger intervention from outside, as it has strong Chinese as well as Indian interests.

This is not an easy game for China. The strategic question is whether the military government can be expected to stay in power or will stumble along the road. Having sided with the current Myanmar Government, China may risk a backlash if or when another government takes over. On top of that the Myanmar Government is suppressing Chinese ethnic minorities in the Northern Shan state (Kokang), which cannot go unnoticed by China, just like it cannot but see the closer links between North Korea and Myanmar. On the other hand, China has invested heavily in building a pipeline (Nansan-Kyaukphyu) to bring oil and gas from the Gulf of Bengal into China bypassing the Malacca Strait.[104]

## Arms Race?

Over the last fifty years Asia, in particular Southeast Asia, has kept its military expenditure at a fairly low level, nurturing armed forces primarily for defensive postures and holding back on the really expensive platforms required for offensive warfare.[105]

This is changing. The rising doubts about whether the U.S. military presence on its present scale will continue, more money flowing from high growth rates, offshore oil fields to be protected, and more assertive nationalism, are elements underpinning higher procurement of increasingly sophisticated weapon systems by a number of countries such as Japan, China, Australia, Korea, and Singapore. There are clear omens, not for an arms race, but for increasing military expenditure by a number of Asian countries outside the traditional spheres of potential conflicts.

It is not easy to say whether this trend will continue. There are other factors in the game than those mentioned above. The necessity to use resources for domestic purposes will pull in the direction of reversing this trend.

The determining factor will probably be the level of integration. If Asian countries manage to build a fairly solid economic integration the feeling of trust will grow and that will influence political decisions.

Conventional thinking says that a higher degree of military capability increases the risk of military conflict, but there is actually not much evidence to support this. The main risk for Asian countries of high military expenditure is lower social expenditure such as care for the elderly, education, infrastructure, etc., all of which are essential ingredients in fostering economic growth.

An analysis[106] from 2008 shows that defence spending in Asia, irrespective of the frequently heard comments from many sources, are still fairly modest, both in absolute figures and as a share of GDP.[107] Chinese spending on the military is estimated to approximate 2 per cent, maybe a little lower or a little higher. In absolute terms it amounts to a strong increase as the share has doubled over the last decade, with an economy growing at about 10 per cent per year. Japan's military spending is approximately 1 per cent, while South Korea has a considerably higher share of GDP going into defence, namely almost 3 per cent.[108]

South Asia depicts a similar picture of fairly modest spending, with India more or less at a little over 2 per cent and Pakistan at about 3 per cent. Southeast Asia shows a similar picture, with Singapore operating at a level almost double that of most other countries in the region, which are also slightly stepping up expenditure on their military.

All in all, the entire picture seems reasonably reassuring. Military spending may be going up measured as share of GDP, but not at a tempo and of a magnitude leading to great anxiety.

Comparing military expenditure is a difficult exercise. Some countries use a conscription army, others a professional army with the consequence that running costs such as salaries and barracks, etc., gobble up a high share of the budget, leaving less for military hardware.

The revolution of warfare changes the parameters for a potential arms race. In the future military potential will be determined by navies, cyberwar, warfare in space, and the ability to absorb the change from saturation bombing to precision-guided munitions (PGMs). All three parameters are much more costly than existing military capabilities and change not only warfare, but also determines which nation states or political entities are capable of making war.

Until recently the destruction of a target required a massive use of bombs as the probability of hitting the target was small. This again required mass armies to drop bombs on the opponent, bringing ammunition up to the front, and mobilizing the nation's resources to provide ammunition, transport, and logistics. Therefore wars in the twentieth century might be labelled wars of the people, wars of attrition, or wars of GDP. With PGM, a target can be hit with a high degree of probability, and therefore it calls for efforts in research and development (R&D) to invent and produce such weapons, plus accompanying technology to find and identify targets. This does not require a large population, but a channelling of money into appropriate industries, which can only be done by nation states sufficiently rich to maintain a high living standard for its population, irrespective of the siphoning off of resources for military R&D purposes. Mass armies become a hindrance as they are costly to maintain while not able to deliver what is needed.[109]

So far the United States is the only nation state that has the capability to switch from mass-scale bombing to precision bombing. In Asia the candidates for entering this game can be narrowed down to China, India, and Japan.

The rest of Asia cannot envisage making war without having access to PGM and the accompanying identification and communication technology/equipment in the hands of one of these three powers. Therefore nation states other than the three mentioned above need to get access to the necessary technology via client-state behaviour vis-à-vis China, India, or Japan, or for that matter, the United States. This means that war in Asia depends on the policies of one or several of these powers.[110] Other nation states may manoeuvre to sidestep this trap by buying cheap technology from others more willing to do technology transfers (Israel, Russia, France, Brazil). You get double bang for the buck, plus higher independence from the above-mentioned dependency policies. All Russian strike airplane sales in Asia[111] come with PGM.

## Asian Powers or Global Powers?[112]

### A Model for Transition

Whether the rising economic clout of Asian nation states will transform them into Asian powers and, if so, also take them a step towards becoming global powers, depends to a large degree on the attitude of the United States and, increasingly, of China. In a long-term perspective — probably beyond twenty-five years — this will happen, but while it is likely that Asian nation states will develop fully into Asian powers in the time frame mentioned, it is by no means certain that they either want to or will become global powers.

The game for power, and in particular the ability to exercise power, is changing fast. So far the evidence is scant that Asian nation states are adapting to that kind of game. The United States and, to a certain extent, Europe are being penalized for conventional behaviour when they engage globally in crises and conflicts, ramming the lesson home that traditional powers cannot accomplish what is expected.

In geographic Asia, the outer perimeter of U.S. defence still goes close to China's borders, and even if the U.S. perspective in the Indian Ocean is less visible, the U.S. navy is able to project power in that part of the world.

A smooth transition will take place under two conditions:

The United States must be willing to relinquish some of its power to other nation states, and rising powers must be willing to play within the rules already in place.

To judge from recent behaviour the problem does not seem to lie so much with rising powers such as China and India, which have actually chosen to join the system, as with the readiness and willingness of the United States to realize that the world is changing.

Maybe U.S. experiences in Afghanistan and Iraq, combined with difficulties over Iran, North Korea and some other hot spots, will bring home the message that the time is past when the United States could run the world on its own. There may be very little China and India can do right now outside a perimeter close to their borders, and some other places recognized as their "sphere of interest", but the new observation is that U.S. ability to solve global crises without having at least a number of the new powers on board is diminishing very fast. In other, and less pleasant, words: the United States can do very little alone; China and India can disrupt U.S. efforts around the globe, but do not have much power to shape things themselves.

For the rising powers in Asia to reach beyond Asia and operate on a global level requires a very simple thing, which is not visible yet: an idea of what they want, a global design, and a strategy. The British Empire had such a strategy even if it is outmoded today. The American Empire or whatever word is preferable also had a strategy even if some people will contest it: the vision of shaping a better world. The United States did not use its overwhelming powers to create an empire or to reign over foreign territories.

When Asian nations speak about reforming the global system they point to voting rights that are out of touch with the existing power structure. That is correct and such a system should be revised much more than already done, but they have not so far conveyed any willingness or indication of shouldering the burden of leadership, except of course for local self interests or ambitions.

What applies in daily life for individual persons also applies to nation states and the global power game. If you have power you are only able to influence other people's behaviour in a coherent way if it is clear what you stand for and what you intend to use the power for. Until this happens, no Asian powers will enter the stage as global powers, however strong they may be economically.

Broadly speaking we may define three stages for rising powers to transform themselves into global power.

The *first* stage is when a rising power can choose between joining the system or continuing to play the role of a marginal power in the political choreography. China decided in the 1990s to join the system. India did so in the second half of the first decade of the twenty-first century. Japan has been in the system a long time, but undercover so to speak.

In the later phases of this stage a rising power may be strong enough to block initiatives put forward by others, but not to shape things. It has power and influence to prevent proposals from being adopted, but not to put its own proposals forward. It is strong enough to be invited into the select group of nation states shaping things, instead of having a fait accompli presented to it.

The *second* stage is growing into a stability power, which is a power working inside the system to maintain the system after having come to the conclusion that it benefits from the system and consequently does not really want anyone to rock the boat. In business language it has become a stakeholder in the system, but one of many. It is ready and prepared to go along with the consensus, but neither strong nor confident enough to shape a consensus. It is being consulted in early phases by the leading power(s) and its opinion is taken seriously, but it does not lead. But each time it opts out or does nothing, its "grade" and standing falls, which can easily turn into a domestic issue as its power base may not agree with, or understand, these shifts.

The *third* stage consists of being strong and confident enough to lead and shoulder the burden of leadership. It does not only require power, but two crucial elements. First, that its basic philosophy or societal model must be applicable outside its borders and other nation states have come to the conclusion that its ideas, principles, and values are universal, and not confined to a specific political and/or geographical environment. Second, that it is willing to sacrifice its own interests or advantages in the endeavours to persuade other and less-powerful nation states to join the system.

Asia's great powers are still somewhere in transition from stage one to stage two. As the U.S. model is in demise, they may transit through stage two quickly, provided that they have a model with universal values to offer.

## A Geopolitical Model

Geopolitics revolves around three kinds of major players: stabilizing nation states, unpredictable nation states, and disrupting nation states.

What is happening in Asia in the first decade of the twenty-first century, probably to dominate the picture for several decades to come, are nation states assuming roles as stabilizing, unpredictable, or disruptive power:

- The new emerging Asian powers move into the role of stabilizing powers not wanting to unsettle the existing system.
- The United States, that used to be the main, and may still for decades be the only, stabilizing power, changes gradually to become an unpredictable power with uncertainty over whether it is ready to see a stronger Asia challenging its position in the region, and asking for a say in global affairs, or resisting that change in power and, if so, possibly by military means. The United States' own interest points to an unpredictability, tilting towards stability, an eroded role, and not disruption.
- Russia may emerge as a disruptive power after finding itself uncomfortable in its new role of seeing Asia moving ahead, leaving it behind as a nation state dependent upon energy export and not much else.
- Japan may also move towards unpredictability. Uncertainty about the U.S. role in Asia presents Japan squarely with awkward, perhaps even agonizing, choices. A benevolent U.S. policy towards Asian integration equals U.S. acquiescence of China as the main Asian power. A belligerent U.S. attitude means mobilizing Japan in an endeavour to unsettle Asia's stability, with far-reaching consequences for Japan. The way for Japan out of this dilemma is to break away from the U.S.–Japan alliance system, but thus raising a whole new string of questions about Japan's behaviour.

Fundamental interests among the major powers point towards a non-war scenario with skirmishes and soft power, albeit they may compete for influence and project power, playing the age-old game of rivals and/or competitors. Miscalculations and ethnic and other issues can change this outlook, but a forecast cannot or should not be built assuming miscalculations take place.

The prospect for threats and how they will evolve in Asia over the next twenty-five years depends on:

- Whether the United States continues to deliver stability and implicit guarantor power.
- Diversion of resources, in particular, water and energy enriching one country, but impoverishing another one.
- The risk posed by failed nation states.
- Terrorism or pandemics undermining the well functioning of globalization.
- Inequality and the unknown repercussions of megacities changing societal behaviour towards confrontational attitudes.
- Risk of growing ethnic and social unrest, nationalism to be reckoned with, and weapons build-up in some countries, in particular, giving them precision-guided munitions.

## THE NEW FRAME FOR CONFLICTS

For Asia to continue on a growth path, two elements are indispensable: *first* to maintain and support the rule of law in relations between nation states, and *second* to understand how the parameters of power are developing. They are linked to each other. The changing nature of armed conflict, transforming it from being a war or armed conflict between nation states, or between nation states and various organizations, to *war among the people*, turns war into a competition to capture people's minds. It is not about being in control of any territory, but of getting and keeping the support of the people.[113] Nation states and other participants in conflicts need to understand that; respect for the law, both domestically and internationally, is condition number one. If not, double standards will be accommodated, giving rise to conflicts about the values the combatants have adopted and pursue.

Outside the law, international relations will inevitably slide into survival, not of the fittest, but of the strongest combatants, be it nation states or organizations. Perhaps it will not even be the strongest one that survives, but the most brutal and ruthless one in rolling out a clear strategy.

If power is used, it will be even more frightening and awesome than most people envisage, for one reason: it is becoming extremely difficult to achieve objectives in today's world by using power.

In 1995 I analysed the three components of power — military, financial, and persuasion — and came to the conclusion that military power is losing weight while financial and, especially, persuasive power were gaining clout: "The decisive factor in the international power game in the 1990s is the diminishing importance of military power and the increasing importance of culture, communication, and a set of values, ethics, and ideas as the spearhead in the struggle for power and influence."[114]

This analysis was followed a decade later by two pieces of work on how the United States actually exercised power and with what effect. The conclusion was the same. Military power is becoming more and more outdated and difficult to use and is being replaced by financial and, in particular, persuasive power.[115]

Rupert Smith[116] puts the nail in the coffin of outright military force saying that:

> the shift in the paradigm of war and the continued resistance to it: Politicians and soldiers are still thinking in terms of the old paradigm and trying to use their conventionally configured forces to that end — whilst the enemy and the battle have changed. As a result, the utility of the effort is minimal: the force may be massive and impressive, but it is not delivering the required results, nor indeed any result that is in proportion to its assumed capabilities. As with the difference between deploying and employing a force, this reflects a lack of understanding of the *utility* of force — which is the core issue at stake...

The challenge for Asia and its political leaders is to grasp this shift of power vectors and shape the inevitable conflicts and disagreements inside this framework.

If they manage this, Asia may actually show the way towards a more "civilized edition of civilization" because it can only be done inside relations among nation states governed by the rule of the law. Congruity may arise between the strategic thinking of political leaders, the population, and various groups rooted in ethics, religion, or ethnicity. They will all speak the same language, thus confining the few extremists finding difficulty in recruiting to a marginal role.

The alternative is a traditional nation state approach, with political leaders and the political system relying on military power to solve conflicts, or at least trying to use military power. As this is ineffective, they will need to upgrade the amount of power, thus painting an unpalatable image of themselves and the policies they pursue. People will gradually dissociate themselves from the leadership and seek refuge inside groups, some of which may be extremists praising terror, which also happens to be the language of the political leaders, so what is the difference? Asian societies will start to crack, accompanied by separatist groups seceding from nation states, but held up by military efforts.

Instead of peaceful developments, Asia may witness armed conflicts, not necessarily among nation states, but organized by political structures outside the framework of nation states playing by their own rules: terror.

Asia's foreign and security policies — peace or conflict or armed conflicts — will be determined by the ability of political leaders to sense the swing in weight of the parameters of powers, degrading military power and instead beefing up persuasive power based on the rule of law.

It is likely that globalization will continue and even strengthen, but encapsulated in a regional framework (Europe, Western Hemisphere, Asia, Africa, Middle East, and some of these broken into segments such as East Asia and Southeast Asia).

The ability to safeguard interests depends on the strength of regional integration and how well the integration is handling extrapolation of national policies. It will be up to various regional integrations to tackle most of the problems threatening national and/or regional stability. Nation states will be too weak, and global powers, too impotent, to intervene thus shifting the burden of predictability, stability, and non-disruption to regional frameworks/ institutions. This will call for policies that in today's vocabulary are labelled soft power, to prevent the boat from capsizing.

There will be no superpower filling the same role as the United States did from 1945 to the beginning of the twenty-first century, but China may want that role and the United States may contemplate handing it over. The alternative is not multipolarity as some observers see it, and some nation states talk about, but a much more unstable, perhaps even irrational, power structure built around global governance and powerful nation states playing a leading role in shaping and administering regional integration.

These powerful nation states may well face the genuine problem of keeping themselves intact as centrifugal forces are at work pulling them apart. It is visible in the United States that the Union of its states is far from being as strong as it looks. There are forces in, for example, California and Texas,[117] floating the idea of seceding from the Union. These voices may not be serious yet, but they may gather strength over the next decade or two, threatening not dissolution in a legal sense, but a severe weakening of the Union. Similar forces are at work in China, India, Russia, Indonesia, and several African states, where the glue holding them together may be thinner and weaker as the idea of nationality becomes old-fashioned.

In contrast, medium-sized nation states such as Brazil, Turkey, Mexico, Pakistan, Egypt, Iran — to mention a few — may start to play a much stronger role than hitherto. Some of them may enter the arena as failed states and play a role in that capacity. This calls for action and policies from other nation states to prevent them from destabilizing a region. Other nation states such as Turkey may gain sufficient economic and political strength to ask for much more say in how the region is run. The current geopolitical steering system is not geared to handle an enhanced role for medium-sized nation states.

Asia enters geopolitics as a player in an era characterized by three grand strategic changes:

- Increasing shortages/scarcities instead of easy access to resources.
- An international/global institutional system that does not realize and, is therefore, not geared to the threats from (failed) nation states or forces harboured by nation states rejecting globalization.[118]
- A threat to governance perceived as less emphasis on objectivity, facts, logic, and rational thinking — the heritage from the age of enlightenment — opening the door to governance systems more dependent on irrational feelings, rooted in sentiments often of a religious, nationalistic nature, and sometimes of extreme character. This can rephrased to say that the secular model, defined in a broad sense to be detached from emotions and beliefs, including religion, does not hold the same control over governance as was the case over the preceding 300 years.

Stability and peace in Asia may depend more on the Asian nations and peoples' ability to chart a course in these uncharted waters, than security policy as defined at the beginning of the twenty-first century.

If Asia can maintain peace for the next twenty-five years, it is likely that the rise of Asia will continue. There are conventional threats inscribed in the well-known zone of armed conflicts, but with a few exceptions, they are unlikely to explode. The main risk consists of threats primarily originating within and among populations, derailing societies and hampering growth. Therefore it becomes of prime importance to get a glimpse of how the many elements influencing Asia's future interact with one another. This is the theme for the following chapter.

## Notes

1 See, for example, the 2nd inaugural address 2005 by President Bush <http://www.whitehouse.gov/news/releases/2005/01/20050120-1.html> and the address by Secretary of State Condoleeza Rice, 19 June 2008, to Council of Foreign Relations <http://www.state.gov/secretary/rm/2008/06/106138.htm>.
2 When speaking about such terrorism we normally look upon it almost exclusively as violent. It can, however, be achieved by non-violent means, such as the hacking

of data systems, disinformation, or other kinds of propaganda. With the surge in new media via the Internet such kinds of terrorism where false perceptions are created may take on a more dangerous character.

3 For an analysis and discussion of armed conflict in the future see, for example, Michael Evan, Russell Parkin, and Alan Ryan, eds., *Future Armies, Future Challenges, Land Warfare in the Information Age* (Allen and Unwin, 2004), in particular, Michael Evans' introduction.

4 Rupert Smith, *The Utility of Force, the Art of War in the Modern World* (New York: Knopf, 2007).

5 For a collection of essays setting out the new conditions for war, including RMA (Revolution in Military Affairs), see Evans, Parkin, and Ryan, *Future Armies* and Michael Evans and Alan Ryan, eds, *The Human Face of Warfare* (St. Leonards: Allen and Unwin, 2000). A complete list of works including from Institute of Strategic Studies (ISS), Institut des hautes etudes de defense nationale (IHEDN), and the U.S. Army War College can be found at <http://www.comw.org/rma/fulltext/overview.html>.

6 For an in-depth analysis of terror based on extremism, see Daniel Benjamin and Steven Simon, *The Age of Sacred Terror* (New York: Random House, 2002). The book looks into how extremist terrorism is born, how it works, and what can be done to counteract it.

7 In the Middle East, suicide attacks are aimed at the civilian population, apparently without much thought given to who is being killed, but it is still far from a general attack on the population as such.

8 In Japan it seems that there is a certain analogy to what is happening in the Middle East.

9 It should not, however, be totally excluded that Marxism and Marxist urban guerillas will stage a comeback. They are operating in India and one wonders whether it is an indicator of what appalling social conditions may give rise to.

10 National Intelligence Council, *Global Trends 2025: The National Intelligence Council's 2025 Project* (Washington D.C.: Government Printing Office, 2008) <http://www.dni.gov/nic/PDF_2025/2025_Global_Trends_Final_Report.pdf> and James R. Locher III, "Forging a New Shield", *The American Interest*, 4, no. 3, Winter (January/February 2009).

11 See, for example, Benjamin and Steven, *The Age of Sacred Terror* or Bruce Hoffman, *Inside Terrorism* (New York: Columbia University Press, 2006).

12 Kim Philby, Guy Burgess, Donald MacLean, and Anthony Blunt — the Cambridge five (the fifth member of the group has never been identified although there are some suspects).

13 The United States Commission on National Security/21ˢᵗ Century, Phase III Report, "Road Map for National Security: Imperative for Change", Washington, 15 February 2001 <http://govinfo.library.unt.edu/nssg/PhaseIIIFR.pdf>.

14 In my book *The End of Internationalism or World Governance* (Westport: Praeger, 2000) I have also examined at length the challenges for globalization.

15 See, for example, Stephen Aguiler-Millan et al., "The Globalization of Crime", *The Futurist* (November–December 2008).

16 See, for example, the international activities of Chinese criminal groups outside China at <http://oai.dtic.mil/oai/oai?verb=getRecord&metadataPrefix=html&ide ntifier=ADA439847> or <http://www.loc.gov/rr/frd/pdf-files/ChineseOrgCrime. pdf>.

17 In an analysis on Mexico on 19 October 2008, Stratfor writes: "Mexico is deeply embroiled in a war against violent drug cartels that control substantial portions of the country. The death toll in 2008 alone has risen to over 3,100 and appears likely to hit 4,000 by the end of the year. And the war is not free. The government's ability to respond effectively to an economic crisis while funding a massive military and law enforcement effort is low — and the scarcity of funds could loosen public support for the cartel war as people look to solve their basic economic needs."

18 <http://news.bbc.co.uk/2/hi/business/davos/7862549.stm>.

19 Mobile networks are in essence closed networks with controlled interfaces and much better protected and defended so far.

20 Edward O. Wilson, *The Future of Life* (Knopf, 2002).

21 For references about biodiversity, see ibid. and <http://www.globalchange. umich.edu/globalchange2/current/lectures/biodiversity/biodiversity.html>, and <http://www.actionbioscience.org/biodiversity/simberloff.html>.

22 Each year government officials, computer hackers, and representatives from law enforcement agencies and the communications industry in the United States meet under the label of Defcon to investigate how to make wireless communication more secure. The website <http://www.defcon.org/> offers insight on various aspects and, in particular, risks, making stronger efforts to secure privacy indispensable, but at the same time, more difficult. There are other global bodies doing work in this area such as the International Telecommunication Union (ITU) and European Telecommunications Standards Institute (ETSI).

23 Available at <http://www.fas.org/irp/ops/ci/docs/2004.pdf>.

24 <http://www.ethicalcorp.com/content.asp?ContentID=2574>.

25 <http://samvak.tripod.com/pp144.html>.

26 In 2004 a BBC investigation showed that in only 3–4 per cent of cases where a corporation asked for a check were bugging devices actually found <http://news. bbc.co.uk/2/hi/business/3853913.stm>.

27 About industrial espionage see, for example, Hedieh Nasheri, *Economic Espionage and Industrial Espionage* (Cambridge: Cambridge University Press, 2004).

28 See, for example, <http://ridgeliner7.wordpress.com/2008/07/17/obama-has-secret-groups-on-his-website-to-smear-cindy-mccain-others/> and <http://www. buzzle.com/articles/200392.html>.

29 <http://www.sun-sentinel.com/business/sfl-090808-sentinel-united-airlines, 0,5067344.story>.

30 I have looked into that trade-off and related issues in Jørgen Ørstrøm Møller,

*Towards Globalism: Social Causes and Social Consequences in the Creative Society of the 21st Century* (Paris: OECD, 2000).

31 Paul A. Samuelson, "Where Ricardo and Mill Rebut and Confirm Arguments of Mainstream Economists Supporting Globalization", *Journal of Economic Perspectives* 18, no. 3 (2004): 135–46.

32 <http://www.globalpolicy.org/nations/sovereign/failedindex.htm>. See also Buzan Barry and Gerald Segal, *Anticipating the Future, Twenty Millennia of Human Progress* (London: Simon & Schuster, 1998), pp. 158–215.

33 Claire Lockhart, *Fixing Failed States: A Framework for Rebuilding a Fractured World* (New York: Oxford University Press, 2008).

34 Marla C. Haims et al., "Breaking the Failed State Cycle", RAND, 2008 <http://www.rand.org/pubs/occasional_papers/2008/RAND_OP204.pdf>.

35 Joergen Oerstroem Moeller, "Protectionism in Reverse", *Asia Times* online, 24 July 2008 <http://www.atimes.com/atimes/Asian_Economy/JG25Dk01.html>.

36 *Foreign Policy*, July/August 2007 <http://www.foreignpolicy.com/story/cms.php?story_id=3865>.

37 For a *plaidoyer* (defence) of international law and global rules, and a critique of recent events undermining such a state of affairs, see Philippe Sands, *Lawless World* (London: Allen Lane, 2005).

38 It does not excuse the behaviour by, for example, the United States and the United Kingdom in not respecting international law, but it does explain why they act as they do.

39 Of ninety-five participating members, twenty-one come from Asia, including parts of the Pacific (2009): Afghanistan, Australia, Brunei Darussalam, Cambodia, Fiji, Japan, Kazakhstan, Kyrgyzstan, Marshall Islands, Mongolia, New Zealand, Papua New Guinea, Philippines, Republic of Korea, Samoa, Singapore, Sri Lanka, Tajikistan, Turkmenistan, Uzbekistan, Vanuatu. Source: <http://cns.miis.edu/inventory/pdfs/psi.pdf>.

40 <http://usinfo.state.gov/products/pubs/proliferation/>.

41 To illustrate, the U.S. National Defense Strategy June 2008 mentions cyberwar five times as a potential threat to U.S. security <http://www.au.af.mil/au/awc/awcgate/nds/nds2008.pdf>.

42 On cyberwarfare, see, for example, <http://www.security-gurus.de/papers/cyberwarfare.pdf>; the CRS Report for Congress, 19 June 2001 <http://www.au.af.mil/au/awc/awcgate/crs/rl30735.pdf>; "Cyber Warfare is Becoming Scarier", *The Economist*, 24 May 2007 <http://www.economist.com/world/international/displaystory.cfm?story_id=9228757>; and a list of incidents where cyberwarfare has been used at <http://staff.washington.edu/dittrich/cyberwarfare.html>. About electromagnetic spectrum, see for example, <http://imagine.gsfc.nasa.gov/docs/science/know_l1/emspectrum.html> and about its role in warfare, see <http://www.globalresearch.ca/index.php?context=va&aid=7681>.

43 One of the first books analysing cyberwarfare and the battlefield in cyberspace is James Adams, *The Next World War* (London: Hutchison, 1998).

44 <http://www.strategypage.com/htmw/htiw/articles/20080520.aspx>.

45 <http://www.defensetech.org/archives/004363.html>.

46 <http://www.computerworld.com/action/article.do?command=viewArticleBasic&articleId=9021663>.

47 See *Christian Science Monitor*, 14 September 2007 <http://www.csmonitor.com/2007/0914/p01s01-woap.html>.

48 Information Warfare Monitor, 20 September 2008 <http://www.infowar-monitor.net/modules.php?op=modload&name=News&file=article&sid=1880> and Technewsworld, 29 May 2007, available at <http://www.technewsworld.com/story/57593.html?wlc=1221909872>.

49 It should be borne in mind that both the United States and the United Kingdom have an interest in signalling high defence posture, which may not necessarily mean that this is the case!

50 "War and PC, Briefing Cyberwarfare", *Jane's Defence Weekly* 45, no. 39, 29 September 2008.

51 Center for Strategic and International Studies (CSIS), "A Report of the CSIS Commission on Cybersecurity for the 44th Presidency" (Washington D.C., 2008) <http://www.csis.org/media/csis/pubs/081208_securingcyberspace_44.pdf>.

52 Louis-Francois Pau, "Business and Social Effects of Denial of Service Attacks in View of Scaling Economic Counter-measures", MPRA paper posted 7 July 2009 <http://mpra.ub.uni-muenchen.de/16115/1/MPRA_paper_16115.pdf>.

53 *Business Week*, 7 December 2008, "US is Losing Global Cyberwar" <http://www.businessweek.com/bwdaily/dnflash/content/dec2008/db2008127_817606_page_2.htm>.

54 *Los Angeles Times* reported on 27 November that "Senior military leaders took the exceptional step of briefing President Bush this week on a severe and widespread electronic attack on Defense Department computers that may have originated in Russia — an incursion that posed unusual concern among commanders and raised potential implications for national security", article headlined "Cyber Attack on Defense Department Computers Raises Concerns" <http://www.latimes.com/news/nationworld/nation/la-na-cyberattack28-2008nov28,0,6441140.story>.

55 See, for example, "Report of the Defense Science Board/Air Force Scientific Advisory Board", Joint Task Force on Acquisition of National Security Space Programs, Office of the Under Secretary of Defense for Acquisition, Technologies and Logistics (Washington D.C., May 2003) <http://www.fas.org/spp/military/dsb.pdf>, "US Leads in Preparing for War in Space", *International Herald Tribune*, 9 March 2008 <http://www.iht.com/articles/2008/03/09/america/space.php?page=1>, and <http://www.wired.com/science/discoveries/news/2004/02/62358?currentPage=1>.

56 It is likely that China will continue to expand its conventional military capabilities, emphasizing *anti-access and aerial denial assets*, including developing a full range of long-range strike, *space* and information warfare capabilities (italics mine), *US*

*National Defense Strategy*, June 2008, mentions cyberwar five times as a potential threat to U.S. security <http://www.au.af.mil/au/awc/awcgate/nds/nds2008. pdf>.

57 BBC, 23 January 2007 at <http://news.bbc.co.uk/2/hi/asia-pacific/6289519. stm>.

58 See, for example, *China Security* 4, no. 1 (Winter 2008): 134–47 <http://www. wsichina.org/cs9_9.pdf>. For a political — and short — analysis, see BBC, 25 September 2008, "What's Driving China's Space Efforts?" <http://news.bbc. co.uk/2/hi/science/nature/7635397.stm>.

59 <http://groups.google.com/group/soc.culture.china/browse_thread/thread/ ab0c9ad38fc3af7b>.

60 Norman Angell, *The Great Illusion*, first published in 1909 under "Europe's Optical Illusion", and then in 1913 under its well-known title. For a short description, see, for example, <http://wwi.lib.byu.edu/index.php/Norman_ Angell's_The_Great_Illusion>.

61 The Hague II Convention of 1899, titled "Laws on Wars: Laws and Customs of War on Land" says in the preamble "Considering that, while seeking means to preserve peace and prevent armed conflicts among nations, it is likewise necessary to have regard to cases where an appeal to arms may be caused by events which their solicitude could not avert". The text of the Convention is available at <http://www.yale.edu/lawweb/avalon/lawofwar/hague02.htm>. At a conference in 1907, the major powers agreed to lay down rules for how "civilized" nations opened hostilities against each other. In the preamble to the Hague III Convention, it says that "The Contracting Powers recognize that hostilities between themselves must not commence without previous and explicit warning, in the form either of a reasoned declaration of war or of an ultimatum with conditional declaration of war." The text of the convention is available at <http://www.yale.edu/lawweb/avalon/lawofwar/hague03.htm>.

62 The common border is also a contentious issue. China has managed to settle all outstanding border problems, except for the land border with India. The stakes, however, do not look sufficiently large for either side to catapult it into a category leading to war, albeit a lot of harassment and accusations will undoubtedly be heard and seen.

63 If water is the criterion the Mekong basin may also be *casus belli* (act or situation provoking/justifying war) for several countries in case one of them implements plans for disrupting the flow of water downstream.

64 Michael Heazle and Nick Knight, eds., *Twenty-First Century: Creating a Future Past?* (Edward Elgar, 2007).

65 <http://www.bangkokpost.com/news/asean-summit2009+/157845/exclusive-interview-with-japanese-prime-yukio-hatoyama>, <http://www.kantei.go.jp/ foreign/hatoyama/statement/200910/10JCKkyoudou_e.html>, <http://www. japantoday.com/category/politics/view/japan-sees-asean-at-core-of-east-asian-community-but-stresses-us-ties>.

66 The Information Office of China's State Council, "China's National Defense in 2008" (January 2009) <http://news.xinhuanet.com/english/2009-01/20/ content_10688124.htm>.

67 China's navy is by far the largest, with 255,000 men, 62 submarines, including 3 SSBN and 6 SSN, 75 surface ships, and 792 naval aircraft. The Indian navy has 55,000 men, 16 submarines, 48 surface ships, and 109 naval aircraft. The Japanese Maritime Self Defense Force has 44,500 men, 16 submarines, 53 surface ships, and 239 naval aircraft (all figures from IISS, *The Military Balance 2008* [London: Routledge, 2008]). Numbers may, however, not tell the whole story as a ship is basically a weapon's platform, implying that the weapons on the ship are more indicative of its combat value than the ship itself. The Japanese navy is probably the most technologically advanced (missile defence and attack capabilities) of the three major navies in Asia.

68 Head of CIA, Michael Hayden, 30 April 2008 <http://afp.google.com/article/ ALeqM5jJVdy3K_8QdPpbZALQoSaTBcRKkQ>.

69 The new U.S. carrier type (CVN 78 Gerald R. Ford class) will be approximately 100,000 tonnes in size, and take more than ten years to build — and there is only one shipyard capable of doing that — at a cost of $11 billion, on top of which comes expenditure for ships to protect the carrier and aircraft etc. The U.S. Navy's new class of surface combatant (DDG-1000 Destroyer) is set at $5 billion per ship.

70 Economic Strategy Institute, "China–Taiwan Economic Ties", 8 April 2005 <http://www.econstrat.org/index.php?option=com_content&task=view&id=9 7&Itemid=59>.

71 Afterwards the true figure was set at not much more than 25 per cent.

72 Economic figures from the following two publications: *North Korean Paradoxes, Circumstances, Costs, and Consequences of Korean reunification* (RAND, National Defense Research Institute, 2005) <http://www.rand.org/pubs/monographs/2005/ RAND_MG333.pdf> and *Straddling Economics and Politics, Cross-Cutting Issues in Asia, the United States, and the Global Economy*, Chapter 38: "Managing the Costs of Korean Reunification if it Occurs" (RAND, 2002) <http://www.rand. org/pubs/monograph_reports/MR1571/MR1571.ch38.pdf>.

73 See the two RAND studies cited in note 72.

74 Seen from the outside, a U.S. attack looks extremely unlikely, but the picture may be different from a North Korean perspective, who have analysed U.S. policies towards the country over decades and have observed what has happened to Afghanistan and Iraq.

75 Pakistan is like many other nation states born under pressure in the wake of decolonization, not rooted in historical facts, but with its people kept together by more ephemeral elements making the identity linked to the nation state less strong, thus leaving the option open for many of its citizens to change their loyalty in case an alternative is offered.

76 Part of this paragraph is sourced from my article, "ASEAN's Relations with the

European Union: Obstacles and Opportunities", *Contemporary Southeast Asia* 29, no. 3 (2007). For an excellent overview see Lay Hwee Yeo, Ian Zaur, and Mette Ekeroth, *Conflict Map of Southeast Asia, Conflict Prevention; Actors, Institutions and Mechanisms* (Singapore, ASEF, 2006).

77  In this context it is permitted to exclude the role of the United States in helping/ forcing Japan to open up towards the outside world in the second half of the nineteenth century.

78  In the U.S. National Defense Strategy 2008, China is the first major power to be mentioned with the words "China is an ascendant state with the potential of competing with the US.... The objective ... is to mitigate near term challenges while preserving and enhancing U.S. national advantages over time" <http://www.au.af.mil/au/awc/awcgate/nds/nds2008.pdf>. When surfing the Internet it is easy to find information and discussion originating in both the United States and China of war between the two countries, see, for example, <http://www.foreignpolicy.com/story/cms.php?story_id=3913> and <http:// theimpudentobserver.com/world-news/doomsday-scenario-china-us-war/>.

79  See, for example, Paul Kennedy, *The Rise and fall of the Great Powers* (New York: Random House, 1987).

80  Condoleeza Rice, "Promoting the National Interest", *Foreign Affairs* 79, no. 1 (January–February 2000): 56.

81  <http://www.mofa.go.jp/region/asia-paci/australia/joint0703.html>.

82  See, for example, Nautilus Institute Austral Policy Forum 07-07A, 15 March 2007, "The New Security Architecture: Binding Japan and Australia, Containing China" <http://nautilus.rmit.edu.au/forum-reports/0707a-tanter.html>.

83  The U.S. policy towards India is enumerated in President Bush's statement of 22 February 2006 heading a White House fact sheet called United States and India: Strategic Partnership, available at <http://www.whitehouse.gov/news/ releases/2006/03/20060302-13.html>.

84  "India, US to Hold Biggest Joint Naval Exercise", Xinhua, 29 September 2003 <http://english.peopledaily.com.cn/200309/29/eng20030929_125192.shtml>.

85  A short analysis of U.S. and Indian interests and where they converge or diverge can be found in *South Asia Monitor*, no. 105 (April 2007) <http://www.csis. org/media/csis/pubs/sam105.pdf>.

86  Eugene A. Matthews, "Japan's New Nationalism", *Foreign Affairs* (November/ December 2003); Japanese Nationalism Links, "World Future Fund" <http:// www.worldfuturefund.org/wffmaster/Reading/Japan/Japanese%20Nationalism% 20Links.htm>; Yumiko Lida, *Rethinking Identity of Modern Japan: Nationalism as Aesthetics* (London: Routledge, 2002); Kevin M. Doak, *A History of Nationalism in Modern Japan* (Boston: Brill, 2007).

87  <http://www.japan-guide.com/e/e2321.html>.

88  <http://news.bbc.co.uk/2/hi/asia-pacific/347224.stm>.

89  See a good summary at Council on Foreign Relations, "Background: Nationalism in China", 23 April 2008 <http://www.cfr.org/publication/16079/>.

90 Jasper Becker, "The Chinese" (New York: The Free Press, 2000). For nationalism in Chinese thinking earlier than the 1930s, see, for example, Jonathan D. Spence, *The Search for Modern China* (New York: Norton, 1991).

91 <http://uk.encarta.msn.com/encyclopedia_781531173/indian_nationalist_movement.html>.

92 <http://en.wikipedia.org/wiki/Islam_in_India>.

93 <http://www.congress.org.in/>.

94 <http://www.bjp.org/>.

95 <http://www.bjp.org/philo.htm>.

96 What was particularly striking was the willingness of the Indian public to give the Congress and other centrist forces an opportunity to revive a democratic political agenda that would emphasize both growth and distributive justice, while steering clear of contentious political projects such as the fomenting of Hindu nationalism. Given that in recent years the battle for the hearts and minds of the Indian voters has been largely dominated by the discourse of the BJP and the left parties, the Congress party's stark failure to capture the national imagination — reduced as it was to a caricature of its former self as the vanguard party of Indian nationalism — had vacated a crucial space in the political field, depriving the Indian voter of an alternative to these two extremes of right and left. *The Hindu*, 8 July 2008, "The Congress Party's Last Chance" <http://www.hindu.com/2008/07/08/stories/2008070854610800.htm>.

97 <http://english.aljazeera.net/news/asia/2008/10/2008101423027693849.html>.

98 See, for example, Adeel Khan, *Politics of Identity, Ethnic Nationalism and the State in Pakistan* (Sage, 2005), refereed with the following words: "A provocative, passionate and stimulating new interpretation of ethnic nationalism" — Dipesh Chakrabarty, University of Chicago, "A significant study that informs us of the politics and group interests in one of the most volatile regions of the world" — Stephen Castles, Oxford University, "Very interesting intellectual and political ideas — refreshing" — Gyan Pandey, Johns Hopkins University, "An informed and lucid work that demystifies the politics of nationalism" — Howard Brasted, University of New England. A major challenge Pakistan has been confronted with since it came into existence is the self-assertion of various ethnic groups, which have actively contested the legitimacy of the state structure. However, despite the seriousness of this ethnic challenge, there exists no detailed study of these movements; Politics of identity fills this vacuum. Ethnic nationalism, the author argues, is a political issue and is essentially a struggle for power between dominant and non-dominant groups. Highlighting the role the state plays in the lives of individuals, the book which studies both the pre-colonial and colonial state system in India and the changes it effected until India's independence and the creation of Pakistan, assesses the state in Pakistan and explains its role in giving rise to ethnic discontent; studies four ethnic movements — Pukhtun, Baloch, Sindhi and Mohajir — demonstrating how their proximity to or distance

from state power have influenced their politics. Available at <http://books.google. com.sg/books?hl=en&id=RYr6cKyF1o0C&dq=pakistan+nationalism&printsec= frontcover&source=web&ots=wXnHtWfLVe&sig=dHIp_UwsMN1LcqT4xE3R tA0Wank&sa=X&oi=book_result&resnum=7&ct=result#PPP1,M1>.

99  See, for example, "Thai-Cambodian Temple Standoff Continues", 21 July 2008, *New York Times* <http://www.nytimes.com/2008/07/21/world/asia/21cambodia. html>.

100 See "Indonesia Tests Ties with 'Arrogant' Neighbour", *Asia Times* online, 19 March 2005 <http://www.atimes.com/atimes/Southeast_Asia/GC19Ae03.html>.

101 See <http://en.wikipedia.org/wiki/Indonesia-Malaysia_Border>.

102 "Pedra Branca Ruling a good start but…", *Straits Times*, 25 May 2008 <http:// www.asiaone.com/News/The%2BStraits%2BTimes/Story/A1Story20080525-66883.html>.

103 Dru C. Gladney, "China's Ethnic Fault Lines", *Wall Street Journal*, 16 July 2009 <http://online.wsj.com/article/SB10001424052970203547904574279952210843672.html?mod=rss_com_mostcommentart#articleTabs%3Darticle>.

104 Ian Storey, "Border Conflict a Test of Beijing's Influence", *Malay Insider*, 3 September 2009 <http://www.themalaysianinsider.com/index.php/opinion/ breaking-views/36746-border-conflict-a-test-of-beijings-influence--ian-storey>.

105 In some countries, such as Indonesia, the role of the armed forces has been linked to the development of society more than to a military proper role. The armed forces have constitutionally been allocated an important role in nation building and devoted a lot of their efforts to non-military activities, for good or for worse.

106 "Defence, Economic Trends in the Asia-Pacific", Defence Intelligence Organisation, Canberra, 2007 <http://www.defence.gov.au/dio/documents/2007_DET.pdf>.

107 These figures do not always allow us to distinguish between weapons acquisition and production and military wages.

108 Japan is still (2007) the biggest spender measured in U.S. dollars with approximately US$45 billion compared with China's approximately US$38 billion, but the gap is closing from US$35 billion ten years ago, to US$8 billion in 2007. A very high share in Japan are weapons, and this share is growing in China too, while Korea's (South) is still dominated by a high share for wages etc.

109 See, for example, George Friedman, *The Next 100 Years* (New York: Doubleday, 2009), Chapter 10.

110 Maybe also Russia.

111 Based on public information, Russia has sold the older MIG 29 design to Bangladesh (8), Azerbaijan (14), India (62), Kazakhstan (36), North Korea (42), Malaysia (19), Myanmar (10), Uzbekistan (30), and Turkmenistan 20). The MIG 35 was first presented in 2007 at the Indian Aero Show.

112 For a collection of essays discussing China in this context, see Kjeld Erik

Brødsgaard and Bertel Heurlin, *China's Place in Global Geopolitics* (London: Routledge, 2002).

113 An example of how military force was used — not to project power — but to gain influence was its deployment in early 2005 by the United States to help Indonesian victims of the tsunami. All in all, 15,000 U.S. military personnel were involved. After the operation, 79 per cent of Indonesians said they had a more favourable view of the United States and its overall favourable rating rose more than 20 percentage points. The need for restructuring military forces in this context is discussed by Lawrence J. Kobb and Max A. Bergmann in "Restructuring the Military", *Issues in Science and Technology* 15, no. 1 (Fall 2008).

114 J. Ørstrøm Møller, *The Future European Model* (New York: Greenwood, 1995), p. 54.

115 "A Nationalistic United States of America", 10 and 17 October 2007, *National Interest* online and "The New Media Inc.", *National Interest* online 27 October 2006, both co-authored with Terence Chong.

116 Rupert Smith, *The Utility of Force, the Art of War in the Modern World* (New York: Knopf, 2007).

117 <http://blogs.abcnews.com/thenote/2009/04/texas-governor.html>.

118 In a philosophical way it can be said that two cornerstones of the international system over the last 350 years are questioned: first, the Westphalian system introducing sovereignty of nation state, sovereignty anchored territoriality, and the exclusion of external actors from domestic authority structures; second, the European nation state concept evolving after the Napoleonic Wars.

# 7

# INTERACTION

The first part of this chapter takes as its starting point the analysis of the main elements classified in three groups in Chapters 3, 4, and 5: those supporting growth and stability; those liable to work for or against these, depending on policymakers' decisions; those seen as obstacles; and as a fourth item, foreign and security policies capable of derailing the development. The stage is then set for examining how the various elements interact with one another and what the decisive issues are for the interaction. This will provide some tools for showing where policymakers have to be vigilant, and also provide a glimpse of some early warning signals indicating in which way Asia is moving.

The second part is an attempt at forward looking analysis based on two assumptions: *first*, that Asia continues to stick to the Western values adopted during its industrialization over the last thirty years, and *second*, that the economic model and political system remain essentially untouched. Fundamentally it is an extrapolation.

## THE FOUR TRIUMVIRATES

Broadly speaking Asia's future can be defined inside four triumvirates of three key issues, each interacting in turn: external environment, domestic policy issues, technology/corporate governance, and environment/quality of life.

The various elements inside these triumvirates interact and the triumvirates interact with one another, pushing Asia towards either a sustainable growth model, or creating obstacles and casting doubts on the future, and even raising the spectre of the implosion of Asian societies, or at least instability.

## The External Triumvirate: Globalization, External Security, and Economic Integration

A *high* commitment to globalization cements Asia's role in economic globalization, opens the door for Asia to take on the role as guarantor of globalization, while at the same time pursuing regional integration. Asia moves from an inactive role to being an active global policymaker. Instead of adjusting to the system as it is now, with policies defined by determining powers such as the United States and Europe, Asia starts to shape or require international/global rules. This will benefit Asia's productivity and competitiveness as rules tune in to favour Asia's production structure and investment patterns. Globalization will still function globally, but gradually turn around to serve as a vehicle for Asia, instead of the United States and Europe. International institutions providing the institutional framework for globalization will tend to be governed by Asia's interests with regard to substance as well as decision making.

This leads to the interesting question of whether Europe (EU) and possibly North America (NAFTA) will in turn adopt similar models of using globalization to serve more regional integration, meaning a two-speed externalization pattern, with high regional interaction complemented by medium (or average) global interaction.

External security depends to a large extent on the commitment to globalization as the plinth for high and sustainable growth among most of Asia's countries and certainly the larger ones. Growth means that there is enough to share, and negotiations among countries to distribute the benefits or enter into the more difficult exercise of burden sharing, become easier to manage. The internal security threat in the form of question marks on globalization, terrorism, and related issues are less likely to arise with economic growth than with stationary economies. The recruitment base for dissatisfied minorities or other groups wanting to attack globalization erodes. Fewer resources need to be diverted to external and internal security, allowing more money to be channelled to other priorities such as research and development (R&D), social welfare, and stakeholder responsibility for globalization.

Economic integration, although it is most likely to take the form of regional integration, rests on a commitment to globalization and external security, removing fears and doubts about neighbouring countries' policies. Growing trust among Asian countries further integration, making it easier to find solutions in common to analogous problems/challenges, and boosting growth through a larger market, the freedom to localize, etc. Gradually a sense of mutual trust and an understanding of a common destiny filter through, creating a political environment to solve Asia's own problems and for it to emerge as a stabilizing global player. Economic integration brings a number of economic advantages and benefits among which the prospect of a synchronized business cycle may be the most important one, but the main benefits are to be found in mutual trust, thus freeing resources hitherto devoted to defence purposes to go into activities furthering economic growth and sponsoring societal values. The impact of the idea that a country knows it can rely on its neighbours, in case of difficulties help will be forthcoming from them, supplemented by the knowledge of a geographical region's capability to solve its own problems without having to fall back on far away countries or global institutions, cannot be overestimated. An issue that may complicate this stems from Asia's cultural, religious, and thus educational heterogeneity which, being higher than say in the European Union, may limit to some extent the abovementioned, mostly economic and trust-based integration.

This positive interaction confirms that commitment to globalization is the right policy that delivers results for the domestic economy and establishes a benevolent political climate in the region. The door opens for even stronger commitment which paves the way for deeper integration, with the advantages such a policy entails.

A *low* commitment confines Asia to inward-looking economic policies, which past experiences show are deemed to give a lower growth rate, with depressing and discouraging consequences for forging a social fabric able to withstand the problems facing Asia in the next twenty-five years. It would be risky to expect domestic growth alone to shoulder the burden of maintaining Asia on a high growth.

Politically and psychologically it would nail down Asia and confine it to policies dominated by uncertainty, perplexity, and irresolution which spill over to domestic policies. It is seen in North America and even Europe, despite a largely shared cultural and historical base, globalization threatens to freeze countries in angst and fear over their ability to compete. Such attitudes emerge as barriers for taking advantage of international trade and international investment, but what is even more worrisome is the impact on the mindset of countries which hampers their competence to adjust and adapt.

A study by Wing Thye Woo[1] focusing on the United States and the fear of globalization among American workers supports this view. It comes to the conclusion that technological innovation and globalization have been good for labour income, but not for job stability as the median job tenure for workers has decreased markedly over the last ten years. The impact of job insecurity is stronger in societies such as the American one, but also in China, where social welfare is less generous than in countries where the social safety net alleviates the economic woes following from unemployment. Despite all declarations about Chinese growth, it should be recalled that the majority of the Chinese population is poor, and that the workers pushed out of towns in 2008 by unemployment due to the global crisis, are quickly exposed to the same insecure feeling. This insecurity has also spread to the Chinese middle class with average incomes of US$5,000 a year, which allows them to consume, but not with a feeling of secure consumer spending.

The fear of globalization cannot be confined to only this feeling of insecurity, but holds countries back from steering a course controlled by change and flexibility. Instead it induces them to be petrified, with negative consequences for their ability to tackle other social, economic, and political problems. They lose confidence in their own performance, thus closing the door for intrepid behaviour.

The fear about a neighbour's intentions will grow and internal insecurity rise as lower growth provides propitious grounds for terrorism and other disruptive activities. Financial resources need to be diverted from growth policies to respond to social problems, with the unavoidable consequence that economic growth falls even more.

There is no strength and will to engage in integration, and less support for globalization makes it difficult to further regional integration, depriving countries of the advantages of living in a solid international environment. The leadership role in globalization is not met, giving other countries the opportunity to shape global rules according to their interests, which enhances the already existing fear of globalization being a racket used by somebody else to further their interests.

A gathering of these forces tends to push in the direction of narrow-minded, even myopic, policies, resembling xenophobia which sow distrust among Asian nations at a juncture where the opposite is called for.

## The Domestic Triumvirate: Growth, Social Stability, and Innovation

The crucial factor is that in today's world change means stability. Theoretically change can take place in a stationary society, but is much more difficult than in a growth society. With growth ideas and entrepreneurship, added resources or production capacity can be channelled into new sectors, balancing out the negative impact on declining sectors, whereas adjustment in a stationary society requires moving production capacity from one sector to another without much time in-between for adaptation. The inability to adjust forces unwelcome and often abrupt changes on societies in a way and time frame not of their own choosing. By adaptation a society keeps the handle of change in its own hand. *High growth* facilitates adaptation and change.

Only if a nation, society, or corporation constantly changes to incorporate new circumstances and conditions from outside (technology, fundamental business opportunities linked to, for example, deregulation, culture, other countries, etc.) will it be possible for a society to be stable, in terms of upholding its basic values. This can be illustrated by two examples, one positive, the other negative.

Positive: *first*, the entry of China in the global economy meant that labour-intensive industries moved from industrialized countries to China. Those industrialized countries trying to hold on to labour-intensive industries were forced to see them leave under acrimonious circumstances, that is, with employment problems, whereas those industrialized countries shifting into another gear and focusing on industries competing on non-wage-sensitive parameters, were able to maintain their social structure relatively unscathed. *Second*, the formation of economic integration forces countries to shift their efforts to shape rules from the domestic to the international arena, to make sure that the framework for political and societal preferences is unchanged. Those understanding this saw their participation in economic integration take shape without much controversy while those clinging to labour-intensive industries have had to deal with the allegation that economic integration lies behind upheavals caused by economic globalization, although integration is an attempt to deal with such problems.

Negative: Saudi Arabia and Russia — where their clinging on to natural resources and trying to hike their prices instead of diversifying and integrating into the global network over a range of economic activities have led to an economic and industrial structure dependent on these resources.

Growth is often misinterpreted and/or misunderstood. Its function is to provide financial resources to implement political objectives. Society's resources are mobilized behind efforts to realize the goals set by the political elite and population. Without growth few political goals stand any chance of being achieved as money is simply not available, or, if available, may be wasted because of the lack of constructive reforms. Consequently growth is not an end in itself, but a set of means to implement policies and achieve social ambitions. The second observation about growth follows from this understanding, meaning that growth is not enough in itself; it may be even more important to see what kind of growth is on the plate. Almost all societies look for growth congruous with political objectives. Some societies may prefer low growth and high income equality; others may be willing to accept high inequality to achieve higher growth. Some countries, especially over the last decades, accept or even want growth, regardless of external diseconomies, such as pollution and the negative impact on the environment. A study calculates the total cost of air and water pollution in China in 2003 to be between 2.68 per cent and 5.78 per cent of gross domestic product (GDP), depending on which definitions are used.[2] A study looking at the United States estimates the total costs flowing from emissions of some air pollutants (particulate matter, nitrogen oxides, ammonia, sulphur dioxide, volatile organic compounds) to be between 0.7 per cent and 2.8 per cent of GDP.[3] For the European Union,[4] the cost of air pollution is estimated at between 0.4 per cent and 1.3 per cent.[5]

One of the most comprehensive studies of the negative impact on society as a whole of environmental damage was undertaken by the Organisation for Economic Co-operation and Development (OECD) in 2008.[6] The verdict is "the costs of policy inaction in a number of environmental areas are significant and are already affecting economies in a manner which shows up in market prices and national accounts both directly and indirectly". The study does not, however, put figures for societies on the costs of inaction to stop pollution.

Social stability and social capital both depend on mutual trust among groups and subgroups in society and the decisive factor for achieving that is a set of common and shared values. Individuals, groups, corporations, and organizations work together to strive towards the same objectives, using the same instruments, not because they have to or are under some kind of threat or pressure to do so, but because they want to as they have what is most essential, namely, common and shared values. Decision making becomes faster and requires fewer resources. Enforcement measures are only brought into play in few and exceptional cases. Trust and confidence among individuals and between individuals and organizations increase productivity. Distribution of income and wealth is not a priority because people are ready to share with those having the same values. It then becomes easier to pursue an economic policy delivering higher growth even if it may be temporarily difficult and requires sacrifices from all or only part of society. Race and religion become less important issues in domestic policy, so these sensitive questions can be removed from the agenda of politics. In Asia, the sharing of values is a key issue as the selection and build-up of these values have been torn in all directions by history (from Maoism to Japanese Imperialism, from Christian values in the Philippines to Muslim extremism in Indonesia).

A political system based on shared values enjoys confidence and legitimacy as its population regards it as theirs and sees shared objectives based on their input. There is money available to guarantee human security, build up a trustworthy defence against potential enemies, increase living standards, and channel resources into developing the society according to the preferences of the population. The majority of the people find that the system delivers what they ask for. Knowing that they enjoy the trust of the population makes political leadership easier. Strategic visions can guide policies.

There are many examples from history of how the feeling among political leaders that they enjoy the confidence of the people makes it easier for them to make what they think are the right choices, irrespective of burdens; and how fear of the people, based on the knowledge that power was not obtained in a legitimate way, or uncertainty about whether people's expectations have been fulfilled, freeze political leaders.[7]

The triumvirate of high growth, social stability, and confidence in the political system serves as a base for a smooth-running society, with few conflicts, but instead a widespread understanding of where it is going, and with people rallying around these objectives and the means to achieve them. The benefits are enormous.

*Low growth* means that irrespective of political goals and their support, they cannot be achieved because the money or trust is not available. Rivalry among policies and sometimes also among political parties/leaders starts to determine priorities, pointing out which policies to divest or downgrade, and which ones to favour. This initiates infighting among groups as policy objectives are normally laid down according to preferences among groups to obtain an equitable distribution of benefits. The underlying social contract binding groups together which form the backbone of society needs to be broken to bring objectives in line with means (growth). Giving up or introducing downsizing policies is synonymous with putting one or several groups' particular interests on the backburner. This struggle could lead to social instability, degrade social capital, and trigger loss of confidence in the political system.

With less total resources available, group members will tend to stay closer together and this raises awareness of other groups' behaviour. Social capital may increase within these groups, but decrease between groups, making it much more difficult for society to function as a whole. Common and shared values as the plinth for society cannot be upheld. The low social coherence and rivalry among groups necessitate a complicated and elaborate set of laws to regulate economic and social life. Societies and countries are transformed into a control-based "organization" gobbling up large resources that might otherwise have been used for productive purposes. Enforcement becomes increasingly frequent, which in turn calls for more and more resources. Social welfare becomes difficult to finance with public budgets, with the inevitable result that people begin to finance their own welfare, leaving those who really need help and assistance adrift, and opening the door for higher inequality of income and wealth.[8]

The political system stumbles when trying to deliver human security, a defence posture against potential foreign enemies, and raising living standards — all at the same time. Increasingly more people lose interest in the national political system, preferring instead to build up regional, sectoral, or group networks. The result is a more decentralized country where power may sometimes glide into the hands of criminal syndicates or political movements, totally breaking with existing norms and/or working for their region's secession from the country in question. Low confidence forces the political system to devote more resources to communicate with the population, or alternatively, to isolate itself in quasi-dictatorships. A gap arises between perception and reality as politicians try to rally support by promising more or painting a more positive picture of what is happening than the realities warrant. Mutual distrust sows the seeds of disruptions as legitimacy wanes. A variant of this are populist policies where politicians, in a vain attempt to gain support, recklessly use what is left of the country's financial resources, or deliberately rob the wealthy part of the population to pay out sums to the majority, hoping to gain their support.

Economic and social life runs into higher friction, augmenting the cost for economic transactions and reducing the incentive to invest for both domestic and external investors.

## The Technology/Governance Triumvirate: Technology, Culture, Organization, and Education

This triumvirate is basically about a positive and mutually stimulating interaction among new technology, new culture, and organization that increases growth potential and focuses upon high-value-added production or services. It has, however, an even more important function and that is to tune society to change and adaptation. So much has been written about the need for change that a repetition sounds like a platitude, but the core of the matter is that new technology forces the mindset of people to change, and during this process, may make change a permanent element of the mindset of the individual and societal behavioural patterns. It is not technology itself that matters, it is the impact of new technology on people's mindsets, opening them up to do things they did not know about before new technology, or to do things differently.

New technology, through interaction with culture/behaviour and societal organization, not only enhances productivity, but transforms society into a risk-taking and sharing society and brings along new products, new consumption patterns, and new production methods. An open society in every sense of that word comes into being.

Education seen as performance of the individual is the key. An education system prioritizing the ability to change, teaching how to handle changes, how to implement them rather than rely on conceptual/dogmatic theories, and preparing the young generation for a constantly changing society, may not only increase productivity, but also reduce the risk of social tensions in the wake of changes. The challenge is to go for the right mix of individualism, creativity, and teamwork. At first glance these may not seem compatible, but without all three a society cannot, in the long run, achieve any of them. Individuality is required because every individual must be aware of where his/her comparative advantage lies. Do what you are best at, is a slogan used by some businesses, but it is of crucial importance for the individual steering his/her way into active life. So individualism is not about keeping a distance from other human beings, but analysing one's own competences, comparing them to competences of others, and then choosing where to concentrate. Creativity enters the picture to find out how to create new knowledge or results, and also how to use new technology to improve performance. This is much more important for a society than creativity in the sense of innovation, which is more likely to take place within corporations and groups than at the individual level. Teamwork is the flywheel for using new technology as its main virtue is that it can be used by many people at the same time and its impact on productivity and social cohesion is proportional to how many people use it — at least for information and communication. It also hangs together with the building of social capital, making individualism more apt at building social capital.

Governance, corporate as well as government, is in itself a competitive parameter. Good governance helps to produce a rule-based society where most of the rules are unwritten and understood by the population and require little or no enforcement. Multinational business, idea makers and entrepreneurs, and the global elite are attracted by such a society which then augments its purchasing power. Transparency is well known as a decisive parameter for economic activities because trust is the foundation of economic transactions. Predictability enhances risk taking as risks can be calculated, and calculations are unlikely to be disturbed by events inside the system, and a societal safety net (e.g. social welfare) applies in case of failure. There will not only be trust between those conducting these economic transactions, but also between them and those providing the underlying societal and government structure. For technology to spread and be applied in a society not confined to pockets of people, good governance is decisive.

Many countries and/or societies are too small and have too limited financial resources to assume leadership in science, humanities, and/or innovation, but they are not too small to smell where new technology emerges and what it is. Many of these societies build up a network via good governance to intercept and subsequently adapt new technology for their own purposes — that is, incorporating new technology into another societal framework which fulfils a role other than the originators had in mind. To do so, governance is necessary because an infrastructure suitable to such activities needs to be at hand and it differs from the kind of infrastructure needed to make technological breakthroughs. Governance may not be able to shape or prevent new innovations, but it may be able to further or block adaptation of new technology suitable for the society in question.

Low contributions to science, culture, and technology, besides aversion to new technological trends, not only keep an economy locked to cost and wages as competitive parameters, but also keep society in a petrified structure, resenting new cultural behaviour and resisting change, thus resulting in a risk-averse society. The interaction of technology-culture-organization is prevented from getting in motion, the society or country remains in the mould of a society heralding past performances — reiterating models, systems, and methods that worked then — but is a complete failure as a modern society. New developments coming from outside meet stiff opposition from structures and norms, thus encouraging the part of the population ready for change and to take risks to leave.

Young people will not only be less adept at handling change, but also grow into a dissatisfied mass, threatening social stability and sometimes family structures. Their education will conform to yesterday's societies, measured by international standards. Information and communication technology opens the window for them to compare things so they will know that they are left behind, compared with similar generations in other countries. A gulf arises between them and progressive political leaders. Reactionary political leaders may get wind in their sails. Businesses may still invest, but less and less investment will be in future-oriented sectors, leaving the country with an inefficient production structure. Low governance, accompanied by nepotism, corruption, and a low-quality legal system, distorts economic fundamentals, thus leading to non-optimal allocation of skills and scaring away multinationals and the global elite.

Apathy or aversion to new technology and cultural creation not only embodies the risk of keeping productivity low, but spills over into a society steered by angst and fear for the unknown and what is coming from outside, which thus resists incorporating all major trends such as technology and globalization. The reward for welcoming new technology is the opening up of opportunities for groups ready and willing to try not only new technology, but also new cultural patterns, thus breaking down barriers for people to mix with others adhering to other cultures having other values.

## The Environmental/Quality of Life Triumvirate: Scarcities, Burden Sharing, and Social Coherence

Scarcity of food, energy, commodities, water, and a clean environment, plus urbanization, cannot be dealt with separately. A global battle about burden sharing is about to begin and Asia, with its rising population and high growth, will be in the eye of the hurricane. It is one of the decisive factors determining whether Asia can turn away from prioritizing economic growth and instead emphasize what kind of economic growth is preferred. Keeping in mind the growing awareness of the costs embedded in "full speed ahead growth" we see hope that Asia may rise to the challenge. The main challenge is neither economics nor technology; it is societal.

The problem is the mindset of individuals, corporations, and communities/groups still engulfed in the conventional belief that growth is good, yes, even indispensable, irrespective of negative side effects. If these are sufficiently big to be addressed it can be done at a later stage when society has grown richer. This attitude neglects the fact that a societal model frames infrastructure. If a society has steered down the road of "growth before environment", the infrastructure has been built to accommodate resource guzzling and polluting systems. Reversing priorities is a costly and time-consuming affair.

The car is the obvious example. If Asia's cities are rebuilt to accommodate the car the costs of transforming transport infrastructure away from the car will be enormous. On top of this comes the problem of reversing consumer preferences. This explains why at this juncture Asia has a chance to set a course avoiding many of the mistakes made by the United States and Europe.

The sustainability industry, perceived in the broad sense of the word, may turn into the next driver of economic growth. This may seem paradoxical, but not if one analyses it thoroughly. As a more "ecological" growth frees resources for other purposes, this kind of growth will increase the financial resources available for solving other societal problems and not diminishing them. Corporations entering the sector of developing and producing sustainability equipment will get an edge not only defined in economic and technological terms, but even more from being on the crest of the wave reshaping local contexts and social interactions. The spillover to the rest of society will be enormous as it becomes clear that high growth can be attained even when reducing pollution. Asia's ability to shape global rules for the environment, including environmental aspects of trade, will weigh heavily on its ability to continue growth.

One of the first steps is increasing energy efficiency. The reason for starting here is the tremendous potential for results in the short run spilling over into other beneficial effects, such as lower energy bills and less dependence on outside suppliers — a factor that may help to reduce military spending. Most important, however, is the fact that a drive for energy efficiency is reaching out to the large majority of people. In the battle for changing mindsets, signs that it works are needed. Reducing pollution of various kinds will be visible and tangible for a large number of people, but the only element really reaching out to almost everybody is energy efficiency, where every citizen can see on the bill that the effort for a better environment pays off. Better energy efficiency reduces energy consumption and people paying less will have more money to spend for other purposes. This is the kind of social engineering playing on many keys at the same time, but experience indicates that as a first step, people must feel and understand that it is profitable for them. The Asian Development Bank (ADB)[9] has analysed the opportunities for energy efficiency for Southeast Asia and concludes that "there are vast, untapped opportunities for energy efficiency improvements". Indonesia, the Philippines, Thailand, and Vietnam together have the opportunity to mitigate up to 40 per cent of their combined, energy-related, carbon dioxide emissions per year by 2020. Another 40 per cent could potentially be mitigated by a variety of measures, such as switching fuel from coal to gas and renewable energy in power generation at a cost below 1 per cent of GDP.

This is not a hidden argument to augment technological imports from the West, or have the West "pay for the changes", but a genuine argument to drive and redirect domestic growth and its social engineering aspects.

If we assume that oil prices and consequently energy prices in the coming twenty-five years follow an upward trend, there is a clear competitive advantage to be reaped by investing in infrastructure and equipment enhancing energy efficiency and conservation.[10] The higher a country's and its domestic corporations' energy efficiency, the lower will be the additional costs to meet energy price increases; and the higher the ratio between a country's energy efficiency and competitors' energy efficiency is, the greater the advantage to be gained. The problem may be that the initial investment requires money now while the benefit is to be gained over a number of years, but there is little doubt that the benefit outweighs the cost.[11] The investment amounts needed for conservation are far less than investments in more new energy generation, so there is ample room for local initiatives.

Ecology can serve as a stabilizing factor enhancing the quality of life and helping to create social stability and social capital. The whole idea of producing more with fewer resources may — if it takes root — initiate another way of thinking, more in conformity with future trends and departing from the age of plentiful resources. Ecological problems, not to mention ecological disasters, create social tensions resulting in recriminations among groups accusing one another of causing the problems, followed by attempts to shift the burden of paying for cleaning up the mess among groups. As very few ecological problems are confined to limited geographical areas — in many cases the pollution deteriorates the environment far away from its technical source — the potential for a negative impact on social capital is obvious.

If the scarcity factor is not solved through a new "ecological" growth model based on sustainability, societies face growing physical scarcity of some commodities and economic scarcity of a large number of commodities, jeopardizing growth. In an attempt to square the circle, countries may be lured towards an even more old-fashioned growth model requiring more financial resources, but as the problem is more output for less input of commodities, more conventional growth will not help — it will aggravate the problem.

Pollution and environmental growth will gradually expose lack of social coherence as citizens and corporations start to compete for resources that grow increasingly scarcer. If other parts of the globe manage to move ahead with a new growth model, Asia will be left behind in an agonizing box of too few resources to satisfy the needs of too many people, asking for too much material welfare, and even asking, as part of an environmental blackmail, other parts of the world to finance in part this wrong spend. Asia's competitiveness will be undermined as the rest of the world cannot be expected to put up with countries producing in what will be labelled un-environmental ways. This would lead to trade restrictions (such as $CO_2$ emission taxes on imports) as the rest of the world introduces standards that Asia cannot meet.

Social capital will be undermined, opening the door for countries, societies, and communities to come in that do not hang together. However, increasingly the seams burst, giving rise to acrimonious recriminations among the groups.

An understanding of "ecological" growth promotes sustainability by saving resources and freeing resources for other purposes, plus it strengthens social capital. At the same time new industries are born in the sector of sustainability, sponsoring new technology and providing the opportunity for setting global standards. Ecological growth can combine growth, new physical landscape, technology, and social capital to show the way towards a new societal model. Alternatively these three elements can stall either separately, or fail to work together, keeping societies within the existing box of industrial growth with all the calamities this implies.

## INTERACTION AMONG THE FOUR TRIUMVIRATES: THE WHEEL OR THE TRAP

For Asia's future one of the determining issues may be whether it manages to combine the four triumvirates to steer the development path towards positive interaction. As the elements inside the four triumvirates support or obstruct one another, the four either work together or against one another — there is no middle way.

While the itinerary from 1980 to the present time has been straightforward, the future seems to hold an "either-or" prospect. Some kind of middle solution, where Asia keeps the ship on an even keel with modest growth, looks like an illusion. It is much more likely that Asia and the world will face a new Asian model or a breakdown of the existing model.

Growth and stability are two sides of the same coin. No growth or low growth endangers social stability; social instability dents growth prospects. The problem is that growth will no longer come to Asia by itself — policies and some new processes or attitudes to that effect must be designed and implemented. If Asia and its political leaders strike the right balance between changes and opportunities, Asia can look forward to an era of stable growth; otherwise the prospect of social unrest framing the lives of three billion people jumps from being of theoretical or localized interest, to a policy perspective to be reckoned with. Also, if no such stability is engineered by proper changes, there is the danger of social differences spilling over to regional conflicts, even wars. In this context growth has to be perceived and defined as the kind of growth that not only increases resources, but frees resources for sustainable productive purposes, instead of having to allocate a share — and a rising share at that — of it to remedy imbalances and social or environmental problems created during the process of growth.

### The Wheel

High growth creates financial resources and confidence to develop society in conformity with political objectives, thus enhancing the legitimacy of the government and making it possible for it to deliver on its promises. Groups or societies or communities find it worthwhile to lay the foundation for nationwide social capital, facilitating the sharing of benefits to make everybody not necessarily happy, but satisfied that the country, community, or society in question offers better terms than if they stand outside.

From this flows the kind of political stability supported by the grass roots (as opposed to political stability enforced from the top), not only as a platform for strengthening domestic cohesion, but also as a signal to other countries in the region that the risk of nationalism or xenophobia is low, thereby building up confidence and trust among nation states. Economic integration becomes easier and nation states realize the obvious advantages as do their various populations. A higher degree of confidence among adjacent countries reduces the need for resources to guard against threats or disturbances coming from the outside, freeing resources for domestic policy goals, thus confirming the benefits of integration.

Social capital works in the same way for domestic policies, moving the country and the population towards a value-based political system where people, organizations, and corporations choose a way ahead in conformity with congruous values. This diminishes the size of resources to be allocated to enforcement or repair patches as conflicting interpretations of what is right and wrong will be exceptions rather than the rule.

If they have confidence in political leaders, the political system and the business sector will be more willing to run risks and the population will be ready to accept this. A more entrepreneurial societal model becomes feasible and workable, opening the door for R&D, accompanied by innovation, inventions, and new products. The people trust that if they stumble in their endeavours to integrate new technology, the government will come to their rescue. With a social safety net, plus a confident political system, the road to technology and cultural-based societies opens up. The ultimate role of pacesetter and trendsetter — to be the place where new behavioural patterns are born — may gradually move from the United States and Europe to Asia.

Education may enjoy the benefits of such a changed attitude in the sense that new forms of education and training will be tested. The system may be more courageous in deviating from the conventional norms and trying to instil adaptability and change in the mindset of students, rather than having academics impose static conceptual theories or dogmas on them. All in all, more daring and bolder societies may follow from such a positive interaction — societies that seek new ways and methods, are open to new ideas, notions, behaviour, and technology and confident enough to reward path-breakers while still caring for those finding it difficult to keep pace.

A better education system intercepting new trends, tolerating creative individuals, delivering good governance, enhancing social capital, and integrating new technologies in society, works in favour of shifting the emphasis of growth from the quantitative aspect to the qualitative aspect, that is, "ecological" growth, which is synonymous with getting growth without much deterioration of the environment and without too high external diseconomies. In practical terms, this means that the overwhelming part of growth is real growth, which does not subsequently need to be redirected to cope with, or alleviate the detrimental effects of purely material growth pushed through without regard to the negative side effects on the economy and society as a whole.

Positive interaction creates bold societies with high social coherence and social capital that are able to free resources from non-productive and, in some cases, counter-productive purposes, channelling them instead into productive use and enlarging the scope for society to attain its objectives. Negative interaction keeps society in an outdated frame with low social coherence, forcing it to use resources for non-productive purposes (enforcement, anti-pollution measures etc.), drawing money away from core policies, and gradually destabilizing society, which threatens to turn social instability into political paralysis.

The crucial question for a society is how it uses and is forced to use its resources and skills. In other words, how much room for manoeuvre it has or, even better, can it create for itself, faced with a limited amount of resources and skills.

One option is that the maximum of resources can be devoted to pursuing objectives high on the list of priorities, established in collaboration between the population, the government, and business, and working in an economic and social environment where obstacles to policy objectives are few and/or relatively easy to remove. The alternative is a social structure defined by exogenous and endogenous factors, pushing it towards the use of resources and skills for non-prioritized objectives, and constantly being diverted from doing what it wants to do by having to address less relevant problems arising as obstacles to its priorities.

The wheel creates growth, enlarging financial resources, marshalling them into productive use in conformity with social and political objectives, enhancing social coherence and social capital, reinvigorating culture, establishing the foundation for solving environmental problems, and strengthening the links based on trust between the population and the political leadership — taken together, all putting Asia in the role where it can shoulder a rising share of global leadership and framing the global development in conformity with Asia's interests.

Asia gains strength, muscle, and confidence to part with the established, conventional model and search for a new model suitable to the problems rising on the horizon and calling for solutions which the existing model forged in the industrial, nation state era cannot deliver.

## The Trap

Low growth or even medium-growth provides too few financial resources and relevant skills to meet all political objectives. Growth will be insufficient to keep social development going according to political objectives tacitly agreed between the population and the political leadership. Most of the growth will be in the mould of the industrial era, accompanied by social imbalances and environmental problems asking for a visible share of the growth to remedy the negative impact created by it. Instead of freeing resources for creative and productive purposes, the resources created by growth need to be channelled back, meaning that real growth perceived as resources for continued development of resources may increase, but at a falling rate. Figures may show high growth, but in reality, growth may decelerate or even turn into sluggish growth strangling further development.

Policymakers (governments) are gradually, but surely, being pushed into a corner where segments and/or groups of society fight for scarce resources, which hinders a flow of resources into growth, keeping productivity growth low. As seen so often, the likely result is that the large majority of people become dissatisfied and build up resentment against the political leadership. Everybody wants more, even if there is less, more precisely, there is less of more to distribute from, leading to an acrimonious domestic battle of distribution not only of income and wealth, but also of the right to use resources or skills and shape life in conformity with the traditional lifestyle dictated by cultural identities.

Trust and confidence between political leaders and the majority of the population fade, to be replaced by rising discontent undermining attempts to build social coherence and a social contract.

The social fabric starts to crack, introducing not only social, but also political problems, with the result that a large part of Asia moves into an "unhappy" scenario where growth begins to follow a downward spiral, and opportunities for turning the development around narrow, while unsolved problems occupy the agenda.

Longer-term prospects for growth and societal development suffer as fewer individuals are motivated or can contribute to creativity and entrepreneurship, less financial resources are available for R&D, technology, innovation, and inventions, starving the economy of investment in activities to deliver tomorrow's growth. What resources are available will be canalized into sectors promising immediate results irrespective of their long-term impact. Not only are future growth prospects being cut, but the economies are pushed down the value-added scale, confining countries to compete more and more on costs and low wages, in itself a blind alley leading to distributional struggles and social confrontations.

The urban districts having attracted labour in times of high growth can no longer deliver jobs and growth. The result is a social urban proletariat as a propitious basis for social unrest, unrest growing out of dissatisfaction, possibly nourishing terrorism or other kinds of groups that contest the prerogative of the government and the state to govern. Parallel societies emerge, attracting disgruntled people and creating their own communities isolated from the rest of society.

Asia loses its position as the most promising part of the world and sees its growth prospects disappear. It turns into a sullen global partner, finding itself uncomfortable inside the existing global system without really knowing what to propose to replace it.

Among the Asian nations an ugly picture of rivalry and agonizing burden sharing starts to grow. Countries try to shift as much of the burden as possible to neighbours, which obviously resist such attempts and try to shift the burden on other countries themselves. Trust among countries breaks down, economic integration stalls, thereafter to crack, and Asia moves into a stage where conflicts, even armed conflicts, triggered by failed burden sharing, leads to a fight for resources.

Asia sees no way out of the straitjacket defined by the industrial, nation state model, and irrespective of disappointments and experience, continues to apply methods offered by that model with the inevitable result that it sinks even deeper into the quagmire.

## INDICATORS

Scenarios and forward thinking are interesting as catalysts for thinking, but as policy instruments they need to be accompanied by a set of indicators (that are not too difficult to access) telling policymakers which one is emerging as the likely one. The indicators themselves have to be studied dynamically for points of inflexion or tilting, and clear aggregation rules must be explained to trace back to root facts.

Economic growth — preferably per capita — is the obvious number one indicator, and as growth figures are available at relatively short notice, it is a reasonably good indicator. For our purpose, the composition of growth ranks as equally decisive, giving a rough indication of consumption (private and public), investment, and exports. Likewise even a crude indicator showing the state of sustainable development would help. If total growth goes up based on investment, and sustainable growth falls, the picture is discouraging. The problem with a more refined growth indicator is the time lag as it is available much later than traditional growth figures.

Asset prices compared with the real economy reveal whether the economy is balanced in terms of whether economic activity is steered by production instead of wealth. The production of goods, and also services, is a solid, long-term basis for growth while wealth is or can be ephemeral. It can be measured in many ways. One of them is the ratio of property prices to real disposable income; another is the price-earnings ratio for stocks compared with historical figures. Asset inflation out of tune with realities not only distorts the economy, but hints that social capital may be low — people prefer assets to bank accounts.

The match between education, skills, and what the economy requires is a prime indicator showing whether a society is on the right course towards growth and harmonious societal development.

The evolution and direction of the education system is reflected by, among other things, the number of students abroad, how many of these return, how many foreign students come to Asia not only to study Asian languages, but other disciplines, and the ranking of Asian universities and number of Asian universities among the top hundred in the world. Asia needs a couple of universities in the top ten to serve as flagship universities, proving that Asia can offer high quality education on a par with the best American universities.

Literacy falls in the same category.

The state of the financial system is a good weathervane. Basic questions such as the number of financial institutions, competition, share of wealth deposited in bank accounts, corporate and private bankruptcies give early warning signals about the economy and social capital.

Environmental yardsticks will unquestionably be a major item in the future.[12] Energy efficiency,[13] solid waste, and air plus water quality are easily measured. Deforestation, coal as share of total energy also come to mind.

Technological progress can be read by, for example, the number of patents,[14] outward versus inward foreign direct investments in high technology, the number of enterprises in high technology, and information and communication technology (ICT) infrastructure (penetration of broadband and mobile). The World Bank has developed a model to help countries identify the challenges and opportunities they face in making the transition to a knowledge-based economy.[15]

Governance has several aspects. The quality of the financial system is dealt with above. Nepotism, corruption, and a lack of transparency are published yearly. Corporate governance is also followed closely by many surveys. An analysis of the adoption of the triple bottom line,[16] or similar accounts, reveals how linked corporations feel to society.[17]

Income disparity indexes and poverty level indexes tell about inequalities and thus indicate the risk of social instability.

The crucial factor for social stability is trust inside the nation state, which is measured frequently. The use of the Internet to voice dissatisfaction is an interesting tool.

Megacities also provide indicators. On the upside, we can see how much talent, purchasing power, etc., are drawn to Asia's megacities. On the minus side we have the crime rate, divorce rate, the number of lonely persons, etc., pointing to social disruption. The crime rate is fairly easy to monitor and available almost without any time lag, giving a good indication of whether megacitities are moving towards stability or instability.

Demographics present a number of good indicators.

A simple and easily available indicator to show that "something" is happening is the fertility rate. It may go up or down for various reasons and it may not be easy to tell why, but it is beyond any doubt if it moves visibly, there are underlying social changes. A broader yardstick is the annual Human Development Index,[18] but its usefulness as a tool to adjust policies is diminished by a time lag of more than two years between its calculation and its publication (the index for 2005 was published at the end of 2007 to mention an example).

The divorce rate reflects, to a certain extent, social stability, especially as children brought up with only one parent are more likely to contest societal values.

Experience indicates that a high percentage of people between fifteen and twenty-five years of age constitute a danger for almost any society. This was seen in France in 1968 and it is seen nowadays in large parts of the Middle East, Iran, and Pakistan. The young people come out of school or finish higher education without much prospect of getting a job and have nothing else to do than voice their discontent, indicating that here is propitious ground for any movement wanting to challenge the established system.

## MAIN FACTORS INFLUENCING THE INTERACTION: FLYWHEELS FOR TAKING POLICY DECISIONS

### The New Industries to Emerge

The common denominator is that industrial development will swing away from traditional manufacturing towards human demand steered by the size and composition of population, quality of life, increasingly longer life as consumers with taste change over the life cycle, and have strong purchasing power.

The *first* vector is the human maintenance sector increasing almost phenomenally in importance. The rising number of people moving into the age bracket where they will need care and health services will change consumption patterns and open the door for new industries and services catering to this segment of consumers. Pharmaceuticals, care, health services, and biotech look like a certain bet for being probably the most dynamic industrial sector. Much depends on the ability of managers to read the demand correctly. Will the Asian population as it grows older follow the same pattern as has been seen in Europe and the United States, or will the world see a different consumption pattern among elderly people in Asia?

The *second* vector is human improvement/performance. Education, learning, skills and the upcoming industry exploiting the change in consumption pattern born out by Book 2 Screen may be a runner-up in the game for the most dynamic industries. Education seems set to be one of the most important industries in the coming decades. The change is to provide not only education as such to a rising number of people, but tune it to future needs. Gone are the days when learning was dominated by the school and a static pool of knowledge. In the future the world will discover learning and teaching to shape human beings to be capable of living and working under new conditions.

The *third* vector may well be human leisure and a meaningful life. Entertainment is one of the sectors under this heading, but in a broader sense, fantasy and dreams enter the picture. The visual world and all the new gadgets have opened a Pandora's Box and the race is on to exploit opportunities by finding out what the consumer wants and in some cases tell the consumer what he/she can get. In a culturally rich Asia, it also means revival and new cultural developments.

Human interaction via the Internet has probably seen its most dynamic days, but will continue to be a strong and dynamic sector offering networks and media channels to people. The challenge is that these networks will not stand alone. They will depend on an element of interaction as have already been seen with Facebook and other hitherto unknown activities.

## The Financial System

Asia's financial system has shown weaknesses most visibly in 1997/98, but perhaps more important, seen when one analyses its ability to channel savings into investment, convert its savings into global assets, and to promote social capital.

Asia's savings will remain high, but not as high as has been the case for the last decades. The financial system as the flywheel for transforming savings into investment projects assumes a much more important role in the next twenty-five years. The analytical ability to screen investment projects must be improved to ensure that the most responsible and sustainable ones receive the capital, while less promising projects do not. For a financial system used to an abundant supply of money, this does not come by itself. The system itself and governments need to put in an effort to that effect. The alternative is a system that receives savings, but continues to immobilize a part of the savings, allowing Asian countries to finance economic activities abroad instead of so-called "structuring" investment in Asia. This has been the case over the last decade or two, as the surplus on balance of payments, in particular for China, bears witness to, but the problem has been surmountable as the savings rate has been sufficiently high to finance both domestic investments and purchase foreign assets, but failed to go into social capital altogether. In short: Asia cannot afford to allow capital to be immobilized/neutralized this way plus screening methods to channel savings into the most responsible and sustainable investment projects are needed.

It is almost a contradiction in terms that countries on the path of rapid industrialization export capital instead of importing capital. Asia's financial systems have not been geared to assume this unexpected task, with the result that a large part of the savings has been used to buy low-performing assets (over a long term horizon) such as U.S. treasury bonds. Only recently, prodded by the subprime crisis, has Asia been alerted to the anomaly and started to purchase better investment assets abroad. This will offer opportunities to increase their international investment activities, but in the long run, the region delivering global savings — and Asia looks likely to maintain that role — must rise to the occasion and shoulder more, much more responsibility, for how the global financial/capital markets are run. The present situation where financial institutions in the United States and Europe shuffle around with Asia's savings is clearly not tenable. Global financial institutions born out of Asia should arise over the next twenty-five years, anchoring Asia firmly in economic globalization not only as a player, but as one of the main players, and perhaps some time in the future, the playmaker, unless the investments become purely regional (a pattern followed by Japan).

Corporate and public governance in the financial and public sector is a weathervane of solidity, confidence, and social capital inside nation states. It is also an indicator of the confidence the rest of the world shows towards the economic powerhouse being born in Asia. This is why well-run financial and public institutions are not only essential for maintaining high economic growth, but also for keeping confidence in political systems and among citizens and citizens institutions at a high level. Experience indicates that the financial sector is among the first sectors to crack if, or when, societal structures crumble. In a way the financial system serves as a litmus test for social capital — people dare trust other people with their savings instead of accumulating cash, foreign currency, and gold.

## Private Consumption

Consumption is the purpose of all economic activity and the role of trendsetter for consumption patterns ensures high profits, but so does the role of cultural centre, from which new cultural behaviour spreads out.

Economic history gives ample proof that high growth depends on high consumption. Exports and investment may for some time drive economic activity, but in the long run, only consumption can fill that role.

Asia has grown used to high savings rates and at the moment they are actually going up because of the developments in countries such as India and Vietnam; but savings can also go down due to population ageing (Japan) or outright poverty (Bangladesh). Unless a better balance is found between savings and consumption, Asia risks being caught in a growth trap with declining exports, an overhang of investment, and a hole in social/pension investments, depressing future economic growth. Based on traditions and social structure it is unlikely to see public consumption rising and in some cases it is politically ruled out.

This leaves private consumption, coupled with pension and medical schemes, as the only thinkable and sustainable driver for economic growth in the next decades and probably even longer. The theory put forward by Walt W. Rostow[19] that economic development falls in stages, ending with mass consumption as the main component of overall demand, is still basically valid as borne out by statistics from OECD countries over the last twenty-five years which show private consumption accounting for approximately 70 per cent (US), 60 per cent (Eurozone), 60 per cent (Japan) of GDP with only minor changes.[20] This, however, serves only as a valid argument when social and pension capital stocks have been built up, as they have in OECD. In short, Asia needs to breed its own consumption culture, coupled with pension and medical schemes, and if unsuccessful the odds are that economic growth will start to level off.

Even more important for the structure of the economies is the ability to move in and act in the pricey segment of brands, reputation, lifestyle, and identity. This is where price does not matter and high profits can be found. To take this step further, this is also where the industries in question start to dominate the rest of the world, radiating tastes and sketching behavioural patterns. Such industries not only emerge as very lucrative ones and manifest themselves as powerhouses attracting talent, ideas, and imagination transforming an economy from manufacturing to meeting the demands mapped out above. Interaction between consumption patterns and new industries guarantees both high growth and the ability to set the pace and direction of consumption.

## Asian Megacities

This is where the biggest and most visible clash between divergent trends may take place. And this may be where Asia's future is decided.

Agglomerations with more than twenty-five million inhabitants may become common in Asia towards the middle of this century. The world has never seen such agglomerations, let alone, many of them. There are no precedents for judging whether they will be able to maintain social coherence, work and function like an entity, solve traffic and other infrastructure problems, keep pollution and emissions at a low and tolerable level, and prevent different layers and/or groups from threatening one another. So far the experience is limited and the examples — of which there are a few in Asia, a few in the Western and South American hemisphere, and maybe one or two in Africa — do not provide definitive clues.[21] The really new thing may not be the size, but the speed with which agglomerations will rise out of cities hitherto with between five and ten million inhabitants.

All the normal patterns keeping people together will be absent. They will come from different social layers, different races and different religions, plus different regions in the home country. In many cases they may not even speak the same language and yet they are supposed to live in peace with one another.

This is unquestionably the largest social engineering the world has ever seen and, though foreseen, its execution is not planned — it is just taking place as people leave rural districts to seek jobs in the cities.

It would be hypocrisy to say that the ingredients for a social implosion are not present, they are. The policy question is whether planning and measures to make it work can prevent such an implosion.

The analysis may go one step further and turn the coin around. Do the megacities perhaps hold the key to a prosperous future for Asia? It is their response to challenge that will decide the issues.

If Asia rises to the occasion and tackles the problems while at the same time exploiting the opportunities offered by higher purchasing power, a critical mass of talented people, possibilities for high consumption, and new consumer behaviour — especially on environment, energy, water, and climate change — megacities may be the card that puts Asia on the right track.

The key to these crucial questions may be the ability to understand that future megacities are not cities in a country, but self-sustaining entities. Sure enough, they are dependent on the rural districts for food supply, but the old pattern with a city interacting with its periphery and hinterland does not work anymore. In the future megacities will interact with other megacities and megaregions anywhere in the world, relying on shared common values to do this, rather than interacting with their hinterland with which the megacities will often not have shared values.

The problems for a national political system are obvious as the paradox poses itself squarely. To prevent megacities from imploding, and the left-behind rural areas from agitating for secession, megacities must be given a high degree of independence to link up with megacities abroad, even if that means political and cultural links to their own periphery and hinterland will loosen. Unless megacities get the freedom to drift away from their geographical periphery, they will drift away politically from the country in which they happen to be located.

Megacities and large multinational and supranational corporations will gradually compel national political systems to accept the consequence that they are losing power.[22] Most people take the present political system anchored in the nation state for granted, but it is actually no more than a couple of hundred years old. Until then allegiance to a prince, a chieftain, or a religious patriarch was the norm and very few citizens felt any loyalty to a country or a nation state.[23]

A rebalancing may happen which could question the existence of megacities, as quality of life becomes better in the hinterlands and creativity may even flourish there. The French policies in the 1960s and 1970s to "decentralize" key universities, research and cultural centres, and high-tech companies away from Paris, and prioritize fast public transport have paid off for Paris as well as the rest of the country. Asia may want to reflect on the economies of scale versus the economies of well-being.

## Changed Family Structure

The family structure, family traditions, and respect/priority for family interests and family members are more ingrained in the Asian way of life — if this term can be used as a broad common denominator.

The implication is, among other things, that social "security" and business life tend to be more dependent on the family than is the case in the United

States and Europe. Very few Asian countries have prepared themselves for a social security system built by the government, whether it is a system offering a minimum of services, or a comprehensive system as seen in some European nation states. It is looked upon as the responsibility of the family and/or private insurance.

China has set up a National Council for Social Security Fund (NCSSF)[24] estimated to be worth US$70 billion, but nevertheless — according to government sources — facing a shortfall of US$350 billion when calculating the pensions to be paid out in the years to come. That calls for much higher funding than the existing sources from the government, lottery, stock market transactions in Hong Kong, and profit from its investment. The Chinese Government is contemplating transferring shares from state-owned companies to the NCSSF to bridge the funding gap. Some observers see this as an interim measure to stabilize Chinese stock markets, and classify this as risky.[25] There is, however, another and much more interesting angle. By shifting the bedrock of the future financing of social security from fixed income such as bonds, to shares, the NCSSF funding ability becomes linked to future production output. If Chinese industry performs well, the funds increase, if Chinese industry performs badly, the funding decreases. In the long run, such a form of financing may turn out to be rather ingenious, as it links a country's level of social security to current output, instead of to a fixed income, and/or running up debts. But it cannot be taken for granted that it will work, or even be approved at all after the global economic and financial crisis. Poor management by public companies as well as corruption may also ruin the efforts.

Many Asian corporations are still run by families. It is unlikely that the family can continue to produce the management skills necessary to keep the corporation dynamic.

It cannot be assumed with certainty, but it is likely that as the families grow smaller and fewer people live in rural districts or have reminiscences of living there, strong family links will weaken.[26]

If so the next question is what will happen to the many people in Asia, as the numbers will grow for those needing some kind of social welfare and a contact network as well. If the family is not ready and if no social welfare system has been put in place to take over from this, a genuine social and political problem arises.

In the same vein the question can be put as to how well Asian corporations still under family control will fare when they are handed over to professional managers.

The depth and speed of changed family structures is difficult to predict and may vary from country to country, and even faster, from social level to social level, or perhaps to be more precise, from cultural/religious groups to other cultural/religious groups. On top of that comes the observation that divergent demographic developments mean that the major Asian countries will not reach the point where demographics start to exercise pressure on the family structure at the same time.

With an element of luck, the transition from strong dependence on families and family structure to a society more dependent on institutions or private economic arrangements may be stretched over a sufficiently long period to ensure a smooth transition.

## ASIA IN THE GLOBAL ECONOMY

We now turn to an extrapolation, analysing possibilities for future economic growth on the assumption that the basic system and global model were fundamentally unchanged:

- Asia participated in the international division of labour. The result was economic globalization instead of predominantly regional economic interaction.
- A global labour market arbitrage emerged, leading to a much larger share of GDP being moved around according to where labour costs weighed against labour productivity was most competitive.
- A growing liberalization of capital movements.
- Acceptance of a free market model (the Washington consensus), irrespective of the rising inequality among individuals inside nation states and a decreasing share of GDP allocated to labour, making room for a higher share to capital.
- American-European readiness to integrate the Asian economies in a global system shaped by the western world and a corresponding wish by emerging countries to join the system even if no genuine steps were taken to adjust decision-making procedures.
- American over-consumption financed by the global economy and Asian under-consumption.
- Asia's willingness to put its savings at the disposal of the rest of the world — in reality, the United States — cementing the Western world's control of international investment, even if the savings invested overseas came from countries outside the Western world.

The crucial question is whether the world can transit into a similarly sustainable model based on growth in Asia under analogous conditions — that is, no major conceptual changes — and if so what the decisive issues will be. The one big change will be a reorientation of the world economy. Until now it has turned around a north-south axis, with the overwhelming trade in goods and services, plus capital movement, going between the rich (industrialized) countries and the rising economic powers. The future axis will be between the now rising economic powers, which will gradually emerge as pacesetters for global economic growth. The world has already seen a growing business cycle among emerging countries and this trend can be expected to continue.

The United States may have lost its seat as the main driver, but that is not the same as saying that it has lost its powers. For the foreseeable future, maybe in the next twenty-five years, the United States will still be influential, although not as powerful as it was over the last fifty years, and consequently not exercising the same power to take part in shaping Asia's future. Politically the Asian countries are still divided and at least some of them will continue to look to the United States as a guarantor or stabilizing power; others will prefer to align with China or India. The main point is to note the continuing U.S. power/influence, but bear in mind that it will probably be accompanied by a lack of will and determination to lead, as it will be drawn towards looking at its own problems, leaving less room for it to exercise global leadership.

Asia will be less dependent on the United States, and Europe will still be there, but having even less influence. On the other hand Asia's interaction with Africa, Latin America, and the Middle East will increase, and over the next twenty-five years, overshadow that with the United States and Europe. Asia will purchase its raw materials, energy, and food in these geographical areas. Asian multinationals will invest there. Gradually markets will emerge that are indispensable outlets for Asia's production. For Asia as well as for Africa, Latin America, and the Middle East the decisive question arises as to whether it will be possible to work out a model based on mutual benefits and mutually-acknowledged sharing of benefits and burdens. If Asia fails in building stable and non-threatening relationships and "image" in these three geographic areas, problems loom ahead. In reality this calls for a new concept of economic globalization, where those hitherto regarded as peripheral players become decisive ones.

It also calls for a new consumption pattern, new global labour arbitrage, and a new global supply chain being created that will have higher commodity prices and higher transport costs and will break the mould that favoured and shaped comparative competitive advantages and the global distribution of labour for the last sixty years.

There is much talk about an Asian model — the term also used in this study — but currently there is no such thing as an Asian model.[27] Differences between nations, regions, races, religions, and values — to name a few — make Asia a geographic term and not much else. Historically rivalries have harassed Asia, as was the case in Europe. The Europeans have managed to overcome these rivalries and set up a political and economic machinery (the European Union) to frame integration. The Asians have not, despite attempts, managed to do so. The point in this context is that underlying animosities and novel challenges (religion, environment, climate change, and water) may surface to spoil the party. So far high economic growth, combined with a preoccupation to solve domestic problems, has prevented rivalries, but over the next twenty-five years, this blessing cannot be counted on as an automatic thing. Some observers point to the race for raw materials, energy, and food, but potentially there are many triggers. A more determined effort to keep together and turn the geographical notion into a political and economic entity seems necessary. A Marshall-like plan to address environmental, climate, and technological infrastructure gaps may be a viable option with Asian countries bearing the bulk of the effort.

Higher consumption in Asia is the paramount economic factor. Asia cannot depend on exports and/or high investment in the longer run. The lower income per capita means that a comparison between Asia and the United States/Europe is tricky, but it still seems fair to say that so far Asia has not adopted nor enabled the notion of mass consumption for its large population.

Without a strong improvement on governance, including public governance, it is unlikely that Asia will manage to create conditions for high growth in an atmosphere of scarcities. Corporate governance, especially corporate financial governance, is moving in the right direction. Some observers take the view that creativity can only thrive if accompanied by democracy. This may be to jump to conclusions. The challenge for Asia is, however, whether diversity and acceptance of different and in some cases divergent attitudes can be reconciled with the political models chosen by the various Asian countries. The method of selecting political leaders may be less important than securing an open society; without conveying the message that basically people with various attitudes are welcome it is difficult to see creativity take root.[28]

Education systems ask for money, but above all, for a lot of new attitudes that reject old ways of thinking because of the realization that students need fundamentals of a new nature and new skills to implement and be made valuable. Perceiving the system as gradually transforming itself into a part of the economy operating on the basis of common business practices will be decisive. Universities face the task of becoming "multinational intellectual enterprises", and not repositories of static theories, and school systems need to develop into teaching how to learn, adapt, implement, and handle change, but not as is too often the case, as proxies for social ranking with no skills to be used. A gradual build-up of kindergartens using children's natural curiosity to nurture creativity will be helpful. The bottom line is that either the education system becomes capable of turning out students prepared for the needs or changes of the future, or it nourishes social discontent by giving academic degrees that are tuned to yesterday's demands, thus producing students unable to get jobs but more than ready to voice their frustrations and anger. Constant upgrading of skills calls for lifelong learning on the part of the labour force, and for the emergence of new grading, diploma granting, and curricula adaptation. It is not surprising to see that Swiss "learning-by-doing" universities and *Fachhochschulen*, as well as French "select-know-manage-implement" *grandes ecoles* are so much in demand.

The world is flat or the world is spiky — according to which high priest of globalization you listen to.[29] Not surprisingly another view taken in this study is that the world is flat *and* spiky, depending on which economic sector we analyse and what we look for. The world is certainly flat in the sense that competitive advantages with regard to labour costs steer production away from high-cost to low-cost countries through labour arbitrage. The world is spiky in the sense that megacities and/or megaregions have emerged attracting talent, creativity, lifestyle, identity, and value-added production, primarily in services. The challenge for Asia is to use both theories to its advantage. Neither of them on its own will do the trick. Labour-intensive production alone confines Asia to manufacturing that competes on costs. Megacities alone may create high value-added production and wealth in selected areas, but not jobs and income in still a large part of Asia kept as developing regions, with a large pool of people with low education. Megacities must play the role of "flagships", pulling Asia along, while manufacturing must provide jobs to the masses. Without jobs, social unrest is to be expected; without megacities, talent, money, and skills will be absent — indeed go elsewhere.

A new global model assuming fundamentally unchanged conditions and operating inside the same intellectual box as the 1980–2005 model could look something like this:

- Asia develops a mass consumption culture sufficiently strong to act as traction, keeping global economic growth at a high level.
- This compensates for lower growth in the United States, Japan, and Europe, allowing global growth to run at 4–5 per cent.
- Economic growth spreads to other regions, first through demand for raw

materials, energy, and food, and next, a much higher level of trade in goods and services.

• The high growth in Asia, accompanied by rising growth in Africa, Latin America, and the Middle East, triggers demand for goods and services from the Western countries, keeping pressure for semi-protectionism at bay.

• Savings in Asia will increasingly flow to Africa, Latin America, and the Middle East as investments in these countries, contributing to their economic growth.

In 1980, the uncertainty would have been whether China could replace a central command economy with a market-driven model and enter the international economy with a market economy; and the attitude of other countries to this potential giant.

In 2008 the main uncertainties are whether Asia can change from managing growth to creating sustainable growth; India can transform into an industrialized country and China transform itself from maintaining economic growth as an industrialized country to being more dependent on the service sector; and Africa, Latin America, and the Middle East will transform themselves into competitive economies, using the rising demand for raw materials for such a tectonic shift; and these regions can be integrated into the global economy.

Asia as the main buyer of raw materials and, gradually, main supplier of capital, plus in the longer run, main trading partner, will decide the outcome.

Analysing the circumstances Asia could be the first example that amalgamates three basic trends to replace capitalism in its American form as the leading economic model.

The *first* trend is the implementation of the steady economy. This notion is in reality an updating of what classical economists such as John Stuart Mill worked with under the heading of stationary economy.[30]

Economic growth in its pure economic definition means higher output, more throughputs in the production process, more use of resources, and a growing, negative impact on the ecology/environment. A steady state economy is not synonymous with zero growth, but signifies that growth is looked at and measured in the context of ecological integrity, environmental protection, and economic sustainability.[31] It is recognized that there are limits to the size of production and, in particular, increase of production in a given ecosystem. For a while this limit may be violated, but not in the long run. Technology and education, plus other societal instruments, may be called upon to enhance efficiency, thus pushing the bar upwards, which indicates that a steady state economy is, far from being a state with no changes, but quite the opposite because the pressure for efficiency requires more and better technology having repercussions on a string of other societal policies. To skirt confrontations with the science of economics and its definition of a steady state economy, I prefer to use the notion of a balanced economy, defined as an economy, which in view of available resources and constraints, continues to be in balance and moves ahead.[32] The yardstick is not economic growth in its conventional definition, but resources, population, and social and capital stock, and the use of all three determines whether the economy is viable and in balance.[33]

The *second* trend is integrating business with societal priorities, regardless of whether the profits of the economic entities go up or down.

The purpose of economic life (production, etc.) switches away from being measured in money and looking at material consumption as the prime objective, to being judged by how much or how little it contributes to a balanced economy. This swing in purpose is linked to the discussion of what happiness there is and how it influences creativity. The more happiness the more creative a society becomes, but, and this is the point, in this particular context, happiness is not synonymous with wealth and income.

Over recent years notions such as corporate social responsibility, corporate citizens, and many others have flourished, especially in the Western world, leading many corporations to publish annual accounts where not only monetary profit is disclosed, but also its impact on labour standards, ecology, the environment, and society. In the Western world corporations are less linked to society than they are in Asia, so over the next twenty-five years it is likely that Asian corporations will see themselves and be seen by the rest of society, not as money earning units, but as supporters of societal development.

The immediate reaction to this is to question what kind of societal development Asia is moving towards? The answer may follow from the first trend if we keep in mind the drain on resources and the use of land by a rising population with a rising income per head. There is no certainty about the evolution of the human mind, but judged from what is happening in China and to a certain extent, India, it is not far fetched to see a model with social and environmental/climate stability and a steady — balanced — economy as Asia's answer to the challenges.[34]

The *third* trend is to integrate the ability to foresee with the ability to adapt to future trends. A society or community's performance in the world we are going to live in may depend to a large extent on its ability and will to prioritize adaptability as an element in societal development. This means several things. *First*, the willingness to define societal development with a time horizon of several decades, maybe up to thirty years or more. *Second*, the readiness to invest in societal development, in particular, education and lifelong learning, knowing full well that the payback for such investments start many years after they were initiated and will become profitable[35] only after several decades during which period society must bear the costs.

Asia did try to emulate the era of industrialization as it was played out in the industrialized countries and was relatively successful in doing so over the last quarter of the twentieth century. This was, however, contrary to Asia's cultural roots which speak against a money-oriented society and in favour of a society more rooted in values and ethics. Asia did break away from its roots to become a modern society and jump out of poverty, intellectual isolation, and not being integrated in global research and technology.

As the world view changes away from the Western model that is anchored in industrialization, it is likely or possible that Asia, as the first major power or biggest continent, will break out of that model and, on the basis of its own cultural values, shape a new economic and political model and political system reflecting the changed conditions and new challenges.

The purpose of the present book has been to analyse the elements pointing in this direction and some of the factors that may derail the process. Nothing can be taken for granted in forecasting, but it is possible for us to sketch, with some trepidation, trends, and weave them together in a coherent framework elucidating why this new political and economic model is likely to happen, and more likely to take place in Asia than elsewhere.

## Notes

1  Wing Thye Woo, "Dealing Sensibly with the Threat of Disruption in Trade with China: The Analysis of Increased Economic Interdependence and Accelerated Technological Innovation" (Washington DC: Brookings Institution), 18 December 2007 <http://www.brookings.edu/~/media/Files/rc/papers/2007/1018_trade_woo/1018_trade_woo.pdf>. There are relevant studies about similar fears of Chinese and Korean workers, but Wing Thye Woo's paper has been chosen as a common denominator for these fears, setting them out in a lucid analytical way.

2  The World Bank, State Environmental Protection Administration, P.R. China (Washington D.C.: The World Bank, 2007) <http://siteresources.worldbank.org/INTEAPREGTOPENVIRONMENT/Resources/China_Cost_of_Pollution.pdf>.

3  Nicolas. Z. Muller and Robert Mendelsohn, "Measuring the Damages of Air Pollution in the United States", *Journal of Environmental Economics and Management*, 54, July 2007.

4   The figures given for China, the United States, and the European Union are not fully comparable, but nonetheless give an indication of the size of the problem.

5   <http://www.epha.org/a/1778>.

6   *OECD Environmental Outlook to 2030* (Paris: OECD, 2008) <http://books. google.com.sg/books?id=8YSB8LMpLaYC&pg=PA256&lpg=PA256&dq=oec d+cost+us+of+pollution+share+gdp&source=bl&ots=e2AzaO9Ci_&sig=7QdN latt7QQfEX9gKeKt7uI0GCU&hl=en&ei=EhItSr3qN4z6kAWQwpDwCg&s a=X&oi=book_result&ct=result&resnum=4#PPP2,M1>.

7   It was not until 1943 that the German economy was switched to full-scale war production because Hitler felt a need to deliver consumption goods to the people. The British economy, however, was quite quickly mobilized after Churchill's nomination as prime minister.

8   It is an intriguing question whether the deregulation starting in the 1980s and gradually extended to a number of activities hitherto under public ownership was due to declining nationwide social capital. Irrespective of the answer, the result was that those who could pay got improved opportunities to look after themselves while those who could not pay were left behind.

9   *The Economics of Climate Change in Southeast Asia: A Regional Review* (Manila: Asian Development Bank, April 2009).

10  Reference is made to Chapter 5 which discusses energy and energy conservation.

11  Denmark has one of the lowest ratios of energy consumption/output, and it has been calculated that a doubling of energy prices improves Denmark's competitiveness by 2 per cent. Source: Erik Haller Pedersen og Johanne Dinesen Riishøj, "Energieffektivitet og konkurrenceevne", Danmarks Nationalbank, Kvartalsoversigt, 2 kvartal (second quarter), 2009.

12  The Yale Center for Environmental Law and Policy (YCELP) and the Center for International Earth Science Information Network (CIESIN) of Columbia University, New York, in collaboration with the World Economic Forum and the Joint Research Center of the European Commission, publish an annual environmental sustainability index. Available at <http://sedac.ciesin.columbia. edu/es/esi/>. It has a time lag of about two years.

13  The International Energy Agency, Paris, is running a database about energy efficiency measures, which also covers China and India. See <http://www.iea. org/textbase/effi/index.asp>. See also Energy Information Administration from the United States, available at <http://www.eia.doe.gov/oiaf/ieo/world.html>.

14  The World Intellectual Property Organization (WIPO), Geneva, publishes these figures. As an indicator they suffer from the slight drawback that they are published with a time lag of about two years. The latest one — available at <http://www.wipo.int/ipstats/en/statistics/patents/patent_report_2007.html> — gives figures for 2005 and shows that out of the top twenty patent offices, eight come from Asia, with Japan topping the list, China (No. 3), Korea (No. 4), India (No. 11), Hong Kong China (No. 15), Singapore (No. 16), and Thailand

(No. 19). Both China and India have a 50–50 distribution of patents filed by residents and non-residents respectively.

15 Worldbank, Washington, D.C., available at <http://web.worldbank.org/WBSITE/EXTERNAL/WBI/WBIPROGRAMS/KFDLP/EXTUNIKAM/0,,menuPK:1414738~pagePK:64168427~piPK:64168435~theSitePK:1414721,00.html>.

16 Economy, social, and ecology.

17 The World Bank publishes an annual rating of governance covering various aspects such as voice and accountability, political stability and absence of violence, government effectiveness, regulatory quality, rule of law, and control of corruption. The figures are published with a time lag of one to two years. Available at <http://info.worldbank.org/governance/wgi2007/sc_country.asp#>.

18 Published by UNDP.

19 W.W. Rostow, *The World Economy, History & Prospect* (University of Texas Press: Austin, 1978).

20 OECD, Paris, *Economic Outlook*, half-yearly publication.

21 Evidence from large U.S. cities about social coherence is discouraging, but may not apply to Asia as it is influenced by differences according to race.

22 Some of these aspects are admirably dealt with in Philip Bobbitt, *The Shield of Achilles, War, Peace, and the Course of History* (Knopf: New York, 2002).

23 Until the seventeenth century, most European wars were fought with mercenaries who followed not the flag, but the purse, fighting for those that offered the highest pay. Civil servants were likewise hired, regardless of their origins, to serve a prince.

24 <http://www.ssf.gov.cn/enweb/Column.asp?ColumnId=39>.

25 "China May Shift Shares to Fund Pension", *Financial Times*, 29 February 2008 <http://us.ft.com/ftgateway/superpage.ft?news_id=fto022920082333060916&page=1>.

26 The divorce rate in Chine rose by 20 per cent in 2007 just to mention an example <http://news.bbc.co.uk/2/hi/asia-pacific/7208385.stm>.

27 We have looked at an Asian future model in Chapter 1.

28 In his book *Cities and the Creative Class* from 2005, Richard Florida selects technology, talents and tolerance as the three decisive Ts. His main point is that talent goes where people feel they will be accepted, regardless of personal behaviour.

29 Thomas Friedman, *The World is Flat* or Richard Florida, *The Rise of Creative Class* and *Who's Your City*.

30 For a relatively modern analysis of the stationary versus the growing economy, see J.E. Meade, *The Stationary Economy* and *The Growing Economy* (London: Unwin University Books, 1965 and 1968 respectively).

31 <http://www.eoearth.org/article/Steady_state_economy>.

32 A definition more or less in line with this is that such economies allow usage of natural resources exactly at the amount of human need. This leads to income per

capita growth at the rate to compensate combined rates of population growth, technological progress, and depreciation. See Risti Permani, "Education as a Determinant of Economic Growth in East Asia", 15 January 2008 <http://www.uow.edu.au/commerce/econ/ehsanz/pdfs/Permani%202008.pdf>.

33  Herman Daly, *Steady-State Economics: Second Edition with New Essays* (Washington, D.C.: Island Press, 1991) and *Steady-State Economics* <http://www.dieoff.org/page88.htm>.

34  The British historian, Arnold Toynbee, who coined the key to development of human civilization with the term "response to Challenge", would say that such a reaction would indeed be a response to challenge. Jareel Diamand who writes about how well-developed societies/communities have committed ecological/environmental suicide by neglecting omens of running down the resource base, might say that this is Asia's way to avoid such a fate.

35  The greatest risk is, of course, that the course is set in a wrong direction, making the societal investment unprofitable, with disastrous consequences. This is why indicators are necessary to inform policymakers whether society moves in the direction originally laid down.

# Appendix 1

# PERCEPTIONS OF ASIA AND ITS FUTURE, 1945 TO 2008

## HISTORICAL ANALYSES

The literature about Asia, its economic rise, and the prospects for the future is vast. In this appendix an attempt will be made to look at some of the many works published to give an idea of the many perceptions and thoughts put forward by various writers and institutions.

Over the last half decade, Asia has turned poverty and a dismal economic outlook to an economic miracle and is now generally looked upon as the new economic superpower, although discrepancies in internal living standards have grown.

This warrants two questions: how did it happen and how solid are the prospects for the prediction that the twenty-first century is Asia's century?

It is said that some years after the end of World War II, economists predicted that Burma, Indonesia, the Philippines, and Vietnam would emerge as winners among the Asian nations to sport strong and viable economies. The basis for this prediction was their endowment with rich resources. It completely missed the industrialization of Asia, propelling nations short of resources such as Singapore, Japan, and Korea, with Hong Kong and Taiwan, to the forefront. This is a classic example of making predictions by extending existing curves, without considering the possibility of abrupt changes forcing the curves to bend.

In 1968 Gunnar Myrdal published *Asian Drama — An Inquiry into the Poverty of Nations*.[1] Myrdal saw two dramas unfolding in Asia:[2] (a) modern ideals confronting the traditional and (b) different economic models being

507

offered to the populations. Its greatest value was to link various trends in a coherent framework not confining itself to a purely economic or sociological study. The book comes in three volumes, and social and sociological issues dwarf the number of pages analysing economics. Myrdal wrote in the mid-1960s, but many of the issues he evokes are still with us. Chapters on the relation of modernization ideals to other values, such as inequality, equality and democracy, corruption, investment in man, health, education, the school system, to mention the most interesting ones, also figure on the agenda forty years later, and Myrdal's observations still give food for thought although they are in many respects outdated. What is not outdated, however, is his approach, which deviates from pure economics.

Even today many economists have not realized the eternal wisdom in Myrdal's blunt statement that:[3]

> Economic theorists, more than other social scientists, have long been disposed to arrive at general propositions and then postulate them as valid for every time, place and culture. There is a tendency in contemporary economic theory to follow this path to the extreme. For such confidence in the constructs of economic reasoning, there is no empirical justification.

He adds a little later:[4]

> That the use of Western theories, models, and concepts in the study of economic problems in the South Asian countries is a cause of bias seriously distorting that study will be a main theme of this book.

Asian values have captured a good many headlines over the last decade or so; therefore it can be useful to look up what Myrdal says about that:

> Insofar as there are considerable and systematic differences in conditions among the several South Asian countries there is undoubtedly something to the concept of a "national character". The same may be said of religions. And as the differences in conditions are much more pronounced between these countries as a whole and the Western world, there is room also for the concept of the "Asian" — or "South Asian" — mind. But these terms are not suitable for scientific use. They have been contaminated by being made to serve — in South Asia as in the Western world — speculative, nationalist, aggressive or apologetic ideologies.

The specific value of Myrdal's study is limited in today's world. But his main contribution to spread the analysis beyond economics, maybe even subordinating economics to social and sociological issues, has withstood the change of time. His firm rejection of transferring Western concepts to Asia is another major contribution.

Myrdal concluded that the countries analysed were likely to be kept at a low stage of economic development as a rigid social structure prevented change and governments were too weak, or simply not willing/prepared to break established structures and norms. He attributed low growth to factors outside a purely economic framework and advocated social policies to stimulate growth.

It is one of the whims of history that at the same time that he published his book, political systems emerged in Southeast Asia setting most of the region on a firm growth pattern for the next thirty years.

Around 1990 the theory of the flying geese emerged showing that the rest of Asia was following Japan and Korea in their development pattern.[5] The basic philosophy was that the strong Japanese economy was pulling the rest of Asia along, based on a primarily export-oriented economic model. And very few then were talking about China from the economic point of view, entangled as it was in its own system and the aftermath of the Cultural Revolution and the war with Vietnam. India was simply not regarded as a serious contender in the big league for many, many years to come.

Looking at how Asia's growth has unfolded over the last fifty years we find it striking that Japan is in the forefront in upgrading education as a vital factor in promoting economic growth, realizing fully that investment in education is a long-term investment that may not realize its full potential until about thirty years later. It has also invested in machinery, following the German model, as no manufacturing economy can stay competitive without productivity and complexity gains from machinery. Korea and Taiwan followed the Japanese example on both counts, which is also the case for Singapore, while it seems doubtful if all other Asian countries have realized the importance of education and are ready to invest now, with the prospect of reaping the benefits over a horizon that may stretch to more than thirty years.[6] In the late 1980s only Japan invested in science, China and India followed in the late 1990s, but only in a few selected areas.

In its 1993 study of East Asian countries,[7] the World Bank[8] highlights the significance of human capital through a determined educational effort and points out that education must span from basic schools to tertiary education.

The key findings are put this way:[9]

> Aside from the ability to sustain rapid growth with fairly equal income distributions, the HPAEs[10] also differ from other developing economies in three factors traditionally associated with economic growth. Elevated rates

of investment, exceeding 20 percent of GDP on average between 1960 and 1990, including remarkably high rates of private investment, combined with rising endowments of human capital because of universal basic education, tell a large part of the growth story. These factors "account" for roughly two-thirds of the growth in the HPAEs. The remainder is attributable to productivity growth. In fact, productivity growth in the HPAEs exceeds that of most other developing and industrial economies. This superior performance comes from the combination of success at allocating capital to high-yielding investments and success at catching up technologically to the industrial economies.

In 1994 Paul Krugman[11] published his analysis about Asia's growth contradicting the conclusion of the World Bank study. He draws on earlier analytical work,[12] saying that basically Asia's growth was not so much due to higher productivity, as to higher input of production factors. He admitted, however, the importance of education.

Turning to the future, John Naisbitt's *Megatrends Asia*[13] published in 1996 is a natural starting point. It deals with Asia as a whole and, contrary to Myrdal's book, takes a strong positive outlook on Asia and its future, possibly inspired by several decades of high growth pulling a large part of Asia out of poverty, albeit a part of the population in most countries still lived near or below the poverty threshold.

Naisbitt's book was certainly not the first to foresee Asia's rise as the dominant economic region and to explain why that would constitute a permanent trend, accompanied by some repercussions, but it may be the first of its kind reaching out to a broad public. Basically he puts forward the thesis and defends it that the modernization of Asia means a decline for the West, not only economically, but also culturally and politically. As a side effect of modernization, Asia will be confronted with many of the social and sociological problems that have harassed the West for decades, such as crime and the breaking up of the traditional family structure.

## FUTURE STUDIES

In 2006 the World Bank published "An East Asian Renaissance: Ideas for economic Growth".[14] The report analyses Asia's economic growth over the last decades and underlines the importance of economies of scale as a driving force.

While it does not explicitly enter into forecasts or recommendations for the future, its selection of issues vital for future economic growth indicates both problems and opportunities for staying on a growth pattern.

The number of people living in the middle-income bracket will rise so strongly that most people in East Asia will live in this income bracket, with consequences for purchasing power and consumer preferences.

In the introduction, the World Bank emphasizes supercities as being probably the most important phenomenon to take place. "Cities are at the core of a development strategy based upon international integration, investment and innovation" is the key phrase. The outlook of the report is primarily economic, and it analyses and discuses the need for investment and how supercities interact in a competitive framework while the social and sociological aspects, such as impact on the traditional family structure, are not dealt with. Environmental consequences are ignored as are natural resources.

The World Bank sees a renaissance in innovation and networking, which leads to the term "A New Asia".

There has been a "renaissance" in innovation, but it has not grown steadily nor consistently as some countries' models espoused outsourcing revenue and job opportunities (China is an example). Such revenues were mapped into productivity improvements and not necessarily long-term investments in know-how infrastructure.

Kishore Mahbubani,[15] who has a knack for saying things bluntly, followed up in 2008 on his other writings about the rise of Asia by pointing to two salient features of our historical epoch. "First, we have reached the end of the era of Western dominance of world history (but not the end of the West, which will remain the single strongest civilization for decades more). Second, we will see an enormous renaissance of Asian societies."

And then, "One key message of this book is that the Asian March to Modernity ... represents a new opportunity both for the West and for the world."

The book is an eloquent and lucid analysis of why Asia is rising and how it happened, but it tends less to offer a futuristic analysis of how Asia and Asian societies may be expected to adjust or react to the continued changes and challenges taking hold over the next twenty-five years.

Sanjeev Sanyal[16] traces India's decline from AD 1000 when its share of world gross domestic production was 29 per cent — even higher than China's — to 1991 when it had fallen to only 3 per cent. From India's independence from the British Empire in 1947, some — albeit limited — progress was made, but a centrally planned economy held it back. In 1991 reforms were introduced and they opened the way for a strong rise in growth and export, admitting India to the global economy and globalization.

Sanjeev Sanyal sees a bright and promising future for India, but does not hide the many obstacles and challenges this vast country faces, and points out with almost acrid clarity that, unless reform policies are pursued, the risk of falling back to lower growth is agonizingly high.

It should be added that even in issues linked to modern infrastructure, such as telecommunications, there is an Indian tradition to build regulation in an awkward way making it prone to lower relative growth.[17]

This book, exclusively on India, is more future-oriented than Kishore Mahbubani's work covering Asia, in that it analyses a number of sectors such as education, law, technology, and savings, to mention a few, pointing out what kind of reforms need to be implemented and what the consequences may be if they are not. The reader sits back with the image of India as having enormous potential, but also with more and deeper problems than conventional wisdom tells us.

According to Sanjeev Sanyal, India will change and enter the hypergrowth phase, which will transform the country over the next few decades. He mentions the following crucial points that may also be of interest to other countries in a comparable situation.[18]

Urbanization will rise as a consequence of growth and will itself stimulate growth. The middle class will grow over its present level of about fifty million (thirteen million families) and promote institutional reforms. The schism between westernization and modernization holding back India's reforms may disappear with the higher growth and the rising middle class. Environmental costs will be high and a real problem for the economy. India will take its place on the global stage, reflecting its economic size and thus also acting as a stimulant for productivity and competitiveness. The growing film industry is an example of how India will project soft power.

A study commissioned by the Asian Development Bank (ADB)[19] concludes that India could go from poverty to affluence in one generation, but not without difficulties and problems.

According to the ADB, India follows China in its development model, but with a ten-year time lag running into the obstacles and problems connected with economic growth that China has encountered. The well-known Indian service-led growth model gives way to a more traditional development with industry and manufacturing as drivers. Problems such as infrastructure, the environment, training of the labour force, and migration from rural to urban districts will dominate the agenda. Basically to succeed India must become a more cohesive country, be a globally competitive economy, and a responsible global citizen. The determining factors are abilities and political willingness to set up institutional machinery mapping out long-term objectives, pursue them, and monitor progress to step in with corrective action in case something starts to go wrong.

Five major challenges are mentioned and of interest because they apply to most other countries trying to get out of the low-income bracket. Cities must be turned into sustainable cities not gobbling up resources, but contributing to growth; the education system must be tuned to future demands, income inequalities must be addressed, combined with equal access to opportunities, and India's geographical environment must be stabilized so as not to disrupt the growth pattern.

Of particular significance for India is the warning of an oligarchic capitalistic system, where the market, under the control of a few large enterprises in conjunction with political power, malfunctions, drawing resources away from growth.

India has the chance to learn from some of the mistakes committed by East Asian countries in their drive to manufacturing. Fundamentally India will go through a strong growth, but the message is that unless it manages the problems and obstacles in an adroit way, growth will level off and leave India in the position of a middle-income country, not capable of moving on to a higher income per capita. If so, India will be caught in a position where it is not sufficiently high-tech to compete with countries such as the United States, the European Union, Japan, and possibly China, while at the same time operating at a wage cost level ruling it out of the competitive league dominated by low-cost producers.

An ambitious attempt to sketch broad lines of development until 2050 (and even further) was made in 1998 by Barry Buzan and Gerald Segal.[20] The book is still very readable and has the added value that after more than ten years it offers an opportunity to test future forecasting. It weathers such a vetting in fine shape.

The following excerpt from the book gives a short summary of its messages:[21]

> We can project with reasonable assurance some of the characteristics of the world.... Political and cultural framework in 2050 will be quite similar to our own. Most of the familiar states and nations and major languages will probably still be there, as will many of the international and transnational organisations (or their recognisable successors). Large parts of Asia will have carried through their process of modernisation, though whether this will have been achieved without wars in the region is less certain. The world will still be heavily divided by patterns of uneven development and inequality. The restraints on war amongst the leading world powers will probably be stronger and somewhat more widespread, but so too will the problem of failed states and the proliferation of privatised violence. The development of the global economy and global

communications will have continued, and be much deeper rooted, and more widespread. The world population will be something like double what we now have, but it will be peaking, with only a few areas still showing sharp growth. A great redistributing of population will have taken place, with the old West having shrunk to a smallish percentage of the world's people, and containing a relatively even mix of age groups; and the rest of the world containing the bulk of humanity, and with a preponderance of younger age groups.

Buzan and Segal dwell on the notion of *mondoculture*,[22] which they see as a staple, pluralist sense of identity embracing most of humankind.[23]

They predict continued nationalism, but in a weaker form, leaving the door open for localism and many non-geographical threads of linkages to communities of shared interests. Cultural identity moves gradually from established nationalism to a feeling of belonging culturally, and with regard to a chosen set of values, to larger communities reaching across political borders and geographical distances. This diversification makes it easier for them to take a welcoming or, at least, tolerant attitude to those belonging to other human communities. In such an environment, *mondoculture* emerges as attitudes making it possible for human beings to live with others more closely, while retaining their myriad of identities.

The first signs of *mondoculture* will be seen in most culturally-mobile forms of the arts and entertainment, music, sports, fashion, and food. This will not harmonize tastes or produce homogenized world products, but instead generate global market segments where consumer groups enjoy the same kind of lifestyle wherever they live, and feel a common bond with consumers enjoying the same services, irrespective of geographical and/or political/religious differences.

Buzan and Segal foresee conflict, even wars, social unrest, terrorism, and various forms of disruption, but offer the conclusion that around 2030, the world will move into what they term "geoeconomic diplomacy" as a result of increasing interplay between business and political global relations.

They discuss population explosion and environmental problems, but conclude by stating that even if these problems and challenges will not be negligible, the world will survive and by year 2050 have weathered the storm.

The National Intelligence Council (NIC)[24] in the United States published in 2008 its report called "Global Trends: A Transformed World", which sketches a geopolitical picture of the world in 2025. Its basic conclusion is that the present global system, anchored in overwhelming U.S. power, will give way to a multipolar world with China and India as rising powers asking for, and getting, influence on the system. China will be the second largest and India the third largest economy. The third Asian power, Japan, will not be able to keep its place, and must accept a slide down in ranking and less economic clout.

The impact on Asia of such a likely scenario is less stability and a more pronounced power game, where a number of players will jostle for position and play one against another — a scenario judged from history to invoke, at best, instability, and, at worst, armed conflict.

A somewhat "inconvenient truth" analysis focusing on the many challenges flowing in the wake of rising populations and limited resources, is found in a classic scenario building published by Forum for the Future.[25] It starts by outlining seven categories of factors shaping the future response to climate change.

- Climate change is a scientific certainty, but we do not know how quickly it will happen and where different impacts will be felt.
- The perception of climate change among the public will have a profound influence over what can and will be done.
- The same goes for how the business community responds, faced with the shift to a low-carbon economy.
- It is still anyone's guess how the global economy will develop over the coming years, including the reaction to the global financial/economic crisis that took hold in late 2008 and is expected to continue until 2010.
- Resource shortages in areas other than climate change will play a major role.
- The political response and its support from the population reflect a wide range of views, keeping us in the dark about which policies will be implemented and based on what kind of philosophies.
- New technology will be developed and implemented, but the time frame is not defined.

The analysis puts forward five scenarios for 2030:

- Efficiency first, with rapid innovation in energy efficiency and novel technologies opening the door for the continuation of present lifestyles and business practices.
- Service transformation, with a high price of carbon, forcing a revolution of how people's needs are satisfied.
- Redefining progress, which introduces new priorities of "well-being" and

"quality of life", putting sustainable forms of living ahead of present day resource-intensive lifestyles.

- Environmental war, with resource shortages pushing the existing model to the limit, and political entities seeking solutions to gaining access to resources, even if that means conflicts with other political entities.
- Protectionist world, where globalization is rolled back and political entities, primarily in the form of nation states, try to shift the burden to others.

This analysis revolves around climate change as the main parameter, but illustrates how important aspects cannot be resolved in isolation and need to be seen in the context of globalization, both geographically and sectorally. No major problem can be singled out and solved without considering repercussions on other countries and other sectors.

An interesting and thought provoking attempt to make a forecast for the next hundred years is made by George Friedman (2009)[26] from Stratfor. Friedman's analysis is exclusively geopolitical, confining itself to the struggle among great powers for supremacy. He does not deal with any kind of domestic, economic, or social issues, although many of these implicitly form part of his analysis and conclusions.

The world Friedman sees is dominated by the United States, which will move into unprecedented power and influence. China and India will not make it as real superpowers and are actually curiously absent from most of his analysis, as are Africa and Latin America. His underlying assumption that they will not be able to modernize themselves into great powers is in itself debatable and highly questionable, but even if that assumption is accepted, it is a long step from seeing them almost as non-players.

In Friedman's scenario the next world war takes place in the middle of the twenty-first century between the United States on the one hand and a coalition between Japanese-led forces in Asia and a Turkish-led conglomeration of forces in Europe, where an emerged Polish sphere of influence is the closest ally of the United States. Germany and France end up more or less on the side of Turkey, while the United Kingdom finally decides to step in and support the United States and the Polish conglomeration of forces. The United States wins this war.

What is more interesting in Friedman's book is his analysis of military conflict, where he points to the importance of space in armed conflict and talks about battlestars as some kind of future battleships from which battles are directed and which are capable of administering enormous fire power.[27]

Irrespective of his scenarios, the analysis setting out in clear text why precision weapons change warfare is undoubtedly right. In traditional warfare, targeting was imprecise, so to destroy a target an enormous number of bombs were needed. The allies dropped almost 600,000 bombs on the German city of Schweinfurt to destroy the factories there that were producing ball bearings, with debatable consequences at least until the end of the war. This required many platforms for delivering bombs, mass armies, and the mobilization of the whole nation. In a future war with precision weapons which hit the target, only one bomb and one platform is needed and the platform may be reusable. Therefore there is no need for a mass army and no need for the mobilization of the whole nation. In Friedman's scenario about a world war, losses of human beings are almost negligible compared with what happened during World Wars I and II.

This is an interesting contribution to the thinking about future warfare, but even more interesting is, of course, how relevant the basic idea of warfare seems to be in the next twenty-five years.[28]

## CONCLUSION

These studies are all valuable and give insights of various kinds. The common denominator is how Asia's vast resources and vast populations influence economic growth. Prior to around 1970, when Myrdal wrote, a large population, especially of the kind in Asia, was seen as a barrier to growth, eating up what economic growth could be mobilized. All the ingredients for a growth pattern, from savings to good governance, were lacking.

After that date, studies shift track and start to analyse the high growth rates afterwards so as to sketch trends for the future in an optimistic environment where Asia is predicted to be the rising power and to be the dominating continent in the twenty-first century.

The common denominator for all the optimistic studies appearing after 1970 and, in particular, in the 1990s and the beginning of the first decade of the current century, is an almost blind acceptance of American-style capitalism as the global model. Asia is seen to be growing by adopting the principles of this market-oriented and export-led growth model. Reservations are confined to non-economic problems such as the environment, without hiding many of the challenges further development poses to the political environment.

## Notes

1  G. Myrdal, *Asian Drama: An Inquiry into the Poverty of Nations. A Twentieth Century Fund Study* (New York: Pantheon, 1968).
2  Although the word "Asia" is prominent in the title, the book actually excludes West Asia, China, Japan, and Korea. It confined itself to India, Pakistan (today's Pakistan, plus Bangladesh), Sri Lanka, Myanmar, Malaysia, Singapore, Thailand, Indonesia, the Philippines, and, sometimes, what was South Vietnam.
3  Myrdal, *Asian Drama*, prologue, p. 16.
4  Myrdal, *Asian Drama*, prologue, p. 19.
5  Edith Terry and Chalmers A. Johnson, *How Asia Got Rich: Japan, China and the Asian Miracle* (Sharpe, 2002).
6  In July 1963 Japan's Ministry of Education (Monbusho) published *Japan's Growth and Education 1963*, sketching the role of education in promoting economic growth and referring to how education already played an important role in the Meji Era modernization of Japan in 1868 <http://www.mext.go.jp/b_menu/hakusho/html/hpae196301/hpae196301_1_001.html>. An analysis of the early modernization of Japan, with emphasis on the role of education and technology, can be found in Wayne. E. Nafziger, *Learning from the Japanese: Japan's Pre-war Development and the Third World* (Sharpe, 1994).
7  It is another whim of history that while Myrdal did not include the part of Asia which took off when he wrote his book, the World Bank concentrated on East Asia, writing one year after the 1992 economic reforms in India that launched that country on a growth pattern.
8  World Bank, *The East Asian Miracle: Economic Growth and Public Policy* (New York: Oxford University Press, 1993).
9  *World Bank Policy Research Bulletin* 4, no. 4 (August–October 1993).
10  High Performing Asian Economies.
11  Paul Krugman, "The Myth of Asia's Miracle", *Foreign Affairs* (November/December 1994).
12  By Alwyn Young of Boston University and Larry Lau of Stanford University.
13  John Naisbitt, *Megatrends Asia: The Eight Asian Megatrends That are Changing The World* (London: Nicolas Brealey, 1997).
14  "An East Asian Renaissance: Ideas for Economic Growth" (Washington, D.C.: World Bank) <http://web.worldbank.org/WBSITE/EXTERNAL/COUNTRIES/EASTASIAPACIFICEXT/0,,contentMDK:21056110~pagePK:146736~piPK:146830~theSitePK:226301,00.html>.
15  Kishore Mahbubani, *The New Asian Hemisphere* (New York: Public Affairs, 2008).
16  Sanjeev Sanyal, *The Indian Renaissance: India's Rise After a Thousand Years of Decline* (Singapore: World Scientific, 2008).
17  <http://portal.acm.org/citation.cfm?id=1359998.1360005&coll=GUIDE&dl=GUIDE&CFID=45063031&CFTOKEN=51826540>.

18  Sanjeev Sanyal, *The Indian Renaissance*, Chapter 8, "How India will change".

19  Asian Development Bank, "India 2039: An Affluent Society in One Generation", prepared for the Emerging Markets Forum (Manila, 2009) <http://www.scribd.com/doc/16761658/India-2039-An-affluent-society-in-one-generation-by-httptrakin>.

20  Barry Buzan and Gerald Segal, *Anticipating the Future: Twenty Millennia of Human Progress* (London: Simon and Schuster, 1998).

21  Ibid., pp. 215–16.

22  The authors define *mondoculture* in this way: "about the move away from a world of tightly bounded and geopolitically separated nations and states, and towards a more complicated multicultural world in which cultures penetrate each other, and up to a point blend and fuse", p. 221.

23  Buzan and Segal, *Anticipating the Future*, p. 220.

24  National Intelligence Council, *Global Trends 2025: The National Intelligence Council's 2025 Project* (Washington D.C.: Government Printing Office, 2008).

25  Forum for the Future, "Climate Futures, Responses to Climate Changes in 2030" (October 2008).

26  George Friedman, *The Next 100 Years* (New York: Doubleday, 2009).

27  The future world war starts with a Japanese surprise attack on the most important of three American "battlestars". The attack comes from Japanese bases on the moon, which have secretly stocked weapons for such an attack, taking the United States completely by surprise as was the case with Pearl Harbor in 1941.

28  See Chapter 6.

# Appendix 2

## WILD CARDS

Wild cards are normally defined as low-probability, but high-impact events. They are used to discuss future events which are unlikely to happen, but if they do, the repercussions will be dramatic. They cannot be ruled out of any futuristic study, but the analyst and the reader must bear in mind that we are talking about low-probability events — a bit like thinking the unthinkable. Typical wild cards from the past would have been, prior to 1979, China's change into a market economy; or prior to the 11 September attacks, a coordinated terrorist attack on the World Trade Center, the Pentagon, the White House, and the U.S. Congress.

Currently some of the global wild cards floating around are enumerated in *The Futurist* issue of spring 2009.[1]

- Spiritual paradigm shift sweeps the world, sponsored by the use of the Internet and the growing complexity of connections and dependency.
- Science is wrong: it is rapid cooling, not global warming, that is the biggest manifestation of climate change. New scientific evidence suggests that the major terrestrial driver of global climate patterns may be wind over the oceans. If the world faces cooling, instead of global warming, not only would a whole string of high profile policies have to be rethought, but confidence in science would fall dramatically, altering societal structures.
- New energy discovery comparable to the control of fire — for example, what is labelled zero point energy (ZPE) with the Casimir Effect. According to a recent article in the science journal *Nature*,[2] this experiment has set the stage for a revolution in energy that will rival the discovery of fire.

- Cloned humans threaten everything, calling into question ethics and politics.
- Intelligent alien life confirmed, confronting humanity with possibly the biggest question ever.
- The possibility of a food crisis — which is less of a wild card as the omens of food shortage are already visible and about 800 million people are living under the threat of famine or close to such a condition.[3]
- A catastrophic weather event rivalling or surpassing Hurricane Katrina.
- A dramatic political shift to the far left in U.S. politics. Alternatively, a massive shift to the right.
- Political upheaval in China.
- A worldwide backlash against fundamentalist religions.
- Widespread illness and death from tainted food (either accidental or deliberate).
- A surprisingly rapid economic recovery — when the experts tell us that the United States may be mired in recession for many months, perhaps years.
- The disabling of the Internet.
- A disruptive new business model on the scale of the Web when it emerged in the mid-1990s.
- The incapacitation of President Obama, through scandal, illness, or assassination.
- Markets imploding and Western capitalism collapsing.

These are examples only to give a general idea of what a wild card is and how the debate among futurists tackles this notion. Some of the above mentioned examples are genuinely wild cards also in the perception of ordinary people, for example, alien life; others are debated within relatively well-known territories of scientific disciplines, for example, cloned humans. The major contribution of futurists will often be to lift the discussion out of a purely scientific, one-sector analysis, and open it up for a discussion on the consequences of a societal and political nature. For a futurist a possible revelation of alien life may, in the first place, be more about its consequences for our own thinking, philosophy, religious beliefs, behaviour, etc., than about finding out what it means for pure science. The consequence for the mindset and mentality weighs more than pure scientific reasoning. If, for example, global warming proves to be the wrong theory, and mankind is faced with global cooling instead, a whole number of consequences for science arises, but it is even more interesting to note that this will probably mean a total loss of credibility for the global establishment for having led humanity into one of the largest ever projects, ranging from infrastructure to the price of electricity for the ordinary consumer.

For our purpose we exclude wild cards such as natural catastrophes and pandemics, that is, we limit ourselves to, let us call it, man-made wild cards and classify them in two groups: wild cards which would help Asia in its future development (such as China's turnaround in 1978–79) and wild cards with deep negative consequences (such as 11 September).

## Positive Wild Cards

A technological breakthrough in the energy field would do wonders for Asia. Examples are coal liquefaction, biofuel on the basis of waste from agriculture, solar power. There are probably more possibilities, but for a wild card to affect development in the short term, it must not need large investments in infrastructure. A more long-term, positive wild card is the ZPE mentioned above.

## Negative Wild Cards

A shift in foreign policy in China that replaces the present policy with a much more assertive stance prompting the United States to mobilize Japan, Australia, and Taiwan in an effort to "keep China in its place", with obvious disruptive repercussions on Asia.

Some kind of breakdown in relations between populations and the political system in heavily populated countries such as China, India, and Indonesia, triggering not only social unrest, but a genuine loss of power for the political system and landing the country in a state of non-government.

A turnaround in policies in Africa or Latin America or the Middle East making them inward looking, and not interested in joining the global economy, thus choking off exports of raw materials.

Rising sea levels because of global warming resulting in dramatic social consequences for several hundred millions of people living in Bangladesh and in major Asian cities such as Jakarta, Bangkok, and Ho Chi Minh City. Just think of fifty or a hundred million people from Bangladesh seeking a new home if their home disappears into the sea.

China and India are often compared and in many ways that makes sense. For our purpose the pertinent observation is that they face similar problems: the need for high growth, inequality, rising pollution, raw materials from abroad, big megacities, governments striving to exercise control over regions/provinces, and a genuine fear of social unrest.

China may be better placed to weather the problems because many of these problems have been on the agenda in China for some time. China's population is expected to fall, not rise; manufacturing has been under way for many years, providing some clue on how to handle pollution, job creation, training, the movement of labour from the rural districts. The nationwide problems are more likely to be tackled in China than in India because the government in China, despite visible difficulties, is more in control of the provinces than is the government in India. Industrialization demands infrastructure and China has taken that route.

India is going to face all these challenges, of which the most delicate are industrialization, job creation, moving people from rural districts to cities, and growing pollution. India is, so to speak, hitting this point of the curve later and is at a point less promising and with less helpful conditions than was the case for China.

This is not to say that India cannot make it or that China has made it. The point is that when we look at the future of Asia in the next twenty-five years, India is the country facing the most acute and difficult problems and with the biggest question mark over its potential to solve them. To our mind this is wild card number one.

## Notes

1    *The Futurist* (May–June 2009): 18–24, with articles by John L. Petersen, John Rockfeller, Brian Pomeroy, Marc Blasband, and Steve Malerich.

2    "Measured Long-Range Impulsive Casimir-Lifshitz Forces", *Nature* 457, 8 January 2009 <http://www.nature.com/nature/journal/v457/n7226/full/nature07610. html>.

3    <http://paperdreamer.files.wordpress.com/2008/04/world_hunger_map.jpg>.

# INDEX

positive interaction, 472
powers, parameters of, 456
precision-guided munitions, 452
Prensky, Marc, 260
Pricewaterhouse Coopers (PcW), 216
private consumption, 492–93
    role of, 219
privatization, 85
    philosophy, 84
production factors, 30
    relative prices, 80
production processes, competitiveness,
    16
production theory, sharing, 74
production and wealth, measuring,
    86–88
Programme for International Students
    Assessment (PISA), 245
progress, redefinition of, 111
Project Society, 258
Proliferation Security Initiative (PSI),
    419
protectionist world, 111
public service, definition blurred, 22

**Q**
Qing dynasty, 59
quality of life, 3
quantum mechanics, 6

**R**
rational thinking, quest for, 6
Reagan, Ronald, 45
recycling process, cost of, 82
regionalization, 13–15, 33
religion, 448
    influence on legal system, 41
    percentage growth in, 343
religious freedoms, 40
religious groups
    as new player, 71
    breakdown according to religion,
        342

religious minorities, symbols, 40
religious symbols, 40
Renaissance, 2
Republican Party, 139
representative economy, 139
research and culture, 13
resources
    pricing, 10
    use of, 485
Ricardo, Mercado, 77
Rice, Condoleeza, 440
rights of freedom, 35
rights of individuals, 32–34
rights of minorities, 43
risk factors, 142
Roman Empire, 127
Rostow, Walt, 8
Roszak, Theodore, 57
Royal Society, Lord Kelvin, 117
rule-based framework, 109
rule of law, 59
    between nations, 456
    history, 59
Russia, 474

**S**
Saddam Hussein, 401
Sanyal, Sanjeev, 199, 256, 512
Saudi Arabia, 474
    exporter of crude oil, 366
savings
    Asia, world's financier, 196–200
    demographics, 197–99
    social welfare, 197–99
savings rate, future, 199–200
scarcity, 383–89
    food, 350
scarcity factor, 482
science of economics, 3
scientific breakthroughs, slow in
    maturing, 108
scientific publications, indicator of
    future technology, 182

www.ingramcontent.com/pod-product-compliance
Lightning Source LLC
Chambersburg PA
CBHW021841020426
42334CB00013B/143